The Gay Nineties in America

The Gay Nineties in America

A Cultural Dictionary of the 1890s

Robert L. Gale

Greenwood Press
Westport, Connecticut • London

Library of Congress Cataloging-in-Publication Data

Gale, Robert L.
The gay nineties in America : a cultural dictionary of the 1890s / Robert L. Gale.
p. cm.
Includes bibliographical references and index.
ISBN 0-313-27819-9 (alk. paper)
1. United States—Civilization—1865-1918—Dictionaries.
I. Title.
E169.1.G26 1992
973.8—dc20 91-47061

British Library Cataloguing in Publication Data is available.

Library of Congress Catalog Card Number: 91-47061
ISBN: 0-313-27819-9

First published in 1992

Greenwood Press, 88 Post Road West, Westport, CT 06881
An imprint of Greenwood Publishing Group, Inc.

Printed in the United States of America

The paper used in this book complies with the Permanent Paper Standard issued by the National Information Standards Organization (Z39.48-1984).

10 9 8 7 6 5 4 3 2 1

For
Maureen Dowd Gale and our children
John, Jim, and Christine

CONTENTS

PREFACE

The American 1890s were the best of times, and they were the worst of times—to paraphrase a memorable statement made about another fin de siècle epoch and another continent. Our 1890s were certainly a time of conflict and contrast.

Conservative religious leaders were buffeted by secular social Darwinians. Traditional romantic literature was popular, but realists were gaining strength and new-fangled naturalism was coming across the Atlantic Ocean from France. Folksy painting and neoclassical sculpture were being challenged by a whole generation of realists. Classical architecture was giving way to functional structures. Travel into the Far West and across the oceans was becoming more common. And through it all, the robber barons—crooked railroaders, industrialists, monopolists, bankers, and politicians—were making fortunes arrogantly and spending them conspicuously; at the same time, low wages or no wages shrouded too many ordinary folks, including the native born, Native Americans, African Americans, newly arrived immigrants, and mostly silent women. The effects of the Civil War were over, just in time for America to be caught up in the Spanish-American War, with expansionist consequences creating problems that would be felt to this day.

The 1890s were a time of momentous contrasts. According to Frederick Jackson Turner, the frontier closed at this time. But at the same time, machines first generated alternating current on a commercial basis, movies lit up in earnest, and radio messages first crackled through space. Stately magazines such as the *Atlantic Monthly* fought against the competition of newcomers like the *Chap-Book* and the *Smart Set*. The Panic of 1893 swept the country and caused untold misery, but in the same year the developers of the World's Columbian Exposition in Chicago spent millions of dollars to praise the glories of the New World. While Walter A. Wyckoff earned 17¢ an hour for a nine-hour day as a janitor in a New York insane asylum, John Pierpont Morgan earned a $7,000,000 commission for loaning the federal treasury gold from his ample reserves. A few rich newspaper owners printed "yellow journalism" to stir the public with the cry "Remember the Maine!" and many less-opulent Americans died of Spanish bullets and yellow fever. George Barr McCutcheon's silly *Graustark* romances enthralled numberless readers, while Theodore Dreiser's serious *Sister Carrie* went unsold. Booker T. Washington made significant progress for African Americans, but Sitting Bull was murdered and the massacre of other Native Americans at Wounded Knee soon followed.

It is my hope that this cultural dictionary of the 1890s in the United States will help readers at all levels, in and out of high schools, colleges, and universities, to a more thoughtful understanding of the excitement and ferment of that turbulent decade just a century ago. In addition, this book offers a quick source of information or review for persons interested merely in looking up a particular name, title, or item, for example, Thomas A. Edison or Theodore Roosevelt, *The Red Badge of Courage* or *The Awakening*, baseball or commemorative stamps.

I expand the 1890s generously to include 1888 through 1901. And since no significant epoch begins and ends crisply, I have chosen to present some events transpiring well before 1888 if their momentum carries them into the 1890s; similarly, I offer some details pushing well into the early twentieth century if their roots are in the 1890s.

The people engaging in these activities in the 1890s display a variety of specialties. Represented are the accomplishments of writers, inventors, painters and illustrators, politicians, sculptors, social workers and critics, explorers, soldiers and sailors, boxers, educators, editors, and photographers, and others. My entries also include titles of especially significant literary works (for example, *A Hazard of New Fortunes*) and magazines (the *Century*, for one). Entries range widely, including general subjects such as "The Genteel Tradition," "Alcoholism," and "Crime"; key events such as "The Pullman Strike" and "Disasters"; and groups such as "The Ash Can School," "Parent-Teacher Associations," and "The Big Four." Miscellaneous entries such as "National Parks," "Medicine and Medical Advances," and "Operettas" should also help to convince readers of the diversity of our Gay Nineties.

Still, although the men and women and their activities discussed here combine to hold up a gigantic mirror to that monster the 1890s, I feel certain that some readers will look in vain for specific items. They may wonder why I bring in Henry Huttleston Rogers but leave out James Fisk, or consider automobiles but omit luxury liners. All I can do is plead ignorance as well as lack of sufficient space and a need to stop somewhere.

Naturally, a work of this scope must build on the much-appreciated labor of previous scholars. The absence of intrusive footnotes at many turns may be partially remedied by my extensive bibliography. Let me hereby thank everyone whose work is mentioned there. The value of a work of this sort is for me threefold in nature: It is gratifying to hope, perhaps fondly, that countless readers over a period of years may gain an increased appreciation of our 1890s and thus come to a more measured understanding of our present glories and confusions; also I am honored to be allowed to add to the body of written material about our country; and, finally, assembling a cultural dictionary of the 1890s in the United States has been an educative experience for me. Before I started this project, I did not know much about—to name a few random examples—Nikola Tesla, *Chita*, Camillus F. Fly, Whitcomb L. Judson, or Nellie Bly. Did you?

A distinguished literary critic, after commenting on dozens of 1890s authors, concludes thus: "When the transforming events of the nineties subsided into the tranquillity of the following ten years, these writers appeared to be part of the temporary disorders which had been thrown off in the now ended spasms of the decade. But these spasms proved in fact to be not the convulsions of rejection but the first strong and sure labor pains of modern American literature."[1] My 1890s reference book attempts to suggest that not in literature alone, but also in other art forms and in political, scientific, philosophical, military, and journalistic activities as well, the big and little people of the 1890s made possible many of the joys, miseries, anguishes, and successes of our entire twentieth century.

This book would not have been possible without the unfailingly amiable cooperation of the librarians of the University of Pittsburgh, especially Laurie Cohen, Anne W. Gordon, and Amy E. Knapp, and of the Carnegie Public Library, Carnegie-Mellon University, and Duquesne University as well, and I thank them all. I also would like to express my appreciation to Marilyn Brownstein, Senior Editor, Humanities, of the Greenwood Press, for her invaluable encouragement, advice, cooperation, and patience, and to Lynn E. Wheeler and Teresa R. Metz for their superb copyediting and production work.

The Index, as well as the *see* references and the asterisks that indicate cross-referencing, will help diligent readers find more information on a subject of particular interest to them. The Chronology assembles fascinating facts, events, and tidbits from the dictionary together with some additional background data in a year-by-year survey. The Classified Appendix and Index should also prove useful.

NOTE

1. Larzer Ziff, *The American 1890s: Life and Times of a Lost Generation* (New York: Viking, 1966), p. 348.

CHRONOLOGY

1888

Nikola Tesla* patents induction motor. William Seward Burroughs* patents adding machine. Marvin Chester Stone patents drinking straw made of waxed manila paper. Kodak hand camera developed by George Eastman.* Marine Biological Laboratory established at Woods Hole, Cape Cod, Massachusetts. State of New York adopts execution by electrocution.* Republican Benjamin Harrison* elected president (1889–1893). *Collier's** founded. Publications: Edward Bellamy,* *Looking Backward: 2000–1887*;* George Washington Cable,* *Bonaventure: A Prose Pastoral of Acadian Louisiana*;* William Dean Howells,* *Annie Kilburn*;* Henry James,* "The Aspern Papers"* and *The Reverberator*.*

1889

United States convenes first International American Conference (resulting in the Pan-American Union). Cabinet status accorded to Department of Agriculture. North Dakota, South Dakota, Montana, and Washington granted statehood (*see* Statehood). Oklahoma "Land Rush" occurs. Sons of the American Revolution formed. Hull House started by Jane Addams* (Chicago). Dr. Charles H. Mayo and his brother Dr. William J. Mayo open Mayo Clinic, in Rochester, Minnesota. Coin-operated telephone patented. First All-America football team chosen. *Arena** and *Munsey's Magazine** founded. Publications: Henry Adams,* *History of the United States during the Administrations of Jefferson and Madison** (9 vols., to 1891); Lafcadio Hearn,* *Chita: A Memory of Last Island*;* William Dean Howells,* *A Hazard of New Fortunes*;* Theodore Roosevelt,* *The Winning of the West: An Account of the Exploration and Settlement of Our Country from the Alleghanies to the Pacific** (4 vols., to 1896); Mark Twain,* *A Connecticut Yankee in King Arthur's Court*.*

1890

United States joins Germany and Britain in establishing protectorate over Samoa. Tariff written by William McKinley* raises duties (to average of 49.5%). Unused lands granted to railroads returned to public domain. U.S. frontier declared closed. Idaho and Wyoming granted statehood (*see* Statehood). Yosemite National Park established (*see* National Parks). Sherman Anti-Trust Act* passed. Sherman Silver Purchase Act (reducing gold reserves) passed (*see* Free Silver). General Federation of Women's Clubs established. United Confederate Veterans organized. Sitting Bull* captured and murdered. Wounded Knee massacre* occurs. Survey finds that over 600,000 U.S. children ages 10 to 14 work. Daughters of the American Revolution founded. Navy wins the first Army-Navy football game to be held. American Tobacco Co. creates near-monopoly. Movie film developed. *Literary Digest** and *Smart Set** founded. George Francis Train sets around-the-world record in balloon (67 days, 13 hours, 3 minutes, 3 seconds). Nellie Bly* circles the globe mainly by train and ship in 72 days, 6 hours, 11 seconds. U.S. population calculated to be 62,947,714. Publications and productions: Thomas Bailey Aldrich,* *Wyndham Towers*;* George Washington Cable,* *The Negro Question*;* Kate Chopin,* *At Fault*;* Emily Dickinson,* *Poems*; Clyde Fitch,* *Beau Brummell*;* Harold Frederic,* *The Lawton Girl* and In the Valley*;* Henry Blake Fuller,* *The Chevalier of Pensieri-Vani*;* Lafcadio Hearn,* *Two Years in the French West Indies** and *Youma: The Story of a West-Indian Slave*;* James A. Herne,* *Margaret Fleming*;* William James,* *The Principles of Psychology*;* Alfred Thayer Mahan,* *The Influence of Sea Power upon History, 1660–1783*;* Jacob Riis,* *How the Other Half Lives: Studies among the Tenements of New York.**

1891

Superintendent of Immigration Office established. New Orleans mob kills eleven reputed Mafia members after police chief is murdered. American Sugar Refining Company creates monopoly. Carnegie Hall opens in New York. Thomas A. Edison* patents movie camera. Whitcomb L. Judson* invents zipper, which Lewis Walker* soon begins to develop with him. James Naismith* invents basketball (*see* Sports). *Review of Reviews** founded. Publications: Thomas Bailey Aldrich,* *The Sisters' Tragedy, with Other Poems, Lyrical and Dramatic*;* Ambrose Bierce,* *Tales of Soldiers and Civilians*;* Emily Dickinson,* *Poems: Second Series*; Ignatius Donnelly,* *Caesar's Column: A Story of the Twentieth Century*;* Mary E. Wilkins Freeman,* *A New England Nun and Other Stories*;* Hamlin Garland,* *Main-Travelled Roads*;* Henry James,* "The Pupil."*

1892

Ellis Island,* in New York harbor, begins processing immigrants (to 1954). Chinese Exclusion Act renewed. Central Conference of American Rabbis condemns Zionism. Robert Edwin Peary* begins Arctic explorations (to 1909). Charles Edgar Duryea and his brother J. Frank Duryea build first American automobile (*see* Automobiles). Nikola Tesla* creates alternating current motor. William Painter invents bottle cap and bottle-capping machine (*see* Inventions). John Muir* establishes Sierra Club. Homestead Lockout* occurs in Pittsburgh. John Pierpont Morgan* organizes General Electric Company.

American Fine Arts Society established. John Philip Sousa* starts concert band. James J. Corbett* gains heavyweight boxing title from John L. Sullivan.* United States indemnifies Italian victims of 1891 New Orleans mob action. Lizzie Andrew Borden accused of killing her father and stepmother with ax in Fall River, Massachusetts. Democrat Grover Cleveland* reelected president (1893–1897, first served 1885–1889). *Godey's Magazine** and *Sewanee Review** founded. Publications: Ambrose Bierce,* *The Monk and the Hangman's Daughter** and *Black Beetles in Amber*;* Rebecca Harding Davis,* *Silhouettes of American Life*;* Henry Blake Fuller,* *The Chatelaine of La Trinité*;* Charlotte Perkins Gilman,* "The Yellow Wall-paper";* James A. Herne,* *Shore Acres*.*

1893

Panic of 1893* (followed by a depression to 1897). Silver Purchase Act repealed (*see* Free Silver). World's Columbian Exposition* held in Chicago. Anti-Saloon League of America formed. Colorado legislates right of women to vote. Alexander Graham Bell* loses monopoly on telephone service. World premiere of Anton Dvorak's *New World Symphony* in New York City. Frank Lloyd Wright* builds first house. Supreme Court declares Chinese Exclusion Act unconstitutional. Lizzie Borden acquitted. *McClure's Magazine** founded by S. S. McClure.* Publications: Henry Adams,* *Memoirs of Marau Taaroa, Last Queen of Tahiti*;* Thomas Bailey Aldrich,* *Two Bites at a Cherry, with Other Tales*;* Ambrose Bierce,* *Can Such Things Be?*;* Stephen Crane,* *Maggie: A Girl of the Streets*;* Henry Blake Fuller,* *The Cliff-Dwellers: A Novel*;* William Demarest Lloyd,* *Wealth against Commonwealth*; John Muir,* *The Mountains of California*;* Frederick Jackson Turner,* "The Significance of the Frontier in American History."*

1894

Bureau of Immigration established. Wilson-Gorman Tariff lowers duties selectively (to average of 39.9%). John Pierpont Morgan* organizes Southern Railroad Company. Pullman Strike occurs.* Eugene V. Debs* imprisoned. Unemployment is widespread, and many strikes are held. Labor Day holiday established. American Federation of Labor disavows socialism. Jacob Sechler Coxey* marches Coxey's Army* on Washington, D.C. Carey Act grants one million acres of federal land to states provided the land will be irrigated and homesteaded. Anti-Saloon League of America* becomes nationwide movement. Milton Hershey develops rectangular chocolate candy bar, in Lancaster, Pennsylvania. Cream of Wheat marketed. Jockey Club founded to improve the image of horse racing (*see* Sports). U.S. Golf Association established. American Protective Association (an anti-Catholic organization) gains power. New York *World* prints color comic strips. *Chap-Book** founded. Publications and productions: Thomas Bailey Aldrich,* *Mercedes: A Drama in Two Acts*;* Kate Chopin,* *Bayou Folk*;* Paul Leicester Ford,* *The Honorable Peter Stirling, and What People Thought of Him*;* Mary E. Wilkins Freeman,* *Pembroke*;* Hamlin Garland,* *Crumbling Idols: Twelve Essays on Art Dealing Chiefly with Literature, Painting and the Drama*;* Lafcadio Hearn,* *Glimpses of Unfamiliar Japan*;* William Dean Howells,* *A Traveler from Altruria*;* Mark Twain,* *Pudd'nhead Wilson, A Tale*.*

1895

United States intervenes in Venezuela-Britain boundary dispute (to 1896). Income tax declared unconstitutional (legalized by Sixteenth Amendment in 1913). Utah legislates female suffrage. Republican Party controls Congress (to 1911). Sears, Roebuck & Co. starts mail-order business. Booker T. Washington* addresses Atlanta Exposition. New York Public Library founded. American Bowling Congress established. Gettysburg National Military Park established. George B. Selden patents clutch-operated automobile. Dorothy Dix (real name: Elizabeth Meriwether Gilmer) starts column in New Orleans *Daily Picayune* offering advice to lovelorn. *American Historical Review*,* *Bibelot*,* *Bookman*,* *The Lark*,* and *The Philistine** founded. Publications: Thomas Bailey Aldrich,* *Unguarded Gates and Other Poems*;* George Washington Cable,* *John March, Southerner*;* Stephen Crane,* *The Black Riders and Other Lines** and *The Red Badge of Courage*;* Ignatius Donnelly,* *The American People's Money*;* Henry Blake Fuller,* *With the Procession: A Novel*;* Hamlin Garland,* *Rose of Dutcher's Coolly*.*

1896

American sympathy with Cuban rebels opposing Spanish rule increases. U.S. Supreme Court decision legalizes segregation via "separate but equal" doctrine (overturned in 1954). Billy Sunday* begins career as evangelist. Rabbi Isaac Elchanan Theological Seminary, first yeshiva in the United States, established in New York City. Rural Free Delivery (of mail) begins. At Olympic Games, held in Athens, Greece, for first time since A.D. 394, American James Brendan Connelly wins first gold medal, for triple jump (*see* Sports). Utah granted statehood (*see* Statehood). X-rays first used to treat cancer. Motion pictures* first shown to paying public. Diamond Match Co. markets matches in pocket-size folders. Silver Republicans nominate William Jennings Bryan.* Gold Democrats form separate ticket. Bryan nominated by Democrats following "Cross of Gold" speech. Republican William McKinley* elected president (1897–1901). Publications and productions: George Ade,* *Artie*;* Thomas Bailey Aldrich,* *Judith and Holofernes: A Poem*;* Abraham Cahan,* *Yekl: A Tale of the New York Ghetto*;* Stephen Crane,* *George's Mother*;* Emily Dickinson,* *Poems: Third Series*; Harold Frederic,* *The Damnation of Theron Ware*;* William Gillette,* *Secret Service*;* Charlotte Perkins Gilman,* *Women and Economics: A Study of the Economic Relation between Men and Women as a Factor in Social Evolution*;* Sarah Orne Jewett,* *The Country of the Pointed Firs*;* Mark Twain,* *Personal Recollections of Joan of Arc*;* Owen Wister,* *Red Men and White*.*

1897

Spain makes concessions to United States regarding Cuba. Dingley Tariff Act puts duties at highest rate in U.S. history (57%). First U.S. subway, in Boston. Coal miners launch successful strikes in Pennsylvania, Ohio, and West Virginia. Parent-Teacher Associations* founded. Gold rush to Alaska occurs (to 1898). Library of Congress completed (first phase). New York Public Library begun (completed 1911). Francis P. Church says, "Yes, Virginia, there is a Santa Claus" to Virginia O'Hanlon in New York *Sun*. Rudolph Dirk's "Katzenjammer Kids" in New York *Journal* is first comic strip to use speech balloons. *Charities** founded. Publications: George Ade,* *Pink Marsh*;* Edward Bellamy,* *Equality*;* Kate Chopin,* *A Night in Acadie*;* Stephen Crane,* "The Open Boat"* and *The Third Violet*;* Richard Harding Davis,* *Soldiers of Fortune*;* Ellen Glasgow,* *The Descendant*;* William Dean Howells,* *The Landlord at Lion's Head*;* William James,* *The Will to Believe, and Other Essays in Popular Philosophy*;* Edwin Arlington Robinson,* *The Children of the Night*;* Charles M. Sheldon,* *In His Steps: What Would Jesus Do?*;* Mark Twain,* *Following the Equator: A Journey around the World*;* Owen Wister,* *Lin McLean*;* Walter A. Wyckoff,* *The Workers: An Experiment in Reality: The East.**

1898

United States declares war on Spain (25 April–10 December—*see* Spanish-American War). United States acquires Puerto Rico, Guam, and the Philippines (for $20,000,000). Hawaii annexed (granted territorial status in 1900, granted statehood in 1959). Anti-Imperialist League founded in Boston. Richard J. Gatling demonstrates machine gun capable of firing 3,000 bullets per minute. The Bronx, Brooklyn, Manhattan, Queens, and Richmond join to form New York City. National Institute of Arts and Letters established. American Impressionist painters formally exhibit works. Eight-hour workday ruled constitutional by U.S. Supreme Court. Supreme Court also rules U.S. citizenship must be decided without regard to race or color. Publications: Edward Bellamy,* *The Blindman's World and Other Stories*;* Winston Churchill,* *The Celebrity*;* Stephen Crane,* "The Blue Hotel,"* "The Bride Comes to Yellow Sky,"* *The Open Boat and Other Tales of Adventure*,* and *Active Service*;* Richard Harding Davis,* *The Cuban and Porto Rican Campaigns*;* Finley Peter Dunne,* *Mr. Dooley in Peace and in War*;* Ellen Glasgow,* *Phases of an Inferior Planet*;* Henry James,* "The Turn of the Screw";* William James,* *Human Immortality: Two Supposed Objections to the Doctrine*;* Walter A. Wyckoff,* *The Workers: An Experiment in Reality: The West.**

1899

Boer War (to 1902). United States occupies Wake Island. U.S. and Germany partition Samoan Islands. John Hay* formulates Open-Door Policy* for China (on into 1900). Filipinos resist U.S. rule (to 1902). Gideon Society established in Boscobel, Wisconsin. Scott Joplin* popularizes his "Maple Leaf Rag." *Everybody's Magazine** founded. Publications and productions: George Ade,* *Doc' Horne: A Story of the Streets and Town*;* Ambrose Bierce,* *Fantastic Fables*;* Kate Chopin,* *The Awakening*;* Winston Churchill,* *Richard Carvel*;* Stephen Crane,* *War Is Kind*,* and *The Monster and Other Stories*;* Clyde Fitch,* *Barbara Frietchie*;* Paul Leicester Ford,* *Janice Meredith: A Story of the American Revolution*;* William Dean Howells,* *Their Silver Wedding Journey*;* Elbert Hubbard,* "A Message to Garcia";* Henry James,* "Europe";* William James,* *Talks to Teachers on Psychology: and to Students on Some of Life's Ideals*;* Edwin Markham,* "The Man with the Hoe";* Frank Norris,* *McTeague: A Story of San Francisco*;* Theodore Roosevelt,* *The Rough Riders*;* Mark Twain,* "The Man That Corrupted Hadleyburg";* Thorstein Veblen,* *The Theory of the Leisure Class.**

1900

Boxer Rebellion occurs in China; U.S. troops are sent to Peking (Beijing). Civil government established in Puerto Rico. United States goes on gold standard. International Ladies Garment Workers established. American athletes win twenty gold medals, sweep Olympics held in Paris (*see* Sports). According to estimates, more than 8,000 horseless carriages are on U.S. highways, 18,000,000 horses and mules are still in service, 1,300,000 telephones are in use, and 4,000,000,000 cigarettes are produced annually. U.S. population calculated to be 75,994,575. *World's Work** founded. Publications and productions: George Ade,* *Fables in Slang** and *More Fables*;* Lyman Frank Baum,* *The Wonderful Wizard of Oz*; David Belasco,* *Madame Butterfly*;* Edward Bellamy,* *The Duke of Stockbridge: A Romance of Shays' Rebellion*;* Stephen Crane,* *Whilomville Stories** and *Wounds in the Rain: A Collection of Stories Relating to the Spanish-American War in 1898*;* Theodore Dreiser,* *Sister Carrie*;* Ellen Glasgow,* *The Voice of the People*;* Robert Grant,* *Unleavened Bread*;* Edwin Markham,* "Lincoln, the Man of the People";* Theodore Roosevelt,* *The Strenuous Life: Essays and Addresses by Theodore Roosevelt*;* Owen Wister,* *The Jimmyjohn Boss and Other Stories*.*

1901

Overseas wireless messages first sent (*see* Radio). Pan-American Exposition* held in Buffalo, New York. President William McKinley* assassinated; Theodore Roosevelt* becomes president (to 1909). Philippines granted civil government (become self-governing commonwealth in 1935, become independent in 1946). U.S. Army War College founded in Washington, D.C. Oil discovered near Beaumont, Texas. Andrew Carnegie* sells steel facilities to John Pierpont Morgan,* who creates U.S. Steel Corporation. U.S. Socialist Party established. Carl Hedstrom displays motorized bicycle in Springfield, Massachusetts. Orville Wright designs wind tunnel to experiment with flight simulation in Dayton, Ohio. Platt Amendment gives United States quasi-protectorate over Cuba. Hay-Pauncefote Treaty permits United States to construct and control Panama Canal (construction begins in 1904, is completed in 1914). Publications and productions: George Ade,* *Forty Modern Fables*;* Winston Churchill,* *The Crisis*;* Stephen Crane,* *Great Battles of the World*;* Clyde Fitch,* *The Climbers** and *Captain Jinks of the Horse Marines*;* William Vaughn Moody,* *Poems*;* John Muir, *Our National Parks*;* Frank Norris,* *The Octopus: A Story of California*;* Booker T. Washington,* *Up from Slavery: An Autobiography*.*

LIST OF ENTRIES

The Gay Nineties in America

A

Abraham Lincoln: A History (1890). A ten-volume biography of Abraham Lincoln and history of the Civil War, by John Hay* and John G. Nicolay. This massive work has 224 chapters, 4,580 pages, many illustrations and maps, and an enormous index. Volume I (1780 to May 1856) concerns the Lincoln family background; Lincoln's childhood and youth and his roles as soldier, surveyor, state legislator, husband, and congressman; and pertinent political background. Volume II (May 1856 to December 1860) features a background of pre–Civil War politics, in front of which is seen Lincoln's rise to national prominence, culminating in his election as president. Volume III (December 1860 to April 1861) combines pre-war activities in the North and the South and Lincoln's actions on the eve of war. Volume IV (April to November 1861) dramatically details the events that took place during the first seven months of the Civil War. Volume V (May 1861 to August 1862) carries the war well into its second year. Volume VI (August 1862 to January 1863) connects the continuing story of the war to international power politics and the problem of emancipation. Volume VII (July 1862 to October 1863) continues the war narrative, stressing generals Ulysses S. Grant and Robert E. Lee, Vicksburg and Gettysburg, and the topic of prisoners of war. This volume is the most absorbing of the entire history. Volume VIII (February 1863 to June 1864) concerns battles, mistakes, and the freeing of five slave states. Volume IX (May 1864 to March 1865) combines military and political history, stressing Lincoln's reelection and the successes of generals Philip H. Sheridan and William Tecumseh Sherman. Volume X (October 1864 to the end of the war and its aftermath) concerns Union victories, the Confederate surrender, Lincoln's assassination, and, finally, his richly deserved fame. *Abraham Lincoln* presents, in an even-handed way, the vast schisms between pro- and anti-Union forces in Europe, between the North and South, in Northern politics, between the civilian and military viewpoints, in Lincoln's cabinet, and in the army itself; the interrelationship of war and politics; aspects of fatalism; and big doses of ironic, sarcastic, and grim humor. Stylistically, this work is most impressive. A priceless history and incalculably influential over the years, *Abraham Lincoln* has been used by numerous later scholars and frequently cited and quoted. It was abridged by Nicolay in 1902 and again by Paul M. Angle in 1966.

Active Service (1899). Novel by Stephen Crane.* Marjory Wainwright timidly tells her father, Professor Harrison B. Wainwright of Washurst College, that she wants to marry Rufus Coleman, the New York *Eclipse* Sunday editor. After forbidding her to do so, the diminutive professor decides to escape from the situation with his pretentious wife Mary and Marjory and eight students on a tour to Greece. Meanwhile, in Coleman's *Eclipse* office, stories about deformed babies and shipwrecked sailors are being processed to increase readership. Marjory sees Coleman again to tell him that they cannot wed and that the Wainwrights are going to Greece. Six weeks later Coleman wangles an assignment to cover the probable outbreak of war between Greece and Turkey. Aboard ship to England, he meets a friend, the gorgeous actress Nora Black, who is scheduled to appear on the London stage but who would prefer to be with him. Coleman, however, slips away to Athens, where he learns from the American minister that the Wainwrights are now trapped in Turkey. Coleman hires a dragoman to guide him across dangerous enemy terrain in varied weather, observes much military activity, and miraculously comes upon the Wainwright group. On their way back to safety, pretty Nora suddenly appears. She has quit acting, has become a correspondent herself, and is relentlessly pursuing Coleman, who, however, after much derring-do and a bit of uncertainty opts for Marjory—through hopelessly, he thinks. Back in Athens, Mrs. Wainwright criticizes Coleman; Marjory and the professor emote; the American minister sings Coleman's praises to the professor; and the professor permits the lovers to wed. This novel spoofs romantic fiction of the sort Crane despised, but it does have elements worth noting. It satirizes sensational journalism (of the kind promoted by William Randolph Hearst* and Joseph Pulitzer*) and contains gripping journalistic descriptions of Greco-Turkish War action. It also includes interesting autobiographical and biographical overtones. Coleman is partly an autobiographical figure and partly a spoof of Richard Harding Davis,* Crane's war-correspondent rival in Greece and elsewhere. Coleman's New York newspaper office reconstructs locales that Crane knew well at Lafayette College and Syracuse University. Wainwright epitomizes the kind of vapid, unrealistic professors Crane judged, though too quickly, in college. A real-life woman was in danger much as was Marjory in *Active Service*. Harriet Boyd, an American student in Greece, became a correspondent for Hearst during the war and was trapped by the Turkish advance. Nora Black is based partly on Crane's so-called wife Cora Taylor. One wonders why in the novel Crane says that Nora's voice suggests "the liquid siren note of a succubus." The name Nora Black echoes that of Dora Clark, a demimondaine whom Crane knew in New York City. Several college students and their antics in the novel owe much to Crane's memories of undergraduate life. The American minister to Greece when Crane was there (early 1897) was Eben Alexander; in *Active Service*, dedicated to Alexander, the man becomes Thomas M. Gordner (from Nebraska).

Adams, Brooks (1848–1927). Historian. Born in Quincy, Massachusetts, Adams was the great-grandson of President John Adams, the grandson of President John Quincy Adams, the son of diplomat-author Charles Francis Adams, Sr., and the brother of railroad reformer and lawyer-author Charles Francis Adams, Jr., and of author Henry Adams.* Brooks Adams graduated from Harvard (1870), studied law, practiced until sickness forced him to retire (1881), became a profound but eccentric historian, and taught law at Boston University (1904–1911). He married Evelyn Davis in 1889. Adams was the author of *The Emancipation of Massachusetts* (1887, an inconoclastic study of the dangers of religious and political conservatism), *The Law of Civilization and Decay: An Essay on History* (1895), *America's Economic Supremacy* (1900, theorizing that, after the Spanish-American War* and during the presidency of Theodore Roosevelt,* America began to emerge as an international force), *The New Empire* (1902, about the rise-and-fall cycles of imperial governments), and *Theory of Social Revolution* (1913, linking political and economic forces). In *The Law of Civilization and Decay*, he espoused the theory that the moral decay of medieval and more modern societies not only was caused by ruthlessly usurious financiers but also could be compared to the immutable laws of the physical universe. This theory influenced his brother Henry Adams to make an analogy between the acceleration of historical events and the second law of thermodynamics.

Adams, Henry (1838–1918). (Full name: Henry Brooks Adams.) Author and educator. Born in Boston, Massachusetts, Adams was the great-grandson of President John Adams, the grandson of President John Quincy Adams, the son of diplomat-author Charles Francis Adams, Sr., and the brother of railroad reformer and lawyer-author Charles Francis Adams, Jr., and of historian Brooks Adams.* Henry Adams was educated at Harvard (graduated 1858) and in Berlin. He enjoyed a Grand Tour (Germany, Austria, Italy, France, and England) and then served as the secretary of his politician father, first in Washington, D.C. (1860–1861) and then in England when that skillful man served as minister to England during and after the Civil War (1861–1868). While in England, young Adams favored Darwinism in its various applications and began his lifelong opposition to imperialism. After he returned home, he launched a phenomenal career that featured journalism, teaching at Harvard (1870–1877), and profoundly serious writing. He concerned himself with various subjects in many forms: politics, medieval history and arts, American history and social and religious life, Oriental mores and Polynesian history, modern physics, and contemporary chaos—in essays, lectures, books, poems, novels, and an incomparable autobiography, *The Education of Henry Adams* (1907, 1918). Adams made himself obscure by adopting the role of a cunning, puzzling, coy poseur. His works have been far more influential after his death than they were during his lifetime. In addition to his autobiography, his major works include *Chapters of Erie* (1871, with his brother Charles Francis Adams, Jr.), *The Life of Albert Gallatin* (1879, which led him to more massive American historical work), *Democracy: An American Novel* (1880, anonymously published), *John Randolph* (1882, a biography), *Esther: A Novel* (1884, as by Frances Snow Compton), *History of the United States during the Administrations of Jefferson and Madison** (9 vols., 1889–1891), *Memoirs of Marau Taaroa, Last Queen of Tahiti** (1893), *Mont-Saint-Michel and Chartres* (1904, 1913), and *The Life of George Cabot Lodge*[*] (1911). Adams was also a fine and dedicated letter writer.

A pivotal event in the life of Henry Adams was the death of his wife Marian "Clover" Hooper Adams (they married in 1872 and had no children). Despondent over her beloved, agnostic father's death in 1885, she committed suicide later the same year, after which Adams became pessimistic, stoical, and restless. He commissioned his friend the sculptor Augustus Saint-Gaudens* to create an enigmatic seated bronze statue for his wife's grave in Rock Creek Cemetery, Washington, D.C. After Adams finished his enormous *History of the United States*, he traveled more widely than ever before, and he often shuttled between Paris, his favorite artistic and intellectual city, and Washington, D.C., which he found to be politically and socially exciting. Adams, who knew many of the most influential thinkers of his time, numbered among his close friends Senator James Donald Cameron (and especially his wife Elizabeth Sherman Cameron), John Hay,* Henry James* (with whom he exchanged brilliant letters), geologist Clarence King, John La Farge* (with whom he traveled widely), Lodge, Theodore Roosevelt* (with whom he socialized in the White House), Saint-Gaudens, and Trumbull Stickney* (to whom he played uncle in Paris). Adams is buried, by his wish, in an unmarked grave beside his wife.

Addams, Jane (1860–1935). (Full name: Jane Laura Addams.) Social reformer, pacifist, and woman's rights advocate. Born in Cedarville, Illinois, Addams was the daughter of a well-to-do merchant. She graduated (1881) from Rockford Seminary (now Rockford College) and visited institutions for social reform in England. With the assistance of Ellen Gates Starr, a former college classmate, she founded a social welfare center in Chicago called Hull House (1889). She and her associates lived there, worked in and out of it, helped ameliorate life for Chicago slum dwellers, and provided day-care services for working mothers. Reformers visited Hull House to obtain ideas for their own work, and other settlement houses throughout the United States were patterned after Addams's establishment. Addams fought for better housing, playgrounds, and public parks in Chicago. She also advocated prohibition, woman suffrage, and reform of labor laws for children and working mothers. She was an active pacifist before and during World War I, and she became president of the Women's International League for Peace and Freedom (1919). She was awarded the Nobel Peace Prize, along with Nicholas Murray Butler in 1931. Addams forcefully expressed her concerns in ten books and in more than four hundred articles—in leading magazines of the time as well as in her own *Hull House Bulletin* (1896–1906). Her two most significant books are *Democracy and Social Ethics* (1902) and *Twenty Years at Hull House* (1910). One of her best-known academic friends in Chicago was Robert Morss Lovett.*

Ade, George (1866–1944). Journalist, humorist, dramatist, and librettist. George Ade was born in Kentland, Indiana. His father, born in England, was a farmer and bank cashier. Ade attended Purdue University, where he enjoyed theatrical productions and edited its only student publication. His closest friend in college was John Tinney McCutcheon, a skillful cartoonist who later illustrated many of Ade's books and who was the younger brother of the popular novelist George Barr McCutcheon.* Ade also knew Booth Tarkington* at Purdue. After he graduated in 1887, Ade became a reporter in Lafayette, Indiana; in 1890, he joined the staff of the Chicago *Morning News* (later named the *News-Record* and finally the *News*). John McCutcheon, who was on the *Morning News* staff as a cartoonist, helped Ade get his job. Ade, who was always observant (especially of the various nationalities in Chicago), articulate, graphic, and wry, started a feature called "Stories of the Streets and of the Town" (1893), which soon became a hit. Ade published *Artie** (1896), *Pink Marsh** (1897), and his first newspaper fable in slang (1 September 1897). From the first, his fables were unique—marked by capitalized nouns, clichés, mordant humor, accurate American slang and vernacular, absence of literary pretentiousness, and end-of-essay morals. Ade traveled widely in Europe (1898) and to the Philippines, China, and Japan (1900). By then he was immensely popular, with *Doc' Horne: A Story of the Streets and Town** (1899), *Fables in Slang** (1899), *More Fables** (1900), and syndication of his fables (from September 1900).

Ade continued to travel, this time to the Middle East (to Egypt, for example, in 1905). Meanwhile, his brother was wisely investing Ade's incredible royalties (up to $5,000 weekly) in Indiana farmland for him. After *Forty Modern Fables** (1901), Ade began to write plays and libretti for musical comedies. One example, *The Sultan of Sulu* (1902), written with composer Alfred Wathall, was a Broadway hit; Gilbert and Sullivan in style, it satirized American conduct in the Philippines. His *Babel* (1903), an instant best-seller, was made up of "Street and Town" columns. In 1904 three Ade shows appeared on Broadway and on national tour: *The County Chairman* (his best, about small-town political campaigning), *The College Widow* (the first drama ever based on American student life and college athletics), and *The Sho-Gun* (musical comedy, satirizing American commercial and social activities in the Far East). Not a success, *The Sho-Gun* marks the beginning of Ade's decline from great public acclaim. That same year, Ade bought Hazelden, an estate complete with a golf course, a tennis court, and a swimming pool, at Brook, near Kentland. He held lavish picnics there for children; once his guests, counting parents, numbered no fewer than

8,000. Ade's *In Pastures New* (1906) is a book of travel sketches that satirize foolish American tourists in England, France, Italy, and Egypt. His novel *The Slim Princess* (1907) gently ridiculed George Barr McCutcheon's romances but still caused a rift between the two friends. Ade continued to write fiction and plays, including farcical one-acters; but during and after the 1920s his production, his quality, and his popularity fell off sharply.

Ade never married (publishing "Single Blessedness" in 1922), became wealthy (*The College Widow* grossed $2,000,000 in its first few years), was generous to Purdue and to other recipients of his largesse, and died in Brook. George Ade is nearly forgotten now; only his fables are read to any great extent. In his day, however, he was famous throughout the English-speaking world, especially in England. He was once praised by William Dean Howells,* who, in a 1904 essay, extolled him as more than a regionalist and who privately urged him—to no avail, as Ade sadly recalled later—to move from popular journalism to realistic American fiction. Mark Twain* regarded *Pink Marsh* as effortlessly wonderful. Ade is now seen as gently satirical, bitterly cynical at times, and best in his unaffectedly vernacular fables. The satirical "Mr. Dooley" pieces by his friend Finley Peter Dunne,* fellow Chicagoan, have enjoyed a more steady fame.

African Americans. In the decade of the 1890s, African Americans made many noteworthy strides toward equality and self-identification. Many individual African Americans contributed to American culture in different ways; however, most were still victimized by racial prejudice, the problems caused by miscegenation, and the hatred and violence spawned by racism. African Americans worked in southern fields, in northern factories, and on western ranges; they held many other types of jobs, too, including those of domestic servants, office workers, and public entertainers. Individual African Americans in the 1890s especially excelled in the fields of education and literature. On the roll call of pioneering African-American educators, the names of Booker T. Washington* and George Washington Carver,* both active in the 1890s, will always remain preeminent. Washington and Carver, both born to slave parents, were, by their own efforts, able to gain national and even international renown. Washington's *Up from Slavery*,* a classic black autobiography, tells, among much else, how he organized an African-American normal school in Tuskegee, Alabama. Carver, an agricultural researcher, developed many products from peanuts and sweet potatoes, and he inspired his students to emulate his accomplishments. African-American writers active in this period of American history include Charles W. Chesnutt,* W.E.B. DuBois,* Paul Laurence Dunbar,* and Frances Harper.* All four worked against white prejudice and the lack of normal and decent opportunities available to black people. In spite of these obstacles, Chesnutt produced enduring fiction, which was at its best and most valuable when it lashed out against racism and segregation; he also dramatized what he knew personally, that is, the joys and sorrows of miscegenation. The first black to earn a Ph.D.

at Harvard, Dubois studied abroad and returned to America to conduct sociological research in Philadelphia. He taught effectively and wrote and edited brilliantly, but eventually he became so bitter at conditions in America that he was wooed by the siren song of international communism. He expatriated himself to Europe and finally to Africa, where he died. Particularly rankling to DuBois was Booker T. Washington's moderate accommodationist attitude toward white policy and prejudice. Dunbar spun prolific, effective fiction and other writings out of a personal life marred by opportunities tragically delayed and love pathetically lost. Harper, who had to overcome being both black and female, wrote brilliantly; she published *Iola Leroy*, the first effective novel written by an African-American woman in the United States. Meanwhile, George Washington Cable,* white novelist, essayist, and lecturer, put himself at personal risk by publishing his liberal book entitled *The Negro Question*,* as well as other controversial works. Even while Cable was writing, Joel Chandler Harris* and Thomas Nelson Page,* among other white writers of fiction long and short, were using sentiment and humor to evoke memories of the Old South. Frederick Douglass,* aged though he was in the 1890s, dismissed both sentiment and humor as weapons; he remained realistically eloquent to the end in seeking to ameliorate the plight of African Americans and women. Among numerous skillful African-American musicians, the name of Scott Joplin* stands out as the first ragtime composer and a performer of unparalleled influence. Finally, the outstanding African-American painter of the 1890s was Henry Ossawa Tanner,* who was best when he memorialized rural American black scenes charmingly but who, like DuBois and others of his time and color, found Europe more palatable than his native land.

Alcoholism. Americans of note in the 1890s who had alcohol problems of varying degrees of severity include Ambrose Bierce,* Grover Cleveland,* Stephen Crane,* Charles Crocker,* Eugene V. Debs,* Paul Laurence Dunbar,* Camillus S. Fly,* Charles Manning Freeman (the husband of Mary E. Wilkins Freeman*), Geronimo,* O. Henry,* Winslow Homer,* Jack London,* James Whitcomb Riley,* Edwin Arlington Robinson,* John L. Sullivan,* Booth Tarkington,* and indubitably many more.

Alden, Henry Mills (1836–1917). Editor and author. Alden, who was born at Mount Tabor, Vermont, moved when he was five years old with his family to Hoosick Falls, New York, where he worked as a cotton-mill bobbin boy until he was fourteen. With almost no schooling up to that time, he undertook seminary study and then obtained a classical education at Williams College (graduating in 1857). While a college student, he taught school in Vermont and New York district schools. He attended Andover Seminary (graduating in 1860) but declined to be ordained. He went to New York City (1861), failed the physical examination to enter the Union Army for Civil War service, and instead taught school. He published a few philosophical essays in the *Atlantic Monthly** and lectured on paganism at the Lowell Institute in Boston (1863–1864). Alden became an assistant editor at *Harper's* (1863), was managing editor of *Harper's Weekly* (1863–1869), and was then editor of *Harper's Magazine* (1869–1919). Alden was deeply religious, decent, and conservative in his literary tastes. He was brilliant, conscientious, and tactful in handling authors. He published works by such distinguished authors as Mary E. Wilkins Freeman,* Lafcadio Hearn,* William Dean Howells,* Henry James,* and Owen Wister,* among others. It is notable that he sanitized Thomas Hardy's *Jude the Obscure* for American serial publication. Alden also wrote three books—*God in His World* (1890), *A Study of Death* (1895), and *Magazine Writing and the New Literature* (1908). Alden married Susan Frye Foster in 1861 (the couple had four children, and she died in 1895) and poetess Ada Foster Murray in 1900.

Aldrich, Thomas Bailey (1836–1907). Novelist, short-story writer, poet, playwright, and editor. Aldrich was born in Portsmouth, New Hampshire. With his family, he spent a few childhood years in New Orleans (1846–1849). His father's death in 1849 prevented Aldrich from attending college. He lived with and clerked for his merchant uncle in New York (beginning in 1852), and soon became a successful reporter, literary critic, free-lance writer, and editor, first in New York (1855–1864, with a brief 1861 stint as a reporter with the Union Army at the front during the Civil War) and then in Boston (from 1866). Thereafter he called himself not Bostonian but "Boston-plated." He published many books of poetry (beginning in 1855) and fiction (beginning in 1870); he is now best remembered for his autobiographical novel *The Story of a Bad Boy* (1870), which takes place in Rivermouth, the fictional counterpart of Portsmouth. Noteworthy also are his short story "Marjorie Daw" (1873), which has a brilliant surprise ending, and the novel *The Stillwater Tragedy* (1880), an antiunion, anti-immigrant labor story which features the first private detective in American fiction. Aldrich succeeded William Dean Howells* as editor of the *Atlantic Monthly** (1881–1890). After publishing *Wyndham Towers** in 1890, Aldrich retired, was honored as one of America's most distinguished writers, traveled to Europe often until 1900, and continued to write thereafter. Notable are *The Second Son* (1888, a novel coauthored with Mrs. M.O.W. Oliphant, cast in England, concerning a squire's three sons), *The Sisters' Tragedy, with Other Poems, Lyrical and Dramatic** (1891), *An Old Town by the Sea** (1893), *Two Bites at a Cherry, with Other Tales** (1894), *Mercedes: A Drama in Two Acts** (1894), *Unguarded Gates and Other Poems** (1895), and *Judith and Holofernes: A Poem** (1896). His works were collected in eight volumes, in 1896.

As a writer, Aldrich displays charm, mild wit, and a polished style, but little depth. He remained a conservative editor who favored traditional Boston values. His sentimentality and espousal of the Genteel Tradition* prevented his evolving into a full-scale realist and meeting the critical challenges of the 1890s. Aldrich is now, to a great degree, forgotten. Praising *The Story of a Bad Boy* in an 1870 review, Howells pointed out that it was the first fiction to describe what an

American boy's life is rather than what it should be. This novel was the first in the now extensive tradition of stories about boys, advanced by Howells himself, but, more important, not only by Mark Twain* (who knew, enjoyed kidding, and admired Aldrich for remaining constantly youthful, and whose depictions of Tom Sawyer and Huckleberry Finn reflect his influence) but also by Stephen Crane.* Howells also praised Aldrich's ''Marjorie Daw,'' in an 1873 critical essay, for its neatly managed surprise ending—an innovative device at that time.

Alger, Horatio, Jr. (1830–1899). Popular writer. Born in Chelsea, Massachusetts, to a Puritan family, Alger graduated from Harvard (1852), rebelled by trying Bohemian life in Paris for a time, returned to New England to write, teach, and edit, and attended Cambridge Divinity School (1857–1860). He was ordained and served as a Unitarian minister in Brewster, Massachusetts (1864–1866), was dismissed from his church on allegations of homosexuality* involving two parish boys (1866), published stories and poems in *Harper's Weekly* during that time, then left the pulpit to go to New York to begin an energetic literary career. He wrote almost a hundred juvenile books (1866–1896), during which time he also tutored (1869–1881), wrote biographies of self-made heroes and also minor works, and traveled extensively (1873, 1877–1878, 1887–1890). He finally fell sick from overwork. Alger's books in the 1888–1901 period include *The Errand Boy* (1888), *Tom Thatcher's Fortune* (1888), *Charlie Codman's Cruise (1894), Victor Vane* (1894), *Adrift in the City* (1895), *Frank Hunter's Peril* (1896), *A Boy's Fortune* (1898), *Rupert's Ambition* (1899), *The Adventures of a Telegraph Boy* (1900), *A Debt of Honor* (1900), *The Erie Train Boy* (1900), *Mark Stanton* (1900), *Tom Tracy* (1900), *Ben Bruce (1901), Lester's Luck* (1901), *A New York Boy* (1901), and others whose dates are uncertain. Alger estimated that by 1897 some 800,000 copies of his books had been sold, with volumes in his *Ragged Dick Series* (beginning in 1867) representing a big fraction. *Luck and Pluck* items (from 1869) and *Tattered Tom* numbers (from 1871) also sold well. Leaders of the conservative establishment did not favor Alger's rags-to-riches books, perhaps because they also carried implications of the author's proper revulsion at the means used and the hypocrisy of the robber barons of the so-called Genteel Tradition.* At any rate, after his death in 1899, Alger's works suffered a decline, until about 1910, after which they once more became incredibly popular, selling more than a million copies a year until about 1925, when his sales, reputation, and even name recognition fell off. In 1928 a debunking, hoax biography (by Herbert R. Mayes) appeared and further damaged Alger's case for decades. Today Horatio Alger, Jr., is regarded as the creator of one of America's most enduring myths: If you work hard and persevere and if you are polite, decent, and frugal, you can evolve from ragged poverty to wealth and moral respectability.

Altgeld, John Peter (1847–1902). Politician. Born in Niederselters, Hesse, Germany, Altgeld moved with his parents to Richland County, Ohio, in 1848 where, as a boy, he worked long hours for his illiterate father and had little schooling. He served (1864–1865) in the Union army during the Civil War, walked from Ohio to Missouri (1869), became an unskilled laborer and then a schoolteacher, studied law, and was admitted to the bar (1872). He was elected state's attorney, Andrew County, Missouri (1874–1875); moved to Chicago (1875), where he practiced law but made more money through building construction; and was elected to the Cook County Superior Court (1886–1891). When he was elected governor of Illinois (1893–1897), Altgeld was the first foreign-born governor of Illinois, the first citizen of Chicago to be elected governor, and the first Democrat to be elected governor since the Civil War. His administration was notable for many reasons. The World's Columbian Exposition* was held early in his term (1893). He gained quick criticism but ultimate praise for pardoning in 1893 three anarchists among the eight arrested, tried, and convicted of murder after the Chicago Haymarket riot of 1886 (one of the others had committed suicide in his cell, and four others had been hanged in 1887). He protested the dispatching by Grover Cleveland,* then president, of federal troops to quell rioters during the Pullman Strike* of 1894. Altgeld took control of the Democratic national convention from Cleveland (1896), and he supported the doctrine of Free Silver,* thus championing the presidential aspirations of William Jennings Bryan* (1896, again in 1900).

Under Altgeld's leadership, many admirable events occurred. Prisons were reformed, an industrial home for the blind was founded, a girls' reformatory school was established, sensible factory labor laws were passed, employers were no longer permitted to lease convict labor, women were first appointed to important government posts, more support was given to the University of Illinois, and a portion of the revenue from the Illinois-Michigan Canal was paid to Illinois. Altgeld lost when he ran again for governor in 1896. He married Emma Ford in 1877. *Live Questions* (1899) is a collection of his interviews, speeches, and essays. Altgeld might have become president but for his often unattractive honesty and—of course—his foreign birth.

American Historical Review. Distinguished professional magazine, founded in October 1895 with private funds and funded by the American Historical Association from 1898. The first two managing editors were John Franklin Jameson, a history professor at Brown University (1895–1900, 1906–1928), and Andrew Cunningham McLaughlin, a history professor at the University of Michigan (1901–1905). The review publishes essays by the best American historians on various aspects of American history and reviews and makes notes on research developments.

The American People's Money (1895). Tract in fictional form by Ignatius Donnelly.* Hugh Sanders and James Hutchinson are passengers on a westbound railroad train. They are discussing money, paper currency, and bimetallism (*see* Free Silver). Sanders is a farmer who espouses Donnelly's position. Hutchinson is a banker from Chicago who is eventually defeated by Sanders's logical parade of evidence and by his gift of gab. Donnelly wrote the little 25¢ paperback as a potboiler at his publisher's request because there was a demand for books about money. It is not a silver tract, since Donnelly favored fiat currency. However, he felt that, as long as a metallic currency was in use, the gold standard should be changed to a bimetallic standard, and silver should be another basis for money. In thus seeming to advocate silver as a standard, Donnelly was popular with the pro-silver element in the Populist Party.* He hoped, to no avail, that he could induce Henry Demarest Lloyd* to provide an introduction for his little book.

Annie Kilburn (1888). Novel by William Dean Howells.* Annie Kilburn, age thirty-one, single and now parentless, returns after many years in Italy to her hometown of Hatboro, Massachusetts. The town has lost its old-fashioned, New England idealism and is now harshly capitalistic, with labor strife. Annie encounters social climber Emmeline Gerrish, wealthy mill-owner George Wilmington and his family, easygoing Dr. James Morrell, widowed minister Julius W. Peck and his small daughter Idella, and alcoholic lawyer Putney, among others at various social strata. Annie becomes interested in staging theatricals to support a social union for local millworkers, but she quickly judges as hypocritical the town's agreeing to "unite" different classes at the theater but then to allow the haves to help the have-nots only by charity. Annie is one of the few in town to applaud Reverend Peck's more pervasive solution of a kind of Christian communism. After a church rumpus, Peck decides to resign, dissuades Annie from accompanying him, and plans to teach elsewhere; however, on his way to a neighboring town, he is killed in a railroad accident. Annie adopts Idella, who when sick is tended by Dr. Morrell, who in time marries Annie. *Annie Kilburn* was Howells's first novel to criticize the American social system, capitalistic competition, and band-aid charity; furthermore, it expresses sympathy for labor. His implicit message is weakened by its being carried by an eccentric minister who is killed toward the end.

Anthony, Susan B. (1820–1906). (Full name: Susan Brownell Anthony.) Woman suffrage advocate. Anthony was born in Adams, Massachusetts, and was educated in a private school in Batterville, New York, and then in a Quaker boarding school. She taught school (1835–1850); became involved in the temperance, woman's rights, and antislavery movements (1852–1969); cofounded the National Woman Suffrage Association (1869); and thereafter was steadily active in the suffrage movement (1869–1906). Anthony came by her temperance philosophy naturally; her father was a dramatic abstainer. It was through her antialcohol work that Anthony was first attracted to other progressive movements. She habitually encountered so much male resistance to all female would-be reformers that she decided that women could be politically effective only if they gained the right to vote.

Anti-Saloon League of America. Interdenominational organization advocating prohibition of liquor traffic. The movement was started by a Methodist minister, Howard Hyde Russell (1893), who began by enlisting the aid of the faculty and students at Oberlin College. Another local movement began in Washington, D.C. (also in 1893). The national Anti-Saloon League of America, which began in Washington, D.C., in 1895, cooperated with the Prohibition Party* and the Woman's Christian Temperance Union to obtain local option, county option, state prohibition, and national prohibition. Most of the backing was Protestant, but some Catholics supported it; others avoided criticizing the league out of fear of a possible nativist backlash. In the 1890s, the league had an annual budget of $2,000,000 and published bulletins through its American Issue Press. The league supported the Eighteenth Amendment to prohibit liquor sales and use nationwide. During Prohibition (1920–1933), the league urged vigorous enforcement. When Prohibition was repealed, the league campaigned in modified ways; later, it changed its name and function.

Arena**.** Monthly journal (December 1889–August 1909). The *Arena*, a crusading reform magazine, founded by B. O. Flower,* at first concentrated on eclectic religious essays but soon turned to matters of social and economic reform. It featured articles, editorials, symposia, and book reviews. Targets of its strenuous attacks included poverty, unemployment, and evil slum conditions and slumlords. Essays promoted the cause of the feminist movement by frankly discussing such topics as female education, labor, dress reform, marital rights, voting rights, and prostitution, as well as divorce, rape, alcoholism, and various other populist causes. The *Arena* supported the political and economic theories of William Jennings Bryan,* Edward Bellamy,* and Henry George,* government and prison reform; antitrust measures (*see* Sherman Anti-Trust Act); better control of public utilities; and many other reform measures. Flower, who was interested in psychical research, accepted numerous essays on spiritualism, mesmerism, astrology, and so on. Included too were essays in the field of literary criticism, for example, by James A. Herne;* poetry, for example, by Edwin Markham* and Joaquin Miller;* and fiction, for example, short stories by Hamlin Garland.* The *Arena* was in financial trouble in 1896, changed ownership several times thereafter, did better for a while but then did worse again, and finally merged with *Christian Work* (1909).

Art Pottery. Aesthetically pleasing pottery. The movement commenced in the United States in Cincinnati, Ohio, when Karl Langenbeck began painting china there in 1871. He was soon assisted by Mrs. George Ward (Maria Longworth) Nichols (Mrs. Bellamy Storer from 1886). Benn Pitman began a china-painting class for women at the Cincinnati School of Art in 1872. His students exhibited their overglaze decoration in Philadelphia in 1876. Mary Louise McLaughlin, one of his students, displayed her work in her native New York (1878) and also in Paris (1878). She started a pottery club in Cincinnati in 1879 and invited Mrs.

Nichols, who, however, evidently never received the invitation, and, miffed, started her own factory in Cincinnati in 1880, which she called Rookwood. Thomas J. Wheatley formed a firm in Cincinnati in 1880 and patented a method of underglaze decoration, but he quit in 1882. Langenbeck ran his own company from 1886 to 1887. Mrs. Nichols's Rookwood creations became preeminent in the field in the 1880s. Her artists experimented with pressed and transferred designs, carved and incised forms, and Japanese-style patterns, but they soon developed their own unique plant and animal motifs and used atomizers to apply colors more subtly (giving a distinctive Rembrandt shading). Mrs. Nichols (now Storer) expanded her company and made it more commercial; she had become the art-pottery leader in the United States by 1889 and she won a gold medal in Paris in that same year. She sold out to her associate William Taylor in 1890. Rookwood products inspired rivals. W. A. Long of Steubenville, Ohio, for example, developed a fine line of Lonhuda pottery (1892) but soon sold it to S. A. Walker of Zanesville, Ohio (1895). J. B. Owens of Cincinnati also imitated the Rookwood products (1896), as did Roseville Pottery of Cincinnati (1900). There have been many other imitators in the field of art pottery, but Maria Nichols's Rookwood offerings remain the best in the eyes of the discriminating.

Artie (1896). A collection of episodic stories by George Ade,* about Artie Blanchard, a fresh, brash, opportunistic Chicago office boy. Artie is materialistic, peppy, shallow, crudely but humorously ambitious, accurately slangy, and altogether too representative of a dangerous type of city-slicker American youth.

Ash Can School. *See* The Eight.

"The Aspern Papers" (1888). Long short story by Henry James.* The narrator is a professionally dedicated but unscrupulous American literary scholar who has come to Venice, Italy, to seek the papers of the dead Jeffrey Aspern, a renowned American poet of the early nineteenth century. Helped by Mrs. Prest, a resident in Venice for some fifteen years, the narrator rents rooms in the musty old palazzo of Juliana Bordereau, Aspern's aged American mistress who supposedly has the papers, and he confides in her niece Tina Bordereau that he wants them. Juliana callously suggests that he take Tina out to see Venetian nightlife, and the seemingly simple younger woman soon agrees to aid him in his quest. Juliana, implying that she knows his game, offers the narrator a portrait of Aspern for £1,000. When old Juliana becomes very sick, the narrator tries to rifle her desk but is caught. Ashamed, he leaves the palazzo for a few days. Upon returning, he learns that Juliana has died. Tina gives him the portrait but says that she can share the Aspern papers only with family members. The narrator refuses the gambit and stalls, but he returns next morning prepared to propose marriage. Tina, however, says that she just burned the papers one by one.

"The Aspern Papers" is full of Jamesian ambiguity. The reader is never certain that there are any Aspern papers. The Venetian scene is beautifully evoked, and the life of American expatriates is sketched in the background. The Bordereaus are American, as is the narrator, and so may be Mrs. Prest, who is thought to be modeled on James's friend Katherine De Kay Bronson, from New York and Newport, Rhode Island, before she and her husband moved to Venice, where they bought a house and entertained lavishly.

Astor, John Jacob IV (1864–1912). Capitalist, inventor, and dull personality. (He is the Astor who touches on the most significant number of 1890s events.) Jack Astor, as he was called, was born in Rhinebeck, New York, into the fabulously wealthy Astor family, whose fortune was founded by the original John Jacob Astor (1763–1848). Legendary fur trader, merchant, and Manhattan real estate investor, this patriarch married Sarah Todd, and their children included John Jacob Astor II (1791–1869) and William Backhouse Astor (1792–1875). William married Margaret Armstrong, and their children included John Jacob Astor III (1822–1890) and William Backhouse Astor, Jr. (1830–1892). These two brothers disliked each other. John Jacob Astor III married Charlotte Augusta Gibbs, and their children included William Waldorf Astor (1848–1919). William Backhouse Astor, Jr., married Caroline W. Schermerhorn, and their children included John Jacob "Jack" Astor IV. Jack Astor was thus the great-grandson of the original John Jacob Astor and the cousin of William Waldorf Astor. Jack attended St. Paul's School (Concord, New Hampshire), earned a B.S. from Harvard (1888), and patented a bicycle brake, a marine turbine, a vibrating machine to extract power gas from peat, and a pneumatic machine to blow dirt off roads, which won a prize at the World's Columbian Exposition* in Chicago in 1893.

In 1894 Astor published a science fiction novel entitled *A Journey to Other Worlds*. Set in the year 2000, it features pumping the Arctic to balance the globe, leveling the Aleutian Islands to let Japanese waters warm the Arctic, high-speed automobiles, magnetic railroads, a primitive television system, and much else. Astor built hotels in New York: the Astoria (next to and merging with his hotel-building cousin William Waldorf Astor's 1893 Waldorf Hotel, on the old Astor mansion site), the Knickerbocker, and the St. Regis. The lavish, ostentatious Waldorf-Astoria Hotel opened in 1897, complete with a ground-floor promenade, reception rooms, the Palm Garden, polyglot waiters, a thousand rooms (with 750 private bathrooms), a roof garden, a skilled manager (George C. Boldt), and a unique chef (Oscar Tschirky—"Oscar of the Waldorf"). The most lavish of the lush private balls held here was a fancy dress affair hosted by Bradley Martin and his wife for 900 guests on 10 February 1897, at a cost of $250,000. Jack Astor was also on the board of directors of several important companies, including the Equitable Life Assurance, the Illinois Central Railroad, and the Mercantile Trust. His extravagant life-style, and that of other Astors as well, was the subject of many columns in *Town Topics*,* whose owner William D'Alton Mann blackmailed many of the beautiful people to pay him handsomely for his silence. Astor owned a luxury yacht named the *Nourmahal*, enjoyed Caribbean cruises on it, placed it at the disposal of the U.S. Navy during the Spanish-American War,* outfitted an artillery battery at a personal cost of $75,000 for use in the Philippines, and was appointed inspector general (through contacts with William McKinley* and Theodore Roosevelt*) with the rank of lieutenant colonel. Finley Peter Dunne* satirized the appointment. Astor saw duty in Cuba, observed the Rough Riders' San Juan Hill charge and the bombing of the Spanish naval fleet, caught malaria, and was shipped home.

During the next few years, Astor loosely supervised his family business holdings (valued in 1900 at $200,000,000, with annual rentals of $9,000,000—exposés by Jacob Riis* caused Astor to sell fifty Fifth Avenue tenement buildings in 1900), toyed with the idea of entering politics, socialized in Manhattan and at Newport, Rhode Island, bought and raced in a number of new-fangled automobiles, yachted here and there (on his new *Noma*), experienced difficulties with his glittering, sporty wife Ava Willing Astor, was divorced by her (1909), and happily married a teenager named Madeleine Force (1911). Jack and Madeleine were on the *Titanic* when she sank on 15 April 1912. Jack drowned. Madeleine was rescued and gave birth to John Jacob Astor VI a few months later.

John Jacob Astor IV left a huge estate, $87,000,000 of which went to Vincent Astor, his son (1891–1959) by Ava. Vincent Astor became a civic-minded property owner, a friend of Samuel Gompers,* an associate of President Franklin D. Roosevelt, and the founder of *Today* magazine (which merged with *Newsweek*). He left (childless after three marriages) a $120,000,000 estate—half to his widow and half to the Vincent Astor Foundation (1948), dedicated to alleviating human suffering. The mother of John Jacob Astor IV was the Mrs. William Astor who threw unbelievable parties and long dominated New York's high-society Four Hundred, written about by Ward McAllister.* Astor's cousin William Waldorf Astor became U.S. minister to Italy (1882–1885), moved to England (1890), became a British subject (1899), and was markedly successful in British journalism and aristocratic society thereafter. The wife of his son Waldorf Astor (1879–1952) was the fabulous Lady Astor (1879–1964), the Viscountess Nancy Langhorne Shaw Astor.

Astronomers. As in most other decades throughout history, astronomy made steady strides forward in the 1890s. Six American astronomers active in the 1890s, selected from among dozens probably nearly as competent, are Edward Emerson Barnard (1857–1923), Samuel Pierpoint Langley (1834–1906), Percival Lowell (1855–1916), Albert Abraham Michelson (1852–1931), Simon Newcomb (1835–1909), and Edward Charles Pickering (1846–1919).

Barnard was born in Nashville, Tennessee, graduated from Vanderbilt University (1887), and was named junior astronomer at Lick Observatory, Mount Hamilton, California (1887–1895), and then professor of astronomy and astronomer of the Yerkes Observatory, Lake Geneva, Wisconsin, administered by the University of Chicago (1895–1923). He went with personnel from the U.S.

Naval Observatory in Washington, D.C., to observe the solar eclipse visible in Sumatra in 1901. An enthusiastic, incredibly keen-sighted visual observer and a talent photographer, he discovered sixteen comets, located the fifth through ninth satellites of Jupiter, contributed to celestial photography, and tracked what may be the fastest star in the cosmo
: was also a competent author and editor.

Langley, born in Roxbury, Massachusetts, was educated in Boston high schools and briefly abroad. After practicing civil engineering and architecture, he became the assistant director of the Harvard College Observatory (1865), the director of the Naval Academy Observatory (1866), and the director of the Allegheny Observatory in Pittsburgh, Pennsylvania, and professor of physics and astronomy at what became the University of Pittsburgh (1867–1887). Langley invented the bolometer, an instrument to ascertain exceedingly small differences in temperature, especially in solar rays and spectra. He was appointed secretary of the Smithsonian Institution in Washington, D.C. (1887–1906). While there, he helped found the Astrophysical Observatory (and the National Zoological Park as well). His work, beginning in 1887 and with Alexander Graham Bell* in 1891, concerning the movements of surfaces through the air helped strengthen national belief in the feasibility of heavier-than-air flight, and he launched two unmanned airplanes (1896) and developed bigger ones which failed (1898, 1903).

Lowell, born in Boston, graduated from Harvard University (1876), was active in the business world, and traveled extensively in the Far East. He wrote about his experiences in the Far East where, incidentally, he associated with Ernest Fenollosa.* Lowell suddenly grew interested in the theory that the planet Mars had canals built by intelligent beings. He devoted his fortune to the establishment of the Lowell Observatory in Flagstaff, Arizona (1894), mainly to study the possibility. He founded a journal (1898) to promulgate the now totally discredited theory and published widely on the subject, for example, *Mars* (1895). More significantly, he predicted the approximate position of an unknown planet that was discovered and named Pluto fourteen years after his death.

Michelson, born in Strzelno, Poland, migrated as an infant with his family to California, graduated from the U.S. Naval Academy (1873), taught chemistry and physics there (1875–1879), and resigned from the navy (1881) to pursue further study abroad. He later taught at what became Case Western Reserve (1883–1889), at Clark University (1889–1892—*see* Universities), where he determined the speed of light with great accuracy, developed the interferometer for measuring astronomical distances by means of light-wave lengths, and conducted ether-drift experiments (with Edward M. Morley) which helped lead to Albert Einstein's theory of relativity. Michelson was also interested in precise measurements of lengths and weights, was president of the American Physical Society (1901), and was the first American to receive the Nobel Prize in physics (1907).

Newcomb, born in Wallace, Nova Scotia, ran away from home (1853), graduated from Harvard's Lawrence Scientific School (1858), and became a mathematics professor at the U.S. Naval Observatory (1861–1897; he ultimately held the rank of rear admiral), where he was also superintendent of instruments and procedures relating to astronomy (1877–1897). He also taught at the Johns Hopkins University (1884–1894, 1898–1900). He was a dedicated astronomical observer, mathematician, and scientific writer, concerned primarily with the positions and movements of astronomical bodies, particularly planets. He summarized much of his vast work in *The Elements of the Four Inner Planets and the Fundamental Constants of Astronomy* (1895) and continued to publish research about the moon, asteroids, and the outer planets. After his retirement, he wrote *The Stars* (1901), which became immensely popular. He also wrote about economics, finance, and politics, in the realm of science fiction, and an autobiography—*Reminiscences of an Astronomer* (1903).

Pickering, born in Boston, graduated from Harvard's Lawrence Scientific School (1865), taught at Harvard University (1865–1867) and the Massachusetts Institute of Technology (1867–1876), and then returned to Harvard to teach astronomy, where he became director of the college observatory (1877–1919). While there, he engaged in innovative stellar photometric and spectroscopic studies, invented the meridian photometer, with it supervised gauging the brightness of some 80,000 stars, and undertook the classification of star spectra. In 1891 he also helped establish Harvard's observatory at Arequipa, Peru, with his young brother William Henry Pickering, who, also an astronomer, discovered Saturn's ninth satellite and erected Lowell's Flagstaff telescope.

At Fault (1890). Novel by Kate Chopin.* Thérèse Lafirme, a young Creole Catholic woman, inherits a plantation from her deceased husband and takes over its management. She faces changes. She moves and rebuilds the house because a railroad is encroaching. Needing money, she permits a lumber mill to invade the pastoral scene. She remains staunchly moral, even after David Hosmer, the tall northern mill manager, enters the picture and proves upsettingly attractive. A point against him is his divorce from his alcoholic wife Fanny, whom Thérèse persuades David to remarry. Next, David's sister, the naive Unitarian Melicent, and Thérèse's nephew Grégoire fall briefly in love, but after Grégoire shoots a mill arsonist he flees to Texas where he dies, and she moves out. The remarriage of David and Fanny does not go well, despite visits from some of Fanny's vapid St. Louis friends. Fanny, jealous of Thérèse, suddenly drowns in the nearby Red River. Time passes. Thérèse goes abroad. One day, on a trail up from New Orleans, David and Thérèse meet again and soon wed. *At Fault*, Chopin's first novel, is autobiographical and weak. Widowed Thérèse resembles widowed Kate Chopin in several obvious ways. Thérèse's Place-du-Bois plantation is a mirror of the Chopin family holding at Cloutierville, Natchitouches Parish, in north-central Louisiana. Further, the romantically happy ending, prepared for by a drowning, is troublesome. Nevertheless, *At Fault* valuably explores such problems as divorce and conservative ethics and the need of an individual—particularly a woman—to confront change, social strictures, and passion with personal honesty. As such, *At Fault* led directly to Chopin's masterpiece, *The Awakening*.*

***Atlantic Monthly*.** Distinguished magazine devoted to literary, artistic, and political matters. It was founded in Boston in 1857 by leading New England cultural spokesmen and then edited by a sequence of important establishment writers, including James Russell Lowell, James T. Fields, William Dean Howells,* Thomas Bailey Aldrich* (1881–1890), Horace Elisha Scudder (1890–1898), Walter Hines Page* (1898–1899), and Bliss Perry (1899–1909). At first the *Atlantic Monthly* favored Boston Brahminism, but it became more political during the Civil War; gradually, it accepted more non–New England writing and broadened its coverage to include non-belletristic departments. Aldrich made the *Atlantic Monthly* more conservative again; he published works by Henry James* and Sarah Orne Jewett,* for example, among many others. Scudder again broadened the magazine's interests to include political items by Theodore Roosevelt* and others. Page and then Perry accepted controversial political and sociological essays by Jacob Riis* and others.

Austin, Mary (1868–1934). (Full name: Mary Hunter Austin.) Writer. Mary Hunter was born in Carlinville, Illinois, graduated from Blackburn College there (1888), and then homesteaded with her widowed mother and her brother in the Tejon district of the southern San Joaquin Valley, California (beginning in 1888). She taught school in Mountain View (1889–1891) and married Stafford Wallace Austin in 1891. Through the 1890s, her husband managed a failing irrigation project in Owens Valley, taught school in Lone Pine, became a superintendent of schools, and then the registrar of the Land Office at Independence. The couple had a mentally retarded daughter born in 1892. Meanwhile, Mary Austin published a short story in the *Overland Monthly* (1892), and taught school again (at Bishop, 1895–1897; Lone Pine, 1897–1999; and Los Angeles, 1899–1900). Upon returning to Independence, she published further (in the *Atlantic Monthly*,* *Cosmopolitan Magazine*,* *Munsey's Magazine*,* and *Out West*—edited by her friend Charles F. Lummis*) and developed friendships with various West Coast writers, including Ambrose Bierce,* Charlotte Perkins Gilman,* Jack London,* Ina Coolbrith,* Edwin Markham,* John Muir,* and Charles Warren Stoddard.*

Mary Austin had an illustrious literary career. Her total production included thirty-five books, in addition to hundreds of shorter items—novels, short stories, plays, poems, and essays. As for her marriage, it suffered; she was estranged (1906) from her husband, who charged her with desertion (1907) and divorced her (1914—the year their institutionalized daughter died). By this time, Austin had visited England, where, in 1909, she met Henry James* and other celebrated writers, and had become involved in the woman's rights movement (from 1912). She moved to Santa Fe, New Mexico (1924), where she undertook reform work for Native Americans of the Southwest (from 1925). Austin's best work, much of which is rooted in her 1890s experiences, includes *The Land of Little Rain* (1903), a classic, composed of sensitive sketches about the desert, its people, animals, and plants; *Isidro* (1905), a melodramatic novel featuring an abandoned child and racial overtones in a southern California setting; *The Flock* (1906), nonfictional studies of shepherds' habits; *Santa Lucia: A Common Story* (1908), a novel of manners about marriages in California Anglo society; *Lost Borders* (1909), fictional sketches showing that desert inhabitants must adjust to their environment to survive; *The Arrow Maker* (1911), a play about a Native American medicine woman and her revenge; *No. 26 Jayne Street* (1920), about New York radicalism; *The American Rhythm* (1924), concerning Native American poetry; *The Land of Journeys' Ending* (1924), nonfictional sketches of New Mexican and Arizona landscapes; and *One Smoke Stories* (1934), tales in which the land and its peoples interact. Her autobiography, *Earth Horizon* (1932), reveals her mystical love of nature and the importance she placed on individualism and personal freedom.

Automobiles. Steam-driven horseless carriages were in operation in England and on the Continent in the second half of the eighteenth century and in the nineteenth century until the 1880s and beyond. But, beginning in the 1860s, experiments in Germany, France, and Austria were conducted with internal-combustion engines, using volatile liquids as fuel. Gottlieb Daimler, an engineer and manufacturer, began with a motorcycle and developed an internal-combustion, one-cylinder, hot-tube engine (1885). Karl Benz, another engineer and manufacturer, began with a tricycle and developed an internal-combustion, one-cylinder, spark-ignition engine (also 1885). Daimler and Wilhelm Maybach, an engineer, patented a V–2 engine (1889) and demonstrated a real automobile at the Paris Exposition (also in 1889). Within a few years, great progress was being made in France, Germany, and England. Engineers, often working independently and far apart, created numerous innovations. Races were held to popularize the automobile. Emile Constant Levassor won a Paris-to-Rouen race in 1894 and, the next year, drove 740 miles from Paris to Bordeaux in forty-eight hours, averaging fifteen miles an hour.

The United States, with a restless population, would have seemed to be more than ready for independence, which the automobile could provide, at least as early as 1890, the official date of the closing of the frontier, according to historian Frederick Jackson Turner.* Cars would obviously have been a welcome alternative to bicycles and horse-drawn vehicles. Bicycles had limited speed, range, and carrying capacity; horses created unbearable pollution (manure, urine, carcasses, flies) in big cities. And yet American inventors remained mysteriously behind their European counterparts. Still, George B. Brayton, an engineer, developed an early two-cycle engine in 1872 and exhibited it in Philadelphia in 1876. In 1879 George B. Selden, a patent attorney and inventor in Rochester, New York, applied for a patent on his so-called road engine (issued in 1895, subsequently causing a lawsuit with Henry Ford,* resolved in 1911). Charles

Edgar Duryea, assisted by his brother J. Frank Duryea, both of whom were bicycle mechanics, drove a one-cylinder, gasoline-powered car of their design and manufacture on the streets of Springfield, Massachusetts (21 September 1893). Charles Duryea had read about Benz's car in a magazine (1889), invented the spray carburetor (1892), was the first to put pneumatic tires on automobile wheels (1893), and with his brother founded the Duryea Motor Wagon Company (1895). Frank Duryea won an automobile race in Chicago the same year, driving a two-cylinder Duryea car. He negotiated a fifty-five-mile route in eleven hours. The Duryeas participated in a motorcade from London to Brighton in 1896. Soon thereafter, the brothers quarreled and stopped working together.

Meanwhile, other Americans were experimenting and producing better than their counterparts in Europe. Josiah Dallas Dort and William Crapo Durant, carriage makers, formed a corporation in Flint, Michigan, to build cars efficiently by controlling all aspects of the production of parts and their assembly (1893). Elwood G. Haynes, an engineer, developed a one-cylinder internal-combustion engine (1894), with the help of Elmer Apperson and his brother Edgar Apperson, machinists, and also Jonathan D. Maxwell, an automobile enthusiast (1894). Haynes and the Appersons drove it at six miles an hour in Kokomo, Indiana, built Haynes-Apperson cars until 1904, split up over long-standing disputes, and then continued separately to sell Haynes models and Apperson models for years thereafter. Hiram Percy Maxim, automotive pioneer son of the Maxim gun inventor and himself the inventor of the silencer (and the author of *Horseless Carriage Days* [1937]), experimented with little internal-combustion engines on a tricycle in Lynn, Massachusetts (1892–1895). He was hired by Albert A. Pope, ex-Civil War colonel and later manufacturing head of America's largest bicycle company, to join him in his Hartford, Connecticut, factory and produce great numbers of cars (1895).

Detroit, soon to dominate the automobile industry, became involved next. Charles Brady King, automotive pioneer, drove the first gasoline-powered car there in 1896. Henry Ford,* a Detroit electrical engineer and inventive genius, tested his quadricycle there (1896), and with friends financed the Detroit Automobile Company (1899). Other prominent names emerged at the very end of the 1890s. Ransom Eli Olds, a machinist, built cars in Lansing, Michigan (1896–1899), then moved to Detroit (1899), and soon was ordering parts from John Dodge and his brother Horace Dodge, both machinists. Alexander Winton, a bicycle manufacturer, produced automobiles in Cleveland (from 1896); he was the first person to take a long-distance trip by car (Cleveland to New York in 1898). David D. Buick, an engineer and plumbing-fixtures manufacturer, built cars (1899–1902), failed commercially, but started again with new backers. James Ward Packard, a businessman, started his car business in Warren, Ohio (by 1900). Of course, there were many others.

The early twentieth century saw enormous changes and growth in the automobile industry. Some, 4,192 cars were manufactured in 1900. Olds, the most successful manufacturer at this time, built 600 Oldsmobiles in 1901, far more thereafter; but, when he disagreed with his financial backer Samuel L. Smith, a copper and lumber magnate, he returned to Lansing to build cars called the Reo after his initials (1905). Henry B. Joy, son of a railroad magnate, and some wealthy friends, including William F. Murphy, a lumberman, gained control of the Packard Company and established it in Detroit (1903). The backers of Ford criticized him for racing too much, released him, and reorganized with Henry M. Leland, a toolmaker, to manufacture a new car—called the Cadillac—in 1902. Leland was so precise that his automotive parts were the first to be interchangeable. With fresh support, Ford started the Ford Motor Company in 1903, with John and Horace Dodge as stockholding suppliers of parts, and soon produced his Model T (1908). Meanwhile, William Crapo Durant, head of the Durant-Dort Carriage Company of Flint, Michigan (from 1886), gained control of Buick's floundering company (1904), moved it to Flint, and soon was a leading manufacturer. Maxwell, who had helped build Haynes-Apperson cars, worked thereafter for Olds and still later for the highly successful Briscoe brothers Benjamin and Frank (1903), Detroit steel-metal manufacturers. The Big Four as of 1908—Buick, Ford, Maxwell-Briscoe, and Reo—all got their start in the turbulent 1890s.

Not to be forgotten are two salient facts. Through these early years of the evolution of gasoline-powered automobiles, steam-driven cars were also temporarily popular, and so were electric cars. But they could not long compete with the gas-guzzlers of the early twentieth century. As for trucks, John M. Mack, a teamster with exceptional mechanical ability, and his younger brother August F. Mack invested in a Brooklyn wagon factory (1893), repaired wagons and carriages (1894–1895), expanded (1897), and incorporated as the Mack Brothers with their oldest brother William C. Mack in 1901 (between William and John was another brother, Charles W. Mack; between John and Augustus, another, Joseph S. Mack). John and Augustus Mack built a steam car (1894) and an electric car (1896), but then their firm began to manufacture buses and trucks. Their first truck, which had four cylinders and thirty-six horsepower, could go from twelve to twenty miles an hour. The Mack Brothers—all five of them—soon built fifteen trucks (1900–1903) and were well on their way to success.

Incidentally, the horseless carriage was first called an "automobile" in the New York *Times* (3 January 1899).

The Awakening (1899). Novel by Kate Chopin.* Edna Pontellier is the wife of Léonce Pontellier. Now twenty-eight years of age, Edna is tall, graceful, vibrant, and sensual, with a Presbyterian background from her family's old Kentucky and Mississippi days. Léonce is a Creole businessman in New Orleans. Though he married outside his Catholic and French background, he values tradition, An authoritarian, he is cold, stiff, and rather uncommunicative, but he is a good provider. The couple have two sons, sickly Raoul, age five, and temperamental Etienne, age four. During a little vacation on Grand Isle in the sun-drenched

Gulf, Edna meets and is attracted to Robert Lebrun, a twenty-six-year-old Creole, who finds her desirable but predictably restrains himself. When the Pontelliers return to New Orleans, Edna begins to revolt. She stops receiving callers. She seeks comfort from Adèle Ratignolle, a friend who has devoted herself exclusively to her husband and their children—four in number to date. Further, Edna turns more seriously to her hobby of painting and associates more confidentially with Mademoiselle Reisz, a skillful, sensitive, nonconformist pianist. Edna's stuffy, male-chauvinist father and her wise old physician Dr. Mandelet talk with the uneasy woman. When her two little boys are at the Pontellier family plantation at Iberville and Léonce is in New York on business, Edna daringly attends the horse races at the Jockey Club, where she meets Alcée Arobin, a lawyer, man about town, and rake. Although she recalls Robert with deeper affection, she and Alcée begin a brief passionate love affair. Edna moves into a smaller house, paints more—not very well—and then welcomes Robert home after his long business trip to Mexico. When Léonce returns, he is puzzled by his wife's conduct, but he does little except try to preserve appearances for the sake of his reputation and business. One night, urgent word comes to interrupt Edna and Robert at conversation: Her friend Adèle is in labor and needs her. In the pain of childbirth, Adèle warns Edna to remember her own children. Edna returns, but Robert has left. His ultimate rejection of her is owing to timidity, business, and family morality. Soon therafter, Edna visits Grand Isle again, tells some friends she is going for a chilly swim, disrobes, and deliberately swims too far and drowns herself.

The Awakening is partly autobiographical. Kate Chopin must have had many of the peppy qualities of Edna Pontellier, whose husband Léonce, sadly, may have been modeled to a degree after Chopin's husband Oscar. It is certain that Dr. Mandelet is patterned after Chopin's family physician and friend Dr. Frederick Kolbenheyer. And Chopin must have known many earth-mothers as restricted and dull as poor Adèle Ratignolle. *The Awakening* was ahead of its time. Chopin was reviled for it. Widely banned, it earned its author only $145 in three years. Nevertheless, it is a novel of consummate artistry and a woman's liberation document of primary importance. Several of its scenes are beautifully staged, and much of its imagery is stunning. The message is vital and timeless: A "safe" marriage can be stifling, loneliness is deadly, and a woman may be defeated but still win.

B

Baker, George Pierce (1866–1935). Educator. Born in Providence, Rhode Island, Baker graduated from Harvard (1888) and taught literature at Harvard (1888–1924) and at Yale (1925–1935). Baker is remembered today for having held playwriting classes with great success for such Harvard students as Philip Barry, Sidney Howard, Eugene O'Neill, and Thomas Wolfe. Baker invited well-known dramatists, including Clyde Fitch,* to visit his classes and discuss their techniques with his students.

Barbara Frietchie (1899). Play by Clyde Fitch.* Union Captain Trumbull meets and falls in love with Confederate sympathizer Miss Frietchie in Frederick and Hagerstown, Maryland (where the playwright's parents first met). After the captain is wounded at the Battle of Frederick, he is hidden and tended to in the heroine's own bedroom, but he dies. Now preferring the Union cause, Barbara waves the Stars and Stripes from her balcony. General Stonewall Jackson gallantly orders that no shots be fired, but a disgruntled rival for Barbara's hand enters and shoots the heroine dead. *Barbara Frietchie* proved a popular play, although it is overly melodramatic, even silly, and the historical Barbara Frietchie was ninety-six years old and sick when Jackson made his appearance in town.

Barber, Charles Edward (1840–1917). Engraver. Born in London, he accompanied his family to America when his father, a skilled engraver, obtained a position at the Philadelphia mint. Young Barber became his father's assistant in 1869. After his father's death in 1880, Barber received a presidential appointment as chief engraver. He designed the 50¢, 25¢, 10¢, and 5¢ coins that were in use from 1892 to 1916. He designed the back of the World's Columbian Exposition* commemorative silver half dollar coin in 1893, which was accepted in preference to the design submitted by the renowned Augustus Saint-Gaudens.* Barber's Columbian design shows a ship over two hemispheres. Barber also designed coins for China, Hawaii, Japan, fourteen Pan-American countries, and the Philippine Islands, and was also a sculptor in miniature and a fine musician. He married Martha E. Jones in 1875 (the couple had one child; Mrs. Barber died in 1898) and Caroline Gaston in 1902. Charles Barber's work was always held in the highest esteem.

Barton, Clara (1821–1912). (Full name: Clarissa Harlowe Barton.) Humanitarian. Born in Oxford, Massachusetts, Barton taught school for a while but quit because of a throat ailment and then worked in the Patent Office in Washington, D.C. (1854–1861). She became a battle-site nurse during the Civil War (1861–1865), where she abundantly earned her sobriquet "The Angel of the Battlefield," and then established a bureau of records to collect data on missing and dead Union soldiers (1865–1869). Barton went to Geneva, Switzerland (1869), to improve her health, but soon became a volunteer in the International Red Cross to aid victims of the Franco-Prussian War. When she returned to the United States in 1873, she organized various groups to affiliate with the International Red Cross, formed them into the American Association of the Red Cross (1881), and became the first president of the American Red Cross (1882–1904). She represented the United States at international conferences; for example, in Geneva, 1884; Karlsruhe, Germany, 1887; Rome, Italy, 1892; Vienna, Austria, 1897; and St. Petersburg, Russia 1903. She also organized the shipment of relief supplies for victims of yellow fever in Florida (1887), the flood in Johnstown, Pennsylvania (1889), a famine in Russia (1891), a South Carolina hurricane (1893), and a massacre in Armenia (1896); for American soldiers during the Spanish-American War* (1898); and for victims of a hurricane at Galveston, Texas (1900). Her personal style and accounting methods were criticized (1900), but she stayed on (until 1904). Barton wrote *An Official History of the Red Cross* (1882), *The Red Cross in Peace and War* (1902), *A Story of the Red Cross* (1904), and *Story of My Childhood* (1907).

Baseball. *See* Sports.

Basketball. *See* Sports.

Baum, Lyman Frank (1856–1919). Author. Born in Chittenango, New York, Baum became a journalist in South Dakota (1880), edited a trade magazine for decorators of store windows, published a popular book entitled *Father Goose: His Book* (1899), and then struck it rich with *The Wonderful Wizard of Oz* (1900). In this immortal classic a Kansas farm girl named Dorothy is carried by a tornado to the fantastic land of Oz. To get home again, she must travel to the Emerald City, capital of Oz. On her way there, Dorothy encounters a tin woodsman, a talking scarecrow, and a cowardly lion. Many adventures cause her to wonder whether life in Oz is more fun than life in Kansas. *The Wonderful Wizard of Oz* was adapted into a successful play in 1902. Baum took profits from Oz and moved to Pasadena, California, where he wrote thirteen more Oz books, including *The Woggle-Bug Book* (1905), *Ozma of Oz* (1907), *The Emerald City of Oz* (1909), *The Road to Oz* (1909), *Tik-Tok Man of Oz* (1914), *The Lost Princess of Oz* (1915), and *The Scarecrow of Oz* (1915). He also wrote twenty-four girls' books using Edith Van Dyne as a pen name and six boys' books using Floyd Akers as a pen name. Baum wrote more than sixty books in all and died in Hollywood.

Bayou Folk (1894). A collection of twenty-three short stories by Kate Chopin.* They are unified by locale and by the common theme of love, its mutations, and its consequences. Some stories feature reappearing characters. The best story in *Bayou Folk* is "Désirée's Baby." Orphaned Désirée is adopted by a loving family, grows into a beautiful and charming young woman, marries Armond Aubigny, and bears his child. When the proud, hot-tempered father discerns Negroid features in the son, he rejects Désirée and her baby, and she disappears into the swamp with her child. Soon thereafter, Armond finds among his family papers evidence that his mother was an African American. The central character of "Old Aunt Peggy" is a freed slave, aged 125, who declines to leave the family of her former owners. In "La Bella Zoraïde," a slave-owning woman refuses to let her light-skinned slave Zoraïde marry field-worker Mézor, her African American lover. She gives away their child and sells Mézor. Instead of marrying the man her mistress has capriciously selected for her, Zoraïde goes insane and fondles a doll that substitutes for her missing child. "A Lady of Bayou St. John" is also valuable. In it, the heroine misses her Confederate soldier husband during the Civil War, falls in love with a neighbor man, and plans to leave with him for France—until, that is, word comes that her husband has been killed. Then planned-for love gives way to memories of past love. Other stories in *Bayou Folk* are also powerful, ingeniously plotted, and often sad in tone. This book, published by Houghton, Mifflin in Boston and New York, was well received and was enthusiastically reviewed. Chopin's second volume of short stories, *A Night in Acadie*,* published in 1897 by a less well-known firm, proved to be less successful.

Beard, Dan (1850–1941). (Full name: Daniel Carter Beard.) Illustrator, author, and pioneer worker with boys. Beard was born in Cincinnati, Ohio, into a family of artists. His father was a successful portrait painter. An uncle was an animal painter. Two sisters were illustrators (and authors). Three brothers were painters and cartoonists. After graduating from Worrall's Academy in Covington, Kentucky, as a civil engineer, Beard practiced in Cincinnati and then was hired as a Mississippi Valley surveyor for a New York map company. When he suddenly sold an illustration of a fish to *Scribner's Magazine** (1878), he decided to study at the Art Students League in New York (1880–1884), and he began to place illustrations in books, literary journals, and comic magazines. He published an essay in *St. Nicholas* magazine on tentless camping (1882) and followed it with a book entitled *What to Do and How to Do It: The American Boys Handy Book* (1882, his most popular work), which included his own illustrations. He became an instructor in illustration at the women's school of Applied Design (1893–1900). His continued interest in boys, and in books and pictures for them regarding woodcraft and camping, led to his fame in this field and—early in the twentieth century—to his concentrating on boys' organizations, and culminated in an organization called Boy Pioneers. This group became the inspiration for the Boy Scouts, which was founded in England in 1908 and soon spread to America and then worldwide. (Ernest Thompson Seton* cooperated with Beard in this endeavor.) To millions of American boys, Beard became known as Uncle Dan. He wrote more than twenty books in all. His 1890s works are *Moonlight and Six Feet of Romance* (1892) and *Outdoor Games for All Seasons* (1896). One of his best accomplishments was the spirited and satirical illustrations for the first edition of *A Connecticut Yankee in King Arthur's Court** by Mark Twain.* Beard married Beatrice Alice Jackson in 1894 (the couple had two children). He was long a Swedenborgian and later a Quaker. Beard was professionally active into his nineties. His autobiography is *Hardly a Man Is Now Alive* (1939).

Beau Brummell (1890). Play by Clyde Fitch.* Its episodic action divides into four main parts: Brummell's succeeding in the court of King George IV, his fall from grace into poverty because of the treachery of former friends, his ruined old age in Calais, and his being cheered by the king and his courtiers at the end. Fitch gained his understanding of Beau Brummell by reading Captain William Jesse's biography of Brummell and William Blanchard Jerrold's play deriving from that biography. Fitch's play is well written, with sharp characterization and witty dialogue. A smash hit when it was first performed, it starred the popular but temperamental actor Richard Mansfield, who had commissioned Fitch, then unknown, to write it but who then selfishly took most of the plaudits.

Belasco, David (1853–1931). Dramatist, theater manager, producer, and actor. He was born in San Francisco of English Jewish parents. The family resided in Victoria, British Columbia, Canada, during the Civil War. Part of this time, young Belasco was taught in a monastery under the supervision of a Catholic priest. Back in San Francisco again, he worked in his father's fruit store and attended school irregularly (until 1871). While still a teenager, he wrote plays based on cheap novels. He put on one such drama in a noisy beer garden when he was fourteen. He became an itinerant actor along the California coast, then a stage manager at Maguire's Theater in San Francisco (1874), an assistant to James A. Herne* at Baldwin's Theater there (1876), and finally its director (1878). Meanwhile, Belasco was cobbling revisions of old plays, writing numerous plays of his own, directing, and acting. He and Herne, among other collaborative ventures, rewrote an English drama as the popular *Hearts of Oak* and took it to New York, where it failed (1880). Belasco returned two years later with a smash revival of *The Octoroon; or, Life in Louisiana*, Dion Boucicault's popular 1859 melodrama. The rest of Belasco's 1880s in New York were filled with low-paid hack work, successful directing for others (notably at the Madison Square Theater and the Lyceum Theater), and collaborations. Best was his *May Blossom* (1884, domestic drama, a variation of the *Hearts of Oak* plot).

Then came the 1890s. He coauthored *The Girl I Left Behind Me* (1893, Indian and U.S. Army melodrama) and profited handsomely with his *The Heart of Maryland* (1895, a complex Civil War play). Next came his famous *Madame Butterfly** (1900). He followed his lavishly mounted historical play *Du Barry* (1901) with *Adrea* (1904, a romantic tragedy, coauthored with J. L. Long). Belasco's later career confirmed his stage genius. In addition to producing works by others and starring his professional discoveries and friends, Belasco wrote and presented *The Girl of the Golden West* (1905, made into Giacomo Puccini's 1910 *La Fanciulla del West*) and *The Return of Peter Grimm* (1911, a play about a ghost). In 1907 Belasco developed his own Belasco Theater at West 44th Street. By this time, the colorful, eccentric, genially demanding workaholic was the most successful independent writer-producer of plays in the United States. His contributions to the American theater include the use of bizarre sets, combined with realistic stage devices and innovative special effects. After World War I, the evolution of the American stage pretty much left him behind. David Belasco married Cecilia Loverich in 1873 (the couple had two children). He often wore a clerical collar, in loyalty to his early Catholic education; this eccentricity earned him the title of the Bishop of Broadway. His autobiography is *The Theatre through Its Stage Door* (1919).

Bell, Alexander Graham (1847–1922). Inventor and physicist. Bell was born in Edinburgh, Scotland, to a family concerned with elocution and also problems of deafness. His mother was deaf. His father and grandfather trained him to teach deaf persons to talk. He also studied anatomy and music. He and his parents moved from London to Ontario, Canada, for reasons of family health. Bell taught vocal physiology at Boston University (from 1873) and experimented with harmonic telegraphy. He received his first patent on the telephone in 1876. (His claims were completely validated only in 1893, by a U.S. Supreme Court decision.) He experimented successfully with telephones in his own laboratory (1876), married a deaf woman (1877), and became an American citizen (1882). Remaining active through the 1890s and well into the twentieth century, he became concerned with aviation (1891, working part of the time with Samuel Pierpont Langley—*see* Astronomy), inaugurated telephone service between New York and Chicago in a much-publicized ceremony (1892), was named regent of the Smithsonian Institution (1898), was president of the National Geographic Society (1898–1904), and began (1907) to encourage a group of scientists who later developed the hydrofoil. Bell tried to induce Mark Twain* to invest in his new-fangled invention, the telephone, but the humorist would have none of it.

Bellamy, Edward (1850–1898). Author and social reformer. Born in Chicopee Falls, Massachusetts, Bellamy was the son of a Baptist minister. Young Bellamy had a religious experience followed by baptism (1864); failed the physical examination for West Point (1867); studied briefly at Union College, where he became interested in socialism; visited and studied in Germany (1868–1869); read for the law in Springfield, Massachusetts; and was admitted to the bar (1871) but did not practice. Instead, he turned to free-lance journalism in New York (1872) and in Springfield (1872–1877 and 1880–1882); sickness and travel caused the hiatus. While still a newspaperman, Bellamy wrote considerable fiction, always romantic and usually dull, and often based on theories of spiritual brotherhood, social equality, and commonsense economics. In 1884 Bellamy retired in order to write. Along came *Looking Backward: 2000–1887** (1888). He had employed the dramatic device of hypnosis in his 1880 novel *Dr. Heidenhoff's Process*, and he used it again at the outset of *Looking Backward* when its narrator-hero is hypnotized in 1887 and awakens in the year 2000 in what has become a socialist utopia.

The immense popularity of this novel had several results. Clubs were established, beginning in 1889, to promote its tenets. A "Nationalist Movement" followed in 1889, partly led by Bellamy himself, who also founded the *New Nation* (1891–1894) to crusade for economic betterment through nationalization of industries. Bellamy and his cohorts influenced the Populist Party* from 1891 to 1894; the policies thus promulgated found their way into the 1892 platform of the People's Party. Finally, Bellamy published *Equality** (1897), which, though partly a romantic novel, is mostly a tract. Never strong and in addition suffering from chronic tuberculosis, Bellamy died the following year. His minor works include *The Blindman's World and Other Stories** (1898) and *The Duke of Stockbridge: A Romance of Shays' Rebellion** (1900). Henry George* deplored Bellamy's *Looking Backward* as a castle in the air with clouds for its only foundation. On the other hand, Thorstein Veblen* regarded the book as an inspiration; William Dean Howells wrote in a "Biographical Sketch" for *The Blindman's World* that Bellamy's romantic imagination almost equalled that of Nathaniel Hawthorne; and John Dewey* praised Bellamy as "the American prophet," for being the first to understand democracy in human terms.

Bennett, James Gordon (1841–1918). Editor. Born in New York City, Bennett was the son of the distinguished editor and publisher of the same name. Young Bennett was educated mainly in France, was a U.S. Naval lieutenant during the Civil War (1861–1865), and then entered the world of journalism. He was named managing editor of his father's New York *Herald* (1866), and, when his father retired in 1871 he became its director (1867–1918). During his long tenure, the *Herald* stressed military, navy, and shipping news. He developed scoops by dispatching correspondents to seek out the news. He sent Henry M. Stanley to Africa to find Dr. David Livingstone (1870–1871), financed an expedition to seek the Northwest Passage (1871), sent Januarius Aloysius MacGahan to the Crimea and elsewhere (1873–1875), and financed an Arctic expedition (1879–1881). When Bennett broke his engagement to marry, he was horsewhipped and then involved in a harmless duel with his ex-financée's brother (1877). After these events, Bennett lived mostly in France, but he foolishly continued to manage his paper and other publishing ventures by cable and without permitting subordinates to have sufficient independence. He and a partner formed the Commercial Cable Company, laid transatlantic cables (1883), broke the monopoly of Jay Gould* thereby, and profited handsomely in the process. Bennett established a Paris edition of the *Herald* in 1887. Even though the New York *Herald* was not doing well financially, he moved its headquarters to Broadway and Sixth Avenue (Herald Square) and thus increased circulation. During the Spanish-American War* (1898), he spent about $300,000 on war news services. The yellow journalism tactics of William Randolph Hearst* and Joseph Pulitzer,* however, at this time and at other times, hurt Bennett. In 1899 he hired Guglielmo Marconi to report the America's Cup races by radio.* Taking and spending about $1,000,000 annually from *Herald* profits, Bennett was devoted to polo and to racing yachts, automobiles, airplanes, and balloons. He married widowed Baroness de Reuter in Paris (1914). He is remembered as a domineering, eccentric, crotchety, and notorious man.

Berenson, Bernard (1865–1959). Art scholar, critic, connoisseur, and author. Born near Vilnius, Lithuania, to a Jewish family, he migrated with them to Boston (about 1872), studied under Charles Eliot Norton* and William James* at Harvard, graduated (1887), and married Mary Logan Whitall Smith Costello (1900), the sister of author Logan Pearsall Smith. The Berensons settled at Settignano, just northeast of Florence, Italy, where they bought, restored, and decorated a huge eighteenth-century villa, called Villa I Tatti (1900), in which Berenson amassed a collection of art works, books, and photographs. He became the world's leading authority on Italian Renaissance paintings. He was sequestered in Tuscany during World War II. His publications include *Venetian Painters of the Renaissance* (1894), *The Study and Criticism of Italian Art* (1901, 1902, 1915), *The Drawings of Florentine Painters* (1903, rev. 1938), and many later works. Beginning in 1894, Berenson helped Isabella Stewart Gardner* amass her art collection at Fenway Court, Boston. He also was a major influence on Edith Wharton,* from the time of their first effective meeting (Paris, 1909).

Best-selling Books, 1888–1901. The following have been tabulated by statistical researchers as the books by American authors selling best within their first ten years of publication: James Lane Allen, *The Choir Invisible* (1897); Irving Bacheller, *Eben Holden* (1900); Lyman Frank Baum,* *The Wonderful Wizard of Oz* (1900); Winston Churchill,* *Richard Carvel** (1899) and *The Crisis** (1900);

Ralph Connor, *Black Rock* (1898); Stephen Crane,* *The Red Badge of Courage** (1895); F. Marion Crawford,* *Don Orsino* (1892) and *In the Palace of the King* (1900); Richard Harding Davis,* *Soldiers of Fortune** (1897); Margaret Deland, *John Ward, Preacher* (1888); Paul Leicester Ford,* *The Honorable Peter Stirling, and What People Thought of Him** (1894) and *Janice Meredith: A Story of the American Revolution** (1899); Archibald Clavering Gunter, *Mr. Barnes of New York* (1888) and *Mr. Potter of Texas* (1889); Annie Fellows Johnston, *The Little Colonel* (1896); Mary Johnston, *To Have and to Hold* (1900); Hamilton W. Mabie,* *My Study Fire, Second Series* (1894); George Barr McCutcheon,* *Graustark* (1901); Charles Major,* *When Knighthood Was in Flower* (1898); S. Weir Mitchell,* *Hugh Wynne, Free Quaker* (1898); Opie Read, *The Jucklins* (1895); Alice Hagan Rice, *Mrs. Wiggs of the Cabbage Patch* (1901); Amélie Rives, *The Quick or the Dead?* (1888); Margaret Marshall Saunders, *Beautiful Joe* (1894); Charles M. Sheldon,* *In His Steps: What Would Jesus Do?** (1897); F. Hopkinson Smith, *Caleb West* (1898); Booth Tarkington,* *The Gentleman from Indiana* (1899); Maurice Thompson, *Alice of Old Vincennes* (1901); Ralph Waldo Trine, *In Tune with the Infinite* (1897); Mark Twain,* *A Connecticut Yankee in King Arthur's Court** (1889); Charles Wagner, *The Simple Life* (1901); Lew Wallace,* *The Prince of India* (1893); and Edward Noyes Westcott, *David Harum* (1898). It is of interest not only that few significant writers made the above list but also that most of the authors and titles on it are forgotten today.

Bibelot. (Full title: *The Bibelot: A Reprint of Poetry and Prose for Book Lovers, Chosen in Part from Scarce Editions and Sources Not Generally Known.*) Unique monthly journal founded by Thomas Bird Mosher, a self-educated, voracious, and discriminating reader living in Portland, Maine. His magazine was cheap at 5¢ a copy but beautifully printed, and it ran from January 1895 through December 1914. Its title makes Mosher's intentions fairly obvious. Reprinted were classical and recent poetry and prose, Celtic revival material, and contemporary items—often foreign in origin.

Bierce, Ambrose (1842–1914?). (Full name: Ambrose Gwinett Bierce.) Soldier, writer, and cynic. He was born in Meigs County, Ohio. During the Civil War, Bierce served in the Union Army (1861–1864), was severely wounded in the head at Kenesaw Mountain (1864), and was demobilized as a first lieutenant. His harrowing war experiences, probably the worst of any writer to come out of the Civil War, colored the rest of his long and bitter life; he was obsessed with thoughts of death and suicide, became an alcoholic, and probably deliberately caused his own mysterious death—now the subject of legend. Bierce worked in Alabama as a federal treasury agent (1865), joined a military mapping expedition proceeding from Omaha, Nebraska, to California (1866–1867), brevetted major), and worked in the federal treasury in San Francisco (1867). He became a professional writer there and nearby. He established a thirty-year pattern of writing columns for three San Francisco weeklies (*Newsletter*, *Argonaut*, and *Wasp*) and a weekly column for the San Francisco *Examiner*. In time, he became a kind of West Coast literary dictator, earning the nicknames "Almighty God Bierce" and "Bitter Bierce." He married Mary Ellen "Mollie" Day in 1871 (the couple had three children).

Bierce and Mollie moved to England where they lived and worked in London, Bristol, and Leamington (1872–1875). Bierce wrote for publication and was happy, popular, and successful. Home again, he was employed briefly in the San Francisco mint (1875), did editorial work (1877), and continued to write. He worked honorably for an incompetent, corrupt Dakota Territory mining company (1880), then returned to San Francisco a year later to write and try to cure his chronic asthma. One of the targets of his vitriolic satire was The Big Four,* the rapacious Central Pacific and Southern Pacific Railroad robber barons Charles Crocker,* Mark Hopkins,* Collis P. Huntington,* and Leland Stanford.* Bierce called these men "railrogues" and spelled the last one's name as "£eland $tanford." Bierce and his wife permanently separated in 1888 when he incorrectly thought that she had reciprocated another man's affections. Bierce's teen-age son Day was killed, as was the lad's opponent, in a duel over a girl (1889). Bierce collaborated with a German Jewish dentist named Gustav Adolph Danziger, who in the early 1890s changed his name to Adolphe de Castro. When he quarreled with Danziger, Bierce became the subject of Danziger's inaccurate critical comments. During these years of misery, Bierce wrote many of his most representative and gruesome tales. He successfully lobbied in Washington, D.C. (1896) for William Randolph Hearst,* for whose San Francisco *Examiner* he had written (from 1887) and for whom he wrote in other ways (until 1909), against a railroad funding bill proposed by Huntington. Bierce deplored the Spanish-American War* and inveighed against it in print. In his later years, he lived mostly in Washington (1909–1913).

One of his numerous vituperative poems got Bierce into serious trouble. It seems that when Governor William Goebel of Kentucky was assassinated (February 1900), Bierce published the following quatrain in Hearst's New York *Journal*: "The bullet that pierced Goebel's breast / Can not be found in all the West; / Good reason, it is speeding here / To stretch McKinley on his bier." President William McKinley* was assassinated in September 1901. Bierce was embarrassed by his seemingly prophetic lines and explained lamely that all he had meant by them was that security measures against assassins were inadequate. All the same, Hearst's plans to run for governor of New York as an avenue to the White House were wrecked by his poet's verse. Misery continued to dog Bierce. His son Leigh, who married in 1900, died of pneumonia the next year. Bierce's daughter Helen, who married in 1902, was divorced four years later. Bierce and his wife, long separated, were also finally divorced in 1905; she died later the same year. Bierce began to prepare, and uncritically inflate, his *Collected Works* (1908). After visiting Civil War battlefields (October 1913), Bierce went south to Juarez, Mexico (November 1913) and then probably proceeded to Ojinaga and got himself killed during the battle there, which occurred in January 1914.

Ambrose Bierce's major works are *The Fiend's Delight* (1873), as by Dod Grile; *Nuggets and Dust Panned Out in California* (1873), as by Dod Grile; *Cobwebs from an Empty Skull* (1874), as by Dod Grile; much admired by Mark Twain*; *Tales of Soldiers and Civilians** (1891); *The Monk and the Hangman's Daughter** (1892), with Danziger; *Blacks Beetles in Amber** (1892), satirical poems; *Can Such Things Be?** (1893); *Fantastic Fables** (1899); *Shapes of Clay* (1903), satirical poems; *The Cynic's Word Book* (1906), enlarged as *The Devil's Dictionary* (1911); *Write It Right* (1909), a grammar handbook; *The Shadow on the Dial and Other Essays* (1909); and *The Collected Works of Ambrose Bierce* (12 vols., 1909–1912). These works all directly or indirectly reflect Bierce's unhappy childhood, grisly war experiences, personal sorrows, professional difficulties (including publishers going bankrupt and colleagues getting greedy), and hence unrelieved bitterness and cynicism. With his many casual friends, for example, Mary Austin* and Ina Coolbrith* in California, Bierce could be completely charming.

The Big Four. The rapacious Central Pacific Railroad and Southern Pacific Railroad robber barons Charles Crocker* (1822–1888), Mark Hopkins* (1813–1878), Collis P. Huntington* (1821–1900), and Leland Stanford* (1824–1893). All born in the East, they migrated to Sacramento, California, during the Gold Rush days, not to become miners, however, but wealthy merchants, politicians, and power brokers instead. Their profitable railroad ventures resulted from the vision of Theodore Dehone Judah (1826–1863), who developed the first workable plan for a transcontinental railroad, beginning in California and going northeast through the Sierra Nevada to Reno, Nevada. He persuaded The Big Four to incorporate the Central Pacific (1861) and then went to Washington, D.C., and pushed an aid bill through Congress (1862). The Big Four bought out Judah's interest (1863), lobbied and bribed congressmen for more federal money that year and the next, and became shadowy figures behind dishonest fiscal schemes such as the Crédit Mobilier (established 1863, exposed 1872). Crocker, nicknamed "Bull," was huge, profane, and alcoholic, but he got things done, in part by hiring reliable Chinese coolies to join his brawny Irish laborers. Hopkins was a stubborn financial wizard. Huntington was a hard-working, autocratic, tactless businessman. Stanford, a master politician, was a vain man.

Well known is the epic story of the construction of the transcontinental line, climaxing at Promontory Point, Utah, on 10 May 1869, when The Big Four's Central Pacific rails from the West connected with Union Pacific rails that had started from Omaha, Nebraska. A year earlier, The Big Four had bought up the Southern Pacific Railroad to augment their West Coast monopoly. By 1883, the Southern Pacific added lines into Arizona, Texas, and Louisiana. In 1885 The Big Four, reduced to three by the death of Hopkins, merged the Southern Pacific and the Central Pacific. The ruthless trio of Crocker, Huntington, and Stanford controlled coastal business and politics and profited unconscionably by charging "all the traffic will bear" for shipping commercial and agricultural products. Ambrose Bierce,* writing in the San Francisco *Examiner* (owned by William Randolph Hearst*) and elsewhere, called Crocker, Huntington, and Stanford "railrogues" and spelled Stanford's name as "£eland $tanford." When Edwin Markham* published "The Man with the Hoe"* as a warning that the day would come when labor would rise in violent protest against exploiters, Huntington offered a prize of $750 for the best literary rebuttal.

By the time Frank Norris* excoriated the rich railroaders in *The Octopus*: *A Story of California** (1901), The Big Four were all dead, but their legacy of exploitation and conspicuous consumption stained the 1880s, 1890s, and beyond. Examples are numerous. In 1884, when Huntington was married for a second time, he tipped Henry Ward Beecher, the minister in charge, the sum of $4,000. Later in the 1880s, Huntington, who had informally adopted his first wife's deceased sister's daughter Clara Prentice (later called Clara Huntington), bought Clara's marriage to a disgusting German prince for more than $2,000,000 (*see* Travel and Travelers). In 1886 Crocker bought and furnished a New York mansion for $250,000 but, the next year, disliked it and gave it to his daughter as a wedding present. After Hopkins's death, his rich widow built a $150,000 mausoleum for his corpse in Sacramento; driven by bad publicity to the East Coast, she built a $2,000,000 mansion for herself in Great Barrington, Massachusetts, and other lush residences elsewhere. She married an eccentric furniture expert twenty-two years her junior in 1886; when she died, in 1891, she left him all of her estate and disinherited Timothy Hopkins (Mark Hopkins's nephew and their adopted son). Timothy contested the will and accepted $8,000,000 or so in an out-of-court settlement. Meanwhile, permission was given in the 1890s to open the Hopkins mansion on Nob Hill for art classes conducted by the San Francisco Art School. Some Big Four money served better purposes. Leland Stanford financed Eadweard Muybridge* in his experiments to photograph animals in motion. After Leland Stanford, Jr., died of persistent fever (1884, at age fifteen), Stanford and his wife Jane Lathrop Stanford used part of their ill-gotten fortune to establish Stanford University, the campus of which was designed by Frederick L. Olmsted* and which opened in Palo Alto, California, in October 1891. The university was in jeopardy when Stanford died. He left much money but also many railroad company obligations which were complicated by the enmity of his old friend Huntington, who called the university "Stanford's circus." Nor would childless old Collis Huntington have approved of what happened to part of the inherited wealth of his older brother Solon Huntington's son Henry Edwards Huntington (1850–1927). Collis Huntington had made his nephew Henry Huntington a California railroad executive (1881–1900) and willed him substantial stock (1900). Henry Huntington continued to do well in business and then, for good measure, married Uncle Collis's rich widow (1913), thus enabling him to continue his habit of picture and book buying on an incredible scale, in England, on the Continent, and in the United States. He deposited everything in his San Marino library, near Pasadena, California, and endowed the world-famous Huntington Library with $8,000,000 in 1919.

Black Beetles in Amber (1892). Collection of poems by Ambrose Bierce.* Mostly reprinted from West Coast newspapers and periodicals, these poems include scathing, vitriolic, and vituperative lampoons of the illustrious—all in polished, clear, graceful, but brutal lines. For example, he asks Andrew Carnegie* why Carnegie insists that "black and red are similarly white / And you and God identically right." He also castigates Chauncey M. Depew, railroad attorney and executive, and popular after-dinner speaker, for converting banquet knives and forks into oars by means of which he rows "his way to eminence."

The Black Riders and Other Lines (1895). Book of poetry by Stephen Crane.* The sixty-eight poems, mostly quite short and written in free verse, are telegraphic in their brief bursts of words—unmusical, metaphoric, bitter in tone, sometimes parabolic, usually anarchical in content. Naturalistically, Crane denies God, rails at Him, longs for Him, and misses Him. In one poem, the poet fears that his lifelong search may reveal "nothing . . . [b]ut a vast blue." In another, when a spirit denies God, "[a] sword from the sky" kills him. Another poem explains that "God fashioned the ship of the world carefully," only, however, to let it "slip . . . slyly down the ways." Aiming always at personal honesty, Crane in evident frustration offers this poem: "Yes, I have a thousand tongues, / and nine and ninety-nine lie. / Though I strive to use the one, / It will make no melody at my will, / But is dead in my mouth."

Blaine, James G. (1830–1893). (Full name: James Gillespie Blaine.) Politician. He was born in West Brownsville, Pennsylvania, graduated from Washington and Jefferson College in Washington, Pennsylvania (1847), and taught mathematics in Kentucky (1848–1852) and in a school for the blind in Philadelphia (1852–1854), during which time he also studied law. In 1850, while in Kentucky, he married Harriet Stanwood (the couple had seven children). Next, Blaine settled in Augusta, Maine, in his wife's native city and near his well-to-do in-laws (1854). He was active as a newspaper editor in Maine (1854–1860), became involved with politics, was a delegate to the first Republican convention (1856), and was elected to the Maine legislature (1859–1862), then as a congressman (1863–1876) and senator (1876–1881). During his bid for the presidential nomination, which went to Rutherford B. Hayes (1876), a friend dubbed Blaine the "Plumed Knight." Blaine lost the nomination when he inadequately answered an accusation that he had profiteered in an Arkansas railway bond scandal during the administration of President Ulysses S. Grant. Blaine always associated politics and big business. He served as secretary of state under President James A. Garfield (1881), resigned when Garfield was assassinated (1881), but remained in Washington, D.C., where he wrote *Twenty Years in Congress, from Lincoln to Garfield* (first volume 1884; second, 1886). He was nominated as a presidential candidate but was defeated by Grover Cleveland* (1884), partly because his friend Samuel D. Burchard foolishly galvinized the opposition by defining the Democrats as a party of "rum, Romanism, and rebellion." Blaine neither repudiated nor used the opprobrious term.

Blaine declined to be considered for the presidential nomination in 1888; instead, he supported the successful Benjamin Harrison* and became his secretary of state. Blaine presided over the helpful first Pan-American Conference (1889), supported the reciprocal trade provisions in the tariff act that bore the name of William McKinley* (1890), handled a ticklish situation when American sailors were murdered in Chile (1891), encouraged a U.S. Naval buildup, and expanded American interests in Central and South America, the Caribbean, the Isthmus of Panama, the Pacific Ocean, and the Bering Sea. He also favored the annexing of Cuba, Hawaii, and Puerto Rico. Falling out with Harrison, in poor health, and grieving because three of his children had just died in a two-year period, Blaine resigned from the cabinet (1892) and, a few months after Harrison was renominated, died. Blaine, who had a dignified appearance, a charismatic manner, and magnetic oratorical skills, was the most popular Republican politician in national politics in the 1880s and early 1890s, and he had a significant say in his party's policies and successes.

Blakelock, Ralph Albert (1847–1919). Painter. He was born in New York City, graduated from the College of the City of New York (1867), was self-taught in art, disliked the soft and sentimental aspects of the Hudson River School of landscape painting, and instead created eerie, highly imaginative pictures. They are notable for their subjective quality, poetic luminosity, and haunting moodiness, often with dreamy moonlight, mystical, diffuse foliage, and frequent use of yellow and brown. Blakelock's one great adventure was an inspiring trip into the Far West to observe scenery and Native American life there (1869). He grew morose when success was slow in finding him. Even though he won a prize (1899), he went insane because of poverty, poor sales, and a growing family to support. He was placed in a mental asylum in 1899. He hardly knew that critics and the public alike began to appreciate his work from 1900. When he was released from the asylum in 1916, he returned to New York (1916–1918) but was unable to paint well again. He was reinstitutionalized in 1918 and died in 1919. His works have been compared to those of Albert Pinkham Ryder,* but they are both more representational and less well composed.

The Blindman's World and Other Stories (1898). Collection of ingeniously imaginative short stories by Edward Bellamy.* In the title story, the spirit of an astronomer voyages to Mars, where he finds beings blessedly untroubled by the past through having weak memories and also possessed of the ability to see the future perfectly. Another story, "The Old Folks' Party," depicts a little group of young people enjoying a celebration in which they become the ghosts of their future beings. In yet another story, "Two Old Lovers," the protracted courtship of an aged couple is livened by a peppy twosome who are themselves in love and who change partners with the fogies.

"The Blue Hotel" (1898). Short story by Stephen Crane.* A Swedish tailor from New York gets off a train one snowy morning in Fort Romper, Nebraska, and takes a room in a blue-colored hotel run by Pat Scully. A cowboy and a quiet Easterner named Blanc are there too. Pat's son Johnnie and an old farmer quarrel over a game of cards, and the farmer walks away. A new game starts, with the noisy cowboy, Blanc, and the Swede joining in. The Swede begins to talk uneasily about violence in the West—probably right here too. Johnnie denies that anyone has been killed in this room. When the Swede says that the cowboy probably wants to fight, Pat mollifies him, lectures him about the progressive nature of Fort Romper, gives him some whiskey, and induces him to have supper. Soon after a new card game starts, the pot-valorous Swede accuses Johnnie of cheating. Blanc turns pale, and the cowboy's jaw drops. The Swede and Johnnie settle their dispute by means of a flailing fistfight in the whirling snow. The Swede knocks his adversary down twice, swaggers to his room, packs up, leaves, and gloatingly storms through the night snow to a saloon. He boasts there that he thumped Johnnie Scully, asks a group of card players to have a drink with him, and, when a professional gambler in the group politely refuses, the Swede grows violent and tries to drag the smaller man to the bar. The gambler deftly stabs the Swede to death.

Months pass, and Blanc and the cowboy meet again. To the astonished cowboy, Blanc explains that Johnnie was indeed cheating, that Blanc was not man enough to say so, that the cowboy simply puffed around and wanted to fight, and that Pat was partly responsible too. Blanc concludes: "Every sin is the result of a collaboration . . . and that fool of an unfortunate gambler [given a three-year prison sentence] . . . gets all the punishment." The sluggish cowboy replies, "Well, I didn't do anythin', did I?" "The Blue Hotel" is a naturalistic masterpiece.

Bly, Nellie (1867–1922). (Real name: Elizabeth Cochrane Seaman.) Journalist. Born at Cochrane Mills, Pennsylvania, a town founded by her father, who was a judge, she was educated locally and at Indiana, Pennsylvania. While working for the Pittsburgh *Dispatch* (about 1880–1887), she took the name Nellie Bly, from the song of that name by Stephen Collins Foster. She wrote theater and art notes; pieces about slum life, conditions of women and children working in factories, and divorce; and travel sketches that were sent back during a trip to Mexico (1887). She applied to Joseph Pulitzer,* owner of the New York *World*, and was hired (1887–1895). She attained renown with two scoops. First, she pretended to be insane, got herself committed to the asylum at Blackwell's Island, and wrote an exposé of the horrible conditions there (1887). Second, she toured the world (14 November 1889–26 January 1890), setting a record, from New York to New York in 72 days, 6 hours, and 11 minutes. Her *World* columns on these two adventures were reprinted in book form as *Ten Days in a Mad House* (1887) and *Nellie Bly's Book: Around the World in 72 Days* (1890). Bly married a rich manufacturer named Robert L. Seaman in 1895. After his death (1904), she had trouble with his employees and was in litigation often; the concern went bankrupt in 1915. During World War I, Bly went to Europe (1914) as a reporter but was interned (until 1918). She then wrote for the New York *Evening Journal* (1919–1922). One of her last assignments was covering an execution; she used her report to argue against capital punishment. In writing, Bly used the first person, was forceful and sensational, but was intellectually shallow.

Bok, Edward (1863–1930). (Full name: Edward William Bok.) Editor. Bok was born in Den Helder, Netherlands, and migrated to the United States at the age of six. He attended Brooklyn schools, was a Western Union office boy, went to night school, and began to work for New York publishers (1882). In 1886 he organized a syndicate to handle the publication of Henry Ward Beecher's sermons. Next, he was hired by Cyrus H. K. Curtis, successful publisher in Philadelphia, to edit the *Ladies' Home Journal*,* a position Bok held from 1889 until his retirement in 1919. By adding many new features, he made this magazine one of the most attractive and influential popular journals in America. Calling himself "Ruth Ashmore," Bok in 1889 started what became a popular column of advice to young and presumably vulnerable women. Later he hired a woman to conduct the column and also encouraged Eugene Field* to spoof him in print elsewhere—for publicity. Bok's other writings include *Successward* (1895), *The Young Man in Business* (1900), and his prize-winning autobiography *The Americanization of Edward Bok* (1920). Late in life, Bok became involved in the international peace movement.

Bonaventure: A Prose Pastoral of Acadian Louisiana (1888). Three long stories by George Washington Cable.* The stories—"Caranco," "Grande Pointe," and "Au Large"—are only slightly related; they have distinct plots and some different characters, although they are set in the same locale and although their characters all descend from the Acadians expelled from Canada in 1755. In their new region, they cherish their language, traditions, and pastoral life-style. In the first story, Bonaventure Deschamps finds his identity through decency. In the third, his student Claude St. Pierre practices what his teacher has taught him about the joys of renunciation. These saccharine stories are noteworthy mainly because of their accurate landscape description and their reproduction of the Creole accent.

Bookman. Monthly magazine, founded by Frank Howard Dodd, president of New York publishers Dodd, Mead, and Company, which ran from February 1895 through March 1933. The first editor (until 1907) was Columbia Latin professor Harry Thurston Peck, who established a scholarly but light tone. The *Bookman*, which was sparsely illustrated, featured biographical and critical essays about authors and their work (old and new, American and foreign), book reviews (including early notices of Edwin Arlington Robinson* and Edith Wharton*), serial fiction (including items by George Barr McCutcheon*), poetry (by Stephen Crane* and Richard Hovey,* among others), publishers' news items, a department called "Best Selling Books" (started in 1897 and new in American journalism), and letters from readers.

Boyesen, H. H. (1848–1895). (Full name: Hjalmar Hjorn Boyesen.) Novelist, educator, and critic. Boyesen was born in Frederiksvärn, Norway, where his father was a naval academy mathematics teacher in a Norwegian fishing town. The boy happily lived there and also at times with his maternal grandfather near a fjord, amidst natural beauty, and close to peasants full of folklore. Boyesen was excellently educated at a Latin school, a gymnasium, the University of Leipzig, and the University of Christiana (where he earned his Ph.D., 1868). Following the wish of his unselfish father, who had lived briefly in the United States and admired American-style freedom, young Boyesen migrated with his brother in 1869. Boyesen became editor of a Norwegian-language weekly in Chicago and tutored classical languages at the Swedenborgian college in Urbana, Ohio. He wrote *Gunnar*, a romantic novel about a Norwegian cattleboy turned artist, which William Dean Howells* read and accepted for serial publication in the *Atlantic Monthly* (1873; published book form 1874). When Boyesen decided to teach in the United States, he first brushed up on philosophy and linguistics in Leipzig (1873) and then taught at Cornell, free-lanced in New York, published *Falconberg* (1879, an autobiographical novel), and taught German and Scandinavian literature at Columbia (1881–1895). In 1878 Boyesen married Elizabeth "Lillie" Keene, the daughter of wealthy, divorced Chicago parents (the couple had one child).

Boyesen's early books, *Goethe and Schiller* (1879) and *Story of Norway* (1886), were followed by respectable academic publications in the 1890s—including *Essays on German Literature* (1892), *Commentary on the Writings of Henrik Ibsen* (1894), *Literary and Society Silhouettes* (1894, often nobly idealistic), and *Essays on Scandinavian Literature* (1895). Boyesen also wrote two books for children, *The Modern Vikings* (1887) and *Boyhood in Norway* (1892). His 1890s novels are *Mammon of Unrighteousness* (1891), which castigates America's excessively high evaluation of education and satirizes hypocritical educators by contrasting an idealist and his politician brother in an urban setting (especially praised by Howells); *The Golden Calf* (1892), which portrays the fall of a decent man tempted by money; and *Social Strugglers* (1893), which, dedicated to Howells, tars, with one bold brush, members of both the middle class and the upper class who callously seek money, status, and conspicuous leisure. Heavy-handed Boyesen was once more popular than he is now. He is now seen as a sturdy friend of innumerable writers of his time who are now regarded as more significant than he.

Brann, William Cowper (1855–1898). Journalist, author, and lecturer. He was born in Humboldt, Illinois. His mother died when he was two years old, and his father let a neighboring farm family raise him. Brann ran away at age thirteen, worked at various jobs, educated himself by voracious reading, and became a reporter in St. Louis and then in Texas. Perhaps understandably opposed to the high, mighty, and pious, Brann established a monthly journal provocatively called the *Iconoclast* in Austin (1891–1894; he knew O. Henry* there) and restarted as *Brann's Iconoclast* in Waco (1895–1898). After 1898, his periodical had a checkered career, but by then the fiery Brann did not care. He had taken a sarcastic position against Baylor University in a campus scandal involving a foreign coed (1894). Furthermore, his editorials against Christianity and Christian preachers, promiscuous sexual behavior here and there, local political hypocrites, prohibition, and African Americans in the South—the last in opposition to liberal writings at the time by George Washington Cable*—raised circulation to at least 50,000 but also made the establishment seethe. When the editor of the Waco *Times-Democrat* refused to print a defense of Brann written by a friend, the editor and his brother were both killed in a gunfight (1897). Brann, though not directly involved, was blamed. A few months later, he was shot without warning on a downtown street, but he lived long enough to kill his cowardly assailant. Brann's works include *Brann's Speeches and Lectures* (1895?), *Potiphar's Wife: The Story of Joseph Revised* (1897, separately published short narrative), and *Brann's Scrap-Book* (1898, selection of articles). After his murder, some of his wildest essays were collected as *Brann, the Iconoclast* (1898); much later, his collected works were issued (12 vols., 1919). Brann married Carrie Martin (1877).

"The Bride Comes to Yellow Sky" (1898). Short story by Stephen Crane.* Jack Potter is escorting his bride from San Antonio, Texas, where they were married just this morning, to his home in the town of Yellow Sky, where he is the marshal. He did not tell anybody about his impending marriage and is now beginning to wonder what his friends will think. Meanwhile, Yellow Sky troublemaker Scratchy Wilson, drunk again, is out on the streets, shooting up various establishments and deciding that to challenge his nemesis Potter would be real fun. Behold, that heroic figure alights from the train with bride on arm. Scratchy confronts him and waves his revolver at him but is nonplussed when Potter says that he is unarmed and newly wed. Scratchy presumes that their old feud is off now and slouches away along the sandy road. "The Bride Comes to Yellow Sky" is a masterpiece of naturalistic irony and anticlimactic drama.

Brisbane, Arthur (1864–1936). Journalist and editor. He was born in Buffalo, New York, the son of the Fourierist Albert Brisbane. Arthur Brisbane was educated in New Jersey, Brooklyn, France, and Germany. He became a New York *Sun* reporter (1883) and then the London correspondent for the *Sun* (1886). His dispatches were so effective that they were soon syndicated. Brisbane became the first managing editor of the New York *Evening Sun* (1887), then took that position with the New York *World* of Joseph Pulitzer* (1890–1897). William Randolph Hearst* persuaded Brisbane to become the editor of his New York *Evening Journal* (1897–1921). Brisbane's pithy, moralistic editorials immediately became phenomenally popular and influential, and they were printed in more than a thousand newspapers. His columns were called "Today" and "This Week." Later in his career Brisbane bought the Washington, D.C., *Times* (1917) and the Milwaukee *Evening Wisconsin* (1918), then sold both to Hearst (1919). Brisbane was involved in real estate and agricultural science. His mental quickness was legendary. He gave much to many charitable causes. He knew most of the reporters of the 1890s, including Richard Harding Davis.* He married Phoebe Cary in 1912 (the couple had six children).

Brownell, W. C. (1851–1928). (Full name: William Crary Brownell.) Journalist, literary critic, and editorial consultant. He was born in New York City, graduated from Amherst (1871), and worked for the New York *World* (1871–1879), the *Nation* (1879–1881), and Charles Scribner's Sons (from mid–1880s). In addition to advising innumerable contributors (for example, Edith Wharton*) to the firms for which he worked, Brownell also wrote *French Traits, An Essay in Comparative Criticism* (1889), *French Art* (1892), *Victorian Prose Masters* (1901), and much else. His overriding thesis was that Americans needed to study European art and manners in order to grow out of their provinciality. Brownell married Virginia S. Swinburne in 1878 (she died in 1911) and poet-novelist Gertrude Hall in 1921.

Bryan, William Jennings (1860–1925). Politician and lawyer. He was born in Salem, Illinois, and graduated from Illinois College (1881). He practiced law in Jacksonville, Illinois, from 1883 to 1887, then moved to Lincoln, Nebraska, where he combined law and Democratic politics. He was a member of the U.S. House of Representatives from Nebraska (1891–1895), quickly became a renowned orator, was known as "The Commoner," adopted the cause of the advocates of Free Silver* (from 1894), and edited a pro-bimetallism Omaha newspaper (1894–1896). Although he lost every election in which he ran from 1894 on, Bryan became enormously influential in national politics. His "Cross of Gold" speech, in favor of Free Silver, at the 1896 Democratic Convention earned him the presidential nomination, but he was defeated by Republican William McKinley,* who advocated the gold standard and high tariffs. During the Spanish-American War,* Bryan was a colonel in the Third Nebraska Volunteer Regiment but saw no active duty. He was stationed in Florida, where he and many others in his unit suffered from typhoid. Nominated for president again in 1900, he campaigned against the expansionist, imperialist policies of McKinley and Theodore Roosevelt,* but he lost once more. In his later years, Bryan founded and edited the *Commoner*, as a weekly out of Lincoln, Nebraska (1901–1913), then a monthly (to 1923), to promulgate his reform programs; traveled around the world (1905–1906); ran unsuccessfully for president against William Taft (1908); aided in the nomination of Woodrow Wilson for president (1912); served briefly as Wilson's secretary of state (1913–1915, resigning because of his pacifism); and supported Wilson's renomination (1916). Bryan is best known now not only for his stand on Free Silver but also for his creationist opposition to the brilliant Clarence Darrow, the defense attorney for John T. Scopes, who was indicted for teaching evolution in a Tennessee public school in 1925. Many influential people supported Bryan's opposition to McKinley's imperialistic policy toward the Philippines and Roosevelt's later jingoism. Bryan's political cohorts included Andrew Carnegie,* Eugene V. Debs,* Samuel Gompers,* William Dean Howells,* and Mark Twain.* Bryan married Mary Elizabeth Baird in 1884 (the couple had three children).

Bunner, H. C. (1855–1896). (Full name: Henry Cuyler Bunner.) Editor, fiction writer, and poet. Bunner was born in Oswego, New York. Because he could not afford advanced education, he got a job with an import firm in New York City, worked briefly for the *Arcadian* (a weekly), and then became assistant editor of *Puck** (1876). From 1877 until his death, Bunner was editor of *Puck*, contributed to and otherwise improved its contents, and converted it from a flimsy comic weekly into a forceful sociopolitical magazine. In addition, he steadily wrote light poetry (collected in *Rowen* [1892] and *Poems* [1896]), early novels cast in New York (*The Midge* [1886] and *The Story of a New York House* [1887, a three-generation historical romance]), and urbane short stories (*''Short Sixes'': Stories to Be Read While the Candle Burns* [1890], *Zadoc Pine* [1891], *More ''Short Sixes''* [1894], *Jersey Street and Jersey Lane* [1896], *Love in Old Cloathes* [1896]). Bunner's poetry is light, coy, technically dextrous, and often parodic. His short fiction resembles that of Guy de Maupassant. In fact, when Bunner assembled *''Made in France'': French Tales Retold with a United States Twist* (1893), he inserted one of his own stories and was pleased when readers and critics alike regarded it as another fine little French classic.

Burbank, Luther (1849–1926). Horticulturalist. Born in Lancaster, Massachusetts, he was raised on a farm and had only minimal local schooling. At age nineteen he was permanently inspired by a reading of Charles Darwin's *The Variation of Animals and Plants under Domestication*. Thereafter, Burbank taught himself techniques of plant crossing, hybridizing, and selecting. He bought farmland in Lunenberg, Massachusetts (1870), experimented with local potato seeds, and soon produced what became the superior Burbank (or Idaho) potato. With the profits, he moved to California (1875), bought four acres in Santa Rosa and eight more acres nearby, and established a nursery garden, a greenhouse, and an orchard. He successfully experimented to create bigger, hardier, tastier, more vivid, and more fragrant products in a tremendous profusion. He practiced multiple cross-breeding of foreign and native strains in improved and controlled soils and environments, grafted seedlings onto sturdy plants, and carefully and patiently noted results, selected the best, and ruthlessly destroyed unsuccessful plants. He unprofessionally failed to save potentially useful negative notes. He worked on a vast scale with wonderful results. For example, he worked through 65,000 bushes to produce his variety of blackberry-raspberry, and he experimented with 30,000 varieties to bring into being 113 useful types of plums and prunes. He is responsible for some 800 varieties of fruits, vegetables, grains, grasses, and flowers, including 50 varieties of lilies, 10 varieties of commercially valuable berries, many kinds of roses, the Shasta daisy, the Fire poppy, and so on. Burbank rarely theorized, but he did prefer notions concerning inheritance of acquired plant characteristics over certain more modern principles of plant genetics. He wrote many catalogues, called *New Creations* (1893–1901), as well as *Luther Burbank, His Method and Discoveries and Their Practical Applications* (12 vols., 1914–1915). He also coauthored an autobiography beautifully entitled *Harvest of the Years* (posthumously published 1927).

Burgess, Gelett Frank (1866–1951). Author, illustrator, and editor. Born in Boston, Burgess graduated from the Massachusetts Institute of Technology (1887), was editor of *The Lark** in San Francisco (1895–1897), and contributed to it the notorious four-line nonsense jingle ''The Purple Cow'' (1895). He published a sequel to it (1900) expressing sorrow that he ever ''wrote it,'' ending, ''I'll kill you if you quote it.'' Of Burgess's many books, which include fiction, light verse, and drawings, the most famous is a children's humorous manual of etiquette entitled *Goops and How to Be Them* (1900). Goops are floppy, semihuman creatures of two sorts: sulphites (independent thinkers) and bromides (platitudinous bores).

Burnham, Daniel Hudson (1846–1912). Architect and city planner. Born in Henderson, New York, he moved with his family to Chicago (1855) and, during his education there and then at Waltham, Massachusetts (to 1866), mainly evinced a proficiency in drawing. He spent a year with Chicago architects, a year in a Nevada mining camp, then several more years in Chicago with other architectural firms and finally with a firm that employed John Wellborn Root, a skilled draftsman. The two became friends and established their own partnership (1873–1891), each complementing the other's style. Root favored Romanesque; Burnham preferred neoclassical. They drew plans for the country's first skyscraper (the Montauk Block, Chicago, 1882) and then similar Chicago buildings using steel-skeleton building frames, all with exterior walls of masonry. The firm of Burnham and Root was awarded the contract (1891) to oversee all of the architecture for the World's Columbian Exposition* held in Chicago in 1893. When Root died (1891), Burnham became the architectural administrator and chief of construction for the exposition. Ultimately he employed almost 20,000 men (including Walter A. Wyckoff,* who wrote about the experience in *The Workers: An Experiment in Reality: The West**) and was responsible for disbursing $20,000,000 in construction costs. The exposition was completed on schedule (1893) and showed a profit.

Burnham was elected president of the American Institute of Architects (1894), was chairman of the U.S. Senate Park Commission (1901), and designed many more fine buildings (1902–1911). For example, he planned Filene's (Boston), the Flatiron Building (New York), the Pennsylvania Railway Station (Pittsburgh), the Rookery and the Railway Exchange (Chicago), and Selfridge's (London). He was also city planner for Baguio and Manila (in the Philippines), Baltimore, Chicago, Cleveland, San Francisco, Washington, D.C., and elsewhere. In the course of his active professional life, Burnham met and impressed many people in different fields of endeavor, for example, Frederick L. Olmsted* Charles Eliot Norton,* and Lorado Taft.*

Burroughs, John (1837–1921). Naturalist and author. He was born near Roxbury, New York, taught school (1854–1863), clerked in the Treasury Department in Washington, D.C. (1863–1873), and then lived on a farm near Esopus, New York (beginning 1873). He built a cabin in the hills nearby (1893) and often stayed there in seclusion. After he published a book on his friend Walt Whitman (1867), he began to write distinguished essays on nature, often concerning animals, birds, flowers, and trees in the Catskill Mountains, in the tradition of Ralph Waldo Emerson and Henry David Thoreau. Burrough's later books include *Indoor Studies* (1889), *Squirrels and Other Fur-Bearers* (1900), and *Camping and Tramping with* [Theodore] *Roosevelt*[*] (1907). *My Boyhood* and *The Heart of Burroughs's Journals* appeared posthumously (1928). Burroughs accused Ernest Thompson Seton* of falsifying his descriptions of animal habits (in a 1903 *Atlantic Monthly** essay) but qualified his criticism in a follow-up essay (*Atlantic*, 1904).

Burroughs, William Seward (1857–1898). Inventor. He was born in Rochester, New York. After brief schooling, Burroughs became self-supporting from age fifteen, at first clerking in a bank. Starting in 1881, he worked in his mechanically ingenious father's St. Louis shop, where he built casting models. He constructed an initially impractical calculating machine (1885), helped organize the American Arithmometer Company in St. Louis a year later, and patented a working model of an adding machine in 1888. He received a Franklin Institute medal for his achievement in 1897. In time, the machine succeeded commercially, but Burroughs died before he could gain much profit from it. The Burroughs Adding Machine Company, situated in Detroit, Michigan, was a 1905 outgrowth of his original St. Louis firm.

C

Cable, George Washington (1844–1925). Author. He was born in New Orleans, Louisiana. After his father died (1859), young Cable quit school and clerked in a New Orleans warehouse and then for a grocer to support his mother and sisters. He served in the Confederate cavalry during the Civil War (1863–1865), was wounded twice, clerked again, was sick with malaria, then worked off and on for cotton businessmen (1869–1881) and also as a newspaperman (from 1869) before becoming a popular short-story writer and novelist, and then an unpopular defender of the rights of Southern blacks. He published sketches in the New Orleans *Picayune* and began in the 1870s to gain national prominence by publishing the first local-color stories focusing on the postbellum South in *Scribner's Magazine** (edited by Richard Watson Gilder,* later Cable's friend) and *Appleton's Journal*. Cable began to correspond with H. H. Boyesen* (1877). Cable's *Old Creole Days* (1879) is a collection of stories. The success of his powerful novel *The Grandissimes: A Story of Creole Life* (1880, rev. 1883), concerning slavery and voodooism, mixed-blood angers, and a feud between aristocratic families at the time of the Louisiana Purchase, gave Cable confidence enough to devote himself full-time to writing (from 1881). Resentment of his study *The Creoles of Louisiana* (1884, illustrated by Joseph Pennell*) helped to persuade Cable to move with his family to Connecticut (1884), then Northampton, Massachusetts (1885). (Cable's mother was from New England.)

Cable and his friend Mark Twain* went on a rollicking lecture tour together (1884), managed by James B. Pond;* Twain paid Cable $450 a week plus expenses for a twenty-week run. Cable's essays "The Convict Lease System in the Southern States" (1884) and "The Freedman's Case in Equity" (1885) caused him to be further disliked in certain Southern quarters for espousing the cause of African Americans. He even invited (though without success) the African-American writer Charles W. Chesnutt* to be his private secretary (1887). Cable's later books are *Bonaventure: A Prose Pastoral of Acadian Louisiana**

(1888), three linked stories featuring a teacher who helps exiled Acadians in Louisiana; *The Busy Man's Bible* (1891), on how to read and teach the Bible; *John March, Southerner** (1894), about Reconstruction problems in the New South; *Strange True Stories of Louisiana* (1899), polished anecdotes collected from letters, diaries, and legal records; and *The Cavalier* (1901), an immensely popular Civil War historical romance, which Cable dramatized in 1902 for Broadway. None match his masterpieces—*Old Creole Days* and *The Grandissimes*—and all show a falling off in quality.

While he was still writing *John March, Southerner*, Cable was asked to prepare an essay about his methods of composition. The result was "After-Thoughts of a Story-Teller" (*North American Review*, January 1894). This led to Cable's being asked to participate in a symposium on realism and romanticism with Hamlin Garland* and Hamilton W. Mabie* (New York, 13 March 1894). This in turn led to several lectures (New Haven, Connecticut, and Boston, 1895–1896) and essays by Cable on literary aesthetics (1896–1897, in *Atlantic Monthly*,* *Chap-Book*,* etc.). In these critical items, Cable advocated fiction which is "supposable" (because it is often based on facts so selected, "pruned," and stylized as to become romantic and religious in appeal), characters whose emotions the author has felt or can feel, and the sort of reader "entertainment" which ends in reader "profit." *The Negro Question** (1890), which collects six earlier journal essays, remains uniquely significant for readers of Cable to this day. For a brief time, Cable also edited the *Letter* (1896; it became the *Symposium* in 1896) and also *Current Literature* (New York, 1897). He toured England and Scotland reading from his works; while there, he met Andrew Carnegie* (1898). Cable was married three times: to Louise Stewart Bartlett (the couple had eight children [two predeceased Cable]; Louise died in 1904); to Eva Colgate Stevenson in 1906 (she died in 1923); and to Hanna Cowing in 1923.

An unpleasant experience in Cable's life should be mentioned. For years Cable helped a somewhat inept Louisiana writer named Dora Richards Miller by advising her, trying to get her work published, buying her Civil War diary for possible useful data, loaning and giving her money, hiring her as a research assistant, and finally editing her essay entitled "A West Indian Slave Insurrection" (anonymously published in *Scribner's Magazine*, December 1892, but with Cable's introductory note that Dora in the narrative was the authoress). Miller repaid his kind efforts by rebuking him in a letter published in a New Orleans newspaper and thus drawing him into an unpleasant exchange in print.

Cable was steadily active in Home Culture clubs and Bible study, editing, travel, and until 1918 in writing. Though remaining a delight as a local-color stylist, Cable was influential in the 1890s largely because of his controversial book *The Negro Question*.

Caesar's Column: A Story of the Twentieth Century (1890), as by Edmund Boisgilbert, M.D. Utopian novel by Ignatius Donnelly.* The place is New York; the time, September 1988. Gabriel Weltstein writes a series of letters back home to his brother Heinrich. The two are members of a Swiss family long settled in Uganda, in Africa, and are wool merchants there. At first, Gabriel relishes seeing the technological wonders of this brave new world—a lighting system powered by Northern Lights, electronic communications, airplanes, a grand hotel (significantly named the Darwin) with televised menus and computerized newspapers, and so on. But joy turns to horror when he rescues a beggar being beaten by a servant of a Jewish Italian Industrialist named Prince Cabano and learns that the beggar is Maximilian Petion, disguised leader of a worldwide anarchistic movement known as the Brotherhood of Destruction. Its mission is to save a vast underclass of oppressed and now brutal workers from the grimy toil that makes this pseudo-utopia possible. The government is in the hands of an oligarchy. Gabriel now hides in Maximilian's slum district, where he meets and observes the revolutionaries and lectures to them about his notion of a better society, but he is scoffed at as a dreamer and is forced to hear Maximilian's summary of two late-nineteenth-century political failures: the rejection of the single tax proposal of Henry George* and a Marxist revolution which ended in ruin for the workers and was followed by the establishment of the present oligarchy. Gabriel sneaks into a meeting of the oligarchical council, led by Cabano. Gabriel also associates with huge Caesar Lomellini and his cohorts, who are the force behind the revolutionaries. All of Gabriel's efforts as a peacemaker fail, war breaks out, and oligarchical airplane pilots are bribed to defect to the revolutionaries. Civilization collapses instantly when these pilots use poison bombs on government troops. Bloodthirsty Caesar commemorates the victory by building a monumental column filled with a quarter of a million corpses, of the guilty and innocent alike, but he is soon beheaded himself by a mob of terrorists he cannot control.

Caesar's Column has subplots involving Gabriel's love for Estelle Washington, who was destined to become Cabano's concubine, and Maximilian's love for Christina Jansen, an innocent young singer. These good people all escape by an airplane to Uganda, where they establish a genuine utopia based on Gabriel's idealistic sociopolitical philosophy.

After Donnelly was defeated in his campaign for the U.S. Senate in January 1889, he wrote *Caesar's Column* in five months, failed to place it with any big publisher, let a small Chicago firm issue it, and was vindicated by sales of 60,000 in less than a year and hundreds of thousands thereafter, by legitimate and pirated editions in England, and by translations into German, Norwegian, and Swedish. Donnelly was undoubtedly inspired in large part by *Looking Backward: 2000–1887*,* published in 1888 by Edward Bellamy.* The description of slum life appearing in the first part of *Caesar's Column* anticipates similar effects in *Maggie: A Girl of the Streets** published in 1893 by Stephen Crane.* *Caesar's Column*, though powerful, is inartistic in the extreme. Hastily written, it repeatedly violates the epistolary point of view, and it is grotesquely melodramatic and tediously didactic. Its author was motivated by fear that in America, and in much of the rest of the world too, much of the wealth was increasingly in too few hands, with poverty dangerously brutalizing more and more people. Most of the novel is a hellish vision of the consequences of this situation unless changes are made. Aspects of Populist Party* ideas undergird the little that is positive in the work—mainly its utopian conclusion. There, Donnelly espouses universal suffrage; nationalization of mines, utilities, and rail transportation; paper currency and a demonetizing of gold and silver; elimination of privilege, tariffs, and interest; and fair employment and decent wages for all.

Cahan, Abraham (1860–1951). Journalist, fiction writer, socialist activist, and labor union organizer. Born in Podberezy, near Vilnius, Lithuania, to a scholarly Jewish family, Cahan lost his faith and turned from a study of the Talmud to atheism. He favored Russian culture, and, to avoid being drafted into the Russian army, he became a shy student at the Jewish Teachers' Institute in Vilnius (1877–1881), where he read Russian classics and underground socialist tracts and attended secret socialist meetings. He taught in a Jewish school in Velizh, in White Russia (1881), but he was suspected by the police there and migrated to New York City (1882). Cahan was part of a mass exodus of East European Jews at this time. He settled in the Jewish Lower East Side ghetto. In New York, he gave the first speech in Yiddish on socialism (August 1882), worked in a cigar factory, taught Yiddish and Hebrew, learned English quickly and well, and soon published articles on immigrant urban life in the New York *Sun* and the New York *Evening Press*. He cofounded, coedited, and wrote for *Di Neie Tseit* (The New Era), the first Yiddish socialist newspaper; it folded in a month (1886). In the next several years, Cahan edited the *Arbeiter Tseitung* (The Worker's Gazette, New York, 1891–1894) and was a reporter on the New York *Commercial Advertiser* (1897–1901), where he knew Lincoln Steffens* and Norman Hapgood,* among others. He cofounded and then edited the *Jewish Daily Forward* (Yiddish, 1897, 1902, 1903–1951). He improved its circulation from 7,500 early in the twentieth century to 250,000 and made it the world's leading newspaper in its restricted field—amusing, informative, and persuasive.

In the 1890s, Cahan gradually changed from a stubborn radical to a pro-labor pragmatist amenable to realistic compromise. He continued to associate with Steffens and began to write fiction. His first short story, "Mottke Arbel and His Romance" (1895, in Yiddish), was about a Jewish immigrant's loneliness; he translated it into English and republished it as "A Providential Match" (also 1895). His popular short novel *Yekl: A Tale of the New York Ghetto* * followed (1896). Cahan's other works include *Social Remedies* (1889), *The Imported Bridegroom and Other Stories of the New York Ghetto* (1898), *The White Terror and the Red: A Novel of Revolutionary Russia* (1905), *The Rise of David Levinsky* (1917, an autobiographical novel), a history of the United States in Yiddish (2 vols., 1910, 1912), a huge autobiography in Yiddish (5 vols., 1926–1931), and much else. In 1886 Cahan married an immigrant from Kiev named Anna Bronstein (the couple had no children).

California Midwinter International Exposition. The first West Coast international exposition, held in San Francisco, 27 January–30 June 1894. This exposition was inspired in part by the successful World's Columbian Exposition* (Chicago, 1893). Michael H. De Young, the owner and publisher of the San Francisco *Chronicle*, had been impressed by the Chicago fair, where he was the California exhibit commissioner. He organized a fund-raising committee, helped choose the site at Golden Gate Park, and otherwise directed plans for construction of a quadrangle surrounded by five main buildings: the Administration Building, the Horticulture and Agriculture Building, the Fine Arts Building (the only structure to remain permanently), the Manufactures and Liberal Arts Building, and the Mechanical Arts Building. In the center was a searchlight atop a 226-foot tower. Smaller exhibits featured such attractions as buffalo and ostriches, a Chinese pagoda and a Japanese tea garden, and a mockup of an original gold-rush camp. The hodgepodge of eclectic buildings (including a neo-adobe hall) was overshadowed by foreign exhibits, including the first impressionist paintings by Édouard Manet and Auguste Renoir available to the Western American public. More than 1,350,000 ticket buyers enabled the exposition to exceed its $1,193,000 cost by just over 50 percent.

Can Such Things Be? (1893). A collection of eerie short stories by Ambrose Bierce.* The best and most complex story in the book is "The Death of Halpin Frayser." In it, Frayser, long devoted to his mother, whom he affectionately called Katy, is now, years later, a sailor far from their old Tennessee home. He does not know either that she remarried or that her second husband killed her. Frayser awakens from a midsummer night's nap in a graveyard in California's Napa Valley, speaks out the name "Catherine Larue" without knowing whose it is or was, falls asleep again, and becomes the victim of an oneiric murder, occasioned by his seeing a horrible "apparition . . . so like, yet so unlike his mother." The killer is his mother's murderer. The scene is near her grave, properly marked "Catherine Larue," since her second husband was named Larue. The tale, which is a tangle of reality and dream, and which contains a generalization about "the dominance of the sexual element in all the relations of life," has challenging Oedipal and Freudian overtones.

Candler, Asa Griggs (1851–1929). Manufacturer and philanthropist. Born near Villa Rica, Georgia, he became a practicing pharmacist. In 1887 he bought a formula for what became Coca Cola from Dr. J. S. Pemberton, who specialized in making patent medicines. Pemberton's product contained a small amount of cocaine, as did many other contemporary elixirs and nostrums. Candler improved the recipe (beginning in 1889 and continuing through the 1890s), was sued in federal court by the Pure Food and Drug Administration (1909–1917), and defended his phenomenally popular soft drink by claiming that he had brought it into conformity with legal standards. Candler sold his secret recipe for $25,000,000 (1917) and became mayor of Atlanta (1917). He subsequently devoted his energies to supporting numerous churches and schools, notably Emory College, of which his younger brother Warren Akin Candler was president (1888–1898).

Captain Jinks of the Horse Marines (1901). Play by Clyde Fitch.* This charming period piece is set in New York in 1872. Captain Robert Jinks, Charlie La Martine, and Augustus Van Vorkenburg are dashing young men about town. They wager as to who will first flirt successfully with European opera star Madame Trentoni, who is about to disembark for her American debut. When Jinks is smitten by the woman's profound goodness, he cheerfully forfeits his bet by writing the other men a $1,000 IOU, which one of them uses as evidence to discount Jinks's sincerity in an unsuccessful attempt to sabotage Jinks's acceptance by the lovely singer. Though superficial, *Captain Jinks of the Horse Marines* was a hit because of its snappy dialogue, suspense, and pleasing moral: Good wins. (It was made into a musical comedy during the Roaring Twenties.)

Carman, Bliss (1861–1929). (Full name: William Bliss Carman.) Poet and essayist, born in New Brunswick, Canada, to an Anglican New England family which, out of loyalty to England, had migrated to Canada during the American Revolution. Carman was an excellent student in Canada, then at Oxford and Edinburgh, and finally at Harvard (1886–1888), where he studied English literature and philosophy, and where he also met Richard Hovey.* Carman worked for several New York and Boston publishers (from 1888), most happily with the *Chap-Book** (1894–1897). His first book, *Low Tide on Pré: A Book of Lyrics* (1893) contains as fine verse as he ever wrote. It is delicate, melancholy, elegiac, mystical, and escapist. The title poem, in rhythmical five-line stanzas rhyming ababb, is especially appealing. Carman and Hovey coauthored *Songs from Vagabondia* (1894), which helped establish both young men as popular poets; *More Songs from Vagabondia* (1896); and *Last Songs from Vagabondia* (1900). To these works Hovey contributed an open-road, Whitmanesque quality, and Carman injected traces of melancholy. Later came Carman's *Echoes from Vagabondia* (1912). In 1896, after a vacation in England and France, Carman met Mary Perry King (histrionic, domineering, possessive, and exactly his age) and her hard-working physician husband in New Canaan, Connecticut. Carman adopted her philosophy of Unitrinianism—the integration of body, emotions, and mind. The well-to-do Kings wined, dined, housed, clothed, and flattered Carman, who was a somewhat effeminate poseur in their presence, for the rest of his life. The relationship between Carman and Mary is an enigma to this day.

Carman's other collections of poetry in the 1890s are *Behind the Arras: A Book of the Unseen* (1895), more philosophical, less popular; *A Seamark: A Threnody for Robert Louis Stevenson* (1895); *Ballads of Lost Haven: A Book of the Sea* (1897), weaker; and *By the Aurelian Wall, and Other Elegies* (1898), uneven. Of his twenty or so books after 1900, the best may be the five volumes of *The Pipes of Pan* (1902–1905), in which Pan combines matter and spirit as do both human beings and nature, and *Sappho* (1904), reconstructions and modifications of the puzzling Greek poetess's fragments. Carman's two favorite authors were Robert Browning and Matthew Arnold. The year before he died, Carman was named Poet Laureate of Canada. His fatal flaw was that he never outgrew his predilection for a lyricism which became vapid and a mystical yearning for universal harmony which seems rather precious.

Carnegie, Andrew (1835–1919). American industrialist, humanitarian, and philanthropist. Carnegie was born in Dunfermline, Scotland, the older of two sons, to liberal, reform-minded parents. When the father failed as a weaver, he migrated with his family to Allegheny, then a suburb of Pittsburgh, Pennsylvania (1848). Young Carnegie worked in a cotton mill, became a telegraph messenger (1850), taught himself telegraphy (1851), and became the personal clerk and telegraphist of the superintendent of the Pittsburgh division of the Pennsylvania Railroad (1853). He worked his way up, and when his supervisor advanced, Carnegie was named division superintendent (1859). During the Civil War he was in Washington, D.C., organizing and supervising the military telegraphy department (1862); however, he took time off to visit Scotland (1862) for the first of numerous trips out of the United States. Though offered a major promotion by the Pennsylvania Railroad (1865), Carnegie resigned and turned to steel making. His formula was to surround himself with able associates. He helped establish the Keystone Bridge Company (1865), built a mill to manufacture steel rails, established a residence in New York City and an office on Wall Street (1867), sold millions of dollars worth of bonds overseas to make enormous commissions and expand his Pittsburgh steel mills (from 1869), took a trip around the world (1878), organized a newspaper syndicate in England (1880, expanding it in 1881, but selling it in 1885), gave a library to his old Scottish hometown of Dunfermline (1881), bought heavily into the H. C. Frick Coke Company of Henry Clay Frick* (1882), controlled through substantial shareholding many steel-making requirements (such as coal, iron, railroads, and lake steamships), bought the Homestead Steel Works of Pittsburgh (1888), named Frick the chairman of the board of Carnegie Brothers & Company (1889), was out of the country when the violent Homestead Lockout* of 1892 occurred (Carnegie blamed Frick for hiring Pinkerton strikebreakers and thus instigating bloodshed, and he sent Charles M. Schwab* to Homestead to restore harmony), and leased iron-rich Mesabi land in Minnesota (1896). By this time, Carnegie's art of flattering, cajoling, and using other men was consummate, and his personality was a combination of ruthlessness and optimism.

In 1899, a group headed by Frick attempted to buy Carnegie out for $175,000. The deal collapsed because of insufficient funding, and Carnegie kept option money totaling more than $1,000,000. He then organized the Carnegie Steel Company, ousted Frick a year later, and in 1901 sold the company to the United States Steel Company, headed by John Pierpont Morgan* and engineered by Schwab for nearly $500,000,000. Carnegie declined to stay on as a partner and accepted instead $300,000,000 or so as his share. Thereafter, Carnegie, who had been interested in cultural affairs as early as 1867, devoted himself to scholarly and humanitarian endeavors.

Some of Carnegie's many books are *Round the World* (1879, rev. and enlarged 1884); *An American Four-in-Hand in Britain* (1883); *Triumphant Democracy, or Fifty Years' March of the Republic* (1886, enlarged as *Triumphant Democracy Ten Years Afterward, or Sixty Years' March of the Republic* [1893]); *The Gospel of Wealth and Other Timely Essays* (1900), which argues that wealthy men have an obligation to live unostentatiously, to provide moderately for their immediate dependents, and while still living to help the less fortunate to understand themselves and the world around them better; *The Empire of Business* (1902); *Problems of Today, Wealth, Labor, Socialism* (1908); and his autobiography (1920).

Early in his public career, Carnegie learned to appreciate the power of persuasive writing, and at first he was more widely known internationally as an author before it was clear that he was a manufacturing genius. Ultimately more important than his written works or his industrial wizardry was his devotion to humanitarian, pacifist, philanthropic, and allied causes. He donated $350,000,000 for the following: some 7,500 church organs; some 2,800 libraries in the United States and elsewhere in the English-speaking world (on the condition that the recipient locale provide land, books, and maintenance funds via taxes; the first such library in the United States was funded in Pittsburgh in 1886); New York Music Hall (1891, renamed Carnegie Hall in 1898); Carnegie Trade Schools (1900, later Carnegie Institute of Technology, finally Carnegie-Mellon University); Carnegie Institute of Pittsburgh (1896); Carnegie Trust for the Universities of Scotland (1901); Carnegie Institute in Washington, D.C. (1902); Carnegie Dunfermline Trust Fund (1903); Peace Palace at the Hague (1903); Carnegie Hero Fund Commission (1904); Carnegie Foundation for the Advancement of Teaching (1905, evolving into the Teacher's Insurance and Annuity Association in 1917); Carnegie Endowment for International Peace (1910); Carnegie Corporation of New York (1911, with an endowment of $135,000,000); and Carnegie United Kingdom Trust (1913).

Carnegie's father died in 1855; his mother, to whom he was devoted, and his brother, died in 1886. Carnegie married Louise Whitfield in 1887 (the couple had one child). He bought Skibo Castle, in northern Scotland, in 1898, and regularly summered and entertained there. He knew and was generally liked and respected by innumerable persons in the United States and abroad who were significant in various fields in the 1890s and later. The Americans include James G. Blaine,* William Jennings Bryan,* George Washington Cable,* Richard Watson Gilder,* John Hay,* Whitelaw Reid,* John D. Rockefeller,* and Mark Twain.*

Andrew Carnegie is still a controversial figure. He has been criticized for exploiting labor and defeating competition by ruthless tactics. However, he made numerous mill workers his partners without requiring them to invest, and he established pension plans for this employees. Furthermore, his innovative techniques outdistanced his rivals and made the United States the steel leader of the world. (It had begun to outproduce England by 1890.) And the scale and variety of his philanthropy is unique in the history of the world.

Carver, George Washington (1861?–1943). Botanist, chemurgist, and educator. He was born a slave on the farm of Moses and Susan Carver, near Diamond Grove, Missouri. He was orphaned early when his father was killed in an accident and his mother was stolen by slave kidnappers. He was freed in 1865, was educated in a one-room school for African Americans at Neosho, nine miles from the Carver home, and then did odd jobs to support himself while attending high school in Minneapolis, Kansas (graduating in 1885). After homesteading unsuccessfully in the West for a time (1886–1889), he attended Simpson College, at Indianola, Iowa (1889, working as a cook), transferred to Iowa State College of Agriculture and Mechanic Arts, at Ames, and was the first African American to graduate from there (B.S., 1891; M.A. 1892). Carver displayed talent as a painter, exhibited at Cedar Rapids, Iowa (1892), and received an honorable mention for work shown at the World's Columbian Exposition* (Chicago, 1893). He became the first African American to teach at Iowa State (1894–1896). He made his best move when he accepted the invitation of Booker T. Washington* to join the faculty at the Tuskegee Institute in Alabama (1896) as head of the agriculture department.

Carver began experimenting to enrich local Southern soils, depleted by one-crop cotton farming, through planting peanuts, sweet potatoes, and soybeans. He developed some three hundred by-products of these new crops, thus dramatically changing the South's farm economy. He also took to the field, with his famous "school on wheels," to instruct regional farmers in fertilizing and crop rotation. The U.S. Department of Agriculture and many foreign countries adopted this concept of mobile instruction. Thomas A. Edison* tried without success to employ him at a salary far above his Tuskegee pay. Carver assisted the Department of Agriculture in compiling a catalogue of medicinal flora (1897). His first published article was "Feeding Acorns to Livestock" (1898). He won many awards in the United States and abroad. Among his finest accomplishments are the Carver Research Foundation (Tuskegee, 1940), funded at first by his own life savings of $33,000, and the Carver Museum (Tuskegee, 1943). Carver never married.

Cassatt, Mary (1845–1926). Painter and printmaker. She was born in Allegheny, then a suburb of Pittsburgh, Pennsylvania, the daughter of a prosperous merchant. Cassatt spent much of her childhood with her parents in France and Germany (1851–1858), then moved with them to Philadelphia (1858), where she studied at the Pennsylvania Academy of Fine Arts (1861–1865). After the Civil War, Cassatt went to France (1866–1870), returned to the United States, and then went to Europe again (1872). This time, she studied in Parma, Italy (1872), Seville, Spain, and Belgium (1873). At this time, she especially revered the works of Correggio, Diego de Silva y Velázquez, and Peter Paul Rubens. Cassatt's paintings began to be exhibited annually at the Salon in Paris (1872–1876), where they attracted the attention of Edgar Degas (beginning in 1874). She established her studio in Paris in 1874. She and Degas met (1877), and he invited Cassatt, the first and only American, to exhibit with his fellow Impressionists (1877–1881, 1886). Both artists began to be influenced by Japanese printmakers (from 1880), and more forcefully so after a big print show in Paris (1890). She was also influenced by the works of Édouard Manet. In her turn, she was influential in gaining French painters recognition in the United States. She enjoyed two one-person shows at the Durand-Ruel Galleries in Paris (1891, 1893).

Cassatt was somewhat imitative in the 1870s, but she became more "American" in the 1880s and later, with sharper colors, broader strokes, more rounded solidity and detail, and greater clarity and liveliness. She painted two of her finest works in the 1890s: *The Bath* (1892), depicting a mother in a striped robe, helping her serious, chubby little girl bathe her feet in a basin on an uptilted floor; and *The Boating Party* (1893), showing a mother and child being rowed by a man, all presented in an asymmetrical composition of firm, rakish, curved lines, with vivid, unusual colors. Cassatt created some two hundred prints; the most famous was a set of ten color aquatints in the Japanese style (1891), including *Maternal Caress*. She painted a mural for the Women's Building at the World's Columbian Exposition* (Chicago, 1893). It was big and broad, and unfortunately is now lost. In the last years of the 1890s and later, her works became drier, less charming, with diminished clarity. She traveled in Italy and Spain (1901) with wealthy American friends, including art patroness Louisine Elder Havermeyer. Cassatt visited America a final time (1908–1909), developed severe eye trouble, had cataract surgery (1912), and was forced to quit painting (1914).

Mary Cassatt is remembered most fondly for her picutres of women—with babies, at the bath, reading, and at the theater. Her brother, Alexander Johnston Cassatt, was a wealthy and generous railroad executive, who became president of the Pennsylvania Railroad Company. Cassatt advised wealthy Americans in search of good European art. For example, she was responsible for the purchase of four Renoirs for $5,000 by Bertha Palmer, wife of Chicago merchant Potter Palmer.*

Catt, Carrie (1859–1947). (Full name: Carrie Lane Chapman Catt.) Reformer. Born in Ripon, Wisconsin, she graduated from Iowa State College (1880), was a school administrator in Mason City, Iowa (1880–1885), then married Leo Chapman, a Mason City newspaper editor (1885). Widowed the following year, she married George Catt in 1890. He worked as a civil engineer in New York City (until his death in 1905). Carrie Catt had already begun woman's suffrage work in Iowa (1887). She continued her work in New York, succeeded Susan B. Anthony* as president of the National American Woman Suffrage Association

(1900–1904), became president of the International Woman Suffrage Alliance (1904–1923), was reelected president of the national association (1915–1947), and founded the League of Women Voters (1920). Carrie Catt was an excellent speaker and administrator.

The Celebrity (1898). Satirical novel by Winston Churchill.* In this light work, influenced by the popular Courtlandt Van Bibber stories of Richard Harding Davis,* Churchill pokes fun at the too-quick success of a celebrated, foppish, cocky author (like Davis himself) who seeks to avoid troublesome lionizers by assuming a seemingly protective false identity, that of a real person who then steals money and becomes a pursued felon. Friends embarrass the celebrity by declining to corroborate his tardy protestations of innocence. A notable feature of *The Celebrity* is Churchill's pleasant gallery of female characters, most of whom are mirror images of the Gibson girls of Charles Dana Gibson.*

***Century*.** (Full title: *Century Illustrated Monthly Magazine*.) Distinguished continuation of *Scribner's Magazine*,* a literary journal established in 1870 and running until 1881, at which time it became the *Century*. *Scribner's* featured serial novels, short stories, poetry, nonfictional prose, and excellent engravings. The *Century*, edited by Richard Watson Gilder* from 1881 to 1909, brilliantly but in time too conservatively, published material in various genres. Fiction included works by George Washington Cable,* Joel Chandler Harris,* John Hay,* William Dean Howells,* Henry James,* Jack London,* S. Weir Mitchell,* Frank R. Stockton,* Mark Twain,* and many other fine writers. Poetry included the work of Thomas Bailey Aldrich,* Edwin Markham,* Joaquin Miller,* William Vaughn Moody,* Edwin Arlington Robinson,* Edmund Clarence Stedman,* and Walt Whitman, as well as too many second-raters, including several women devoted to Gilder's predilection for ideality. Also published were nonfictional prose, notably a popular Civil War series, followed by *Abraham Lincoln: A History** by Hay and John C. Nicolay and a series on the Spanish-American War*; literary criticism, by Howells, Stedman, and a few non-American experts; art and architecture notes; a few essays by Theodore Roosevelt*; items by several writers of humor, including George Ade* and Finley Peter Dunne*; and editorials on civil service, conservation, fiscal policy, immigration, international copyright, labor, municipal, and tax policies, activities, and reforms. The best illustrators for the *Century* were Charles Dana Gibson,* Winslow Homer,* Joseph Pennell,* and Frederic Remington,* as well as a few non-Americans. After Gilder's death in 1909, the *Century* declined in significance. In 1929 it was published only quarterly, and in 1930 it merged with the *Forum*.

***Chap-Book*.** Semimonthly magazine, started in Cambridge, Massachusetts, by Herbert S. Stone* and Hannibal Ingalls Kimball when the two were seniors at Harvard. The first issue appeared on 15 May 1894. The two young men were inspired to start their little magazine after reading such forward-looking American writers as H. H. Boyesen,* Bliss Carman,* Hamlin Garland,* Richard Hovey,* and Henry James,* and works by many contemporary English, Irish, and French authors, all of whom they wished to popularize in the United States. At first planned as a means to advertise their small publishing house, the *Chap-Book* immediately gained favor with the intelligentsia because of its attractive appearance and the originality of its contents. The first issue included an illustration by Aubrey Beardsley and a critical essay by Carman, who was editor for the first two months. When Stone and Kimball graduated from Harvard, they took their *Chap-Book* to Chicago and put it under the wing of Stone's father, who had founded the Chicago *Daily News* and was both the Associated Press general manager and a wealthy banker. Although praise was always high for the *Chap-Book*, its circulation was never substantial. Kimball left for New York in 1896, taking the publishing firm of Stone & Kimball along with him and publishing books. Stone stayed in Chicago, retained control of the *Chap-Book*, and published it and books via Herbert S. Stone & Co. The *Chap-Book* published fiction, poetry, criticism, and artwork by the following Americans, among many others: Thomas Bailey Aldrich,* John Burroughs,* George Washington Cable,* Carman, Stephen Crane,* Paul Laurence Dunbar,* Clyde Fitch,* Henry Blake Fuller,* Garland, Lewis E. Gates,* Ellen Glasgow,* Joel Chandler Harris,* Hovey, James, Hamilton W. Mabie,* William Vaughn Moody,* Joseph Pennell,* Edmund Clarence Stedman,* and Lincoln Steffens.* In addition, it published contributions from numerous non-Americans. The final issue of the *Chap-Book* appeared on 1 July 1898. The *Chap-Book*, regarded from the outset as both a rebel and an establishment organ, set high standards and inspired at least two hundred other, usually short-lived, literary magazine imitations within the next several decades.

Charities. (Full title: *Charities: A Monthly Review of Local and General Philanthropy.*) Magazine reporting on various charitable social services and advocating liberal political reforms. It had a curious evolution. It was started in New York by Edward Thomas Devine, secretary of the Charity Organization Society of the City of New York (1897); became a weekly (1898); and absorbed *Charities Review: A Journal of Practical Sociology* in 1901, after the ten-year existence of *Charities Review* as a monthly. It changed its name several times in the ensuing years: *Charities and the Commons* (1905–1909), *The Survey* (1909–1937), and so on. Publication stopped in 1952.

The Chatelaine of La Trinité (1892). Novel by Henry Blake Fuller.* While in Switzerland, Aurelia West, from Rochester, New York, attempts tyrannically to modernize Bertha, the so-called Chatelaine, who is an innocent girl living at a farm called La Trinité. Miss West persuades Bertha to develop along American lines—materialistic, militant, and domineering of males—rather than along more typically European lines. Aurelia's efforts are opposed by Baron Zeitgeist, who (like Fuller himself) deplores the new culture of America—industrialism, urbanization, and high-finance society—and criticizes Americans for expecting the men to toil too hard and the women to play too irresponsibly. Aurelia, however, turns Bertha's head to such an extent that the once-sweet girl loses three suitors, who dislike the changes in her and abandon the chase for her hand. But Bertha is sufficiently corrupted to leave for Paris and the attentions of other men. Thus, although Aurelia has failed for the moment in Switzerland, Fuller implies his deep-seated fear that some Europeans may already be fatally eager to emulate American social and industrial behavior. This novel, like *The Chevalier of Pensieri-Vani** two years earlier, has minor characters with allegorical names, for example, Fin-de-Siècle, Pasdenom, Saitoutetplus, and Tempo-Rubato; but *The Chatelaine of La Trinité* has sharper, more bitter edges of realism than the earlier work. Reviews of it were so unsatisfactory that Fuller cancelled his plans for a third transatlantic romance, to be based on his 1892 working vacation in Spain and already partly composed, and became more realistic in his artistic orientation. Nevertheless, he retained affection for *The Chatelaine of La Trinité* and once called it his best work.

Chesnutt, Charles W. (1858–1932). (Full name: Charles Waddell Chesnutt.) African-American writer, teacher, lawyer, and stenographer. Born in Cleveland, Ohio, Chesnutt was one-eighth black. After the Civil War ended, his family moved back to Fayetteville, North Carolina, their former hometown. Chesnutt was educated in public schools in Cleveland and Fayetteville, but only to age fourteen. He then taught and soon became a principal in segregated normal schools in South Carolina and North Carolina (1872–1883), read widely in his spare time, married Susan Utley Perry in 1878 (the couple eventually had five children), was a reporter in New York (1883), became a legal stenographer for a railroad company lawyer in Cleveland (1884–1889), published some short stories for the S. S. McClure* newspaper syndicate (1885), passed the Ohio bar (1887), and joined a Cleveland law firm (1887–1890). Thomas Bailey Aldrich,* editor of the *Atlantic Monthly*,* accepted some short stories by Chesnutt (1887, 1888). George Washington Cable* helped him publish his first essay—"What Is a White Man?"—in the *Independent* in 1889 and tried unsuccessfully to hire him as his private secretary (1889).

Chesnutt decided to try supporting his growing family by opening a stenographic service and by writing fiction (1890). *The Conjure Woman* (1899), eagerly purchased by Walter Hines Page* of the Houghton Mifflin publishing firm, is a collection of seven dialect tales, some of which grimly focus on the miseries of slavery, others on voodooism and folk magic both comic and tragic. *The Wife of His Youth and Other Stories of the Color Line* (also 1899) contains nine tales about the plight of dark-skinned persons snubbed by their uppity mulatto relatives. William Dean Howells* and Hamilton W. Mabie* reviewed the collection favorably, but most other critics did not. Also in 1899, Chesnutt published a schoolroom biography of Frederick Douglass.* Chesnutt closed his lucrative stenographic office to rework a novel he had completed earlier. Originally called *Rena Walden*, the book was rejected (1890) by timid Richard Watson Gilder* of the *Century*,* but it was accepted by Houghton Mifflin and published as *The House Behind the Cedars* (1900). It is a tragedy about miscegenation and trying to "pass for white." In the first half, stunning Rena Walden, the daughter of a Southern white man and his light-skinned slave concubine, pretends to be white. She is wooed by an aristocratic Carolinian, but she is dumped when her suitor discovers her racial background. In the second half, Rena becomes a schoolteacher among African Americans, is subjected to sexual harassment, and eventually dies. Chesnutt's second novel, *The Marrow of Tradition* (1901), is based on a bloody 1898 race riot in Wilmington, North Carolina. The plot dramatizes the opposition of a post-Reconstruction North Carolina blueblood family headed by intolerant newspaper editor Carteret to a mixed-blood family headed by Dr. Miller. Soon after his only son is killed by a white mob, Dr. Miller is asked to tend Carteret's only son, who is desperately sick. The outraged man refuses—at first. Climactically, it is revealed that Mrs. Carteret's father was once married to Mrs. Miller's mother; hence the two women, on opposite sides of the color line, are half-sisters. Neither the critics—not even Howells—nor the public welcomed this work. Its financial failure impelled Chesnutt to return to court reporting. A pair of essays Chesnutt published at about the same time as *The Marrow of Tradition* are of interest. He prematurely theorizes in "The Future American: A Complete Race-Amalgamation Likely to Occur" (in the Boston *Evening Transcript*, 1 September 1900), but he is delightfully informative in "Superstitions and Folk-Lore of the South" (*Modern Culture*, May 1901). Chesnutt struggled too hard, published another novel, *The Colonel's Dream* (1905), suffered a nervous collapse (1910), and was debilitated by appendicitis and peritonitis (1920).

Charles W. Chesnutt was a pioneer in writing mature, serious fiction and hard-hitting essays treating racial hatred, forced segregation, and the complex problems generated by miscegenation.

***The Chevalier of Pensieri-Vani*. . .** (1890). As by Stanton Page, 1890, rev. and expanded ed., 1892. Allegorical, episodic, travel novel by Henry Blake Fuller.* (The expression "pensieri vani" means "idle thoughts.") The chevalier, called the Cavaliere, is a kind of autobiographical character, or perhaps the sort of neutral observer Fuller wished to be. Echoing Fuller's happy vacations in Italy in 1879–1880 and 1883, the Cavaliere relishes travel to town after town in Italy, meets a variety of people, and reports and comments on conversations he has with them. The two most important characters the Cavaliere meets are the Prorege of Arcopia [Arcadia utopia?] and young George W[ashington?]. Occident, of Shelbyville, Shelby County, U.S.A. Less central characters, often symbolically or humorously named, include the Princess Altissimi, the Duke of Avon and Severn, Gregorianius, the Seigneur of Hors-Concours, the Madonna Incognita, the Contessa Nullaniuna, the Margravine of Schwahlbach-Schreckenstein, and the Signorina. The Prorege, who beneficently rules the agrarian island of Arcopia and dislikes the inhumane consequences of industrialization, tries to persuade Occident, his young, wealthy, thoughtful, democracy-loving student from the United States, that Europe is better politically, socially, and culturally than industrial, materialistic, barbaric America. The death of Gregorianius, an expatriate German medievalist, symbolizes the fatal effect of living in the past. Occident's return home may be equated with Fuller's own determination to emulate his idol, William Dean Howells,* that is, to return from the Old World to fight America's cultural battles on the home front.

Fuller published *The Chevalier of Pensieri-Vani* at his own expense through a Boston publisher. Conservative Boston critics such as James Russell Lowell and Charles Eliot Norton* were pleased with the stylish book. Reviews soon touched off debates as to whether Chicago, Fuller's native city, could really produce such a skillful romancer. After a second edition and then a third had been exhausted, Fuller added a chapter for a fourth, published in New York City by the Century Company. By that time, he had already published his second transatlantic romance, entitled *The Chatelaine of La Trinité*.*

Chicago, University of. *See* Universities.

Chicago World's Fair of 1893. *See* World's Columbian Exposition.

The Children of the Night (1897). Collection of poems by Edwin Arlington Robinson.* At his own expense, Robinson had published *The Torrent and the Night Before* (1896), containing forty-six poems, all in precise rhyme or blank verse, his habitual forms. (Copies of the little forty-four-page book are now exceedingly rare.) A year later, a friend financed publication through a vanity press of *The Children of the Night*. It repeated forty-four poems from *The Torrent and the Night Before* and added forty-three new ones. Robinson's best 1890s poems are ''Credo,'' which voices faith that light will end all of this chaotic contemporary darkness; ''George Crabbe,'' praising the British poet who though now denied by most readers beats on with a pulse of truth; ''John Evereldown,'' about a man who though aging and wearing out cannot resist the siren call of women; ''Luke Havergal,'' who goes to the western gate, where ''the dark will end the dark'' and where he will hear her call if he listens and trusts; ''Richard Cory,'' who the townspeople think has it all but who, ''one calm summer night, / Went home and put a bullet through his head''; and ''Zola,'' who, since he finds ''the divine heart of man'' in the terrifying truth, must be neither feared nor hated. Robinson was right when he said that by 1889 he was doomed, elected, or sentenced to life as a poet. The poems in his two 1890s books attracted little critical attention at the time but marked the beginning of modern verse in America. One admiring contemporary reader was Theodore Roosevelt,* who praised *The Children of the Night* in print and saw to it that the poet obtained an easy job in New York's federal Custom House (1905–1909).

Chita: A Memory of Last Island (1889). Novel by Lafcadio Hearn.* *Chita* has three parts: "The Legend of L'Île Dernière," "Out of the Sea's Strength," and "The Shadow of the Tide." The first part contains bold impressionistic description. The reader is taken from New Orleans through canals and bayous to the Gulf, observes the desolate islands nearby, notes that the sea constantly gnaws at them, and sees birds, fish, sunbathers, and swimmers. On 10 August 1856 a titanic hurricane savagely rakes natives, guests, and crops from Last Island. Captain Abraham Smith, whose *Star* survives the roiling waters, saves almost "twoscore souls." In the aftermath, gulls fly in to eat the dead fish, and two-legged marauders sail in to rob the human corpses of their *objets de luxe*. The second part tells how Carmen, the wife of a Spaniard named Feliu Viosca, who fishes off Louisiana's coasts, dreams one night of their child Conchita, buried back in Barcelona. In the morning, evidence from Last Island floats nearby. Feliu goes to help, finds and rescues a lone survivor, a tiny, lovely Creole girl, and takes her to the ecstatic Carmen. Authorities query the timid child, learn little, vainly seek her family, and let the Vioscas adopt her. Many months later, young Dr. Julien Raymond LaBrierre, thought to have drowned with his wife, whose body was recovered, and with their missing child, turns up in New Orleans, having been rescued by a sea-going vessel. Missing his wife and child dreadfully, he takes up his life again. In the third part, Chita, as Carmen and Feliu call the girl, grows, plays along the beach, dreams of her mother, respects but also fears the sea, and learns to swim. In 1867 New Orleans is visited by the plague. A sick man named Henry Edwards flees to where the Viosca family lives and then summons his friend Dr. Julien La Brierre to tend him there. Though chronically ill himself after Confederate Army service during the Civil War, Julien takes a sailboat through slimy bayous and then the pleasant open sea, to Last Island, where Feliu tells him that old Edwards has died and Julien falls victim to fever. Chita pops in, and Julien sees his dead wife's features in the child. Soon, with Chita kept safely away from the sickbed, verbosely delirious Julien, tended by devout Carmen, dies.

In 1883, George Washington Cable* told Lafcadio Hearn about the 1856 hurricane which destroyed L'Île Dernière and killed everyone there except one little girl, who was adopted by a fisherman and his childless wife. When the girl was identified years later she was returned to her New Orleans family, but later she went back to her preferred island life. Hearn vacationed in Grand Isle (August 1884), researched details of the 1856 hurricane in pertinent New Orleans newspapers (especially the *Picayune*), began writing his novel on Grand Isle (1886), and finished it a year later while visiting Grand Isle again. He based Chita and her adoptive parents loosely on fact and her real father on his New Orleans friend Dr. Rodolfo Matas, to whom he dedicated *Chita*. Hearn changed the ending of the story from happy to tragic. Harper's editor Henry Mills Alden* accepted *Chita* in 1887 and published it in *Harper's Monthly Magazine* (April 1888) and then as a much-revised book (1889). In style, the novel deliberately echoes features of Hearn's favorite author, Pierre Loti, an impressionistic word painter of exotic places. The great success of *Chita* lies in its superb depictions of the air and the sea, in calm and stormy moods. The sea has a Darwinian message. It throws up life and smashes it down with sublime indifference.

Chopin, Kate (1851–1904). Novelist and short-story writer, minor poet, and essayist. Kate Chopin was born Katherine O'Flaherty, in St. Louis, Missouri. Her father was an Irish immigrant and a successful businessman; her mother was of French-Creole ancestry. Kate's father was killed in a railroad accident in 1855. In the household, Kate admired both her storytelling, intellectually liberal maternal great-grandmother, who supervised her music and her French lessons, and also her maternal grandmother, who taught her the Creole language. Kate was educated in Catholic schools and became a charming socialite; in 1870, she married Oscar Chopin, a conservative Louisiana Creole. After a honeymoon in Europe, they established a residence in New Orleans, where Kate bore five sons and then a daughter and where Oscar Chopin was a cotton merchant until 1879. They moved to Cloutierville, Natchitoches Parish, in north-central Louisiana; there, they lived on inherited land, he managed several farms, and they relished the local social life. Oscar died of swamp fever in 1883, and two years later Kate returned to St. Louis with rather little money. Dr. Frederick Kohlbenheyer, who was her obstetrician, and also an author and an anarchist, encouraged her to study and write. Guy de Maupassant's short stories were her first model. In 1889 she broke into print with a fine lyric poem, "If It Might Be" (in *America*, 10 January), followed at once by two short stories.

From the start, Kate Chopin maintained an unconventional and "unrespectable" position concerning ethical absolutism, women's rights, traditional social mores, sex, and marriage. This position is revealed in her first novel, *At Fault*,* privately printed in St. Louis in 1890. She tried unsuccessfully in 1891 to place a second novel, which she later destroyed. Selling her significant short story "Désirée's Baby" to *Vogue* in 1893 encouraged her to write many more short stories. Some were collected in *Bayou Folk*,* published by the Boston and New York firm of Houghton, Mifflin in 1894 (and often reprinted). Other stories were issued by equally respectable magazines in the East, including more in *Vogue*. Her second short-story collection, *A Night in Acadie*,* was published by a little-known Chicago firm in 1897. By this time, her unconventionality made it difficult for Chopin to place yet another collection of stories, some of which had been published in *Vogue*. Next came Chopin's forward-looking masterpiece, *The Awakening*.* Published by the company of the distinguished Chicagoan Herbert S. Stone* in 1899, this novel too honestly depicted the power of sex and criticized society's mistreatment of women. The result was that Chopin was adversely viewed by most readers and reviewers and by many of her friends as well. Although she was hurt, she continued to write, though at a slower pace. She died soon after at the age of fifty-three.

Churchill, Winston (1871–1947). Novelist. Churchill was born in St. Louis, Missouri. Within weeks, his mother had died, and he was adopted by his mother's sister and her husband. Churchill graduated from the U.S. Naval Academy at

Annapolis (1894) but resigned from the navy three months later. In 1895, he went to work for *Cosmopolitan Magazine*,* resigned the same year, married Mabel Harakenden Hall (the couple had three children), and moved to Irvington-on-the-Hudson, New York, to devote himself to writing. Churchill published two short stories in the *Century** (1896, 1898); a biography of George Dewey,* the naval hero, and a sketch of the Spanish-American War* naval battle off Santiago, Cuba, both in the *Review of Reviews** (1898); and his first novel, *The Celebrity** (1898). This piece of light fiction was followed by three historical romances, of a planned but unfinished five-volume series: *Richard Carvel** (1899), dramatized by E. E. Rose in 1900, set during the American Revolution; *The Crisis** (1901), dramatized by Churchill in 1902, about divided loyalties in St. Louis during the Civil War; and *The Crossing* (1904), featuring the George Rogers Clark expedition. The first two were phenomenal bestsellers in the United States, England, and elsewhere. In fact, in the summer of 1899, the novelist received a letter from the British Winston Churchill, who was no relation, explaining that henceforth he would sign his books Winston Spencer Churchill. Mediocre sales of *The Crossing* convinced Churchill the novelist that romantic historical fiction was giving way to problem novels of a more serious nature. The Churchills bought property in the art colony of Cornish, New Hampshire (1899) and made their permanent home, called Harakenden House, there. It was destroyed by fire in 1923. Churchill combined more writing with reform politics and foreign travel, was in the state legislature (1903–1907), failed in a gubernatorial bid (1912), and published an incredibly popular religious novel entitled *The Inside of the Cup* (1913) but then nothing of note after 1917. (It is a curiosity that the title of each major work by Churchill has a capital letter "C" in it.) Churchill is to be praised for doing careful historical research, presenting detailed background, and offering the public significant themes to ponder; however, almost never did he create notable characters or unusual plots.

Clark University. *See* Universities.

Clark, William A. (1839–1925). (Full name: William Andrews Clark.) Capitalist and politician. Born in Connellsville, Pennsylvania, he moved with his parents to Van Buren County, Iowa (1856), studied law at Iowa Wesleyan College, taught school in Missouri, and then went to the mining fields of the West (1861). He worked in the Colorado and Montana gold mines, opened a store in Virginia City, Montana, and another in Elk City, Idaho, carried the mail from Missoula, Montana, to Walla Walla, Washington, and got into banking and wholesale trading at Deer Lodge and Butte in Montana (to 1877). He took a year off to study mining at the Columbia University School of Mines, and he returned to make a fortune by founding the Colorado and Montana Smelting Company, by starting the first stamp mill and the first smelter in Butte, and by buying up adjacent and distant mines (mainly containing copper). He developed enormous holdings in bronze, city lighting systems, copper, dams, electricity, flour, gold, lumber, newspapers, railroads, sawmills, silver, streetcars, sugar, timber, waterpower, wireworks, and zinc, in Arizona, California, Colorado, Idaho, Montana, New Jersey, New York, and Utah. Clark and Marcus Daly,* for a long time friends, became bitter enemies over politics (1888–1900). Clark wanted to run for political office; Daly sought only to control the politicians. When Daly wanted Anaconda to become the capital of Montana, Clark agreed on the condition that Daly would support him politically. When Daly refused, Clark helped to get Helena named as capital instead. Even though Clark had been president of the 1884 convention to write a constitution for the new state of Montana (and would be chairman of the 1889 convention), he was defeated as a candidate for delegate to the U.S. Congress because of Daly's secret adverse influence (1888). Because of Daly, Clark also lost his bid to be the Democratic senator from Montana (1890 and again in 1893). When he was finally elected senator (1899), Daly saw to it that charges of bribery were leveled against Clark—he admitted spending $140,000 on his campaign—so he resigned (1900).

Clark was able to serve as a senator later (1901–1907) because, by then, Daly had died. In the senate, Clark opposed the federal conservation efforts of Theodore Roosevelt.* Clark married Kate L. Stauffer of Pennsylvania in 1869 (the couple had six children; Kate Clark died in 1893) and Anna E. La Chapelle of Butte in 1901 (the couple had two children). Clark donated a beautiful park, an orphanage, and a working-girls' home to Butte, partly to counter the adverse influence of another enemy, F. Augustus Heinze.* Clark filled "Clark's Folly," his ornate Fifth Avenue Mansion in New York City, with valuable paintings, statues, tapestries, laces, and carpets—all donated to the Corcoran Art Gallery, in Washington, D.C., by his widow. S. S. McClure* published a biased exposé of Clark in his magazine (1906).

Clemens, Samuel Langhorne. *See* Mark Twain.

Cleveland, Grover (1837–1908). (Full name: Stephen Grover Cleveland.) Twenty-second and twenty-fourth president of the United States. Cleveland, born in Caldwell, New Jersey, moved with his family to Fayetteville, New York, in 1841. After his father's death, in 1853, Cleveland worked in New York City in a general store and at an institution for the blind; later, he resided with a well-to-do uncle in Buffalo, New York (1855), where he clerked and studied in a law firm and was admitted to the bar (1859). Rising fast in politics, Cleveland became an assistant district attorney of Erie County, New York, as a Democrat (1863). He avoided serving in the Civil War by explaining that he was his widowed mother's sole support and by paying a substitute to serve for him. He became Erie County sheriff (1871–1873), but mostly he practiced law and in time was elected Democratic mayor of Buffalo on a platform promising honesty and efficiency (1881). Supported by Harold Frederic,* among innumerable others, he was elected governor of New York in 1883 as a nonmachine candidate, and he earned public confidence by vetoing legislation favoring the spoils system as controlled by Tammany Hall.* After a campaign marked by mudslinging on both sides, Cleveland became the first Democratic president in twenty-four years. He antagonized office-hungry supporters by opposing a continuation of the patronage system—but only for a while. He refused to augment Civil War veterans' pensions, arguing that they were sometimes of questionable authenticity. He advocated lower tariffs to avoid selective subsidizing of manufacturers, to diminish the power of trusts, and to reduce the treasury surplus. He repealed the Tenure Act (1887) in order to have the power to dismiss incompetents without congressional approval.

All of these admirable but unpopular moves caused Cleveland's defeat for reelection by Republican Benjamin Harrison* (1888). Cleveland returned to law practice in New York. Four years later, he defeated Harrison, who favored the Silver Purchase Act (*see* Free Silver) and the McKinley Tariff Act, sponsored by William McKinley,* to become president again. During his second administration, which was marred by the Panic of 1893* and its aftereffects, Cleveland caused the repeal of the Silver Purchase Act, which distressed Free-Silver Democrats, and let pass without signing a weak new tariff measure, the Wilson-Gorman Tariff (1894). He opposed the expansionists who favored annexing Hawaii and supporting insurgents in Cuba, but he also pleased them by forcing England to substitute arbitration for intervention in the boundary dispute between British Guiana and Venezuela (1895). Cleveland started a controversy when he favored the selling of bonds through New York syndicates (headed by the pitiless John Pierpont Morgan*) to prop up the unstable gold standard. It was also costly to his reputation when Cleveland opposed Coxey's Army* (1894) and later ordered federal troops to break up the Pullman Strike* (1894). Cleveland was repudiated by the Democratic Party, which nominated William Jennings Bryan* for president (1896). McKinley defeated him, and Cleveland returned to law practice, lecturing, and writing. Cleveland married Frances Folsom, age twenty-two, in the White House in 1886 (the couple had five children).

Grover Cleveland is extolled by many for being honest and impartial, for permanently strengthening the executive branch of federal government, for opposing paternalistic favors to special interest groups (businessmen, railroaders, veterans, farmers, workers), for lowering tariffs, for preserving the gold standard and therefore national economic stability, and for exemplifying conscience in dealing with foreign governments. It has been thought that the titular hero of *The Honorable Peter Stirling, and What People Thought of Him*,* the popular 1894 novel by Paul Leicester Ford,* was partly based on Cleveland. Shortly after Cleveland died, Richard Watson Gilder* published a biography of him (1910).

The Cliff-Dwellers: A Novel (1893). Novel by Henry Blake Fuller.* This novel grew out of a novella drafted by Fuller, entitled "Between the Millstones," unpublished, and now lost. The central fact and symbol of *The Cliff-Dwellers* is the Clifton, an eighteen-story office building owned by Arthur J. Ingles and caging some four thousand workers. Most of the characters are employed in the building or are otherwise associated with it. Erastus M. Brainard, the rich, demanding president of the Underground National Bank, located in the Clifton, is a crooked financial manipulator. He is also the massively frigid husband of an ailing wife. Their quite different children are the heartlessly ambitious Burton Brainard, who marries upward-bound Cornelia McNabb; gentle, nonmaterialistic Abigail "Abbie" Brainard; Mary Brainard, who is enamored of, marries, and is abandoned by sinister J. Russell Vibert; and sensitive young Marcus Brainard, who is interested in art and music and, hence, is both disliked by his father and unsuited for heartless Chicago commerce. The central character in *The Cliff-Dwellers* is George Milward Ogden, a recently transplanted young New Englander who works in Brainard's bank and coolly admires Abbie, who steadfastly loves him. Dislike of her shady family combined with a desire to improve his social status turns George Ogden's head, and the callow man marries Jessie Bradley, whose parents are unpretentiously reputable. Jessie, though pretty, is shallow, frivolous, and sickly. With ruinous extravagance she seeks to emulate Cecilia Ingles, the unseen but much-envied wife of the skyscraper owner, and she is thus the indirect cause of Ogden's stealing money from Brainard's bank. In the melodramatic climax, weak Marcus argues with his cruel father, mortally stabs him, and hangs himself. These events keep Ogden from being charged with embezzlement. Jessie's death then clears the way for Ogden to marry faithful, patient Abbie.

Fuller's twin topics in *The Cliff-Dwellers* of commercial greed and marriage for money blend into a naturalistic picture of life in Chicago that is repellent, as the author found much of his native city to be. Action centers in and near the Clifton but is not limited to that locale. Subordinate characters abound elsewhere in the city and its suburbs. Failures in the Brainard family—especially Erastus's hatred of his son Marcus—may mirror Fuller's disgust at his own father's commercialism and at the man's unsuccessful attempts to make his son into a copy of himself. A skillful device is Fuller's use of Brower, Ogden's bookish roommate early in the novel, who is a mordant commentator on much of the action. *The Cliff-Dwellers* was immediately disliked by conservatives, such as Fuller's friend Charles Eliot Norton,* a Boston brahmin, but also praised by forward-looking critics such as H. H. Boyesen,* Hamlin Garland,* and William Dean Howells.* In an 1893 review of the novel, Howells so praised Fuller for joining the camp of the realists at last that Fuller, remaining partly romantic in orientation, took offense.

The Climbers (1901). Social comedy by Clyde Fitch.* *The Climbers* dramatizes the effects of hedonistic social and financial climbing in Manhattan's high society. Widowed and bankrupt Mrs. George Hunter has three daughters—Blanche, Clara, and Jessica. Mrs. Hunter improves her position by marrying Johnny Trotter, younger and appropriately named, since he is on the move socially. Blanche's husband, Richard Sterling, age thirty-eight, is addicted to gambling.

He loses heavily, but he is rescued from financial ruin by Edward Warden, his chum from college days. Warden and Blanche love each other, but she will not divorce her husband for him. When Sterling discovers their profound affection for one another, he kills himself with an overdose of opium. In the effective closing scene, Blanche and Warden see Sterling apparently asleep and are puzzled about what he intends to do. Warden says, "We will know when he wakes." Several minor characters are well sketched. One is Ruth Hunter, Mrs. George Hunter's sister-in-law. Miss Hunter is in love with a man whose wife is hopelessly insane. She tells Blanche early in the play, "Heartbreak comes from the sorrow of doing wrong, not from the pain of doing right." The moral beneath the quick and sparkling lines of *The Climbers* is that climbing to enhance one's social and financial position can result in a fall.

Cochrane, Elizabeth. *See* Nellie Bly.

Cody, William F. (1846–1917). (Full name: William Frederick Cody; nickname: Buffalo Bill.) Frontier scout and showman. Cody was born in LeClaire, Iowa, moved with his family to Kansas Territory (1854), was a Pony Express rider, served briefly in the Union army as a teamster during the Civil War (1864–1865), married Louisa Frederici in St. Louis in 1866 (the couple had two children), and held various jobs in the Far West. He contracted to supply meat to railroad construction workers (1867–1868), scouted for the U.S. Cavalry (1868–1872), and was a guide for an aristocratic Russian hunting party in the Far West. Cody was the subject of sensational writing by prolific dime-novelist Ned Buntline, who also talked him into appearing in a ridiculous (but popular) Buntline play *The Scout of the Prairie*, which fictionalized his hero's exploits (Chicago, 1872, then elsewhere). Hundreds of additional fictional pieces—many of the most lurid by Prentiss Ingraham—starring Buffalo Bill poured forth. Cody put together his own fabulous Wild West show (Omaha, Nebraska, 1883), took it to London as part of Queen Victoria's Jubilee (1887) and then to the Continent, and appeared at the World's Columbian Exposition* (Chicago, 1893). One of his most attractive and durable stars was Annie Oakley, who toured with him for seventeen years (1885–1902). The show began to slip financially (1902) but continued sporadically for decades thereafter. During the chronic unrest involving the American army and Native Americans preceding the murder of his friend Sitting Bull* (1890) and the Wounded Knee* massacre (1890), Cody placed himself at the service of General Nelson A. Miles,* commander of the Military Division of the Missouri; but Cody was not able to intervene to make peace. Buffalo Bill's various "autobiographies," some ghostwritten, are too unreliable to list.

Coins. American coins have had a long and fascinating history. To regularize and simplify matters of coinage, the U.S. Congress passed a law in 1890 restricting changes in the design of coins to periods of not less than twenty-five years. In 1892 Charles Edward Barber,* chief engraver at the Philadelphia mint, designed a half-dollar silver coin, with a new Liberty head in right profile on its front, which was minted until 1915. Barber also designed the back of the World's Columbian Exposition* commemorative silver half-dollar coin in 1893. In response to a presidential order from Theodore Roosevelt* (1905), the distinguished sculptor Augustus Saint-Gaudens* designed new $10 and $20 gold pieces (1907, minted until 1932). The $10 coin has a Native American head in left profile on the front and a standing eagle on the back. The $20 coin has a standing Liberty on the front and a flying eagle on the back. Saint-Gaudens' $20 gold piece is regarded as one of the most beautiful coins ever struck.

Collier's. Illustrated magazine founded by the successful, Irish-born publisher Peter Fenelon Collier, which enjoyed a long run as a weekly, beginning on 28 April 1888. Its early titles were *Collier's Once a Week* (until 1889), *Once a Week, An Illustrated Weekly Newspaper* (1889–1895), and *Collier's Weekly, An Illustrated Journal* (1895–1904). The magazine was cheap (7¢ a copy at first), popular (with a circulation of 250,000 within four years), and varied, with fiction, factual news, and humor. Collier's son Robert J. Collier became editor (1898) and immediately improved post-panic circulation, partly by serializing "The Turn of the Screw"* by Henry James,* by covering the Spanish-American War* with reports and photographs by James H. Hare* (among other correspondents), and by hiring other talented contributors, including Richard Harding Davis,* Finley Peter Dunne,* Charles Dana Gibson,* Frank Norris,* Frederic Remington,* and James Whitcomb Riley.* *Collier's* had an interesting later history, was edited by Norman Hapgood* (1902–1912), but discontinued publication on 4 January 1957.

Commemorative Postage Stamps. In the 1890s the United States Postal Service began its now common practice of issuing postage stamps to commemorate events and persons important in American history. The first set of such stamps was the beautiful Columbian Commemorative Issue created to celebrate the quadricentennial of the discovery of America by Christopher Columbus and timed to advertise the World's Columbian Exposition* (Chicago, 1893). The series of stamps consists of sixteen different values. Fifteen were issued on 2 January 1893; the 8¢ stamp 1 March 1893. The stamps are as follows: 1¢, deep blue, "Columbus in Sight of Land"; 2¢, brown-violet, "Landing of Columbus"; 3¢, green, "Flag Ship of Columbus"; 4¢, ultramarine, "Fleet of Columbus"; 5¢, chocolate, "Columbus Soliciting Aid of Isabella"; 6¢, purple, "Columbus Welcomed at Barcelona"; 8¢, magenta, "Columbus Restored to Favor"; 10¢, black-brown, "Columbus Presenting Natives"; 15¢, dark green, "Columbus Announcing His Discovery"; 30¢, orange-brown, "Columbus at Rabida"; 50¢, slate blue, "Recall of Columbus," based on a painting by Augustus George Heaton*; $1, salmon, "Isabella Pledging Her Jewels"; brown-red, "Columbus in Chains"; $3, yellow-green, "Columbus Describing Third Voyage"; $4, crimson lake, ''Isabella and Columbus''; and $5, black, ''Columbus,'' based on the souvenir Columbian half-dollar issued for the exposition. The 2¢ stamp was issued in the greatest number, some 1,464,590,000. The $5 stamp, the scarcest today, is, of course, the most valuable; only 21,844 were issued. Its 1991 catalogue values are $2,850 unused, $1,100 used. The Columbian Commemorative Issue was the first, and probably is still the most prized, of the American commemorative postage stamp issues.

Next in the 1890s came the Trans-Mississippi Exposition* Issue of 1898. Placed on sale on 10 June 1898, the set, designed to celebrate the exposition held in Omaha in 1898, consists of nine stamps: 1¢, dark yellow-green, ''Marquette on the Mississippi''; 2¢, copper red, ''Farming in the West''; 4¢, orange, ''Indian Hunting Buffalo''; 5¢, dull blue, ''Fremont on Rocky Mountain''; 8¢, violet-brown, ''Troops Guarding Train,'' based on a drawing by Frederic Remington;* 10¢, gray-violet, ''Hardships of Emigration,'' from a Heaton painting; 50¢, sage green, ''Western Mining Prospector,'' from a Remington painting; $1, black, ''Western Cattle in Storm'' (regarded by experts as one of the best-designed stamps ever issued); and $2, orange-brown, ''Mississippi River Bridge [at St. Louis].'' The 2¢ stemp was issued in the greatest number, some 159,720,800. The $2 stamp is today the scarcest—only 56,200 were issued—its 1991 catalogue values are $1,800 unused, $700 used.

The Pan-American Exposition* held in Buffalo, New York, in 1901 was commemorated in a series of six stamps, each with a central design in black and with a frame in color. Offered for sale beginning on 1 May 1901, the stamps are as follows: 1¢, green and black, ''Fast Lake Navigation''; 2¢, carmine and black, ''Fast Express''; 4¢, deep red-brown and black, ''Automobile,'' based on a photograph of an electric automobile (one of only 8,629 automobiles built in the United States by 1 January 1901 [*see* Automobiles]); 5¢, ultramarine and black, ''Bridge at Niagara Falls''; 8¢, brown-violet and black, ''Canal Locks at Sault de [sic] Ste Marie''; and 10¢, yellow-brown and black, ''Fast Ocean Navigation,'' from a picture of the *St. Paul*, a passenger vessel and the first ship commissioned as an auxiliary cruiser for the American navy during the Spanish-American War.* The 2¢ was issued in the greatest number,—209,759,700; the 8¢, the fewest—4,921,700. Three stamps in this series—the 1¢, the 2¢, and the 4¢—were accidentally printed with inverted centers and hence are now among the most famous rarities in the philatelic world. The 2¢ is the very rarest, with probably no more than 155 unused copies and three cancelled copies now in existence; its 1991 catalogue values are $35,000 unused, $13,500 used.

In the twentieth century, the Postal Service has issued stamps commemorating more than sixty persons whose activities were significant in the 1890s.

Comstock, Anthony (1844–1915). Anti-vice crusader. Comstock was born in New Canaan, Connecticut, completed high school, and served in the Union army during part of the Civil War (1863–1865). He joined the Young Men's Christian Association (New York, 1872) and for the rest of his life worked to suppress what he regarded as salacious literature. He organized the New York Society for the Suppression of Vice in 1873, serving as secretary to 1915; was appointed its chief special agent, with arrest powers; caused the passage of the so-called federal Comstock Laws (1873); and became a special agent for the postal service. A list of books, the sales of which he opposed, sometimes unsuccessfully, includes *The Decameron* by Giovanni Boccaccio, *Gargantua* and *Pantagruel* by François Rabelais, *The Heptaméron* of Marguerite d'Angouleme, *Tom Jones* by Henry Fielding, and *The Triumph of Death* by Gabriele d'Annunzio (all listed in 1897). Comstock was also active in suppressing the sale of contraceptive pamphlets and devices on the grounds that they were immoral and harmful to the public. Comstock conducted raids on publishers and bookstores, frequently testified in court, and wrote books with such revealing titles as *Traps for the Young* (1883) and *Morals versus Art* (1887).

A Connecticut Yankee in King Arthur's Court (1889). Satirical novel by Mark Twain.* The Yankee is Hank Morgan, an intelligent, mechanically inclined foreman of the Colt Arms Factory, in Hartford, Connecticut. He is knocked unconscious during an argument in the factory, awakens in the year 528, is captured by Sir Kay and taken to King Arthur's Round Table at Camelot, and is aided by a page named Clarence. The Yankee saves himself from the machinations of the evil magician Merlin by correctly predicting a solar eclipse and thus impressing everyone. He gains more stature by blowing up Merlin's tower. Called the Boss, the Yankee undertakes to modernize the benighted and church-dominated kingdom by establishing a network of secret schools and factories (supervised by Clarence) to improve the lot of the oppressed people and by running a liberal press and establishing a telephone and telegraph system. Required to go grailing, the Boss accepts Alisande de Carteloise's request that he rescue a certain ogre's victims. He and "Sandy," as he dubs the talkative but charming girl, ride through the countryside. On the way, he recruits able fellows for his training programs, rescues cruelly mistreated prisoners (including some held by King Arthur's beautiful but vicious sister Morgan le Fay), sees that the ogre's castle Sandy has led him to is a mere pigsty and the ogre's prisoners pigs (which he frees), and repairs a leaky well in the Valley of Holiness (thus further discomfiting old Merlin).

The Boss persuades King Arthur to go with him in disguise as pilgrims and see for themselves under what wretched conditions the common people live, suffer, and die. King Arthur agrees. Arthur is appalled by the conditions he sees and behaves well in a sequence of melodramatic episodes. He and the Boss are finally captured and sold as slaves. The Boss escapes, telephones Clarence, and rejoices when knights, led by the redoubtable Sir Launcelot of the Lake, mount a bicycle attack and rescue Arthur and his fellow slaves, who had turned homicidal and were all condemned to be hanged. Back in Camelot, the Boss must now duel Sir Sagramore, whom he unwittingly offended; circumstances oblige the Boss, dressed in circus tights, to shoot to death the foolish knight in glittering but ineffective armor.

Three years now pass, during which the Boss has made commerce flourish (railroads, machines, electric power plants, baseball, and the Round Table converted into a stock exchange) and has married Sandy and fathered a daughter (named Hello-Central after his telephone operator back home). When the child grows sick, a doctor in Merlin's pay encourages the family to vacation in France, during which time the wily magician darkens the whole of England under a church interdict and thus reverses the Boss's republican improvements. Sir Lancelot has also misbehaved, by participating in a railroad stock swindle but more importantly by loving King Arthur's Queen Guenever then murderously rescuing her when she was caught. King Arthur killed his nephew Sir Mordred, would-be usurper to the throne; but Arthur has also died, and Guenever has become a nun. Clarence reports all this to the Boss, who returns, engages in a desperate battle with Merlin and his forces, electrocutes thousands of the enemy, but is stabbed. Merlin casts a spell over him but then backs into an electrified wire and dies cackling. Clarence hides the Boss in a cave along with a manuscript account of everything.

Twain long enjoyed reading Sir Thomas Malory's *Le Morte D'Arthur* (his immediate literary inspiration), recorded the idea for his *Connecticut Yankee* in a notebook entry in 1884, gradually changed his plan from easy-going burlesque to pervasive satire of established British aristocracy, and on the surface plumps for democracy, liberty, and a market economy, rather than monarchy, social castes, and governmental economic control. Beneath the surface, however, boils Twain's bitter awareness that Yankee ingenuity, American machine culture, and any dictatorial form of government (whether that of King Arthur, Merlin, or Sir Boss) hurt the masses and—worst of all—that education (even when conducted in the Boss's Man Factories) cannot enlighten "the damned human race." Dan Beard,* Twain's good friend, provided highly effective illustrations for the first edition of *A Connecticut in King Arthur's Court*, which, incidentally, belongs in the same class as *The Prince and the Pauper* (1881), Twain's earlier and equally popular satire of British monarchical government.

Coolbrith, Ina (1842–1928). (Real name: Josephine Donna Smith; full legal name: Ina Donna Coolbrith.) Poetess. Born near Springfield, Illinois, she was a niece of the Mormon prophet Joseph Smith, was taken by her mother and stepfather William Pickett by covered wagon to California in 1852, and settled with her family in tiny Los Angeles. She married Robert B. Carsley, an evidently deranged minstrel player and ironmonger (1858), had a daughter who died early, and obtained a divorce from Carsley in 1861. Her stepfather protected her one time by wounding her wildly shooting husband in the hand, which then had to be amputated. Pickett later disappeared (1874). Coolbrith made her home in San Francisco (from 1865), helped Bret Harte edit the *Overland Monthly* (1868), and worked long, hard, and effectively as a librarian in Oakland (1873–1906, except when she was sick, 1893–1897). She was friendly with numerous celebrities, including Gertrude Atherton, Mary Austin,* Ambrose Bierce,* Isadora Duncan, Jack London,* Charles F. Lummis,* Edwin Markham,* Joaquin Miller* (she suggested his pseudonym), John Muir,* Edmund Clarence Stedman,* George Sterling, Charles Warren Stoddard,* and Mark Twain.* Her several books of thin, subjective, inspirational lyrical poems about love, land, and sea include *The Singer of the Sea* (1894), a short elegy, and *Songs from the Golden Gate* (1895), a collected edition. She lost all of her worldly goods in the San Francisco earthquake and subsequent fire in 1906, after which she was saved by the charity of friends. Coolbrith always took herself, as well as her decorous, rather Victorian literary salon, with profound seriousness. She was named California's first Poet Laureate by an official act of the California legislature (1915). She was also the nation's first state laureate. But her name will be more lasting as a genial influence upon writers far better than she was. Coolbrith may be equated with the scintillating but unselling poetess Elaine in *For the Pleasure of His Company*, Stoddard's 1903 roman à clef.

Copeland, Charles Townsend (1860–1952). (Nickname: Copey.) Educator, anthologist, and editor. Copeland was born in Calais, Maine, graduated from Harvard (1882), where he was a classmate of Owen Wister,* became a drama critic, then taught English literature and composition at Harvard (1893–1932). He was too young in the 1890s to have greatly influenced the students who attended his popular classes; but his twentieth-century students included Robert Benchley, S. N. Behrman, Van Wyck Brooks, Malcolm Cowley, Bernard DeVoto, John Dos Passos, T. S. Eliot, and John Reed, among other notables. Copeland was witty, read aloud beautifully, but could be ruthless in class. William James, son of the philosopher William James,* painted Copey's portrait.

Copyright Laws. The first significant copyright law was enacted in England in 1700. Several other countries followed suit in due time—Denmark, 1741; France, 1793; Spain, 1847; and Germany, 1870. The Berne Convention (1887) established the first international copyright and created the International Copyright Union, by which each unionist country granted foreign authors the same rights as those enjoyed by its nationals provided their work was first published in the given unionist country. Meanwhile, individual states in the United States adopted their own laws or none, until Congress passed a national copyright law in 1790. Modifications followed. Protection was extended to prints in 1802. The first term of protection was fixed at twenty-eight years, renewable for fourteen more (1831). Musical compositions were protected (1831), as were dramas (1856), photographs (1865), fine-art works, translations, and nondramatic literary works converted to dramas (1870). Responsibility for handling copyright matters was shifted from the State Department to the Department of the Interior (1859) and later to the Library of Congress (1870). Next, chromos, designs, drawings, models, paintings, and statues were protected (1870), then cuts and engravings

(1874). The Chace Act first protected foreign writers, but only if their books were manufactured and registered in the United States (1891). This requirement kept the United States from becoming part of the International Copyright Union. The United States established a Register of Copyrights, which functioned in the Library of Congress (1897). Music performed in public was protected (1897). In the last decade of the nineteenth century, many American writers, including Richard Watson Gilder,* William Dean Howells,* Robert Underwood Johnson,* and Mark Twain,* argued passionately for changes in the laws, to protect authors' and their heirs' rights. Twentieth-century modifications of copyright laws have been numerous; mainly, they have extended coverage to new media—motion pictures, radio programs, sound recordings, television programs, and computer-generated material—and have lengthened the period of protection (as of 1978, for the life of the "author" plus fifty years).

Corbett, James J. (1866–1933). (Nicknames: The Dude, Gentleman Jim, Handsome Jim, Pompadour Jim.) Professional heavyweight boxer. Corbett, one of the ten surviving children of his Irish-born parents, was born in San Francisco. His father was a livery stable owner. Young Corbett excelled as a runner and gymnast, left school at age sixteen, worked in a San Francisco bank (progressing from messenger to assistant teller in six years), and took boxing lessons at the Olympic Club in San Francisco. Dapper Corbett (at 6 feet, 1 inch, 180 pounds) began to box professionally in 1889. He fought tough Joe Choynski three times that year—the first decision was a draw, then Corbett won the second by a knockout in the twenty-seventh round and won the third by decision in four rounds—defeated Jake Kilrain (1890, sixth round), and attracted national attention by fighting Peter Jackson, a redoubtable Australian black, to a sixty-one round draw (1891). Corbett began touring in vaudeville shows and often publicly sounded off about the hesitancy of John L. Sullivan,* whom he had seen twice on tour in the Bay area in 1884 and 1886, to defend his championship title. Corbett met and drank with Sullivan in Chicago, harmlessly sparred with him on stage in San Francisco for money, and began to raise the challenge money of $10,000 Sullivan demanded of any opponent (1891).

Corbett and Sullivan signed in March 1892 for a winner-take-all purse of $45,000. While Sullivan casually trimmed his weight from 246 to 217 pounds, Corbett trained conscientiously, partly in Asbury Park, New Jersey, where Stephen Crane* observed him hobnobbing with Hamlin Garland,* among other important people. The fight, held on 7 September 1892, was the first heavyweight championship event to be sponsored by an athletic club rather than by gamblers, to be held in a legal urban ring, and to be fought under the Marquis of Queensbury rules (with gloves, three-minute rounds, ten-second knockouts, and so on). Western hero Bat Masterson was timekeeper. Corbett had speed, nimbleness, youth, and scientific training in his favor. He broke Sullivan's nose in the third round, was easily in control through the fourteenth round, danced all about the helpless champion through the twentieth round, and knocked him out in the twenty-first round. Fifty Western Union telegraphists flashed the blow-by-blow news, which went across the country and abroad. Corbett sent his parents $10,000 to pay off the mortgage on their house and stable.

Corbett defended his title in 1894 but then lost it to Robert Fitzsimmons by knockout in 1897. Family tragedy struck during the following year: Corbett's father murdered Corbett's mother and then committed suicide. Corbett was knocked out twice more in vain attempts to regain the title (from James J. Jeffries, 1900, 1903); became a stage, movie, and radio celebrity; and wrote his autobiography, *The Roar of the Crowd: The True Tale of the Rise and the Fall of a Champion* (1925). Corbett was the first of a long line of scientific heavyweights who used intelligence, speed, and finesse, instead of pile-driver strength, and who helped lift professional boxing somewhat from its earlier, more shadowy scenes. He was divorced in 1895 from his first wife, then married Jessie Taylor (a.k.a. Vera Stanwood) later the same year. In the final months of his life, he wasted away to 140 pounds. He died of liver cancer and left an estate of $100,000 to Jessie.

***Cosmopolitan Magazine*.** Popular magazine, founded in Rochester, New York, in 1886 as an illustrated home monthly, at $4 a year. It quickly evolved into a literary journal; for example, early issues included works by H. H. Boyesen* and Mary E. Wilkins Freeman,* among other established figures. *Cosmopolitan* moved to New York City, got into financial difficulties (1888), and was purchased by the dazzlingly versatile John Brisben Walker, who cut the price (1889, $2 a year; 1895, 10¢ a copy; 1898, $1 a year), changed its format, and even induced William Dean Howells* to become coeditor briefly (1892). Howells attracted works by Hamlin Garland,* John Hay,* Henry James,* Sarah Orne Jewett,* Theodore Roosevelt,* and Edmund Clarence Stedman,* and contributed articles himself. Illustrators eventually included Frederic Remington,* Charles Dana Gibson,* and Howard Pyle.* By 1898, *Cosmopolitan* enjoyed great circulation, advertising, and therefore financial success, moving, for example, from an 1888 circulation of 20,000 to 300,000 in 1898. It developed departments concerned with socioeconomic and American and international political issues, notably articles on Cuba and South Africa (by Stephen Crane,* Theodore Dreiser,* and Julian Hawthorne), and also with educational, transportation, and scientific issues. Later writers included Harold Frederic,* Jack London,* Mark Twain,* Edith Wharton,* and numerous tip-top foreign authors. Walker, who had many other interests, sold his magazine to William Randolph Hearst* in 1905.

Cotton States and International Exposition. International exposition held at Atlanta, Georgia from 18 September to 31 December 1895. It was planned, beginning in December 1893, to encourage the economy after the Panic of 1893;* to exhibit products and resources of the so-called cotton states (as well as thirty-six other states and thirteen foreign countries); to demonstrate appliances used to cultivate, manufacture, and use those products and resources; to attract outside investors to the South; and to encourage trade with Latin American countries. Obtaining funds totaling almost $2,500,000 proved difficult. Citizens of Atlanta and Fulton County contributed, as did a local banker, the federal government, exhibitors, and concession owners. Piedmont Park was chosen as the site of thirteen main buildings (devoted to agriculture, arts, African-American concerns, electricity, forestry, machinery, manufactures, minerals, transportation, women, and so on), mainly romanesque and forming a kind of amphitheater. The Women's Building and the Negro Building proved to be especially attractive. In the latter, Booker T. Washington* gave his famous Atlanta Compromise Speech, which argued for what amounted to a separate-but-equal status for African Americans. Smaller buildings represented several states, Mexico, Japan, and several Central and South American countries. Bernhard E. Fernow,* the renowned forester, was an exhibit judge. The exposition featured a popular midway. The fair attracted 780,000 people, lost 1 percent of its investment, but in the process proved an economic boon to the South.

The Country of the Pointed Firs (1896). Loosely integrated novel by Sarah Orne Jewett.* The unnamed narrator is a woman writer from the city who is visiting Dunnet Landing, a town on the coast of Maine. In a series of twenty-one local-color cameos, she tells how, in the course of a summer there, she learns to appreciate the rugged independence of its citizens. They have a seafaring, fishing, and island tradition, but the region is now an economic backwash, devitalized but still quietly proud and independent. The narrator rooms and boards with widowed Almira Todd, who is the local herb doctor and the repository of much lore. Almira grows some of her own herbs, collects others elsewhere locally, concocts nostrums, and talks to friends all over the region. The narrator decides to write in the empty schoolhouse, where one day retired old Captain Littlepage calls on her, mentions his favorite authors, then launches into an anecdote about a town near the North Pole which he heard about from a fellow seaman and which is thought to be a haven for souls on their way to heaven. Mrs. Todd takes the narrator to Green Island, a pine-wooded herbal sanctuary, where her octagenarian mother Mrs. Blackett and her aging bachelor son William Blackett live. William, though chronically shy, opens up to the quietly receptive narrator. Back home, Mrs. Todd tells the narrator the story of Joanna, her drowned husband's cousin, who was frustrated in love long ago and decided to live on Shell-heap Island. When Mrs. Todd accompanied the minister on a visit to Joanna there once, they found her happy enough, living partly on fish supplied by friendly fishermen, and when she died she was buried there. Toward the end of summer, Mrs. Todd favors the narrator by letting her accompany her and her mother to their Bowden ritualistic family reunion, held some distance inland. Old Mrs. Blackett is a respected matriarch of the clan. When the unobtrusive narrator impresses widowed Elijah Tilley, one of Dunnet Landing's oldest fishermen, he invites her to his tidy home, where she observes his knitting and listens to his stoical reminiscence about his beloved wife. When the time comes for the narrator to leave the village and return to her own home, Mrs. Todd, suddenly taciturn, cannot say goodbye, but instead packs everything for her departing guest and leaves a valuable little gift for her.

Jewett gained her love of "Dunnet Landing" and the kinds of people who lived there through accompanying her father, a country physician, on his rounds. The scenery depicted is a composite of the Berwick and Boothbay regions of coastal Maine. *The Country of the Pointed Firs* is a masterpiece of its sort. Its appeal lies not in action but in subtle characterization and charming description. The tangy characters and their sometimes dour but often startlingly beautiful living space of land, water, and sky are memorably linked in marvelously evocative poetic prose. Jewett wrote four more Dunnet Landing stories, some or all of which are sometimes incorporated, not very harmoniously, into later editions of *The Country of the Pointed Firs*. "The Queen's Twin" (1899) is about an old woman who was born the same day as Queen Victoria and hence feels a psychic identity with her. In "A Dunnet Shepherdess" (1899), Mrs. Todd introduces the narrator to William Blackett's aging girlfriend Esther Hight. "The Foreigner" (1900) tells about the woman from whom Mrs. Todd learned her herbal wizardry, and "William's Wedding" (uncompleted, 1910) concerns the wedding of Esther and William.

Coxey, Jacob Sechler (1854–1951). Manufacturer and politician. He was born in Selinsgrove, Pennsylvania. After working as a young man in a rolling mill, he established a company in Massillon, Ohio, that furnished high-grade silica sandstone sand for steel mill use (1881–1929). He also founded a lucrative steel mill in Ohio (1889), which he sold to the Pittsburgh Plate Glass Company (1909). He also became a well-to-do horse breeder. When he had to lay off forty quarry laborers during the Panic of 1893,* he was inspired to become a permanent champion of the cause of the unemployed. He was imprisoned for twenty days for organizing and leading Coxey's Army* of unemployed men on a job-demanding march into Washington, D.C., in the spring of 1894, during the second presidency of an unsympathetic Grover Cleveland.* Coxey later proposed the issuance of noninterest-bearing bonds and extensive appropriations to improve county roads. Under his plan, a given county wanting better roads could issue bonds to be deposited with the secretary of the treasury for legal tender notes, the bonds to be retired by taxes over a twenty-five-year period. Such public improvements would be built by otherwise jobless men at $1.50 per eight-hour day. Coxey's Good Roads Bill proposed financing roads nationwide by the issuance of $500,000,000 in legal tender. Coxey reasoned that his plan would lower interest rates, inflate currency, especially improve backward rural areas, and provide work for the unemployed. In later years, Coxey was an unsuccessful Populist Party* candidate for various state and federal offices. He also led a later march of the jobless on Washington in 1914.

Coxey married Caroline Amerman in 1874 (the couple had four children). They were divorced in 1888, and Coxey married Henrietta Sophia Jones in 1890 (this couple also had four children, including a son ridiculously named Legal Tender Coxey). Henrietta and Legal Tender were recruits in Coxey's famous army and were part of its march on Washington.

Coxey's Army. A march of unemployed workers into Washington, D.C. The march was organized by Jacob Sechler Coxey,* at Massillon, Ohio, in the spring of 1894. Carl Browne, a religious zealot and charlatan, joined the group. Browne asserted that he and Coxey were living parts of Christ's mind: Coxey was the cerebrum and Browne himself was the cerebellum. Coxey's wife, Henrietta, and their baby boy, Legal Tender Coxey by name, were both part of the army, which aimed to present the president, Grover Cleveland,* with a "petition in boots." Coxey led off with the boast that 100,000 men would follow him. Although only 100 started with him, Coxey had attracted about 500 by the time he reached Washington, where he and Browne were arrested and fined for walking on the grass. Coxey's Army inspired seventeen other such marches of the disaffected jobless.

Crane, Stephen (1871–1900). Short-story writer, novelist, poet, war correspondent, and literary hack. Born in Newark, New Jersey, Crane was the fourteenth and last child of an old-fashioned Methodist minister and his wife. Only eight of his siblings were alive when Stephen Crane was born. The Crane family lived in various places in New Jersey and then, from 1878, in Port Jervis, New York. Crane's father died in 1880. The mother, a religious essayist, temperance advocate, and reporter, moved the family to Asbury Park, New Jersey, in 1883. She died in 1891. By this time, Crane had gained some journalistic experience by relaying vacation news to his brother Jonathan Townley Crane, who managed a news agency for the New York *Tribune*. Crane's formal education was brief and uninspired. He attended a New Jersey Methodist boarding school (1885–1887) and a military academy at Claverack, New York (1888–1890), then went for a term in 1890 to Lafayette College, and for another in 1891 to Syracuse University. In college he excelled only in boxing and baseball. He was employed as a Syracuse stringer for the New York *Tribune*; he also accomplished some early private writing. By the spring of 1891 he abandoned all plans for further schooling. That summer he met and was influenced by Hamlin Garland* and also camped briefly with friends in Sullivan County, New York. In the fall he lived with his brother Edmund Brian Crane in Lake View, New Jersey, bummed around in New York City, and began his full-time literary career.

At first Crane was an impoverished free-lance reporter, living in the seedy Bowery, and often imposing on the hospitality of other writers, and also artists and medical school students, some of them little better off than he was. Crane called the rowdy bunch "Indians." His most important host benefactor at this time was the painter-photographer Corwin Knapp Linson,* who was then a National Academy of Design student and a magazine illustrator. With these loyal Bohemian friends, Crane smoked incessantly, drank too much, played cards, and ate injudiciously because of poverty. In the summer of 1892 he was a reporter at Asbury Park, New Jersey, and, among other items, covered a lecture by Jacob Riis,* author of *How the Other Half Lives: Studies among the Tenements of New York*,* on New York slum life. Crane published the first version of *Maggie: A Girl of the Streets** in 1893, privately and pseudonymously. This harsh, Zola-esque novel impressed William Dean Howells,* who through Garland met Crane, favorably reviewed him, and provided other help. In the summer of 1894, Crane camped briefly in Pike County, Pennsylvania. Late that same year, he published an abridgement of *The Red Badge of Courage*.*

The years 1895 and 1896 were busy ones for Crane. In 1895, he journeyed to the American West and down into Mexico as a reporter and writer (January–May), then published *The Black Riders and Other Lines** and *The Red Badge of Courage* in full-length form. In 1896, he published a revision of *Maggie, George's Mother*,* *The Third Violet** (as a serial in October and November), and *The Little Regiment and Other Episodes of the American Civil War*.* By this time, Crane was established as a skillful writer not only of fiction but also of features and special journalistic reports. He sent an inscribed copy of *George's Mother* to Theodore Roosevelt,* who was then New York police commissioner and who, in a letter of acknowledgment, praised Crane's work, especially *The Red Badge of Courage*. However, Crane soon got himself hounded out of New York City by gossip and the police. He had written some muckraking "Midnight Sketches" describing Manhattan derelict life and police corruption. Then, in September, he staged an evening chat with two chorus girls and Dora Clark, a woman known by a nearby plainclothes detective to be a prostitute. When the detective collared her, Crane objected, insisted on appearing in court to help her, gained bad publicity by doing so, incurred the enmity of the authorities, and was intimidated by them. In November he decamped for Florida to await transportation to Cuba to report the rebellion against the Spanish government there. First, however, in Jacksonville he met Cora Ethel Eaton Howorth (1865–1910). Known as Cora Taylor for business purposes, this Massachusetts-born woman had divorced one husband (Thomas Vinton Murphy), was separated from a second (Captain Donald William Stewart), and became the proprietress of a brothel doubling as a nightclub.

While attempting to run guns to Cuban rebels, Crane and others were shipwrecked fifteen miles off the Florida coast below Daytona, on 2 January 1897. He converted this experience into his short story "The Open Boat,"* again sought passage to Cuba, but soon gave up and by March was in England on his way to cover the Greco-Turkish War for the New York *Journal* (owned by William Randolph Hearst*) and the London *Westminster Gazette*. Cora Taylor joined him in London and accompanied him to Munich; by train, she went on to Greece, where she was billed as the first female war correspondent (for the *Journal*), using the pen name Imogene Carter. Crane soon got himself to Greece via Marseilles and Crete. He vividly reported the one-month debacle of the Greeks (ending late May), vacationed a little, joined Cora in Marseilles, and by

June began a bizarre residence with her in Surrey, England. They socialized with the Scottish novelist Robert Barr, expatriate American novelist Harold Frederic* (and Kate Lyon,* the second of his two concurrent "wives"), British publisher William Heinemann,* Polish-born novelist Joseph Conrad, and others. (Crane especially liked Frederic's Civil War short stories and was grateful to Frederic for a discerning 1896 review of *The Red Badge of Courage*.) While in England, Crane scribbled frantically to minimize debts incurred by "Cora Crane." His best products were "The Monster,"* "Death and the Child," "The Bride Comes to Yellow Sky,"* and "The Blue Hotel."*

Soon after he heard that the *Maine* had been blown up in Havana harbor on 15 February 1898, Crane left England and Cora for New York and war. He tried to join the U.S. Navy in April but failed the physical examination because he had tuberculosis. So he became a reporter for the New York *World*, owned by Joseph Pulitzer,* in Cuba in April and May. He told war photographer James H. Hare,* with whom he became friendly, that his only purpose in signing with the *World* was to get a military pass so that he could observe the war and write a book about it. During the conflict, Crane also associated with correspondents Richard Harding Davis* and Sylvester Scovel.* While in Cuba, Crane added typhoid and malaria to his list of ailments. Still, he went on to become a reporter for the *Journal*, very briefly in Puerto Rico in August. His Spanish-American War* dispatches are considered among the best of their sort, especially "Marines Signaling under Fire" (*World*, 1 July 1898). After the war, Crane holed up for three months in Havana to write newspaper articles and fiction. Not knowing his whereabouts, Cora asked John Hay,* then American ambassador to England, to trace him.

In January 1899 Crane returned from New York to England, picked up with Cora again, this time in Sussex, where he wrote and also made the acquaintance of many nearby writers, including George Gissing, Edmund Gosse, Ford Madox Hueffer (later Ford Madox Ford), Henry James,* and H. G. Wells. Fighting tuberculosis and more unpaid bills, Crane wrote on and on, usually less well but sometimes with the same old gaunt power. He and Cora took in two of the children of Kate Lyon and Harold Frederic after Frederic died in October 1898. (Cora kept them until October 1900.) Foolish entertaining strained Crane's health dangerously. Severe lung hemorrhages in December 1899 and April 1900 slowed and then stopped his last literary efforts. The results of his death-defying writing include *War Is Kind** (published in May 1899), *Active Service** (October 1899), *The Monster and Other Stories** (December 1899), *Wounds in the Rain: A Collection of Stories Relating to the Spanish-American War of 1898** (1900), *Whilomville Stories** (1900), *Great Battles of the World** (1901; Harold Frederic and Kate Lyon helped with the research, and Lyon did much of the writing); *The O'Ruddy* (an Irish parody-romance potboiler completed in 1903 by Barr in accordance with Crane's deathbed instructions); and numerous shorter items. Cora took Crane to the Continent in May 1900, and he died in Badenweiler, Germany, in June.

Stephen Crane was a careless, pioneering literary genius who wrote with many sustained flashes of brilliance, especially in fiction, but who was addicted to alcohol and nicotine and led a suicidally undisciplined life. Aiming from the start at personal honesty, he presented a jaundiced view of the world and its people, as he evolved an ever more satirical, detached, ironic tone. *Maggie* is both the first significant literary treatment of slum life in America and America's first naturalistic novel. *The Red Badge of Courage* remains the best literary interpretation of the psychology of Civil War soldiers. His short stories "The Blue Hotel," "The Bride Comes to Yellow Sky," and "The Open Boat" are classics. His poetry is usually shocking and often unacceptably bitter. He called them "pills." Because of his impressionistic responses to embattled human beings' illusions, he is variously interpreted as an awkward determinist and as a sarcastic Christian idealist. Although Crane read a good deal, other authors offer more comparisons than evidence for source study. *Maggie* may have been influenced by Gustave Flaubert's *Madame Bovary*. War scenes in Leo Tolstoy and Émile Zola may have affected *The Red Badge of Courage* to a degree, although Crane's work is less repertorial than Zola's and although Crane called *War and Peace* "Peace and War."

Many American writers touch Crane's professional and personal life. His *Whilomville Stories* are in the same vein as *The Story of a Bad Boy* by Thomas Bailey Aldrich.* The unromantic war stories of Ambrose Bierce,* as well as his cynicism, have inevitably inspired comparisons to Crane, who greatly admired "An Occurrence at Owl Creek Bridge" and much else by the older man. Although Bierce praised *The Red Badge of Courage*, he must have been jealous of the success of this novel, by a youth who, unlike Bierce, had never seen combat. Richard Harding Davis, initially more famous than Crane, disliked him personally in many ways, envied him his genius but honestly acknowledged his ability both in print and privately, disapproved of and gossiped about Cora, and was Crane's able rival as a war reporter first in Greece and then in Cuba, where they were often together. For his part, Crane regarded Davis as a conscientious reporter but a snobbish, foolish man. The two satirized each other in fiction: The snobbish journalist Rufus Coleman in Crane's *Active Service* is based partly on Davis, whose characterization of Channing, the mordant journalist in his 1901 story called "A Derelict," owes something to Crane. Crane and Harold Frederic were kindred spirits: both advocated realism and despised cant. In London, Frederic read *The Red Badge of Courage* and praised it extravagantly in a dispatch to the New York *Times* (26 January 1896). When Crane first arrived in England on his way to Greece, Frederic helped him socially and did so again after Crane had returned to England. Bigamous Frederic and Kate Lyon, one of his two wives, were later hospitable to both Crane and his "wife" Cora. The foursome enjoyed a working vacation in Ireland in September 1897. Crane praised Frederic's work in general in a *Chap-Book** essay (15 March 1898). Frederic, in the New York *Times*, 1 May 1898, extolled Crane's powers of observation as evidenced in *The Open Boat and Other Tales of Adventure*.* Frederic disliked "The

Monster'' by Crane and argued with him about it. Frederic and Kate Lyon aided Crane in his research for the *Great Battles of the World*. Hamlin Garland, one of the first to recognize genius in Crane, was a major influence on him. Crane attended a lecture by Garland at a New Jersey resort on Howells and realism, and he reported the main points so intelligently in a New York *Tribune* review (18 August 1891) that Garland arranged to meet him. Garland also arranged for Crane to meet publisher S. S. McClure* (January 1893), praised *Maggie* when it first appeared, persuaded Crane to send Howells a copy, was impressed by Crane's uncanny ability to write fine poetry spontaneously, and read and was thrilled by a draft of *The Red Badge of Courage*. Garland steadily reinforced Crane's determination to depict life truthfully, as Howells was advising the whole new generation of realists to do. Howells invited Crane to his home beginning in April 1893, championed him all he could and on a regular basis, granted him a significant interview in which they discussed realism and which Crane published in the New York *Times* (28 October 1894), and in his preface to the 1896 London edition of *Maggie* boldly compares its theme to fatalism in Greek tragedy. *The Third Violet* is, in a sense, Crane's contribution to the subgenre of the summer vacation novel popularized by Howells for decades. More significantly, in *The Red Badge of Courage*, Crane availed himself of the third-person, objective point of view that Howells, as well as Henry James, had been perfecting in popular magazines available to him. In a perfunctory way, Crane admired some of the works of James but more often regarded them as tiresome. Crane and especially Cora were more interested in socializing with James in Sussex. The painter C. K. Linson, Crane's Bowery friend, was a significant influence, and his *My Stephen Crane* is a valuable reminiscence; however, it was not published until 1958, late in the artist's life. Linson is partly a model for Billie Hawker in *The Third Violet*, Crane's novel about a Bohemian painter. Frank Norris* reviewed *Maggie* in 1896 and compared its painterly effects to flashlight photographs; however, he felt that Crane was more concerned with style than with content, and he regarded Crane's handling of his heroine's downfall as too brief. Riis probably influenced Crane's *Maggie* to a degree. Roosevelt never liked Crane after the Dora Clark incident, and, during the Spanish-American War, he preferred chesty war reporter Davis to slovenly Crane, who, however, praised in print both Teddy and his Rough Riders in Cuba. Crane and Mark Twain* met briefly in New York (1895) and again in London (1899). Crane liked neither what he regarded as the sometimes clownish figure the celebrated humorist cut nor very much of his writing. He thought that *Adventures of Huckleberry Finn* had a ridiculous ending and that *A Connecticut Yankee in King Arthur's Court* * was as ''inappropriate as a drunken bride.'' Only *Life on the Mississippi* pleased him, but he found this too long, as indeed he found most books.

Crawford, F. Marion (1854–1909). (Full name: Francis Marion Crawford.) Novelist, historian, and literary critic. He was born in Bagni di Lucca, Italy, the son of Thomas Crawford, the expatriate American sculptor with studios in

Rome. His mother was Louisa Ward Howe Crawford, the sister of the politician-lobbyist Samuel Ward and of the authoress Julia Ward Howe. One of his many cousins was Ward McAllister.* F. Marion Crawford lived mostly in Rome until 1879, but he was also a student at St. Paul's School (Concord, New Hampshire, 1866–1869); in Essex, England (1870–1873, intermittently); at Trinity College, Cambridge (1873–1874); and in Karlsruhe and Heidelberg, Germany (1874–1877). He edited a newspaper in Allahabad, India (1879–1880), returned to Rome, then went to Boston (1881) to seek work as a writer. He quickly wrote two popular novels: *Mr. Isaacs: A Tale of Modern India* (1882) and *Dr. Claudius: A True Story* (1883). From this time on, his life became a romantic legend. Using Sorrento and Rome as his main bases, Crawford wrote more than forty novels. He married Elizabeth Christophers Berdan in Constantinople in 1884 (the couple had four children), purchased and personally redesigned a Sorrentine villa for himself and his family and numerous guests (1887), traveled widely, enjoyed annual visits to the United States (1892–1907), bought a large yacht (1896), wrote a romantic play called *Francesca di Rimini* (1902), and started multivolumed histories of Rome, Venice, and southern Italy and Sicily.

Crawford's main talent lay in fiction writing, particularly novels. In all, Crawford published more than fifty book-length works, several in two and three volumes each. The twenty-two novels and five other books that he published between 1888 and 1901 show his spectacular fecundity and diversity. *With the Immortals* (1888) is a curious fantasy in which the spirits of Julius Caesar, Frédéric Chopin, Francis I of France, Heinrich Heine, Dr. Samuel Johnson, Leonardo da Vinci, and Blaise Pascal discuss many problems with persons of this age. *Greifenstein* (1889), based on a real case, is a powerful tragedy cast in Germany that projects fear of German militarism. *A Cigarette-Maker's Romance* (1890) details the love of a Russian count and a poor Polish girl in Munich. *Sant' Ilario* (1889), *Don Orsino* (1892), and *Corleone: A Tale of Sicily* (1897) are the last volumes of Crawford's acclaimed Saracinesca tetralogy which began with *Saracinesca* (1887) and which details the life of a great Italian family in Papal Rome from 1865 to Republican Rome in the 1890s. (*Corleone*, incidentally, is a Mafia romance.) *Khaled: A Tale of Arabia* (1891) is an Arabian Nights fantasy about a genie seeking a soul through love. *The Witch of Prague: A Fantastic Tale* (1891) is an original blend of Gothic horrors, occultism, and pseudo-science. *The Three Fates* (1892) details the struggles of a modern writer, like Crawford himself, in well-depicted New York City. *The Children of the King: A Tale of Southern Italy* (1892) and *Pietro Ghisleri* (1893) are melodramatic Italian romances. *Marion Darche: A Story without Comment* (1893) is a socially conservative, antimaterialistic novel set in contemporary New York City. *Love in Idleness: A Tale of Bar Harbor* (1894) is a summer love story. *Katharine Lauderdale* (1894) and its sequel, *The Ralstons* (1895, included in the first best-seller list to be published in the United States, by *Bookman*,* January 1895—*see* Best-selling Books, 1888–1901), deplore decadence in dehumanized New York. *Casa Braccio* (1895) is a fiery Italian tragedy involving a nun, love, and murder. *Adam Johnstone's Son* (1896) and *Taquisara* (1896) are southern Italian melodramas of intrigue. *A Rose of Yesterday* (1897) is an antidivorce novel. *Via Crucis* (1898) is a Sir Walter Scott–like Crusade romance. *In the Palace of the King: A Love Story of Old Madrid* (1900) is a melodrama cast in the time of Philip II of Spain. *Marietta: A Maid of Venice* (1901) is a fifteenth-century love story and, incidentally, describes glassmaking in an authoritative manner.

In addition, Crawford wrote *Constantinople* (1895) and *Bar Harbor* (1896), both of which are travel books, and *Ave Roma Immortalis: Studies from the Chronicles of Rome* (1898) and *The Rulers of the South: Sicily, Calabria, Malta* (1900). Finally, Crawford's *The Novel: What It Is* (1893) sets forth his thesis that the novel should amuse and interest the reader by creating the illusion of reality rather than reality itself, should strive for universal appeal—by stressing love, for example, and not local-color peculiarities—and should not aim to preach religion, social change, or politics. Obviously, these tenets set Crawford apart from most of other significant writers of the 1890s. Still, he catered to his vast reading public with enormous success. He is the best example of the historically and scenically accurate romantic novelist in the entire late nineteenth century.

Crawford was handsome, debonair, and gracious. He knew fifteen or more languages, was at home in the "best" Italian and American society, was knowledgeable about various forms of art, was a master seaman, and thoroughly understood European history. Many more critically acclaimed contemporary writers accepted his hospitality but envied his facile success.

Crime. By 1890, if not earlier, most of the American public had grown aware that something was amiss in this land of opportunity. Fortunes had been made by Civil War profiteering. Huge industrial and other businesses had combined in restraint of competition. The American idle rich, inheritors of unearned wealth, were living extravagantly on both coasts and in Europe. City, county, state, and federal politicians received and dispensed bribes. The discrepancy was dramatically vast between the rich, in their mansions in and out of town, and the huddled masses that froze or sweltered in city tenements. Violent labor strikes were on the rise. Lawlessness formerly thought by the Eastern reading public to be confined to the plains and saloons of the Far West was rampant in inner cities, where not only street gangs but also armed citizens roamed out of control. Statistical reports proved that murder, blackmail, extortion, and theft were increasing drastically. Mafia soldiers and Tong warriors were growing menaces, and anarchists (mostly "foreigners") were openly advocating the use of dynamite. So-called coroners, often political appointees, were amateurish and lax. Bribe-taking, racist police, including private police, and other law enforcement officers were usually minions of the high and mighty. Vigilantism and even political assassination were frequent and dramatic responses to the people's sense of frustration.

What to do? Intrepid and sensation-seeking journalists and editors—William Randolph Hearst,* S. S. McClure,* Joseph Pulitzer,* and Lincoln Steffens* the most notable of dozens—wrote and published exposés in inexpensive magazines and newspapers of wide circulation (especially *Collier's,* Cosmopolitan Magazine,* Harper's Monthly Magazine,* McClure's Magazine,** the New York *Journal*, the New York *World*, *Munsey's Magazine,** and the San Francisco *Examiner*). The Society for the Prevention of Crime (founded in 1870) became more active. Tammany Hall* villainy in New York was vigorously investigated for the first time, as were political corruption and police brutality in other seamy cities, including Chicago, Denver, Indianapolis, New Orleans, Philadelphia, Pittsburgh, and San Francisco. Better, if now and then ridiculous, methods of detection were tried, including the use of pseudo-scientific criminal profiling (after Cesare Lombroso, Alphonse Bertillion, and others), the establishment of the National Bureau of Criminal Identification (in Chicago, 1897), chemical analysis of evidence (including blood and poisons), and finally the science of fingerprinting (but not until the turn of the century).

Crime fiction was another response, an indirect cry for help. Many of Sir Arthur Conan Doyle's stories of Sherlock Holmes, the world's most famous fictional detective, were republished in the United States (beginning 1890) and helped popularize the publication of reports about real-life American detectives (from the mid-1890s) and also short stories centering on crime and detection. At first these were written by journalists (for example, Richard Harding Davis* and Steffens) who frequently made reporters their antiestablishment, science-minded narrators. Four authors of crime fiction in the 1890s deserve special mention: Rodrigues Ottolengui, Melville Davisson Post, Josiah Flynt (real name: Josiah Flynt Willard), and Francis Walton (real name: Alfred Hodder). Ottolengui's *A Conflict of Evidence* (1893) features an experienced detective and his dumb assistant, a murderer staging his own murder and implicating his enemy, misleading circumstancial evidence, disguises, a secret room, a written confession, and true love. Ottolengui, a dentist, also wrote *Methods of Filling Teeth: An Exposition of Practical Methods . . .* (1892). Post, an attorney, wrote *The Strange Schemes of Randolph Mason* (1896, seven short stories) and *The Man of Last Resort; or, the Clients of Randolph Mason* (1897, five more short shories). These popular works feature crimes, the law, and minor detective action, the purpose of which is to show that by legal maneuvers the guilty rich can usually avoid punishment. Post wrote much other fiction, on into the 1920s. Flynt and Walton together published *The Powers That Prey* (1900), a reprinting of ten of their short stories that had originally appeared in *McClure's*, showing, by the use of bitter irony, not only that power corrupts politicians, policemen, prison authorities, detectives, and criminals, but also that being corrupt pays handsomely. Flynt, after much research, also wrote *Tramping with Tramps: Studies and Sketches of Vagabond Life* (1899, paralleling research by Walter A. Wyckoff*; often reprinted; translated into German in 1904), *Homosexuality among Tramps* (1900), *Notes of an Itinerant Policeman* (1900), *The World of Graft* (1901), and *The Little Brother: A Story of Tramp Life* (1902). Thus Flynt came by his cynicism naturally. His autobiography, *My Life*, was published posthumously (1908). Walton earned a Ph.D. at Harvard in philosophy and also published a sociological study entitled *The New Americans* (1901).

The Crisis (1901). Novel by Winston Churchill.* Set in and around St. Louis, Missouri, before and during the Civil War, *The Crisis* depicts the dramatic clashes between powerful conservative pro-Confederate leaders and German immigrants, other migrants, and other common citizens, all of whom favor abolition and the Union cause. Hero Stephen Brice is a Boston-bred lawyer, practicing in St. Louis in 1856. Brice works for Republican abolitionist Judge Whipple, whose fine old friend is Colonel Comyn Carvel (grandson of Richard Carvel, hero of Churchill's 1899 novel *Richard Carvel**). Colonel Carvel is an aristocratic Southern Democratic merchant. The colonel's daughter Virginia admires Brice, though not his Northern political opinions, and hence becomes engaged instead to dashing, fiery, pro-Southern Clarence Colfax. War splits Brice and Virginia. Colfax becomes a Confederate soldier. Brice, who was impressed by Abraham Lincoln during the Lincoln-Douglas debates, enlists in the Union army, serves under General William Tecumseh Sherman, is wounded and is then nursed back to health by Virginia, and becomes an aide to President Lincoln. At war's end, the president—to Virginia's delight—pardons Colfax, who is about to be shot as a Confederate spy.

Two subplots are secondary to war matters but are related to them. One subplot concerns Brice's friend Karl Richter, a St. Louis resident who escaped from unstable Germany in the late 1840s and who exemplifies numerous Missouri Germans favoring unionism now. The other subplot concerns Eliphalet Hopper, a wily, greasy war-profiteer from New England who impoverishes Colonel Carvel and nearly makes off with his daughter Virginia.

The Crisis, an even better popular success than *Richard Carvel*, sold 100,000 copies the first week after publication. Theodore Roosevelt* praised it publicly. The vignettes of Lincoln, Sherman, and also General Ulysses S. Grant, and other aspects of the historical background, were much admired. More forward-looking critics, such as William Dean Howells* and Frank Norris,* however, labeled its romantic historical tendencies outmoded.

Criticism and Fiction (1891). Essays by William Dean Howells.* Howells selected and assembled these pieces quickly, from items published while he was conducting "The Editor's Study" (*Harper's Monthly Magazine*, January 1886–March 1892). He contends that the critic's function is "to discover principles . . . [and] report," not to create or to pass judgment; he admires the efforts of the best American writers of fiction for realistically picturing life instead of scientifically mapping it; and he applauds those writers for "concern[ing] themselves with the more smiling aspects of life, which are the more American," and for avoiding what is wrongly overemphasized by European novelists (namely, sexual relationships of various types) and for excelling in the short story. Howells felt that America, unlike Europe, was an area of more happiness than tragedy and also that American novelists rightly avoid topics "not usually talked of before young people, and especially young ladies." Howells uses a memorable metaphor when he suggests that fiction writers should look at reality in ordinary daylight and present it, just as a scientist seeking to explain a grasshopper would study real specimens rather than an ideal one artistically constructed by others.

Crocker, Charles (1822–1888). Railroad builder and one of The Big Four.* (The three others are Mark Hopkins, Collis P. Huntington, and Leland Stanford.)

Croker, Richard F. (1841–1922). Politician. He was born in Clognakilty, County Cork, Ireland, into a Scottish-English family. An uncle was governor of Bermuda; another, a member of the British Parliament. His parents and his eight brothers and sisters migrated to Cincinnati, Ohio, and soon thereafter to New York City (1844), where Croker attended school for three years, quit at age thirteen, and became a blacksmith and a machinist, then a rowdy gang member, a prizefighter, and an upward-bound member of Tammany Hall* (1862). He was a court clerk, an election district captain, a fireman, and a Young Democrat alderman opposed to William Marcy Tweed and under the tutelage of anti–Tweed Democrat John Kelly. When Tweed fell (1871) and was jailed (1873), Croker was elected coroner (1873–1879) and took $20,000 or more a year in fees, was charged with murdering a political enemy but was freed for lack of evidence after brief jail time (1874), and was an alderman again until he became a fire commissioner (1883–1886). After Kelly's death (1886), Croker became chairman of the Tammany Finance Committee (1886–1902) and hence the undisputed boss of Democratic (i.e., city) politics in New York. He engineered a dramatic mayoral race in which Democrat Abram S. Hewitt defeated Republican Theodore Roosevelt* and United Labor Party Henry George* (1886). When Hewitt displeased Croker, he was not renominated because Croker controlled 90,000 political workers organized into thirty-five districts, all loyal because of the spoils systems and intimidation. Croker was city chamberlain (1889–1890), which netted him $25,000.

After Croker had been temporarily discredited by disclosures of police corruption in 1894, he decamped to England, where he stayed until 1897 to avoid having to testify before state legislative investigators. He then returned to New York to put his candidate, Robert C. Van Wyck, into office (1898) as the first mayor of Greater New York (including Brooklyn, Staten Island, and parts of Queens and Westchester counties). Croker asserted under oath during a hearing held in 1899, before a legislative committee appointed by Governor Roosevelt, that he had handpicked Van Wyck's administrative subordinates and did so to enrich himself—and handsomely—by what friends called "honest graft." Croker's New York residence cost $200,000 and a stock farm cost $250,000 more, not to mention his racehorses, which cost another $100,000. Joseph Pulitzer* saw to it that his newspaper, the New York *World*, constantly blasted Croker, who returned to England in 1901 when a fusion movement replaced the crooked Van Wyck with honest Seth Low as mayor. Thereafter, Croker was finished as a political force, and he stayed mostly in his mansions in Wantage, England, and Glencairn, outside Dublin, where he bred horses and lived at ease. He married Elizabeth Frazier in 1873 (the couple had two sons), but he was later estranged from her. Upon her death in 1914, he married Beula Benton Edmondson, a Native American Cherokee fifty years his junior. Croker's last three years were soured when his family squabbled over rights to his property. Alfred Henry Lewis's novel *The Boss* (1903) is based on Croker's career.

Crook, George (1829–1890). Army officer. Born near Dayton, Ohio, Crook graduated from the U.S. Military Academy at West Point (1852), was stationed on the Pacific Coast with an infantry unit fighting Indians, and then served gallantly during the Civil War. Crook spent most of his many remaining years as a brilliant Indian fighter in the West and Southwest (1866–1886). He obtained the surrender of Apache chief Geronimo* (March 1886), who, however, escaped again. (Camillus S. Fly* accompanied Crook and his troops to photograph Geronimo.) Crook resigned his command rather than comply with a dishonorable change in surrender terms, and it remained for the more ruthless General Nelson A. Miles* to capture Geronimo a final time (later in 1886). Thereafter, Crook tried conscientiously to ameliorate the harsh treatment of the Apaches at the hands of the American government. He was promoted to major general in 1888. He died two years later, shortly before the occurrence of the massacre at Wounded Knee,* of which he would have been ashamed. Crook is usually regarded as the most competent, most honest, most humane Indian fighter of them all. His autobiography was published in 1946.

Crumbling Idols: Twelve Essays on Art Dealing Chiefly with Literature, Painting and the Drama (1894). Critical manifesto by Hamlin Garland.* The essays are entitled "Provincialism," "New Fields," "The Question of Success," "Literary Prophecy," "Local Color in Art," "The Local Novel," "The Drift of the Drama," "The Influence of [Henrik] Ibsen," "Impressionism," "Literary Centres," "Literary Masters," and "A Recapitulary Afterword." Four of the essays, substantially rewritten, first appeared in the *Arena*,* edited by B. O. Flower* (1890, 1892, and 1893). The title of Garland's little book is meant to suggest that classical, traditional, conservative models in the arts must yield to here-and-now productions. Herbert S. Stone,* who published the book, produced a fine example of a devoted bookmaker's skillful experimental art. Garland feels that the cultural center of America, which has moved from Boston to New York, is now shifting again, to Chicago, and will continue to drift farther west. He defines his proto-realistic doctrine of "veritism" as "the truthful statement of an individual impression corrected by reference to the fact." (The term may have been inspired by Garland's reading of Eugène Véron's 1877 *Aesthetics* [*L'Esthétique*, 1876]. Later, Garland conflated realism, veritism, and Americanism.) Hence, he favors realism, the Midwest, local color, and evolutionary determinism over their respective opposites. He prefers gentle and optimistic realism over romantic art, since the latter promotes economic "feudalism," to the continued detriment of agrarian and industrial laborers. Specifically, Garland favors modern fiction by Stephen Crane,* Harold Frederic,* and Henry Blake Fuller,* for example, over old-fashioned romantic sentimentality. Garland also likes local-color stories but only if written by natives and with regional knowledge used only for "texture and back-ground." Garland knows that no artist can control his environment, but he can support efforts at social betterment and honest creativity, and hence he can retain his self-respect. Garland theorizes that truth can be revealed better by way of impressions than by realistically recorded data. Therefore, he admires "open-air painting," names a few masters of Impressionism, and naturally includes an American—Childe Hassam.* Garland deplores contemporary "society plays," which feature "sexually diseased" characters, and much prefers works by Richard Harding Davis,* Clyde Fitch,* and James A. Herne,* for example.

Crumbling Idols was adversely reviewed by Eastern critics and even by a few Chicagoans; however, Flower defended it well, and the controversy helped to increase the sales of Garland's later works.

The Cuban and Porto Rican Campaigns (1898). An eight-chapter book about the Spanish-American War* by Richard Harding Davis.* "The First Shot" reports on the taking of prize ships. "The First Bombardment" concerns the shelling of Matanzas. "The Rocking-Chair Period" comments on army delays at Tampa, Florida. "The Voyage of the Transports" discusses moving 16,000 soldiers in thirty-one vessels to Santiago de Cuba. "The Guasimas Fight" details the battle. "The Battle of San Juan" follows. "In the Rifle Pits" describes the wretched combat conditions, the strategy used, and the casualties incurred. Finally, "The Porto Rican Campaign" stresses the well-planned nature of the quick climax. Davis saw much during the Spanish-American War and reports details honestly and graphically, with many human-interest touches. Depicting one fatal wound, he adds that it "made the yellow stripes and brass insignia of rank seem strangely mean and tawdry." The book is enhanced by many excellent brownish photographs and a few drawings. Davis writes about the American army of the able but indifferent regulars and the enthusiastic but inexperienced volunteers in Tampa, traveling with the efficient navy to Cuba, early military conferences, the Battle of Guasimas, Theodore Roosevelt* and his Rough Riders, the Battle of San Juan, Guantanimo Bay, good General Nelson A. Miles,* inept General William R. Shafter, and glorious American imperialism. The inadequacy of the accounts in *The Cuban and Porto Rican Campaigns*, though often compellingly graphic, results from the fact that Davis was an amateur, without knowledge of military science. Since he was knowledgeable with respect to drama and sports, he perhaps pardonably saw war as theatrical and athletic.

D

Daly, Augustin (1838–1899). (Full name: John Augustin Daly.) Theater manager and playwright. He was born in Plymouth, North Carolina. After the death of his father, a sea captain and shipowner, the family moved to New York City, where Daly loved to attend plays, did some acting, but soon preferred writing and directing. He became a drama critic for New York newspapers (1858–1869), rewrote a German play and produced it as *Leah the Forsaken* (Boston 1862, New York 1863), adapted numerous French and German plays and British and American novels for stage presentation, and then wrote and produced *Under the Gaslight* (New York, 1867), in which the heroine saves a wounded soldier from being run over by a train. He took the play to receptive London audiences (1868), added other suspense dramas and also some Shakespeare to his repertoire, and wrote and produced two timely plays—the realistic frontier drama *Horizon* (1871), which is regarded as his best original work, and *Divorce* (1871), a play with twenty-four characters, including two contrasting couples. Daly brought several managers together into a cooperative theatrical trust to avoid the complications of competition (1873). A producer-manager of three New York theaters during part of the early 1870s, he put on *Roughing It* (1873), a silly satire inspired by *Roughing It* by Mark Twain*; *Pique* (1875), in which a girl marries someone else because her lover marries her stepmother for money; and *The Dark City* (1877), a melodrama about disinheritance.

The failure of *The Dark City* caused Daly to go to England (1878–1879) to recoup; he then returned to convert an old Broadway playhouse to Daly's Theater (1879). He produced a few plays by fellow Americans but, for the most part, continued to adapt French and German ones (until 1896), usually shifting their scenes to American locales. Daly took his troupes abroad several times. He went to London (1884, 1886, 1888—for the first American production of Shakespeare—and 1890); to Berlin (1886—only British and American residents attended); and to Paris (1886, 1888, and 1891—audiences only gradually approved). The Irish-born, American actress Ada Rehan was sensational under his direction in Shakespeare's *As You Like It* (London, 1890). Encouraged, Daly built his own theater in London in 1891. Alfred, Lord Tennyson so admired Daly's work that he authorized the American to convert the Tennyson poem *The Foresters* into a play (London, 1892). Daly continued to mount Shakespearean productions in New York and London (1896–1898). He returned to London to look into commercial problems there (1899), but he grew sick and died in Paris. In all, Daly wrote, adapted, and produced about ninety plays. Daly married Mary Duff in 1869 (the couple had two children, both of whom predeceased their parents).

Daly, Marcus (1841–1900). Miner and industrialist. Born in Ireland into a poor family, Daly migrated to the United States in 1856, worked briefly in New York, and then worked as a pick-and-shovel miner in California, Nevada, and Utah, until he had gained extensive knowledge of mining processes. He went to Butte in the Montana Territory (1876), where he became a mining partner, sold his interest for $30,000, and with California investors bought the Anaconda Silver Mine. Daly, who saw beneath the exhausted silver veins vast copper deposits, quietly closed the mine to lull potential competitors, bought adjacent mines, started enormous copper-mining operations in and around Butte, and built the town of Anaconda. He exploited nearby coal and timber regions, developed interests in banks, irrigation facilities, newspapers, power plants, and railroad lines, and emerged a multimillionaire. Daly was always loyal and generous to his employees.

Daly and William A. Clark,* his friend of long standing, became bitter enemies over business and politics (1888–1900). When Clark gained control of Butte's reduction plants and became uncooperative, Daly built the town of Anaconda and a smelter there. When Clark seemed to be in political control of Missoula, Daly built Hamilton, a rival town up the Bitter Root Valley. When Clark ran for various political offices, Daly, who avoided political office himself but wanted behind-the-scenes power, thwarted Clark's national ambitions, although they were fellow Democrats. When Clark was finally elected senator from Montana (1899), Daly gave financial support to the Senate Committee on Elections and thus helped engineer his enemy's resignation. Daly lavished hundreds of thousands of dollars through the 1890s in a vain effort to have Anaconda named the capital of Montana. In addition to Clark, Daly had another rival in the copper business—the redoubtable F. Augustus Heinze.* Daly supported the 1896 campaign of William Jennings Bryan.* Daly married Margaret Evans in 1872, and the couple built a lavish mansion at Hamilton, with an adjacent ranch and orchards, excellent racehorses, and a horse-training center. Curiously, Margaret Daly's sister was married to the brother of William Clark, Daly's perennial enemy. S. S. McClure* published a biased exposé of Daly in his magazine (1906).

The Damnation of Theron Ware (1896). Novel by Harold Frederic.* Theron Ware, a young Methodist minister, is disappointed when he is assigned to Octavius, New York, a rural community, rather than to the larger church in Tecumseh. He and his wife Alice are soon criticized by his quasi-fundamentalist congregation for their allegedly superior ways: Theron Ware's preaching is too fancy, and so is Alice's bonnet. Feeling intellectual, Theron decides to write a treatise on Abraham. When he helps a mortally injured Irish-Catholic laborer, he happens to meet the local priest, Father Forbes, and also Celia Madden, his beautiful, red-haired friend and church organist. When Theron calls on Father Forbes for advice about his Abraham research, he learns that both of these Catholics, members of a religion that he has nominally criticized, are charming, amiable, and highly cultivated. Through Father Forbes, Theron meets Dr. Ledsmar, a nonpracticing physician, scholar, and observant bystander. Both Forbes and Ledsmar know a great deal more about biblical times than does Theron, who feels rather humbled. He walks toward home by way of the Catholic church, where he hears Celia playing the organ. Theron escorts her to her well-appointed home and learns about her several interests, which include literature and art.

Time passes. At a Methodist church revival, Theron is helped in a money-raising effort by pragmatic Brother Soulsby and his wife Sister Soulsby, who employ high-pressure sales techniques. Distressed, Theron tells Sister Soulsby that he is tempted to quit the church, but she tells him that most people are hypocrites, that he could not do well in the outside world, and that he ought to shape up. Wrongly suspecting Alice of being fond of a church trustee named Gorringe, Theron now feels the urge to love Celia. He confers with her about buying a home piano; he also discusses early church history with rationalist Dr. Ledsmar, whom, however, he offends by hinting that Father Forbes is too intimate with Celia. Theron grows weary of the religious fervor displayed at a Methodist camp meeting, wanders through the woods, and comes upon a Catholic picnic. Celia is there. They talk and kiss, and he complains of his professional and marital condition. He soon spoils his friendship with Celia, first by telling her that they must keep their friendship a secret and then by telling Father Forbes that Dr. Ledsmar thinks little of Celia. Theron accuses Alice of misbehavior with Gorringe; her proper denial sends Theron over to Celia's home, where her brother Michael, dying of tuberculosis, candidly tells the troubled minister that he looks untrustworthy, has manifestly lost his innocence, and should stay with his own supportive religious group.

Learning that Celia has gone to New York City—with Father Forbes?—Theron tells Alice that he must hasten to Albany on business. He goes furtively to New York instead, where he sees Celia and Father Forbes and follows them to a hotel. When the priest is away, he visits with Celia. She rebukes him, calls him a bore, and says she saw him following her. Father Forbes returns with other men and explains to Theron that they are all trying to extricate Celia's other brother Theodore from a troublesome situation. Crushed, Theron wanders off, tries to commit suicide by overindulging in alcohol, and accepts help from the practical Soulsbys, who, now in New York, summon Alice. After a long sickness, the minister quits his former line of work. He decides to accept the Soulsbys's help to get into Seattle real estate; if that fails, he will try politics.

The town of Octavius is a mirror image of several 1870s Mohawk Valley towns that Harold Frederic knew well. Father Forbes is closely patterned after Father Edward Terry, a liberal, Irish-born Catholic priest whom Frederic knew, to his intellectual benefit, in Utica in the late 1870s. Friends of Father Terry and Frederic were Thomas McQuade, his pretty, red-haired daughter Josephine, and his pianist daughter Catherine. Frederic combined these two girls into the character of Celia Madden. *The Damnation of Theron Ware* was published in London as *Illumination* (a title Frederic preferred), a month ahead of its American release, by the Chicago firm of Stone and Kimball, headed by Herbert S. Stone.* The novel hit every best-seller list late in 1896, and it was also well received by critics on both sides of the Atlantic. For example, William Dean Howells* in an 1897 essay praised it, though only in passing, as powerful; in an 1899 essay, he regarded it as outstanding.

Davis, Rebecca Harding (1831–1910). (Full name: Rebecca Blaine Harding Davis.) Author. She was born in Washington, Pennsylvania. When she was a child, she moved with her parents to Alabama and then to Wheeling (then part of Virginia), where she observed first-hand the deplorable living and working conditions of coal miners and iron mill employees. Early in her life, she published short stories but gained notice only with "Life in the Iron Mills," an 1861 *Atlantic Monthly** story, which was quickly followed by the mill town novel *Margret Howth: A Story of To-Day* (1862). Davis's early pioneering work is realistic, grim, and sympathetic toward the plight of workers exploited by the moneyed classes; hence, it was a generation ahead of the American naturalists. She married L. Clarke Davis, a lawyer in Philadelphia (1863) and subsequently made that city her home. Her husband later became an editor. The two had three children, the first and most famous of whom was Richard Harding Davis,* the journalist, war correspondent, and fiction writer. In later years, Mrs. Davis visited and closely observed the life-style and the scenery of Kentucky, North Carolina, and New Jersey. Continuing to write, she next produced harshly realistic short stories dealing with the psychology of women as well as men during the Civil War. The novel *Waiting for the Verdict* (1868) sympathetically treats interracial love and African Americans' crossing the color line. *John Andross* (1874) bravely concerns political corruption, the Whiskey Ring, and lobbying in Pennsylvania. *Silhouettes of American Life** (1892) collects thirteen of her short stories. By the 1890s she was being naively regarded as sentimental. In reality, her so-called didactic sentimentality is undercut by wry humor and a valuable implication that humility is often victorious. *Bits of Gossip* is her autobiography (1904). Rebecca Harding Davis was a pioneering realist who was insufficiently appreciated by the critics in her lifetime. William Dean Howells,* for example, ignored her completely, and the public let her son Richard Harding Davis, though inferior as a writer, outshine her vastly.

Davis, Richard Harding (1864–1916). Journalist, war correspondent, fiction writer, and playwright. He was born in Philadelphia. His mother was the pioneering realist Rebecca Harding Davis.* Richard Harding Davis had a fascinating life. He was a flamboyant, indifferent, degreeless student in many schools, including Lehigh University (1882–1885) and Johns Hopkins University (1885–1886). By then, he had written a first book, *The Adventures of My Freshman* (1884). Always a flashy dresser, Davis was fired from his first job, as a reporter with the Philadelphia *Record* (1886), for working with yellow kid gloves on his hands. He did well with the Philadelphia *Press* (1886–1889) and became coeditor of the *Stage* (1888–1889). He began to publish short stories during these years. He gained national fame in June 1889 when he reported the Johnston Flood (*see* Disasters) and then later that summer when he covered the international cricket matches in England. His career was enhanced when he began late in 1889 writing for the New York *Evening Sun* under the famous editor Arthur Brisbane.* In its columns, Davis published popular stories featuring the handsome Courtlandt Van Bibber, who, like Davis, enjoyed plays, operas, sporting events, and high society, and not only did noble but also occasionally foolish things. Davis's 1890 *Scribner's Magazine** story "Gallegher, A Newspaper Story," inspired by a streetwise *Press* copyboy, was also a popular success.

The famous publisher S. S. McClure* tried to hire Davis, who declined, however, when the man offered him a New York post instead of the one in London he really wanted. So, instead, Davis became managing editor of *Harper's Weekly* (1891–1893), for which he traveled on assignment throughout the West (1892). The literary result was Davis's *The West from a Car-Window* (1892). In addition, he got his first alluring taste of military action when, during this trip, he joined an American cavalry unit helping Mexican authorities find a Mexican bandit in Texas. Next, he went to southern Europe on another working vacation, which resulted in *The Rulers of the Mediterranean* (1894). With an enviable reputation by this time, Davis cut loose from specific publishers to turn to free-lance writing. He published *Our English Cousins* (1894), coverd the coronation of Nicholas II in Moscow (1894), earned $500 from William Randolph Hearst* for reporting the 1895 Yale-Harvard football game, went with two colleagues to Central and South America (1895), and published *Three Gringos in Venezuela and Central America* as a result (1896). His best novel, *Soldiers of Fortune*,* appeared in 1897.

Davis's next important chore was covering Cuban insurrectionists (1896–1897). When Davis learned of Hearst's false, yellow-journal account—complete with a drawing by Frederic Remington*—of body searches of some Cuban women by Spanish soldiers, Davis countered by filing a veracious dispatch with the New York *World*, owned by Joseph Pulitzer.* Next, Davis was sent by the London *Times* to cover the 1897 Greco-Turkish War. Here, he and fellow journalist Stephen Crane* operated out of Athens. When the Spanish-American War* loomed, Davis signed on with the New York *Herald*, *Scribner's Magazine*, and the London *Times* as a war correspondent and went to Florida, where, awaiting action, he was impressed by Theodore Roosevelt* but tangled with the bungling General William R. Shafter. During hostilities in Cuba and then in Puerto Rico, Davis filed graphic and informative reports and associated with, among many others, photographer James H. Hare,* correspondent Sylvester Scovel,* and again with Crane, whom he greatly admired. (In Davis's 1901 short story "A Derelict," the newsman Channing is based, to a degree, on Crane.) Davis's thoughts on the war are recorded in *Cuba in War Time* (1897), *The Cuban and Porto Rican Campaigns** (1898), and *A Year from a Reporter's Note-Book* (1898).

After the war, Davis married Cecil Clark, a Massachusetts dog breeder (1899). The couple honeymooned aboard a ship bearing them to Capetown, South Africa, and the Boer War. Though anti-British, Davis covered hostilities at first by accompanying the British to see a modern army in action. Then he attached himself to the Boer forces, whose bearded soldiers, fighting for their farms, reminded him of biblical heroes, and whose rag-tag international volunteers intrigued him. He and his wife left in April 1900 for France and then New York. He published *With Both Armies in South Africa* (1900). In 1901 he seems to have been catching his breath, but his last years were also full of activities. *Collier's** sent him to Japan and elsewhere in 1902. He wrote popular plays and more fiction, covered coronations in Spain and England, and reported on the troubled Belgian Congo and the Russo-Japanese war. He was separated and then divorced in 1910, sold some plots to the movies, married a young singer-dancer named Elizabeth Genevieve McEvoy, whose stage name was Bessie McCoy, in 1912 (the couple had one child), and covered another trouble spot in Mexico and another war—World War I. Incredibly, when he died in 1916, he was not yet fifty-two.

Richard Harding Davis is not highly regarded by modern critics. His fiction, often melodramatic, may be likened to comic opera. Much of his facile reporting may be downgraded as superficial. He deliberately cut a swashbuckling figure. And his Manifest Destiny philosophy has long been out of fashion. But, at his best, he was a daring, energetic correspondent who could be grippingly graphic. Furthermore, he was a role model for several better writers who followed him, among them Crane, Ernest Hemingway, Jack London, Frank Norris,* Ernie Pyle, John Reed, Vincent Sheean, and John Steinbeck.

Debs, Eugene V. (1855–1926). (Full name: Eugene Victor Debs.) Socialist and labor leader. He was born in Terre Haute, Indiana. He worked in a railway paint shop, as a locomotive fireman, for a wholesale grocery company, and as a city clerk (1870–1883). From 1871 he was active in the International Brotherhood of Locomotive Firemen of the United States and Canada, at first as a member, then as editor of the union journal, and finally as a skillful union secretary and treasurer (1880–1890). Debs ably served as a Democratic member of the Indiana legislature (1884–1886), then turned to labor organizing full-time. He helped found the American Railway Union and was elected its president (1893). He led his union to victory in the Great Northern Railway strike (1894). While he was helping to direct the Pullman Strike* (1894), he was convicted of conspiracy to obstruct the mails and served a six-month jail term with several union associates (1895). Young Clarence Darrow was their attorney. The U.S. Supreme Court upheld Debs's conviction. His prison reading turned Debs into a socialist. He supported William Jennings Bryan* for president in 1896. The American Railway Union became part of the Social Democracy of America (1897), which Debs served as an executive officer. He helped steer the 1897 striking coal miners to victory. He ran unsuccessfully for president on the Social Democratic Party ticket in 1900. (He ran four more times for president, always unsuccessfully.) Debs remained controversial and active in political causes during and after World War I. His several books include *Liberty* (1895). He was praised by friends (Eugene Field* and James Whitcomb Riley,* among them) as gentle and sincere, though passionately eloquent in his beliefs.

Depression of 1893. *See* Panic of 1893.

The Descendant (1897). Novel by Ellen Glasgow.* *The Descendant* spins a naturalistic plot about a vibrant New York painter named Rachel Gavin who quits painting an immense Mary Magdalen, sacrifices her career, and gives her total love to Michael Akershem, an editor of the radical *Iconoclast*. Michael soon tames down and reforms. He comes to regard Rachel as sinful, but—because he is a man—can discreetly step up into conventional and influential social and professional circles and even court a respectable young schoolteacher. However, Michael (mentioned as an illegitimate Southerner), in a burst of atavistic anger, kills a former iconoclastic pal, is imprisoned for seven years, and finally returns when dying to Rachel. By this time, she is a successful painter, and her *Magdalene* is on exhibit. *The Descendant*, not a great novel, hints at Glasgow's developing strength. A Macmillan editor rejected the manuscript and advised Glasgow to go home and have babies. The novel was published by Harper, as by an anonymous author, once thought to be Harold Frederic.*

Dewey, George (1837–1917). Naval officer. Born in Montpelier, Vermont, Dewey attended Norwich University in Northfield, Vermont, transferred to and graduated from the U.S. Naval Academy at Annapolis (1858), and was on active duty during the entire Civil War (1861–1865). During the next several years, he performed excellent service off the California coast, on lighthouse duty, and at European stations; he rose to the rank of captain in 1884. He was appointed chief of the Bureau of Equipment (1889), was promoted to commodore (1896), was named president of the Board of Inspection and Survey (1896–1897), and became commander of the Asiatic Squadron (January 1898), taking command in the harbor at Nagasaki, Japan. Theodore Roosevelt,* then assistant secretary of the navy in the cabinet of William McKinley,* alerted Dewey to danger in the Pacific Ocean because of Spanish forces in the Philippine Islands, ordered him to Hong Kong (February), advised him to be in contact with the U.S. consul at Manila to augment outdated U.S. intelligence reports concerning the Philippine Islands, and approved of his establishing a munitions base at Mirs Bay on the coast of China. This step was necessary because, in the event of a war with Spain, America would be denied harbor facilities by neutral Britain.

When the Spanish-American War* began in April 1898, Dewey, under orders, took his fleet to Manila Bay, through mined waters and under ineffective fire from shore batteries, and launched an attack on the Far Eastern Spanish Fleet off Cavite (1 May). He sank, burned, or captured the entire enemy squadron with no loss of American lives or ships. European historians immediately defined America as a major sea power. Next, Dewey (by now a rear admiral) blockaded Manila, challenged (and outfaced) a large German fleet seeking to land supplies to aid Spanish contingents ashore, and in conjunction with U.S. Army forces captured Manila by amphibious assault (August). He cooperated in the suppression of Filipino resistance to American occupation, thus bitterly antagonizing rebel leader Emilio Aguinaldo (who was later defended eloquently by Mark Twain*). Dewey (by now an admiral) left the Philippines in May 1899, returned a towering hero to the United States, was promoted to the rank of admiral of the navy, and was repeatedly asked to run for president. To this request, he said in one interview (1900) that if the people wanted him to do so he was more than willing; furthermore, the job was not a difficult one. Never nominated, Dewey was instead appointed president of the new General Board of the Navy Department to advise the navy secretary (1900–1917). In this position, he supervised the development of big ships and also naval war plans against both Germany and Japan. Dewey married Susan B. Goodwin in 1867 (the couple had one child). His wife died in 1872, and he married Mildred McLean Hazen in 1899. Dewey published his autobiography in 1913. His famous order in Manila Bay—"You may fire when you are ready, Gridley"—was delivered from the bridge of his flagship to Captain Charles Vernon Gridley, who was fighting the ship from the conning tower. Gridley, chronically ill at the time, was advised that the shock of combat would be fatal to him, but he was eager to participate. He was injured, invalided, and sent to Hong Kong and then Japan, where he died on 5 June 1898.

Dewey, John (1859–1952). Philosopher, psychologist, educator, and writer. Born in Burlington, Vermont, he studied at the University of Vermont (graduating in 1879), taught high school classes (1879–1882), and studied at Johns Hopkins University (Ph.D., 1884), under G. Stanley Hall.* Dewey then taught at the universities of Michigan (1884–1888, 1889–1894), Minnesota (1888–1889), and Chicago (1894–1904), and at Columbia University (1904–1930). While at the University of Chicago, he was chairman of the department of philosophy, psychology, and pedagogy, and he helped develop the anti-Hegelian Chicago school of philosophy. His book *Psychology* (1887), which shows the influence of William James,* theorizes that, to be meaningful, education must include vocational training and encourage intellectual responses to experience. He wrote a study of Gottfried Wilhelm von Leibnitz (1888). In *The School and Society* (1899), Dewey used his knowledge of psychology to advocate that all schools should develop children's ability and need to talk, whet their innate curiosity, and teach them to build things and otherwise express their artistic proclivities. Dewey put these concepts into practice in his progressive Laboratory School at the School of Education, at the University of Chicago (from 1896), and thus helped to modernize American education nationwide. James praised Dewey as a pedagogical pragmatist. James also admired *Studies in Logical Theory* (1903), a collection of essays by Dewey and seven of his associates.

In later years (into the 1940s), Dewey was prolific as a publishing scholar. He lectured and traveled widely both in the United States and abroad, and he advocated many liberal political causes. He reasoned that since reality, which is based solely on experience, is mutable and evolutionary, knowledge and intelligence must function to enable human beings to exert beneficial control over their environment, and that ideas are of value only as "instruments" for social betterment here and now. Dewey praised Edward Bellamy* as an "American prophet" for first understanding democracy in human terms. Dewey married Harriet Alice Chapman in 1886. The couple had six children; after two of them died, they adopted an infant in Italy.

Dick, A. B. (1856–1934). (Full name: Albert Blake Dick.) Manufacturer and inventor. He was born in Bureau County, Illinois. The family moved to Galesburg, Illinois (1863), where Dick received a public school education. He worked for companies manufacturing agricultural implements and lumber companies in Illinois (1872–1883), organized his own lumber company (1883), and incorporated the A. B. Dick Company with himself as president and treasurer (1884–1934). The time-consuming task of writing and rewriting inquiry and inventory sheets inspired him to invent a process of quick and multiple duplication of such memoranda. He wrote form letters on waxed sheets with a stylus, inked them by a hand roller on a flatbed press, and found that he could print hundreds of copies from each sheet (1887). When he learned that Thomas A. Edison* had invented an electric pen to duplicate original writing, he obtained a license from Edison and was encouraged in his efforts by Edison. The result was the Edison-Dick mimeograph. Dick's company sold its lumber interests (1887) and turned to improving mimeograph machines in various ways, through the 1890s and beyond, by adapting stencils (including forms made of Japanese hazel-brush fibers) to the typewriter, devising rotary machines to replace the flatbed press, and using electricity in place of hand power. Dick was prominent in social, civic, educational, and commercial activities in Chicago and New York. He married Alice Sheldon, a Galesburg banker's daughter in 1881 (the couple had one child). Alice Dick died in 1885, and he married Mary Henrietta Sheldon Matthews, his sister-in-law, in 1892 (the couple had four children).

Dickinson, Emily (1830–1886). Poet. Born in Amherst, Massachusetts, she studied for a year at Mount Holyoke Female Seminary and spent most of the rest of her life reclusively in her parents' home. She enjoyed intellectual friendships with Benjamin F. Newton, a lawyer in her father's office; Reverend Charles Wadsworth, of Philadelphia and then San Francisco; Thomas Wentworth Higginson, a talented Boston editor; and very few others. Emily Dickinson wrote more than 1,700 poems, mostly short ones. She showed very few of them to anyone. Only five were published in her lifetime. Her works burst upon the public in the 1890s, as follows: *Poems*, in 1890; *Poems: Second Series*, in 1891, and *Poems: Third Series*, in 1896. The first book sold more than 10,000 copies; the second, over 5,000; the third, about 2,000. In addition, a few of her letters were published in the *Atlantic Monthly** (October 1891), and many more appeared in book form (1894).

The public in the 1890s was ready for her experimental poetry, whether the literary establishment was ready or not. Traditional literary criticism was weakening, and the strangeness and oddity of her style caused delight and was widely appreciated. Higginson, one of her editors, prepared the public by a sensible preface to the 1890 edition and also by an anonymous review published in the *Nation* (27 November 1890). Further, William Dean Howells* opined in a *Harper's Monthly Magazine* review (January 1891) that her verse added valuably to the literature of the world. Many traditional critics fought back, however; for example, Thomas Bailey Aldrich* commented on Dickinson adversely in the *Atlantic Monthly* (January 1892). Later in the decade, professional and popular interest declined somewhat. In general, established New England, New York, Western, and British critics and reviewers in conservative monthly journals were adverse and often caused timid reviewers to follow their lead. Younger critics and women critics, including those who reviewed for family and religious weeklies, dared to be complimentary.

Emily Dickinson is now acclaimed throughout the world for her technical innovations, compression, subtle ambiguities, and daring thematic values.

Disasters. Every country in every decade of every century has had its natural and human-caused disasters. In the period 1888–1901 the following American disasters were particularly grievous. The 11–13 March 1888 New York City blizzard killed about 200 people and caused enormous property loss and damage. The 31 May 1889 Johnston, Pennsylvania, flood caused the death by drowning of 2,295 people; when oil spilled from an overturned freight car caught fire, about 300 more people burned to death. The 27 March 1890 tornadoes hitting western and central states destroyed Bowling Green, Kentucky, with a loss of 300 lives; in nearby Louisville 300 buildings were demolished. On 13 July 1890 the steamer *Sea Wing* capsized on Lake Pepin, Minnesota, causing the death by drowning of 147 people. The 22–30 August 1893 hurricane in the Caribbean and southern United States killed nearly 1,000 people and ravaged Charleston, South Carolina. The 1 September 1894 forest fire in and near Hinckley, Minnesota, killed 418 people, destroyed Hinckley and eighteen other towns, and burned more than 160,000 acres of timber. The 27 May 1896 tornado that hit St. Louis and also East Moline, Illinois, killed 306 people and caused $13,000,000 in property damage. On 15 February 1898 the U.S. battleship *Maine* was blown up in the harbor at Havana, Cuba; 264 men were killed. The attack helped precipitate the Spanish-American War.* The 26 November 1898 Long Island and New England gale destroyed or damaged 213 vessels, including the *City of Portland*, which sank off Cape Cod, Massachusetts, with a loss of 157 lives. On 1 May 1900 the mine explosion at Scofield, Utah, killed 200 miners. The 30 June 1900 Hoboken, New Jersey, pier fire killed more than 300 people and caused $4,627,000 in property damage. During the period from 27 August to 15 September 1900 a hurricane and high tides at Galveston, Texas, killed more than 6,000 people and caused damage amounting to $30,000,000 in the city.

Doc' Horne: A Story of the Streets and Town (1899). A collection of episodic but unified stories by George Ade.* The stories feature an old codger named Calvin ''Doc' '' Horne, an experienced Chicagoan, now retired. He is neat, bald, and bright, with a white chin beard, and he has an inexpensive room in the Alfalfa European Hotel. He spins excellent, somewhat vernacular yarns full of wind and didacticism, brag, and wit. They include unforgettable sketches of friends, antics, and sorrows, and they delight an assortment of only partly taken-in listeners, including a ''lightning dentist'' and a ''lush.''

Donnelly, Ignatius (1831–1901). Politician, novelist, essayist, and editor. He was born in Philadelphia. His father, born in Ireland, was a physician. Donnelly was admitted to the bar in 1852. Three years later, he declined to enter the Democratic political arena, married Katharine McCaffrey (and was widowed in 1894), and moved to a boomtown near Hastings, Minnesota, where he practiced law, obtained property, became a Republican, and ran for the territorial senate without success. In 1859, a year after Minnesota acquired statehood, Donnelly, now living in St. Paul, was elected lieutenant governor. He was subsequently reelected and later became a Republican member of the U.S. House of Representatives (1863–1869). In Minnesota state politics again, Donnelly evolved from Liberal Republican to Granger to Greenback Democrat and finally to a member of the Populist Party.* He may be defined as a third-party liberal leader, who fought for the individual against railroad magnates, wheat mill kings, and lumber barons. He steadily favored agrarian and other reforms. He founded and edited his own weekly newspaper, *The Anti-Monopolist* (1874–1879). As a Populist, he wrote the party preamble to the Omaha Platform, in 1892. During the intervening years, Donnelly published *Atlantis: The Antediluvian World*

(1882); *Ragnarok: The Age of Fire and Gravel* (1883); *The Great Cryptogram: Francis Bacon's Cipher in the So-Called Shakespeare Plays* (1887); *Caesar's Column: A Story of the Twentieth Century** (1890); *Doctor Huguet* (1891); and *The Golden Bottle: Or the Story of Ephraim Benezet of Kansas* (1892). Soon to follow were *The American People's Money** (1896) and *The Cypher in the Plays, and on the Tombstone* (1899).

Donnelly ran unsuccessfully for vice president on the Populist ticket with William Jennings Bryan,* who was nominated for the presidency in 1900. Donnelly's writings display intellectual virtuosity but also compositional haste. His purpose, as he often stated, was not to be careful and artistic, but to make people think and thus improve themselves and others. *Atlantis* theorizes that the island of Atlantis was real, was the first seat of civilization, that a ''convulsion of nature'' destroyed it and most of its inhabitants, and that myths about floods and deluges, and also real Ice Ages, followed. *Ragnarok* combines pseudo-science and myths to suggest that terrestrial clay, sand, and gravel are the debris of a prehistoric comet. Both *The Great Cryptogram* and *The Cypher in the Plays* theorize that Sir Francis Bacon was the author of William Shakespeare's plays. *Doctor Huguet*, a science fiction novel, criticizes racial prejudice by showing the consequences of having a liberal white doctor and an oppressed black man exchange minds and personalities. *The Golden Bottle* is a utopian fantasy in which a poor farm lad, given a magic liquid that can transmute iron to gold, improves mankind's lot by putting the resulting gold to good use, in accordance with Populist principles.

Donnelly married Katharine McCaffrey in 1855 (she died in 1894) and Marian Hanson in 1896 (she was then age twenty-one). It is curious that Donnelly, who fretted so greatly about what would happen once the twentieth century began, died on 1 January 1901.

Douglass, Frederick (1817?–1895). (Original name: Frederick August Washington Bailey.) African American abolitionist, orator, and author. Born in Tuckahoe, Maryland, he was son of an unknown white man and Harriet Bailey, a black slave, was ''illegally'' taught the alphabet by his owner's wife, learned ship caulking in Baltimore, escaped a slave breaker by using a black sailor's papers (1838), took the name Douglass, worked as a laborer in New Bedford, Massachusetts, joined the Massachusetts Anti-Slavery Society, and spoke eloquently at abolitionist meetings beginning in 1841. He published *The Narrative of the Life of Frederick Douglass: An American Slave* (1845), went to England for two years and lectured there, was legally freed through purchase by his friends, returned to America and made his home in Rochester, New York, and founded a newspaper called the *North Star* (later *Frederick Douglass's Paper*, 1847–1863). During the Civil War he advocated the enlistment of black soldiers in the Union army and advised President Abraham Lincoln. In his later years, Douglass held government positions in Santo Domingo (from 1871) and in Washington, D.C. (1877–1886). He became the U.S. minister to Haiti (1889–

1891), in which capacity he befriended Paul Laurence Dunbar.* His later publications also include *My Bondage and My Freedom* (1855) and *Life and Times of Frederick Douglass* (1882). Douglass married Anna Murray, a free African American in 1838 (the couple had four children). After she died in 1882, he married Helen Pitts, a white woman, in 1884. His death came when he collapsed after participating in a women's suffrage meeting.

Dow, Herbert Henry (1866–1930). Chemist. Dow was born in Belleville, Ontario, Canada, where his father managed a sewing machine factory. The family moved to Cleveland, Ohio, and young Dow went to the Case School of Applied Science (now Case Western Reserve). His senior thesis concerned the chemistry of Ohio brine. After graduating (1888), he taught chemistry and toxicology at a Cleveland hospital college (1888–1889) and invented a process to extract bromine from brine (1889). This procedure (patented in 1892) was a method of obtaining bromine from brine through electrolysis with air blown through the vapor to speed the exit of the bromine therein. Dow built a laboratory in Midland, Michigan, and established the Dow Process Company there, and then other companies, to produce bromine, bromides, chlorine, and other derivatives from brine (1890–1897). Next, he organized the Dow Chemical Company (1897), which, at first, manufactured chlorine and caustic soda. Soon it absorbed the other companies Dow had established and produced magnesium carbonate, magnesium chloride, and magnesium sulphate (by 1900). In the early twentieth century, Dow began to manufacture chloroform by a method he had devised, and soon he produced carbon bisulphide and carbon tetrachloride as well. He supervised a great expansion of his product line and, during World War I, advised governmental agencies and also produced mustard gas and other potent war chemicals. Dow married Grace Anna Ball in 1892 (the couple had seven children). He was issued more than one hundred patents for various chemical processes. His hobby of gardening enabled him to become a close friend of Luther Burbank.* Dow was a generous philanthropist. By the time of his death, his vast company was a leading producer of aromatic, industrial, and pharmaceutical chemicals, and also dyes, insecticides, magnesium, and solvents.

Dreiser, Theodore (1871–1945). Fiction writer, nonfictional prose writer and poet. Born in Terre Haute, Indiana, Dreiser was the ninth of ten children, three of whom died in infancy. His father, born in Germany, was a narrow-minded Catholic zealot who worked in an Indiana wool mill; his mother was a Bohemian Mennonite of Czech background. Injuries, death, poverty, debt, and bad luck dogged the family, which partly separated and moved to Vincennes, Sullivan, and Evansville, all in Indiana (1879–1884), then Chicago (1884), and then Warsaw, Indiana (1884–1886), where Dreiser was encouraged by a talented and generous teacher, Mildred Fielding. Meanwhile, his energetic, fun-loving siblings had been evolving. Paul Dreiser was jailed for forgery before success came his way as musical composer Paul Dresser (*see* Songs). Rome Dreiser was a drunkard and a gambler. Mame Dreiser was seduced as a teenager, but her lover provided the family with grocery money. Emma Dreiser lived with an older married man in Chicago, where Claire Dreiser had some rich lovers. Unwed Sylvia Dreiser's baby was fathered by a Warsaw family scion. Theodore Dreiser grew tall, was awkward and seemed ugly. He hid behind a wall of solitude and brooded on the meaninglessness of his father's bigotry and the impermanence of his mother's and sisters' warmth.

Dreiser went on his own to Chicago to seek work (1887). After he had worked as a dishwasher, a cleaner in a hardware store, an artist's studio assistant, a boxcar tracer, and a stock boy, Mildred Fielding persuaded him to attend Indiana University for a year at her expense (1889–1890). Declining her offer of further generosity, he returned to Chicago, where he worked as a realtor's runner and a bill collector and again lived with his mother, who soon died (1890). After working at other miscellaneous jobs, Dreiser began to cover political news for the Chicago *Globe* (1890), and then he moved to St. Louis to work first for the *Globe-Democrat* and then the *Republic* (1892–1894). While visiting the World's Columbian Exposition* in Chicago (1893), he met and began to like Sara Osborne "Jug" White. He worked in Toledo, Cleveland, and Buffalo, and finally for the *Dispatch* in Pittsburgh (all 1894), where he was profoundly affected by some serious spare-time reading, especially works by Honoré de Balzac and Herbert Spencer. Dreiser moved to New York, poverty, and depression (late 1894); but, in the following year, he initiated his productive New York phase, which lasted into the 1920s and, sporadically, even later. (Dreiser wrote about his experiences as a reporter in Chicago, St. Louis, Pittsburgh, and New York, from 1892 to 1895, in *A Book about Myself* [1922].) He began to edit and write for *Ev'ry Month*, which he and his brother Paul Dresser started late in 1895; wrote briefly for the *World*, owned by Joseph Pulitzer;* succeeded as a free-lance writer (1896–1899); and married Sara White (1898) after a six-year celibate engagement. He soon regretted surrendering to the conventions of marriage.

On a dare from a journalist friend with whom he was briefly staying in Ohio in 1899, Dreiser impulsively began to write *Sister Carrie*,* which Doubleday, Page & Company published in 1900, but, growing timid, failed to promote. The company's conduct was partly responsible for the chronic nervous breakdown Dreiser suffered from 1901 to 1903. During this time he became a railroad crew worker. Thereafter he turned to editorial work in New York, separated from his wife (1910), quit editing, and began to produce the great novels and other naturalistic works for which he is famous, including *Jennie Gerhardt* (1911), *The Financier* (1912), *The Titan* (1914), *The "Genius"* (1915), and *An American Tragedy* (1925). In the 1920s he established a residence in Hollywood and associated with actress Helen Richardson (whom he married in 1944, two years after his first wife's death). In his later years, Dreiser was active politically, traveling to and writing about Russia and the Soviet experiment, and lecturing on behalf of labor unions and pacifism.

Dreiser was the first significant American novelist who was not Protestant,

Anglo-Saxon, middle class, and desirous of respectability. He wrote verbose, ponderous, sprawling novels, dealing for the most part with commonplace characters and their drab and often seamy lives. His naturalistic view of life is frank and insightful; his piling up of significant details is moving; and his compassion for humankind is unsurpassed. *Sister Carrie* is considered a naturalistic document of unparalleled importance and influence; *An American Tragedy* is assuredly an American classic.

DuBois, W.E.B. (1868–1963). (Full name: William Edward Burghardt DuBois.) African-American writer, editor, and educator. Born in Great Barrington, Massachusetts, to a single-parent mother of Dutch-African heritage, he enjoyed his New England environment as a lad and youth. He attended Fisk College, in Nashville, Tennessee (B.A., 1888), and Harvard (B.A., 1890; M.A., 1891; Ph.D., 1896), where he was the first African American to earn a Ph.D. While at Harvard, DuBois was influenced by and attracted the attention of William James* and George Santayana,* among other professors. DuBois undertook postgraduate studies in economics and sociology at the University of Berlin (1892–1894) and then accepted a position as a teacher of Greek and Latin at Wilberforce College, in Wilberforce, Ohio (1894–1896) before an invitation came too late from Booker T. Washington* to teach at his Tuskegee Institute. When DuBois began to dislike Wilberforce, he became an assistant instructor in sociology at the University of Pennsylvania (1896–1898), specifically to study the social condition of African Americans in a Philadelphia political ward. The result of this research was *The Philadelphia Negro: A Social Study* (1899), a revolutionary, data-filled racial-history study together with a history of Philadelphia as related to that subject. The book conservatively admonished African Americans to cooperate with the larger community to ensure progress instead of using memories of former oppression to make demands on and to menace that community. *The Philadelphia Negro* was DuBois's third book. Earlier ones are his excellent Harvard dissertation, entitled *The Suppression of the African Slave-Trade to the United States of America, 1638–1870* (1896) and *The Conservation of Races* (1897).

Next, DuBois taught economics and history at all-black Atlanta University (1897–1910). He associated with Booker T. Washington, admired him, and praised him, but he opposed him when Washington proposed accommodationist solutions to African-American problems. DuBois felt that, since whites were responsible for the enslavement of African Americans that had caused past repression and present misery, whites must help African Americans gain real freedom and equality and social, economic, and political improvement. In his best book, *The Souls of Black Folk: Essays and Sketches* (1903), DuBois criticizes Washington for condoning "class distinctions." His split from Washington resulted in DuBois' cofounding the Niagara Movement (1905) to promote African-American freedom and development. The National Association for the Advancement of Colored People (the NAACP), which DuBois helped organize (1909), soon overshadowed the Niagara Movement and attracted many members. While at Atlanta University, DuBois headed several Conferences for the Study of Negro Problems and had much to do with twenty volumes of conference publications (1896–1917). Later in his long, active, and controversial life, DuBois was the director of publicity and research for the NAACP (1910–1934); edited the NAACP's protest periodical entitled *Crisis* (1910–1934); wrote assiduously in a variety of genres (sketches and poetry concerning African-American life, sociological studies, pieces against imperialism and for pacificism and the rights of small nations, novels, and so on); became a target of Senator Joseph R. McCarthy; and joined the Communist Party (1957), renounced his American citizenship, moved to Ghana (1960), became an African citizen, and died in Accra.

W.E.B. DuBois married Nina Gomer in 1896 (the couple had two children; she died in 1950) and Shirley Graham in 1951. DuBois's autobiographical volumes are *Dusk of Dawn* (1940) and *The Autobiography of W.E.B. DuBois: A Soliloquy on Viewing My Life from the Last Decade of Its First Century* (1968).

The Duke of Stockbridge: A Romance of Shays' Rebellion, 1900. Historical novel by Edward Bellamy.* In *The Duke of Stockbridge*, Bellamy presents a well-researched, veracious picture of the 1786–1787 insurrection of distressed and exploited Berkshire farmers, led by Daniel Shays, in justifiable opposition to high land taxes, imprisonment for debt, and foreclosures on land. The work is humanized to a degree by a rather weak subplot of tragic love. The posthumously published novel was first serialized in the *Berkshire Courier* in Barrington, Massachusetts (1878–1879).

Dunbar, Paul Laurence (1872–1906). African-American writer. Dunbar was born in Dayton, Ohio, to parents, former slaves, who separated in 1874 and divorced in 1876. The father died in 1884. The mother taught Paul to read. The only African American in his high school class, Dunbar served as president during his senior year; he graduated in 1891. He had started a black newspaper, called the Dayton *Tattler* (1889–1890), which was printed by Orville Wright, a friend and fellow classmate. Lack of funds caused the paper to fold. Although ambitious to study law at Harvard, Dunbar for lack of funds sought challenging work in Dayton, only to be denied because of his color. He became an elevator operator. He read standard English and American poetry assiduously; sold several poems, some in plantation dialect, and a little prose fiction (1891–1892); and, with the encouragement of white friends, including James Whitcomb Riley,* who admired his verse, published his first book at his own expense: *Oak and Ivy* (Dayton, 1893). This volume contains fifty-six poems, including "Ode to Ethiopia," which praises African Americans' tangible achievements and their stoical courage in the face of abuse and worse, and "Sympathy," which begins "I know why the caged bird sings, ah me, / When his wing is bruised and his bosom sore, / When he beats his bars and he would be free." Dunbar found brief employment and solid professional contacts in Chicago (1893). Frederick Douglass,* newly appointed consul general to Haiti, obtained work for him at the World's Columbian Exposition* at the Haitian Pavilion.

Dunbar returned to Dayton and his elevator job in 1894, but he continued to read and write. White friends sponsored his *Majors and Minors* (Toledo, 1894), which contains ninety-three poems, some of which are reprinted from *Oak and Ivy*: sixty-nine, called ''Majors,'' are in standard English; twenty-four, ''Minors,'' are in black dialect. The year 1896 was Dunbar's most splendid. James A. Herne* reported his admiration of *Majors and Minors* to William Dean Howells,* whose *Harper's Weekly* review (27 June 1896) gave Dunbar great publicity, even though Howells unduly stressed the poet's Robert Burns–like genius. Through friends, Dunbar met lecture-manager James B. Pond,* who arranged for Dunbar to give readings in New York City and also to publish *Lyrics of Lowly Life* there instead of in Ohio (1896, with an introduction by Howells). Fine sales of this collection—of the 105 poems, only 8 were new—made the poet financially independent. An English edition soon appeared (1897). Dunbar spent six months in England (1897), where he met John Hay,* who, as American ambassador, arranged a reading before influential people in London. Dunbar was generally disappointed, however, by his reception by the British and as a consequence published his negative essay entitled ''England as Seen by a Black Man'' (*Independent*, 16 September 1897). Next, Dunbar clerked in the Library of Congress, Washington, D.C. (1897–1898); and in 1898, he married Alice Ruth Moore, a fair-skinned Creole short-story writer and teacher (they separated in 1902). In 1898 Dunbar published *Folks from Dixie*, an important collection of twelve short stories: Five are cast in antebellum days and the rest focus on African-American dilemmas occurring during Reconstruction; all show the influence of Joel Chandler Harris* and Thomas Nelson Page.*

Dunbar's first novel, *The Uncalled* (1898), is a disappointing story that stresses religious zeal and trouble in an all-white family. Dunbar wrote the book and lyrics for *The Origin of the Cake Walk; or, Clorindy* (1898), the first all-black minstrel show to be performed for white audiences (*see* Musical Comedies). Next came *Lyrics of the Hearthside* (1899), which contains 110 poems, including 37 in humorous dialect. Always frail, Dunbar contracted pneumonia and sought better health in the Catskills and then the mountains near Denver, Colorado (1899). He published *The Strength of Gideon and Other Stories* (1900), including some twenty pieces, the best of which concern political corruption, racist violence, and pro-white injustice. He returned to Washington, D.C. (1900–1902), where he felt frustrated as a result of being dangerously stereotyped because of the success of his dialect verse and also because of writing for minstrel shows and musicals. His next novel, *The Love of Landry* (1900), is a saccharine Western of no consequence. The next one, *The Fanatics* (1901), is a thin historical novel cast during the Civil War, which features whites almost exclusively, dramatizes sectional violence, and indirectly satirizes racial and political hypocrisy. His last novel, *The Sport of the Gods* (1902), is a naturalistic melodrama showing that, in the environment created by unjust white men, African Americans are inevitably dehumanized, whether in the South or in the North. This powerful, pioneering novel was the first to portray blacks in Harlem. When his wife left him, because of his alcoholism and pressure her family put upon her, Dunbar grew despondent and sicker; but he rallied to publish two more books of poetry, two more collections of short stories, and some minor items.

In 1903 Dunbar moved back to Dayton, where he lived with his mother in a home he had purchased for her; he later died there of tuberculosis. His epitaph, taken from one of his poems, ends "tek yo' res' at las'." Always self-divided, sometimes Dunbar expressed the accommodationist position of his friend Booker T. Washington;* at other times, he was almost as radical as another friend, W.E.B. DuBois.* Dunbar was black but wrote mainly for a white readership. He wrote not only to entertain but also to instruct. He wrote about blacks and whites, in the South and in the North. He was quaintly humorous and deadly serious. He wrote poetry and prose. He was easily the most significant African-American poet of the entire nineteenth century.

Dunne, Finley Peter (1867–1936). Journalist, humorist, and editor. Dunne was born in Chicago, where his father was an Irish-American carpenter, landowner, and activist in Chicago Democratic politics. His mother, twenty-five years her husband's junior, was a cultivated Irish-American woman. Both parents retained a sympathetic awareness of the difficulties the Irish suffered back home because of British rule. Young Dunne was the fifth of seven children. His twin died while a baby. After a mediocre showing in the public schools (ending in 1884), Dunne worked his way up on several Chicago newspapers. He was office boy at the *Telegram* (1885), city editor of the *Times* (1888), editorial page editor of the *Evening Post* (1892), political writer and then editor of the *Evening Post* and for the *Times-Herald* (1892–1897), and finally editor of the *Journal* (1897–1900). During all this time, he associated with a group of liberals called the Whitechapelers. One of his Chicago newspaper friends at this time was George Ade.*

Dunne stumbled upon the idea of writing timely, humorous columns in Irish-American dialect for the *Post* (1892) and then the *Journal*. It was surprising that these pieces were a success, even though writers, such as Ade, George Washington Cable,* Sarah Orne Jewett,* Mark Twain,* and many others, had popularized local-color and regional literature often flavored with homespun accents. Against Dunne would seem to be anti-Irish prejudice, temperance writers inveighing against Irish fondness for alcohol, and a nationwide gentility at odds with the sort of down-to-earth, commonsense, antiestablishment pronouncements of Dunne's persona. At first, his mouthpiece was Colonel McNeery, based so closely on a well-to-do saloon keeper named James McGarry that Dunne renamed him Dooley in an October 1893 column. Fictitious Mr. Martin J. Dooley, age about sixty, has come from Roscommon, Ireland, to Chicago in the early 1850s, and he now lives and owns a saloon in the Sixth Ward, known as Bridgeport, a solid, moral, loyal, patriotic neighborhood. Every Irishman in Bridgeport is now ''enough like a native American to burn a witch,'' as Mr. Dooley asserts. Malachi Hennessy, a mill worker, is his straight man; John McKenna, his handy Republican strawman; and Schwartzmeister, a nearby saloon-owning competitor. At first, Mr. Dooley's subjects and targets include Bridgeport social and religious life, unfair labor practices against Chicago's railroad and meat-packing workers, corrupt city politicians, the literary affectations of Chicago's nouveau riche, woman's rights advocates, and even the World's Columbian Exposition* of 1893. During the Spanish-American War,* Mr. Dooley aimed his satirical barbs at American commercial imperialism, the ineptness of the army, and the vanity of most high-ranking officers. He exempted ''Tiddy Rosenfelt'' (Theodore Roosevelt*) and also George Dewey,* who he claimed was his cousin George Dooley. Dunne's ''On His Cousin George,'' which concerns Dewey and the likely dire consequences of American victory in the Philippines, achieved phenomenal success for Dunne. He began to earn $1,000 a week for his essays. His first two books, *Mr. Dooley in Peace and in War** (1898) and *Mr. Dooley in the Hearts of His Countrymen* (1899), collections of his best newspaper columns, were runaway best-sellers, with sales of 10,000 copies a month. Dunne vacationed in England twice (1899, 1901). As Mr. Dooley, Dunne reviewed *The Rough Riders** by Roosevelt, suggesting that its title ought to be *Alone in Cubia* inasmuch as the account of the war in it ''fell fr'm th' lips of Tiddy Rosenfelt an' was took down be his own hands.'' Roosevelt wrote Dunne joyously and started their long friendship.

Dunne went to New York as *Collier's** editor (1902). He was part owner of the New York morning *Telegraph* (1902–1904). He did editorial work for many magazines (1904–1919), including *McClure's Magazine*,* founded by S. S. McClure.* All of this work brought Dunne into contact with Lincoln Steffens,* Ida M. Tarbell* (whom Mr. Dooley called ''Idarem''), and Norman Hapgood* (whom Mr. Dooley called ''Normal Slapgood''). Dunne married Margaret Abbott, a Boston Protestant Brahmin lady in 1902 (they lived on Long Island and had four children, including twins). Dunne's later works are *Mr. Dooley's Philosophy* (1900), *Mr. Dooley's Opinions* (1901), *Observations by Mr. Dooley* (1902), *Dissertations by Mr. Dooley* (1906), *Mr. Dooley Says* (1910), and *Mr. Dooley on Making a Will and Other Necessary Evils* (1919). One of his sons, Philip Dunne, compiled a kind of autobiography of his father entitled *Mr. Dooley Remembers: The Informal Memoirs of Finley Peter Dunne* (1963).

E

Eakins, Thomas (1844–1916). (Full name: Thomas Cowperthwaite Eakins.) Painter. His father was a professional penman and calligrapher. Eakins was born in Philadelphia and studied drawing at the Pennsylvania Academy of the Fine Arts there and also anatomy at the Jefferson Medical College (1861). He spent three years at L'Ecole des Beaux-Arts in Paris (1866–1869), toured in Italy and Germany (summer 1868), and spent some eye-opening months in Spain, where he came to respect the refreshing naturalism of Jusepé de Ribera and Diego de Silva y Velázquez (1869–1870). Home again, Eakins opened his own studio in Philadelphia (1870) and realistically painted a variety of subjects—family members, friends, athletes, African Americans, professional persons, hunters, and people in boats. Eakins taught at the Pennsylvania Academy (1876–1886), where one of his students was Henry Ossawa Tanner,* an African American. An innovator in using the camera as a painter's aid, Eakins experimented with Eadweard Muybridge* in photographing humans and animals in motion (1884–1885). When Eakins insisted on using totally nude models in mixed classes when he lectured on human anatomy at the Pennsylvania Academy, he was forced by its conservative trustees to resign (1886). He began to teach at the newly established Art Students League of Philadelphia (about 1886–1893).

Opposition to his insistence on nude models finally obliged him to quit teaching; poor sales of his splendid outdoor and domestic genre scenes forced him to turn exclusively to portraits. Because these portraits were usually of students and other friends—in his uncompromising warts-and-all style—they did not bring in much revenue; for example, *Mrs. Letitia Bacon* (1888); *Miss Amelia Van Buren* (c. 1889–1891); *Professor Henry A. Rowland* (1897), the thoughtful, stern physicist is pictured seated holding a rainbow-colored card, with instruments in a darkened background; *Addie (Miss Mary Adeline Williams)* (1900), a strange woman with thick eyebrows and a wide mouth; *Mrs. William D. Frishmuth* (1900); *The Thinker: Louis N. Kenton* (1900); and *Professor Leslie*

Miller (1901). Several of these works reveal Eakins's knowledge of sculptural composition; not surprisingly, Eakins also created a few statues (1880s, early 1890s). He also liked to depict athletes, as in *Between Rounds* (1899), which shows a boxer resting on his stool, being tended by two trainers but not looking optimistic. Although Eakins's reputation was secure among professionals by the time of his death, it has grown considerably since. His two most famous paintings are *Max Schmitt in a Single Scull* (1871), with a magnificent use of perspective, and *The Surgical Clinic of Professor [Samuel D.] Gross* (1875), presenting a gory operation, to the squeamish discomfort of Eakins's contemporaries. The skill exhibited in the latter is reflected in a later painting, *The Agnew Clinic* (1889). His candid, psychologically revealing, and straightforward work is notable for reserved vitality and the wonderful turns given to heads.

Earp, Wyatt (1848–1929). (Full name: Wyatt Berry Stapp Earp.) Western peace officer, gunfighter, gambler, and saloon keeper. He was born in Monmouth, Illinois, and spent his early years in Illinois and Iowa with his family, which included older brothers James and Virgil, younger brothers Morgan and Warren, an older half-brother Newton, and a baby sister Adelia. The Earp family went to California (1864), where Wyatt Earp began a career which is now the stuff of legend. In the 1860s, 1870s, and early 1880s, he was a stage driver and freight hauler (in California, Utah, and the Dakota Territory), buffalo hunter, and town marshal (in Missouri and Kansas and in Tombstone, Arizona Territory).

Earp was marshal of Tombstone at the time of the famous gunfight at the O.K. Corral (26 October 1881). Bad blood had been building between Earp and nearby ranchers, mainly members of the Clanton family, who were probably minor rustlers. But rumor also had it that Earp was in league with certain stage robbers. Matters soon came to a head. The shoot-out involved Wyatt Earp and two of his brothers, Morgan (who was wounded in the shoulder) and Virgil (who was wounded in the leg), and their friend John Henry "Doc" Holliday (who was grazed on the hip)—all in opposition to William "Billy" Claiborne (who fled early), Joseph Isaac "Ike" Clanton (who fled even earlier) and his young, teen-aged brother William "Billy" Clanton (who was mortally wounded in the chest and stomach), and their friends Frank McLaury (who was mortally wounded in the stomach) and his brother Tom McLaury (who was killed by a shotgun blast). Ike Clanton and Billy Claiborne escaped through the photographic gallery in Tombstone owned by Camillus S. Fly* and his wife. The aftermath of the shoot-out was gory. When Virgil was severely wounded from ambush and Morgan was later murdered, Wyatt Earp exacted a series of gory revenges (1881–1882).

Wyatt Earp's later life was a long anticlimax. In the later 1880s Earp failed at gold mining in Colorado and Idaho, worked in a Texas saloon, and became well-to-do in San Diego real estate. He gambled in San Diego (1889–1890), was a bodyguard for a San Francisco editor, and was in demand as a boxing-match referee. He officiated at the prize boxing fight between Robert "Ruby

Robert'' Prometheus Fitzsimmons and ''Sailor Tom'' Sharkey (San Francisco, 2 December 1896). Earp awarded the prize to Sharkey when it was medically determined that Fitzsimmons had caused his knocked-out adversary ''genital trauma'' by a low blow; the decision precipitated an international controversy. Earp later opened a saloon and dance hall in Nome, Alaska, to capitalize on the gold rush in the territory (1898), tried gold mining in Nevada (1901–1906), and then resided in Los Angeles. In his later years, Earp worked as a bank guard, dabbled in oil and mineral properties, horsed around on movie lots with cowboy stars, consented to be interviewed by Stuart N. Lake (1927 and 1928), returned briefly to Tombstone (1928), and died soon after in Los Angeles. Earp married two or perhaps three times: Willa Sutherland (1870), who died the same year; probably a girl named Mattie (late 1870s), who died in 1888); and Josephine Sarah Marcus (1897), with whom Earp had two children, both of whom died in childhood.

Eastman, Charles (1858–1939). (Full name: Charles Alexander Eastman; Indian name: Ohiyesa.) Native American, a Santee Sioux. His maternal grandfather was a white man from New England; his maternal grandmother, part French. After an uprising of Minnesota Sioux in 1862, Eastman was taken to Dakota Territory and then into Canada, where he was kept from contact with whites until 1873. He then attended school in Dakota Territory, graduated from Dartmouth (1887), and received a medical degree from Boston University (1890). In November 1890 he became agency physician at Pine Ridge (Dakota Territory), just in time to tend the survivors of the massacre at Wounded Knee* (29 December 1890). In 1890 Eastman met Elaine Goodale, a Massachusetts woman who had taught African Americans and Native Americans in Virginia before her appointment as superintendent of Indian schools in Dakota. The two were married in 1891. The couple had six children, but when one daughter died the parents separated (in 1921). Meanwhile, Eastman had resigned (1893) as the Pine Ridge doctor, worked elsewhere with Native Americans in the region—including at Crow Creek, South Dakota, from 1900 to 1903—and moved to Detroit and then Ontario. He was appointed to aid in the revising of Native American names (1901–1909) and was active later in Boy Scout work (from 1914).

Eastman, who became a distinguished Native American writer, began his publishing career with an autobiographical essay (1894), continued with *An Indian Boyhood* (1902), and later wrote many fine works about Indian religious beliefs, ways of life, virtues, customs, history, leaders, and reservation life and white-induced problems.

Eastman, George (1854–1932). Manufacturer, inventor, and philanthropist. He was born in Waterville, New York. His father, a penmanship instructor, founded the first commercial college in Rochester, New York, and moved his family there in 1860 but died soon thereafter (1862). After seven years of schooling, young Eastman clerked in an insurance office and then a bank. When he became interested in photography, he bought a great deal of equipment (1877) and began to experiment with dry-plate emulsions. He patented a process of preparing gelatin dry plates (1879) and began to manufacture them in Rochester (1880). He pioneered mass-production techniques, extensive advertising campaigns, and international sales. He and an associate formed the Eastman Dry Plate Company, capitalized at $10,000, and built a small factory (1880) and a larger one a year later. He patented a method of putting a sensitized emulsion on paper-backed collodion, to be sold in strips (1884). He and another partner devised a holder which could house such film in twenty-four-exposure rolls and which could be attached to the back of a camera (1884). Eastman expanded his firm into the Eastman Dry Plate & Film Company (1884, capitalized at $200,000) and soon thereafter introduced the Kodak camera, which could hold a 100-exposure roll of film making circular pictures 2½ inches in diameter (1888). Meanwhile, a man named Hannibal W. Goodwin invented a celluloid film and sent Eastman samples in confidence (1887). Eastman's company applied to patent this type of film (1889) but years later, after a court case (1914), had to pay the holders of Goodwin's patent $5,000,000 in damages. Thomas A. Edison* ordered from Eastman's company this innovative type of film (beginning 1889) and thus was able to start the motion-picture business. Eastman reincorporated as the Eastman Company (1889, capitalized at $1,000,000).

Throughout the 1890s, Eastman sought, by buying up patents and even rival companies, to monopolize the camera and film markets. He developed a film that was shielded by black paper and could therefore be loaded into a camera in daylight (1891). He changed the name of the firm to the Eastman Kodak Company (1892, capitalized at $5,000,000). He discharged a brilliant research chemist, along with his two associates, from his company when he learned that they planned to form a rival business (1892; he later sued the three). He developed the pocket Kodak (1895), then a $5 model (1896). Despite the Panic of 1893,* he recapitalized yet again (1898, at $8,000,000) and distributed more than $178,000 in the ensuing profits among his executives and employees (1899). He renamed the firm the Eastman Kodak Company of New Jersey (1901, capitalized at $35,000,000; it was later found to be in violation of antitrust laws—*see* Sherman Anti-Trust Act). By the turn of the century, Eastman had established manufacturing plants, wholesale branches, and subsidiary companies in several states and in foreign countries around the world. One, in Harrow, England, employed 3,000 people (1900).

In the early decades of the twentieth century, Eastman's company pioneered with new film-developing processes, large flexible films to replace glass plates in professional photographic studios, films for x-ray use, amateur movie cameras and projectors, and color movie film. The company also developed synthetic chemicals, trained photographers during World War I, and afforded its employees unprecedented fringe benefits. In addition, Eastman was an enlightened philanthropist. His first sizable gift was $200,000 to the Rochester Mechanics Institute (1899). His main beneficiaries over the years were the University of Rochester and the Massachusetts Institute of Technology. He donated more than $75,000,000 to universities, medical and dental facilities, and cultural organizations in Rochester, elsewhere in the United States, and abroad. He studied art and collected paintings, was fond of music, was an avid hunter and was an amateur horticulturalist and farmer. He never married but lived with his mother and made her very comfortable in his Rochester mansion until her death in 1907. He was a modest but generous host. Late in his life, Eastman grew more reserved and lonely, and he felt that even his own younger researchers were developing processes beyond his ability to comprehend. He inexplicably committed suicide.

Eddy, Mary Baker (1821–1910). (Full name: Mary Morse Glover Patterson Eddy.) Religious leader, church founder, and author. She was born in Bow, New Hampshire. Her father was a farmer and a Calvinist. She married George Washington Glover, an architect, in 1843. He died of fever in 1844, shortly before she bore their child. She married Daniel S. Patterson, a dentist and homeopathist, in 1853, but the couple separated in 1866 and were divorced in 1873. She was treated by mental healer Dr. Phineas Parkhurst Quimby of Portland, Maine, for chronic invalidism (1862). On 1 February 1866 she critically injured herself in a fall on icy pavement in Lynn, Massachusetts. She turned to the Bible for help (Matt. 9:1–8). When she felt cured, she assiduously studied the Bible (1866–1869), began to spread the word concerning spiritually aided self-healing, and established her practice of faith healing in Lynn (1870). She was convinced that she could, by careful readings, cure herself and help others to cure themselves. She wrote *Science and Health with Key to the Scriptures* (1875, often revised), which became the text of Christian Science and which she used as her basic document for lecturing and healing. In 1877 she married one of her disciples, the devoted but not especially bright Asa Gilbert Eddy, who had heart trouble. In 1882 he died of what Mrs. Eddy called "mesmeric poisoning" by an enemy.

Mrs. Eddy founded the Church of Christ, Scientist, in Boston (1879); obtained a charter for the Massachusetts Medical College, in which to train Christian Science practitioners (1881); began to publish the *Journal of Christian Science* (1883); opened the first of innumerable Christian Science reading rooms (1888); established, with a dozen of her followers, her mother church, the First Church of Christ, Scientist, in Boston (1892); began her own Christian Science Publishing Society, a board of lecturing, and a board of education (1898); and founded the *Christian Science Monitor* (1908). In 1891, she had a dramatic falling out with an associate named James Henry Wiggin, a Boston-born Unitarian minister turned music critic, drama critic, and book editor. Wiggin had helped her prepare new editions of *Science and Health* (1885, 1890) and had helped her edit the *Journal of Christian Science* (1887–1889) and her autobiographical *Retrospection and Introspection* (1891); shortly after, she accused him of becoming influenced by animal magnetism (1891). Mrs. Eddy changed her base of activities several times: Boston (1882–1892), Concord, New Hampshire

(1892–1908), and finally Chestnut Hill, Massachusetts (1908–1910). Some of her seventeen books, in addition to those mentioned above, are *The People's Idea of God* (1886), *Unity of God* (1891), *No and Yes* (1891), *Manual of the Mother Church, the First Church of Christ, Scientist, in Boston, Massachusetts* (1895), *Miscellaneous Writings* (1896), *Pulpit and Press* (1898), *Messages to the Mother Church* (1900, 1901, 1902), and *The First Church of Christ, Scientist, and Miscellany* (1913). The most sensational criticism of Mrs. Eddy's intellectual position is contained in *Christian Science with Notes Containing Corrections to Date* (1907) and "Secret History of Eddypus, the World-Empire" (published posthumously in 1972), both by Mark Twain.*

Edison, Thomas A. (1847–1931). (Full name: Thomas Alva Edison.) Inventor. Edison was born in Milo, Ohio, but the family moved to Port Huron, Michigan, in 1854. Edison had only three months of formal schooling because his teacher rejected him as dreamy and "addled." His mother taught him thereafter. He studied physics at age nine, had his own little chemistry laboratory at age ten, sold newspapers and candy on the railroad running between Port Huron and Detroit, suffered a grievous hearing loss as a result of an accident, and became a vagabond telegraph operator in the Middle West (from 1863). He patented a vote recorder (1869); went to New York (1869); improved a stock-ticker system (1870), which he sold for $40,000; opened a laboratory in Newark, New Jersey, to make tickers and other electrical devices; improved telegraphic transmitters (1873–1874); discovered an electrical phenomenon called the "Edison effect" (and later "thermionic emission"), which resulted in the development of the radio and led to twentieth-century electronics (*see* Radio). Edison opened a laboratory in Menlo Park, New Jersey (1876), where he invented the microphone (1876), an improved telephone transmitter (1877), a device to measure solar rays (1877), the phonograph (1877), a carbon-filament incandescent lamp (1879), new dynamos to generate and transmit electricity from a central light power station (1882), and much else. He opened plants in Schenectady, New York, which merged with the rival Thomas-Houston Electric Company and became the Edison General Electric Company (1892), a huge manufacturing concern. One of his employees, Nikola Tesla* (1884), patented an alternating current system (1888) despite Edison's early opposition to it in principle. (George Westinghouse* also rightly preferred alternating current, unlike Edison.) Edison moved to West Orange, New Jersey, in 1887. He cooperated with A. B. Dick* in the development of the mimeograph machine (1887). Edison consulted with Eadweard Muybridge* about his zoöpraxiscope, a device designed to project images of animals in motion (1888). Edison instead used a patent purchased from Thomas Armat; developed the kinetoscope and vitascope, devices that projected primitive motion pictures; ordered an innovative type of movie film from George Eastman* (beginning in 1889); and finally patented the kinetoscope and vitascope in 1891. Edison showed the first commercial movies in New York

City (23 April 1896); he later demonstrated that movies could be synchronized with a sound track (1913), which Muybridge had suggested to him earlier.

Edison was invited to the Paris Centennial Exhibition (1899) and was awarded the French Legion of Honor; he was also honored in Rome, London, and Berlin. During and after World War I, Edison was intensely active, working for the U.S. government and for himself on acids, airplanes, automobiles, cameras, drugs, dyes, explosives, radios, and rubber. He received more than a thousand patents for his inventions, which also include an electric railroad train, alkaline storage batteries, and a magnetic process to separate low-grade iron ore. Edison has been criticized for preferring the practical process instead of the theoretical discovery, but he was one of America's greatest geniuses. He married Mary G. Stillwell in 1871 (the couple had three children; Mrs. Edison died in 1882) and Mina Miller in 1884 (they also had three children).

The Eight. (More formally called The Eight Independent Painters.*) A group of eight American painters who first exhibited together at the Macbeth Gallery in New York City in February 1908. The leader was Robert Henri,* and the others were Arthur Bowen Davies, William James Glackens, Ernest Lawson, George Benjamin Luks, Maurice Brazil Prendergast, Everett Shinn, and John Sloan. All had been active artists, who had enjoyed various degrees of success in the 1890s. The Eight were the first group of American artists to depict ordinary people in their unpretentious urban habitats and in routine actions. The painters were later called the Ash Can School because of their frequent depiction of shabby urban areas; they were also called the Revolutionary Black Gang, partly, perhaps, because Henri promulgated some of the theories of Leon Trotski and other Russian radicals. Despite the names, the paintings of The Eight were usually optimistic in tone. Most of their human figures were depicted as warm, friendly, and peppy, not as denisons of filthy tenements and sweatshops.

The Eight Independent Painters. *See* The Eight.

Electrocution, Execution by. The first execution by electrocution was that of William Kemmler, a.k.a. John Hart, at Auburn Prison, Auburn, New York, on 6 August 1890, for a murder committed on 29 March 1889. The first woman to be executed by electrocution was Martha M. Place; the sentence was carried out at Sing Sing Prison, Ossining, New York, on 20 March 1899, for a murder committed on 7 February 1898.

Ellis Island. A 27½-acre island in New York Harbor. Several original buildings on Ellis Island were used, beginning in 1892, to house, feed, examine, and process immigrants to the United States. Between 1892 and 1954, the Immigration Service processed 17,000,000 men, women, and children, mostly from Europe, who sought a better life in the United States (*see* Immigration). After passing physical and mental health inspections, the new and often bewildered arrivals collected their baggage, changed what money they had, and started on their way. About one-third of them settled in New York City; others went by ferry to New Jersey and then by railroad to various places throughout the country. About 2 percent of the applicants failed inspection and were sent back. The Great Hall replaced an original processing building, which burned in 1897; it was opened in 1900. Abandoned in 1954, the hall suffered water damage and was also systematically vandalized for thirty years. Now refurbished as a museum and opened in September 1990, it features photographs, video shows, and documentary movies, and plays host to 1,500,000 visitors annually.

Equality (1897). A utopian novel by Edward Bellamy,* a follow-up of his *Looking Backward: 2000–1887.** More tract than fiction, *Equality*, which mainly counters objections raised against *Looking Backward* by conservatives, explains how the transition from past and present socioeconomic injustice to a future utopia could come about without violence or even undue confusion. Bellamy's scenario for twenty-first-century happiness is relatively straightforward: Capitalism and monopolies will give way to one monopoly, controlled by a government that is federal in organization, democratic in spirit, and socialist in politics; all citizens will share dividends through ownership of stock in nationalized industries and can spend stipends therefrom as they wish but cannot bequeath any financial residue; government workers will evolve from soldiers, policemen, judges, and wardens to agents active in promoting human freedoms (of speech and worship, and from fear and want); and the final effect will be the unique elimination of divisions separating rich, superior masters and poor, subservient dependents.

"Europe" (1899). Short story by Henry James.* Back from Europe, the narrator visits old Mrs. Rimmle and her three aging daughters in a Boston suburb. Each time that Becky, Jane, and Maria plan for one of the sisters to care for their mother while the other two visit Europe, the old woman dashes their hopes by getting sick. Once, however, a friendly couple escort Jane to Europe, which she loves too much ever to return. When the narrator visits next, Mrs. Rimmle tells him that Jane has died in Europe (not so) and that Becky (who is quite sick) is going next. During his final visit, the old woman explains that Becky has gone to Europe. Evidently, the wretched Maria lets her mother think so rather than tell her that Becky has died. By such stories as "Europe" and many others, James dramatizes both parental selfishness and the spell Europe cast on Americans in the late nineteenth century.

Everybody's Magazine. Ten-cent magazine founded by Wanamaker's store in New York as a house organ in 1896. At first the magazine reprinted material bought from the London *Royal Magazine*; soon it also published American writing, was sold in 1903 to three businessmen, and became an illustrated bestseller of varied contents and much advertising. Featuring essays on finance and muckraking pieces, it was highly successful in the early years of the twentieth century.

Exploration. In the 1890s, Americans continued to extend their physical boundaries and to satisfy their limitless curiosity by exploring the Far West, the Middle East, the Orient, the North Pole, and numerous other areas of the globe. John Muir,* nonpareil naturalist and conservationist, made the Far West his reverently adored home and the subject of his inspiring books. Continuing the work of geologist-surveyor Clarence King and his team, the redoubtable John Wesley Powell,* though maimed in the Civil War, explored the Rocky Mountain region and beyond, did anthropological work under the auspices of the Smithsonian Institution, and then directed the U.S. Geological Survey well into the 1890s. In his own way, Theodore Roosevelt* was also an explorer; among the many accomplishments of this versatile, active man may be listed ranching in the Dakotas and hunting as far away as Brazil. Ellsworth Huntington,* who was born in Illinois, became a teacher in Turkey and so loved the region that he explored and wrote about that country, as well as about Iraq and Afghanistan, then India, China, Siberia, and elsewhere. The most intrepid explorer of this period was Robert Edwin Peary,* who made the Far North and the Arctic his challenge. Homer Lea* and William Woodville Rockhill* did not intend to be explorers, but their exploits in China qualify them as such. Many others could be listed as explorers, perhaps even Nellie Bly,* who after all set a world's record for a fast tour of the world, at just over seventy-two days (ending 26 January 1890).

F

Fables in Slang (1900). The first collection of "fables" by George Ade.* This book was issued in Chicago by the progressive publisher Herbert S. Stone.* Unique from the first, these fables were marked by capitalized nouns, slang, clichés, mordant humor, accurate American vernacular, absence of literary pretentiousness, and end-of-text morals. A good example is "The Fable of the Caddy Who Hurt His Head Thinking," in which a caddy watches rich and outlandishly dressed duffers awkwardly hammering golf balls from one flag to another. The lad painfully wonders why his father, who works in a lumber yard, rarely has a spare dollar. Moral? "Don't try to Account for Anything."

Fantastic Fables (1899). A collection of fables by Ambrose Bierce.* These more than 300 tiny, acidic fables castigate in terse, precise, often archaic language a variety of objects, including religion, authority, soldiers, politicians, lawyers, policemen, lovers and spouses, writers, thought processes, and most emotions and so-called virtues. Many appear in Aesopian animal- and bird-fable form. They are endlessly ingenious, witty, cynical, bitter, and negative.

Farmer, Fannie Merritt (1857–1915). Cookery expert and author. Born in Boston, the daughter of a printer, she was crippled by an inexplicable malady at age seventeen. She helped her mother at home and attended the Boston Cooking School for teachers, from which she graduated in 1889. She remained at the school as a teacher and became its director (1891). She taught a course at the Harvard Medical School in cooking for invalids. Her first cookbook, privately published, sold only within the school. Fanny Farmer's famous book, *The Boston Cooking-School Cook Book*, issued in 1896, included 557 pages and sold for $2. She had to pay for the first printing, of 3,000 copies. The book, a runaway success, made its author rich and famous and had exhausted twenty-one editions by the time of her death; it has now sold well over three million copies. She founded Miss Farmer's School of Cookery (1902) to train housewives, not teachers or chefs, and she lectured widely and, with her sister, coauthored the *Woman's Home Companion* cookery column. She also wrote *Chafing Dish Possibilities* (1898) and later books. A stroke left her paralyzed in both legs (1907), after which she lectured on crutches or in a wheelchair until shortly before her death. Her famous cookbook, which begins with a prefatory quotation from John Ruskin concerning the mythological aspects of cookery, is aimed at the woman who heads a family of six and has one servant or none. The book tells how to build a variety of fires and offers, as the pièce de résistance, a battery of high-calorie recipes and full-course menus. Notable is her insistence on "level" teaspoon, tablespoon, and cup measurements rather than pinches or heapings. Efficient, utilitarian, and comprehensive, she stresses the wholesome but includes recipes calling for wine or brandy and offers suggestions for recycling leftovers into casseroles and hashes.

Fenollosa, Ernest (1853–1908). (Full name: Ernest Francisco Fenollosa; Buddhist name: Tei-Shin; Japanese name: Kano Yeitan Masanobu.) Orientalist, educator, and author. He was born in Salem, Massachusetts. His father was a Spanish musician who enlisted in an American frigate band, arrived in the United States (1838), settled in Salem, and married an American in Salem. Fenollosa attended Harvard, where he studied art (under Charles Eliot Norton*), philosophy, and sociology, took painting lessons, and was the 1874 class poet. He married Lizzie Goodhue Millett in 1878 (the couple had two children and were later divorced) and accepted his first position in Japan (1878). Thereafter, he taught economics, logic, philosophy, and political science at the Imperial University of Tokyo (1878–1886); was appointed fine arts commissioner for the Japanese government (1886–1887); and taught aesthetics at, and also managed, the Tokyo Fine Arts Academy and the art department of the Imperial Museum of Tokyo (1887–1890). During this time, he made himself an expert in Oriental art and worked to preserve neglected Japanese shrines, temples, and art treasures; he even salvaged fragments of sculpture in junkyards and discarded paintings in furniture stores. He taught the Japanese to appreciate their own art. (The Japanese poet Yone Noguchi says that Fenollosa was "the very discoverer of Japanese art.") Fenollosa became a professing Buddhist.

When he returned to the United States, Fenollosa gave public lectures on Japanese and Chinese history and art, was appointed curator of the Department of Oriental Art at the Boston Museum of Fine Arts (1890–1896; the museum had purchased earlier his collection of some thousand Oriental paintings), and represented Japan at the World's Columbian Exposition* (Chicago, 1893). He persuaded many educators to teach Far Eastern art and aesthetics in American schools. On returning to Japan, Fenollosa was treated disdainfully by suddenly jingoistic Japanese scholars of their own art, was assigned to teach English literature at the Imperial Normal School in Tokyo (1897–1900), and therefore returned to the United States, where he taught intermittently at Columbia (1901–

1908). He planned another trip to Japan, with a group of students, but en route he suffered a fatal heart attack in London.

Fenollosa's publications include *East and West: The Discovery of America and Other Poems* (1893); *An Outline of Ukiyo-e* (1901), on seventeenth-century Japanese wood-block prints; and *Epochs of Chinese and Japanese Art* (1912), a valuable volume left in chaotic form with numerous errors, which was assembled by his second wife, Mary McNeill Fenollosa, a novelist who used the pen name Sidney McCall (they were married in 1895). Fenollosa also studied the parallels between Greek drama and the Japanese Nō theater. He associated with numerous American artists and intellectuals, many of whom visited Japan, stayed to work in Japan, or came to appreciate Oriental art, including Henry Adams,* Bernard Berenson,* Sturgis Bigelow, Isabella Stewart Gardner,* Lafcadio Hearn,* John La Farge,* Percival Lowell, Edward S. Morse, and Theodore Roosevelt.* Among many later writers influenced by Fenollosa are Ezra Pound and William Butler Yeats.

Fernow, Bernhard E. (1851–1923). (Full name: Bernhard Eduard Fernow.) Forester, author, and educator. Born in Inowrazlaw, Posen, Germany, he was educated at Bromberg, Posen, the University of Königsburg, and the Hanover-Münden Forest Academy. He served during the Franco-Prussian War (1870) and then worked for the Prussian forest service (to 1876). Fernow emigrated to the United States in 1876 and immediately discovered that scientific management of forests was unknown in America. He established a tin-scrap plant in Brooklyn (1876–1878) and then, fortunately, obtained a job managing a Pennsylvania mining company's land holdings (1878–1885). His early writings on forestry, which attracted attention in scientific and government circles, led to his cofounding the American Forestry Congress (1882, later named the American Forestry Association), of which he was secretary (1882–1894). He was named head of the U.S. Department of Agriculture's Division of Forestry (1886–1898), during which time he concerned himself with forestry research, studies of various trees and their wood, means of avoiding forest destruction by fire and disease, and legislation not only to protect forests in the public domain but also to set aside acreage to establish national forests (1891–1897).

Fernow organized and taught at the first American college forestry school, the New York State College of Forestry, which was connected with Cornell University (1898–1903). He was an exhibit judge at the World's Columbian Exposition* (1893), the Atlanta Exposition (1895), and the Pan-American Exposition* (1901). He became a timber consultant and explorer in the United States, Mexico, and the West Indies (1903–1907), lectured at Yale (1904), started forestry studies at Pennsylvania State College (1906–1907), and founded and administered a forestry department at the University of Toronto (1907–1919). In addition to numerous articles, Fernow published several books, including *The White Pine* (1889), *Report upon Forestry Investigation of U.S. Department of Agriculture, 1877–98* (1899), *Economics of Forestry* (1902, the first book of its kind in English), *A Brief History of Forestry in Europe, the United States, and Other Countries* (1907), and *The Care of Trees, in Lawn, Street and Park* (1910). Fernow established the *Forestry Quarterly* (1902) and edited it (1902–1916) and the *Journal of Forestry*, its successor (1916–1922). He married Olivia Reynolds in 1879 (the couple had five children).

Ferris, George (1859–1896). (Full name: George Washington Gale Ferris.) Engineer and inventor. Ferris was born in Galesburg, Illinois, and studied at the California Military Academy and the Rensselaer Polytechnic Institute. He built bridges in Kentucky (1883–1885), did consulting work nationwide, organized his own metallurgical company in Pittsburgh (1885), and added an engineering branch to the company three years later (1888). Then, ignoring all ridicule, Ferris devised plans for ferris wheels and built a huge one for the World's Columbian Exposition* (Chicago, 1893). As the whole world now knows, the ferris wheel is a popular ride for amusement parks, carnivals, and fairs. It is a large, upright double wheel supported by a single or double tower, with enclosed or open seats attached at regular intervals to the wheel and usually hanging so as to remain parallel to the ground while swinging somewhat. It is powered to revolve, thus carrying seated customers up, high into the air, and down again. The Columbian Exposition model could carry 2,000 people at a time 264 feet up into the air. George Ferris later suffered business reverses and died in poverty in Pittsburgh. His Columbian Exposition wheel was moved to the Louisiana Purchase International Exposition (St. Louis, 1904). An 1894 ferris wheel erected in London was 328 feet high and accommodated 1,200 persons in 40 cars. One of the largest modern ferris wheels is located at the Prater in Vienna, Austria.

Field and Stream. Magazine. John P. Burkhard and Henry W. Wack started the magazine, originally known as *Western Field and Stream*, in 1896, moved it to New York in 1898, retitled it *Field and Stream*, and made it into the premier American magazine devoted to all aspects of hunting and fishing. Its finances were shaky until Eltige Warner became the business manager. The editorial staff stressed conservation not slaughter, collected films of wildlife, and commissioned wildlife paintings by first-rate artists.

Field, Eugene (1850–1895). Author of poetry, humorous pieces, and prose stories. He was born in Saint Louis, Missouri. His parents came from Vermont. When his mother died in 1856, young Field and his brother (later the novelist and journalist Roswell M. Field) were sent to relatives in Amherst, Massachusetts. Eugene Field attended Williams College (beginning in 1868). When his father, a successful Saint Louis lawyer, died in 1869, Field transferred first to Knox College, in Galesburg, Illinois, and then to the University of Missouri. He left the University of Missouri without a degree; tried acting briefly; spent most of his inheritance on travel in England, France, Ireland, and Italy (1872); and returned to marry Julia Sutherland Comstock, his sixteen-year-old sweetheart, in 1873. The couple had eight children, and Mrs. Field, long a widow, died in 1936. From 1875 to 1883, Field worked on editorial staffs of newspapers in Saint Joseph, Saint Louis, Kansas City—all in Missouri—and the Denver of gold-rush times. In 1883 he began his long association with the Chicago *Morning News* (called the *Record* from 1890). His *Sharps and Flats* columns contained a mishmash of material—poetry, sketches, parodies, humorous reviews, hoaxes, personal items, and so on—and, despite their ephemeral nature, they were reprinted nationwide.

Field was a tall, bald, eccentric, ever-boyish practical joker. He loved the poet Horace and named his suburban Chicago home "Sabine Farm" because of Horace's property in the Sabine Hills, northeast of Tivoli, Italy. Field also loved old English ballads and was an avid book collector. He was such a popular writer of light, familiar verse, often marked by folksiness and a funny Midwestern dialect, that he was embarrassed by his more serious efforts. He even tried to fool the public into believing that some of his splendid lyrics had been written by others. Still, his best poems, such as "Wynken, Blynken, and Nod" and "Little Boy Blue," are of permanent value. (*See* also Songs.) At his best, Field combines Western vigor and Eastern refinement. He never responded to the example of such socially conscious Chicago writers as Jane Addams,* Finley Peter Dunne,* Henry Blake Fuller,* Robert Herrick,* and Thorstein Veblen,* as well as others who passed through Chicago and recorded the injustices they saw there. Field regarded the realism of William Dean Howells* as bad art and a pernicious influence. Field's works include *A Little Book of Western Verse* (1889), privately printed; *A Little Book of Profitable Tales* (1889), weak; *Second Book of Verse* (1892); *With Trumpet and Drum* (1892); *Echoes from the Sabine Farm* (1893), verse translations from Horace, with Roswell M. Field; *The Holy Cross and Other Tales* (1893); *Love Songs of Childhood* (1894); and *The Love Affairs of a Bibliomaniac* (1896). Field died at an early age, of heart failure. His works were reprinted in a ten-volume collected edition in 1896.

Field, Marshall (1852–1906). Merchant and philanthropist. He was born near Conway, Massachusetts. After a limited formal education, he clerked in a store in Pittsfield, Massachusetts (1852–1856), moved to Chicago, and became a salesman for Cooley, Wadsworth & Co., a wholesale dry goods firm. He became a junior partner of Cooley, Farwell & Co. (1862) and then a partner of Farwell, Field & Co. (1862), which was reorganized as Field, Palmer & Leiter (1865) when merchant genius Potter Palmer* offered to sell his wholesale dry goods firm to Field and Levi Zeigler Leiter. After Palmer retired from the firm, Field reorganized as Field, Leiter & Co. (1867). Field and Leiter moved their store from Lake Street to the corner of State and Washington streets, and other commercial firms soon followed. Leiter withdrew, and the firm became Marshall Field & Co. (1881). (Leiter invested in commercial real estate in Chicago, became a multimillionaire, and among other activities financed his daughter Mary Victoria Leiter's wedding to Lord Curzon—*see* Travel and Travelers.)

Field experienced much trouble but also enjoyed steady commercial expansion. The Chicago Fire of 1871 burned his store and its stock of goods. The Panic of 1873 caused more disruption. Then Field's retail store burned (1877). Despite all these setbacks, Field's success continued because of his policies, many of which were innovative. He offered high-quality merchandise, courteous service, home delivery, a personal shopping service, a one-price system with clearly tagged prices, and a generous return policy; he also installed a store restaurant. When Field split his wholesale and retail departments, his retail store became the largest in the world. He bought on a cash basis, extended credit wisely, but demanded prompt payments. He expanded his activities to include manufacturing of dry goods, with factories in the British Isles, on the Continent, and in Australia, Brazil, and Japan. He stocked on a gigantic scale, often buying out all the products of a particular factory. By 1891, he employed 12,000 people (mostly paid hardly more than subsistence wages), and his sales totaled $35,000,000. Annual business had increased to $40,000,000 by 1895. Field invested wisely in banks, railroads, and steel companies.

A hard-driving, single-minded worker, Field never cared much for high society or politics, although in later years he was generous to many causes. For example, he gave $1,000,000 to the Columbian Museum at the World's Columbian Exposition* (Chicago, 1893); the museum became the Field Museum of Natural History when he later gave $8,000,000 more for its new, permanent building in Chicago. (It has since been sustained by gifts from the Field family and other donors. The museum, with anthropology, botany, geology, and zoology departments, displays well over ten million objects.) In addition, Field donated land valued at $450,000 to the incipient University of Chicago (*see* Universities) and later gave the school another $100,000; built a library in Conway, Massachusetts, where he had been born; and was generous to various Presbyterian Church programs. Field married Nannie Douglass Scott in 1863 (the couple had two children before Mrs. Field died) and Delia Spencer Caton in 1905. At his death, Field's estate was valued at $100,000,000. His son Marshall Field II (1868–1905) showed little inclination toward the family business and died of an accidental or self-inflicted gunshot wound. His son Marshall Field III (1893–1956) was educated in England; served in France during World War I; founded, bought, and merged various liberal newspapers; undertook other publishing ventures; and established the Field Foundation to consolidate his many admirable philanthropic organizations. His son Marshall Field IV (1916–1965), educated at Harvard and the University of Virginia, admirably carried on and extended his father's publishing and philanthropic endeavors. His son Marshall Field V (born in 1941) has been active in publishing and also in paper manufacturing.

Film. *See* Motion Pictures.

Fiske, John (1842–1901). Historian, philosopher, and lecturer. He was born in Hartford, Connecticut. His father was Edmund Brewster Green, a lawyer, newspaper editor, and politician, who died in Panama when his only son was ten.

Fiske's mother, Mary Fisk [*sic*] Bound Green, was a teacher who remarried in 1855. The boy was reared by his maternal grandmother from his earliest years. In 1855 he legally adopted the name John Fisk after his grandmother's father. (He added the "e" in 1860.) Fiske was a child prodigy who read voraciously and widely and studied mathematics and languages. He was schooled at a Connecticut academy (1855–1857) and was tutored (1857–1860) in preparation for Yale, but instead went to Harvard. Coming under the influence of Auguste Comte and Herbert Spencer, he was intellectually too independent to suit the Harvard faculty, where he made mediocre grades, but he graduated (1863) and obtained a Harvard law degree (1864). Fiske married Abby M. Brooks in 1864 (the couple had six children), quit the practice of law (1866), obtained work at Harvard as a lecturer (from 1869) and then as a librarian (1872–1879), and began to write feverishly to support his family. Fiske's first two books were *Myth and Myth-Makers* (1872), dedicated to his close friend William Dean Howells,* and *Outlines of Cosmic Philosophy* (1874), an attempt in an unoriginal but engaging manner to correlate evolutionary theories and theism. For the latter work, Fiske went to England and conferred with Spencer, Charles Darwin, and Thomas Henry Huxley. Spencer disliked Fiske's insistence that evolution proved the existence of God; Darwin, however, praised the book.

Early in 1879, having turned from philosophy to history, Fiske began a successful career as a lecturer. His first thesis was that American history and Anglo-American law are proof of the beneficence of social Darwinism. Later in 1879, and again in 1880 and 1883, he went to England to lecture. During this time, he also lectured widely in the United States, part of the time under the management of James B. Pond.* In the mid–1880s Fiske gave a series of lectures theorizing that, out of the "germ" idea of Anglo-American self-government, grew the American Constitution, which carried federalism throughout North America and is destined to spread worldwide. Fiske's *The Critical Period of American History, 1783–1789* (1888) evolved from those lectures. Next came *The Beginnings of New England* (1889, rev. ed. 1898), which praises New England, in an ultimately unpopular way, for being the seedbed for democratic political action in the United States. In 1892 Fiske accepted an invitation to go to Oregon to speak at the centennial anniversary of the discovery of the Columbia River.

Fiske's writings through the 1890s are in the main exciting narratives of heroic and skillful American deeds in war, politics, and diplomacy. His overriding theses were that early empires failed because their leaders, after their conquests, did not incorporate or allow representation, whereas the Anglo-American system, especially as modified by the New England puritans, permitted representation; furthermore, that, owing to the American Constitution and the spread of its effects as a result of the transcontinental railroads, the congressmen's baleful sectionalism could be restrained by federalism. During this decade, Fiske was paid an annual salary by his Boston publisher Henry Houghton, starting at $5,000 and ending at $12,000, in the shrewd and correct expectation that a guaranteed income would free Fiske to develop a series of popular, money-making tomes. Some of his many titles include *The War of Independence* (1890), *The American Revolution* (1891), *The Discovery of America* (1892), *Old Virginia and Her Neighbors* (1897), *The Dutch and Quaker Colonies in America* (1899), and *The Mississippi Valley in the Civil War* (1900). Of his many philosophical books, *Through Nature to God* (1899) is the last and perhaps the best. In it, Fiske suggests that the world contains evil and sorrow so that we can know good, happiness, and progress. Nature's seemingly utter cruelty, which destroys the many to develop the few, improves not only certain species but also certain social groups and even races. We must accept, sometimes with a love that is self-sacrificial, the march of events toward spiritual progress in accord with God's cosmic plan.

John Fiske, who at the close of his life weighed over 300 pounds and was wildly bewhiskered, is remembered as a successful popularizer of the original thinking of others. He skillfully, if superficially, blended masses of data into a sequence of books, which display range, clarity, and vividness with enough concrete examples to make accessible to the common reader the belief that the evolution of American political institutions is divinely and grandly willed and that, ultimately, all will be right with God's entire world. Many forward-looking thinkers of Fiske's era were not so sure about this prediction.

Fitch, Clyde (1865–1909). (Full name: William Clyde Fitch.) Dramatist. He was born in Elmyra, New York. His father served during the Civil War as a Union army officer. His mother, Alice Clark, was a Union sympathizer from Hagerstown, Maryland. The two met and were married there in 1863. Young Fitch lived with his parents on several different army posts. When he was ten, in Schenectady, New York, he put on his own neighborhood skits. He went to school in Connecticut and New Hampshire and entered Amherst College in 1882. While at Amherst, he displayed signs of eccentricity and independence, took female roles in productions of a few eighteenth-century plays, helped design costumes and settings, and directed plays. After he graduated (1886), Fitch went to New York, failed to obtain work as a newspaper reporter, and became a tutor and a free-lance fiction writer.

In 1889 he met the famous actor Richard Mansfield, who asked him to write a play for him based on the life of Beau Brummell but with the historical facts altered to make the character of the English dandy and gambler more appealing. Fitch did so, and *Beau Brummel** was a great success when it was first performed in 1890. Mansfield, who kept it in his repertoire for years, received most of the credit for its initial popularity, but the professional world knew better. Later in the 1890s and beyond, Fitch was asked to write other plays for specific actors and actresses: John Drew and Maude Adams in *The Masked Ball* (1892), an adaptation of a French play; Otis Skinner and Maud Durbin in *His Grace de Grammont* (1894); Maxine Elliott in *Nathan Hale* (1898), Fitch's first play based on an event in American history; Julia Marlowe in *Barbara Frietchie** (1899);

Ethel Barrymore in *Captain Jinks of the Horse Marines** (1901); and Annie Russell in *The Girl and the Judge* (1901). Fitch often altered history to suit his theatrical purposes. Thus, *Nathan Hale* absurdly manipulates events in the doomed hero's final days to stress his love for Alice Adams, the heroine. (Hale's dramatically expressed patriotism pleased audiences during the ongoing Spanish-American War.*) History and John Greenleaf Whittier's popular poem are ignored even more in *Barbara Frietchie*. *Captain Jinks of the Horse Marines* is a light, popular, and charming period piece. Then came a more serious play, *The Climbers** (also 1901), which contains a serious warning against social and financial climbing. *Lovers' Lane* (also 1901) represents another attempt by Fitch to deepen his writing; it dramatizes the decency of an old-fashioned, upstate New York minister whose admirable righteousness not only triumphs over small-minded church administrators and members but also gains for him the love of a good woman.

In a 1904 *Smart Set** essay, entitled "The Play and the Public," Fitch defends his use of melodrama by citing Shakespeare as an exemplary predecessor, argues that the advocates of realism should not sweep imaginative and poetic effects from the stage, and states that, to be satisfactory, a play should have an uplifting moral. Fitch unsuccessfully adapted *The House of Mirth* (1906), the splendid novel by Edith Wharton,* for the stage. Several of Fitch's last plays address darker moral problems and include harsher language, which puzzled his loyal American followers but pleased more advanced audiences abroad. *The Truth* (1906) is an example.

Fitch was amazingly fecund. He wrote thirty-three plays and twenty-three adaptations of plays by others. He could write so fast that he once dashed off an adaptation of a French drama in three days. His popularity brought material rewards. In 1901, four of his plays were running on New York stages at the same time. His income through the 1900s was at least $250,000 annually. In 1907, 500 New York theater workers of all categories earned salaries and wages totaling more than $500,000 as a direct consequence of plays by Fitch. But such intense work took its toll. Fitch was dangerously stressed in 1902, went to Europe in 1902 but became ill abroad, was in worse health in 1907, and, while in Europe again in 1909, suffered an appendicitis attack, had an appendectomy, and died in France. (*See* also Songs.)

Flower, B. O. (1858–1918). (Full name: Benjamin Orange Flower.) Editor and social reformer. Flower, who was born in Albion, Illinois, was educated in public schools in Evansville, Indiana, and at the University of Kentucky. He founded and edited a weekly journal in Albion (to 1880), moved to Philadelphia to work as his physician brother's secretary, and moved to Boston, where he published progressive journals and, in other ways, strove zealously to improve the plight of the disadvantaged. Flower founded and edited the *American Spectator* in Boston (1886–1889), combined it with his crusading, reform monthly *Arena** (founded in 1889), and edited the new *Arena* (to 1896). The *Arena* welcomed many important progressive writers, many of whom Flower knew and all of whom wished to present their positions on religious, social, moral, educational, economic, aesthetic, and political issues.

Earlier, Flower and his friend Minot J. Savage founded the American Psychical Society (Boston, 1892); Hamlin Garland,* whom Flower had been publishing in the *Arena* and had encouraged, was an officer. Flower coedited the Chicago *New Time* (1897–1898), which was pledged to promote "social progress." He also coedited the *Coming Age*, based in Saint Louis and Boston, until it too combined with the *Arena* (1900). Thereafter he was on the editorial staff of the *Arena* until 1904, after which he was the editor in chief and a frequent contributor until its last owner declared bankruptcy (1909). Flower then founded and edited the *Twentieth-Century Magazine* (Boston, 1909–1911), which favored voting, legislative, labor, and public utility reforms. Still later, Flower studied and wrote about Queen Victoria's early reign, Christian Science, and woman's rights; he opposed Catholicism and criticized antidemocratic cliques within government. Flower wrote many books; those published in the 1890s, didactic, biographical, and critical in nature, include studies of Charles Darwin (1892), Gerald Massey (1895), Sir Thomas More (1896), and John Greenleaf Whittier (1896). Other titles, often hinting at their contents, are *Civilization's Inferno; or, Studies in the Social Cellar* (1893), *The New Time: A Plea for the Union of the Moral Forms for Practical Progress* (1894), *Persons, Places and Ideas: Miscellaneous Essays* (1896), and *Equality and Brotherhood . . .* (1897). He also reprinted many of his *Arena* articles in pamphlet form. Flower was far more important as an editor who welcomed new writers than as a writer. He encouraged all sorts of progressive writers. A significant tragedy in his life was that, not long after he married Hattie Cloud in 1885, she became unstable and had to be institutionalized.

Fly, Camillus S. (1849–1901). (Full name: Camillus Sidney Fly; nickname: Buck.) Photographer. Born in Andrew County, Missouri, he was reared in California. With his wife Mary E. Goodrich Fly, also a photographer, he moved from San Francisco (1879) to live in Tombstone, Arizona Territory, in order to photograph the people there and to do some mining. (The mining proved profitless.) The two set up shop in a tent, then built an adobe-walled combination lodging house and photographic gallery and studio at the Fremont Street entrance to the O.K. Corral. Fly witnessed the famous shoot-out there (26 October 1881), which took place between the brothers Morgan, Virgil, and Wyatt Earp* and Doc Holliday, on the one hand, and Billy Claiborne, brothers Ike and Billy Clanton, and brothers Frank and Tom McLaury, on the other. After Ike Clanton and then Claiborne escaped through Fly's gallery, Fly darted from his studio to disarm Billy Clanton. Fly later accompanied General George Crook* to photograph the Apache chief Geronimo* on the occasion of his surrender in March 1886. Fly sold four pictures of Geronimo to *Harper's Weekly* (April 1886) and copyrighted fourteen surrender pictures in all (1886). Two years after he was commissioned by a British syndicate to photograph the Chiricahua Mountains (1892), he moved his studio to Phoenix (1894) and became sheriff of Cochise County (1894–1896). In his time, Fly photographed lawmen, cardplayers, gunfighters, robbers, prisoners, Native Americans, Indian camps, and military meetings. He also occasionally published his photographs in the Tombstone *Epitaph* (from 1880). After his death from acute alcoholism, his wife brought to publication his *Scenes in Geronimo's Camp; the Apache Outlaw and Murderer, Taken before the Surrender to Gen. Crook, March 27, 1886, in the Sierra Madre Mountains of Mexico* . . . (1905).

Following the Equator: A Journey around the World (2 vols., 1897). Autobiographical travel book by Mark Twain.* Dedicated to Henry Huttleston Rogers,* the rambling book includes two parts. I. In midsummer [15 July 1895], Twain and two family members [his wife Olivia and their daughter Clara] start from New York and proceed to British Columbia to commence his lecture tour around the world. A long voyage takes them past Hawaii, across the equator and under the Southern Cross, to the Fiji Islands, and down to Sydney, Australia. They proceed by rail to Melbourne, Adelaide, and other Australian locales. They travel by boat to Tasmania and New Zealand and then by rail and boat to Christchurch and other spots. II. On 23 December 1895, Twain and his party leave Sydney bound slowly for Ceylon. In January, they visit Bombay—full of sights. By rail they travel to Baroda and back, then to Allahabad past the Ganges, Benares, Calcutta, Darjeeling in the Himalayas, and other places, including Lucknow and Lahore, the Taj Mahal, the Afghanistan border, Delphi, and Jeypore. At the end of March, the three voyage from Calcutta to Madras and go on lazily to Mauritius; in mid-April, by slow train, they travel from Port Louis to Curepipe. In early May, they take a boat to Mozambique. After resting in Durban, South Africa, the trio goes to Cape Town in mid-July. At last, they return to England, completing a circumnavigation of the globe in thirteen months.

In *Following the Equator*, Twain discusses fun with and foibles of fellow passengers; occasionally dilates on personal experiences from his past; often recalls, humorously summarizes, and satirizes his extensive reading; praises the hospitality of various hosts; describes native beliefs, customs, foods, and speech patterns, flora and fauna, and colorful servants hired (one in Bombay he nicknamed "Satan"); expresses horror at poverty, disease, and wretched deaths (especially in India); and bitterly inveighs against European colonial policies (especially the British in Australia and South Africa—Cecil Rhodes was a particular nemesis). Twain lectured along the way for large sums of money—in Australia, New Zealand, India, and South Africa. During their happy stay in London, however, Twain and his wife received word that their daughter Susy was sick in Connecticut. Twain remained to work on *Following the Equator*; Olivia and Clara hurried home, but Susy died before they got there. Twain buried himself in writing to complete his book, which, published in November 1897, made a great deal of money. More important, *Following the Equator* points to the future, bitterly denounces colonialism in particular and man's inhumanity to man generally, and includes heartrending expressions of Twain's own personal misery.

Football. *See* Sports.

Ford, Henry (1863–1947). Manufacturer. Henry Ford, who was born near Dearborn, Michigan, repaired watches as a hobby. He had little formal schooling (to 1878) and walked nine miles to Detroit (1879), where he worked as a machine and engine shop apprentice during the day and a watch repairman in the evening. He installed, repaired, and tinkered with steam-powered farm machinery (to 1884) and operated a sawmill (1884). He obtained a job as engineer and machinist for the Edison Illuminating Company in Detroit (1887) and married Clara Bryant in 1888 (the couple had one child, Edsel Bryant Ford [1893–1943]). In his spare time, Henry Ford built a two-cylinder, four-horsepower, gasoline-powered automobile (to 1892), drove it (1893), sold it, experimented further, and quit his Edison Company job (1899). Ford then associated with the Detroit Automobile Company (1899–1902). He held a small amount of the stock of the company, which made custom-built cars. Because he wanted to create a universal car that could be mass-produced, he left the company, went into business for himself, perfected a few cars, manufactured two four-cylinder, eighty-horsepower racing cars (the 999 and the Arrow), won all the races he entered, and organized the Ford Motor Company (1903).

In the ensuing years, Henry Ford produced a two-cylinder, eight-horsepower, chain-drive model (1,708 cars in 1903), four- and six-cylinder models, and countless strong but lightweight Model T cars (from 1908). He regularly plowed the profits back into construction. He evolved assembly-line methods, introduced the eight-hour workday at a daily minimum wage of $5, tried (1914–1915) to halt the onset of World War I, but then manufactured gun carriages, Liberty motors, and many other products during the war. He ran unsuccessfully for the U.S. Senate (1918) and retired from the presidency of his company (1919). When his son Edsel, who succeeded him, died, he again became president until the year of his own death. Henry Ford opposed paternalism and charity; instead, he established a trade school and a Detroit hospital. (*See* also Automobiles.)

Ford, Paul Leicester (1865–1902). Novelist, historian, bibliographer, and expert chess player. Born in Brooklyn, New York, Ford, a hunchback, was educated by tutors and by browsing in the library of his father, Gordon Lester Ford, a well-to-do lawyer, businessman, journalist, independent political figure, and world-renowned collector of Americana. His library ultimately contained 100,000 books and 60,000 manuscripts (in his forty-one-room mansion). Ford's mother, Emily Ellsworth Fowler Ford, knew Emily Dickinson* in Amherst, Massachusetts, and was herself a publishing poet. Gordon and Emily Ford had five daughters and three sons; Paul was the youngest son. At age eleven, he wrote and printed on his own press a genealogy of the Webster family, which included his great-grandfather Noah Webster. Paul Ford, his father, and Worthington Chauncey Ford, one of his brothers, founded the Historical Printing Club in Brooklyn and through it reprinted historical documents, including *Winnowings in American History* (15 vols., 1890–1891). Paul Ford also edited the writings of Thomas Jefferson (10 vols., 1892–1899), Christopher Columbus (1892), and John Dickinson (1895); edited *Essays on the Constitution* (1892); and wrote biographies of George Washington (1896) and Benjamin Franklin (1899).

More important, Ford wrote several novels, including *The Honorable Peter Stirling and What People Thought of Him** (1894); *The Great K. & A. Train-Robbery* (1897), a Western; *The Story of an Untold Love* (1897); *Tattle Tales of Cupid* (1898); *Janice Meredith: A Story of the American Revolution** (1899); *Wanted: A Matchmaker* (1900); and *Wanted: A Chaperon* (1902). *The Honorable Peter Stirling*, inspired by Ford's unsuccessful attempts to enter Brooklyn politics, depicts shoddy political life in the 1890s. Its popularity was due partly to the belief that its hero was based on the early career of Grover Cleveland.* *Janice Meredith*, a best-seller, sold 200,000 copies in the first few months and earned its author $48,000 during that period. (Sales continued well for a generation.) Ford married Grace Kidder in 1900 (the couple had one child). Worthington Ford, handicapped by deafness, became a manuscript curator and edited Washington's complete works (12 vols., 1899) and some of the letters of Henry Adams* (2 vols., 1930, 1938). Paul Ford vacationed in the West Indies (1887), enjoyed a research trip to England and the Continent (1890), and visited Europe again (1900).

After their father died (1891), Worthington and Paul Ford inherited his library, which they gave to the New York Public Library (1899); its estimated value was almost $200,000. Under the terms of the presentation, John Pierpont Morgan* bought the manuscripts for $35,000, kept what he wished, and gave the bulk to the library. Malcolm Webster Ford, who was indifferent to scholarship, was exiled from the family (1882), became a semiprofessional athlete, was disinherited (1891), unsuccessfully sued after his mother's death (1893) for one-seventh of the family estate (1894), and was given $4,500 by his brothers in settlement of all claims. After the unbalanced man became involved in financial difficulties, he visited Paul Ford in his Manhattan home. When he asked for more money and was refused, Malcolm Ford shot his brother to death and immediately committed suicide in front of a witness.

Paul Ford, brilliant and versatile, possessed almost superhuman energy. He produced nearly seventy books, of which only his historical works are now considered first rate. Henry James* said in a 1898 review that the enormous sales success of *The Honorable Peter Stirling* keeps one from saying more than merely that the work is both formless and tasteless.

Forty Modern Fables (1901). More "fables" by George Ade. These fables capitalize on the great success of *Fables in Slang** (1900) and *More Fables** (1900). From the first, these unique fables were marked by capitalized nouns, slang, clichés, mordant humor, accurate American vernacular, absence of literary pretentiousness, and end-of-text morals.

The Four Hundred. A term designating the high-society leaders in the United States and referring to a list of guests supposedly shortened by Ward McAllister* at the request of Mrs. William Astor.

Fox, Richard Kyle (1846–1922). Journalist. Born in Belfast, Ireland, Fox worked as an office boy for a religious paper, paid for his own schooling, and worked for the *Belfast News Letter*. He married Annie Scott in 1869 and, in dreadful poverty, migrated with her to New York City in 1874. After selling advertising for the *Wall Street Journal*, Fox became the business manager of the *National Police Gazette* (1875), got the sixteen-page weekly (founded in 1845 and especially popular in barber shops) out of debt, became its sole proprietor (from 1877), and ran it with spectacular success until his death. The lurid *National Police Gazette* featured advertisements for products for males, animal fights, atrocities, biographies, crimes (burglary, forgery, murder, rape, robbery, seduction—especially when committed by clergymen), executions (under the heading of "Noose Notes"), scandals, sports events (mainly boxing), theater notes, and violence. The *Gazette* with its sensational illustrations was, from the 1880s, printed innovatively on pink-tinted paper (5¢ a copy; regular circulation, 150,000; sales in twenty-six foreign countries). Fox spent $250,000 erecting his own office building (1882). He began to live lavishly, sporting silk hats, Prince Albert coats, and canes about town; giving lavish office parties, featuring champagne, whiskey, and barbecued oxen; chartering trains to take fans to prizefights; bailing out expugilists; enjoying high life now and then in London society; and collecting expensive furniture and rugs for his lush home in Red Bank, New Jersey. He bought a ranch in California and gave an estimated $250,000 to athletes both amateur and professional. For example, he presented John L. Sullivan* with a $4,000 bejeweled belt (1889) even though he had always disliked Sullivan, had reviled him in print, and had imported and backed boxers in the hope that one would defeat him. Fox and his first wife had six children. Years after her death (1890), he married Emma Louise Raven Robinson (1913). Fox left an estate of more than $1,500,000.

Frederic, Harold (1856–1898). (Original name: Harold Frederick.) Fiction writer. Born in Utica, New York, he was an only child. His father, a freight conductor, was killed in a railroad wreck in 1858, and his hard-working, religious mother remarried in 1861. Frederic, who relished history and drawing, left school at age fourteen, worked as a photographer's assistant in Utica and Boston, thought of becoming a painter, but returned to Utica (1875) and began a newspaper career there. He started as a proofreader for the *Morning Herald* and then the Democratic *Daily Observer*; for the latter, he became a reporter, editorial writer, and then its editor (1880). Meanwhile, he had published some Revolutionary War fiction, and in 1877 he married Grace William of Utica. The couple had four children, one of whom died in infancy. Frederic was appointed editor of the Republican *Evening Journal* in Albany (1882), effected a change in its Republican policy, supported Democratic Grover Cleveland* for governor of New York, and became his friend. Frederic and his family went to England (1884), where he had been named as London correspondent for the New York *Times*. The accuracy of his article on cholera in southern France and northern Italy, along with his gruff charm and great energy, won him respect and popularity in clubs and among British writers and politicians. He soon became an internationally known European correspondent, especially for his pro–Home Rule stance for Ireland—he knew Charles Stewart Parnell—but his ambition was to devote himself exclusively to literature.

Frederic's efforts to become a belletristic writer, which included a trip back to America in 1886—as well as two later visits—never truly succeeded. Frederic continued to combine work as a foreign correspondent in London with energetic novel writing. His first novel, *Seth's Brother's Wife*, was serialized and later published in book form by Scribner's (1887). A partly autobiographical, bitter portrayal of life in a small, upstate New York town and its harsh rural environs, it features a journalist named Seth Fairchild, his vicious older brother, his brother's sexy wife, and several unscrupulous state politicians. Although *Seth's Brother's Wife* attracted the favorable notice of Hamlin Garland* and William Dean Howells,* it was a commercial failure. It was soon followed, however, by two more novels: *The Lawton Girl** (1890) and *In the Valley** (1890), both also cast in upstate New York. In 1890 (or perhaps a little earlier), Frederic fell permanently in love with Kate Lyon.* Soon thereafter he began, incredibly, to maintain two English households, one with his wife Grace (who died of cancer in 1899) in the outskirts of London, and a second with his other "wife" Kate, in London and later in Kenley, Surrey. By Kate, he eventually had three children. To support his two "wives" and families, Frederic wrote too much too fast: *The Young Emperor, William II of Germany: A Study in Character Development on a Throne* (1891), about the young kaiser; *The New Exodus: A Study of Israel in Russia* (1892), exposing and denouncing Russia's persecution of Jews; *The Return of the O'Mahony* (1892), a comic potboiler novel praising the Irish temperament; *The Copperhead and Other Stories of the North during the American War* (1894), set during the Civil War; and *Marsena and Other Stories of the Wartime* (1894), set again during the Civil War. Frederic even wrote a weekly column for stamp collectors. Domestic circumstances, politics, conditions of employment, and his own contentious nature combined to keep Frederic from becoming a greater novelist than he was. Nevertheless, next came his masterpiece, *The Damnation of Theron Ware** (1896). It was well reviewed, became a best-seller, and provided Frederic with considerable financial relief. In 1897

Frederic and Kate met Stephen Crane* and his so-called wife Cora Taylor, and the four delighted in each other's company. (Crane was grateful for Frederic's laudatory review of *The Red Badge of Courage*,* published early in 1896.) Frederic and Kate also made the acquaintance of Robert Barr, George Gissing, Thomas Hardy, John Hay,* Henry James,* and H. G. Wells, among other influential writers.

Frederic's last years were mostly sad and bitter. In addition to considerable other writing, Frederic completed two more novels: *Gloria Mundi* (1898) and *The Market-Place* (1899). Set in England, both novels concern problems caused by money and both appeared after Frederic had died from a series of strokes brought on in part by a reckless regimen of too much work, food, and tobacco. Kate Lyon, a Christian Scientist, did not summon proper medical help for him and was arrested and tried for manslaughter (1898) but was acquitted.

Free Silver. A late nineteenth-century fiscal policy. Debtors, farmers, silver-mining interests, and common laborers combined to advocate the unlimited minting of silver coins by the United States government, at no charge to the owner of the silver except for the cost of the base metal added to it to make the coins. Until some time after the Civil War, the United States was bimetallist; in other words, it valued currency on the basis of both gold and silver. The silver standard was abandoned in 1873 because silver had become comparatively worth more than the government's arbitrary evaluation of $1.292 per ounce; therefore, silver coins no longer circulated. But when silver not only dropped in relative value during the mid–1870s depression but was also mined in the Far West in greater quantities, silverites again advocated unlimited federal coinage of silver. They felt that the inflation that would result would alleviate debts and poverty. Two unsatisfactory compromises, the Bland-Allison Act (1878) and the Sherman Silver Purchase Act (1890), represented partial surrenders to the free-silver forces. The Bland-Allison Act, which remonetized silver in a limited manner, pegged its value at one-sixteenth that of gold. The law was in force until the Sherman Silver Purchase Act repealed it and ordered the purchase of 4,500,000 ounces of silver per month at market price, payable in either gold or silver treasury notes at the option of the secretary of the treasury. Following the Panic of 1893* and despite the efforts of the Populist Party,* gold-Democrat Grover Cleveland,* early in his second presidential term, caused the repeal of the Sherman Silver Purchase Act (1893). William Jennings Bryan* twice campaigned unsuccessfully for president against William McKinley* (1896, 1900) and in the process created his famous oratorical sentence—"You shall not crucify me on a cross of gold!" The passage of the Gold Standard Act (1900) effectively assured the demise of the free-silver movement.

Freeman, Mary E. Wilkins (1852–1930). (Full names: Mary Eleanor Wilkins and then Mary Eleanor Wilkins Freeman.) Fiction writer. Born in Randolph, Massachusetts, Mary Wilkins was the daughter of Warren Wilkins, a God-fearing

Calvinist carpenter, originally from Salem, and his wife Eleanor, who came from another old-line Massachusetts family. Mary had three siblings, all of whom died very young. She enjoyed school, played with Mary Wales in the nearby Wales farmhouse, and read a great deal. She moved with her parents to Brattleboro, Vermont (1867), where her father worked as part owner in a store. She went to high school and attended Mount Holyoke Female Seminary for one year (1869–1870). Shy and distressed by the rigid religious and work discipline, she disliked the food and became ill. She returned home, continued a reading program with a girlfriend, and fell in love with a dashing young naval officer named Hanson Tyler, who was the son of a local minister and who jilted her. Mary's father, who was a commercial failure, became a carpenter again; eventually, he had to room and board with his family in the Tyler home (by 1877). When Mrs. Wilkins, who became the Tyler family servant, died three years later, Mary and her father moved out, and she began to write for pay. Her father took a job in Florida but died of fever (1883).

Mary E. Wilkins, single, lonely, and insecure, lived briefly with a Brattleboro family and then with the Waleses back in Randolph (beginning in 1884). She earned a name for herself as the author of children's stories, but with *A Humble Romance and Other Stories* (1887) and *A New England Nun and Other Stories** (1891), both published by Harper & Brothers, her national reputation was secure, and she was much in demand by editors. In 1892, word came that Hanson Tyler had married in California. During that same year, while she was visiting her Harper's editor Henry Mills Alden* in Metuchen, New Jersey, Mary met another dashing man, a hard-drinking, horse-loving physician named Charles Manning Freeman, who was in his early thirties. Mary alternately wanted and hesitated about marriage; the doctor steadily thought negatively about the subject. Ten uncertain years later, however, they were married (1902).

In the intervening decade, much had happened. Dr. Freeman had quit working for the Bureau of Pensions in Washington, D.C. (1899) and had returned to Metuchen to work in the family coal and lumber business. Mary published more collections of short stories, a play, and several novels, the best of which is her solid, dour masterpiece, *Pembroke** (1894). Some of her many other titles from this period are *Jane Field* (1893), a novel in which a New England woman impersonates her dead sister to gain property but then has an attack of New England conscience; *Giles Corey, Yeoman: A Play* (1893), about a real-life Salem witchcraft victim; *Madelon* (1896), a novel about a strong-willed brunette loved by two men, one of whom jilts her for a blonde; *Jerome: A Poor Man* (1897), a long novel about poverty stifling love; *Silence and Other Stories* (1898), mostly about New England history, including the 1704 Deerfield Massacre; *The People of Our Neighborhood* (1898), sketches of stereotypical villagers; *The Jamesons* (1899), a novel pitting busybody summer visitors against native New Englanders; *The Love of Parson Lord and Other Stories* (1900), in which the poignant title story concerns a parson who promised God that his daughter Love Lord will be a missionary but she falls in love; *The Heart's Highway* (1900), a historical novel cast in seventeenth-century Virginia and featuring unbridled love; *Understudies* (1901), stories of characters told partly by the use of flower and animal symbolism; and *The Portion of Labor* (1901), a naturalistic, workers'-rights novel, cast in a New England mill town.

During the first years of their married life, Dr. Freeman moderated his drinking and was a helpful husband; however, his wife continued an addiction to sedatives for insomnia and slowly grew deaf. Nevertheless, she wrote and published steadily—until 1918. By this time, however, Dr. Freeman had returned to drinking and was a hopeless alcoholic; he was committed to a mental institution in 1920 and died three years later.

At her best, Mary E. Wilkins Freeman depicts New Englanders trapped by a harsh environment and puritanical social and moral codes, and displaying stoicism, self-esteem in the face of solitude and loss, and even humor, often expressed in tangy dialect and gossip. Her best characters are women, sometimes wrongly dominated by men, often neurotic, frequently frustrated, but almost always heroic. Mary Freeman was highly regarded by the most discerning of her contemporaries, including Hamlin Garland,* William Dean Howells,* Henry James,* and Edwin Arlington Robinson.*

French, Daniel Chester (1850–1931). Sculptor. Born in Exeter, New Hampshire, French was the son of a highly cultivated lawyer. Young French moved with his family to Cambridge, Massachusetts (about 1860), then to nearby Concord (1867). He exhibited talent at modeling, soon made a name for himself locally, and was commissioned to create a bronze *Minute Man* (Concord, 1874), which depicts a handsome, strong, accurately costumed American Revolutionary farmer-rifleman in the pose of the *Apollo Belvedere* (it is now accessible to the public in a park setting). Next, French studied in Florence (1875–1877); returned from abroad to establish a studio in Washington, D.C., where he executed portraits (including one of Ralph Waldo Emerson [1879]) and massive figures representing ideals (starting in 1877); and went to Europe again, this time to Paris (1886–1888), to do a marble bust of Lewis Cass for the state of Michigan. French established a studio in New York (1888–1930), where he combined professional success, married life, with his cousin Mary Adams French (1888; the couple had one child), and considerable socializing, including friendships with Richard Watson Gilder,* William Dean Howells,* Augustus Saint-Gaudens,* and many others. The best work by French from this period is his marble group entitled *The Angel of Death and the Sculptor* (1892), which dramatically shows death in the act of stopping the hand of Martin Milmore, French's cohort who had recently died. French also created several objects for the World's Columbian Exposition* (Chicago, 1893), including an allegorical figure entitled *The Republic* for the lagoon. In addition, a bronze of French's *Death and the Sculptor* was triumphantly exhibited at the exposition.

French was active through the rest of the 1890s, both in his New York studio and at a studio on a farm near Stockbridge, Massachusetts. Among works from this period are *Rufus Choate* (Boston, 1898), cosculpted equestrian statues of Ulysses S. Grant (Philadelphia, 1899) and George Washington (Paris, 1900), and personifications of abstractions (some as part of memorials). More distinguished and rewarding work (including busts, full-length portraits, equestrians, idealistic memorials, and allegorical groups), several national and international honors, and a busy and happy private life (including much travel) mark French's career in the first decades of the twentieth century. The culmination of his admirable professional life is his *Abraham Lincoln*, the gigantic, seated, pensive marble figure located in the Lincoln Memorial in Washington, D.C. (1922).

Frick, Henry Clay (1849–1919). Manufacturer and philanthropist. He was born in West Overton, Pennsylvania. His grandfather was Abraham Overhold, the whiskey distiller. Frick, always serious and with few friends, had limited schooling, then clerked in an uncle's retail store (1865), and invested savings in Connellsville coal land, which the owners soon discovered to be uniquely rich in the sort of coal suitable for coke. Borrowing funds from Judge Thomas Mellon of Pittsburgh, Frick established a coke company (1868), organized H. C. Frick & Company (1871), acquired more and more coal deposits by dispossessing farmers, gradually established 12,000 coke ovens, and furnished vast quantities of coke to Pittsburgh's modern steel industry. Andrew Carnegie,* who admired Frick's pitiless efficiency, made the young man a partner (1881). For a long while their relationship flourished. Frick reorganized his company as H. C. Frick Coke Company with Carnegie and his associates as major shareholders (1882). He became the highly paid chairman of the board of Carnegie Brothers & Company (1889) and was in large part responsible for advancing the company's interests by streamlining administrative procedures, absorbing the competition, integrating and expanding company activities, and leasing iron-rich Mesabi lands in Minnesota (1896).

Frick and Carnegie had different temperaments, however, as had become evident at the time of the Homestead Lockout* (1892), during which, while Carnegie was out of the country, Frick hired Pinkerton men and thus instigated much bloodshed and several deaths. Carnegie blamed Frick for the ensuing difficulties. Frick gained undeserved sympathy when he was shot and stabbed, not fatally, by a New York anarchist, Alexander Berkman (1892). Frick refused to lower his price for the coke shipped to Carnegie's steel mills and connived with rivals offering to buy Carnegie out (1899). Carnegie pocketed $1,000,000 in unexercised options tendered in the attempt and ousted Frick as chairman of his Carnegie Steel Company (1899), paying him $15,000,000 for his shares. Frick then helped organize the United States Steel Company, which was headed by John Pierpont Morgan* and which bought Carnegie out for nearly $500,000,000 (1901). Frick was a director of several railways and also of U.S. Steel.

Frick married Adelaide Howard Childs in 1881 (the couple had two children). Frick was long an avid art collector, amassed splendid objects in his magnificent

New York mansion (built 1913–1914) on Fifth Avenue, and made generous contributions to schools, hospitals, and charitable institutions in Pittsburgh and New York City. At his death, his estate was estimated at $50,000,000. His New York residence now houses the fabulous Frick Museum (opened in 1935).

Fuller, Henry Blake (1857–1929). Fiction writer, playwright, poet, and amateur musical-score writer. Born in Chicago, Fuller was the son of a banker; that man's father was a New England judge who had settled in Chicago in 1849 and had become an unscrupulous and wealthy entrepreneur and real estate holder. Fuller's mother came from a distinguished old New England family. Fuller interrupted humdrum Chicago high school studies by spending a pleasant year at a classical academy in Oconomowoc, Wisconsin, but, after graduation from the Chicago high school (1875), he went to work in a crockery store and then a bank. In 1879, having amassed sufficient savings, he went to Europe for a delightful year in England, France, Italy, Switzerland, Germany, and the Netherlands. He took voluminous notes in preparation for a book. Upon his return, he found Chicago depressing. Determined now to become a writer, he paid Italy another visit (1883); this time, however, he found the Old World less appealing but, even so, more attractive than commercial, uncultured Chicago. After sailing home in the fall, he tried Boston for a time. He began to publish satirical items (1884). A year later, his father's death called him back, permanently, as it turned out, to Chicago, where he managed the properties the family owned and rented. At this time, and indeed later, Fuller vacillated between admiration for the writings of Europeanized Henry James* and somewhat greater respect for the American realism of William Dean Howells;* both authors represented contrasting—even conflicting—ideals for Fuller.

While grinding away at the family business in Chicago, Fuller wrote a charming travel novel, *The Chevalier of Pensieri-Vani** (published in Boston in 1890, at his own expense, under the pen name Stanton Page). The novel reflects Fuller's America/Europe schizophrenia. The thinking of the three main characters, the Prorege of Arcopia, George W. Occident, and the chevalier, represent, respectively, a Jamesian aesthetic and political position, a Howellsian philosophical orientation, and the bewildered, unsettled Fuller. When *The Chevalier of Pensieri-Vani* proved to be popular, Fuller wrote another transatlantic romance, entitled *The Chatelaine of La Trinité*,* which Richard Watson Gilder* serialized in the *Century* Magazine* before its book publication (1892). When it appeared, Fuller was again in Europe on a half-year tour, this time in Spain. He started to write a third romance, this one based on Spain; but adverse reviews of *The Chatelaine of La Trinité* turned him toward realism. Once back in Chicago, he began to write essays in praise of the architecture of the World's Columbian Exposition* (1893). Next came the publication of his bitter masterpiece, *The Cliff-Dwellers: A Novel** (1893). In 1894 he again went to Italy, and the following year he published *With the Procession: A Novel.** In 1896 came *The Puppet-Booth: Twelve Plays*. "At Saint Judas's," a one-acter in this collection, reflects his homosexuality.* He went to Europe yet again; this time he also sampled Africa and Sicily (1896–1897). Out of these adventures came *From the Other Side: Stories of Transatlantic Travel* (1898).

Fuller now entered a final phase. In response to American imperialism during the Spanish-America War,* Fuller published an acerbic work entitled *The New Flag: Satires* (1899). Early in the new century, Fuller was very busy. He published a weak romance cast in Sicily, entitled *The Last Refuge* (1900); wrote nonfictional pieces for the *Saturday Evening Post* and the Chicago *Post* (1900–1901); and published *Under the Skylights* (1901). In his last decades, he retreated into an abiding alienation, pessimism, and homosexuality (*Bertram Cope's Year: A Novel*, published at his own expense in 1919, deals with gay life), and, although he wrote much else, he became more significant as a reviewer and an adviser of younger writers. Fuller was a close professional friend of several important authors and artists, including Hamlin Garland* (whom, however, he satirized in "The Downfall of Abner Joyce," a 1901 short story), William Dean Howells,* Harriet Monroe, and Lorado Taft;* he was greatly admired by them all and also by Theodore Dreiser.*

G

Garden, Mary (1877–1967). Operatic soprano. Born in Aberdeen, Scotland, she immigrated with her family to Montreal, Canada, to Chicago, and then Milwaukee. She played the violin at age eight, sang beautifully by age fourteen, and in time went to Paris to study voice (1897). Garden was a member of the Opera Comique staff (1900–1907), was understudy to the lead in Gustave Charpentier's *Louise*, and filled in with spectacular success (1900). She captivated all audiences thereafter with her vivid, sultry voice and superb dramatic technique. Another early role for her was that of Mélisande, which Claude Debussy created for her in his *Pelléas and Mélisande* (1902). Returning to the United States in 1907, Garden debuted in Jules Massenet's *Thaïs* at the Manhattan Opera House in New York and shocked American audiences with her performance in Richard Strauss's violent *Salome*. She enjoyed a glamorous, controversial career with the Chicago Opera Company (beginning in 1910), became director during its financially disastrous final season (1921–1922), retired (1934), published *Mary Garden's Story* (coauthored in 1951), and died in Aberdeen.

Gardner, Isabella Stewart (1840–1924). (Nickname: Mrs. Jack.) Art patroness. She was born in New York City into a wealthy family. She went to a girls' school in Paris, visited Italy with her father (1857), and married John Lowell Gardner (1860), who was a school chum's rich brother and with whom she settled in Boston. The Gardners had a son who died in his late twenties. Mrs. Jack inherited $2,750,000 from her father when he died (1891). A graceful, beautiful hostess, also publicity seeking and daring, she was abetted by her indulgent, adoring husband. She became interested in the arts (by 1867), studied art history under Charles Eliot Norton* of Harvard, traveled extensively (in Europe, the Middle East, and Japan), collected European and Oriental objets d'art, sponsored musical soirées in her lavish home, and supported celebrated musicians. She took the advice of such artists and art experts as Bernard Berenson,* John La Farge,* John Singer Sargent,* and James Abbott McNeill Whistler* to augment her ever-growing private collection, which contained mostly American, English pre-Raphaelite, Flemish, Italian, and Spanish paintings. Sargent and Whistler both painted portraits of her. When her husband suddenly died (1898), his will revealed that the two had been planning a Boston museum, which (starting in 1899) became an Italianate palace called Fenway Court and opened with much fanfare on New Year's Day, 1903.

Mrs. Jack continued to entertain spectacularly. After a final tour of Europe (1906), she continued to collect works of art (until 1921). She suffered a paralytic stroke and died in Boston. Isabella Stewart Gardner knew many establishment figures of great wit, charm, and significance, including Henry Adams* and his wife, F. Marion Crawford* (who almost accompanied the Gardners to Japan in 1883), Henry James,* John L. Sullivan,* and Edith Wharton.* When the Gardners briefly rented a Venetian palace (1892), the place became an instant mecca for expatriate Americans.

Garland, Hamlin (1860–1940). (Full name: Hannibal Hamlin Garland.) Fiction writer, literary critic, autobiographer, dramatist, and poet. Born in West Salem, Wisconsin, he worked as a farm boy in Wisconsin, Minnesota, and Iowa, doing backbreaking work with his heroic but unsympathetic father and his sad mother. Garland intermittently attended Cedar Valley Seminary, in Osage, Iowa, where he learned to appreciate standard literature, and graduated in 1881. He traveled to the East, worked at odd jobs for several years, taught school in Illinois for a year, and then staked a claim in Dakota Territory (1883), a claim he sold a year later for money to finance a literary pilgrimage to Boston. Once in Boston and at first in dreadful poverty, he read the works of many writers, including Charles Darwin, John Fiske,* Henry George* (who later became Garland's personal friend), Herbert Spencer (whom he defined as his philosopher and master), Hippolyte Taine (for critical theory), and Eugène Véron (for aesthetics). Later Garland supported himself by teaching at the Boston School of Oratory and by lecturing on literature to private classes. In 1887 Garland met William Dean Howells,* who encouraged him to write about what he knew best, that is, oppressive Midwestern farm life, with its violent weather, unending work, quilting bees, quick romances, loneliness and sorrow, absence of much Eastern culture, and the constant lure of the Far West.

Garland made an extended visit back to his homeland, and, when he passed through Chicago, he met Joseph Kirkland,* whose *Zury: The Meanest Man in Spring County* he had enthusiastically reviewed. Back in Boston again, Garland published six fictionalized autobiographical pieces entitled "Boy Life on the Prairie" (1888), republished in book form as *Boy Life on the Prairie* (1899). In 1889, Richard Watson Gilder* accepted a story by Garland for publication in the *Century** (1891); in 1890, B. O. Flower* accepted another Garland story for his *Arena*.* Since Gilder was both slower and more genteel than the radical Flower, Garland began to send his harsh prairie stories to the *Arena*. Acting on

Flower's suggestion, Garland collected six stories for 1891 publication as *Main-Travelled Roads*,* by far his finest work. Later that year, while lecturing in New Jersey, Garland met Stephen Crane.* (He later reviewed Crane's *Maggie: A Girl of the Streets*,* admiring much in it but deploring it for not depicting the families who lived next door to the heroine whose lives were purer and more heroic.) Influenced by George's theories, Garland campaigned for agrarian and Populist Party* movements in Iowa and elsewhere (1891, 1892). His novel *Jason Edwards: An Average Man* (based on his 1890 play) appeared in 1892. In that same busy year, he also published three other works of fiction: *A Member of the Third House* (also based on his 1890 play), *A Spoil of Office* (commissioned and published by Flower), and *A Little Norsk; or Ol' Pap's Flaxen. Jason Edwards* is little more than a naturalistic tract on the economics of Western farming. *A Member of the Third House* inveighs against political lobbying by corrupt railroad interests. *A Spoil of Office* weakly combines blasts against congressional chicanery, hypocrisy, and cant, and also praise of feminist activism. *A Little Norsk*, a money-maker, tells how bachelor homesteaders befriend a sweet orphan girl. Also in 1892, Garland became an officer in the American Psychical Society, founded by Flower and a friend.

In 1893 Garland helped his aging parents to move from their South Dakota farm back to a more comfortable Wisconsin home. In that same year, he delivered a lecture entitled "Local Color in Fiction" at the World's Columbian Exposition* in Chicago, where he established his residence (until 1916). In 1893 he also published *Prairie Folks*, a collection of nine stories which feature several characters first encountered in the stories in *Main-Travelled Roads*. Garland soon associated with a number of creative Chicagoans, including George Ade,* Finley Peter Dunne,* Eugene Field* (whose sentimentality he deplored), Henry Blake Fuller* (who satirized Garland, in a 1901 short story entitled "The Downfall of Abner Joyce," for turning socially conventional), Robert Herrick,* Kirkland, and Lorado Taft,* whose sister, Zulime Taft, Garland married in 1899. Garland continued to write extensively; from 1893 to 1896, Herbert S. Stone* of Chicago was his publisher. Stone's firm, Stone & Kimball, issued Garland's controversial manifesto entitled *Crumbling Idols: Twelve Essays on Art Dealing Chiefly with Literature, Painting and the Drama** (1894) and his best novel, *Rose of Dutcher's Coolly** (1895, rev. ed. 1899), both major works in his long career.

Following the defeat of the Populists by William McKinley* (1896) and after much restless traveling during that year and the next two, Garland began to decline as a serious writer. Weaker are all of the following: *Wayside Courtships* (1897), *Ulysses S. Grant: His Life and Character* (1898), *The Trail of the Goldseekers* (1899), *The Eagle's Heart* (1900), and *Her Mountain Lover* (1901). *Wayside Courtships* collects eleven stories, some previously published, featuring loss of love as well as youthful romance and including few farm folks. The Grant biography is workmanlike and patriotic, but not probing. *The Trail of the Goldseekers* reflects Garland's disappointing 1898 trip to Alaska. *The Eagle's Heart*, a catchall romantic novel, depicts a strong hero's character changed by a multitude of Western experiences. *Her Mountain Lover* is an unsuccessful yarn, supposedly humorous in part, about a Western miner seeking British financial backing; it reflects Garland's 1899 trip to England. Being a householder, husband, and father of two daughters motivated Garland to become conservative and to write works for popular consumption and big royalties. He published twenty-eight books between 1902 and 1939. Most are weaker than his significant production during the 1890s. Two concern inexplicable phenomena. The best honestly depict yet again the harshness of life beyond the Mississippi River, especially in the Southwest and California, in the old days. *A Son of the Middle Border* (1917), which covers Garland's life to age thirty-four, deserves praise for honestly recalling his boyhood miseries and his determination to have an intellectual and creative life. (He wrote seven other autobiographical volumes.) *The Book of the American Indian* (1923) collects fourteen excellent short stories and one novella (first published 1899–1905), based on his detailed and repeated observations of Native Americans (1892, 1895, and 1897); the book, which sympathetically portrays the dignified red man's problems in adapting to white "civilization," includes illustrations by Frederic Remington,* whose work Garland chose to deplore, however, as stereotypical.

Garland moved to Los Angeles (1930) and died there ten years later. In the course of his long career, he wrote articles about, reviewed works by, and offered comments on numerous friends and associates, including John Burroughs,* Crane, Ignatius Donnelly,* Field, George, James A. Herne,* Howells, Kirkland, Edward MacDowell,* Joaquin Miller,* Frank Norris,* James Whitcomb Riley,* Theodore Roosevelt,* Ernest Thompson Seton,* Taft, Mark Twain,* and Walt Whitman. In his autobiographical volumes, Garland added personal notes on many of those just named as well as others, including several he met in England, for example, Henry James.*

Gates, Lewis E. (1860–1924). (Full name: Lewis Edwards Gates.) Professor of English and comparative literature. Born in Warsaw, New York, Gates graduated from Harvard (1884) and remained there to teach (1884–1887, 1890–1902), with time off to do advanced study in England, France, and Germany (1887–1890). He then resigned because of poor health. His books include *Three Studies in Literature* (1899), on Francis Jeffrey, John Henry Newman, and Matthew Arnold; and *Studies and Appreciations* (1900), essays on general literary topics, specific non-American authors, and two (previously published in the *Chap-Book**) on Nathaniel Hawthorne and Edgar Allan Poe. Gates taught and wrote to the effect that romantic writing ought to be grounded in actuality. One of Gates's teaching assistants was William Vaughn Moody.* Gates's most notably successful composition student was Frank Norris,* who wrote part of *Vandover and the Brute* (1914) and part of *McTeague: A Story of San Francisco** (1899) in Gates's class and dedicated the latter to Gates. Another of Gates's composition students was Trumbull Stickney.*

Gays and Lesbians. *See* Homosexuality.

The Genteel Tradition. The dominant, refined, upper middle-class culture of the post–Civil War era. A culture that extended into the 1890s and later, it was a combination of effete Puritanism, Americanized Victorianism, and discreet materialism. Its leaders set moral, social, and aesthetic standards. Under its aegis, success was to be judged by one's wealth, social status, and visible property. (Have money, let others know about it, but don't talk about it.) If one remained self-reliant, worked hard (at a respectable job, not as a common laborer), kept one's nose to the grindstone, and conformed to perceived norms, one could get ahead and prove oneself successful by marrying well, having an admirable and well-appointed residence and praiseworthy children, and showing off with spectacular parties, vacations, and a few nice charity activities. If, on the other hand, a person did not get ahead, he or she was probably lazy, immoral, and not an Anglo-Saxon Protestant. If one failed, it was one's own fault, because America was the land of opportunity. One had to display the virtues of commercial acumen plus probity, religiosity, patriotism and hero worship, clean conduct and proper talk, steadiness and reliability, ultramoderate drinking, respect for the property of decent folks, visible respectability, and manifest good "breeding." Charming manners could best be shown by courteous treatment of women—unless they were servants, immigrants, African Americans, or prostitutes—and by avoiding any obvious sexual activity outside marriage. Although one should prefer urban life with its commercial challenges, one should remember one's humble, preferably rural, background fondly and nostalgically, especially the part one's mother played.

Religion promoted all of these virtues, as did the arts, especially painting and literature—the finest form of which was poetry, which at its best extolled God and country, motherhood, hard work, self-reliance, temperance and chastity, good manners, domestic bliss, and negative morality. Male writers could be more outward and objective than female writers, whose inwardness and subjectivity would be gently tolerated. One's sons (not daughters) should go to the best colleges and universities, preferably in the East, and study the classics rather than modern, liberal, or vocational subjects. The conservative writers and artists of the 1890s, too numerous to name here, supported the Genteel Tradition; the progressives of the era—again, too numerous to mention—did battle against it. To the traditionalists, literary naturalism* was especially anathema. Obviously, gentility survived well past 1900 and indeed into the Roaring Twenties and beyond. George Santayana* is responsible for the term "genteel tradition," which he used in a 1931 essay entitled "The Genteel Tradition at Bay."

George, Henry (1839–1897). Economist and reformer. He was born in Philadelphia. His father was a publisher of religious books and a customs-house worker; his mother, a former teacher. At age thirteen, George quit school, became an errand boy and then a clerk, shipped (1855) for a year as a foremast boy to

Australia and India, returned home (1856) to become an apprentice printer, and sailed (1857) as a steward to the West Coast to try the gold fields of British Columbia (1858), became a San Francisco typesetter (1858–1860), and finally entered the fields of journalism and politics in San Francisco and Oakland (1860–1875). He married Annie Corsina Fox (an Australian-born Catholic) in 1861, fathered four children, and endured deep poverty for several years—partly because of his long-standing animosity toward vested interests. He published *Our Land and Land Policy* (1871), which was an overture to the masterwork of his life, *Progress and Poverty* (1878), one of the most significant documents ever written on economic theory. George's observations from Calcutta to New York led to the conclusion that economic progress increases poverty. He reasoned that landowning individuals become prosperous through rents that rise as their property is improved, whereas laborers and investors alike are held back by receiving low wages and marginal interest. George's solution was to free both labor and capital from the burden of being exploited to benefit the landowner. How? By levying a "Single Tax" on all land and on virtually nothing else.

George had visited Philadelphia and New York (1868) and later moved to New York (1880). He published *The Irish Land Question* (1881), then visited England and Ireland (1881–1882), then England again (1883, 1884–1885, 1889), to lecture effectively there on his controversial single-tax theory. George's later publications include *Social Problems* (1883), concerning public ownership of industries and utilities; *Protection or Free Trade* (1886), antitariff but procapital; *The Condition of Labor: An Open Letter to Pope Leo XIII* (1891), urging labor reform and the regarding of all people as equal; *A Perplexed Philosopher* (1892), an attack on Herbert Spencer's agnostic, materialistic theories of social evolution; and the unfinished, flawed, posthumous book *The Science of Political Economy* (1898). Throughout his writings, George advocated Christian socialism and the welfare state. His unsuccessful political efforts include running for mayor of New York City as the United Labor Party candidate (1886, 1897; the machinations of Richard F. Croker* caused his defeat) and for New York secretary of state (1887). He also unsuccessfully supported William Jennings Bryan* for the presidency in 1896 (which election he covered as a special writer for the New York *Journal*). George suffered a stroke in 1890 and was urged to conserve his energy; however, while he was running for mayor of New York late in 1897, he died from a second stroke. The outpouring of public sympathy was unparalleled in the history of the city. Well over 100,000 people—perhaps more than twice that number—passed by his body, which was placed in state at Grand Central Palace.

Henry George's theories, presented simply, cogently, logically, and fervently, were enormously influential. In the United States, Edward Bellamy,* John Dewey,* Hamlin Garland* (note his short story "Under the Lion's Paw," in *Main-Travelled Roads**), James A. Herne,* William Dean Howells,* Elizabeth Peabody, and Thorstein Veblen,* among innumerable others, adopted them, at least in part; abroad, John Stuart Mill, George Bernard Shaw, Sun Yat-sen, Leo

Tolstoy, Beatrice and Sidney Webb, among others, followed them, as did political leaders less well known in several other countries. *Progress and Poverty* soon enjoyed more than 100 editions and innumerable translations; by 1906, it had been read by at least 6,000,000 people.

George's Mother (1896). Short novel by Stephen Crane.* The scene is the same slum region memorialized by Crane in *Maggie: A Girl of the Streets*,* published three years earlier. In fact, the central character George Kelcey lives in the same tenement as does Maggie Johnson, heroine of the earlier novel. George's mother is Mrs. Kelcey, an alternately fierce and pathetic "little old woman." Her husband is dead, as are four of her five sons. She is grateful that her one surviving son, George, an indecisive, weak-willed, menial laborer, still lives with her. But he distresses her almost all the time. He is slovenly, whereas she is orderly. He drinks too much beer, whereas she hates the brewery that towers nearby and the damage it spews out. He swears "tangled . . . oaths" and regards religion as a "blackening" process, whereas she goes alone to "prayer-meetin'," sighing like a martyr. Oddly, although George evinces no steady or worthy ambition, she clings to the belief that he is just about "perfect." When his brief daydreams about a love affair with his neighbor Maggie come to nothing, he has a stormy argument with his mother, gets belligerently drunk down the street, lies to her about it, then agrees to accompany her to church—which experience makes him feel damned. George soon backslides, joins a truculent, beer-swilling neighborhood gang, and loses his job. When his mother gets sick he is temporarily contrite. She seems better but has a sudden relapse, and dies in their little hovel.

Like *Maggie* and *The Third Violet*,* this short novel draws heavily on Crane's personal life. George's mother resembles Crane's to a degree, and George owes something to Crane himself. Both pairs, one in real life and the other in fiction, suffered similarly ambivalent love-dismay relationships. Furthermore, Crane knew George's Bowery environment well, as proved by the well-sketched scenes in *Maggie*. In many ways, George's neighborhood is even better drawn than Maggie's because after *Maggie* came *The Red Badge of Courage*,* by means of which Crane improved his mastery of a true word-painter's palette. Crane sent an inscribed copy of *George's Mother* to Theodore Roosevelt,* who replied in a gracious letter of thanks and praise.

Geronimo (1829?–1909). (Apache name: Goyathlay or Goyakla, "One Who Yawns." He was called Geronimo, Spanish for Jerome, by a panic-stricken Mexican soldier during an 1850s battle.) Chiricahua Apache Indian leader. Geronimo was born and grew up near the Gila River headwaters, in what is now Arizona. While he was harmlessly drinking with some friends in Janos, Chihuahua, across the border, some Mexican soldiers attacked the Apache camp and killed his mother, wife, and three children (1858), turning him against all persons not Native American. He developed a fiercely vicious temper, which was often exacerbated by *tiswin* (a native alcohol). He remarried and fathered more children, but he remained a wild warrior. He operated out of a Sierra Madre base in northwestern Mexico, was arrested by American authorities in southwestern New Mexico Territory, and was imprisoned with numerous other members of his band in a squalid reservation in eastern Arizona Territory (1877). He and some fellow warriors escaped (1878–1880), returned to the reservation (1880), and escaped again (1881)—this time to terrorize the region and raid south into Mexico. He was tracked by General George Crook* and his scouts and was persuaded to surrender (1883). Although he surrendered on easy terms (1884), he broke out again (1885), defied a ban on *tiswin*, parleyed with Crook but got drunk and disappeared again (1886), and at last was captured by troops under Crook's replacement, General Nelson A. Miles* (4 September 1886). Leonard Wood,* then a young army officer, was also involved in the capture.

Geronimo did not fully understand the terms of his surrender and was wrongly sent to confinement in Florida. While in Florida (1886–1888), then in Alabama (1888–1894), and finally in Oklahoma (1894), he earned a little money by selling pictures of himself and bows and arrows with his name on them. He also displayed himself at the Trans-Mississippi Exposition* (Omaha, 1898), the Pan-American Exposition* (Buffalo, 1901), and elsewhere. He dictated his self-vindicating autobiography, which was considerably reshaped before publication by S. M. Barrett as *Geronimo's Story of His Life* (1906). At the time of his death (after an alcoholic spree and a fall from his horse), he was a paid army scout at Fort Sill, Oklahoma. Geronimo is remembered as the last Indian leader to surrender to the U.S. Army, but not until after outmaneuvering as many as forty-two well-equipped American cavalry and infantry companies, and some 4,000 Mexican soldiers, for months at a time—with at most fifty braves, who often were accompanied by their Apache wives and children.

Gibson, Charles Dana (1867–1944). Illustrator. Born in Roxbury, Massachusetts, Gibson studied at the Art Students League in New York City. He sold a sketch to *Life*, the old weekly humor magazine, when he was nineteen years of age, and later became its staff artist and then editor. Beginning in the early 1890s, Gibson drew pictures satirizing social life. He contributed illustrations to such prestigious magazines as the *Century*,* *Harper's Monthly Magazine*,* and *Scribner's Magazine*.* He illustrated many popular books, including *The Prisoner of Zenda* (1894) by Anthony Hope and *Soldiers of Fortune** (1897) by Richard Harding Davis.* Later in his career, Gibson painted oil portraits, now less admired than his superb line illustrations. He published *The Education of Mr. Pipp* (1899), *The Americans* (1900), and *The Social Ladder* (1902). Gibson is now best known for pen-and-ink drawings of the so-called Gibson Girl, who typically was glamorous, athletic, and reserved, and who set hair and dress styles for two decades, starting about 1890. (He was not above satirizing her, however, if she crossed the Atlantic Ocean in search of a European title through marriage—*see* Travel and Travelers.)

Giddings, Franklin Henry (1855–1931). Sociologist and educator. He was born in Sherman, Connecticut. He preferred outdoor activities in the Berkshires to public school, but as a youth he read and was inspired by the works of Herbert Spencer and was thus early influenced to believe in social evolution. He attended Union College (1873–1875), hoping to become a civil engineer, but poor health prompted him to start teaching instead (1875–1877). He tried journalism in Springfield, Massachusetts, and elsewhere in New England (1877–1888). In his spare time he studied social, economic, commercial, political, and welfare problems in America, and he made himself such a scholarly expert that Union granted him two degrees (B.A., 1888, as one of his 1877 class; M.A., 1889). Giddings returned to teaching, this time in social science, at Bryn Mawr College (1888–1894). He coauthored *The Modern Distributive Process* (1888) and edited *Annals of the American Academy of Political and Social Sciences* (1890–1892) and *Publications of the American Economic Association* (1891–1893). Columbia University appointed him the first American professor of sociology (1894–1928). Giddings published twelve books and more than 200 articles.

Giddings's major works are *Philanthropy and Social Progress* (1892), *The Theory of Sociology* (1894), *The Principles of Sociology* (1896, widely translated), and *Inductive Sociology* (1901). Giddings also wrote a book of mystical poetry (1914). A pioneer in sociology, he made it a scientific and inductive study rather than a theological one, encouraged scientific and statistical research methods in investigating social ills, and stimulated curiosity concerning the subject. He defined society by categories and systems, and he theorized that people respond to stimulation by acting on their fellows via imitation, suggestion, and example. These actions create a communal sense of being like-minded, which in turn permits more sophisticated associations managed by emerging customs and norms. A given society is thus a group bonded by "consciousness of kind"; the interplay of its discrete minds creates a culture. Giddings married Elizabeth Patience Hawes in 1876 (the couple had three children).

Gilder, Richard Watson (1844–1909). Editor and poet. He was born in Bordentown, New Jersey, the son of a Methodist minister and Union army chaplain who died of smallpox while aiding sick men in his regiment during the Civil War (1864). Young Gilder himself served briefly with a Philadelphia artillery unit. After the war he clerked in a New Jersey railroad office and became a newspaper reporter in Newark, New Jersey. He edited a small magazine published by Charles Scribner and Sons (to 1869) and became managing editor when it grew into *Scribner's Magazine** (1870–1881). By the mid–1870s, he was making many editorial decisions, and, when the magazine was converted into the *Century**—he suggested the new name—he became its conscientious editor (1881–1909). Robert Underwood Johnson* was his assistant editor. In 1871 or so, Gilder met Helena De Kay, an artist and linguist. They shared interests in painting, literature (especially Dante and Omar Khayyám's *Rubaiyat*), and "ideality" (revelation of moral, religious truth aesthetically intertwined with formal beauty). When the two were married in 1874, their home offered hospitality to a variety of artists and writers. (Helena Gilder cofounded the Art Students League of New York.)

As he gained power, Gilder offered friendship, encouragement, advice, and sometimes publication to most of the best and some of the next-best American writers of the times, including Thomas Bailey Aldrich,* George Washington Cable,* Kate Chopin,* Richard Harding Davis,* Mary E. Wilkins Freeman,* Hamlin Garland,* Joel Chandler Harris,* Bret Harte, William Dean Howells,* Henry James,* Sarah Orne Jewett,* Joaquin Miller,* Thomas Nelson Page,* Edwin Arlington Robinson,* Edmund Clarence Stedman,* Mark Twain,* Edith Wharton,* and Walt Whitman. To many of these Gilder gave their start. Under Gilder, the *Century* circulation increased to more than 200,000; however, even though he was a would-be reformer, he was too idealistic, too genteel, and even too sweet to be a substantial influence on the forward-looking young writers emerging in the 1890s. Gilder is the embodiment of the Genteel Tradition.* It is significant, for example, that he was chairman of the Tenement House Commission in 1894 but refused to accept fiction or nonfiction describing the horrors of tenement life. He rejected *Maggie: A Girl of the Streets** by Stephen Crane* and muckraking exposés of the big trusts and other national sociopolitical ills. Gilder did, however, support civil service reform, the Young Women's Christian Association, kindergartens, public monuments, and the international copyright law (*see* Copyright Laws). He is no longer extolled for his sixteen books of poetry or for his biographies of Abraham Lincoln (1909) and Grover Cleveland* (1910). Gilder's letters, edited by his daughter Rosamond Gilder, were issued posthumously (1916). Anecdotes are numerous about Gilder's firm if tactful editorial hand. But the truth remains that Gilder was the finest literary editor that basically genteel America produced during the years of his influence.

Gillette, King Camp (1855–1932). Inventor, manufacturer, and would-be reformer. He was born in Fond du Lac, Wisconsin. The family moved to Chicago (1859), where the father, a businessman and inventor, was wiped out by the Chicago Fire (1871) but eventually recovered. After completing his public school education in Chicago, young Gillette worked for hardware companies there and in New York and Missouri. He went briefly to England on business, returned home (1889), and worked in the United States and abroad for a huge bottle-stopper company established by William Painter* in Baltimore (1889–1899). At one point, his employer happened to tell Gillette, who like his father and brothers was of an inventive and tinkering turn, that he ought to invent something that could be used and then thrown away (1895). In his spare time, he began to work on the idea of a two-edged shaving blade clamped between plates with a handle. He founded the Gillette Safety Razor Company and named himself president in 1901. Within three years, he had sold 12,400,000 blades for 90,000 razors and was soon manufacturing 3,000 razors and 3,000 packages of extra blades a day

(1908). His main plant was in Boston, but, in time, he opened plants in Canada, England, France, and Germany.

Gillette published *The Human Drift* (1894), *The Ballot Box* (1897), and *Gillette's Industrial Solution* (1900); in addition, he coauthored *Gillette's Social Redemption* (1897). His writings were designed to explain his social philosophy concerning industrial inefficiency and waste, the dangers of competition, and the usefulness of an international cooperative trust and of a utopia run by humane engineers. He established a world corporation in the Arizona Territory (1910) and offered Theodore Roosevelt* $1,000,000 to head it for four years. Roosevelt declined (1910). Only Gillette's ideas for government-offered work in time of unemployment and for air-conditioned buildings have proved acceptable. Gillette retired (1913), continued his social theorizing with *The People's Corporation* (1924), and remained president of his company (until 1931) and director (1931–1932); meanwhile, he went into real estate ventures in Los Angeles. Gillette married Alanta Ella Gaines in 1890 (the couple had one child). Gillette's mother, Fanny Lemira Camp Gillette, wrote *The White House Cook Book* (1887) and *Mrs. Gillette's Cook Book* (1897). The latter sold more than three million copies, in five languages.

Gillette, William (1853–1937). (Full name: William Hooker Gillette.) Actor and playwright. Born in Hartford, Connecticut, he was the handsome son of a U.S. senator from Connecticut who was one of the founders of the Republican Party. Against family wishes, Gillette became an actor, first in New Orleans and then in Boston (1875). He became a successful playwright when he wrote and took the title role in *The Professor* (opening in New York, 1881). Ultimately he wrote or adapted twenty plays, which were usually melodramatic or farcical; he performed in nine of them. Two of his most memorable plays concern the Civil War: *Held by the Enemy* (Brooklyn, 1886), the first successful play about the Civil War; and *Secret Service** (Philadelphia, 1896), Gillette's best work, which he took to London (1897) and which was also produced by others in Paris. Other Gillette plays in the 1890s include *All the Comforts of Home* (Boston, 1890), about a man who thinks the hero loves his wife, but the hero really loves the man's daughter; *Mr. Wilkinson's Widows* (Washington, D.C., 1891), a farce about bigamy; *Settled out of Court* (New York, 1892), another farce; *Too Much Johnson* (Holyoke, Massachusetts, 1894), a philanderer farce; *Because She Loved Him So* (New Haven, Connecticut, 1898), about real and feigned jealousy; and finally *Sherlock Holmes* (Buffalo, 1899), based on Sir Arthur Conan Doyle's character (and including Dr. Watson and Moriarty) but mostly Gillette's plotting, about mysterious documents sent by German royalty to a woman now dead. Gillette created the public's permanent notion of the immortal detective—an observant, hawk-faced man, smoking an oversized pipe and wearing a hunter's flapped cap. Gillette enjoyed great success in this role in the United States and in England (1899–1903).

In the twentieth century, Gillette continued to act successfully in his own plays, original and adapted, and those of others, and he wrote a new Sherlock Holmes one-acter (New York, 1905). His writing, production, and acting, which stressed logical plots and realistic details, helped lift the American theater out of the sentimental doldrums in which it had become partly enmeshed in the 1880s and 1890s. He also adopted the quiet scene ending introduced by James A. Herne* and pioneered the resourceful stage hero—cool and calm under stress. His Hartford neighbor and family friend Mark Twain* got Gillette a part in *Colonel Mulberry Sellers*, a drama based on Twain's *American Claimant*, which was playing in Boston (1875). Gillette also acted in a stage version of *The Gilded Age*, by Twain and Charles Dudley Warner, in New York (1877). Gillette married Helen Nickles in 1882.

Gilman, Charlotte Perkins (1860–1935). (Full name: Charlotte Anna Perkins Stetson Gilman.) Sociologist, fiction writer, lecturer, and poet. She was born in Hartford, Connecticut, one of three children borne by her mother in three years. A fourth child died in infancy (1866), after which the mother was told that bearing another child would kill her. The father abandoned his wife (1869), and the two were soon divorced (1873). Charlotte, who showed early evidence of precocity, was distressed by her father's conduct and by its effects on her permanently distraught mother. She made a role model out of Harriet Beecher Stowe (Charlotte's father's aunt), read voraciously, attended the Rhode Island School of Design (1878–1880), and then began to support herself as a teacher and commercial artist. She married artist Charles Walter Stetson in 1884 but with many misgivings because she valued personal independence more than conventional marriage. She gave birth to a daughter (1885), felt stifled by domesticity, became involved in feminist activities (1886), and finally had a nervous breakdown. She was treated patronizingly by Philadelphia physician and author S. Weir Mitchell* (1887). In 1887 she separated amicably from her husband and moved with her daughter to Pasadena, California, the following year.

Charlotte Stetson supported herself by teaching adult education classes, by placing poems in magazines, and by selling didactic short fiction dramatizing the plight of women. She always advocated more justice, freedom, and happiness for women. She moved to Oakland and joined the Pacific Coast Women's Press Association (1891). She published her best-known short story, "The Yellow Wall-paper,"* in 1892. She collected her poetry into *In This Our Life* (1893), divorced Stetson and moved to San Francisco, met a number of West Coast authors (for example, Mary Austin*), and became editor of the *Impress* (1894). As the official magazine of the Pacific Coast Women's Press Association, the *Impress* was a woman's paper, a protest journal, and a Populist Party* mouthpiece. It blasted government corruption and robber barons, and praised such writers as Edward Bellamy,* Eugene V. Debs,* Hamlin Garland,* Henry Demarest Lloyd,* and Jacob Riis.* Charlotte Stetson attended the Women's Suffrage Convention in Washington, D.C., and the International Socialist and Labor Congress in London (1896), and published her monumental *Women and Eco-*

*nomics: A Study of the Economic Relation between Men and Women as a Factor in Social Evolution** (1898). She began to associate with George Houghton Gilman (a cousin) in 1896, initiating a three-year premarital correspondence with him during which she wrote him twenty- to thirty-page letters almost daily. These letters are now of inestimable value to scholars. She attended the International Women's Congress in London (1899), married Gilman, began a New York residence with him, and published *Concerning Children* (1900).

Charlotte Gilman's later work includes much additional significant writing (novels, nonfictional books, and essays), lecturing and conference participation (including tours abroad), and editing. When her husband died in 1934, she moved again to Pasadena to be near her daughter. A year later, suffering from inoperable breast cancer, she committed suicide. *The Living of Charlotte Gilman: An Autobiography* appeared posthumously (1935). Charlotte Perkins Gilman, an intellectual feminist of enormous significance, wrote persuasively on the evils of patriarchal religion, the patriarchal family, poverty, the plight of African Americans, woman's rights, woman's economic dependence, domestic budgeting, woman's work, female superiority in the natural scheme of things, love, marriage and/or career and divorce, motherhood, children, prostitution, birth control, modesty and dress fashions, and urban betterment.

Glasgow, Ellen (1873–1945). (Full name: Ellen Anderson Gholson Glasgow.) Fiction writer. She was born in Richmond, Virginia, where she lived her entire life, apart from several years she spent in New York City (1911–1916). Evidently too delicate to attend school on a regular basis, Glasgow educated herself to a great extent through self-disciplined reading at home, in literature, economics, philosophy, and science. She suffered partial deafness when she was about sixteen years of age. She blamed her stern, philandering father, whom she hated, for causing profound nervousness in her mother, who bore ten children and then died in 1893. She became depressed after her mother's death and was saddened by the suicide of a mentor-like brother-in-law in 1894 (a brother also committed suicide, in 1909). In 1895 she published her first short story, "A Woman of Tomorrow," in which a successful female lawyer is glad to have avoided marriage when she sees what it did to her whilom lover's used-up wife.

After a trip to England (1896), Glasgow published the first three of her nineteen novels: *The Descendant** (1897), *Phases of an Inferior Planet** (1898), and *The Voice of the People** (1900). All three concern the tragically ruinous difficulties of women in a man's world and thus made Glasgow an early protagonist for woman's rights. She had barely started her illustrious career by the turn of the century. She wrote steadily, and with increasing brilliance and popularity, marked by such classics as *Virginia* (1913), *Barren Ground* (1925), *The Sheltered Life* (1932), and *Vein of Iron* (1935). Glasgow involved herself in such activities as the prevention of cruelty to animals (her father had neglected his wife's pets), suffered through several broken engagements, took an overdose of sleeping pills after one such disappointment (1918), maintained a celebrated poise by developing an ironic view of life, and finally won out when she received critical acclaim and many awards later in life. Her autobiography and letters were posthumously published (1954, 1963). Ellen Glasgow should be remembered as a pioneering Southern novelist, who, just before the twentieth century, began to overcome the double burden of being a product of the Old South and of being a female writer. Her several novels portraying the postbellum South are among the finest that have been produced in America.

Glimpses of Unfamiliar Japan (1894). Sketches by Lafcadio Hearn.* This two-volume collection contains twenty-seven essays, averaging about twenty-five pages each. Four of the essays were originally syndicated in various newspapers, and six first appeared in the *Atlantic Monthly** (1891–1893). Hearn dedicated the volumes to Mitchell McDonald, his American naval friend in Yokohama, and to Basil Hall Chamberlain, professor of philology and Japanese at the Imperial University of Tokyo.

Glimpses of Unfamiliar Japan was the first of Hearn's dozen books on Japan. It has no firm unity but is instead a series of fourteen impressionistic travel pieces and thirteen essays on specific topics. "My First Day in the Orient" reveals the narrator's excitement, thoughts, and impressions upon leaving disliked Western civilization behind and encountering the Orient. "A Pilgrimage to Enoshima" concerns shrines, bell sounds, and statues. "At the Market of the Dead" describes various items and indicates their use. "Bon-Odori" features a dance performed during a festival of the dead, beside a faraway temple. "At Hinomisaki" presents another temple in more detail. "The Chief City of the Province of the Gods" impressionistically sketches Matsue, the city where Hearn first taught in Japan. "Kitsuki: The Most Ancient Shrine of Japan" conveys any newcomer's puzzlement and then concludes, "I trust . . . that I may presume some day to speak of the great living power of that faith now called Shintō." "At Mionoseki" contrasts villagers who believe in their traditional chicken-hating god, on the one hand, and sailors serving on a modern Imperial man-of-war, on the other. "From Hōki to Oki" describes Hearn's trip to the islands of the Oki archipelago on a "squabby" steamer past "phantom-color, delicate, elfish, indescribable" scenery. The best of the substantive essays concern images of the god of children ("Jizō"), the suicide of lovers ("Shinjū"), foxes ("Kitsune"), gardens ("In a Japanese Garden"), the Japanese woman's "richest ornament" ("Of Women's Hair"), a Japanese gardener with four souls ("Of Souls"), and "the generally happy and smiling character of the native faces" ("The Japanese Smile"). Of unique biographical interest is the chapter entitled "From the Diary of an English Teacher." There is much else of interest in *Glimpses of Unfamiliar Japan*. The prose is slow and careful, intricate, and rich; the contents are always informative and often entertaining.

Godey's Magazine. Continuation of the popular and influential old *Godey's Lady's Book*, a magazine of fashion, manners, and miscellaneous pieces, started in Philadelphia in 1830. It moved to New York (1892), changed its name, published fiction by important writers (including H. H. Boyesen*), went bankrupt (1898), and was bought by Frank A. Munsey* and absorbed into his new magazine, the short-lived *Puritan* (1897–1901).

Golf. *See* Sports.

Gompers, Samuel (1850–1924). Labor leader. Gompers, who was born in London of Jewish and Flemish parentage, immigrated to the United States with his parents in 1863. He was introduced to the American labor movement when he got a job making cigars (as his father had done in London) in New York City and especially when he joined the Cigarmakers' Union in 1864. Gompers married Sophia Julian in 1866. He and his wife knew much poverty and slum living, at that time and on through the 1870s. He marched with 25,000 New York workers demanding an eight-hour workday (1871). He became president of a cigarmakers' union local (1875). By 1881 he and fellow labor intellectuals had formulated plans to use unions for the immediate purpose of demanding more money for shorter hours. In 1881 he helped found the organization that became the American Federation of Labor (AFL) in 1886. He recruited 140,000 members for the AFL, became its first president, and held that position with great distinction for the rest of his life (except 1894–1895). He corresponded with Friedrich Engels concerning socialist rivals (1891).

By 1892 Gompers had become successful enough to state that his purpose was to gather and concentrate the forces of labor into national unions, and added that his work had been crowned with unique success. Setbacks included the Homestead Lockout* in 1892, AFL political agitation for popular collective ownership of the means of production and distribution (1894), the Pullman Strike* in 1894, unsuccessful support of William Jennings Bryan* for the presidency (1896); furthermore, criticism of American expansionist policy during the administrations of William McKinley* and Theodore Roosevelt* proved unpopular (from 1898). Despite the setbacks, by 1900 the AFL had 548,000 members. Gompers, who had cooperated with industrialists and financiers, including Mark Hanna,* became vice president of the National Civic Federation (1901). Its purpose was to reduce the amount of labor unrest and the number of strikes. Ultimately, the AFL became the largest labor union in the United States; it succeeded by being pragmatic and opportunistic, whereas the Knights of Labor (founded in 1869 and the rival of the AFL in the early days), was idealistic and political. Gompers was always skillful at reconciling internal differences in the union. His realistic aim was always to improve the workers' wages and working conditions, and hence their morale and efficiency. He once brushed aside a critic who asked him whether he thought American workers got the "full product" of their toil by saying that because of unionism they were receiving a larger share than ever before in history. He urged passage of the labor provisions of the 1914 Clayton Act, in the unrealized hope that doing so would minimize governmental interference. By 1914, the AFL had well over 2,000,000 members, with 111 national unions, 762 city central bodies, and 26,761 locals. During World War I, Gompers was an adviser to the Council of National Defense. After the war, he advocated the participation by labor in peace conferences, condemned the Soviet government (1919), and petitioned federal authorities to pardon Eugene V. Debs* and others convicted of sedition.

Gompers's steady aims as a labor leader were as follows: the autonomy of the national union; the levying of dues high enough to cover all expenses, benefits, and welfare programs during times of hardship; the promotion of business unions rather than industrial unions; the setting of one union per trade; bargaining with employers for better wages, more favorable hours, and better working conditions, and not for explicit political reforms; and opposition to governmental injunctions and other forms of intervention. Gompers did not favor offering union membership to women, African Americans, or the unskilled. Gompers is now regarded as an essentially conservative American labor leader.

Gould, Jay (1836–1892). (Christened name: Jason Gould.) Railroad owner and builder, and stock speculator. Gould was born in Roxbury, New York, a poor farmer's son. After little schooling, he became a clerk, a blacksmith, and a surveyor (1854–1857). He went into the tanning business in Pennsylvania, sold leather in New York, and began ruthlessly speculating in and dishonestly manipulating railroad stock and made great profits in New York, Pennsylvania, and Ohio (1859–1860). The first man who financed him was wiped out and committed suicide. During the Civil War, Gould was a stock trader in New York City. By 1867 he and his partners were directors of the Erie Railroad, and they competed successfully against Cornelius Vanderbilt for its continued control (to 1869). During this so-called Erie War, Gould and his henchmen issued fraudulent stock, bribed New York state legislators to legalize it, and reaped millions. Gould and his associates tried to corner the gold market, which scheme resulted in a panic (24 September 1869) until the U.S. Treasury released government gold. In 1872, one of his partners—the ebullient, fun-loving James Fisk—was murdered by his mistress's pimp; in addition, William Marcy "Boss" Tweed, who had abetted Gould, began his fall from power. Gould resigned from the Erie Railroad (1872) and bought the Union Pacific Railroad (in the 1870s and 1880s), the Missouri Pacific, the Kansas Pacific, the Denver and Pacific, and the Wabash (all in the 1880s). He also bought the New York *World* in 1879 (and sold it to Joseph Pulitzer* in 1883), the Western Union Telegraph Company (1881), and the Manhattan Elevated Railroad (1887); in addition, he found time to dabble in coal, oil, and timber. James Gordon Bennett* and a partner broke Gould's transatlantic cable monopoly in 1883. By 1890 Gould controlled half the railroad mileage in the Southwest.

Jay Gould was somber, joyless, diabolical, and fiendishly clever at shaking up the industrial system and then stepping in to reap enormous profits. He is a prime example of the ruthless, unscrupulous "robber baron." He liked only money, books, and gardening. He married Helen Day Miller in 1863 (the couple had six children). When he died in New York, his estate was valued at $77,000,000. One of his daughters, Anna Gould, married the worthless Count Boniface of Castellane (1895) and lived unhappily abroad. (*See* Travel and Travelers.) One of his sons, Edwin Gould, headed a Saint Louis railroad company, organized the Continental Match Company (1894), and consolidated it with the Diamond Match Company (1899). Another son, George Jay Gould, lost the railroad interests he had inherited to various financiers far more clever than he. Another daughter, Helen Miller Gould, who married Finley Johnson Shepard in 1913, gave money to American army hospitals during and after the Spanish-American War* and made other, later philanthropic donations.

Grant, Robert (1852–1940). Lawyer, judge, novelist of manners, essayist, and poet. He was born in Boston, attended the Public Latin School (1863–1869), and went to Harvard for a decade (B.A., 1873; Ph.D., 1876—the first Ph.D. in English given there; LL.B., 1879). He practiced law in Boston briefly (from 1879), traveled in England and on the Continent (1881), and became the private secretary of Boston's mayor (1882–1883). He served as a water commissioner (1888–1893), became a county probate and insolvency judge (1893–1922), earned and enjoyed various honors, and served on the Massachusetts governor's Sacco-Vanzetti advisory committee in 1927 (Grant recommended execution). In 1904, Grant published the first of his three novels dramatizing divorce and satirizing divorce laws. In 1905 and for years thereafter, he campaigned for a uniform federal marriage and divorce law. He knew that feminist demands for changes were just, but he deplored disorder and frivolity, the weakening of the family, and the sexual promiscuity that would inevitably follow their implementation. Grant married Amy Gordon Galt in 1883 (the couple had four children).

Although Grant published many books, in a variety of genres, beginning in 1879 and continuing until *Fourscore: An Autobiography* in 1934, he is best known as a novelist of manners. His best works in this vein include *Face to Face* (1886), which depicts high-society life in New York City and the Northeast, dramatizes the clash of capital and labor, and presents a young, idealistic British woman caught amid vigorous male representatives of both sides; *Unleavened Bread** (1900), which features a ruthless "heroine" and is by far Grant's most hard-hitting novel; and *The Chippendales* (1909), about the thinning of the blue blood of an aristocratic, old Boston family as new democratic, social, and economic forces imperil its rectitude. In the 1890s, Grant also published four collections of essays: *The Reflections of a Married Man* (1892), about family and social life; *The Opinions of a Philosopher* (1893), concerning changes in the American psyche; *The Art of Living* (1895), on many subjects, from housing to vocations to woman's liberation; and *Search-Light Letters* (1899), on vulgar democracy versus aristocratic elitism in modern politics and society. (In 1912 Grant published *The Convictions of a Grandfather*, an autumnal summing up.)

Grant enjoyed the friendship of many important people of his era, including Theodore Roosevelt* and Edith Wharton.*

Great Battles of the World (1901). History book by Stephen Crane.* Its eight chapters cover various battles, sieges, stormings, and campaigns, including Bunker Hill (American colonists vs. British, in Massachusetts, 17 June 1775); Vittoria (British vs. French, in Spain, 21 June 1813); Plevna (Turks vs. Russians, in Bulgaria, July–December 1877); Burkersdorf Heights (Prussians vs. Austrians, in Germany, 21 July 1762); Leipzig and Lützen (Swedes vs. French, in Germany, 8 September 1631 and 6 November 1632); Badajos (British vs. French, in Spain, 19 March 1812); New Orleans (American vs. British, in Louisiana, 14 December 1814–8 January 1815); and Solferino (Italians and French vs. Austrians, in Italy, 24 June 1859).

Each chapter begins dramatically, sketches historical and political background, and narrates the conflict in graphic, reportorial style, occasionally with dialogue and laced with irony and mordant humor. Crane is especially commendable in presenting weather and ground conditions, supply problems, tactics, and the personalities of leaders. On the other hand, he includes too many details, often quotes excessively from various sources, and sometimes uses curiously prissy diction. Crane undertook this work strictly for money while he was mortally sick in England and was aided in his research by Harold Frederic* and especially by Kate Lyon,* Frederic's second wife. She did much of the writing (without being given proper credit), especially toward the end of Crane's life. The essays were published in *Lippincott's Magazine* (March–October 1900) and then in book form (in different order) in Philadelphia and in London (1901).

The Great White City. *See* World's Columbian Exposition.

H

Hall, G. Stanley (1844–1924). (Full name: Granville Stanley Hall.) Psychologist, philosopher, and educator. He was born in Ashfield, Massachusetts, to a religious, rather restrictive farm family. After schooling in a preparatory academy in Ashfield and then a seminary in Easthampton, Massachusetts, he attended Williams College (B.A., 1867, M.A., 1870), where he was a friend of Hamilton W. Mabie*, and Harvard (Ph.D., 1878), where he studied under William James.* In between, he was a Union Theological Seminary student in New York (1867–1868, degree in 1871) and a teacher and tutor in New York (1867–1868, 1871–1872); he also studied in Germany (1868–1871 and again 1878–1880, 1888–1889). During the Franco-Prussian War, he was a war correspondent for American newspapers and periodicals (1870–1871). This energetic, versatile man taught at several institutions of higher learning: literature and philosophy at Antioch (1872–1876), English and pedagogy at Harvard (1876–1878, 1880–1882), and psychology and pedagogy at Johns Hopkins (1882–1888), where one of his students was John Dewey.* During his first years at Johns Hopkins, Hall established the first formal psychology laboratory in the United States. His early work there rivaled that of James at Harvard. Finally, Hall worked at Clark (1889–1920—*see* Universities); he was appointed the first president of this newly established university and remained its head during his long tenure there. Before he went to Clark, however, he founded *The American Journal of Psychology* (1877), the first in its field, and edited it (1887–1921). He also helped to found the Child Study Association of America (1888). Then, to prepare for his manifold duties at Clark, he visited various European universities (1888–1889). Thereafter, he stimulated his faculty to promote interest in experimental psychology.

Hall specialized in culture-epoch theory. He helped to found the American Psychological Association (1891) and became its first president. He edited *The Pedagogical Seminary* (1891–1924). He was chairman of a conference on experimental psychology held at the World's Columbian Exposition* (Chicago,

1893). Beginning in 1893, he became a lecturing head of his Psychology Department at Clark and also offered a three-year course in the history of philosophy. He edited *The American Journal of Religious Psychology and Education* (1904–1915). Hall invited Sigmund Freud and Carl Gustav Jung to lecture at Clark (1909), thus introducing America to psychoanalysis. Hall edited *The Journal of Applied Psychology* (1917–1924). He was a revered member of numerous professional associations. Hall wrote many books, but most of them were published either before 1888 or after 1901. Among his best are *The Contents of Children's Minds* (1883), *Adolescence, Its Psychology and Its Relation to Physiology, Anthropology, Sociology, Sex, Crime, Religion and Education* (2 vols., 1904, abridged as *Youth; Its Education, Regimen and Hygiene* [1906]), *Educational Problems* (2 vols., 1911), and *Jesus, the Christ, in the Light of Psychology* (2 vols., 1927). Hall is now regarded as a major contributor, if an occasionally unscientific one, to the development of psychology and pedagogy.

Hanna, Mark (1837–1904). (Full name: Marcus Azonzo Hanna.) Wealthy Ohio businessman and politician. He was born in New Lisbon, Ohio, but as a teenager moved with his family to Cleveland (1852). He knew John D. Rockefeller* when both were boys there. Hanna left Western Reserve College after a few months to go into the grocery and commission business with his father (1858–1867). Briefly during that period, in 1864, Hanna served in the Union army during the Civil War. He married Charlotte Augusta Rhodes in 1864 (the couple had three children) and entered into coal and iron ventures with his father-in-law in 1867. He also was involved in the shipbuilding business, bought the Cleveland *Herald* and the city opera house, became a bank president, and influenced city councilmen to favor streetcar franchises that he owned. In the 1880s Hanna became active in Republican Party politics and steadily favored the gold standard and protective tariffs. He organized support in Cleveland for James A. Garfield's successful presidential campaign (1880). After failing to engineer Ohio Senator John Sherman's nomination for president (1888), Hanna turned his attention to William McKinley,* helped make him governor of Ohio (1892–1896), and even repaid his immense financial losses in the Panic of 1893.* Hanna discontinued being an active businessman in 1894, maneuvered McKinley's first-ballot nomination for president (1896), and, during the campaign, persuaded bank and corporation officials to contribute funds.

During McKinley's administration (1897–1901), Democratic opponents rightly accused Hanna of having undue control over the president, who gratefully appointed Hanna senator from Ohio (1897). Hanna was reelected (1897, 1903) amid recurrent charges of bribery. As a behind-the-scenes McKinley adviser, Hanna handled patronage in such a way as to increase the hold of big business on national politics. He favored subsidies to American shipowners and supported early Panama Canal efforts. Hanna only briefly opposed U.S. intervention in Cuba (1898). He opposed Theodore Roosevelt* as vice president under McKinley in the 1900 campaign. Although Hanna promoted commercial interests, he treated his employees well and also notably aided the National Civic Federation, as its chief executive officer, in mediating capital-labor disputes, helping, for example, to settle the 1902 anthracite coal strike. It is possible that he would have sought the nomination for president instead of Roosevelt at the 1904 convention, but he contracted typhoid fever and suddenly died in Washington, D.C. Hanna's daughter, Ruth Hanna McCormick Simms, was active in political, civic, and commercial affairs, and she served as a member of the U.S. House of Representatives (1929–1931).

Hapgood, Norman (1868–1937). Author and editor. Hapgood was born in Chicago and attended Harvard (B.A., 1890; LL.B., 1893). While at Harvard, he edited the *Harvard Monthly* and was friendly with Bernard Berenson,* Robert Herrick,* Robert Morss Lovett,* William Vaughn Moody,* and Trumbull Stickney,* among others. Hapgood tried law in Chicago, then journalism there and in Milwaukee (1893–1894), but soon moved to New York City. He became a book review editor, drama critic, and editorial writer on the New York *Commercial Advertiser* (1897–1902). Among his associates were Abraham Cahan* and Lincoln Steffens.* Hapgood published several books on history and on drama, including *Literary Statesmen* (1897); biographies of Daniel Webster (1899), Abraham Lincoln (1899), and George Washington (1901); and *The Stage in America, 1897–1900* (1901), of special interest because of its sensible praise of Clyde Fitch* and James A. Herne,* among others. Hapgood was active as the reform-inclined editor of *Collier's** (1902–1912), was liberal in a rational way (although he was satirized as "Normal Slapgood" by Finley Peter Dunne*), was involved in a libel suit with the tawdry *Town Topics*,* edited *Harper's Weekly* (1912–1915), preferred Woodrow Wilson as a presidential candidate to Theodore Roosevelt* (1912), was named minister to Denmark by President Wilson (1919), and later continued to write courageous, sane editorials supporting liberal political figures. Hapgood married Emilie Bigelow in 1896 (the couple had one child and were divorced in 1915) and Elizabeth Kempley Reynolds in 1916 (the couple had three children).

Hare, James H. (1856–1946). News photographer and war correspondent. Hare was born in London. Because he was a poor student, he began to work for his father, who manufactured fine cameras by hand. The son soon advanced beyond the father in the technique of photography and began to take pictures of public meetings and sports events. By chance, he started taking excellent snapshots with a hand-held camera. He adopted advanced American film techniques, immigrated to the United States (1889), and became a photographer for the *Illustrated American* and also a free-lance photographer for various newspapers. When the *Maine* was blown up and the Spanish-American War* was imminent, Jimmy Hare got himself hired to furnish *Collier's** with pictures from Cuba (1898). He earned a high reputation for his daring and capable battlefield photographs. With the zestful New York *World* correspondent Sylvester Scovel,*

Hare interviewed rebel General Maximo Gomez. He photographed numerous sieges and battles close up and also provided pictures of the Cuban coast for American naval commanders. Hare met Stephen Crane* and Richard Harding Davis,* and the three were in several precarious spots together. Hare looked over Crane's shoulder in awe once while the tired correspondent slowly wrote one of his finest war essays, which later found its way into *Wounds in the Rain: A Collection of Stories Relating to the Spanish-American War of 1898*.* When President Theodore Roosevelt,* at one point, voiced criticism of Crane (September 1902), Hare, who was present, rushed noisily to Crane's defense.

Later in his career, *Collier's* sent Hare to cover revolutions in the Caribbean, Mexico, and Central and South America, the Russo-Japanese War (1904–1905), and various Balkan conflicts. He edited and arranged *A Photographic Record of the Russo-Japanese War* and included in it an account of the battle of the Sea of Japan by Alfred Thayer Mahan* (1905). Hare, a pioneer in aerial photography, beginning as early as 1906, used his expertise during World War I, at which time he was employed by *Leslie's Weekly*. In his later years, he lectured in person and on radio, wrote about his daring and impudent exploits, and continued to photograph. Hare married Ellen Crapper, who was from Yorkshire, in 1879 (the couple had five children). He died in New Jersey.

Harper, Frances (1825–1911). (Full name: Frances Ellen Watkins Harper.) African-American writer and activist. Frances Ellen Watkins was born free in Baltimore, attended an all-black school there, worked in a Baltimore bookstore, taught domestic science near Columbus, Ohio (from 1850), worked on the Underground Railroad in Philadelphia (from 1854), and lectured widely in New England and also in Canada on the subject of abolition. She published *Poems on Miscellaneous Subjects* (1854, enlarged in 1855 and again in 1871). This book, containing mostly narrative verse either opposing slavery or deriving from the Bible, and echoing Felicia Dorothea Hemans, Henry Wadsworth Longfellow, Harriet Beecher Stowe, and John Greenleaf Whittier, proved immensely popular. Its twentieth edition (1871) included an introduction by William Lloyd Garrison. (Watkins wrote an earlier book of poetry, entitled *Forest Leaves*, c. 1845, of which no copy is now extant.) She married widower Fenton Harper in Cincinnati in 1860 (the couple had one child, and the husband died in 1864). She became a professional writer, lecturer, and reformer.

Frances Watkins (later Frances Harper) had a distinguished publishing record. She published "The Two Offers" (1859), which, featuring a white woman who opts for antislavery work rather than marriage, was probably the first short story written by an African-American woman. She lectured off and on in the South after the Civil War (1867–1871) and then resided in Philadelphia, where she wrote steadily and engaged in work through the African Methodist Episcopal Church to promote social and political reforms. She associated with the American Equal Rights Association, the National Council of Women, and the Women's Christian Temperance Association (to about 1892). Her colleagues included

Susan B. Anthony,* Frederick Douglass,* and Elizabeth Cady Stanton.* Harper cofounded the National Association of Colored Women, in Washington, D.C. (1895), and served as its vice president (1897). She went into semiretirement in about 1902. As for her writings during these decades, she published *Moses: A Story of the Nile* (1869), which was enlarged in 1889 and again in 1901, retitled *Idylls of the Bible*. The work is ably dramatic but insignificant. Then came *Poems* (1871), along the lines of *Poems on Miscellaneous Subjects*. A professional associate of Harper's said that 50,000 copies of her two books of poetry had been sold by 1878. Far better is Harper's *Sketches of Southern Life* (1872, often reprinted), black-diction narrative poems mostly featuring witty old Aunt Chloe and mystical old Uncle Jacob. *The Sparrow's Fall and Other Poems* (1890?) includes "Double Standard," in which a sexually abused woman asks why society "so coldly crushed me down, / And excused the man?" Later came *The Martyr of Alabama and Other Poems* (1894?), the title poem of which narrates the murder by callous whites of an African-American lad who politely refuses to dance for them. Next was a book again called *Poems* (1895, enlarged in 1898 and again in 1900).

The most significant book Harper ever wrote, and the one that deserves detailed comment, is her novel *Iola Leroy; or, Shadows Uplifted* (1892). Although it is a sentimental work involving stereotypical characters and a hackneyed search plot, it forcefully treats the subjects of white violence against slaves, sexual exploitation of slave women, and enforced silence among African Americans. The octoroon heroine, Iola Leroy, thinks that she is white until the death of her planter father, who had bought a slave named Marie, educated her, and married her. Iola is now torn from her slave mother, sold into domestic slavery herself, released to become a Civil War army nurse, and then preyed upon sexually by gross white men. But Iola survives, rejects a white doctor's love, marries a mulatto physician, finds her mother at last, and dedicates her life to the improvement of African Americans—and all women as well.

Iola Leroy was not the first novel by an African-American woman, although it is the first viable one. Earlier came *Our Nig* (1859), by Harriet E. Wilson; *Clarence and Corinne; or, God's Way* (1890), by Harriet E. Wilson; and *Megda* (1891), by Emma Dunham Kelly. These novels are important only historically. Frances Harper was a trailblazer who was followed, in most cases appreciatively, in the 1890s by Amelia Johnson, who wrote *The Hazeley Family* (1894) and *Martina Meriden; or, What Is the Motive?* (1901); Victoria Earle Matthews, who wrote *Aunt Lindy* (1893); and Emma D. Kelly-Hawkins, who wrote *Four Girls at Cottage City* (1898); not to mention other African-American women who also wrote novels and short stories during this period.

Harper's Monthly Magazine. Distinguished magazine founded in New York (1850) as *Harper's New Monthly Magazine*. Its name later changed to *Harper's Monthly Magazine* (1900), then *Harper's Magazine* (from 1925). It lowered its price per issue from 35¢ to 25¢ in 1899. At first *Harper's* printed much British writing, but Henry Mills Alden,* who was its excellent editor from 1869 to 1919, welcomed contributions by numerous American authors of the first rank, including Mary E. Wilkins Freeman,* Hamlin Garland,* William Dean Howells,* Henry James,* Sarah Orne Jewett,* and Owen Wister,* and contracted for artwork by Winslow Homer,* Howard Pyle,* and other fine artists. Some of the best literary criticism of the age appeared under the long-standing rubric of the "Editor's Easy Chair," which was long occupied by Howells (1901–1921). Beginning about 1900, *Harper's* featured more material on sociopolitical issues.

Harriman, Edward Henry (1848–1909). Railroad speculator, magnate, and administrator. Born in Hempstead, New York, he was a sharp-eyed Wall Street quotation boy (1862–1869) who was helped by family money to buy a seat on the New York Stock Exchange (1870). He established his own brokerage firm (1872) and soon began to reorganize bankrupt railroad lines, first in upstate New York. He became a director of the Illinois Central Railroad (1883) and then one of its vice presidents (1887). He foresaw (1890) the coming of the Panic of 1893* and survived it by early retrenchment. He ultimately controlled 60,000 miles of tracks, including those of the Illinois Central, the Union Pacific—of which he was an executive committee member in 1898 and president five years later—and the Central and Southern Pacific; his miles of track even extended into the Oregon and Navigation Company. Harriman and James J. Hill, of the Northern Pacific Railroad, locked horns over control of the Chicago, Burlington, and Quincy (1901); Hill bought the Burlington and Harriman countered by investing in the Northern Pacific, which controlled part of the Burlington. Their greed precipitated the Wall Street Panic of 1901. A Supreme Court decision awarded control of the Burlington and Northern Pacific to Hill in 1904. Furthermore, Harriman was censured by the Interstate Commerce Commission for engaging in shady practices (1907).

Although Harriman was seen as a ruthless speculator indifferent to bad publicity, it should be noted that he favored conservation, organized a scientific expedition to Alaska (1899), and founded and supported an active New York boys' club. Harriman married Mary W. Averell in 1879. The couple had six children, including William Averell Harriman (1891–1986), a New York governor, statesman, and diplomat.

Harris, Joel Chandler (1848–1908). Author. Born in Putnam County, Georgia, Harris was distressed all his life by the fact that his unwed mother had been deserted by her Irish laborer lover. After working as a teenager and a little later for publishers in Georgia and New Orleans (1862–1870), Harris joined the editorial staff of the Savannah *Morning News* (1870–1876) and then the Atlanta *Constitution* (1876–1900). Beloved in his day, he is still remembered for his Uncle Remus stories, the first of which was published in the *Constitution* (1879). Collections include *Uncle Remus: His Songs and His Sayings* (1881), which, when revised in 1895, gained Harris international fame; *Nights with Uncle Remus: Myths and Legends of the Old Plantation* (1883); *On the Plantation: Uncle Remus and His Friends* (1892); *Mr. Rabbit at Home* (1895); and still later titles. Harris started his own *Uncle Remus's Magazine* (1900).

Of Harris's many other published works, those in the 1890s, his busiest decade, are *Joel Chandler Harris' Life of Henry W. Grady* (1890), a biography of Harris's *Constitution* associate and persuasive, liberal New South lecturer; *Balaam and His Master and Other Sketches and Stories* (1891), stories about love of the land, black-white relations, strong blacks, the Civil War, and miscegenation; *Evening Tales Done into English from the French of Frédéric Ortoli* (1893), translations by Harris and his wife of French folktales; *Little Mr. Thimblefinger and His Queer Country* (1894), fairy tales for children, some redacted from European sources; *Sister Jane: Her Friends and Acquaintances . . .* (1896), a semiautobiographical novel about the narrator's sister Jane's caring for a friend and her illegitimate baby; *Stories of Georgia* (1896), a narrative history of Georgia, chronologically arranged, for high school students; *The Story of Aaron . . .* (1896), stories for children about a full-blooded Arab slave; *Aaron in the Wildwoods* (1897), stories about the earlier life of the same Arab, again for children; *Tales of the Home Folks in Peace and War* (1898), melodramatic, sentimental yarns often in praise of blacks; *Plantation Pageants* (1899), children's stories at the time of General William Tecumseh Sherman's march through Georgia during the Civil War; and *The Chronicles of Aunt Minervy Ann* (1899), comic stories as told by a peppy black woman.

Harris advocated the postbellum, progressive New South, but he also satirized some of its values, looked back nostalgically to Edenic old plantation days, and accurately and sensitively differentiated several levels of Middle Georgia speech patterns. He is most memorable when he probes human characteristics in animal allegories. He created two immortal characters: Uncle Remus, the freed slave, white-family servant, and fabulous storyteller; and Brer Rabbit, the crafty, cynical survivor in a dog-eat-dog world. Among lovable, shy Harris's many friends were George Washington Cable,* Richard Watson Gilder,* William Dean Howells,* Thomas Nelson Page,* James Whitcomb Riley,* and Mark Twain.* Harris married Esther LaRose, a French-Canadian woman, in 1873 (the couple had nine children, three of whom died in infancy).

Harrison, Benjamin (1833–1901). Twenty-third president of the United States. Born in North Bend, Ohio, he was the son of a Whig congressman and the grandson of William Henry Harrison, the ninth president of the United States. He graduated from Miami University of Ohio (1852), studied law, and married Caroline Lavinia Scott in 1853 (the couple had one son and one daughter). Harrison and his wife moved to Indianapolis, Indiana (1854), where he joined the Republican Party and was elected city attorney (1857) and also state supreme court reporter for Indiana (1860, 1864). He served during the Civil War on the Union side (1862–1865; he was promoted from colonel to brigadier general).

He practiced law (1865–1881) and was elected a U.S. senator (1881–1887), in which capacity he was active but unsuccessful in seeking statehood for several Western territories. When nominated as the Republican candidate for president, he campaigned mainly from his Indianapolis front porch, speaking informally to more than eighty audiences totaling almost 300,000 persons. He defeated Democratic incumbant Grover Cleveland* and served one term as president (1889–1893).

During his tenure, Harrison was an energetic administrator but an aloof, cold, and tactless politician. He organized the first Pan-American Conference (1889, in Washington, D.C.); signed the Sherman Anti-Trust Act* (1890), the Silver Purchase Act (1890–*see* Free Silver), and the McKinley Tariff Act (1890, promoted by William McKinley*); and advocated a treaty to annex Hawaii (withdrawn by President Cleveland in 1893). Harrison steadily advocated a strong national economy, the development of a large two-ocean navy and a bigger merchant marine service, reciprocal trade agreements with Latin American countries, civil service reform—he appointed Theodore Roosevelt* civil service commissioner in Washington, D.C., in 1889—civil rights for African Americans, and federal regulation of railroads. Harrison ran for reelection in 1892; but Cleveland projected an image of more vigor, and Cleveland's supporters combined with anti-Republican farmers and laborers to defeat Harrison, whose wife died two weeks before the election. Thereafter, having published his speeches (1892), Harrison practiced law again, married his deceased wife's niece, Mary Lord Dimmick, in 1896 (the couple had one daughter), wrote a popular book about federal government procedures entitled *This Country of Ours* (1897), argued as senior counselor the Venezuela position against England in the Venezuela boundary dispute (1898–1899), and completed *Views of an Ex-President* (1901), which was edited by his widow and published posthumously.

Hassam, Childe (1859–1935). (Full name: Frederick Childe Hassam.) Painter and etcher. Born in Dorchester, Massachusetts, he started his career in Boston as a wood engraver and free-lance illustrator. He traveled to Europe (1883), returned to Boston, married Kathleen Maud Doane in 1884, and went back with her to Paris to study (1886–1889) and again later (1897–1898). He helped to found a group of fellow Impressionistic painters called The Ten* (1898). Hassam was greatly influenced by the French Impressionistic painters and also by James Abbott McNeill Whistler.* Upon his return to America, Hassam attempted to transplant French Impressionism, concentrating on people rushing or promenading along streets (especially those of lower Manhattan) and also in sunny landscapes in luminous air in New England and rural New York. Hassam's painting *The Flower Garden* (1888) presents massive, dark garden growth at the left, a delicately blossomy garden section at the right, and a young woman on a brightly neutral pathway in the center. His *Washington Arch in Spring* (1890), a Frenchified, blotchy, Impressionistic rendering of the wooden arch designed by Stanford White* at the foot of New York's Fifth Avenue, illustrates the arch obscured by trees, and also with horse-drawn carriages, a few promenaders, and a street sweeper in a white uniform and cap. *Mount Vesuvius* (1897) shows the Bay of Naples with its castle and the volcano rather close and oddly dominated by puffy clouds. *Late Afternoon, Winter, New York* (1900) reveals a wide, lightly trafficked street blurred by heavy snow, with a tall, ugly, rectangular Manhattan skyscraper happily obscured by even more snow.

Hay, John (1838–1905). (Full name: John Milton Hay.) Statesman, journalist, poet, travel writer, fiction writer, and biographer. He was born in Salem, Indiana. After he graduated from Brown University (M.A., 1858), he studied law in Illinois (1859–1861); campaigned for Abraham Lincoln (1860) and worked for him (1861–1865), living in the White House as Lincoln's assistant private secretary; and served in diplomatic posts in Paris, Vienna, and Madrid (1865–1870, intermittently). He became a newspaper editor in New York City and married Clara Louise Stone in 1874 (the couple had four children, one of whom predeceased them). The Stone family enjoyed great wealth in Cleveland. Hay and his family moved to Washington, D.C. (1879), where they lived in a mansion adjoining that of his close friend Henry Adams* and his wife. Hay served President Rutherford B. Hayes as assistant secretary of state (1879–1881), President William McKinley* as ambassador to England (1897–1898) and as secretary of state (1898–1901), and President Theodore Roosevelt* as secretary of state (1901–1905). Hay formulated the Open Door Policy* in China (1899, conferring with William Woodville Rockhill* in the process) and negotiated the first Panama Canal treaties (1900–1903).

Hay's major literary works are *Pike County Ballads* (1871), *Castilian Days* (1871), *The Bread-Winners* (1884), *Poems* (1890), and *Abraham Lincoln: A History** (10 vols., 1890, with John G. Nicolay). Hay and Nicolay also edited Lincoln's works (2 vols., 1894; 12 vols., 1905). Hay's closest friends included Adams, William Dean Howells,* Henry James,* and Mark Twain.* When he turned fifty-two in 1890, he was exceedingly rich and generally unsympathetic toward the liberal political and social movements that were disturbing the status quo. In fact, in *The Bread-Winners*, an early labor novel, he favors corporate authority, champions property rights over civil rights, and makes his villain a criminally inclined labor organizer. As the ambassador to England, Hay met several of the forward-looking American writers of the 1890s, including Stephen Crane,* Paul Laurence Dunbar,* and Harold Frederic.* Hay never recovered his good spirits after his son Adelbert Hay, President McKinley's assistant secretary (from 1900), accidentally fell from a hotel window in New Haven, Connecticut, to his death (1901).

A Hazard of New Fortunes (1889). Novel by William Dean Howells.* After years of unpalatable employment with a Boston insurance company, Basil March resigns to become editor of *Every Other Week*, a new literary magazine which his Western friend Fulkerson is starting in New York City. March convinces his reluctant wife Isabel and their teenage children Tom and Bella that New York has possibilities; after much searching, they find an apartment and move. With Fulkerson's help, March soon has a strange staff and other uncertain support: Talented but selfish Angus Beaton is engaged as the art director; irritable Jacob Dryfoos, a natural-gas millionaire from Indiana now in New York seeking investment opportunities, becomes the magazine's backer; his son Conrad Dryfoos acts as nominal publisher; and Berthold Lindau, a German refugee maimed during the Civil War, serves as the foreign language consultant. The magazine does well, but social life for its main participants soon gets very complicated. Old Dryfoos hopes that his countrified wife Elizabeth and especially their son Conrad and their daughters Christine and Mela can penetrate Manhattan society, but they are all misfits in one way or another. Conrad would rather be a minister than a businessman. Christine falls in love with Beaton, who does not reciprocate. Mela remains rather silly. Fulkerson admires peppy Madison Woodburn, who with her father, a courtly, unreconstructed colonel from Virginia, boards where Fulkerson does. The colonel wants Fulkerson to publish his proslavery essays.

Next comes trouble. At a celebratory banquet given by Dryfoos for key magazine personnel, Lindau voices radical opinions and angers his host, who orders March to fire him. March would be in a moral dilemma except that the high-principled Lindau resigns. Dryfoos continues his destructive ways, however, by arguing with his son and by snubbing Beaton. In a general streetcar strike, Lindau is fatally clubbed by the police and Conrad is accidentally killed by a stray bullet. Remorseful now, old Dryfoos has Lindau's funeral service held in the Dryfoos home. He persuades Beaton to call again on Christine, who, however, despite a lingering affection for him, rebuffs and even claws him. Dryfoos sells *Every Other Week* to Fulkerson and March on easy terms and takes his family to Paris, which relishes American plutocrats. Fulkerson weds Miss Woodburn. March has a fine magazine to edit. It is reported that Christine is engaged to an impoverished French aristocrat.

Howells, in *A Hazard of New Fortunes*, capitalizes on the popularity of Basil and Isabel March, who appeared in one of his earlier novels (*Their Wedding Journey* [1872]) as well as in three short stories and who would appear again in three later novels (*The Shadow of a Dream* [1890], *An Open-Eyed Conspiracy* [1897], and *Their Silver Wedding Journey** [1899]). March's gentle lectures to his uneasy wife, which combine secular Christianity and a kind of fatalism, are echoes of Howells's own social philosophy. Conrad Dryfoos's radical Christian socialism springs from Howells's excited reading of Leo Tolstoy (beginning in 1885). March's chancy move from respectable Boston to vibrant but slum-blighted New York parallels Howells's identical move in 1888; the dark tones of the novel owe much to the fact that during its composition, the novelist's daughter died at the age of twenty-six. Several well-drawn minor characters figure in the social, political, and artistic background. The banquet and the strike are pivotal dramatic scenes. *A Hazard of New Fortunes* is a panoramic novel that exposes levels of Manhattan life, presents a diversity of characters, and defines (but does not solve) America's problems with respect to social justice and artistic expression. When it first appeared, it came close to being regarded as "The Great American Novel." It and *The Rise of Silas Lapham* (1885) are now regarded as Howells's two best novels. (The title of *A Hazard of New Fortunes* comes from William Shakespeare, *King John*, II, i, 71).

Hearn, Lafcadio (1850–1904). (Full name: Patrick Lafcadio Hearn.) Irish-Greek miscellaneous writer. Born on Lafcadio, an island off the west coast of Greece, he had a wretched childhood. His father, Charles Bush Hearn, was an Anglo-Irish surgeon in the British army. His mother, age seventeen when he was born, was an Ionian beauty named Rosa Cassimati. When Dr. Hearn was ordered to go to the British West Indies, he tardily admitted his marriage and sent his wife and son to Dublin to his widowed Anglo-Irish mother and her widowed, rich Catholic sister Sarah (Mrs. Justin) Brenane (1852). Dr. Hearn finally visited his family in Dublin late in 1853 but soon left for duty in the Crimea (early in 1854). Lafcadio Hearn's mother suffered a mental breakdown and returned to Greece, where she gave birth to Daniel James Hearn (late in 1854). Dr. Hearn callously obtained an annulment on the technicality that Rosa, who was illiterate, had not signed the marriage certificate. He then abandoned his offspring and married a former Irish sweetheart (1857). When Rosa married another man in Greece, she sent her second son, Daniel, to Mrs. Brenane. That woman soon sent the boy to England to school. Lafcadio Hearn's father died of malaria, near the Gulf of Suez, in 1866; his mother died in a mental asylum, in Corfu, in 1882. Early in 1890, his brother Daniel wrote from Ohio to Lafcadio, who was then in New York City; they exchanged a few letters but never met.

Left in Ireland, young Lafcadio Hearn remembered his beautiful mother fondly but his seldom-seen, stuffy father with distaste, and he was informally adopted by Mrs. Brenane. He suffered nightmares but enjoyed swimming and reading. Advised by Henry Hearn Molyneux, a relative with whom she was living, Mrs. Brenane sent Hearn to Catholic schools, first near Rouen, France (1862) and then near Durham, England (1863–1867), where he was prankish and bookish. When he was sixteen he was blinded in one eye during a playground accident, and forever thereafter he felt deformed. Mrs. Brenane lost her fortune through Molyneux's unwise investments (by 1867); she took Hearn out of school and sent him to live with a former maid who was married to a dockworker in London, which city the lad hated. Molyneux gave Hearn enough money to go to Cincinnati and get temporary help from Molyneux's sister (1869). First, Hearn worked in New York City, probably as a typesetter, until 1871. After going to Cincinnati, where he suffered poverty but enjoyed voracious public library reading, he became a bohemian writer (on books, painters, spiritualists, and sensational scenes and crimes) for the *Enquirer* (1872–1875) and the *Commercial* (1875–1877). In 1874 he "married" Mattie Foley, a beautiful, illiterate, daughter of a Kentucky slave woman and her white owner. The contract was illegal because

Mattie was a "Negress." The couple parted forever several years later (1877). (Mattie married another man in 1880.)

Hearn went to New Orleans and, after enduring poverty, dengue fever, and fear of blindness, became a columnist, a book reviewer, a French language translator (of works by Théophile Gautier, Pierre Loti [ultimately his favorite author], and Guy de Maupassant), and even a cartoonist for various newspapers there. These newspapers included the *Item* (1878–1881), often with woodcuts by Hearn; the *Democrat* (1880–1881); and the *Times-Democrat* (1881–1887), where Hearn was literary editor, essayist, and translator of works by François Coppée, Alphonse Daudet, Loti, and Émile Zola. (Much later, he translated works by Gustave Flaubert and Anatole France.) He enjoyed contact with Creoles, brothel ladies, and French Quarter exoticism. At the same time, he sought out George Washington Cable,* whose *Old Creole Days* he admired; through Cable he gained access to polite society and the *Century*.* Soon various Harper's magazines opened up to him as well. He published a book of his translations of stories by Gautier (1882) and then a larger book, entitled *Stray Leaves from Strange Literature* (1884), which retells folktales from almost a dozen cultures, from Arabic to Eskimo. In 1884, he came upon Japanese art at the World Industrial Exposition, in New Orleans, where he met Ichizo Hattori, the manager of the Japanese exhibit there. Hearn also relished a vacation at Grand Isle, south of New Orleans. In 1885, he published a Creole cookbook and a book of Creole proverbs, vacationed in Florida, and dug into the works of Herbert Spencer, John Fiske,* and the great Russian novelists. In 1887 he published six of his poetic little stories as *Some Chinese Ghosts*, finished *Chita: A Memory of Last Island*,* and cruised to Martinique, French West Indies. To Hearn, Martinique, unspoiled by modern civilization, was ripe for literary plucking. He roamed the island—even climbed Mount Pelée—in sickness and health, often in poverty; made and observed friends; and stayed until the spring of 1889, when he published several of the many sketches that became *Two Years in the French West Indies** (1890).

Hearn left Martinique with regret and went to Philadelphia and then New York. At a dinner party to which Harper's editor Henry Mills Alden* had invited him, he met William Dean Howells.* When Hearn's novella *Youma: The Story of a West-Indian Slave** was published (1890), Howells praised its impressionistic word pictures. By the time the book came out, Hearn, with little money and only a vague agreement with Alden, had gone to Japan. From Yokohama early in 1890 he sent Alden an essay but then wrote to break his agreement for more work. Hearn was soon aided in Japan by recipients of letters of recommendation from American friends of his, including Mitchell McDonald, U.S. Navy paymaster in Yokohama; Basil Hall Chamberlain, British scholar of Japanese culture; and Ichizo Hattori (now in the Japanese Ministry of Education). In September 1890, Hearn began teaching English, at a respectable salary, to middle-school and normal-school students at the remote, attractive coastal town of Matsue, west of Tokyo and northeast of Hiroshima.

Hearn fell in love with the Japanese—their appearance, customs, scenery, songs, art, food, faults, temples, superstitions, and gods. In 1891 (probably in January) he participated in a tactfully arranged marriage to Setsu Koizumi, age twenty-two, of a samurai family. The two, who had four children, came to respect, love, and help each other tremendously. In November, Hearn—with wife, in-laws, and servants—moved to the southern island of Kyushu and began teaching English and Latin, for better pay but less happily, at a secondary school in the more modern, less pleasing city of Kumamoto. In February 1892 he began syndicating articles through the New Orleans *Times-Democrat.* In 1893 he finished his best book, *Glimpses of Unfamiliar Japan,** published in two volumes in Boston (2 vols., 1894). In 1893, 1894, and 1895, several of his sketches appeared in the *Atlantic Monthly.** In October 1894 Hearn moved to the port city of Kobe to edit the *Kobe Chronicle*, an English language newspaper, but, when he got sick, he quit and decided to become a free-lance writer. Soon thereafter he was invited to accept the chair as professor of English language and literature at Tokyo Imperial University. Hearn became a Japanese citizen (to protect his family's fortune), changed his name to Koizumi Yakumo (Yakumo means eight clouds), and accepted the chair in 1896. By then, both *"Out of the East": Reveries and Studies in New Japan* (1895) and *Kokoro: Hints and Echoes of Japanese Inner Life* (1896) had appeared.

Hearn lectured hypnotically, cajoled and encouraged students, and eventually was adored though always puzzled over too. He met Ernest Fenollosa* and his wife, but he was too shy to respond much to their friendly advances. In his ample free time, Hearn continued to publish steadily, as follows: *Gleanings in Buddha-Fields: Studies of Hand and Soul in the Far East* (1897), *Exotics and Retrospectives* (1898), *In Ghostly Japan* (1899), *Shadowings* (1900), and *A Japanese Miscellany* (1901). These are all books of essays and tales, much like his previous work, and all are informative, delightful, and often scary. He continued to write. In 1903 he resigned from the university rather than take a pay cut. His invitation to lecture on Japanese culture at Cornell University was cancelled the same year because of an outbreak of typhoid fever in Ithaca; Hearn converted his planned lectures into *Japan: An Attempt at Interpretation* (1904). In the spring of 1904, he began to lecture at Waseda University in Tokyo. His summer vacation was troubled by seeing former students marching off to the ominous Russo-Japanese War. In the early fall of 1904, he suffered a fatal heart attack.

A great number of Hearn's splendid letters have appeared in many publications (beginning in 1907). His wife Setsu Koizumi published *Reminiscences of Lafcadio Hearn*, translated by others (1918). A fine edition of his works was later published (16 vols., 1922). His oldest son, Kazuo Koizumi, published *Father and I: Memories of Lafcadio Hearn* (1935). Hearn's brilliantly styled impressions of the Japanese people, their traditional and more modern ways, and their beautiful land will long be admired and treasured. In addition, the French West Indies stories he wrote and the scenes he sketched have an important place among his writings.

Hearst, William Randolph (1863–1951). Newspaper chain owner. Hearst, born in San Francisco, was the son of George Hearst, a mine owner and then a U.S. senator. His mother Phoebe Apperson Hearst was a philanthropist. (She co-founded the Parent-Teacher Associations,* 1897.) While William Randolph Hearst attended Harvard (1882–1885), he haunted the Boston *Globe* offices. He left school (late in 1885), worked as a reporter for the New York *World* (recently purchased by Joseph Pulitzer*), then returned to San Francisco (1887) to manage the *Evening Examiner*, which his father had purchased in 1880. William Randolph Hearst became a reforming crusader who fought against government corruption, against the bribing of officials by the Southern Pacific Company, and against mismanagement by the utility companies that controlled water and electricity. Hearst went to New York in 1895, bought the *Morning Journal* and improved its circulation, hired Julian Hawthorne and Stephen Crane* (among others) to write for him, and even raided the *World*. Hearst established the New York *Evening Journal* (1896) and built up its circulation enormously. (On the day after William McKinley* was elected president, despite Hearst's support of William Jennings Bryan,* the *Journal* printed 1,506,000 copies.) Hearst's constant demand for war against Spain (1897–1898) was partly responsible for the ensuing Spanish-American War* (1898). Hearst again unsuccessfully supported Bryan against McKinley during the next presidential campaign (1900), calling McKinley and his friend Mark Hanna* servants of the big commercial trusts. Hearst began to advocate numerous reforms in utilities, as well as in politics and education. He bought the New York *Morning Advertiser* and combined it with the *Morning Journal*. In Chicago, he established the *Evening American* (1900) and then the *Examiner* (1902); in Boston, the *American* (1904). He continued to buy, found, and consolidate city newspapers in several states; ultimately, he owned twenty-three in eighteen widely separated cities. He established the Hearst News Service (1900) with news-gathering reporters scattered around the world. His news service and its numerous subsidiaries became the world's largest.

Hearst was also, by acquisitions, the leading publisher of magazines, beginning with *Motor* (1903) and later including *Cosmopolitan Magazine*,* *Good Housekeeping*, and *Harper's Bazaar*. He also bought up radio stations and motion-picture companies. He was president of the National Association of Democratic Clubs (1900–1901). He also represented New York in Congress (1903–1907).

Hearst is now in considerable disrepute for being an advocate of sensational journalism, for advocating war against Spain and later against Mexico, and for being generally ultranationalistic and also racist. Hearst married dancer Millicent Willson in 1903; the couple had five children. In 1917 William Randolph Hearst met dancer-actress Marion Davies, who became his longtime mistress in their palatial San Simeon because his wife would not give him a divorce. One of his sons, Randolph Apperson Hearst, was the father of Patricia Campbell "Patty" Hearst Davies (born 1954).

Heaton, Augustus George (1844–1930). (Alternate name: Augustus Goodyear Heaton.) Painter and author. Born in Philadelphia, Heaton manifested an interest in art from childhood and was sent by his wealthy parents to Paris (1863–1865), where he became the first American to study at L'Ecole des Beaux-Arts. When he returned to Philadelphia, he taught at the School of Design for Women (1865–1867). He then began to enjoy success as a popular painter of portraits and historical scenes. Heaton moved to New York, married Ada W. Griswold in 1874 (the couple had three children), and, in a few years, took his family to Paris (1878–1884). He enjoyed his association with his fellow expatriates. He also enjoyed working vacations to Spain (1881) and Italy (1882–1883). While in Spain, he studied background material for his most famous painting, *The Return of Columbus* (1883). It was bought by Congress for the U.S. Capitol and was exhibited at the World's Columbian Exposition* (Chicago, 1893). Another excellent work of his is *Hardships of Emigration*. Both of these paintings were the basis of American postage stamps (*see* Commemorative Postage Stamps). In later life, Heaton resided in Washington, D.C. (from 1884), where he painted many portraits, some of them of political celebrities. Heaton was also the author of *A Treatise on the Coinage of the United States Branch Mints* (1893), *The Heart of David—The Psalmist King* (1900), and several other works including a book of poetry.

Heinemann, William (1863–1910). Publisher of fiction, drama, and translations. Born in Surrey, England, he studied music in England and Germany and later worked for an English publisher. He founded his own firm (1890) and published and republished works by many significant American writers, including his friends Stephen Crane,* Harold Frederic,* and Henry James.*

Heinz, Henry John (1844–1919). Manufacturer of prepared food. Born in Pittsburgh, he worked as a bookkeeper and general helper in his father's brickyard and took courses at Duff's Business College (in Pittsburgh). From the age of eight, he sold fruit and vegetables grown in the Heinz family's four-acre garden. He steadily improved production, made frequent deliveries by wagon to local grocers, and ran an unsuccessful company selling horseradish (1869–1875). In 1876 Heinz, with a brother and a cousin for a time, began his world-famous business with the manufacture of pickles, condiments, and other processed food. In 1888 he reorganized the company as the H. J. Heinz Company, built its main plant (1889, with later additions), received medals and other prizes for his products at the Paris Exposition (1889) and the World's Columbian Exposition* (Chicago, 1893), adopted the catchy advertising slogan "57 Varieties" (1896), and led his flourishing company into the twentieth century.

Heinz pioneered in American pure-food movements and was known for his excellent relations with labor. At the time of his death, the company was the largest of its kind in the world. It had many American branches and three outside the United States—in Canada, England, and Spain. Heinz was a Sunday-school superintendent for twenty-five years; served on many civic, charitable, and educational committees; was generous to educational institutions; traveled widely in his later years; and collected watches, canes, and art objects made of ivory. Heinz married Sarah Sloan Young in 1869 (the couple had five children, and Mrs. Heinz died in 1894). H. J. Heinz's fortune at his death was valued at $4,000,000. Their third child, Howard Covode Heinz (1877–1941), was the father of Henry John Heinz II (1908–1987), who was the father of Senator Henry John Heinz III (1938–1991) of Pennsylvania.

Heinze, F. Augustus (1869–1914). (Full name: Frederick Augustus Heinze.) Miner and industrialist. He was born in Brooklyn. His father was German, Jewish, and Lutheran in descent; his mother, Connecticut-Yankee and Irish. Heinze was educated at the Brooklyn Polytechnic Institute, in Germany, and at Columbia University's School of Mines. After graduating from Columbia (1889), he became a mining engineer in Butte, Montana, returned briefly to New York to help edit the *Engineering and Mining Journal* (1891), then returned to Montana to vie with William A. Clark* and Marcus Daly* for control of copper production in the West. Heinze leased a mine, manipulated it in a crooked manner to give himself all the profits, organized his own ore-purchasing firm (1893), built his own smelter, leased an abandoned mine and bought a working one (1895), made millions, contrived other deals, and extended his operations (including railroads) into Canada. When the Amalgamated Copper Company sued him, Heinze used the law, bribes and other tricks, powerful eloquence, public sympathy against established companies, well-treated workers, and friendly judges to defeat his big rival. Then he legally exploited copper veins lying beneath Amalgamated's own closed mines. Amalgamated fought back (1903) in less biased courts and bought most of Heinze's holdings for $10,500,000 (1906), whereupon Heinze proceeded to found the United Copper Company (1906). The Standard Oil Company, directed in large part by Henry Huttleston Rogers,* controlled Amalgamated and fought Heinze's new company, which was weakened considerably by the Panic of 1907. Heinze married a divorced actress named Berenice Golden Henderson in 1910; they had one child, were divorced, but became reconciled the year of her death (1913). S. S. McClure* published an exposé of Heinze in his magazine (1907).

Henri, Robert (1865–1929). (Original name: Robert Henry Cozad.) Painter. He was born in Cincinnati. His father, a retired professional gambler, founded Cozad, Nebraska, to which he had moved his family in 1873. He shot and killed a man, and although the act was in self-defense he fled anyway (1882). The family reassembled in Denver, moved to New Jersey, and took new names. Henri attended the Pennsylvania Academy of the Fine Arts in Philadelphia (1886–1888), studied in Paris (1888–1891), was admitted to L'Ecole des Beaux-Arts (1891), but soon rebelled against its methods, and returned to the Pennsylvania

Academy (1891–1892). Henri became an intermittent member of the faculty at the Philadelphia School of Design for Women (1892–1900). He proved to be an influential thinker and conversationalist during informal gatherings at his studio. Until the mid–1890s he was an Impressionist, after which, because of more study and work in Europe (1896–1900), he developed the use of darker, less sunny colors and broader strokes. He exhibited portraits at the Paris Salon (1896, 1897) and also enjoyed a huge one-man show in Philadelphia (1897).

In Paris in 1899, Henri painted four especially fine and representative works. *La Neige* shows a horse-drawn wagon and pedestrians dominated by heavy snow on awnings and an ominous sky. Its being sold to the French government for the Luxembourg Museum was the thrill of the painter's life. *On the Marne* depicts a boat moored, with the river off to the far right. *Quay at Carcarneau* offers blotchy figures and strong, vertical background lines. *Sidewalk Café* reveals chic, seated patrons, mostly with their backs turned toward the viewer. Henri visited Spain (1900) and then returned home to open a studio in New York. He painted several American landscapes and cityscapes, including *East River Embankment* (1900), illustrating a precarious walkway on a cliff-like hill at the left and tiny tugs on the right—all viewed from 58th Street. Then Henri concentrated on portraits, taught influentially at the New York School of Art (1902–1909) and at his own Henri School (1909–1912), served as an art judge, grew discontent with his unwanted role as establishment spokesman, and helped plan independent and counterculture exhibitions.

Henri seems always to have been restless and uneasy. In his later years he went to the Far West, Europe, and Ireland for new subjects; and he taught in New York at the ultraprogressive Ferrer Center School (1914–1918)—while there, he admired the revolutionary theories of Leon Trotsky, a student of his—and also at the Art Students League (1915–1928). Henri's book *The Art Spirit* (1923) assembles many of his eclectic lectures and pronouncements. Henri was most famous for helping to form an art show (1908) at the Macbeth Gallery in New York of the highly liberating group of artists called The Eight* (and later called the Ash Can School). He wanted to help artists show the lives and activities of the masses rather than either the effete members of the Genteel Tradition* or the idealistic forms envisioned by an ungrounded imagination. Hence he and his cohorts depicted New York waterfronts, cheap restaurants, messy backyards, slums, and their habitués. Henri followed the Macbeth show with the Independent Artists Exhibition (1910—no prizes to be awarded). Henri's work was often too facile, but it was always warmly humane and usually optimistic.

Henry, O. (1862–1910). (Real name: William Sydney [earlier Sidney] Porter.) Short-story writer. Porter was born in Greensboro, North Carolina. When his mother died (1865), he and his father and older brother lived with her sister and mother. Porter read voraciously from his early teen years, worked in his uncle's drugstore (1879), was licensed as a pharmacist (1881), lived on a Texas cattle ranch (1882–1884), began drinking excessively (his father and paternal grandfather were both alcoholics), and moved to Austin (1884), where he met the ill-starred editor William Cowper Brann.* In 1887 in Austin he married Athol Estes (the couple had one child), settled down, and became a draftsman and skillful cartoonist.

The 1890s were the beginning of his personal ruination and professional success. Porter became a teller in the First National Bank of Austin (1891); founded, wrote for, and published a humorous weekly entitled *The Rolling Stone* (1894–1895); was indicted for embezzling $5,500 in bank funds but seemed to have been exonerated by virtue of a grand jury no-bill (1894); became a feature writer for the Houston *Post* (1895); and was arrested when his case was reopened but escaped to Honduras before his trial (1896). When he learned that his wife was grievously sick, he returned home to comfort her until she died in 1897. His first short story was accepted in 1897 by editors under S. S. McClure.* In 1898 he was tried and found guilty of the embezzlement charge and served part of a five-year sentence in a federal penitentiary in Columbus, Ohio (1898–1901). (The Austin bank vice president and one cashier certainly had manipulated illegal overdrafts, and Porter may have been an innocent fall guy.) While in prison, Porter became "O. Henry," the facile, cynical genius of the short story. He used the pen name to conceal his identity. In prison, where he had time to hone his literary skills, he wrote steadily and saw into print fifteen or so stories in several national magazines.

The rest of O. Henry's career is easily summarized. O. Henry lived in Pittsburgh (1901–1902); moved to New York (1902), where he wrote a hundred short stories for the mass audience of the *Sunday World* (1903–1904); collected stories set in Central America as *Cabbages and Kings* (1904); gained international celebrity with *The Four Million* (1906), twenty-five New York–based stories, and later collections; married Sara Lindsay Coleman (1907); and died of alcoholism three years later. Today, the name O. Henry, author of 272 stories, is synonymous with a compact tale that features scenic accuracy; conventional plots, such as mistaken identity, triangular affairs, and bitterness of fate; stereotypical characters, such as the sad lover, poor artist, plucky shop girl, downtrodden worker, rich man, gentle cheater, and sympathetically treated tramp; clever diction, including precise phrasing, colloquial dialogue, and deliberate literary misallusions; wit and irony; and a surprise ending.

Herbert, Victor (1859–1924). Music composer, concert cellist, and orchestra and band conductor. Herbert was born in Dublin, Ireland. His father died when the boy was three. His mother married a German physician, and the family went to Stuttgart, where young Herbert studied music. After playing the cello for some years in various orchestras, he met and married Royal Opera soprano Therese Föster (1886) and migrated to the United States when the couple were both hired by the Metropolitan Opera of New York (1886). Herbert played in that orchestra, composed and played two of his own concerti, and became a bandmaster of the New York's 22nd Regiment Band (1893), conductor of the

Pittsburgh Symphony (1898–1904), and operetta composer. His 1890s operettas include *Prince Ananias* (1894), *The Serenade* (1897), *The Fortune Teller* (1898), and *The Singing Girl* (1899). (*See* Operettas.) Four of his best-loved songs are "Ah! Sweet Mystery of Life," "Just a Kiss in the Dark," "Kiss Me Again," and "Thine Alone." His *Babes in Toyland* (1903) was a later popular operetta. He tried his hand at writing grand operas, but with limited success. Herbert sued for libel and won $15,000 in damages from the *Musical Courier** when it called him a plagiarist (1902). He actively lobbied for legislation to enable composers to copyright their material (1909); he cofounded the potent American Society of Composers, Authors and Publishers (ASCAP) in 1914 and was ASCAP's vice president (1914–1924); and he composed the musical score played by a traveling orchestra for the movie *The Birth of a Nation* (1916). Herbert was rich, admired by many friends, and lavishly hospitable.

Herne, James A. (1839–1901). Playwright and actor. Born in Cohoes, New York, he quit school at the age of thirteen, worked in a brush factory, and read widely. He joined a touring theatrical company and took a role in an 1859 performance of *Uncle Tom's Cabin* in Troy, New York, from which city after two seasons he moved to Baltimore as an actor. He married Helen Western in Baltimore in 1866, continued his acting career there, then was divorced and went to California on tour in 1868. In San Francisco, he acted in several popular, sentimental plays, including adaptations of novels by Charles Dickens. He managed a theater in New York (1869–1870), acted there and in Montreal, and became a director in San Francisco (beginning in 1874), and then a director and leading man in another theater (1876). He helped start the career of Irish-born actress Katharine Corcoran, whom he married in 1878 and who thereafter was his beloved inspiration, coworker, and often his leading lady. (They had four children, including daughters Julie and Chrystal Herne, both of whom became actresses.)

In his early efforts as a playwright, Herne was not successful, but then, collaborating with young David Belasco,* he wrote and starred in *Chums* (San Francisco, 1879—retitled *Hearts of Oak*) and took it successfully to Salt Lake City, Chicago, Philadelphia, New York, and Boston. Next came *The Minute Men of 1774–1775* (Philadelphia, 1886), a critical success but a financial failure; and *Mary, the Fisherman's Child* (New York, 1888—retitled *Drifting Apart*), which, about alcoholism, was another financial failure. In 1890 Herne offered the controversial *Margaret Fleming*,* first in Lynn, Massachusetts, then in a rented Boston auditorium. Hamlin Garland,* who had admired *Drifting Apart* and had introduced the playwright to the writings of such forward-looking thinkers as Henry George,* William Dean Howells,* and Henrik Ibsen, helped Herne produce *Margaret Fleming*. About marital infidelity, this play was too daring for its time, even though Thomas Bailey Aldrich,* B. O. Flower,* Mary E. Wilkins Freeman,* William Lloyd Garrison, Garland, and Howells,* among others, recommended it in various ways. A commercial failure in Boston, New

York, and Chicago, it was not produced after 1894 in Herne's lifetime. Herne's next noteworthy play was *Shore Acres** (1892, with alternate titles), which started uncertainly in Chicago and Boston, but then became a huge success in New York. It ultimately earned the playright one million dollars. Next came *The Reverend Griffith Davenport* (New York, 1899), an unpopular but gripping drama about slave ownership and conflicting loyalties during the Civil War. Finally, Herne wrote and starred in the popular *Sag Harbor* (Boston, 1899), a substantial revision of *Hearts of Oak*, which presents the love two brothers have for one woman, who marries one but loves the other. While on tour Herne came down with rheumatism and an infected foot; he convalesced in New York but developed pneumonia there and died.

Herne's career mirrors the changes occurring in America's critical taste. His first works, regardless of formal genre categorizing, are romantic and stiff. His best and later works are more realistic in the portrayal of the psychology of plain, ordinary, humble characters. Herne's attitude toward drama is indicated in the content—and even the title—of his essay "Art for Truth's Sake" (published in 1897 in the *Arena** of B. O. Flower).

A fire in the Long Island home of James and Katharine Herne destroyed much invaluable material, including unique manuscripts of both *Margaret Fleming* and *Griffith Davenport*. Herne's widow was able to rewrite the former from memory, but the latter is now gone.

Herrick, Robert (1868–1938). American novelist and educator. He was born into an old New England family in Cambridge, Massachusetts, and was soon temperamentally torn between his weak father, who was a lawyer and an academic author, and his domineering mother, who greedily sought money, status, and fame for the family. Herrick graduated from Harvard (1890), taught writing at the Massachusetts Institute of Technology (1890–1893), then joined the English faculty of the University of Chicago (1893), where he taught until 1923. In 1894 he married his first cousin, Harriet Peabody Emory; the couple had three children, but only one survived to adulthood.

In 1894 Herrick published a short story in the *Atlantic Monthly*;* in the next three years, he published three more stories in *Scribner's Magazine*;* in 1900 and 1901, he published four more in the *Saturday Evening Post*, *Lippincott's Magazine*, and the *Atlantic Monthly*. By 1901, he had also published two books of stories and four novels: *Literary Love-Letters, and Other Stories* (1897), *The Man Who Wins* (1897), *The Gospel of Freedom* (1898), *Love's Dilemmas* (1898, a collection of stories, published in Chicago by Herbert S. Stone*), *The Web of Life* (1900), and *The Real World* (1901). The two story collections are notable for several bright, upper-class, tangled love plots, highlighting articulate, emotionally mature females and often related in ironic tones. *The Man Who Wins* presents a physician whose pure love of research is tainted by marriage to a money-demanding woman but who wins by persuading his sheltered daughter's artist fiancé to opt for professional success rather than yet another miserable marriage. *The Gospel of Freedom* presents a modern heroine who inherits wealth, tries but then rejects the culture-vulture world of expatriates in Paris, marries a Chicago businessman, divorces him because of his drive for money and power and his notion that women are not true partners, and opts for a philanthropic idealism. This novel contains an acid portrait of Bernard Berenson,* Herrick's friend from Harvard days. *The Web of Life* counterpoints plot and current events. The plot concerns a physician who prefers an old-fashioned practice to a cushy Chicago clinic and a high-society marriage; events include a fire at the World's Columbian Exposition,* the Pullman Strike,* the Spanish-American War,* and problems associated with Chicago's unprincipled financiers. *The Real World* has a hero whose childhood (oppressive home), education (Harvard), and escape from the East to the Middle West mirror Herrick's own life closely. More significantly, however, the hero after an unsatisfying Eastern love affair finds an idealistic (and rich) wife and the willpower to aid hard-working, less fortunate people.

After 1901, Herrick produced more fine writing, which, however, builds upon his earlier work by continuing to dramatize the desire for success versus personal probity, and the need to fight political graft and dehumanizing effects of modern industrialization. After about 1908 his literary power diminished. Later in his uneasy life, he scored some successes, lost his idealism and much of his public, was divorced (1916), quit teaching (1923), lost heavily in the 1929 Wall Street crash, and in 1935 became governor secretary of the Virgin Islands in St. Thomas (where he died). His University of Chicago friend Robert Morss Lovett* then replaced him in that office (1939).

History of the United States during the Administrations of Jefferson and Madison (1889–1891). A history of the United States by Henry Adams.* The nine-volume history covers major events between 1800 and 1817. It opens with a definition of the physical nature (huge, undeveloped) and character of America in 1800 by sections (New England, the Middle States, and the South). Adams then provides an account of the diplomatic, political, military, and naval events of President Thomas Jefferson's and then President James Madison's administrations, concentrating on the Louisiana Purchase (Jefferson vs. Napoleon), the Embargo, and the War of 1812 (stressing naval successes). Finally Adams presents a view of the United States in 1817, in relation to economics, religion and politics, literature and art, and "national character." His tone is often ironic and bleak (though lightened by wit); in his view, America's early leaders were pushed by chance and seeming need into making decisions based on expediency, thus diminishing the freedom of its people and somewhat tarnishing their manifest prosperity. Adams feared, even at this point in America's history and his own career, that the American Dream might sour. The new country might have grown too big too soon to avoid European-style failures (wars, class tensions, prejudices, tariffs, and defeatism). But he still hoped that out of America's conditions and resources, and because of Americans' intelligence, quickness, and mildness, a superior race might evolve.

Adams was doing research on and writing this work at the time of his wife Marian Hooper Adams's depression over the death of her father and then her suicide later the same year (1885). By doggedly completing the work, he made himself the only American historian of the 1890s who not only continued the tradition of William Hickling Prescott, George Bancroft, John Lothrop Motley, and Francis Parkman, but also became at least their equal. (An 1890s near-equal of Adams's *History* is the massive biography of Abraham Lincoln coauthored by John Hay.*) Adams often compared his efforts to those of British historians Edward Gibbon and Thomas Babington Macaulay; despite Adams's characteristic self-deprecation, the comparison seems valid. Adams's *History* is "scientific" and pro-Darwinian in approach, tracing causes and effects objectively and favoring a notion of inevitable progress. Often narrative in style, it is also dramatic and intriguing where possible.

Holmes, Oliver Wendell (1841–1935). Jurist. He was born in Boston, the son of Oliver Wendell Holmes, Sr., the famous man of letters and physician. Young Holmes was educated at Harvard (B.A., 1861; LL.B., 1866). Between those two degrees, he served as a Union army combat officer during the Civil War (1861–1864), thrice wounded and rising to the rank of lieutenant colonel. He was admitted to the Massachusetts bar (1867), practiced in Boston (intermittently from 1867), taught law at Harvard (1870–1872, 1882), edited *The American Law Review* (1870–1873) and Kent's *Commentaries* (12th ed., 1873), lectured at the Lowell Institute on common law (1880), and served on the supreme court of Massachusetts (1882–1902). President Theodore Roosevelt* appointed Holmes to be associate justice of the U.S. Supreme Court (1902–1932), an appointment Roosevelt later regretted because of Holmes's many antigovernment dissenting opinions. In his capacity as the war-hero son of an intellectual leader and then as a profoundly intelligent and quite witty professional himself, Holmes associated with the best minds and liveliest personalities of his age. They include Henry Adams,* Thomas Bailey Aldrich,* Isabella Stewart Gardner,* William Dean Howells,* Henry James,* William James,* Charles Eliot Norton,* Roosevelt, Josiah Royce,* George Santayana,* and John Singer Sargent.*

Holmes wrote *The Common Law* (1881), which was internationally acclaimed for its combination of logic and style. His other published works include *Speeches* (1891, enlarged 1913), *Collected Legal Papers* (1920), *The Dissenting Opinions of Mr. Justice Holmes* (1929), his war papers *Touched with Fire: Civil War Letters and Diary of Oliver Wendell Holmes, 1861–1864* (published 1946), and especially his magnificent correspondence with British jurist Sir Frederick Pollock (2 vols., 1941), British political scientist Harold J. Laski (1953), and American diplomat-scholar Lewis Einstein (1964). These letters are filled with candid and brilliant if conservative comments on personalities and cultural aspects of his epoch. Holmes married Fanny Bowditch Dixwell in 1872.

Homer, Winslow (1836–1910). Painter. He was born in Boston. His mother, an amateur painter, encouraged her son. He became an apprentice under a Boston lithographer (1855–1857) and then a free-lance magazine illustrator, moved to New York (1859), and was sent by *Harper's Weekly* during the Civil War to be an artist correspondent on the Virginia front. Focusing on camp life rather than on combat scenes, his work there was starkly realistic, graphic, direct, and objective. A stint of oil painting in France (1866–1867) did little to alter the essentially American thrust of his work. He painted many authentic, convivial rural and urban scenes in the 1870s, worked near the North Sea coastal village of Tynemouth in England (1881–1883), rendered harsh life there in subtle watercolors, established a residence at remote Prouts Point, Maine (1883), painted coastal scenes and rugged fisherfolk there, and then began regularly spending time in Florida and the Bahamas (1880s, 1890s). During these years, Homer stressed nature more than man versus nature, and moved from a muted romanticism to a bleak, potent naturalism.* He won a gold medal at the Paris International Universal Exposition in 1890.

Homer's best oil paintings include *Huntsman and Dogs* (1891), showing predators about to range for sport through a scene already ravaged by careless humanity; *The Fox Hunt* (1893), depicting crows about to attack a hungry fox in a snowy scene, in which nature is revealed as both indifferent and enduring; *Northeaster* (1895), illustrating a wave smashing the rocky Maine shore and raising foam above creamy waters; and *Gulf Stream* (1899), depicting a black sailor on the deck of a ruined little boat with sharks close by, a waterspout in the offing, and another boat too far away to help.

Homer felt that he was best in watercolor. Some of his glorious works in this medium are *An October Day* (1889), showing glassy water rippled by the antlered head of a deer swimming; *Guide Carrying Deer* (1891); *Mink Pond* (1891), a delicate combination of floating blossom, fish, and frog in dark water; *Deer Drinking* (1892); *On the Trail* (c. 1892), a hunter and a dog half smothered by fall foliage; *Under the Coco Palm* (1898), a black lad seated beneath a steamy tree; *The Turtle Pound* (1898), two individualized black lads with a grabbed turtle; *Sloop, Bermuda* (1899), wavy waters and a swaying boat under an angry sky; and *After the Hurricane, Bahamas* (1899).

The message in most of Homer's most gripping pictures is that nature displays a disinterested fury or an ironic calm in the face of puny mankind. By 1900, if not earlier, Winslow Homer was recognized by critics, the public, and buyers alike as one of America's greatest painters. In his last years, he changed not a whit his crusty ways and his everlasting love of and professional and personal need for celibate solitude. In the last year of his life, Winslow Homer went blind.

Homestead Lockout. Violent clash between steel manufacturers and laborers in 1892. The event took place in Homestead, Pennsylvania, on the Monongahela River, seven miles east of Pittsburgh. Adversaries in the dispute were the Carnegie Steel Company, newly established by Andrew Carnegie,* and the Amalgamated Association of Iron and Steel Workers. Carnegie owned twelve steel and coke works in and near Pittsburgh, with 13,000 employees; the national labor association, with 25,000 members, was a powerful trade union. Homestead was a steel town of from 10,000 to 12,000 inhabitants, 3,800 of whom were employed by Carnegie and his antiunion plant manager, Henry Clay Frick,* to manufacture boiler and armor plate and structural components. Wages ranged from 14¢ an hour for the majority to $280 a month for a few skilled workers. An earlier strike (1889), which had been called in a dispute over the employment of nonunion workers and over a profit-sharing, guaranteed minimum three-year wage scale, resulted in a union victory (with an agreement to stay in force until December 1982) but had left much bad blood. Negotiations opened for a new contract in February 1892. The laborers were told that the price of steel had fallen, that new machinery recently installed was expensive, that the men must accept a wage reduction (with no safety minimum), that their wage loss would be only 18 percent, and that the old contract would expire six months early (30 June 1892). Meanwhile, built around the works was an ominous wooden fence, topped by barbed wire, and with searchlights on platforms. (The men called the place ''Fort Frick'' and its owner ''Carnage-y''.) The union argued that Carnegie's recent lowering of prices to destroy competition would cost them profit-sharing benefits if they had to give up a wage minimum, and that their losses would be fully 26 percent.

Frick met with union representatives but stonewalled them and, when the men hanged him in effigy and water-hosed his superintendent's forces, locked them out (30 June). Nonunion mechanics and common laborers supported the union, which blocked owners' men and scabs from entering and working in the plant. Meanwhile, even before the lockout, Frick had begun negotiations (20 June) to hire 300 armed Pinkerton detectives (at $5 per day). They tried to land secretly by barge on the company beach, where they were met by workers and exchanged gunfire with them (6 July). Seven workers and three Pinkertons were killed—many more on both sides were wounded—before the detectives surrendered to the incompetent county sheriff and were charged with murder. (None was convicted.) Company spokesmen stated that certain union members would be charged with murder and that the company would never employ union members again. The governor sent 8,000 Pennsylvania national guardsmen to occupy Homestead (12 July). Workers at some branches of Carnegie's steel company started sympathy strikes. The company hired hundreds of scabs, began evicting union workers from their company-owned homes, and saw to it that several strikers were arrested for murder while more were charged with other crimes. The purpose of these company maneuvers was to exhaust the savings of workers by their having to post bail and retain attorneys. (None was convicted.) The company also enjoyed a procompany press and gained nationwide sympathy when New York anarchist Alexander Berkman shot, stabbed, and seriously wounded Frick, but did not kill him (23 July). Berkman was soon sentenced to a long prison term. The workers' efforts in the end came to naught. The Carnegie Steel Company clearly won.

Some workers sought jobs elsewhere; others voted to work for Carnegie and Frick again, on company terms (November). Not all were rehired, although many scabs were discharged. Carnegie sent Charles M. Schwab* to the Homestead Steel Works to restore order. Fifteen years later, its common laborers were being paid just under 17¢ per hour and worked 10 to 12 hours per day, 6 or 7 days a week.

Homosexuality. Homosexual activity existed in America from the beginning. It was condoned by Native Americans, was punished in puritan times, and remained underground in the United States until the end of American Victorianism. Walt Whitman, who died in 1892, wrote about what he called "manly love" in many of his poems, especially those in the *Calamus* series; but he became furtive about it all in later years. Still, he exerted a wide influence, at first abroad, for example, with British homosexual writers and theorists (including Edward Carpenter and John Addington Symonds). The probable tendencies of Emily Dickinson* toward lesbianism found no overt outlet in either her friendships or her writings. The sensational trials of Oscar Wilde in London (1895) shook American complacency and caused much editorializing, usually negative, on the subject.

Well-known American writers who practiced or had tendencies toward homosexuality in the last years of the nineteenth century and a little later include Horatio Alger, Jr.,* Henry Blake Fuller,* Henry James,* Charles Warren Stoddard,* and George Santayana.* The novel *A Marriage below Zero* (1899) by Alfred J. Cohen, who used the pen name Alan Dale, is the first American work of fiction to present explicit homosexuality; however, it negatively dramatizes the subject of naive women falling into marriage with gay men, and it concludes with what became a stock plot situation in early gay fiction, namely, the suicide of the homosexual hero. In the 1890s, Cohen published other novels and also books about actresses. Edward Irenaeus Prime-Stevenson, using the pen name Xavier Mayne, wrote *Imre: A Memorandum* (1908, published in Naples), probably the first explicit gay novel by an American. It celebrates the joys of homosexual love between a young Hungarian cavalry officer named Imre and his young lover, who is a language student in Hungary. Mayne also wrote *The Intersexes: A History of Similisexualism as a Problem in Social Life* (1908, privately published in Rome). This book, based on much research conducted during the 1890s, is the first extensive survey in English of homosexuality in its widest practice. It theorizes that homosexuality is inborn, cannot be altered in a person, and should be accepted rather than persecuted. It lists Boston, Chicago, Milwaukee, New Orleans, New York, Philadelphia, Saint Louis, San Francisco, and Washington, D.C., as "homosexual capitals." Next may be mentioned Stoddard's *For the Pleasure of His Company* (1903) and Fuller's

Bertram Cope's Year (1919). A nonfictional work of the period is Josiah Flynt's *Homosexuality among Tramps* (1900—*see* Crime).

The 1920s and 1930s did little to advance the cause of homosexual fiction, but after World War II much progress was made, although McCarthyism applied a temporary damper by equating homosexuality with communism. No American lesbian fiction of consequence appeared before Gertrude Stein treated the subject, though only obliquely, beginning in the 1920s.

No important homosexual poetry appeared in the United States between Whitman and the 1920s. Plays in the 1890s presented occasional gays or lesbians on stage, but with extreme ambiguity or as objects to be ridiculed by the audience.

The Honorable Peter Stirling, and What People Thought of Him (1894). Novel by Paul Leicester Ford.* Born in New England, Peter Stirling attends Harvard. While there, he becomes friendly with rich, effete Watts D'Alloi and often helps him get out of trouble. D'Alloi is engaged to Helen Pierce, a banker's daughter. Peter falls in love with her, but she makes the mistake of marrying D'Alloi. Aided at first by his widowed mother, Stirling becomes a successful New York lawyer and gains prominence in municipal politics by exposing the deliberate sale of tainted milk which caused the death of many children in New York's slums. Despite being a "practical idealist," he rises through ward work to the position of Democratic Party boss. He is sensibly willing to change with the times, if he can do so honestly. When D'Alloi sires an illegitimate child elsewhere, Stirling, to keep Helen from learning that her husband is unfaithful, lets it be thought that he is the father. Stirling continues to rise in politics, to the state level, despite pettiness and corruption all about him, and he becomes a benevolent "boss." His honor is tested when, campaigning for governor, he feels obligated to reveal his sincere, fundamental conservativism during a strike and thus loses the labor vote. He leads his militia regiment against the strikers, is wounded by a bomb, and is nursed back to health by Helen D'Alloi and by Leonore, the daughter of Helen and Watts. When Stirling falls in love with Leonore, he must gain her mother's approval of the match without revealing her husband's ancient sin. Virtue triumphs, and the novel ends happily: Stirling is elected governor and marries Leonore.

Peter Stirling is an admirable role model for pragmatic political leaders. At one point he says, "I have taken the world and humanity as it is. . . . I admire men who stand for noble impossibilities. But I have given my life to the doing of small possibilities." Clearly, Ford hoped that this novel would improve the America of the 1890s, with its slums, labor unrest, corporate and political dishonesty, and anarchy. *The Honorable Peter Stirling* was inspired by Ford's unsuccessful attempts to enter Brooklyn city politics and his consequent observation of the shoddiness therein. Its great popularity resulted in part from the belief, based on shaky evidence, that Ford deliberately patterned his incorruptible hero on the early career of Grover Cleveland.* Both Stirling and Cleveland were forceful, courageous, and honest; in addition, Cleveland was accused in the 1884 presidential campaign of having sired an illegitimate daughter.

Hopkins, Mark (1813–1878). Railroad builder and one of The Big Four.* (The other three are Charles Crocker, Collis P. Huntington, and Leland Stanford.)

Hopkins, Sarah Winnemucca. *See* Winnemucca, Sarah.

Hovey, Richard (1864–1900). Poet. He was born in Normal, Illinois. His father, a Vermont-born Dartmouth graduate, had been the principal of the Framington Academy in Massachusetts and had then married a teacher there and moved to Illinois, where he became the first president of the teachers' college in Normal, Illinois. Soon after the Civil War, in which the father served and attained the rank of major general in the Union army, the Hovey family moved to Washington, D.C., where young Richard was mostly taught by his mother. He graduated from Dartmouth (1885), acted in amateur theatrical shows in Washington, entered a New York seminary to train for the Episcopal priesthood (but soon quit), met Bliss Carman* and took a New England walking tour with him (1887), and knocked about as a lecturer and an actor here and there (1888–1891). Hovey met Henrietta Knapp Russell in Washington in 1890 and traveled abroad with her (1891–1892). She was fourteen years his senior and in addition was married to an actor named Edmund Russell. She bore Hovey a son in Paris (1892). She was an established literary lioness and an expert on Delsartism (advocating loose clothes, body poise, breathing control to improve speech, and exercise). After her divorce (1893), she married Hovey in Boston (1894), amid much gossip and uneasiness. But theirs was a happy marriage on the physical, psychological, intellectual, and spiritual levels. It began with two years in England and France (1894–1896). In Paris Hovey associated with the Symbolists, especially Stéphane Mallarmé. Richard and Henrietta Hovey returned to the United States, where for a long while Hovey struggled in poverty to continue his literary career. He began to teach English literature at Barnard College, New York (1898) but became sick, was hospitalized, and died of testicular varicocele and a blood clot in the heart.

Hovey and Carman coauthored their *Songs from Vagabondia* (1894), which helped establish both young men as popular poets; *More Songs from Vagabondia* (1896); and *Last Songs from Vagabondia* (1900). (*See* Songs.) To these works Hovey contributed an open-road, Whitmanesque quality; Carman injected traces of melancholy. Later came Carman's *Echoes from Vagabondia* (1912). In 1891, Hovey had issued his own *Launcelot and Guenevere: A Poem in Dramas* as the first volume of a project originally planned as six plays and three masques, all presenting the story of King Arthur's wife and his—and her!—favorite knight. This whole idea was surely a serious artistic mistake. Hovey could have written poetry, drama, and perhaps even fiction reflecting America's many problems in the 1890s. In love himself like Launcelot with a married woman in 1891, Hovey wanted to present the dilemma of a man torn between a desire to satisfy established society and his own personal aims. In this book and in *The Marriage of Guenevere: A Tragedy* (1895, published by Herbert S. Stone* of Chicago), *Birth of Galahad* (1898), *The Quest of Merlin* (1898), *Taliesin: A Masque* (1899), and the posthumous volume *The Holy Graal and Other Fragments by Richard Hovey, Being the Uncompleted Parts of the Arthurian Dramas* (1907, edited and annotated by Hovey's widow), Hovey rearranged the plot already altered by Alfred, Lord Tennyson and others from the plot of Sir Thomas Malory and others. In Hovey's version, Arthur is a harsh ruler, Launcelot a tender lover, Guenevere a domineering rebel (like Mrs. Russell), Galahad the son of Launcelot and Guenevere, and Taliesin a poetic prophet (such as the ambitious Hovey thought himself to be).

Other works by Hovey are *Seaward: An Elegy on the Death of Thomas William Parsons* (1893)—Parsons (1819–1892), a minor Boston poet and translator of Dante, was Hovey's friend—*Along the Trail* (1898), and *To the End of the Trail* (1908), also handled by Henrietta Hovey. Hovey also published his translations of the plays of Maurice Maeterlinck: four in 1894 and four more in 1896. Hovey had met Maeterlinck—the distinguished Belgian dramatist, poet, and essayist—in London and was greatly impressed by him. Worth commenting on today are a few of Hovey's poems in *Along the Trail*. His superpatriotic lines in praise of America's idealistic mission during the Spanish-American War* are now an embarrassment. For example, "Great is war—great and fair! / The terrors of his face are grand and sweet." Better are the liberal love poems in the collection and Hovey's sensitive translations from Mallarmé and other French poets. But best are his so-called Dartmouth Lyrics, which include some of the most rousing college songs ever composed in America; for example, "Ho, a song by the fire! / Pass the pipes, fill the bowl! "

How the Other Half Lives: Studies among the Tenements of New York (1890). Book-length, illustrated, socioeconomic study of poverty in New York by Jacob Riis.* This volume grew generally out of Riis's twenty-year observation of New York slum life (partly as a police reporter) and specifically out of several of his 1889 essays, including "How the Other Half Lives" (*Scribner's Magazine*,* December). *How the Other Half Lives* begins by tracing the genesis of tenement buildings. Riis describes life in these horrible tenements, the streets and alleys just outside, the saloons, sweatshops, and cheap lodging houses, the tramps, and the crime. He specifically discusses Italians, Chinese, Jews, "Bohemians," Irish, and other groups (with occasional tinges of racial prejudice); laments the plight of children (underage workers and trained beggars, hungry "waifs" and "Arabs"); adverts to the modicum of reform in the past twenty years; and concludes with "How the Case Now Stands."

Riis's immediate intent in writing the book was to urge better housing for the disadvantaged, so that the miseries of slum life might be mitigated. His focus is on the impoverished immigrant section of Manhattan, with its dark and crowded tenement rooms, rattletrap churches and schools, cramped sweatshops, tawdry little stores, corrupt ward politics and police brutality, and stale-beer dives and opium joints. His hope was to strengthen the Christian family, to promote acculturation of diverse ethnic groups, to minimize if not eliminate the dishonesty of municipal leaders, to provide opportunities for willing workers to afford better housing, and to give little boys and girls a better childhood. Riis was outraged by the paradox of a rich and democratic nation ignoring the masses and tolerating poverty. *How the Other Half Lives* is a gripping classic, which thrusts its contents on the reader by a combination of graphic, reportorial narration and compelling, unassailable statistics.

Howells, William Dean (1837–1920). Novelist, short-story writer, travel writer, playwright, poet, editor, literary critic, and autobiographer. Born in Martin's Ferry, Ohio, Howells worked as a typesetter before he was a teenager. He became a journalist in Columbus (1851), published his first poem (1851) and first short story (1853), read assiduously and studied several languages on his own, became a legislative reporter (in Columbus in 1857) and a newspaper city editor (Cincinnati, 1857; Columbus, 1858), and published *Poems of Two Friends* (1859), with John J. Piatt. Howells got his first real break when in 1860 he wrote the campaign biography of Abraham Lincoln, who as president named him U.S. consul to Venice (1861–1865). During this period, in 1862, Howells married Elinor Gertrude Mead in Paris. From Brattleboro, Maine, she was the cousin of President Rutherford B. Hayes, whose campaign biography Howells also wrote (1876). She and Howells had three children: Winifred, John Mead, and Mildred Howells. When Winifred developed anorexia, vertigo, and hypochondria, she was incorrectly diagnosed as neurasthenic by physician-novelist S. Weir Mitchell,* and she died in 1889, which caused Howells much agony and remorse. John grew up to become a distinguished architect.

After the Civil War, Howells and his wife returned to the United States, and he soon became a successful and influential editor of several important periodicals, including the *Nation* (1865–1866), the *Atlantic Monthly** (1866–1881), the *Century*,* *Harper's Monthly Magazine** (1886), and *Cosmopolitan Magazine** (1892). He also contributed regularly to these magazines. Howells is vitally important in any history of American realism, beginning in the 1880s and continuing into and beyond the 1890s. Chronic violent labor unrest, the Haymarket Massacre in 1886 in Chicago, and his eclectic reading (of Henry George,* Jacob Riis,* Leo Tolstoy, and innumerable other writers) caused Howells to favor labor unionism and political socialism and to revile American imperialism. His restless energy is perhaps indicated by the frequency of his moving to different residences (New York; Cambridge, Belmont, and Boston, Massachusetts; and finally New York). He wrote indefatigably (137 volumes, including 35 novels), traveled to Europe often (1861–1865, 1882–1883, 1894, 1897, 1904, 1908, 1910, and 1911), knew too many of the established American writers of his time to list here, and encouraged innumerable younger ones, including Edward Bellamy,*

H. H. Boyesen,* Stephen Crane,* Harold Frederic,* Mary E. Wilkins Freeman,* Henry Blake Fuller,* Hamlin Garland,* Lafcadio Hearn,* Robert Herrick,* Sarah Orne Jewett,* Frank Norris,* Ernest Thompson Seton,* and Thorstein Veblen.* Howells's three closest friends were John Hay,* Henry James,* and Mark Twain,* who regarded Howells as America's best novelist.

Howells's major works, with emphasis on those of the 1890s, include *Venetian Life* (1866); *Italian Journeys* (1867); *Suburban Sketches* (1871); *Their Wedding Journey* (1872); *A Chance Acquaintance* (1873); *A Foregone Conclusion* (1874); *The Lady of the Aroostook* (1879); *A Modern Instance* (1882), a daring novel about divorce; *The Rise of Silas Lapham* (1885), a realistic novel about an honorable businessman; *Annie Kilburn** (1888); *A Hazard of New Fortunes** (1889), reflecting Howells's 1888 move from Boston to New York; *The Shadow of a Dream* (1890); *Criticism and Fiction** (1891), favoring the depiction of actuality, credible characterization, and ''smiling'' aspects of American reality; *An Imperative Duty* (1891); *The Quality of Mercy* (1892); *Christmas Every Day and Other Stories Told for Children* (1893); *The World of Chance* (1893); *The Coast of Bohemia* (1893); *A Traveler from Altruria** (1894), social criticism via Utopian fiction—a best-seller in 1895; *My Literary Passions* (1895), about his love of Miguel de Cervantes, Oliver Goldsmith, and Washington Irving; his response to some Italian writers, Alexander Pope, William Shakespeare, and Sir Walter Scott; and then discussions of Robert Browning, Geoffrey Chaucer, Charles Dickens, Heinrich Heine, Henry Wadsworth Longfellow, James Russell Lowell, Alfred, Lord Tennyson, William Makepeace Thackeray, Leo Tolstoy, Ivan Turgenev, and others; *The Day of Their Wedding* (1896); *A Parting and a Meeting* (1896); *The Landlord at Lion's Head** (1897); *An Open-Eyed Conspiracy: An Idyl of Saratoga* (1897); *The Story of a Play* (1898); *Ragged Lady* (1899); *Their Silver Wedding Journey** (1899); *Literary Friends and Acquaintance* (1900), about his first visits to various New England writers, mainly Oliver Wendell Holmes, Longfellow, and Lowell, but also Ralph Waldo Emerson, James T. Fields, Nathaniel Hawthorne, and Henry David Thoreau, and to New York writers, including Walt Whitman (the 1910 edition adds an essay on Bret Harte and includes Howells's magnificent ''My Mark Twain''); *Heroines of Fiction* (1901), on characters in Jane Austen, Fanny Burney, Daniel Defoe, Maria Edgeworth, Henry Fielding, and Henry James; *A Pair of Patient Lovers* (1901); *The Kentons* (1902); *The Son of Royal Langbrith* (1904); *Through the Eye of the Needle* (1907), a sequel to *A Traveler from Altruria*; *My Mark Twain* (1910); *The Leatherwood God* (1916); *Years of My Youth* (1916); and *The Vacation of the Kelwyns* (1920).

Howells critically defined and creatively illustrated realism in American fiction, but he squeamishly deplored French novelists' emphasis on sex and Russian novelists' ingrained pessimism. Through Garland he met Crane, whose *Maggie: A Girl of the Streets** he admired immensely and provided an introduction for in 1896; he preferred *Maggie* to *The Black Riders and Other Lines** and to *The Red Badge of Courage*.* Howells unaccountably failed to notice Theodore

Dreiser,* who regarded Howells as a greater person than his works or fame. Howells favorably reviewed Frederic's *Seth's Brother's Wife* and *The Lawton Girl*,* but he was enthusiastic only about his *The Damnation of Theron Ware*,* calling it one of America's best novels. Howells saw in Garland's *Main-Travelled Roads** the promise of better work to come and later called Garland's *A Son of the Middle Border* uniquely true to life and shot through with honest feelings. Howells revered *Castilian Days* by Hay and memorably wrote to Hay once (18 March 1882) that he himself had to avoid putting "palpitating divans" in his fiction since his children were his "censors" and "safe-guards." Howells regarded *Margaret Fleming** by James A. Herne* as remarkable and virtually unequalled on the American stage. *McTeague: A Story of San Francisco** by Norris puzzled Howells, who found it new and unsettling, but whose review saying so encouraged Norris immensely. Howells let the fact that the American reading public in his day was dominated by young women limit his fiction, which in his later years younger critics wrongly downgraded.

William Dean Howells, the most important literary force in the United States in the 1890s, will be permanently remembered for his Christian socialism, his social protest novels, a commonsense espousal of realism in his literary criticism, and his timely encouragement of other American authors.

Hubbard, Elbert (1856–1915). (Full name: Elbert Green Hubbard.) Author, publisher, editor, and commune founder. Hubbard was born in Bloomington, Illinois. In his early adulthood, he was a salesman and advertising copywriter for a Buffalo soap company and also a free-lance journalist. He sold his company interest for a large sum (1893), entered Harvard briefly, visited Europe, and while tramping around in England met and was inspired by William Morris to found a commune and press of his own. Returning to America, Hubbard published the first of his "Little Journeys to the Homes of Good Men and Great" (1894). Combining information and adulation, and proving immensely popular, these little essays were issued monthly (to 1909) and finally totaled 170 in number. When collected in book form (1915), they filled fourteen volumes. Hubbard went ahead and established his commune, called the Roycroft Shop (later the Roycroft Corporation), in East Aurora, New York, near Buffalo (1895). It incorporated a studio where artists and artisans made and sold art objects (paintings, sculpture, and pottery), an art school, a furniture shop, a leather goods shop, a smithy, and, most important, the Roycroft Press. Hubbard capitalized on the success of his *Little Journeys* by founding *The Philistine*,* an artsy, radical, popular monthly magazine (1895–1915), printed by his press and including many of his own articles. In 1900 the press assumed the publishing of *Little Journeys*. It also issued another journal, similar to the *Philistine*, called *Fra* (1908–1917) (Hubbard's nickname for himself was "Fra Elbertus"). Hubbard's greatest triumph was his unbelievably popular 1899 essay "A Message to Garcia"* (1899). His posthumous works are his *Scrap Book* (1923) and his *Note Book* (1927). He met his death when the *Lusitania* was torpedoed and sank.

Hubbard was a strange, eccentric combination of liberal and conservative, sincere and otherwise, in thought and in action. He was a versatile and efficient worker, and an often vigorous, crisp writer.

Human Immortality: Two Supposed Objections to the Doctrine (1898). Short treatise by William James.* The two objections to the belief in human immortality are that the mind is dependent upon the physical body and dies with it, and that universal human immortality would be too widespread and too promiscuous. James answers by theorizing that the brain does not produce the mind, which is only temporarily dependent upon it, but instead filters and directs the mind's products, which come from a primal, conscious source capable of surviving an individual's physical dissolution; and, further, that God has created a vast reservoir, a "mother-sea," which is capable of containing and preserving the vital spirit of everything once physically alive.

Huneker, James (1857–1921). (Full name: James Gibbons Huneker.) Critic of music, art, drama, and literature. He was born in Philadelphia into an art- and poetry-loving family. After only seven years of private schooling, with an emphasis on French (he later learned German as well), he followed an ambition to become a concert pianist by going to Paris (1878–1879) to study—and to enjoy himself. He returned to Philadelphia to teach piano, then moved to New York City (1886). In 1885, Huneker began to write criticism of several forms of artistic expression, publishing his work in *Étude* (1885–1886), a magazine for music teachers; the *Musical Courier** (1887–1902); the New York *Recorder* (1891–1895); the *Morning Advertiser* (1895–1897); *M'lle New York** (1895–1899), of which he was associate editor part of the time; *Town Topics** (1897–1902); the New York *Sun* (intermittently, 1900–1917); and the *Metropolitan Magazine* (1905–1906), a ten-center starting in 1895 which, at first, featured nude illustrations. In later years, Huneker also wrote for the New York *Times*, *Puck** (a weekly humor magazine), the Philadelphia *Press*, and the New York *World*.

In the 1890s, much of Huneker's varied literary criticism focused on contemporary French, British, and German novelists, and some on American novelists as well. His predominant influences included Théophile Gautier, Joris-Karl Huysmans, and Arthur William Symons. Huneker liked to show how the best artists in various media reflect their age, have subtle and sometimes romantic styles, are psychologically realistic, handle sexual topics honestly, and interrelate. He wittily rebuked academicians and pedants. The American writers whom he admired most are as follows: Theodore Dreiser,* whose *Sister Carrie** he praised for verisimilitude but whose heavy style he deplored; Henry Blake Fuller;* William Dean Howells,* for his formal balance and restrained language; Henry James,* whom he regarded as the master; Frank Norris,* whose novel *The Octopus: A Story of California** he lauded; Edgar Allan Poe, whom his father had known; Edgar Saltus,* whom he cast as a minor figure in his own 1920 novel *Painted Veils*; Mark Twain;* Walt Whitman (whom he knew slightly); and certain muckrakers, whose criticism of American life he welcomed but whose occasionally cumbersome style he deplored. Huneker felt that foreign writers, including dramatists Gerhart Hauptmann, Henrik Ibsen, and August Strindberg, were substantially in the vanguard. Huneker's earliest books are *Mezzotints in Modern Music* (1899) and *Chopin: The Man and His Music* (1900). Later came twenty or so more books, many of which were collections of earlier essays, reviews, critiques, and the like. Huneker, a great though neglected critic, helpfully countered much moralistic, provincial, dull-styled work of established critics of the 1890s and those following them into the first years of the new century.

Huneker married Elizabeth Holmes in 1878 (the couple had two daughters, both of whom died in infancy). They divorced in 1891, and Huneker married sculptress Clio Hinton in 1892 (the couple had one child). They divorced in 1899, and Huneker married Josephine Ahrensdorf Laski in 1899.

Huntington, Collis P. (1821–1900). (Full name: Collis Potter Huntington.) Railroad builder and one of The Big Four.* (The other three are Charles Crocker, Mark Hopkins, and Leland Stanford.)

Huntington, Ellsworth (1876–1947). Cultural geographer and explorer. His father was a Congregational minister. Huntington was born in Galesburg, Illinois, graduated from Beloit College (1897), then taught at Euphrates College in Turkey (1897–1901). During his summers there, he explored the canyons of the upper Euphrates River. He returned to the United States to begin a varied professional career. Huntington was a researcher at the Carnegie Institution, Washington, D.C. (from 1901, intermittently). He explored Russian Turkestan, Iraq, and Afghanistan (1903–1904), then Chinese Turkestan, India, China, and Siberia (1905–1906). He studied at, taught at, and did research in and out of Yale University (from 1907, intermittently; he earned his Ph.D. in 1909). He traveled in Syria, Palestine, and Asia Minor (1909), and in Mexico and Central America (1910). He was on the Yale faculty until the year of his death. Huntington's early books are *Explorations in Turkestan* (1905) and *The Pulse of Asia* (1907). The main topic of the latter is the influence of pulsatory changes in climate on history, civilization, diseases, and death. He continued his discussion in *Civilization and Climate* (1915). He wrote many other later works.

I

Immigration. According to reports by the Commissioner General of Immigration, in the period from 1891 to 1900 a total of 3,687,564 immigrants entered the United States: roughly 48 percent were from Northwestern Europe, 50 percent from Southeastern Europe, and 2 percent from elsewhere. In 1890, 9,249,560 foreign-born persons lived in the United States; in 1900, 10,341,276 (an increase of 1,091,716, or almost 12 percent). Of the total of those coming to the United States between 1890 to 1900, only 2,609,173 were documented in 1900, or 71 percent of the total number who entered. Thus, some 29 percent had evidently returned to their respective homelands. The 1890–1900 immigrants were distributed thus: to North Atlantic states, about 80 percent; North Central, 9 percent; Western, 7 percent; South Central, 3 percent; and South Atlantic, 1 percent. In 1900, about 66 percent of all foreign-born people dwelling in the United States lived in cities of 2,500 or greater in population. Almost 65 percent of the so-called new immigrants—mainly Russians, Italians, and Poles—lived in cities of 25,000 or greater in population. In the period between 1892 to 1905, 59,647 would-be immigrants were debarred; 6,117 immigrants who had entered were deported—all for reasons (occasionally trivial) of background, criminal conduct, faulty documentation, inadequate finances, lack of family or friends to report to, "moral turpitude," or poor health. In more general terms, during the peak immigration year (1882), a third of the more than 750,000 immigrants arrived from Germany; about 32,000 came from Italy, and fewer than 17,000 came from Russia. On the other hand, during the peak year of the early twentieth century (1907), immigrants from the Austro-Hungarian empire numbered 338,000; from Russia and the Baltics, 250,000; from Italy, 285,000; but from Germany only 37,000. During the period between 1881 and 1910, people from the following groups immigrated to the United States in these numbers: Italians, about 3,000,000; Jews (mostly from Russia), about 2,000,000; and Poles, almost 1,000,000. About 80 percent found work in Boston, Chicago, Cincinnati, Cleveland, New York, Philadelphia, Pittsburgh, and other large cities in the Northeast and Middle West.

A completely separate group of immigrants late in the nineteenth century came from the Orient, mostly China. Some 19,118 Chinese entered the United States, preponderantly California, in the period between 1888 and 1901. At first, they found work on the railroads and in mines, also on farms and in land reclamation, then in cigar and woolen factories, domestic service, laundries, and restaurants.

Prejudice was rampant in the eastern United States, especially when native-born Americans in Boston, Chicago, and New York became aware that 75 percent of their fellow residents in the 1890s were immigrants or offspring of immigrants. On the West Coast, Chinese stood out by reason of their yellow skin, Oriental dress, pigtails, and enviably clean and loyal living and reliable work habits; they became the objects of shameful and sometimes violent prejudice. Conservatives in the United States were concerned that, whereas the so-called old immigrants, those mainly of Anglo-Saxon or Teutonic descent, were experienced in manufacturing, usually earned adequate wages or better, had relatively small families, sent their children to school when they could, and rather quickly sought to be naturalized, the new immigrants were less experienced in manufacturing, earned less money, had more children and could send fewer of them to school, and delayed being naturalized. Conservatives were also fearful of losing their grip on national political, social, and religious controls.

In His Steps: What Would Jesus Do? (1897). Novel of thirty-one short chapters by Charles M. Sheldon.* In the city of Raymond, sick and unhappy Jack Manning calls a rich church congregation hypocritical for singing "All for Jesus" but denying Christian charity to those in need. Henry Maxwell, the young minister, takes Manning home but Manning soon dies. Maxwell, recalling his latest text, "For hereunto were ye called: because Christ also suffered for you, leaving you an example, that ye should follow in His Steps" (*I Peter* 2:21), challenges his congregation the next Sunday as follows: "Ask yourselves, 'What would Jesus do?'—then be guided, for this next year, by your best answer to that question." Surprisingly, fifty members take the pledge. Maxwell helps common workers and fights for prohibition of alcohol. Edward Norman, the owner and editor of the local newspaper, cleans up his coverage of sensational news, bans tobacco and liquor advertisements, pays his employees better wages, and loses money. A rich woman named Virginia Page bails him out, finances a settlement house, helps an alcoholic woman, inspires her idle-rich brother Rollin Page to reform, and is happy when his fiancée Rachel Winslow then accepts him. Rachel gives up a lucrative comic-opera career to sing for tenement dwellers. And so on. Reform proves contagious—with an exception or two. For example, novelist Jasper Chase disavows the pledge he took and continues to chase fame and fortune by writing popular but unchristian trash. In the last third of the novel, Maxwell's friend Dr. Calvin Bruce observes the effects of the "What would Jesus do?" movement and carries it to Chicago—with great success. When a doubtful bishop reminds an enthusiastic woman there that "this is not an age of miracles," her reply is typical: "Then we will make it one." At the end of the novel, Maxwell has a vision of a worldwide dawn of the millennium.

Owing to a defective copywright, *In His Steps* was pirated by ten publishers in 1899 (more followed later), and Sheldon thereafter enjoyed poor royalties. The book was translated into more than twenty languages; it sold throughout the world, according to varied estimates, anywhere from eight to twenty-five million copies, making it perhaps the most popular modern novel. Sheldon published a sequel entitled *In His Steps Today* (1921). *In His Steps* was dramatized (1923). Sheldon's booklet *The History of "In His Steps"* (1939) discusses his most popular work, which was but one of a number of social gospel best-sellers of the late nineteenth and early twentieth centuries. Runners-up in the 1890s were *Black Rock: A Tale of the Selkirks* (1898) and *The Sky Pilot: A Tale of the Foothills* (1899), both by Ralph Connor, the pen name of the Reverend Charles William Gordon (1860–1937). A notable social gospel author in the next decade (and well beyond) was Harold Bell Wright (1872–1944), whose *The Shepherd of the Hills* (1907), *The Calling of Dan Matthews* (1909), and so on sold phenomenally well.

In the Midst of Life (1892). The British title of *Tales of Soldiers and Civilians** (1891) by Ambrose Bierce.*

In the Valley (1890). Novel by Harold Frederic.* Illustrated by Howard Pyle,* this book is set in the Mohawk Valley of upstate New York, in the period from 1757 to 1777. Climactic action occurs at the Battle of Oriskany, in August 1777. Douw Mauverensen, a good Dutch-American settler and the narrator-hero, opposes haughty Tory Philip Cross. Both love Douw's adopted sister Daisy, a Palatine German orphan. When Cross marries the girl, Douw leaves for Albany, joins General Nicholas Herkimer's army, which opposes Colonel Barry St. Leger's British and Tory forces, at Oriskany. When Cross is wounded, he is generously saved by Douw but later dies. The love story is vapid, but the Dutch-German local-color touches and the historical accuracy are noteworthy. Frederic's underlying belief is that the American Revolution pitted classes, not governments, against each other. William Dean Howells* disliked *In the Valley*, as he did most historical fiction, for stressing events at the expense of character.

The Influence of Sea Power upon History, 1660–1783 (1890). History book by Alfred Thayer Mahan.* He followed it with *The Influence of Sea Power upon the French Revolution and Empire, 1799–1812* (2 vols., 1892), *The Interest of America in Sea Power, Past and Present* (1897), and *Sea Power in Its Relations to the War of 1812* (2 vols., 1905). The general thesis of Mahan's *Sea Power* volumes is that a strong navy, together with strategically located overseas bases, numerous colonies and protectorates, and a vigorous merchant marine, promotes national strength and commercial prosperity through exports and consequent invaluable prestige abroad. He pointed to the British Empire, whose navies had caused an increase in its industrial development back home, as a positive example; and he pointed to the decline of Spain and France as naval powers and thereafter as international commercial forces as negative examples. Mahan's *Sea Power* books greatly influenced professional military strategists not only in America but also especially—at first—abroad, particularly in England, Germany, and Japan, in the years before World War I.

Inventions. As in almost any other decade in American history, the 1890s saw the work of a number of inventors come to fruition. Yankee ingenuity was in evidence in the specific endeavors of William Seward Burroughs,* who invented the adding machine; A. B. Dick,* who developed the mimeograph machine; George Ferris,* who invented the perennially popular ferris wheel; King Camp Gillette,* who devised the incalculably helpful safety razor; and Whitcomb L. Judson,* who first designed the lowly zipper. Even wealthy John Jacob Astor IV* was ingenious enough to patent a bicycle brake, a marine turbine, a vibrating machine, and a pneumatic blower. James Naismith* invented the game of basketball, which, although once somewhat ridiculed, now enjoys worldwide popularity. William Painter invented the cork-lined bottle cap. The inventions of other men in the 1890s proved to be of even greater significance. Alexander Graham Bell,* justifiably famous for his early invention of the telephone (with patent validation, however, only in 1893), did pioneering work in the field of aviation, as did astronomer Samuel Pierpont Langley (*see* Astronomers). George Eastman* revolutionized the field of photography with improvements in cameras and films for them. (*See also* photographer Eadweard Muybridge.) George Westinghouse,* famous for inventing the railroad airbrake well before the advent of the 1890s, followed with many other achievements in this decade, even as George Pullman* was perfecting his railroad sleeping car. Michael Pupin* combined university teaching, laboratory experiments, and inventions of significance in the field of electricity. Nevertheless, the two premier inventors active during the 1890s (and before and after), particularly but not exclusively in the application of electricity to practical ends, were Thomas A. Edison* and Nikola Tesla.* The accomplishments of Edison have been acclaimed and popularized almost to the exclusion of those of Tesla, who was his distinct superior in theoretical accomplishments. The inventions of both men are too numerous to list here. Suffice it to say that Tesla is probably still the most bafflingly brilliant inventor who ever worked in the United States—or anywhere else, for that matter. Mention should also be made of Charles Proteus Steinmetz,* the uncanny electrical engineer and mathematical genius. Advances in astronomy, the automobile industry (*see* Automobiles), the motion picture industry (*see* Motion Pictures), and radio,* were made possible by the combined efforts of countless intelligent and dedicated scientists, laboratory technicians, and workers, many of whose names are forgotten today.

J

James, Henry (1843–1916). American novelist, short-story writer, critic, essayist, playwright, and expatriate. Born in New York City, he was the son of Henry James, Sr., a wealthy Swedenborgian who published and lectured on religion, social problems, and literature, and who supervised his children's travel-interrupted and hence eclectic education. Henry James's older brother was William James,* the distinguished philosopher and psychologist. Henry James lived with his indulgent family in England and France (1843–1845) and in the United States (1845–1855); attended schools in Geneva, London, and France (1855–1858), then Geneva and Bonn (1859–1860); took art classes in Newport, Rhode Island (1860); and dabbled at studying law at Harvard (1862–1863). He began publishing numerous reviews, critical notes, and short stories (1864–1874), with much travel in between in England and on the Continent (1869–1870, 1872–1874), then moved from his parents' home in Cambridge, Massachusetts, to Paris (1875), and finally made England his permanent residence (from 1876)—with an enormous amount of traveling to pace his incredible fecundity. He spoke flawless French, felt completely at home in France, especially in Paris, and left London to spend parts of at least fourteen years in France (1877–1908, intermittently). His favorite foreign country was Italy, which he visited at least nineteen times, often for months on end in Florence, Rome, and Venice (1870–1907, intermittently). He also vacationed in Germany, Ireland, and Switzerland. He was an incredibly observant traveler. He bought and resided in Lamb House, in Rye, Sussex (from 1898); became a legendary host there of the literati and others; and held his guests spellbound by his powers of conversation. He never married, although he was greatly esteemed by innumerable intelligent women; he evidently had passive homosexual tendencies.

James published unremittingly, but sales were generally poor. His major books, with emphasis on those of the 1890s, include *The American* (1877); *French Poets and Novelists* (1878); "Daisy Miller" (1879); *The Portrait of a*

Lady (1881); *A Little Tour in France* (1885); *The Bostonians* (1886), concerning feminism; *The Princess Casamassima* (1886), concerning international anarchism; "The Aspern Papers"* (1888); *The Reverberator** (1888); *The Tragic Muse* (1890), contrasting the lure and demands of art on the one hand, and of politics and marriage on the other; *The American* (1891), a play based on James's 1877 novel, contrasting a rich, socially naive American and a corrupt French family into which he tries but fails to marry; "The Pupil"* (1892); *The Spoils of Poynton* (1897), about acquisitiveness versus personal honor; *What Maisie Knew* (1897), about a child victimized by her divorced parents and their successive lovers; "The Turn of the Screw"* (1898); *The Awkward Age* (1898), on British- and French-educated adolescents entering decadent British society; "Europe"* (1900); *The Wings of the Dove* (1902); *The Ambassadors* (1903); *The Golden Bowl* (1904); *English Hours* (1905); *The American Scene* (1907); *A Small Boy and Others* (1913), which is autobiographical; and *Notes of a Son and Brother* (1914), also autobiographical. James also wrote other short stories too numerous to mention. He published fifty-two stories in the period from 1888 to 1901.

James's central subjects were rich but naive Americans in cultured but corrupt Europe, the plight of the artist in modern society, and accommodation by sensitive individuals of the rights of others, however rapacious. His forty-year residence abroad (he became a British subject in 1915) distanced James from most of the problems of the American 1890s. Nevertheless, in his best travel book, *The American Scene*, which reflects his 1904–1905 tour back home, he expresses alarm at capitalistic greed, urban squalor, uncontrolled immigration, and threats to the beauty and riches of the Far West. Most of James's closest professional friends were European, including Joseph Conrad, Alphonse Daudet, Gustave Flaubert, Sir Edmund Gosse, Frances Kemble, Rudyard Kipling, Robert Louis Stevenson, Ivan Turgenev, H. G. Wells, and Émile Zola. But he also intimately knew such distinguished Americans as Henry Adams,* John Hay,* William Dean Howells,* John La Farge,* James Russell Lowell, Charles Eliot Norton,* and Edith Wharton.* Turning forty-five in 1888, James was a little too old to appreciate sufficiently the literary innovations of the younger American writers emerging in the 1890s. Still, he socialized in London and southern England at that time, and, during his 1904–1905 return to America, he socialized with Arthur Brisbane,* Stephen Crane,* Harold Frederic,* Henry Blake Fuller,* Hamlin Garland,* Sarah Orne Jewett,* Theodore Roosevelt,* Booth Tarkington,* and Mark Twain,* among others. Furthermore, he offered occasional critical aperçus concerning the works of many of them, and also the works of Mary E. Wilkins Freeman,* Owen Wister,* and other writers of the 1890s.

For a few examples, Crane and his so-called wife Cora Howorth Steward, then calling herself Cora Taylor and later Cora Crane, rented a house in Oxted, Surrey, outside London (1897) and later rented Brede House in Sussex (1899). Crane soon met James, who lived in nearby Rye and who had already met Cora in London. The two novelists frequently socialized. James gave the younger man several of his books, was photographed as a tea party guest at Brede House, and participated there in a Christmas Eve party, complete with a multiple-author ghost play. When Frederic died in London (1898), James sent Cora some money to help her care for Frederic's children. James saw in Frederic's *The Market Place* what its author might have accomplished if he had had a different lifestyle. When Crane was dying in Germany, James sent Cora £50 to help out. Once he got wind of her unsavory reputation, however, he wrote to Cora—fresh from renewed brothel work in Jacksonville, Florida, yet another marriage, and subsequently back in England—not to call on him again (1907). James, who liked Crane as a person, regarded his naturalism* as too Zolaesque and professionally admired only his potential. In a review, James praised Freeman for handling details of rustic New England well, but privately he deplored her sentimentality (1898). James was an early influence on Fuller, whose work he read (from the late 1870s). On his trips to Europe (and especially when in Italy), Fuller often compared locales with James's descriptions of them. Fuller parodied James in a dull spoof as by "Bret James and Henry Harte" (1884). After Howells had argued in print for James's preeminence in American fiction, Fuller wrote (1885) but never published an essay entitled "Howells or James?", in which he opted for the former as more pro-American and more middle class. In a review, James praised Garland for his use of pervasive detail (1898). The two met at a dinner party hosted in New York by George Harvey, the president of Harper and Brothers (1904). In Chicago later that winter, Garland was James's dinner host and introduced him at that time to Fuller, among others. Garland visited James in Rye (1906), and the two discussed expatriation. James entertained Jewett at Rye (1898), at which time he praised her local-color writing as being elegant, exact, true, and restrained. In a famous letter to her (5 October 1901), he blasted her 1901 historical romance *The Tory Lover* for being a cheap, misguided effort to present consciousness in a bygone time, and advised her instead to depict such locales as those in *The Country of the Pointed Firs** (1896). He saw her again, in Maine, toward the end of his 1904–1905 American tour. Roosevelt and James, who first met in Boston (1882), were social friends but intellectual adversaries. Roosevelt disliked James's expatriation and supposed snobbishness. James preferred Roosevelt's adventure writing to his didacticism and especially to his jingoistic foreign policy. James knew Wister from the latter's boyhood, watched his professional evolution from afar, corresponded with him, offered page-by-page professional criticism of his *Red Men and White** (1896), wrote him to express the wish that the hero of his *The Virginian* (1902) had stayed single and died nobly, and was escorted by Wister around Charleston, South Carolina (1905) during his 1904–1905 American tour.

James, William (1842–1910). Psychologist, philosopher, and spokesman for pragmatism. He was born in New York, the son of Henry James, Sr., Swedenborgian lecturer and writer, and the older brother of Henry James,* fiction writer and literary critic. William James was educated in New York; France; England; Newport, Rhode Island; Germany; and Switzerland. He studied painting in Newport (1860–1861) and became a student of science and then medicine at Harvard (beginning in 1861), although at this time he was more interested in philosophy. He interrupted his course work to assist naturalist Louis Agassiz on zoological work in Brazil (1865–1866), studied in Germany (1867–1868), and earned his M.D. (Harvard, 1869). Chronic depression followed (1869–1872), lessened by a self-willed declaration of moral freedom (1870). James taught physiology, then anatomy, physiological psychology, and spiritually grounded philosophy, all at Harvard (1872–1907, intermittently). His many students and colleagues at Harvard included W.E.B. DuBois,* G. Stanley Hall,* Josiah Royce,* and George Santayana.* James traveled in Italy (1873–1874). He had a happy marriage (beginning in 1878) with Alice Howe Gibbens, a Boston schoolteacher; they had five children.

James slowly composed his massive, classic *The Principles of Psychology** (2 vols., 1890) and thereafter often traveled to England and the Continent (1892–1893, 1899–1901, 1901–1902, 1905, 1908–1909, 1910) to confer with other leading intellectuals of his age, to lecture, and for reasons of health. Through the 1880s and 1890s, James associated with members of the Society for Psychical Research. He was a visiting lecturer at various American universities (1896, 1898, and 1906). It was in 1898 that he announced his concept of pragmatism at the University of California, Berkeley. He opposed the Spanish-American War,* favored the defense of Alfred Dreyfus, criticized those who sought to limit the activities of Christian Scientists and spiritualists, and advocated voluntary temperance. His 1901–1902 University of Edinburgh lectures were published as *The Varieties of Religious Experience: A Study in Human Nature* (1902). His book *Pragmatism* (1907) stimulated many followers (including John Dewey*) but also much opposition. His 1908–1909 Oxford University lectures resulted in *A Pluralistic Universe* (1909). Some of William James's other writings are *Psychology: Briefer Course* (1892), *The Will to Believe, and Other Essays in Popular Philosophy** (1897), *Human Immortality: Two Supposed Objections to the Doctrine** (1989), *Talks to Teachers on Psychology: And to Students on Some of Life's Ideals** (1899), and several posthumous collections.

James's career may be divided into several phases. At first James taught physiology and then shifted to an interest in physiological psychology and psychological philosophy. He reasoned that emotions are feelings that accompany body changes caused by perceiving things that excite. Then he turned to religion, ethics, and the supernatural considered from practical points of view. He defined and refined his theory of pragmatism: Ideas are true and valuable only if they influence behavior in practical ways. Finally, he applied practicality to transcendental realms.

Janice Meredith: A Story of the American Revolution (1899). Historical novel by Paul Leicester Ford.* First serialized in *Collier's** (28 January–24 June 1899) in forty-seven chapters, *Janice Meredith* was then expanded to sixty-seven book chapters. The time of action in the novel is 1774, when tensions were mounting just before the American Revolution, to 1781, when the Battle of Yorktown signaled the colonists' success. The plot combines historical events with the hero Jack Brereton's pursuit of heroine Janice Meredith. At the outset, she lives in Brunswick, New Jersey, but she is obliged to move with the tides of battle, suffers during the occupation of Philadelphia, observes the famous crossing of the Delaware River and the British surrender at Saratoga, and even turns up at Yorktown. She encounters various historical figures, including John André, John Burgoyne, Lord Cornwallis, Alexander Hamilton, William Howe, Charles Lee, Friedrich Adolph von Riesedel, and George Washington, and the wives of Thomas Jefferson, Joshua Loring, and Riesedel. Brereton, who begins as an indentured servant, joins the American forces and becomes a dashing colonel and finally a general on Washington's staff. Various squires switch their allegiance as military exigencies require and opportunities permit. A British villain named Lord Clowes is loyal only to himself; he seeks all the graft possible and also goes after the pure heroine. Minor characters abound. The love plot of *Janice Meredith* is cloyingly sentimental, but Ford's grasp of history is firm. He admirably evokes the atmosphere of eighteenth-century America and beautifully sketches various historical personages, especially Washington.

Janice Meredith was an early best-seller; 200,000 copies were snapped up in the first few months. The novel spawned "The Janice Meredith Waltz," and the description of the heroine's coiffeur inspired the once-fashionable "Meredith curl." It was dramatized (1900) with considerable success.

Jewett, Sarah Orne (1849–1909). (Full name: Theodora Sarah Orne Jewett.) Fiction writer. She was born in South Berwick, Maine, on the coast southwest of Portland. Her father, the son of a sea captain, was a well-to-do country doctor, who took his somewhat sickly daughter along in his buggy when he made calls on his town and coastal patients. These experiences inspired her love of rugged Maine people, their backgrounds, and the animals and flowers of the region. She learned more of value from such a childhood and youth than she did in classes at private school and then at Berwick Academy, from which she graduated in 1865. Always an assiduous reader, she was especially delighted by Harriet Beecher Stowe's Maine-coast, local-color novel *The Pearl of Orr's Island* (1862). Jewett visited Boston, New York, and Cincinnati (1868), and in that same year began publishing short stories. In 1869 William Dean Howells* accepted one of her stories for publication in the *Atlantic Monthly.** She traveled as far west as Chicago and Wisconsin (1875) and assembled several stories for a collection entitled *Deephaven* (1877), in which two outsiders visit a Maine coastal town and learn to appreciate its various residents. This immature work prefigures her later masterpiece, *The Country of the Pointed Firs** (1896).

In the course of writing and publishing several more books, Jewett met and impressed many established men of letters, Boston publisher James T. Fields among them. Soon after Fields died (1881), his widow Annie Adams Fields and Jewett became intimate companions. In the 1880s, Jewett traveled, wrote, and published steadily. In 1882, she took the first of four trips to Europe with Mrs. Fields. (Each time they made contact with illustrious writers. Their later trips occurred in 1892, when Jewett met Mark Twain,* 1898, when she met Henry James,* and 1900.) Jewett memorialized her father, who had died in 1878, in *A Country Doctor* (1884). In 1886 two of her most celebrated stories appeared: ''A White Heron'' and ''The Dulham Ladies.'' In 1888 ''Miss Tempy's Watchers,'' another of her most poignant pieces, was published. It tells how the spirit of Tempy Dent, who has just died and is being watched over on the night before her funeral by rich Mrs. Crowe and poor Miss Brinson, inspires the two women to reconcile their differences. In 1889 Jewett visited her friend Henry Wadsworth Longfellow's daughter Alice, at Boothbay, northeast of Portland, Maine. This region became the setting for *The Country of the Pointed Firs*. First, however, in 1890 Jewett published two books of short stories. One was *Tales of New England*, which reprinted eight pieces assembled from earlier books. The other was *Strangers and Wayfarers*, with eleven stories, the best of which heartbreakingly depict poor but proud old women whose possessions are taken away by time and cruel people. Next appeared *A Native of Winby and Other Tales* (1893); the best of this collection of nine stories is not the title piece but ''The Flight of Betsey Lane.'' Old Betsey Lane, who lives in the poorhouse, receives an unexpected little windfall of money, escapes her confined quarters, and goes to the Philadelphia Centennial. Two friends fear that she has drowned herself, but all is well when feisty Betsey returns, bringing little gifts for them. *The Life of Nancy* (1895) is a grouping of ten stories, including ''The Only Rose,'' in which a multiple widow wonders which of her three dead husbands most deserves the one rose she has—for one grave.

Then in 1896 came *The Country of the Pointed Firs*, on which Jewett's reputation essentially rests. After it, her production shows a falling off, with *The Queen's Twin and Other Stories* (1899) and *The Tory Lover* (1901). The former includes a pair of sketches, ''The Queen's Twin'' and ''A Dunnet Shepherdess,'' often reprinted in later editions of *The Country of the Pointed Firs*. The latter is Jewett's unsatisfactory attempt at writing a historical romance; in it, a fine Tory becomes loyal to the colonies during the American Revolution, joins John Paul Jones's crew, is captured and jailed in England, and must be rescued by both his mother and his loyal American girlfriend. In a now-famous letter (5 October 1901), James criticized this novel for being ''misguided'' and even ''cheap,'' and James advised Jewett thus: ''Go back to the dear country of the *Pointed Firs*.'' Unfortunately, a carriage accident in 1902 injured her head and spine so severely that Sarah Orne Jewett neither fully recovered nor was able to write effectively again.

The Jimmyjohn Boss and Other Stories (1898). Collection of varied short stories by Owen Wister,* illustrated by his friend Frederic Remington.* The weak title story dramatizes the trouble Dean Drake, a teenaged but able trail leader, has with his hard-drinking, disorderly, brutal crew. He establishes order by shooting up their illicit ''jimmyjohn'' (demijohn) of liquor. Better are both ''Hank's Woman,'' Wister's first published story (1892), and ''Padre Ignazio.'' Hank is a no-good cowboy who abuses his religious Austrian mail-order bride until, one day, he destroys her crucifix and she brains him with an ax, drags his corpse to the mountains, and suffers a fatal fall there. Ignazio is a culture-starved priest in the California of the 1850s who, when an experienced traveler named Gaston Villeré stops briefly and tells him about recent musical compositions in Europe, is tempted to quit his mission and return there himself. Later, a bequest from Gaston, recently dead, for a church organ renews the padre's faith. Wister's talent for comedy comes to the fore in ''Twenty Minutes for Refreshments,'' which concerns the dangers of judging a baby contest. Together, the items in *The Jimmyjohn Boss and Other Stories* reveal Wister's view of the Far West as a dangerous but beautiful region in which good and bad individuals clash, and Indians and whites do so as well.

John March, Southerner (1895). Novel of seventy-eight titled chapters by George Washington Cable.* John March is the only child of Powhatan March, an idealistic, naive judge and the owner of Widewood, a plantation near the town of Suez, beside the Swanee River, in the state of Dixie, the capital of which is Pulaski City. John's mother Daphne is a delicate, religious, querulous poetess. The action starts in 1865, when coddled John is eight years old. The slaves in the region are free now. Major (and Reverend) John Wesley Garnet returns home from service in the defeated Confederate army. He greets his pretty daughter Barbara (age five) and plans to run again his private school called Rosemont. When he flogs an unruly, liquor-loving, gamey ex-slave named Cornelius Leggett, Leggett secretly whips little John and departs, founds Leggettstown, officiates in its new homestead league for African Americans, gets into politics, and in time commits bigamy. General Launcelot Halliday also returns, sells his holdings, and becomes a cotton broker in New Orleans. When his business fails, he returns to Suez in 1869 and is elected to Congress. His coquettish daughter Fannie attracts John but also Confederate veteran ''Colonel'' Jeff-Jack Ravenel, Garnet's former adjutant (and later a dishonest local editor). Reconstruction politics, soon in full swing, are thus defined: ''The ex-master spurned political fellowship with his slave at every turn; the ex-slave laid taxes, stole them, and was murdered.'' All of this because ''it's a war between decency in the wrong, and vulgarity in the right.''

Seven years later, Judge March mortgages part of his land to send John to Rosemont, where he associates with Barbara. Five more years pass. Fannie spurns John, who graduates; the judge dies on graduation day. Another year passes, while March teaches school. In 1878 a railroad, bankrolled by Northerners Gamble and Fair, pushes through from Suez to Pulaski. (The line is nicknamed Susie to Pussie.) John argues with the capitalists and Garnet and is morose when Fannie accepts Jeff-Jack's proposal. He innocently plans to make money from his land by organizing an improvement company to sell water power and minerals, with Fair's aid and that of others, including Leggett, who helps develop the land and also uses tax money to subsidize Garnet's school and a segregated one for African Americans. After Jeff-Jack marries Fannie, John takes his mother's poems to a New England publisher, seeks Northern capital for his land venture, and sees Barbara, in the North for a year of advanced schooling (at what must be Smith College). He declares his love, but they agree that each must be exclusively devoted to a surviving parent. John finds the Ravenels in their hotel, where alcoholic Jeff-Jack is abed with pneumonia. John observes a sick mare harnessed to a carriage, nurses her to health, and persuades her rich and grateful (and dishonest) owner to invest in March land. Jeff-Jack goes alone to Washington on business. John returns home with Fannie. Gossip about their train ride together drives him north again—to Barbara. When he learns that a coalition of Northerners and his Southern "friends," including Garnet, has double-crossed him, he bids Barbara farewell and spends a year in Europe.

During this time, Suez prospers in mining and industry; Garnet writes Ravenel's favorable editorials; and manipulations by Garnet further impoverish March, as he learns from Proudfit, a boozy friend he meets in London. John rushes home but gets sick for a year and feels even worse when he learns that his mother is now engaged to Garnet. He recuperates, however, when Garnet kills Proudfit, who had discovered that Garnet had been dallying with Mrs. Proudfit, had shot at Garnet, but had missed. Reverend Garnet is exposed and feigns repentance; he argues with his daughter and leaves—to marry again and become a popular lecturer in the North. Barbara discovers the evidence that Leggett has regularly used to blackmail her father and tells John: Because of a mistake in deeds, Garnet's school is on the land that legally belongs to the Marches. John and Barbara will marry and thus share the land—if his mother approves.

Cable thought first of giving *John March, Southerner* the title *Johnny Reb*, then *Widewood*. The novel is based partly on a real-life confusion of deeds resulting in the loss of "Colonel" John Moffat's Tennessee lands and a school called Fairmount. Cable knew and got the story from Moffat's daughter Adelene in the 1880s. John March's devotion to his wishy-washy mother, as well as Barbara Garnet's to her hypocritical father, may owe much to Cable's obedience to his mother. John's staying in the South may be Cable's apology to the South for his moving to New England in 1884. The main virtues of *John March, Southerner* are its fine nature description, careful and often sparkling (if sometimes tedious) Southern white and ex-slave black dialects, nice dramatizing of old-fashioned battles between the sexes, subtle and witty stylistic twists, and a few wise and pithy little maxims. But the prolix novel mixes serious and trivializing tones and is weakened by archaic interior monologues. The most admirable character is Johanna, Barbara's African-American maid and companion, six years her senior and six times the woman of any white female in the entire novel. When Richard Watson Gilder,* editor of the *Century*,* rejected the manuscript, Cable sold it to *Scribner's Magazine** for serializing (January–December 1894). H. H. Boyesen* favorably reviewed *John March, Southerner*, in the *Cosmopolitan Magazine** (March 1895), despite a tiff between the two authors caused by Cable's tactless criticism of Boyesen to a publishing interviewer. It would appear that Gilder was more astute critically than Boyesen in regard to *John March, Southerner*, which was never a popular work. Still, it has much stylistic charm and solid sociological value.

Johnson, Robert Underwood (1853–1937). Editor, author, and conservationist. He was born in Washington, D.C., moved to Centreville, Indiana, where his father was a county judge, graduated from Earlham College in nearby Richmond, Indiana (1871), clerked in Chicago for Charles Scribner's Sons, publishers, and then joined the firm in New York (1873). He did editorial work for *Scribner's* which *Monthly*, became the *Century** later (1881). He was associate editor of the magazine under Richard Watson Gilder;* and when Gilder died in 1909, he became the editor (to 1913). Johnson coedited several Civil War volumes and persuaded Ulysses S. Grant to write essays, published in the *Century* in 1884 and 1885, which became the nucleus of his later memoirs. Johnson became a staunch conservationist after taking a camping trip with John Muir* in California (1889). Johnson worked to reform Copyright Laws* (in the early 1890s). He started the movement to organize the Keats-Shelley Memorial in Rome (1903). As secretary of the National Institute of Arts and Letters, he helped to organize its American Academy of Arts and Letters (1904). In later life, Johnson did fine relief work during World War I and then served as ambassador to Italy (1919–1921).

Johnson's books include *The Winter Hour and Other Poems* (1891); *Songs of Liberty*... (1897); *Saint-Gaudens, an Ode* (1910), in praise of the sculptor Augustus Saint-Gaudens;* *Poems of War and Peace* (1916); *Poems of Fifty Years* (1931), reprinting seven previous volumes of verse; *Aftermath* (1933); and *Heroes, Children and Fun* (1934). In his *Remembered Yesterdays* (1923), Johnson writes fondly and valuably of his many professional and personal friends, including Thomas Bailey Aldrich,* William Jennings Bryan,* John Burroughs,* F. Marion Crawford,* Gilder, Joel Chandler Harris,* John Hay,* William Dean Howells,* Henry James,* William James,* Sarah Orne Jewett,* Edward MacDowell,* Thomas Nelson Page,* Joseph Pennell,* Gifford Pinchot,* Theodore Roosevelt,* Saint-Gaudens, Edmund Clarence Stedman,* Frank R. Stockton,* Nikola Tesla,* Mark Twain,* Henry Van Dyke,* and James Abbott McNeill Whistler.* Johnson married Katharine McMahon in 1876; the couple had a son, Owen McMahon Johnson, the novelist, and a daughter. Mrs. Johnson died in 1924.

Jones, John Luther (1864?–1900). (Nickname: Casey.) Railroad engineer and folklore hero. Casey Jones worked for the Illinois Central Railroad and died in a railroad wreck, probably when he was driving the so-called Cannonball Express between Chicago and New Orleans. His death in 1900 occasioned the "Casey Jones" ballad about an engineer who dies in a collision caused by his loyal effort to deliver delayed westbound mail. The first version of the song may have been composed by Wallace Saunders, Casey's African-American engine wiper. The song was revised (1909), was popular on vaudeville stages, and was later further revised. Jones is buried in Jackson, Mississippi, where his home is now a museum.

Joplin, Scott (1868?–1917). African-American composer and performing musician. He was born in Texarkana, Texas. His father, a former slave, played the fiddle at his owner's dance parties. His mother was a singer and banjo player. The couple had six children, five of whom sang and played musical instruments. When the father deserted the family, the mother took young Scott to homes in which she worked as a domestic and was allowed to encourage his innate musical talent by letting him play on various parlor pianos in white Texarkana. A German music teacher is said to have inspired him by training him on the piano and in harmony. While still a teenager, Joplin played at church services and perhaps also in brothels. When his father reappeared and demanded that he get a steady job on the railroad, Joplin argued bitterly and chose instead to become a wandering Mississippi Valley pianist and then the leader of a five-man singing troupe, which included his two younger brothers. Joplin played honky-tonk and early ragtime—then called "jig music"—in Saint Louis saloons and dives (1885–1893), at the fairgrounds of the World's Columbian Exposition* (Chicago, 1893), and in clubs in Sedalia, Missouri (1894). He attended advanced musical classes at the George R. Smith College for Negroes in Sedalia. At about this time, he played the cornet in the Queen City Concert Band, perhaps the first black unit to play real ragtime. Doubling the size of the Texas Medley Quartette, he took it on the vaudeville circuit into New England (to 1896).

By 1895 Joplin had started writing his own musical compositions and published the first one that year. Early works, including "Combination March" and "Harmony Club Waltz" (published in Temple, Texas, in 1896), led to "Original Rags" (published in Kansas City, Missouri, in 1899) and his celebrated "Maple Leaf Rag" (published in Sedalia in 1899). "Maple Leaf Rag," the most popular piano rag ever composed, sold phenomenally well, made Joplin financially secure, and helped popularize "ragtime madness" around the otherwise civilized world. Rag was influenced by Euro-American dances, such as the quadrille, the polka, and the schottische, and by Civil War marches, with repeated strains plus subdominant key in two-beat rhythm—properly played slowly.

Joplin married a young widow named Belle Hayden in 1900, but the marriage ended in 1905. He moved from Sedalia with his reliable white publisher John Stark to Saint Louis, where he began to teach and continued to compose. He wrote prolifically between 1900 and 1905, mainly for piano, but he also wrote songs and, more ambitiously, "The Easy Winners" (1901, ragtime) and "The Ragtime Dance" for piano and voice (1902). *A Guest of Honor*, a ragtime opera, followed but failed (1903). Joplin's later years include some ill-traced wanderings, marriage to Lottie Stoke (1909), and lack of success in producing his own ambitious grand opera entitled *Treemonisha*. Its message is the need for African Americans to achieve freedom by way of education. Joplin published it privately (1911) and produced an unstaged and shortened version of it in New York City's Harlem, with himself at the piano in lieu of an orchestra (1915). (No score of either *A Guest of Honor* or *Treemonisha* is extant.) Joplin was hospitalized for syphilis in 1916 and died the next year. Now recognized as a ragtime musical genius, Joplin was posthumously awarded a Pulitzer Prize for his creative accomplishments in 1976.

Journalism. Some American editors and publishers in the 1890s, like their counterparts in other places and ages, were conservative and timid, as were Richard Watson Gilder* and Hamilton W. Mabie.* Others such as William Dean Howells,* B. O. Flower,* and S. S. McClure* were liberal, even brave. Most, however, were situated somewhere between these two extremes, for example, the distinguished Henry Mills Alden* and the versatile Thomas Bailey Aldrich.* Gilder would have stifled Stephen Crane,* whereas Howells encouraged him, as he did a host of other young writers. Flower and McClure were crusaders; they founded their own magazines and advocated important changes of a progressive nature. During this period, several men established new or improved already existing magazines: Edward Bok,* William Cowper Brann,* W.E.B. DuBois,* Elbert Hubbard,* Frank A. Munsey,* and Herbert S. Stone,* among others. Examples of academic editors in the 1890s are Norman Hapgood,* Robert Morss Lovett,* William Vaughn Moody,* and Charles Eliot Norton.* The most sensational newspaper editors of the epoch were James Gordon Bennett,* William Randolph Hearst,* and Joseph Pulitzer.* Perhaps the most brilliant, most stable American newspaper editor of the nineteenth century was Adolph Simon Ochs,* of the *New York Times*. Journalists in the 1890s were of two opposing types: competent professionals, striving for honest reporting and literary excellence on the one hand, and sensational writers eager to exploit lurid news items on the other. The most distinguished straight journalist was probably Arthur Brisbane.* Among the many daring reporters covering the Spanish-American War* were Crane and Richard Harding Davis.* Many writers of what is too restrictively called literature started as or worked double for years as journalists, including H. C. Bunner* and Joel Chandler Harris* and, of course, so did many better writers of the age, notably Crane, Davis, Theodore Dreiser,* and Howells. A few in this category were also humorists, for example, George Ade,* Gelett Frank Burgess,* Finley Peter Dunne,* and Mark Twain.* A special group of journalists was the muckrakers, who, though trained at the end of the 1890s, came into their own only in the next few years, and who include Lincoln Steffens* and Ida M. Tarbell.* Several unusual men combined editing and other activities; for example, Ignatius Donnelly* was a politician and fiction writer; Edmund Clarence Stedman* was a poet and stockbroker; and Alfred Stieglitz* was mainly known as a world-famous photographer. (*See also* James H. Hare, the photographer-journalist.) Two especially noteworthy book publishers were Stone and Walter Hines Page.*

Judith and Holofernes: A Poem (1896). Three-part narrative poem, almost entirely in blank verse, by Thomas Bailey Aldrich.* With many Homeric figures of speech, Aldrich recounts the story of widowed Judith's saving the Israeli city of Bethulîa by charming its besieger, the Assyrian Holofernes, and—though briefly pitying him—beheading him in his drunken sleep. *Judith and Holofernes* is a revision of Aldrich's poem "Judith" (1865). Aldrich also dramatized the story as *Judith of Bethulîa* (1904). It played successfully in Boston that fall but failed soon thereafter on Broadway, in New York City.

Judson, Whitcomb L. (?–?). Chicago inventor of the zipper, in 1891. The zipper was demonstrated at the World's Columbian Exposition* (Chicago, 1893); thereafter, Judson was financed by Lewis Walker.*

K

Keeley, Leslie Enraught (1834–1900). Physician. He was born in Kings County, Ireland. His soldier father moved with his family to Quebec in 1835. Young Keeley went to Beardstown, Illinois, where he studied medicine under a physician; served during the Civil War as an assistant surgeon with an Illinois regiment (1861–1864); and then attended Rush Medical College in Chicago (1864). On receiving his degree, he moved to Dwight, Illinois, where he advertised that he had discovered a cure for alcoholism (1879), opened the Keeley Institute in Dwight (1880), and began receiving streams of patients. He theorized that drunkenness is caused by alcoholic poisoning of the nerve cells, which when addicted require more and more alcoholic stimulation. He prescribed intravenous injections or oral doses of his ''double chloride of gold,'' a secret nostrum evidently made up of a gold salt plus vegetable compounds. He also prescribed good food, fresh air, exercise, and rest. He organized the Leslie E. Keeley Institute (1880), of which he was president until his death. He got a boost in business when the Chicago *Tribune* praised both him and his cure (1891). He established branches of his institute in every state, and also in Canada and Mexico (through the 1890s). Allegedly cured patients, called graduates, formed the Keeley League, held annual conventions (through 1897), and lectured. Keeley also formed a league of graduates' wives. His organization held a Keeley Day at the World's Columbian Exposition* (Chicago, 1893). Later in the decade most of his branch offices began to close, and Keeley died in 1900. In all, his institutes treated some 200,000 patients for alcoholism and addiction to other drugs. Unfortunately, innumerable patients relapsed and took to drink again. Keeley married Mary Elizabeth Dow in 1888. He also wrote and published two pamphlets: ''A Popular Treatment on Drunkenness and the Opium Habit, and Their Successful Treatment with Double Chloride of Gold, the Only Cure'' (1890) and ''The Non-Heredity of Inebriety'' (1896).

Kirkland, Joseph (1830–1894). Novelist, historian, journalist, and lawyer. He was born in Geneva, New York. His father was a well-educated, devout schoolmaster. His mother, Caroline Matilda Stansbury Kirkland, was a popular writer whose principal subject was the rugged Michigan frontier where the family lived for several years (1835–1843). When the family moved to New York City, his parents started a girls' school, and also taught Kirkland personally. His father accidentally drowned in 1846, and a year later Kirkland worked his way on a packet to England. He traveled in England and on the Continent, returned to New York (1848), held a variety of jobs, became a clerk reader for *Putnam's Monthly Magazine* (1852–1855), and went west again, this time to Chicago. He worked for a railroad and then a coal company (1855–1861). Through Illinois Republican political activity, he met Abraham Lincoln. When the Civil War began, he enlisted in the Union army (1861), rose to the rank of captain, and became General George McClellan's aide-de-camp in Washington, D.C. (1862), where he associated with John Hay* and also with Lincoln again. Kirkland requested a return to combat and was brevetted major in 1862, but he resigned when his commanding general was court-martialed and cashiered (1863).

Kirkland married witty, charming Theodosia Burr Wilkinson in 1863 (the couple had four children) and started an Illinois coal business in Tilton, then in Chicago. Next, the mercurial Kirkland worked for the Internal Revenue Department and studied law (1873), filed for bankruptcy (1877), passed the bar, and practiced law (from 1880). Late in his rather short life, he became seriously interested in miscellaneous writing. He published *Zury: The Meanest Man in Spring County, a Novel of Western Life* (1887) and its sequel *The McVeys (An Episode)* (1888), became the Chicago *Tribune* literary editor (1889), published *The Captain of Company K* (1891) and *The Story of Chicago* (2 vols., 1891); rev. ed., 1 vol., 1892), became a member of the World's Columbian Exposition* committee (1893), published *The Chicago Massacre of 1812* (1893), and was active with librarian John Moses in continuing work on editing *The History of Chicago, Illinois* (containing essays and newspaper accounts) when, after severe tooth trouble, he died of a heart attack. His daughter Caroline Kirkland helped finish this work (2 vols., 1892, 1894).

Zury details the tightfisted progress of Usury ''Zury'' Prouder from an early nineteenth-century Illinois pioneer to a Spring County plutocrat. It is a groundbreaking combination of accurate pictures of harsh Illinois actuality (bitter labor, dour sex, death, rough dialect, humor) and romantic local-color melodrama. Hamlin Garland* praised *Zury* in a Boston *Transcript* review (1887) as an example of graphic treatment of native American material. (He and Kirkland later became close friends.) William Dean Howells* also commented on its clear-eyed realism. *The McVeys*, a weaker effort, concerns Philip and Margaret McVey, twins of Anne Sparrow, who marries McVey when she is pregnant by Zury Prouder. The novel takes Zury into politics and even includes a cameo appearance of young Lincoln. Growing directly out of Kirkland's experiences in the Civil War, *The Captain of Company K* places melodramatic episodes alongside realistic vignettes of an ineptly prepared infantry in combat. A precursor to *The Red Badge of Courage** by Stephen Crane,* it has been compared to it because of their similar depictions of bewildered individual soldiers. Kirkland's soldier is Captain William Faregon. *The Story of Chicago*, a workmanlike account, concerns geology, Indians, activities during the Revolutionary War and the War of 1812, and controversial later events, including financial panics and labor unrest, for example, the Haymarket Massacre of 1886 (Kirkland was antilabor). *The Chicago Massacre of 1812* is the result of careful research into the massacre of the American garrison by pro-British Indians at a fort on the site of Chicago. Kirkland began to write too late in life and then did not live long enough to become of first-rate importance in literary history.

L

Ladies' Home Journal. Popular monthly illustrated magazine. Started as a department of Cyrus Hermann Kotzschmar Curtis's *Tribune and Farmer* in 1879 in Philadelphia, it split off as the *Ladies' Journal* (1883, 5¢ a copy) and then as the *Ladies' Home Journal* a year later. Curtis's wife Louisa Knapp Curtis edited it skillfully and raised its circulation to more than 400,000 copies by 1889, at which time Edward Bok* took it over and made it into the premier journal (10¢ a copy) in its field, with serial and other fiction, poetry, essays, biographies of special appeal to women, and features about the Bible, important people's homes, interior decoration (including flowers), house plants, outdoor beautification projects, music, the dangers of patent medicine, and much else. Among the notable contributors that may be mentioned are Jane Addams,* F. Marion Crawford,* Mary E. Wilkins Freeman,* Hamlin Garland,* Joel Chandler Harris,* William Dean Howells,* Sarah Orne Jewett,* James Whitcomb Riley,* Theodore Roosevelt,* and Mark Twain.* Illustrators included some of the best, for example, Charles Dana Gibson,* Maxfield Parrish, and Howard Pyle.* Calling himself Ruth Ashmore, Bok in 1889 started what became a popular column of advice to young and vulnerable women. Later he hired a woman to continue the column. In 1900, circulation was 800,000; in 1903, 1,000,000. The *Ladies' Home Journal* has retained its beauty, vigor, and importance in the twentieth century.

La Farge, John (1835–1910). Painter, stained-glass designer, and author. Born in New York City into a Roman Catholic family, his father was a French-born naval hero who gained wealth in America through shipping, banking, and real estate. Young La Farge was precocious in languages and reading, took art lessons at an early age from his maternal grandfather (a miniaturist), graduated from Mount St. Mary's College in Emmitsburg, Maryland (1853), and studied law. His father encouraged him to pursue art studies in France, Germany, the Low

Countries, and England (1856–1858) before returning to read more law at home. But when he returned from Europe, he studied art in Newport, Rhode Island (1858). He married Margaret Perry in 1860 (the couple had nine children). His brother-in-law was Thomas Sergeant Perry, Newport-born scholar, author, educator, and translator. In 1866 La Farge began to suffer from some malady from which he never completely recovered. He painted pre-Impressionistic landscapes (beginning in 1866) and was invited by the architect H. H. Richardson to prepare murals for the Boston Trinity Church (1876).

La Farge experimented with stained-glass, with particular success in Quincy, Massachusetts; he is credited with reviving this art, as well as that of mural painting, in the United States. He and fellow artists Augustus Saint-Gaudens* and Louis Comfort Tiffany* organized the Society of American Artists in reaction to the conservative National Academy of Design in New York (1877). La Farge followed his Trinity Church murals with murals in New York, including his masterpiece *The Ascension* (1887) in the Church of the Ascension, at Bowdoin College, and in the lavish New York mansion of Whitelaw Reid.* La Farge received the French Legion of Honor (Paris, 1889) for his work, notably in opaline glass. Two of La Farge's closest friends were Henry James,* who praised his work in several art reviews (from the 1870s), and Henry Adams,* who regarded his mind as uniquely complex. La Farge and Adams traveled together extensively—to Japan (1886) and to Hawaii, Samoa, Tahiti, Fiji, Australia, and Sri Lanka (1890–1891).

These leisurely cultural expeditions, early for any American artist, yielded superb oil paintings and watercolors by La Farge. His lectures at the Metropolitan Museum in New York (1893) were published as *Considerations on Painting* (1895). In addition, he published *An Artist's Letters from Japan* (1897), a survey of the Fenway Court beaux-arts collection of Isabella Stewart Gardner* in Boston (1904), and *Reminiscences of the South Seas* (1912). Among La Farge's watercolors may be mentioned *Afterglow, Tantira River, Tahiti* (1891), which presents a spear fisherman wading in placid, luminous waters in the foreground, with friends, the shore, sun-tipped trees, gently jagged peaks, and rosy-brown clouds in a receding background; and *Maua, Our Boatman* (1891), which shows a native seated in tree shade with flowers in his hair and sunlight dappling the background vegetation. La Farge may have been too versatile and too mannered to focus sharply and simply.

The Landlord at Lion's Head (1897). Novel by William Dean Howells.* Mrs. Durgin and her tubercular husband have a farm near Lion's Head, an imposing peak in the White Mountains of New Hampshire. Her son Jeff, age thirteen, teases a neighbor girl named Cynthia Whitwell and also bedevils Jere Westover, an earnest, so-so, somewhat effeminate Boston artist who comes by, boards with Mrs. Durgin, and paints a picture of the mountain. After studying for five years in France, Westover returns to the region and finds that the widowed Mrs. Durgin is now running a hotel in her former home. Westover helps amiable Jeff get into Harvard, but the fellow is soon suspended for drinking. Jeff goes to Europe to study hotel management and then bothers Westover back at the hotel by attracting pretty Cynthia, who is now working, as is her old father, for Jeff's mother. Uppity Mrs. Vostrand and her daughter Genevieve stay at the hotel and later go to Cambridge, where Jeff, readmitted to school and smoother now, shows them around; but he is unsuccessful in proposing to Genevieve, who eventually marries a penniless Italian count.

Two summers later, Westover finds Jeff at Lion's Head ambitious to expand its facilities. Prim Cynthia agrees to marry Jeff if he finishes at Harvard, where, however, he meets Bessie Lynde, who comes from a rich but out-of-fashion Boston family. Bessie's alcoholic brother Alan is an obstacle to Jeff's amorous aims. Westover visits the Lion's Head region to paint the mountain in winter. Curiously he defends absent Jeff's amorality to the fellow's mother; he also admires Cynthia and praises her as finer than the girls in Boston. Back in Boston, he and Jeff argue after Jeff has given neurotic Bessie false encouragement by kissing her. When Cynthia rejects Jeff, he returns to Bessie, but she now declines his advances and her brother Alan horsewhips him. Jeff visits the hotel to help his mother, who soon suffers a stroke; both he and Cynthia remain. Jeff beats up Alan dreadfully, lets Cynthia and her father handle the hotel, and goes to Europe. In the fall, Westover learns that the hotel has burned. When Genevieve's Italian husband dies, Jeff proposes marriage to her, and the young woman's mother writes to Westover for his opinion of Jeff. She surprisingly regards his critical response as a recommendation, and the marriage takes place. In the aftermath, Jeff rebuilds the hotel with fire-insurance money and his wife's wealth, Cynthia and her father move to Cambridge where she begins to teach school, and Westover proposes to her. She will see.

In *The Landlord at Lion's Head*, Howells offers his first seminaturalistic novel. Jeff Durgin is subtly characterized as an amoral, successful competitor amid a family of losers, and the product of a harsh environment dominated by the silent mountain, which is not only a symbol of nature's indifference but also a challenge to the artist. Howells's liking for this fellow may be understood as a kind of envy of his savage masculinity.

The Lark. Humorous little magazine. Edited by Gelett Frank Burgess* in San Francisco, it was issued monthly from May 1895 through April 1897, followed by a final installment called *The Epilark*. It was printed on fragile, brown, bamboo paper and featured pleasant illustrations and humorous poems, the most famous of which was Burgess's "Purple Cow" nonsense quatrain.

The Lawton Girl (1890). Novel by Harold Frederic.* The action takes place in upstate New York, as does Frederic's other 1890 novel, *In the Valley*.* The heroine of *The Lawton Girl* is Jessica Lawton, an unwed mother. Instead of remaining away, she bravely returns home to Thessaly—the main town in Frederic's first novel, *Seth's Brother's Wife*—the scene of her "disgrace," to help other oppressed young women. Her seducer, Horace Bryce, having meanwhile enjoyed a long trip to Europe, also returns, this time to try to cheat Mrs. Minster, a widow, and her two daughters out of the local iron factory they have inherited. A lawyer named Reuben Tracy (a teacher in *Seth's Brother's Wife*) exposes the villain's attempt. Frederic uses several minor characters to reveal small-town social strata. Most memorable is his depiction of the threat the town faces when opposing forces compete for control of the ironworks (located near the Oriskany battlefield of *In the Valley*). Frederic favors enlightened social planning over despotic capitalism, and he shows here that social Darwinism need not triumph. William Dean Howells* admired *The Lawton Girl*, especially for the characterization in it of the villainous Bryce.

Lea, Homer (1876–1912). Soldier and author. Born in Denver, Colorado, with a spinal deformity, Lea was a hunchback and never grew to normal physical maturity. As an adult, he was five feet tall and weighed eighty-eight pounds. He had only an intermittent formal education, owing to poverty as well as sickness, in a Los Angeles high school, at Occidental College, at the University of the Pacific, and finally at Stanford University (1897–1899). From his early years, he read voraciously in military science, especially Napoleon's campaigns, and he dreamed of a military career despite his physical limitations. His acquaintance with Chinese students in California inspired him to study Chinese history and politics and to seek military prowess in China. When an attack of smallpox prevented him from graduating from Stanford, he rushed off to China (1899) and became an officer in the army of K'ang Yu-wei, who sought to rescue Emperor Kwang-hsu, who had been imprisoned in Beijing (from 1898) by the dowager Manchu empress. The Boxer Rebellion (1900) stimulated K'ang Yu-wei's ambition. With two daring fellow officers, Lea sought to aid K'ang Yu-wei by trying, at immense personal risk and without success, to muster recruits far to the south. When Lea learned of K'ang Yu-wei's failure and escape from Beijing, he went to Hong Kong to confer with Sun Yat-sen. The two became close friends and fled together to Japan, from which Lea departed for San Francisco (1901).

In California, Lea trained anti-Manchu Chinese volunteers on the West Coast and corresponded with Sun Yat-sen and K'ang Yu-wei (who was by then the head of the Empire Reform Association). He returned to China in 1904 to command a New China army division (with the rank of lieutenant general), later accompanied K'ang Yu-wei on tour in the United States and Europe to enlist support for the establishment of a Chinese republic (1904–1905), studied German army maneuvers in Europe and advised the British government on defense strategy (1911), returned to China as Sun Yat-sen's confidential advisor (1911–1912), and was offered the position of chief of staff in the Chinese revolutionary army. Because of deteriorating health, Lea was obliged to decline. He suffered a paralytic stroke and died in Oak Park, near Los Angeles.

Lea wrote *The Vermillion Pencil* (1908), a novel about secret societies in

China during the Manchu regime; *The Valor of Ignorance* (1909), detailing plans by means of which Japan could conquer the Philippine Islands and Hawaii, invade the American West Coast, dictate peace terms to a crippled United States, and take control of the entire Pacific area; *The Crimson Spider* (1909), a play; and *The Day of the Saxon* (1912), warning that the British Empire was also ripe for attack by Oriental forces. Death prevented his completing *The Swarming of the Slav*, yet another warning, this one anti-Russian in nature. Lea was a unique phenomenon. Despite tragic physical limitations, he combined inordinate ambition and courage, prophetic intelligence, military acumen, and an almost hysterical racist attitude against the bellicose Japanese and later against Germans and Russians as well. He inveighed irrationally against decadent America's unpatriotic commercialism and racial mongrelization.

Lease, Mary Elizabeth Clyens (1853–1933). (Alternate name: Mary Ellen Lease; nickname: Mary Yellin.) Populist. The daughter of an exiled Irishman, she was born in Ridgeway, Pennsylvania, was reared on a farm near Allegany, New York. Lease graduated from St. Elizabeth's Academy in Allegany, then moved to Kansas (about 1860), where she later taught in a parochial school. She married pharmacist Charles L. Lease in 1873 and farmed with him in Kingman County, Kansas. After spending some time in Texas, the couple returned to Wichita, Kansas (about 1883), where she studied law, became an attorney, and began to lecture successfully (1885–1887) on the anti-British subject of "Ireland and Irishmen." She became notorious for allegedly telling farmers "to raise less corn and more hell." Lease joined the Knights of Labor, campaigned vigorously for the Union Labor Party in Kansas (1888, 1889), made 160 speeches for the Farmer's Alliance and the People's Party candidates (1890), supported the Populist Party* (1891, 1892), was appointed president of the Kansas Board of Charities (1893), represented Kansas at the World's Columbian Exposition* (Chicago, 1893), and steadily supported agrarian reform, birth control, Free Silver,* government supervision of corporations, nationalization of railroads, pacifism, popular election of senators, temperance, and woman suffrage.

Lease went to New York as a political writer for the New York *World* of Joseph Pulitzer* (1896). She and her husband had four children, but she divorced him for nonsupport (1902). Late in her life, she lectured for the New York Board of Education (1908–1918). In a weird book entitled *The Problem of Civilization Solved* (1895), Lease called both for the colonizing of the tropics with Caucasian owners and black- and yellow-skinned laborers—as tenants by occupancy—and for the elimination of war by partitioning the world among Americans, British, Germans, Latins, and Russians.

Lesbians and Gays. *See* Homosexuality.

Lin McLean (1898). Episodic novel by Owen Wister,* illustrated by his friend Frederic Remington.* Lin McLean, picaresque cowboy and rancher in Wyoming in the 1880s, returns home to Boston only to become convinced that his heart is now in the West, where he subsequently meets and marries a boisterous, worthless waitress named Katie Peck. He soon discovers that she was married earlier (*sans* divorce) and happily dumps her. Lin befriends Billy Lusk, an abandoned little boy in Denver, learns that the waif is Katie's son from her previous—and real—marriage, but still adopts him. Lin's love affair with Jessamine Buckner, a decent Eastern girl from Kentucky, is put on hold when she discovers about his earlier "marriage." But all is well again when Katie reappears to bless Lin's new love relationship and little Billy and then takes a fatal dose of laudanum. The literary merits of *Lin McLean* lie not in its unexceptional plot but rather in its cinematic rendering of Western landscape and speech patterns. Further, *Lin McLean* in many ways was a dress rehearsal for *The Virginian*, in which Lin figures as a friend of the hero.

"Lincoln, the Man of the People" (1901). Blank-verse poem by Edwin Markham.* Mother Nature created Abraham Lincoln by taking warm clay and adding prophecy, tears, laughter, and "a flame to light / That tender, tragic, ever-changing face." Lincoln's virtues include patience, good will, courage, pity, tolerance, and Western strength. Lincoln aimed to correct wrong, and "The grip that swung the ax in Illinois / Was on the pen that set a people free." When Civil War "split the house," he "spiked" the ridgepole and the rafters back again. His death was like the fall of "a lordly cedar" which "leaves a lonesome place against the sky." Markham wrote this poem for a Lincoln Day banquet, given by the Republican Club of New York City, at Delmonico's, in 1900. It was steadily popular, and Markham's *Lincoln, and Other Poems*, the 1901 book in which it was reprinted, was popular as well. In 1922, Markham, at the invitation of Chief Justice William Howard Taft, read this revered poem on the occasion of the dedication of the Lincoln Memorial in Washington, D.C., which featured the massive statue of Lincoln by Daniel Chester French.*

Linson, Corwin Knapp (1864–1934). Painter, illustrator, and writer. Born in Brooklyn, New York, he studied in Paris, where Paul Gauguin was one of his fellow students. He returned to New York and began a successful career. Linson became a member of the New York Water Color Club and also the Allied Artists of America. He met Stephen Crane* there (1893) and in the next few years often provided him shelter, food, money, tobacco, card games, and drink in his studio. Soon thereafter, Linson worked in Athens and Palestine, married an American diplomat's daughter in France (1901), and returned with her to the United States. He exhibited many of his landscapes and portraits, including a portrait of Crane, and also was active in executing church murals and memorial windows. Linson wrote a series of valuable impressions and recollections of Crane, which were assembled, edited, and published as *My Stephen Crane* (1958).

Literary Digest. Weekly magazine. As its first subtitle suggests, it was started in 1890 as "A Repository of Contemporaneous Thought and Research as Presented in the Periodical Literature of the World." It ran until 1938, then merged with *Time*. The *Literary Digest* was founded by Isaac Kauffman Funk, an ex-Lutheran clergyman turned editor and lexicographer, and lawyer Adam Willis Wagnalls. The magazine featured rewritten condensations of religious, sociological, political, scientific, and miscellaneous essays taken from a vast spread of American and foreign periodicals; book reviews and reprints of news items from sundry American presses; indexes to major articles in periodicals, American and foreign; reports on new books and significant up-to-date current events. In late 1893 the *Literary Digest* began to include illustrations. Funk edited the magazine through 1895. He was succeeded by Edward Jewitt Wheeler, who built the circulation from 25,000 to 63,000 by 1900, added a poetry section (1901), and resigned ten years later (1905). The *Literary Digest* expanded its offerings and became an extremely successful magazine.

Literature and Literary Criticism. The 1890s were the most fruitful decade in American literary history, in the production of novels, short stories, drama, and criticism, until the long decade between the end of World War I and the beginning of the Great Depression. In the field of belles lettres in the 1890s, only poetry lagged behind, unable to match the fecundity of poets just before, during, and immediately after the Civil War.

Fiction in the 1890s was of two kinds: either it was reactionary, with a stress on romanticism, sentimentality, and folksy ruralism; or it was marked by realism, grim local color, pessimistic naturalism, and fin-de-siècle cynicism. The battle for realism among intelligent readers and critics had been virtually won by the 1880s, with the superb fiction of William Dean Howells,* Henry James,* Mark Twain,* and several others. At the same time, critical commentary by Howells (notably in his *Criticism and Fiction**), James, H. H. Boyesen,* W. C. Brownell,* Norman Hapgood,* and others also persuaded much of the public that remnants of effete romanticism should not be greatly treasured. To be sure, the Genteel Tradition* still held sway in many quarters, and conservative critics, such as Hamilton W. Mabie,* and ultra-reactionaries, such as Anthony Comstock,* tried hard to hold back the hands of the clock. Much of the reading public continued to opt for sentimental serial fiction and novels in book form rather than anything more challenging. Examples of their preferences are too numerous to list with any kind of completeness here. Best-sellers, some of which had considerable literary merit—by such authors as Winston Churchill,* F. Marion Crawford,* Paul Leicester Ford,* George Barr McCutcheon,* Charles Major,* S. Weir Mitchell,* Charles M. Sheldon,* Frank R. Stockton,* Booth Tarkington,* and Lew Wallace,* among others now more neglected—continued to compete for the dollars if not for the minds of the reading public. The creators of realistic fiction, long and short, unsentimental and often cynical, were gradually persuasive, occasionally, however, not in their own lifetimes. Among them were Ambrose Bierce,* Boyesen, Abraham Cahan,* Kate Chopin,* Stephen Crane,* Harold Frederic,* Mary E. Wilkins Freeman,* Henry Blake Fuller,*

Hamlin Garland,* O. Henry,* Sarah Orne Jewett,* Jack London,* and Frank Norris.* (Theodore Dreiser* followed a little later.)

American drama came of age only in the 1890s, because of the admirable efforts of David Belasco,* Augustin Daly* (who was more accomplished as a manager and producer), Clyde Fitch,* William Gillette,* James A. Herne,* William Vaughn Moody,* and several others. Many of their works are still valuable, lively, and readable, for example, *Beau Brummell** and *The Climbers** by Fitch, *Du Barry* by Belasco, *The Great Divide* by Moody, *Margaret Fleming** by Herne, and *Secret Service** by Gillette.

The only worthwhile American poets of the 1890s are Bliss Carman,* Richard Hovey,* George Cabot Lodge,* Edwin Markham,* Moody, and Edwin Arlington Robinson,* of whom only Robinson is widely read today. Virtually all of their fellow poets continued outworn traditions. The verse of many falls often between dull and atrocious by modern critical standards, for example, that of Ina Coolbrith,* Joaquin Miller,* Edmund Clarence Stedman,* and Trumbull Stickney.* The efforts of several other 1890s poets, to be sure, retain a folksy tang, as in the still-beloved efforts of Eugene Field* and James Whitcomb Riley.* A unique poetic figure is Emily Dickinson.* While she died in 1886, her works first saw book publication in the 1890s. Even so, her real influence was unfelt then and for some decades thereafter.

It bears repeating that the most profound literary expression of the 1890s remains that of fiction. Titles include *The Awakening** by Chopin, *The Cliff-Dwellers: A Novel** by Fuller, *A Connecticut Yankee in King Arthur's Court** and *Pudd'nhead Wilson, A Tale** by Twain, *The Country of the Pointed Firs** by Jewett, *The Damnation of Theron Ware** by Frederic, *In the Midst of Life* by Bierce, *McTeague: A Story of San Francisco** by Norris, *Maggie: A Girl of the Streets** and *The Red Badge of Courage** by Crane, *Main-Travelled Roads** by Garland, *The Reverberator** by James, and *Sister Carrie** by Dreiser, as well as several short stories by Chopin, Crane, Freeman, Garland, Charlotte Perkins Gilman,* James (especially "The Turn of the Screw"*), and Twain. Such works stand as permanent examples of early American realism, as well as examples of the response of America's writers to the towering influence of Émile Zola of France, of several daring Russian fictionists, and of other writers of the school of Naturalism.*

The Little Regiment and Other Episodes of the American Civil War (1896). Collection of six short stories by Stephen Crane.* In the title story, Billie and Dan Dempster, brothers and fellow Union soldiers in a Civil War campaign one muddy December, constantly bicker but like one another. Their affection for each other is proved by Dan's relief when Billie, wounded but alive, returns after a gory engagement. In "A Mystery of Heroism," a soldier on a kind of dare, braves enemy fire to get a bucket of water from a well, knowing that his act is unnecessary. "The Veteran" reintroduces Henry Fleming, hero of *The Red Badge of Courage*,* now an old farmer. He is seen telling his grandson and others that he was terrified during the Battle of Chancellorsville long ago. They are puzzled by his modesty. That night, when the barn on the Fleming farm catches fire, Fleming saves the horses and most of the cows, but, returning for the two colts, is killed in the collapse of the blazing roof. The graphic descriptions and stark imagery of the stories in this collection may be compared to similar effects in *The Red Badge of Courage*.

Lloyd, William Demarest (1847–1903). Influential New York–born publicist, reformer, and author. He graduated from Columbia University (1869), practiced law and opposed Tammany Hall* briefly, and then became the financial editor of and an editorial writer for the Chicago *Tribune* (1873–1885). During this time, he became a serious advocate of social, economic, and political reforms. He traveled abroad (1885), took time off to study philosophy and sociology, and published *A Strike of Millionaires against Miners* (1890), which is a daring exposé of the dictatorial tactics used against labor by the owners of the Spring Valley Company in Illinois. Lloyd's muckraking masterpiece, *Wealth against Commonwealth* (1894), blasts U.S. monopolies, with special attention to the Standard Oil Company of John D. Rockefeller.* In it, Lloyd reasons that, if unchecked by restraints on the philosophy of laissez faire, commercial organizations will, as in a jungle where only the fittest survive, practice ruthless takeovers and become monopolies. He urged instead that political regulation of economic forces become a moral science. Lloyd was a philosophical force behind the Populist Party* until they paid too little attention to his antimonopoly theories and too much to the issue of Free Silver* to suit him. Lloyd again went abroad (1897–1901), this time to research British cooperatives (*Labour Copartnership* [1898]), compulsory arbitration in New Zealand (*A Country without Strikes* [1900]), and Swiss democracy (*A Sovereign People* [1907]). It may be noted that William Dean Howells,* as editor of the *Atlantic Monthly*,* accepted for March 1881 publication Lloyd's pioneering muckraking essay "The Story of a Great Monopoly" (which led to his *Wealth against Commonwealth*); that Lloyd urged compassion toward the "anarchists" sentenced to death after the Haymarket Riot (Chicago, May 1886); and that Lloyd championed the cause of Eugene V. Debs,* who had been jailed (1895) in connection with the Pullman Strike.*

Lodge, George Cabot (1873–1909). (Nickname: Bay.) Poet. Born in Boston, he was the son of Henry Cabot Lodge, the congressman and author. After young Lodge graduated from Harvard (1895), he studied at the Sorbonne in Paris (1895–1896) and in Berlin (1896–1897). He returned to the United States to become his father's private secretary in Washington, D.C. He published *The Song of the Wave* (1898, containing eighty short poems), served as a combat officer in the U.S. Navy during the Spanish-American War* (1898), and then worked again for his father. His later writings include *Poems* (1902), *Cain, a Drama* (1904), *The Great Adventure* (1905), *Herakles* (1908, another drama), and *The Soul's*

Inheritance (1909). Lodge married Matilda Elizabeth Frelinghuysen Davis in 1900 (the couple had three children). His untimely fatal heart attack cut short his curious career. Lodge numbered Henry Adams* and Trumbull Stickney* among his closest friends. Adams published a biography of Lodge (1911). Although his interest in French symbolists made Lodge a minor influence on certain later avant-garde prosodists, his poems—stressing loss, loneliness, and fear—have not stood the test of time. Lodge is now considered a third-rate poet with an egoistic, affected, and simple (though likable) personality.

London, Jack (1876–1916). (Full name: John Griffith London.) Writer of novels, short stories, and nonfictional works. London's mother was Flora Wellman, and his father was most probably William Henry Chaney, a bright but unstable itinerant astrologer, who deserted her before the boy was born in San Francisco. The mother married John London, a widowed father of two daughters (later in 1876). The family lived from hand to mouth on the San Francisco waterfront and on Bay area farms. Helping out by working at menial odd jobs from the age of nine, young London finished grammar school (1891). As the 1890s continued, his real education began. He worked in a pickle cannery in Oakland, California (bottling pickles for eighteen hours a day for a dime an hour), as an oyster pirate (in a sloop bought with $300 borrowed dollars), and then as a fish-patrol worker. He sailed on a sealing schooner (1893) into Japanese waters and worked in a jute mill and then in an Oakland power plant. He planned to march from the West Coat to join Jacob Sechler Coxey* in the march of Coxey's Army* on Washington, D.C., but he quit in Missouri, became an eastbound hobo, and was jailed for vagrancy in Niagara, New York (1894). He returned to San Francisco, attended Oakland High School (1895–1896), joined the Socialist Labor Party (1896), and took classes for one term at the University of California, Berkeley (1896–1897). His favorite authors during this period were Charles Darwin, Karl Marx, and Herbert Spencer. In 1897, London struggled to write full-time (he had won a prize for an essay in 1893). He went to Alaska during the Klondike Gold Rush (1897–1898), but, after an attack of scurvy, he returned again to San Francisco.

A breakthrough came when London sold a story about the Far North to the *Overland Monthly* in San Francisco and another to the *Atlantic Monthly** in Boston (1899). His first book, *The Son of the Wolf: Tales of the Far North*, was published in 1900. He married Elizabeth Mae "Bessie" Maddern on a wrong-headed impulse the day his book of Klondike stories appeared. (They had two children and were divorced in 1905. The next day, London married Clara Charmian Kittredge; the couple had one child, who died in infancy. London's sexual prowess gained him the nickname "The Stallion.") Next came *The God of His Fathers & Other Stories* (1901) and more Northland stories, seventy-eight by 1918. After 1901 came the last fifteen crowded years of this prodigious scribbler. That decade and a half, unparalleled in American literature, has become a legend, to which London's 1890s were a fertile prologue. London wrote novels—including *A Daughter of the Snows* (1902), his first long fiction, set in Alaska; *The Call of the Wild* (1903), on atavism, a best-selling classic in world literature; *The Sea-Wolf* (1904), a best-selling sea adventure; *White Fang* (1906), another best-seller, on environmental determinism; *The Iron Heel* (1908), a futuristic novel against oligarchical capitalism, praised by Eugene V. Debs;* *Martin Eden* (1909), a fictionalized autobiography, praised by Edwin Markham;* *Burning Daylight* (1910), a best-seller about an amoral super-financier, after Frank Norris* and prefiguring Theodore Dreiser;* and *The Valley of the Moon* (1913), an Edenic agrarian love story.

London also wrote sociopolitical documents on degrading slum life in the East End of London (*The People of the Abyss* [1903], London's personal favorite among his books), on hoboing (*The Road* [1907]), and on radical Socialism (*Revolution and Other Essays* [1910]). He wrote an autobiographical, antialcohol novelized tract called *John Barleycorn* (1913). He collected reams of short stories in several volumes. In addition, he ran unsuccessfully twice for mayor of Oakland on the Socialist ticket (1901, 1905), was a war correspondent (for William Randolph Hearst* in Japan and Korea during the Russo-Japanese War [1904] and for *Collier's** during the Mexican Revolution [1914]), lectured at Eastern universities on socialism (1905), sailed on a schooner with Charmian all through the South Seas (1907–1909—the literary results include *The Cruise of the Snark* (1911), an autobiography, *South Sea Tales* (1911), and *On the Makaloa Mat* (1919), more tales—and was a long-time Sonoma Valley rancher and agronomist (from 1905).

London foolishly neglected his health, debilitated by a fistula and skin disease (1908), severe kidney damage (1913), dysentery and pleurisy (1914), and rheumatism (1915)—all exacerbated by alcoholism. During his last six or so years, London worried about money and the decline of his reputation, and he harbored irrational suspicions that some of his friends—including Mary Austin,* Ambrose Bierce,* and Joaquin Miller,* among many others—were disloyal. Finally, uremia and a self-administered overdose of morphine and atropine sulphates caused his death.

In a phenomenal life of outdoor activity and other pursuits, Jack London wrote 200 short stories, 400 nonfictional prose pieces, and more than 50 books—before he died at the age of forty! His wretched childhood, his activities during a vigorous youth and early manhood, and his voracious eclectic reading combined to make him a materialistic monist, a socialist, and a Darwinian, Nietzschean, and Jungian thinker. He was the first lowbrow to rise to such popularity and influence with the middlebrows that he managed to confound the highbrows of his era. He was formed by the forces that buffeted him in the 1890s.

Looking Backward: 2000–1887 (1888). Utopian novel by Edward Bellamy.* Narrator-hero Julian West is a wealthy, aristocratic Bostonian who lives in a fine mansion, in which, however, he is uneasy because factory laborers live in nearby slums. He copes with chronic insomnia by having a doctor hypnotize him in a cement-walled basement room in his house, which is destroyed by fire one night. He awakens 113 years later to a totally new social order. It seems that nineteenth-century mergers created trusts so large that they evolved into one publicly owned, government-run benevolent monopoly.

Julian is told about and shown the numerous fine features of this utopia by a retired physician named Dr. Leete and his daughter Edith Leete. Such features include a well-planned city, pollutionless electric power, no labor unrest, and a socialist-capitalist body politic. In addition, he finds a congress-controlled president, whose educational and health policies are the result of advice from a board of professional seniors. Also an ombudswoman, chosen by women voters, has veto power over bills affecting females. And free education for all. When each student turns twenty-one, he or she enters a three-year period of menial work, followed by vocational-aptitude examinations and government-supervised allocation of adult jobs, each for equal pay, into an industrial army or a professional army. Job switching is, however, easy. Instead of money, people use credit cards. Immediate delivery is made of items (both American and foreign made) ordered at stores that display only samples. Stealing is thus rendered obsolete. Crime is regarded as a mental aberration and is treated in hospitals. Loafers are punished by solitary confinement, on a diet of bread and water. There are early retirement programs. Recreation and culture abound. Royalties to writers and artists are earned by popular endorsement. Music is piped into homes by a nationwide telephone network. At the same time, life for everyone has become a kind of return to arcadian New England village times. Two things happen to Julian: He is made a college professor of history, since he knows the nineteenth century so well; and he falls in love with Edith, who, it turns out, is the great-granddaughter of Edith Bartlett, Julian's fiancée back in the old days.

Bellamy said that he began *Looking Backward* as a literary fantasy, not a book on social reform. He later averred that he wrote it from a Christian protest perspective and that he hoped by it to resolve the dilemma of management versus labor. It sold a respectable 10,000 copies the first year but, with better advertising, almost half a million in 1889. It was many things to its many purchasers. Its utopian message appealed to realistic readers, whereas its love interest and its depiction of a return to village simplicity attracted the romantically inclined. *Looking Backward* was the most influential utopian novel ever published in America. Clubs were formed to discuss Bellamy's ideas and to put them into action, culminating in the short-lived Nationalist Movement. Bellamy edited the *Nationalist* and then founded and wrote for his own journal, the *New Nation* (1891–1894). He also published a sequel, the novel *Equality** (1897), which, however, is more tract than fiction. More important, at least a hundred novelists, essayists, and polemicists capitalized or at least commented on Bellamy's visionary work, usually, at first, in displeasure and even fear. The adverse critics scolded Bellamy for trying to do away with competition, private ownership of property, and individual self-esteem. For example, Henry George* called *Looking Backward* a castle in the air on a foundation of clouds, and the influential

British writer William Morris countered with his *News from Nowhere* (1890). However, Thorstein Veblen* acknowledged its inspiration; John Dewey* called Bellamy "the Great American prophet"; and William Dean Howells* wrote in 1898 that Bellamy's romantic imagination almost equalled that of Nathaniel Hawthorne. In varying ways, Eugene V. Debs,* Ignatius Donnelly,* William Demarest Lloyd,* Jack London,* Mark Twain,* and Frank Lloyd Wright* were also affected by Bellamy's work. The continued later influence, direct and indirect, of *Looking Backward* and of its sequel, *Equality*, was pervasive—on Theosophists, Christian Socialists, Utopian Society members, New Deal advocates, and such thinkers, sensible and otherwise, as Father Charles Coughlin, Huey Long, Upton Sinclair, Norman Thomas, and Dr. Francis E. Townsend.

Lovett, Robert Morss (1870–1956). Educator, editor, and diplomat. Born in Boston, he graduated from Harvard (1892), taught English at Harvard (to 1893), and then joined the faculty at the University of Chicago (1893–1936—*see* Universities). He and his friend William Vaughn Moody* collaborated on two popular academic books: *A History of English Literature* (1902) and *A First View of English Literature* (1905). Lovett later combined a conservative approach to teaching, the writing of undistinguished fiction, and editing with a liberal, even radical, concern for social and political issues. For examples, although his critical book on Edith Wharton* (1925) and his edition of Moody's poems (1931) were both conventional academic exercises, Lovett's friendship with Jane Addams;* his pacifism; his espousal of the American Civil Liberties Union, Russian Bolshevism, and the Republican side in the Spanish Civil War; and his anti-British attitude with respect to India and Ireland forced him to retire from the University of Chicago (1936). Shortly after the death of his friend Robert Herrick* in 1938, Lovett was appointed to succeed Herrick as governor secretary of the Virgin Islands (1939), but his pro-Communist stance incensed Congress and caused his dismissal in 1943. He then taught at the University of Puerto Rico (1944–1946). His book of explanation is *All Our Years: The Autobiography of Robert Morss Lovett* (1948). Lovett married Ida Mott-Smith in 1895. The couple had three children; their only son was killed in action during World War I, in France, in 1918.

Lummis, Charles F. (1859–1928). (Full name: Charles Fletcher Lummis.) Author, anthropologist, and editor. He was born in Lynn, Massachusetts, tried Harvard briefly (1881) and editing in Ohio for a while (1882–1884), then walked quite indirectly from Cincinnati to Los Angeles, where he became city editor of the *Daily Times* (1885–1886) and where he maintained his legal residence thereafter. He was a correspondent for his paper during the Apache War (1886) but then suffered a paralytic stroke (1886). While recovering, he lived among Native American Pueblos in Isleta, New Mexico Territory (1888–1891). He accompanied historian Adolph Francis Alphonse Bandelier on an ethnological expedition to Bolivia and Peru (1892–1894), and became interested in preserving from ruin old Spanish missions and other historical structures and sites in California—for example, the Pala, San Juan Capistrano, and San Fernando missions. He cofounded the Landmarks Club (1895) to aid in this endeavor. When 300 Native Americans were expelled from their homes by court order, Lummis established the Sequoya League to help relocate them (1902).

In addition to earlier and later work, Lummis in the 1890s published fiction, including *A New Mexico David* (1891), *The Man Who Married the Moon, and Other Pueblo Indian Folk-Stories* (1894), *The Gold Fish of Gran Chimu* (1896), *The King of the Broncos* (1897), and *The Enchanted Burro* (1897); personal reminiscence, *A Tramp across the Continent* (1892); and travel and geopolitical essays, for example, *Some Strange Corners of Our Country* (1892), *The Land of Poco Tiempo* (1893) (about native New Mexican culture), *The Spanish Pioneers* (1893), and *The Awakening of a Nation: Mexico of Today* (1898). Lummis also founded, in 1894, the magazine originally called *Land of Sunshine* and edited it until 1909 (it was called *Out West* after 1900), and he worked as a Los Angeles public librarian for five years (1905–1910). He recorded almost a thousand old Spanish and Native American songs (the latter in thirty-seven languages). For his work, he was knighted by the King of Spain (1915). Lummis married three times: Mary Dorothea Roads in 1880 (divorced in 1890), Eva Frances Douglas in 1891 (the couple had four children and were divorced in 1911), and Gertrude Redit in 1915.

Lyon, Kate (1856–?). The mistress and second "wife" of Harold Frederic.* Born in upstate New York, she attended schools in Chicago and taught elementary school there. In England very late in the 1890s, she may have gone there with her sister and brother, Mary and Frank Ritchie, to help take care of the Ritchie children. Kate Lyon met Frederic at about this time, possibly in the British Museum in 1889 or 1890. The two began to live together in 1890 or 1891, first in London and then in Kenley, Surrey, fifteen miles south of London. She soon became known there as Mrs. Frederic, by 1895 was socializing openly with Frederic, and had three children by him. Stephen Crane* knew the couple in Surrey, beginning in 1897. Crane's so-called wife Cora Taylor especially liked and subsequently was of assistance to Kate. When Frederic died (1898), Kate was tried for manslaughter because, owing to her Christian Scientist beliefs, she had neglected to summon adequate medical assistance after he suffered a series of strokes. Following a sensational trial, Kate was acquitted (1898), moved to London, obtained employment with publishers, and aided Crane in the research and composition of his *Great Battles of the World*.* Kate changed her name to Forman, went back to Chicago with her children (1904), and supported herself and them by writing. Frederic had helped their financial situation by willing his American copyrights to her. Kate Forman lived at least until 1934.

M

Mabie, Hamilton W. (1845–1916). (Full name: Hamilton Wright Mabie.) Editor and literary critic. He was born in Cold Spring, near West Point, in New York. His father was a New York City wholesale merchant. Mabie graduated from Williams College (1867), where one of his friends was G. Stanley Hall,* obtained a law degree from Columbia University (1869), and practiced law in New York for several years (1869–1877). He married Jeannette Trivett, an Episcopal clergyman's daughter, in 1876 (the couple had two children). Mabie became a member of the editorial staff of the *Christian Union* (1879–1916). This conservative journal was renamed the *Outlook* (1893). Mabie wrote stories for children, including *Norse Stories Retold from the Eddas* (1882). His books in the 1890s are *My Study Fire* (1890), *Essays in Literary Interpretation* (1892), *My Study Fire, Second Series* (1894, on the 1895 best-seller list), *Nature and Culture* (1896), *Books and Culture* (1896), *The Life of the Spirit* (1899, perhaps his most influential book), and *William Shakespeare: Poet, Dramatist, and Man* (1900). Mabie lectured effectively in Japan (1912–1913). Once lauded for his gentility and serenity, and his earnest and delicate prose, H. W. Mabie is now ridiculed when not ignored. His brand of criticism represents attenuated Victorianism transported late to America. He extolled ideality, branded William Dean Howells* and his fellow realists as atheistic materialists, and ignored the social and artistic value of the emerging naturalists.

McAllister, Ward (1827–1895). (Full name: Samuel Ward McAllister.) Lawyer and social leader. McAllister was born in Savannah, Georgia, practiced law nominally and briefly in San Francisco (1850–1852), and thereafter officially resided in somewhat impecunious splendor in New York City and in Newport, Rhode Island. He became a leader and an arbiter of New York's high society, and was nicknamed "The Autocrat of Drawing Rooms." He originated a group of old New York family leaders called "The Patriarchs" (named Astor, Goodhue,

Jones, King, Phelps, Rutherfurd, Schermerhorn, Van Rensselaer, and—why not?—McAllister). McAllister coined the phrase "The Four Hundred" (first quoted in the New York *Tribune*, in March 1888) to indicate the limited number of truly acceptable New York society folk. He made up his exclusive list, so it is said, when ultra-uppity Mrs. William Backhouse Astor, Jr., mother of John Jacob Astor IV,* asked for his help (1892). It seems that she was obliged to restrict the number of guests to be invited to her annual ball, held each January and costing up to $200,000 each year, to 400 because of the size of the ballroom in her mansion on the site of the Empire State Building. McAllister's book *Society as I Have Found It* (1890) is an episodic, self-aggrandizing little autobiography beginning with praise of his parents, school days in New York, law practice, first experiences in Europe (in London, Florence, Rome, Baden Baden, and Pau), and then social pleasures back in the United States (dining out and hosting dinners and dances, hunting in the South, life in Newport, country life in upstate New York, dressing properly, famous wines, types of cooks, and memorable dinner parties). Then follows "The Present Fashion in Stationery," featuring innumerable examples of calling cards, invitations, acceptance and "regret" cards, announcements, and mourning cards. The entire book, which is so unconsciously snobbish that it offers real fun for tolerant present-day readers, is highly informative and revealing. McAllister was named after his uncle, Samuel Ward, the New York banker. McAllister's cousin was F. Marion Crawford.*

McClure, S. S. (1857–1949). (Full name: Samuel Sidney McClure.) Editor, publisher, and commercial genius. Born in county Antrim, Ireland, he migrated as a youth to the United States, where he founded America's first newspaper syndicate in 1884. He established *McClure's Magazine*,* which flourished from 1893 to 1929 and which was probably most famous for publishing work by muckrakers, notably Ida M. Tarbell* and Lincoln Steffens,* and other critics of society, including Finley Peter Dunne.* McClure started *McClure's Quarterly* in 1895, but it quickly failed. In 1897 and 1899 he established one and then another publishing company. McClure's later career was marked by other grandiose plans, much success, and some failures. He published *My Autobiography* (1914), which was actually written by Willa Cather. McClure made professional contact, sometimes without success, with Stephen Crane,* Hamlin Garland,* Richard Watson Gilder,* William Dean Howells,* Henry James,* Jack London,* Alfred Thayer Mahan,* Theodore Roosevelt,* Booth Tarkington,* Mark Twain,* and many other important writers.

McClure's Magazine. Monthly magazine. Founded by S. S. McClure* and his newspaper syndicate partner John Sanborn Phillips in June 1893, it was originally priced at 15¢ (10¢ from 1895 to 1907). It was abundantly illustrated (later with great brilliance), fell into danger during the Panic of 1893,* but was bailed out by Scottish evangelical writer and lecturer Henry Drummond, Sir Arthur Conan

Doyle, and others. McClure attracted not only able staff members but also great writers. It did not take long for this magazine to succeed—with long biographical installments by Ida M. Tarbell* on Napoleon Bonaparte (1894–1895) and on Abraham Lincoln (1895–1896, 1898–1899); fictional and nonfictional writing by some of the best, most popular British authors and by such Americans as Stephen Crane,* Joel Chandler Harris,* O. Henry,* and Alfred Thayer Mahan;* features on nature, science, and railroads; poetry, usually so-so; and human-interest pictures and illustrations by Charles Dana Gibson,* for one. Special features included "Real Conversations" with celebrities including brief biographies of them. The Spanish-American War* challenged McClure to redouble his efforts, advertising space (the largest in the world between 1895 and 1899), and circulation, which in 1900 stood at 370,000. In 1903 (*McClure's* began to publish some of the greatest, most influential muckraking material ever written—by Ray Stannard Baker, Tarbell, Lincoln Steffens,* and several others—and continued until 1911. Changes, both fortunate and otherwise, occurred and *McClure's* merged with *New Smart Set* in 1929.

McCutcheon, George Barr (1866–1928). Indiana novelist and playwright. He was born near Lafayette, Indiana. He flunked out of Purdue after two years (1883–1885), tried being an itinerant actor, worked as a photographer, and then became a reporter on the *Morning Journal*, in Lafayette (1889–1893) and city editor of the *Daily Courier*, also in Lafayette (1893–1901). He wrote in his spare time, but without much initial success. When financially able, he moved to Chicago (1903). In all, he published nearly forty works in twenty-eight years. The best of McCutcheon's many novels include *Graustark: The Story of Love behind a Throne* (1901), with five sequels; *Castle Cranneycrow* (1902), quite popular; *Brewster's Millions* (1902), a successful farce, later dramatized; *The Sherrods* (1903), a tragic love story set in rural Indiana; *Beverly of Graustark* (1904), dramatized unsuccessfully by David Belasco* in 1905; and *Mary Midthorne* (1911), unusually realistic. The Graustark volumes sold roughly 5,000,000 each. McCutcheon married Marie Proudfoot Van Antwerp Fay in 1904 (it was her third marriage).

McCutcheon had two younger brothers, John Tinney McCutcheon and Benjamin Frederick McCutcheon. John Tinney McCutcheon became a successful Chicago cartoonist, illustrator (of the works of George Ade,* among others), war correspondent for the Chicago *Record*, and big-game hunter (once with Theodore Roosevelt* in Africa). Benjamin Frederick McCutcheon, also a novelist (though a minor one), was the railroad editor for the Chicago *Record*. He suggested the plot of *Brewster's Millions* to his brother George, who gave him a share of its sizable royalties.

George Ade, who knew all three McCutcheon brothers, became friendly with John first, while the two were students at Purdue University, and was John's lifelong friend. Ade had persuaded George to let Herbert S. Stone,* the progressive Chicago publisher, issue his *Graustark: The Story of Love behind a*

Throne under terms favorable to Stone ($500 to the author for publication rights to what became a best-seller). Such a contract could not have endeared the novelist to Ade. Ade later satirized George Barr McCutcheon's Graustark formula in *The Slim Princess* (1907). Although Ade's wit was gentle, McCutcheon took offense and stopped accepting invitations to lavish parties at Hazelden, Ade's estate at Brook, Indiana.

George Barr McCutcheon also wrote a number of plays, many of them serious, satirical, and realistic; but he was unsuccessful in getting any produced and therefore turned some of them into novels. But his creation of the fanciful kingdom of Graustark was a smashing success. In fact, it became so well known to millions of readers that some insisted that they had actually toured there. One man wrote to McCutcheon asking whether it would violate copyright laws for him to name his dog ''Graustark.'' McCutcheon's formula inspired numerous imitators to write about their own pretend kingdoms. A list of such countries would include Altenstein, Altronde, Asturnia, Axphain, Barscheit, Baumenburg-Drippe, Bertrondi, Corconia, Dawsbergen, Doppelkin, Frivonia, Grimland, Hohenphalia, Maasau, Montvilliers, Morovenia, Palatina, Phaetia, Scarvania, Valeria, and Wallaria. Most of these romantic never-neverlands are located two days southeast of Paris or Berlin, with partly Slavic and partly Teutonic populations. McCutcheon's most adept and popular rival was Harold MacGrath (1871–1932), whose Graustarkian novels include *Arms and the Woman* (1899), *The Puppet Crown* (1900), *Hearts and Masks* (1905), and many more. The Graustark vogue declined after about 1907.

MacDowell, Edward (1861–1908). (Full name: Edward Alexander MacDowell.) Composer and concert pianist. Born in New York City, MacDowell had a delightful childhood. His father was a Quaker businessman. Young MacDowell attended public schools, took piano lessons from age eight, revealed an aptitude for drawing, attended courses at a French school as a preteenager, and enjoyed reading literature and history. His mother took him to Paris, where he studied piano and composition (1876–1878); later he studied in Wiesbaden (1878–1879) and Frankfurt (1879–1881). MacDowell began to teach and also to compose in earnest (1881–1882). He played a piano concerto of his own composition before Franz Liszt at Weimar (1882); the master was impressed and recommended his *First Modern Suite* for a Zurich concert (1882). MacDowell continued to compose (1882–1884); married Marian Nevins, an amateur student of his from Frankfurt days, in Connecticut in 1884; and returned with her to Europe (1884–1888), mostly in Germany, where he composed steadily. MacDowell then settled in Boston (1888–1896), where he composed, taught piano, and gave enthusiastically received piano concerts. He became the first professor of music appointed at Columbia University (1896–1904), during which time he taught, lectured, organized an orchestra, formed a male chorus, and gave private lessons. He also composed, usually while on vacation at an eighty-acre farm located in Peterboro, New Hampshire, purchased by his wife (1896).

Disappointed over administrative policy and the inadequate preparation of most of his students, MacDowell resigned. He suffered a nervous collapse in 1904 and, when he was hurt in a carriage accident, he went insane (1905) and died soon after. In the 1890s and later, MacDowell was considered America's premier composer and pianist. His 1888–1901 compositions include the following works for piano, at which he was best: *Marionettes* (1888, 1901); *Four Little Poems* (1888); *Études* (1889, 1890, 1894), among his best works; *Les Orientales* (1889); sonatas (1893, 1895, 1900, 1901); *Air and Rigaudon* (1894); *Woodland Sketches* (1896), including "To a Wild Rose" and "To a Water Lily;" and *Sea Pieces* (1898), among his best. He also composed orchestral works: *Lancelot and Elaine* (1888), *The Saracens* (1891), and *The Lovely Aldâ* (1891); and suites (1891, 1897), among his best. He wrote many pieces for voice and piano in 1889 and 1890 (including "Thy Beaming Eyes"—*see* Songs), 1893 (including "The Sea"), 1894, 1898 (including "The Swan Bent Low to the Lily"), and 1899. He composed songs for male chorus (1890, 1897, 1898) and for mixed chorus (1891, 1892 [with four-handed piano accompaniment]). He even wrote one for violincello and orchestra (1888). He published some of the poems he wrote for his songs (1903, 1908). Some of his Columbia lectures appeared posthumously as his *Critical and Historical Essays* (1912).

Hamlin Garland* met MacDowell in 1894 and later and wrote in praise of him. MacDowell is considered conservative, romantic, lyrical not dramatic, responsive to national and racial impulses, and often charming. His works have been compared (less and less favorably) to those of Edvard Grieg. MacDowell's widow enlarged the Peterboro farm to accommodate an incorporated memorial for writers, composers, artists, and sculptors on MacDowell Colony scholarships.

McKinley, William (1843–1901). Twenty-fifth president of the United States. He was born in Niles, Ohio, attended Allegheny College in Pennsylvania (1860), and taught school briefly in Ohio. He joined the Union army during the Civil War (1861–1865), served gallantly, and was brevetted major (1865). His commanding general was Rutherford B. Hayes, future president. After the war, McKinley studied law in Albany, New York, practiced in Canton, Ohio (beginning 1867), and married Ida Saxton, a neurotic invalid, in 1871. He was elected to the U.S. House of Representatives as a Republican (1877–1883, 1885–1891; chairman 1889–1891). He helped write and pass a protective tariff act called the McKinley Tariff (1890). (Late in his life, McKinley modified his position on tariffs to one favoring international reciprocity.) He was elected governor of Ohio (1892–1896). With the help of Mark Hanna,* he was nominated on the first ballot to be the Republican candidate for president.

McKinley was elected and then reelected (1896–1901). He was always supported by business interests, to the dismay of William Jennings Bryan,* who was twice the progressive Democratic candidate who ran against McKinley. McKinley's campaigns were marked by controversy over bimetallism (*see* Free Silver). Then came the Spanish-American War* (1898), into which he was pressured by Congress, the newspapers (led by William Randolph Hearst*), Theodore Roosevelt* (then assistant secretary of the navy in his cabinet), and the people. The war was a short one (25 April to 12 August 1898). According to peace terms with Spain (ratified on 6 February 1899), Cuba was placed under American jurisdiction; Puerto Rico, the Philippine Islands, and Guam fell to the United States. Victory over the Spaniards enabled McKinley to be easily re-elected; but, in the ensuing conflict with the Filipinos, McKinley was labeled an imperialist by many important writers, including William Dean Howells* and Mark Twain.* During McKinley's administration, the Hawaiian Islands were annexed (1898, then granted territorial status in 1900); the Open Door Policy* was initiated (1899–1900); an American representative attended the First Hague Conference for International Disarmament (1899); parts of the Samoan Islands were annexed (1899); and the United States participated in the quelling of the Boxer Rebellion in China (1900).

In 1901 President McKinley was assassinated in Buffalo, New York, by an anarchist. (Ambrose Bierce* got into trouble for his unmeant poetic prediction that McKinley might be shot to death.) Roosevelt, McKinley's vice president at that time, became president. John Hay* was McKinley's influential secretary of state and remained in that capacity under Roosevelt. McKinley had reflected the people's wants more than he had inspired them to change. Dignified and smooth, he ably administered in part by choosing excellent subordinates, and campaigned competently. His *Speeches and Addresses* were published (1893, 1901).

McTeague: A Story of San Francisco (1899). Novel by Frank Norris.* Before the main action begins, it is reported that McTeague as a child worked in the mines with his dull father, who then died, was sent away by his loving mother so that he could better himself, and he became an apprentice to an itinerant dentist. McTeague, long on brute strength but short on brains, uses a small inheritance from his mother's estate to set up a dental parlor in San Francisco. He is happy with his concertina, steam beer, and a caged canary. Neighbors include friendly Marcus Schouler and his cousin Trina Sieppe. Trina needs dental care, and McTeague soon falls in love with the cute little girl, visits her thifty family, and becomes engaged to her. More good luck comes when Trina wins $5,000 in the lottery. McTeague would like to buy something extravagant, but Trina prefers to invest for their future and continue her job, which is carving and painting little wooden animals. Marcus irrationally accuses McTeague of grabbing Trina for her money. McTeague and Trina get married and are happy for a while, but soon they quarrel about money. Trina becomes miserly. At a picnic, McTeague and Marcus participate in wrestling matches, win, and then compete with each other. Marcus, in a fit of surliness, bites McTeague's ear lobe off and suffers a broken arm in return. Marcus informs the medical officials that McTeague has no dental degree or license, and the poor brute must stop practicing his profession.

McTeague and Trina must move to save money. He manufactures supplies for legitimate dentists, and Trina spends all her time and energy making her tiny toys. McTeague turns to alcohol and becomes abusive. He resorts to biting Trina's fingers to extort money for whiskey, steals her meagre earnings, and disappears. She suffers blood poisoning from her gnawed and paint-infected hands, and the fingers of her right hand are amputated. She becomes a scrub-woman. Wanting to fondle her coins again, she converts the capital from her banked $5,000 into gold coins and wallows in bed with them. McTeague reappears, beats Trina to death, steals her coins, and escapes to the gold mines. Fearful of the law and sensing a posse, he walks into Death Valley with a mule on which are packed his gold, his "chittering" canary, and a canteen. Here he encounters Marcus, who had joined McTeague's pursuers out of a desire to avenge Trina's death. Marcus has a revolver. In an elaborate struggle, the mule is shot dead, falls, and smashes the canteen. McTeague mortally pummels Marcus, but before he dies Marcus handcuffs himself to his now-doomed brutal enemy.

Two significant subplots in *McTeague* concern a junk dealer who marries an insane charwoman for her nonexistent wealth, and two shy tenement dwellers whose lives are separated by a rooming-house wall.

A real-life source for *McTeague* was the 1893 murder of a San Francisco charwoman by her drunken husband. Norris wrote part of the novel while he was a student under Lewis E. Gates* at Harvard (1894–1895), and he dedicated the finished work to Gates. It is regarded as a standard example of Zolaesque naturalism* in American fiction because of its emphasis on heredity, environment, chance, and brutal human nature, and also because of its powerful but clumsy style. William Dean Howells* and Theodore Dreiser,* among other contemporaries, admired Norris's *McTeague*, although they both deplored its Hollywood-Gothic ending.

Madame Butterfly (1900). Play by David Belasco.* Cho-Cho-San is the daughter of a Japanese army officer who committed suicide because he could not carry an imperial order to completion. She meets Lieutenant B. F. Pinkerton of the U.S. Navy, and she forms an intimate relationship with him which she regards as sacred but which he treats casually. He nicknames her Madame Butterfly and toys with her for a while; she loves him profoundly. Promising to return "when the robins nest again," he sails away and soon gets married in America. Cho-Cho-San bears his son and is happy at the news of his tardy return; when she learns of his marriage, she mortally stabs herself with her honorable father's sword and dies in Pinkerton's arms. *Madame Butterfly* opened in New York and enjoyed a successful run in London (also in 1900). It follows the plot line of a short story by John Luther Long and formed the basis of Giacomo Puccini's 1904 grand opera of the same name.

M'lle New York. Fortnightly magazine. Issued from August 1895 to April 1896 and from November 1898 to January 1899, it contains spritely, satirical notices of contemporary events. James Huneker* was associate editor of many of its numbers, and also contributed essays on aesthetics, music, and American foibles. *M'lle New York*, which was well illustrated, praised African-American art and often concerned itself with works by Friedrich Nietzsche and Richard Wagner.

Maggie: A Girl of the Streets (1893). Novel by Stephen Crane.* This first artistically managed American slum novel tells about the miserable life of the Johnson family of Rum Alley, in New York City. The father is a tough laborer; his wife Mary, a loud alcoholic. Their children are Maggie and Jimmie. The father dies. Jimmie matures into a foul-mouthed truck driver and a kind of a Bowery pimp. Maggie, however, "blossomed in a mud-puddle" to become "a most rare and wonderful production of a tenement district, a pretty girl." She gets a job in a sweatshop making collars and cuffs. Jimmie's vicious friend Pete, a bartender, thrills Maggie by inviting her to go to a show one evening. They go out together again. One night, after an argument between Jimmie and his drunken mother, Maggie moves away and begins to live with Pete. After all, as he puts it, "Mag, I'm stuck on yer shape." This turn of events puzzles Jimmie because he fuzzily theorizes that "all sisters excepting his own could, advisedly, be ruined." He has a fight with Pete, at the end of which Jimmie wonders "what's d' use?" So he and his mother curse Maggie instead of discussing her plight. In due time, Pete discards her for a former girlfriend. Maggie tries to return home but is driven away. Pete refuses to assume any responsibility for her. Within a few months Maggie has walked along well-lighted avenues, past saloons, and into shadowy streets and alleys. She has encountered well-dressed gentlemen, rough workers, boys, drunkards, and derelicts. She finally makes her way to black waters and death. Back in her former home, her sloppy mother Mary learns that Maggie has passed away, and she roars out words of forgiveness for her naughty child.

The plot of *Maggie* is highly melodramatic. Its artistry lies in its bold-stroke imagery, its rendering of the chaos of disordered slum existence, and the gruesome irony of its subtle presentation of Christian thought, inadequate here because it is hypocritical. As in the works of Gustave Flaubert and Émile Zola, whom Crane read but often found tedious, the ruling force in Maggie's world is environment. Crane wrote a hasty first draft of *Maggie* during his one semester at Syracuse (early in 1891), revised it in the light of friends' comments on it and his own subsequent Bowery observations, and showed the manuscript to Richard Watson Gilder,* editor of the *Century** and a friend of the Crane family. Gilder rejected it as too cruel and too honest, without sentiment (1892). Crane rewrote *Maggie* once more, peddled it unsuccessfully to several publishers, then published it (1893) under a pen name for $869 of his own money, borrowed against an anticipated inheritance following his mother's death in 1891. The nom de plume Crane chose was Johnson Smith, for its pairing of common names; but the printer made it Johnston Smith, to which Crane agreed. Legends have grown up around the 1,100 copies, largely unwanted, of this edition. Crane gave copies to several friends and sometimes inscribed the following: "It is inevitable that you will be greatly shocked by this book . . . For it trys [sic] to show that environment is a tremendous thing in the world and frequently shapes lives regardless.''

One recipient of a gift copy was Hamlin Garland,* who admired it and passed it along to William Dean Howells.* When Garland reviewed *Maggie* (in the *Arena*,* June 1893, published by B. O. Flower*), he praised it for its ''art impulse'' and ''truthful phrase'' but also criticized it for being fragmentary and for not depicting the heroine's neighbors, whose lives were pure and heroic. Later, however, Garland made negative comments on Crane's Bohemianism. Howells invited Crane to his home (1893), praised *Maggie* in person to him and to other guests, and compared him favorably to Mark Twain.* In a *Harper's Weekly* column (spring 1895), Howells called *Maggie* a wrongly neglected novel. For the 1896 edition, which reduced each ''damn'' and ''hell'' usage to ''d—'' and ''h—'' or deleted them, Howells provided a preface in which he said the novel resembled a Greek tragedy. In general, he judged *Maggie* to be strong stuff but welcome realism, with an uncompromising social and moral purpose.

Mahan, Alfred Thayer (1840–1914). Naval officer and historian. Born at West Point, New York, he was the son of an engineering professor at the U.S. Military Academy. After two years at Columbia, Mahan entered the U.S. Naval Academy at Annapolis, Maryland, and graduated at the top of his class (1859). He was assigned to blockade duty along the Atlantic and Gulf coasts and taught at the Naval Academy during the Civil War. Much later, he published a history of Civil War naval action entitled *The Gulf and Inland Waters* (1883), taught at the Naval War College, Newport, Rhode Island (from 1884, as president 1886–1889), and from his various lectures and courses wrote *The Influence of Sea Power upon History, 1660–1783** (1890) and *The Influence of Sea Power upon the French Revolution and Empire, 1793–1812* (2 vols., 1892). He also published *The Interest of America in Sea Power, Past and Present* (1897). In addition, he published essays on the need for a naval base in Hawaii and on the desirability of a transoceanic canal somewhere across Central America. Mahan retired in 1896, was an American delegate to the first Hague Peace Conference (1899), and was recalled to active duty during the Spanish-American War* (1898, as captain, ultimately listed as rear admiral, 1906), to help direct naval strategy. His *Lessons of the War with Spain* (1899) followed the American victory. He then wrote *Types of Naval Officers* (1901), *Sea Power in Its Relations to the War of 1812* (2 vols., 1905), *Naval Strategy* (1911), biographies of David Glasgow Farragut and Lord Nelson, and an autobiography entitled *From Sail to Steam* (1907). Mahan also provided an account of the battle of the Sea of Japan to be included in *A Photographic Record of the Russo-Japanese War*, edited and arranged by James H. Hare.*

The general thesis of Mahan's major works is that a strong navy promotes vigor and prosperity at home and prestige abroad. He pointed to England as a positive example and to Spain and France as negative examples. Mahan's *Sea Power* books, which preceded America's emergence after the Spanish-American War as a major naval power, greatly influenced professional military strategists not only in America but especially—at first—abroad (particularly in England, Germany, and Japan) in the years shortly before World War I. Mahan is now regarded as one of the most influential writers on the subject of naval policy that America has ever produced. Mahan married Ellen Lyle Evans in 1872 (the couple had three children).

Main-Travelled Roads (1891). Collection of six short stories by Hamlin Garland.* They are "A Branch Road," "Up the Coolly," "Among the Corn-Rows," "The Return of a Private," "Under the Lion's Paw," and "Mrs. Ripley's Trip." The first two stories were first published in this 1891 collection; the other four stories had already been published in *Harper's Weekly* (1888, 1889, and 1890) and in *Arena** (1890), edited by S. S. McClure.* The 1899 edition of *Main-Travelled Roads* added "The Creamery Man," "A Day's Pleasure," and "Uncle Ethan Ripley"—all of less significance. The 1922 edition of *Main-Travelled Roads* added two more stories; the 1930 edition, one more story.

The 1891 collection represents Garland's most powerful writing. The title is unifying and metaphorically significant. The preface explains that "The main-travelled road of the West . . . is long and wearyful and has a dull little town at one end, and a home of toil at the other. Like the main-travelled road of life, it is traversed by many classes of people, but the poor and the weary predominate." In "A Branch Road," Will Hannan after a seven-year absence returns to find Agnes Dingman, his former girlfriend, with a brutal husband and several children. He persuades her to run away with him and start living. "Up the Coolly" tells how Howard McLane, a successful actor, returns to the West to visit his mother, his brother Grant, and Grant's wife. They have had to sell the old Wisconsin family property and are now in wretched poverty on a smaller farm. All is hospitable at first, but Grant soon expresses his bitterness that Howard might earlier have shared his material success and thus prevented family ruin and sorrow. Howard tardily admits as much and offers to help, but it is too late. (This story hints at Garland's uneasiness after having gone East and abandoning his parents to continued rural poverty.) "Among the Corn-Rows" features the almost idyllic courtship by Rob of Julia in a sensual natural setting, but romance is undercut both by the economic side of Rob's desire for a wife and also by the implication that a hard prairie life lies ahead for both. "The Return of a Private" describes the return to his Wisconsin farm of Ed Smith, a Union army soldier so hollowed out by combat during the Civil War that his wife Emma does not even recognize him at first. (Garland's father was a Civil War veteran.) "Under the Lion's Paw" dramatizes the plight of a hardworking farmer named Tim Haskins, who is squeezed by Jim Butler, an unscrupulous, sarcastic landlord. Butler is saved from being murdered by him only when Haskins hears his little daughter's cherubic laughter in the distance. (This story is a parable espousing the single-tax theory of Henry George,* Garland's mentor and friend.) "Mrs. Ripley's Trip" heartbreakingly tells how the drudgery of married life on a lonely farm is mitigated when, after twenty-three years of anticipation, an aging wife goes back to her birthplace, then returns, willingly enough, to resume her burden.

These six stories are notable for fine descriptions of Mother Nature's beauty, resentment that economic determinism seems to control farmers' lives, the accurate use of Midwestern dialect, and effective touches of sentimentality. Urban Midwestern readers and critics resented the honest realism in Garland's *Main-Travelled Roads*, but some of the best reviewers in the East, including William Dean Howells,* praised the work highly.

Major, Charles (1856–1913). Novelist and lawyer. He was born in Indianapolis, Indiana, and moved with his family (1869) to Shelbyville, Indiana, where he finished high school. He studied law in his father's office, passed the bar (1877), was elected to the state legislature as a Democrat (1885), quit after one term, and returned to his law practice. Long interested in sixteenth-century history and literature, Major turned that love into the writing of historical romances. The best of these was his first: *When Knighthood Was in Flower* (1898). Purportedly narrated by Sir Edward Caskoden, court dancing master, it tells about Mary Tudor, the sister of Henry VIII, and her love for Charles Brandon. This work became a best-seller; going into a third edition in its first year, it had sold 400,000 copies by 1904. It was also made into a popular play. Major also wrote *Dorothy Vernon of Haddon Hall* (1902), *A Gentle Knight of Old Brandenburg* (1909), other romances, and some ineffective local-color fiction.

"The Man That Corrupted Hadleyburg" (1899). Short story by Mark Twain.* The town of Hadleyburg is proud of its reputation as virtuous in all regards and likes its motto, which is "Lead Us Not into Temptation." One night a mysterious stranger, offended earlier by the town and now planning revenge, leaves a sack, supposedly containing 160 pounds of gold coins, in the care of bank cashier Edward Richards, with detailed instructions to give the money to the unknown man who befriended the stranger earlier. The deserving recipient may identify himself by quoting the helpful advice he gave to the stranger. The message is in a sealed envelope in the sack. Hadleyburg's nineteen leading virtuous citizens succumb to temptation when they receive identical misinformation from the stranger about the remark. Even Richards fancies he made the statement. The upshot is that Burgess, the former town minister, agrees to conduct a reading of each citizen's statement that he made the remark, and each hypocritical leader (except Richards, whom Burgess spares because of a favor he once did Burgess) is exposed to public ridicule. The true message is an insult to Hadleyburg, which is called worse than hell. The vindictive stranger, disguised, buys up the coins, which are made of gilt lead, sells them to a wealthy citizen, and rewards Richards for his seeming honesty. Soon Richards begins to suffer pangs of conscience, wrongly fears that innocent Burgess plans to expose him soon, raves deliriously, and dies. Town leaders vote to drop "Not" from their motto.

"The Man That Corrupted Hadleyburg," Twain's most skillfully constructed story, is most frequently anthologized, and best illustrates his awareness both of human cupidity and of the effects of a guilty conscience.

"The Man with the Hoe" (1899). Poem by Edwin Markham.* In eloquent blank verse, the poet describes a field laborer so "distorted and soul-quenched" by hard work that he is now "dead to rapture and despair" and "brother to the ox." Let blindly greedy "lords and rulers in all lands" watch out when "this dumb terror shall rise to judge the world." As early as 1886 Markham was inspired by the work of Jean-François Millet, whose painting *The Man with the Hoe* he saw later. Markham read his poem "The Man with the Hoe" at a New Year's Eve party in 1898. The editor of the San Francisco *Examiner* heard it, was deeply moved by it, and published it (15 January 1899). It became an instant hit and the subject of controversy. Ambrose Bierce* ridiculed it and called Markham the laureate of demagogy. But William James* was highly impressed by it, and Frank Norris* gratefully patterned his poet Presley in *The Octopus* partly after Markham. When Markham published *The Man with the Hoe and Other Poems* (1899), it was an enormous financial success, ultimately earning him a reputed $250,000 in the next thirty years or so. "The Man with the Hoe" was one of the most popular nineteenth-century American poems, along with William Cullen Bryant's "Thanatopsis," John Greenleaf Whittier's "Snow-Bound," and Edgar Allan Poe's "The Raven."

Marden, Orison Swett (1848–1924). Journalist. He was born in Thornton, New Hampshire. Orphaned at age two, Marden quickly became used to hard work and faithful study. He went to Boston University (B.A. and B.S., 1877; M.A., 1879; LL.B, 1882), the Boston School of Oratory (B.O., 1879), and Harvard (M.D., 1881). After further study in Europe, he went into business in the Middle West, then returned to Boston (1894) to write a series of little self-help and inspirational books to encourage young people to emulate great role models and thus take charge of their progress toward material success. His books include *Pushing to the Front* (1894), *Architects of Fate* (1895), *How to Succeed* (1896), *Success* (1897), *The Secret of Achievement* (1898), *Cheerfulness as a Life Power* (1899), *Character the Greatest Thing in the World* (1899), *Good Manners and Success* (1900), *The Hour of Opportunity* (1900), *Winning Out* (1900), *Elements of Business Success* (1900), *An Iron Will* (1901), *Talks with Great Workers* (1901), *How They Succeeded* (1901), and later ones with similarly hortatory titles and contents to 1921. Marden founded and edited an illustrated magazine called *Success* (1897–1911), which promoted work toward material gain. Theodore Dreiser* published several essays in *Success*, using pseudonyms. A few years after *Success* failed, Marden found a new financial backer and started up a new *Success* (1918), which did well until he died. He was also editor in chief of the *Consolidated Encyclopedia Library* (10 vols., 1901). Thirty of his books were translated into German, and 3,000,000 or more copies of his books were sold in twenty-five languages. Marden married Clare L. Evans in 1905.

Margaret Fleming (1890). Play by James A. Herne.* Margaret Fleming is the wife of Massachusetts mill owner Philip Fleming and the mother of their tiny baby Lucy. Philip learns through his friend and family physician Dr. Larken that Lena Schmidt, Philip's girlfriend, has just had their illegitimate baby and is dying. Philip goes to them. Meanwhile, Margaret, at home and suffering from glaucoma, is sad that her husband is late in arriving to celebrate Lucy's birthday. Maria, their maid and Lena's sister, knows that the unfortunate girl is dying and vows revenge on the father, unrevealed as yet to her. Dr. Larken privately warns Philip, of whom he is highly critical, that a shock could blind Margaret, who, however, innocently goes with Maria to visit Lena. The girl has written an explanatory letter and dies. Dr. Larken is there but can do little to restrain Maria, who reads the revealing letter, learns of Philip's complicity, and brandishes a pistol. Margaret stops Maria's plans of vengeance by revealing that she herself has suffered more in a few minutes than dead Lena ever did. She ignores the doctor's warning to stay calm, sends for Philip, and nurses dead Lena's hungry infant herself. Philip enters and silently observes. In the final scene, Margaret, now blind, is tending her garden and hears both babies in their common crib. Philip, gone a week, returns home to learn that Margaret is blind. She lectures him poignantly on the double standard, then welcomes him back—but not as a loving wife. He explains that he tried to drown himself in the Charles River, but was revived and hospitalized, and now hopes to regain her respect. She says, "Ah, dreams! Philip! And we must get to work," adding that his babies are in the garden.

In the first version, five years pass before the last act: Lena's child dies, Maria steals Lucy for revenge, and Margaret refuses to forgive her husband. In early productions, Herne, the playwright, took the role of Philip Fleming and his wife Katharine Corcoran Herne played Margaret; in various revivals, their daughters Julie and Chrystal Herne played Margaret. *Margaret Fleming*, which was highly praised by Thomas Bailey Aldrich,* B. O. Flower,* Hamlin Garland,* and William Dean Howells,* among others, greatly advanced the cause of realism and feminism in the American theater. The unique manuscript of *Margaret Fleming* was destroyed when the Hernes' Long Island home burned, but Mrs. Herne rewrote it from memory.

Markham, Edwin (1852–1940). (Original name: Charles Edward Anson Markham.) Poet. He was born in Oregon City, Oregon. His father, from New York and then Michigan, was a hunter and farmer. His mother was a well-read, greedy, religious fanatic. The couple had moved from Michigan to Oregon (1847) and were divorced soon after the birth of the future poet, the last of nine children (including three by the poet's father's first marriage). The mother took the boy to California and tried marriage there two more times. Markham tended sheep at age eight or nine and was doing farm work by the age of twelve. He read widely, obtained haphazard schooling, graduated from Christian College in Santa Rosa (1873), taught school, was unhappily married to Annie Cox (1875–1884), got into politics, became an El Dorado County school official (from 1879), read socialist Christian authors, married again unhappily (1887; this wife, Caroline E. Bailey, was older, had two grown children, and soon left the marriage), and began to publish prolabor poetry in respectable New York and London magazines (by the 1880s). He became a school principal in Oakland (1890) and struck up friendships with such California literary celebrities as Mary Austin,* Ambrose Bierce,* and Joaquin Miller.* He traveled east to the World's Columbian Exposition* (Chicago, 1893) and on to Boston and New York, where he met Hamlin Garland,* among other authors.

About 1895, Markham took Edwin as his first name. He happily married Anna Catherine Murphy, a teacher and poetess, in 1898 (the couple had one child). Inspired by the painting of *The Man with the Hoe* by Jean-François Millet, Markham wrote his famous poem "The Man with the Hoe,"* which when published (1899) was acclaimed as a controversial masterpiece. After its financial success—it garnered a reputed $250,000 in the next thirty or so years—the Markhams moved to New York, where his "Lincoln, the Man of the People"* (1900) was another huge hit. Markham remained sincerely idealistic and continued to be interested in liberal causes, including reform of child-labor laws; but his writings after 1901 are not impressive. He lived on Staten Island, made disastrous investments, took to lecturing, wrote sentimental hack poetry, was widowed in 1938, and died two years later.

Marquis, Albert Nelson (1855–1943). Publisher and editor. Born in Brown County, Ohio, and later orphaned early in his childhood, he was cared for by maternal relatives. He worked in a family store (1873–1876), then sold books in Cincinnati, started his own publishing firm, and moved it to Chicago (1884). He published the first business directory for that city and developed the idea of compiling a biographical directory of Americans along the lines of a successful British *Who's Who* (1897). Marquis's first such volume was called *Who's Who in America* (1899). Successive volumes soon appeared (1901, 1904, 1906), all edited by Marquis's longtime associate John W. Leonard, who had migrated from England to the United States (1868). Marquis himself edited the fifth and later *Who's Who* volumes. Ultraconservative, he included important Americans in the arts, education, government, the military, religion, and the sciences, but not sports figures, persons with suspicious political connections, felons, or divorced people. Contrary to popular belief, one cannot successfully ask to be included, nor is one required to buy a volume to be included. Marquis incorporated his concern and retained a 20-percent interest (1924), remained president (to 1937) and editor in chief (to 1940), with headquarters in Indianapolis, Indiana, but with some offices in Chicago and nearby Wilmette. Marquis married Henriette Rosanna Gettemy Morgan in 1910.

Medicine and Medical Advances. As in every decade, physicians and medical researchers in the 1890s made significant discoveries and advancements in medical science. Relatively few Americans were immediately involved in the late nineteenth century but in the early years of the twentieth century made significant contributions in the field of theoretical and practical medicine. Meanwhile, medical history was being made outside the United States. Emil von Behring, bacteriologist, discovered antitoxins (Berlin, 1890). Alexandre Emile John Yersin and Shibasaburo Kitazato, bacteriologists, simultaneously and independently discovered the plague bacillus (Hong Kong, 1894). Wilhelm Konrad Röntgen, physics professor, photographed x-rays of the human hand (Würzburg, Germany, 1895). Emil H. Grubbe, researcher, discovered that x-rays in heavy doses can kill living cells and experimented on a patient with breast cancer (Chicago, 1896). Ronald Ross discovered the malaria bacillus (India, 1897). Kiyoshi Shiga, having worked with Paul Ehrlich in Germany, discovered the endemic dysentery bacillus (Japan, 1898). These Americans contributed in due course: Walter Reed,* U.S. Army surgeon, discovered that mosquitoes transmit the yellow fever virus (Havana, Cuba, 1900). And John Jacob Abel, an American physician and chemist, and Jokichi Takamine, a Japanese chemist, isolated adrenaline, defined as the first pure hormone obtained from a natural source (Baltimore, 1901). Americans did more in ensuing years.

Memoirs of Marau Taaroa, Last Queen of Tahiti (1893). Biography by Henry Adams.* This work is the literary result of Henry Adams's stay in Tahiti (March–June 1891) during his 1890 to 1892 voyage around the world with his artist friend John La Farge.* Adams loved the climate, beaches and waters, valleys, and native life of this paradise in the Pacific, but he was too restless intellectually to be passive. He made the acquaintance of Tati Salmon, a half-native, half–London Jewish island leader, and through him met and listened to Marau Taaroa, the last queen of the island, narrate its history. Adams took notes and wrote part of his book while on Tahiti, returned to Washington, D.C., where he conducted more research, received more material from Marau and Tati, completed the book, and published it privately (1893, in ten copies). Tahitian friends suggested changes, and Adams published a revised edition, entitled *Memoirs of Arii Taimai E* . . . (Paris 1901; Arii Taimai was Marau's mother, the real "chiefess").

Adams lets Marau narrate, with charm and irony, the island saga, at first more fabulous than scientific, from the thirteenth century to 1850. She discusses the conflicts between early Tahitian clans (love, war, and political jealousy), the importance of women, the effects of cruel European adventurers (from 1767, with respect to politics, weapons, religion, and disease), and native genealogies (Adams presents seven family trees, c. 1650–1877). *Memoirs of Marau Taaroa,*

Last Queen of Tahiti is intriguing and valuable for historians and anthropologists; it is also often boring.

Mercedes: A Drama in Two Acts (1894). Prose tragedy by Thomas Bailey Aldrich.* The action occurs in Spain in 1810, during Napoleon's campaign there. Captain Achille Louvois is ordered to massacre the villagers in Arguano, where, almost two years ago, he had been cured by Mercedes of a wound and then loved by her. The would-be victims poison some wine and flee, but Mercedes stays to tend to her thirteen-month-old daughter and also her feeble grandmother. The men of Laboissière, who is Louvois's lieutenant, find the wine. He forces Mercedes and the baby to sample the wine first, then he shares the rest with his soldiers. When the baby dies, the men learn the truth and rush out. Louvois enters, has a reconciliation with Mercedes, tells her he drank some of the wine outside, and watches her die.

"A Message to Garcia" (1899). Editorial narrative essay by Elbert Hubbard.* During the Spanish-American War,* President William McKinley* orders Lieutenant Andrew S. Rowan to report to Cuban insurgent General Calixto García Íñiguez, to determine how America can help him in his struggle against the Spanish forces. Rowan heroically surmounts many difficulties in accomplishing his mission. The moral of this stirring little work, explicitly stated by Hubbard, is that one should stick to one's mission, through thick and thin, and be efficient in doing so. It is estimated that 40,000,000 copies of "A Message to Garcia" were distributed, often to military personnel, up to the time of World War II.

Miles, Nelson A. (1839–1925). (Full name: Nelson Appleton Miles.) Army officer. Born near Westminster, Massachusetts, he clerked in a crockery store in Boston and served in the Union army during the Civil War (1861–1865), during which he was wounded four times and at the end of which he was major general of volunteers. Remaining in the army (as a colonel, from 1866), he went to the frontier; fought during the Red River War against Native Americans of Kiowa, Comanche, and Southern Cheyenne tribes (1874–1875); campaigned against the Sioux on the Northern Plains (1874–1875); and forced the Nez Percé under Chief Joseph to surrender (1877). By now a brigadier general (as of 1880), Miles was ordered (in May 1886) to capture Geronimo,* on the loose in Arizona Territory. After much difficulty, Miles's subordinate officers brought Geronimo in (September 1886), and the general sent him and some of his band to exile and confinement in Florida. Miles (with the rank of major general beginning in 1890) was in command of the Military Division of the Missouri when the Sioux uprising occurred in the Dakotas (1890). He tried to arrange a peaceful end to the conflict but was nominally responsible when matters got out of hand and ended in the Wounded Knee* massacre (1890). Miles was in command of the troops ordered by President Grover Cleveland* to put down the rioting caused by the Pullman Strike* (Chicago, 1894). Miles was promoted to commander in chief of the U.S. Army (1895). He argued with Russell A. Alger, secretary of war under President William McKinley* (1898), and led a minor expeditionary force against weak Spanish forces in Puerto Rico during the Spanish-American War* (1898). Miles was promoted to lieutenant general in 1900 and retired in 1903.

Miles wrote *Serving the Republic* (1911), an abridged and updated version of his earlier, better autobiography, entitled *Personal Recollections of Nelson A. Miles* (1897, illustrated by Frederic Remington*). Miles's other books are *Military Europe* (1898) and *Observations Abroad* (1899). Miles was skillful, courageous, and aggressive, but also pompous and self-aggrandizing. Theodore Roosevelt,* who disliked and once censured him, called him a "brave peacock." In addition, Miles was jealously critical of fellow officers trained, as he had not been, at West Point.

Miller, Joaquin (c. 1837–1841—1913). (Real name: Cincinnatus Hiner Miller.) Poet, prose writer, playwright, and ridiculous poseur. He was born near Liberty, Indiana, but at an early age migrated with his family to Oregon (1852). He led an adventurous life (later richly embroidered upon to promote his books) as a miner, Indian fighter, horse thief, express rider, editor, lawyer, and judge (to 1869). He published two books of poetry (1868, 1869), got some help from Ina Coolbrith* on how to read his poems in public, and went to London (1870–1871). There Miller dressed outlandishly (to the disgust of Ambrose Bierce* and Mark Twain,* among other serious Westerners), was lionized by important literary personalities as "the Byron of the Sierras," and published two more books of poetry (1871). Miller lived in various places abroad and in the United States until he bought some acreage near Oakland, California, his permanent residence thereafter (from 1887). He went to Alaska and the Yukon as a reporter for William Randolph Hearst* in 1897.

In the 1890s, Miller published *In Classic Shades and Other Poems* (1890), *Songs of Summer Lands* (1892), *The Building of the City Beautiful* (1893), *An Illustrated History of the State of Montana* (1894), and *Songs of the Soul* (1896). Miller's verses are sometimes vigorous and even thrilling, but too often they are hasty, commonplace, and imitative. Miller beckoned non-Western readers to a West that was mostly myth. He was a valuable champion of Western minorities, but he took himself too seriously as an intellectual pioneer. He designed his own granite burial monument, ten feet by ten feet, and eight feet tall, outside Oakland.

Mr. Dooley in Peace and in War (1898). Collection of newspaper columns by Finley Peter Dunne.* Mr. Martin J. Dooley, about sixty years old, migrated from Roscommon, Ireland, to Chicago in the early 1850s. He lives in the Sixth Ward, known as Bridgeport, owns a saloon on "Ar-rchey R-road" (Archer Avenue), was precinct captain from 1873 to 1875 but then "declined to leave the bar for the forum," and now delivers homespun, cracker-barrel comments during innumerable conversations with his straight man Malachi Hennesy, a local mill worker. Rival personalities include those of John McKenna, an Irish Republican politician in Chicago, and Schwartzmeister, the owner of a nearby competing saloon. From the start, in 1893, Dunne's Mr. Dooley essays were a ringing success. They combine satirical use of Irish-American dialect, tortuous misspellings but accurate syntax, bittersweet urban wit, puns, aphorisms, burlesque, horse sense, and down-to-earth moralizing. The humorous lingo, which loses much when translated into standard English, is hard to follow, but it can be understood if read patiently. In a preface, it is explained that the various Irish accents have been modified by "substituting cinders and sulphuretted hydrogen for soft misty air and peat smoke," and that his friends are simple—yes, "like th' air or th' deep sea. Not complicated like a watch that stops whin th' shoot iv clothes ye got it with wears out."

Mr. Dooley pokes fun at William McKinley* (called "Presidint," "Prisident," "Willum," and "Mack") for his "Ph'lippeens" strategy; at preening "Gin'ral [Nelson A.] Miles [*];" and even at "Tiddy Rosenfelt" (Theodore Roosevelt*)." Still, American war prayers ought to succeed because we have "th' most modhern prayin' machines in the warruld," including "a flyin' squadhron iv Methodists, three Presbyteryan monitors, a fleet iv Baptist submarine desthroyers, an' a formidable array iv Universalist an' Unitaryan torpedo boats, with a Jew r-ram." Opposing forces are also ridiculed, including "Gin'ral Garshy" (i.e., revolutionist Calixto García Íñiguez) and his "Cuban pathrite[s']" propensity to eat and smoke. The "Peace" essays blast at a multitude of American topics: golf and football, novels ("th' roon iv people"), political reforms and parades and oratory, urban squalor ("they'se poison in th' life iv a big city"), the fiscal policy of "th' Pops" (i.e., members of the Populist Party*) and their desire for Free Silver*—after all, "[w]hisky is th' [only] standard iv value. It niver fluctuates; an' that's funny, too, seein' that so much iv it goes doen. . . . Goold and silver fluctuates"), and Manifest Destiny ("th' Inyun is bound f'r to give way to th' onward march iv white civilization").

Europe is not spared: its "arnychists," ineffective Greek army ("Whiniver they win, they lose; an', whin they lose, they lose"), Queen Victoria in particular ("She may be a good woman f'r all I know, but dam her pollytics"), and the French in general (since they "ar-re not steady ayether in their politics or their morals. That's where they get done be th' hated British"). The high point of Dunne's anti-European essays may well be his summary in dialect of the trial of "Cap Dhry-fuss" (i.e., innocent Captain Alfred Dreyfus, tried for treason in French military courts), who was defended in 1898 by "[m]e frind [Émile] Zola," whose "Jackuse" (i.e., "J'accuse") was "a mane thing to say to anny man."

Mr. Dooley in Peace and in War was the first and best collection of Mr. Dooley essays; it was followed by *Mr. Dooley in the Hearts of His Countrymen* (1899) and six more Mr. Dooley books. The first two each sold 10,000 copies a month when they first came out. All eight were best-sellers and were republished in England.

Mitchell, S. Weir (1829–1914). (Full name: Silas Weir Mitchell.) Physician, toxicologist, and author. Weir Mitchell, the son of a physician and poet, was born in Philadelphia, attended the University of Pennsylvania but withdrew when he became sick, graduated from Jefferson Medical College (1850), studied neurology for a year in Paris, and during the Civil War was a surgeon and a sanitary commission member. Thereafter, in Philadelphia, Mitchell practiced and taught medicine and did extensive research on snake venom, opium and other pain killers, peripheral nerve paralysis, cerebellum physiology, neurology, psychology, stress and fatigue, and fat and blood. He published articles in medical journals and also the following books: *Gunshot Wounds and Other Injuries of the Nerves* (1864), *Wear and Tear* (1871), *Injuries of Nerves and Their Consequences* (1872), *Fat and Blood* (1877), and *Doctor and Patient* (1888).

Mitchell was regarded as the foremost American neurologist of his time. Sigmund Freud knew and praised Mitchell's work, specifically in 1887 and 1895 reviews. On the other hand, Mitchell deplored Freud's emphasis on sex and tossed one of Freud's books into the fire. Mitchell may be criticized today for physiologically treating symptoms of neuroses without delving into psychological causes. Mitchell was famous in his day for advocating the so-called Weir Mitchell Treatment for nervous breakdowns, which prescribed extreme, prolonged rest in bed in isolation, excessive feeding, and daily massage. He so treated Charlotte Perkins Gilman,* among innumerable others, but modified his method of treatment after reading Gilman's short story "The Yellow Wall-paper."* Mitchell advised Owen Wister* to visit the West to improve his health; treated Winifred Howells, the psychoneurotic daughter of William Dean Howells;* and advised Edith Wharton* that writing fiction had therapeutic value.

Mitchell wrote and published fiction himself, including clinically narrated war and medical stories (beginning in the 1860s) and early historical fiction (from the 1870s). He wrote fifteen novels in all. The best of his 1880s novels are *In War Time* (1885), about cowardice; *Roland Blake* (1886), concerning not only Civil War espionage but also female neuroticism; and *Far in the Forest* (1889), with a Gothic plot cast on the antebellum Pennsylvania frontier. Notable novels by Mitchell in the 1890s are *Characteristics* (1892), in which conversations reveal traits, as is the case with its sequel *Dr. North and His Friends* (1900), very popular; *Hugh Wynne, Free Quaker* (1897), a uniquely fine American Revolutionary War novel cast in Philadelphia; *The Adventures of François* (1898), detailing the picaresque derring-do of a romantic rogue during the French Revolution; and *Circumstance* (1901), dramatizing the effects of circumstances upon character, and also involving alcoholism. Mitchell also wrote stories for children, as well as poetry in several collections, the last being *The Wager* (1900). In the early years of the twentieth century, he published more novels, some concerned with historical events, others with neurotic characters. He wrote *Westways*, his last novel, in 1913, when he was eighty-four.

The Monk and the Hangman's Daughter (1892). Short novel of thirty-six tiny chapters by Ambrose Bierce* with G. A. Danziger. This work is based loosely on a translation by Gustav Adolph Danziger of a story entitled *Der Mönch von Berchtesgaden* (1891) by Richard Voss (1851–1918), who said that he found the original in a Bavarian monastery manuscript. Bierce polished Danziger's translation and amplified the plot. The callow, deluded narrator is a monk named Ambrosius, age twenty-one in 1670, who leaves Passau for a novitiate in Berchtesgaden. Once there, he befriends Benedicta, the daughter of the local hangman, who is widowed, sad, and passive. Ambrosius contends with Rochus, the Saltmaster's tough son, for Benedicta. Ambrosius wants her to avoid dancing with Rochus and instead accept his protection and spiritual guidance. After a night of ecstatic confusion during a mountain retreat, Ambrosius rushes to her hut by Black Lake. He fights Rochus, who defeats but spares him and leaves. He urges Benedicta to repent, die, and be saved; but when she voices preference for Rochus, he stabs her to death, returns to his superior, confesses, and is soon to be hanged.

In some ways, Bierce here anticipates Freudian theory in equating religious and sexual ecstasy. Bierce, in typical fashion, had a huge argument with Danziger over who should get more credit for creating this adaptation.

The Monster and Other Stories (1899). A collection of three reprinted stories by Stephen Crane.* They are "The Monster," "The Blue Hotel,"* and "His New Mittens." "The Monster," of novella length, tells the fate of dapper, cakewalking Henry Johnson, a brave black stableman employed by Dr. Ned Trescott, in Whilomville, New York (patterned after Port Jervis). One day the doctor's house catches on fire. Henry rushes to rescue the man's little son Jimmie. Their only path to safety is through the doctor's laboratory, which the fire has turned into a "garden of burning flowers." Exploding, fiery chemicals spew over the black hero's body and simply eat off his face. Dr. Trescott places the faceless "monster" with a local African-American family. When they become terrified, he cares for Henry in a room over his carriage house. But Henry frightens Jimmie's playmates, scares his former girlfriend, discomfits townspeople, and causes loyal Dr. Trescott to lose much of his practice. Crane sketches town mores deftly, records African-American lingo well, and ultimately depicts the town as more monstrous than the hapless monster. Both Dr. Trescott and Jimmie reappear in several tales collected in Crane's *Whilomville Stories*. "The Blue Hotel" is an intricate, ironic, didactic tale of a Swedish tailor from New York who encounters death in a snowy Nebraska town. The explicitly stated moral, "Every sin is the result of a collaboration," is abundantly dramatized. "His New Mittens," about a sad little boy, is of no great value.

Moody, William Vaughn (1869–1910). Poet, playwright, and editor. He was born in Spencer, Indiana, one of seven children in the family. Their mother, of a pioneering family, died in 1884; their father, a steamboat pilot turned businessman, died two years later. An excellent student, Moody taught school; went to Riverview Academy in Poughkeepsie, New York; and at the age of twenty entered Harvard, where he met Robert Herrick,* George Cabot Lodge,* Robert Morss Lovett,* George Santayana,* and Trumbull Stickney,* among others. (Moody later knew Stickney well and with Lodge and his brother John Lodge edited Stickney's posthumously published poetry.) Moody completed course work in three years with a splendid record, traveled to Europe and the eastern Mediterranean region, returned to Harvard for graduation (1893) and further study (M.A., 1894), and taught English there (1894–1895), where part of the time he was an assistant to Lewis E. Gates* and also Gertrude Stein's instructor. Moody joined the faculty at the University of Chicago (1895–1902) and resumed his friendship with Lovett there. While teaching conscientiously, Moody also prepared editions of works by several standard British writers and began to publish his own poetry (from 1898). During his free time, he traveled widely and vigorously. In Chicago, New York, and Boston, he established friendships with Henry Blake Fuller,* Hamlin Garland,* Edwin Arlington Robinson,* Theodore Roosevelt,* and others. He and Lovett together wrote *A History of English Literature* (1902) and *A First View of English Literature* (1905), both of which enjoyed good financial returns.

Moody planned an ambitious dramatic trilogy (never produced) concerned with mankind's necessary rebellion against God. The plays became *The Masque of Judgment* (1900), praising humankind for properly exercising free will against a wrongful deity; *The Fire-Bringer* (1904), which continues Moody's praise of nature and liberating knowledge by retelling the Promethean myth; and *The Death of Eve* (1912, incomplete), which if finished would have dramatized the reconciliation of God and humanity through His creation of the enduringly Hellenistic female. Of more significance are a few of Moody's timely poems, including "Gloucester Moors" (1900), "The Menagerie," "Ode in Time of Hesitation" (1900), and "On a Soldier Fallen in the Philippines" (1901), all collected in Moody's 1901 *Poems*.* Toward the end of his life, Moody wrote two more plays: *The Great Divide*, successfully produced in New York (1909), contrasting a New England Puritan woman and a free-and-easy Western frontiersman; and *The Faith Healer* (1909), about occultism and levels of love and pain. Moody married Harriet Brainard in Quebec in 1909. The two lived briefly in London, but Moody soon began to go blind and died in California of a brain tumor (1910).

Like his couple in *The Great Divide*, William Vaughn Moody was caught between moralistic, classical, New England conservativism, on the one hand, and modern liberal, scientific, and social philosophies and a freer, even colloquial mode of expression, on the other.

More Fables (1900). Additional "fables" by George Ade,* capitalizing on the great success of *Fables in Slang** (1900). From the first, these fables were unique, marked by capitalized nouns, slang, clichés, mordant humor, accurate American vernacular, absence of literary pretentiousness, and end-of-text morals. *More Fables* was followed by *Forty Modern Fables** (1901).

Morgan, John Pierpont (1837–1913). Banker and financier. He was born in Hartford, Connecticut, the son of Junius Spencer Morgan (1813–1890). At the time, Junius Spencer Morgan was a merchant whose success resulted in his moving to London (1854) as a partner in a bank started by the American merchant George Peabody. Young John Pierpont Morgan accompanied his father to Europe, attended schools in Switzerland and Germany, and worked for his father (from 1857) in a New York bank which represented Peabody in the United States. Young Morgan formed his own bank (1861) and during the Civil War he turned much of his attention to foreign exchange. He and his father combined with Charles H. Dabney to represent Peabody when Peabody retired (1864). J. P. Morgan engineered a coup against Jay Gould* and James Fisk (1869). When Dabney retired (1871), the Morgans and Anthony Drexel of Philadelphia formed a banking firm called Drexel, Morgan & Company. Morgan upset the shifty efforts of Jay Cooke to create a monopoly in government refunding operations (1873). William H. Vanderbilt encouraged Morgan in railroad refinancing operations (1879). When Junius Spencer Morgan died in 1890, with 75 percent of his wealth in his collection of art and allied objects, and then Drexel died in 1893, J. P. Morgan led the old firm and soon renamed it J. P. Morgan & Company (1895). By the end of the 1890s, only Gould and Edward Henry Harriman* rivaled Morgan in the control of railroads.

The Morgans were able to amass their vast fortunes by several strategies. They habitually used their British contacts to sell American corporate securities to enable American businesses to compete and expand. They also financed reorganizations and mergers, greatly to their own profit. J. P. Morgan was a spectacular success on at least three occasions in the 1890s. The Panic of 1893* bankrupted or at least seriously depressed most of the major American railroads, which Morgan soon thereafter invested in, bailed out, and reorganized, especially in the East, to his great advantage. During the depression of 1895 (while Grover Cleveland* was president), Morgan supplied some $65,000,000 in gold to the federal government (for a $7,000,000 commission) and thus prevented the treasury from suspending currency redemption in coin. He also formed the Federal Steel Company (1898), was soon able to buy out Andrew Carnegie* for $400,000,000 (1901), and thereby produced the world's first billion-dollar company—U.S. Steel (1901). Charles M. Schwab* engineered the purchase. During a time of national economic distress, a reporter asked Morgan if a statement to the public might not be in order, to which Morgan made his famous reply: "I owe the public nothing" (1901). But he and some other New York financial wizards combined forces to prevent a near-total Wall Street collapse (1907). Morgan's dangerous power eventually caused federal politicians to see the wisdom of creating the Federal Reserve System as a check (1913).

Morgan was a banking, insurance money, and management titan. He delegated authority cannily. The genius inventor Nikola Tesla* was his client. Morgan was a generous philanthropist. He was an art, manuscript, and book collector. The Morgan Library in New York City owes much to him. He also supported the Metropolitan Museum of Art in New York. He was a sincere Episcopalian. This princely man granted few interviews and left no written articles or autobiographical papers behind. He died in Rome. Morgan married Amelia Sturges in Paris in 1861—she died a few months later—and Frances Louise Tracey in New York City in 1865 (the couple had four children). His only son, John Pierpont Morgan, Jr. (1867–1943), was born in Irvington, New York, graduated from Harvard (1889), became a New York partner in his deceased father's firm (beginning in 1892), in time handled the Morgan empire with undramatic skill, and like his father was an Episcopalian and an art collector. He established the Morgan Library as a magnificent, permanently endowed institution (1923).

Motion Pictures. The American movie industry, which was born late in the 1890s, was the result of the often independent and sometimes cooperative work of many pioneers in the United States, France, England, and Germany. Eadweard Muybridge* analyzed motion by taking a sequence of photographs of a horse galloping past twenty-four cameras (1870s). Étienne J. Marey in France invented a photographic gun and camera to capture phases of motion on film (1880s). Thomas A. Edison* abortively tried to synchronize tiny photographic images, viewed through a microscope, with sounds emanating from a cylindrical phonograph (1888); he also photographed objects and placed the pictures on strips of high-speed emulsions mounted on a celluloid base, designed by George Eastman* (1889). Edison then gave up on sound effects, applied for patents on his kinetograph camera (1891), and marketed his kinetoscope. This peep-show device, actually invented by William Kennedy Laurie Dickson in Edison's laboratory (1888), was fine-tuned to put forty-six images per second on a forty-foot roll of Eastman celluloid film (1894). Edison opened a little movie parlor on Broadway, in New York City, which accommodated one viewer at a time, who could look through a magnifying lens at images lighted by an electric lamp, along one loop of film, for fifty seconds, for one cent (1894). Similar shops soon opened in London and Paris (later in 1894). Edison, who had built his own shack of a movie studio in West Orange, New Jersey (1893), in which to film a variety of vaudeville acts to feed his peep shows, neglected to extend his early patent rights to England and France.

Auguste Lumière and his brother Louis Lumière in France were therefore able legally to improve on the kinetoscope by developing not only lighter weight cameras to photograph on celluloid film but also machines to project the resulting images on a screen, and to a whole audience at once—for the first time on 28 December 1895. Similar inventors were also at work in England and in Germany modifying instruments based on Edison's designs. Edison quickly moved to modify his bulky kinetoscope, developed a vitascope (buying a patent from Thomas Armat to do so), and also began to project images on a screen in New York (1896). While the Lumières were filming and screening real-life incidents—trains, bicycles, firemen, beach scenes, and so on—George Méliès, a French magician and showman who had been intrigued by a Lumière show, bought a camera in England and began to make trick movies (1896–1897)—disappearing and transposed heads and the like—and fairy-tale dramas—*Cinderella* (1899) and *Red Riding Hood* (1901), among others. Meanwhile, precursors of newsreel cameramen were in Cuba and South Africa to shoot action scenes during the Spanish-American War* (1898) and the Boer War (1899–1902). When rivals began making thousands of dollars from what Edison originally regarded as a penny-making toy, he brought many lawsuits against them (1898–1908), and the so-called patent wars ended only when nine major movie companies, including those of Edison and Méliès, were able to join forces and create the Motion Picture Patents Company in 1908 to control most aspects of the U.S. film business.

At the turn of the century, American motion-picture "features" usually lasted about twenty minutes, but they quickly became longer and more sophisticated. These include *The Life of an American Fireman* (1902) and *The Great Train Robbery* (1903), both created by Edwin S. Porter, a former Edison cameraman. The year 1905 marks the approximate date when movies moved from peep-show nickelodeons to ever-larger and more lavish theaters. David Wark Griffith, once an actor under Porter (1907), graduated to directing shows for the Biograph Studio, Edison's principal rival (1907–1912), and then he created the first film epic, *The Birth of a Nation* (1915). Names of other American motion-picture greats, many of whom grew up or were born in the 1890s, include Cecil B. DeMille, Geraldine Ferrar, Lillian Gish, Samuel Goldwyn, Carl Laemmle, Marcus Loew, Hal Roach, Mary Pickford, Max Sennett, and Adolph Zukor.

The Mountains of California (1894). Nature book by John Muir.* This volume contains a set of careful, personal, and charming descriptions of the Sierra Nevada both from a distance and from close up. Muir painstakingly tells about its residual glaciers, snows and "snow banners," passes (including Sonora, Kearsarge, Mono, and Virginia Creek), lakes of many shapes (including Donner, Shadow, Orange, and Starr King), pastures and meadows (including hanging and pothole types), rivers, forests of many types of trees (notably pine, spruce, fir, cedar, and *Sequoia Gigantea*) in calm weather and when buffeted by winds and storms, and birds and animals. A classic chapter is devoted to the captivating Douglas squirrel (*Sciurus Douglasii*). Muir here displays his genius for touching accurate and graphic scientific description into what amounts to poetry, because of his obvious adoration of all things great and small in nature. *The Mountains of California* was the result of ten years of exploration on Muir's part. Muir also prepared a revised edition (1911).

Movies. *See* Motion Pictures.

Muir, John (1838–1914). Naturalist, explorer, conservationist, and author. He was born in Dunbar, Scotland, where his dour Calvinist father tried with incomplete success to hamper his enjoyment of wild outdoor life. Muir immigrated to a Wisconsin farm (1849), attended the University of Wisconsin (1859–1863), and then began his inspiring life as a naturalist. He tramped through Wisconsin, Illinois, and Indiana gathering botanical specimens, walked from Indianapolis to California (1867–1868), settled in the Yosemite Valley (1868–1874), and explored in Nevada, Utah, and Alaska. Once back in California, he married Louie Wanda Strentzel in 1880 (the couple had two children), rented and then bought land from his expatriate Polish horticulturalist father-in-law, and lived on and worked a fruit farm (1881–1891). He successfully lobbied for the creation of the Yosemite National Park (1889, established by Congress in 1890), founded the Sierra Club (1892), and campaigned to have acreage of federal forests vastly increased (from 1897). He was the revered friend of numerous nature-loving authors, for example, Mary Austin.* Muir's best books are *The Mountains of California** (1894, rev. ed. 1911) and *Our National Parks** (1901). More than any other person, although there were many, Muir was responsible for the establishment of National Parks* in the United States. Muir also edited *Picturesque California and the Regions West of the Rocky Mountains from Alaska to Mexico* (1888). His best late writing is contained in *My First Summer in the Sierras* (1911). John Muir is an inspiring example of a nature lover. He adored nature in all of its wild and gentle aspects, observed it as God's living and eternally beautiful system, and wrote about it in fresh, delightful, and informative prose.

Munsey, Frank A. (1854–1925). (Full name: Frank Andrew Munsey.) Publisher. He was born in Mercer, Maine. He worked as a telegraph operator in Maine (to 1882), then started a publishing enterprise in New York (1882). He published several magazines, notably the *Argosy*, *Junior Munsey*, *Munsey's Magazine,** the *Puritan*, and the *Quaker*, and contributed his own fiction to some of these. He also established an agency to distribute his publications. He issued hardbound novels priced at 25¢ and sizable 2¢ paperbacks. Munsey wrote an autobiographical essay entitled "The Founding of the Munsey Publishing-House" (1907), which explained his techniques and boasted that his net profit was $500,000 in 1900. He later bought the New York *Evening Sun* and the New York *Evening Telegram* and a chain of grocery stores. He left most of his estate to the Metropolitan Museum of Art in New York.

Munsey's Magazine. Popular magazine. Begun by Frank A. Munsey* as a weekly entitled *Munsey's Weekly* (1889–1891), this magazine continued as an illustrated, better marketed monthly called *Munsey's Magazine* (1891–1918) and then simply *Munsey's* (until 1929). It was most admired for its fiction, including that of Horatio Alger, Jr.* and F. Marion Crawford,* among others; its poetry, for example, by Bliss Carman,* its essays, including those by William Dean Howells* and Theodore Roosevelt;* and features by competent journalists (often anonymous) about literature, music, drama, public events, and outstanding Americans (including essays by Theodore Dreiser*). *Munsey's*, however, was probably more frequently purchased (at 10¢ a copy) for its seminude pictures and other artwork. Its circulation reached a peak in 1897, at 700,000 copies for each issue. Extensive advertising in *Munsey's* brought the owner big profits. Coverage of the Spanish-American War* was excellent in *Munsey's*. Munsey decried muckraking journalism and had little to do with it.

Music. In the 1890s, most Americans were too busy to be especially creative in the field of serious music. The few memorable American composers active in the decade were Victor Herbert,* Edward MacDowell,* Ethelbert Nevin,* and John Philip Sousa,* who often obtained their inspiration and developed their techniques by European study. Herbert, to be exact, was born in Ireland, not in the United States. Scott Joplin,* African-American composer and musician, had the distinction of inventing ragtime. A few literary figures also wrote libretti, notably George Ade* and Henry Blake Fuller.* Before 1890, only two American cities could point with pride to their own symphony orchestras; five more were established between 1891 and 1900 (*see* Symphony Orchestras). Distinguished singers, the best among them Mary Garden* and Ernestine Schumann-Heink,* graced American operatic and concert-hall stages. Enrico Caruso and others almost as stirring appeared a little later. Perhaps America's greatest contribution to world music in the 1890s was its many and varied musical comedies,* musical reviews,* and operettas* (*see also* Songs). One of the most important American dramas of the decade was *Madame Butterfly** by David Belasco,* which is now most memorable as the source of the plot line for the world-famous Giacomo Puccini grand opera of the same name.

Musical Comedies. The 1890s saw the production of numerous successful and unsuccessful musical comedies. Three of the most popular were *A Trip to Chinatown* (1891), *A Gaiety Girl* (1894), and *The Belle of New York* (1897). The music of *A Trip to Chinatown*, which was the biggest hit of the season, was composed by Percy Gaunt, with book and lyrics by Charles H. Hoyt. The principal songs were "The Bowery," "Reuben and Cynthia," and "After the Ball." The music of *A Gaiety Girl* was composed by Sidney Jones, with book by Owen Hall and lyrics by Harry Greenbank. The principal songs were "Private Tommy Jones" and "Sunshine Above." The music of *The Belle of New York* was composed by the distinguished Gustave Kerker, with book and lyrics by Hugh Morton. The principal songs were "They All Follow Me," "The Purity Brigade," "At ze Naughty Folies Bergère (My Feet Zey Fly up in ze Air)," and "The Anti-Cigarette League." Of incidental interest here is the fact that the music for *The Origin of the Cake Walk; or, Clorindy* (1898) was written by

Will Marion Cook; book and lyrics, by Paul Laurence Dunbar.* *The Origin of the Cake Walk* was the first all-black minstrel show to be performed for white audiences.

Musical Courier. Weekly journal. Published in New York City, beginning in 1880, it was the largest, most thorough, and most profitable weekly concerning music. James Huneker* was the most significant music critic publishing in it (1887–1902). Victor Herbert* was accused of plagiarism by the *Musical Courier*; when he sued for libel, he was awarded $15,000 in damages (1902).

Musical Reviews. The 1890s saw the production of numerous successful as well as unsuccessful musical reviews. Two of the most successful were *The Passing Show* (1894) and *In Gay New York* (1896). The music of *The Passing Show* was composed by Ludwig Englander, with lyrics and sketches by Sydney Rosenfeld. The principal songs were "Old Before His Time" and "Sex against Sex." The music of *In Gay New York* was composed by the distinguished Gustave Kerker, with lyrics and sketches by Hugh Morton. The principal songs were "Girlie Girl," "It's Forty Miles from Schenectady to Troy," "Jusqu'la," and "Molly."

Muybridge, Eadweard (1830–1904). (Full name: Eadweard James Muybridge; original name: Edward James Muggeridge; professional name: Helios.) Photographer. Born at Kingston-on-Thames, England, he worked in the family stationery and papermaking business, then immigrated to the United States (about 1852) and traveled widely as a representative of a British publishing firm. He established a bookstore in San Francisco (by 1856), was badly injured in a stage accident in Texas on his way home (1860), recovered slowly, and returned to San Francisco (1867). Becoming interested in photographing Western scenes (including Yosemite), he took some 2,000 pictures, including many in Alaska (to 1872). He also photographed many railroad scenes (1872–1877). Leland Stanford* of Palo Alto had a theory that galloping horses occasionally had all four hoofs off the ground, and he paid Muybridge to photograph horses in motion to find out for sure (beginning 1872). Muybridge married a girl named Flora Stone who was half his age, in 1872 (the couple had one child). When he caught her later in an act of adultery, he shot her lover to death and was tried and acquitted for the murder (1874). He took photographs in Central America, Mexico, and the Isthmus of Panama, and he photographed the Modoc Indians at war (1873–1874). He began again to photograph horses in motion (1876–1878); this time, he used a set of twelve cameras with stereoscopic lenses and with shutters tripped by threads snapped as the horse galloped by.

Muybridge invented what he called the zoöpraxiscope (also called the zoögyroscope) to project on a screen a rapid sequence of pictures of a variety of animals in motion (1879). He traveled and lectured in Europe (1880–1882). He published *Attitudes of Animals in Motion* (1881) shortly before Stanford and J.D.B. Stillman published *The Horse in Motion* (1882), which mentions Muybridge only perfunctorily in the preface. He sued Stanford but lost. The University of Pennsylvania and Thomas Eakins* financed Muybridge (1884–1885) to photograph the movements of animals and also men (including his cocky self nearly nude). Muybridge consulted with Thomas A. Edison,* without success, about combining the zoöpraxiscope and the phonograph to produce sound movies (1888). When Muybridge, by now lecturing widely, opened his Zoöpraxographical Hall at the World's Columbian Exposition* (Chicago, 1893), it was the first motion-picture theater. Finally, he returned to England, where he published *The Human Figure in Motion* (1901).

N

Naismith, James (1861–1939). Inventor of basketball. Born in Almonte, Ontario, Canada, he was orphaned at age eight and lived with an uncle in later childhood. In 1887 he graduated from McGill University in Montreal, Quebec, where he then taught physical education and coached sports* (1887–1890). He completed a course of study for the ministry at Presbyterian College in Montreal (1890), then worked as a physical-education director and taught at the YMCA Training School (now Springfield College) in Springfield, Massachusetts (1890–1895), where he graduated from the training program in 1891. (He later earned his M.P.E. there in 1910.) While Naismith worked as the physical-education director at the Denver YMCA (1895–1898), he earned his M.D. (1898) at the Gross Medical College (later called the University of Colorado School of Medicine). Finally, he taught physical education and was chapel director at the University of Kansas (1898–1937). While in Springfield, Naismith originated the game of basketball (1891) to provide indoor exercise for his students between the football season and the baseball season. (*See also* Sports.) Luther Halsey Gulick helped him design the game. For starters, Naismith nailed peach baskets overhead at opposite ends of his gymnasium and scheduled nine players on each team. At first, the game was called Naismith ball. The game has been considerably modified since then.

National Congress of Mothers. *See* Parent-Teacher Associations.

National Parks. The Greeks and the Romans set aside squares for public use, but in the Middle Ages the royalty and other rulers decided to reserve well-kept well-stocked open areas for their exclusive pleasure. Democracy-loving reformers in the eighteenth and nineteenth centuries thought anew of parks as natural retreats for the protection of flora, fauna, and scenery, and for public recreation. Urbanized and industrialized centers of population were crowded with ordinary people still more eager for parks. An early American observer of the British and Continental refuges developed in response to these needs was Frederick L. Olmsted,* who with his partner Calvert Vaux designed New York's Central Park. It was an inspiration for many of the city and national parks that followed. Meanwhile, explorers of the Far West, notably John Muir* and John Wesley Powell,* sent back glowing descriptions of what they had seen and thus whetted the curiosity of Eastern seaboard residents. At first national parks were envisioned as a means of protecting monumental scenery more than as faraway sites for recreation. Idealistic and patriotic scientists and writers, artists (especially Albert Bierstadt, George Catlin, and Thomas Moran), photographers (including Camillus S. Fly,* William Henry Jackson, and Eadweard Muybridge*), and various politicians were determined to keep Western scenery from being totally commercialized.

As time passed, the splendors of Yellowstone, Yosemite, and the Sierra Nevada became better known, and the national park concept gained favor. First, Yosemite was a California state park (1864); all the same, it should be regarded as essentially the first national park. (California agreed in 1890 to give the region to the federal government for the purposes of creating a national park.) Second came Yellowstone National Park (1872), in areas of what are now Idaho, Montana, and Wyoming. With the largest geyser area in the world, Yellowstone also boasts a canyon, hot springs, lakes, mountains, rivers, waterfalls, and unique scenery—in all, 3,468 square miles. Yellowstone National Park set the pattern for future national parks. In time came Yosemite National Park in California (1890), with granite peaks and domes, meadows, Sierra Nevada redwood (*Sequoia Gigantea*) forests, valleys, waterfalls, and wildlife—1,189 square miles—and Sequoia National Park in California (1890), with Sierra redwoods and Mount Whitney, the highest mountain peak in the continental United States—629 square miles. Mount Rainier National Park in Washington (1899), which contains the largest one-peak glacial system in the United States, also offers flowers, forests, and meadows, in 368 square miles. These parks were under the administrative supervision of the U.S. Army (1886–1916) but were then transferred to the National Park Service, under the Department of Interior. The twentieth century has seen the establishment of about 300 additional national parks, battlefield parks, battlefield sites, capital parks, lakeshores, military parks, parkways, recreation areas, and seashores. In the process, the birthplaces, homes, and workplaces of many persons of significance in the 1890s have been singled out for memorializing. The purpose of national parks and the setting aside of special locales is to preserve beautiful, spectacular, unique natural features and objects and sites of historical importance. These parks have superintendents, administrative staffs, curators, historians, interpreters, librarians, maintenance people, rangers, scientists, and facilities which aid and comfort millions of visitors annually. The National Park System at present consists of 358 sites in every state (except Delaware), in the District of Columbia, and also in American Samoa, Guam, Puerto Rico, Saipan, and the Virgin Islands. Park rangers at present number 3,200 (of whom 25 percent are women). It has been estimated that 68 percent of the American population have visited at least one national park.

Native Americans. Beginning, as the whole world knows, well before the Civil War, Native Americans were pushed ever farther west by waves of encroaching white settlers, farmers, ranchers, miners, and soldiers. All through the 1870s and 1880s, the process continued until the Native Americans were threatened with virtual extinction, precisely as were their essential and beloved buffalo. By the year 1890, the date according to Frederick Jackson Turner* when the American frontier ''closed,'' most Native Americans had been herded onto reservations, often far from their ancestral lands and under circumstances ranging from unpleasant to heartbreaking. Five Native Americans active in the 1890s illustrate varied responses to their plight. Wovoka,* a Paiute prophet, desperately tried to rally his people and allies but failed. Sitting Bull,* a Teton Sioux chief and holy man, tried in his last years to live a life of accommodation, becoming friendly, for example, with Buffalo Bill (*see* William F. Cody), but was murdered. Charles Eastman,* a Santee Sioux half-breed physician and author, and Sarah Winnemucca,* a Paiute translator, were able to live in partial harmony with whites. Geronimo,* a Chiricahua Apache warrior, fought on with ferocity and cunning until he was captured. The landmark symbol of the misery of Native Americans may be found at Wounded Knee.*

Naturalism (Literary Movement). Although the precise definition of naturalism has been the subject of much critical debate, it may be generally agreed that it is a form of literary realism which presents a considerable degree of objectivity; an amoral, nonjudgmental attitude toward the subjects treated; an advance, initially shocking, in the amount of its crude frankness; a pessimistic tone, often ironic and cynical; and low-life, beastly, neurotic characters who usually have little or no capacity to cope with life's problems. The philosophy of naturalists was generally that of biological and economic determinism; that is, men and women are victims of forces beyond their control, namely heredity, environment, and chance. Hence, free will is decidedly more limited than most people traditionally like to believe. On the other hand, some people, born strong and willful, can push back the forces of fate that hurt, even overwhelm, most puny individuals. It should be noted that such people cannot help being strong and often ruthless, any more than the weak and helpless ask to be so. In any event, passing moral judgment on any human being is not only irrelevant but also impudent. Naturalism came about in Europe as an outgrowth of the diverse promulgations of Sir Isaac Newton, Auguste Comte, Charles Darwin, Herbert Spencer, and Karl Marx, among others; Sigmund Freud was a potent influence later. Naturalism as a literary movement started in France with Émile Zola and Gustave Flaubert, among others. A few Russian novelists, especially Fyodor Dostoyevski and Leo Tolstoy, also advanced the movement. America's most effective naturalists were Stephen Crane,* Theodore Dreiser,* Harold Frederic,* Robert Herrick,* Joseph Kirkland,* Jack London,* and Frank Norris.*

The Negro Question (1890). Six essays by George Washington Cable.* These originally appeared in journals in 1888, 1889, and 1890. Cable here and elsewhere, both in essays and in lectures, made this his general argument: The North fought during the Civil War for the preservation of the Union, not for the abolition of slavery; the South fought for slavery but pretended the struggle was for states' rights; and, with the end of Reconstruction, de facto slavery existed again for Southern African Americans. Branding such a condition both immoral on its face and perilous to American society, Cable steadily appealed for tolerance and understanding of African Americans, for better educational opportunities for them, and for improved interracial relations. More specifically, Cable believed that no government could be ''pure'' if it were not ''true,'' that is, if it did not freely enfranchise all adult citizens. He felt that the nation's well-being and prosperity depended on improving all segments of society, to avoid what would otherwise be an inevitable economic and social caste system. He inveighed against any plan to encourage African Americans to train for trades before seeking civil and political rights. Nor did he favor reserving a distinct territory for African Americans, deporting them to Africa, or making their right to vote depend on literacy. He advocated federal intervention to force states to establish equal rights for all persons. He somewhat reluctantly spoke and wrote against church segregation. In sum, he felt that education was the solution. Earlier essays by Cable of a similar sort helped drive him from his home in New Orleans, where he had been born, into a happy exile in Massachusetts (1884).

Nevin, Ethelbert (1862–1901). (Full name: Ethelbert Woodbridge Nevin.) Composer. Born in Edgeworth, Pennsylvania, Nevin evinced musical talent from age five, took piano lessons from age eight, and studied piano more seriously in Boston (1881–1884) and then in Berlin (1884–1886), where his teachers first encouraged him to become a composer. He held his concert debut in Pittsburgh in 1886. He taught piano, gave recitals, and composed in Boston (1887–1893), after which he and his family lived mostly in Europe and Africa (1893–1897, in Paris, Berlin, Florence, Venice, and Algiers). From 1897 to 1900, he ran a studio in New York. Finally, Nevin moved to New Haven, Connecticut, where he was associated with Yale (1900–1901). Although he also composed piano suites, he is best remembered for his songs, which are simple, graceful, slight, sentimental, and sincere. His piano suites include *Water Scenes* (1891, including the most popular ''Narcissus''), *May in Tuscany* (1896), and *A Day in Venice* (1898). His most beloved piano suite is *In Arcady* (1892); his best songs are ''Little Boy Blue'' (1891), ''The Rosary'' (1898), and ''Mighty Lak' a Rose'' (1901). (*See* Songs.) Nevin's incomplete cantata *The Quest* was finished by Horatio William Parker in 1902.

A New England Nun and Other Stories (1891). Collection of twenty-four stories by Mary E. Wilkins Freeman.* The best of these stories are the title story and "Louisa," "The Revolt of 'Mother,' " and "A Village Singer." "A New England Nun" features Louisa Ellis, engaged for fifteen years to Joe Dagget, who returns from overseas, where he has been working and saving money for their marriage. They now feel little real love but plan to go through with their wedding, until, that is, Louisa innocently overhears Joe and Lily Dyer, his new and suddenly real love, talking hopelessly about the need to be honorable toward Louisa. She is genuinely relieved, releases Joe, weeps only a little, and welcomes spinsterhood as a triumph. "Louisa" concerns a decent, strong-willed schoolteacher, who has been unjustly fired, refuses to marry a cocky suitor whose wealth would comfort both Louisa and her anxious, widowed mother, and instead farms the family plot and hires out as a field hand for neighbors. "The Revolt of 'Mother,' " Freeman's best story, tells of long-suffering Sarah Penn, who quietly seethes when her husband Adoniram Penn promises to build a better house but instead builds a fine new barn. When he leaves to buy a horse, Sarah moves her family and all their possessions into the nice new barn. Adoniram returns, observes, breaks down, surrenders, and reforms. In "The Village Singer," Candace Whitcomb, the aging first soprano in the choir, is harshly dismissed. She shrilly competes through her open window with her replacement Alma Way, who is singing in the church nearby. She has her sturdy say to authorities, but then she repents, becomes mortally sick, and asks Alma to sing for her. After Alma does so, Candace complains that the girl flatted a little.

A Night in Acadie (1897). Collection of twenty-one short stories by Kate Chopin.* The common topic of these stories is sexual passion—its joys, demands, and costs. The title story, "A Night in Acadie," is rather slight. It recounts the ironic fate of a fellow who seeks to escape from his family's insistence that he get married by planning a vacation; on the train, he meets a young lady well worth marrying. The heroine of "Athénaïse" is young Athénaïse Miché, who marries a widower named Cazeau. She soon begins to regard marriage as a kind of bondage, runs away, and has a harmless romantic fling. When she voluntarily returns home, Cazeau, who resisted the standard temptation to pursue her as though she were his slave, wisely and quietly welcomes her back. The central character in "Azélie" is another unusual woman. Azélie Pauché and her sharecropper father are so poor that she resorts to stealing from the plantation store. The store manager, an Acadian named 'Polyte, has long been enamored of her; instead of having her punished when he observes the thefts, he hugs and kisses her and soon regularly gives her supplies for moderate intimacy. Passion so controls him that when the Pauchés leaves the region, he follows them. In "At Chênière Caminada," an awkward Acadian fisherman named Antoine Bocaze falls hopelessly in love with a rich, haughty New Orleans woman who is briefly visiting his island. When he later learns that she has died back home, he is in a way relieved, because he can now keep his memory of her inviolate. (Bocaze reappears in *The Awakening.**) The best story in *A Night in Acadie* is "A Respectable Woman." In it, sensitive Mrs. Baroda is mildly upbraided by her cool husband Gaston Baroda when she seems inhospitable toward Gouvernail, his visitor. Attracted to Gouvernail, Mrs. Baroda has properly restrained herself but now ambiguously promises her husband that she will be "very nice" to their guest. (Gouvernail also reappears in *The Awakening.*)

The stories in *A Night in Acadie* are marked not only by clever old plot twists but also by profound new probings of the female psyche. *A Night in Acadie*, published by a little-known Chicago company, was less well received than Chopin's first volume of short stories, *Bayou Folk*,* published in 1894 by Houghton, Mifflin in Boston and New York.

Norris, Frank (1870–1902). (Full name: Benjamin Franklin Norris, Jr.) Novelist. He was born in Chicago, Illinois. His domineering father was a wholesale jeweler; his doting mother, a former teacher and actress. Young Norris accompanied his family on a vacation to Europe (1878–1879) and moved with them to San Francisco (1885). He studied painting there (1886) and then in Paris (1887–1889); attended the University of California, Berkeley (1890–1894), where he read the works of Charles Darwin and Émile Zola but earned no degree; and then studied French and writing at Harvard (1894–1895), again without obtaining a degree. At Harvard he studied under Lewis E. Gates.* By this time, Norris's parents were divorced (1894). Norris became a reporter for the San Francisco *Chronicle* during the Boer War in South Africa (1895–1896) but contracted tropical fever after a few weeks and returned to California to recover. Having already published (from 1889), he became a subeditor of the *Wave* in San Francisco (1896–1897), contributed numerous stories, critical pieces, essays, and book reviews to it, and then worked in the New York editorial offices of S. S. McClure,* who sent him as a Spanish-American War* correspondent to Cuba (1898), where he contracted malaria and, once again, returned to California to recuperate. Next he rented a New York apartment and wrote steadily (1898–1899). After a short visit to San Francisco (1899), he returned to New York, wrote steadily, read for Doubleday, Page, & Company (a successor to McClure's firm), and married Jeannette Black in 1900 (the couple had one child). Norris, with his wife, went to Chicago to study grain speculation there, moved to San Francisco and then New Jersey, then returned to New York and wrote more (1901). Finally, he returned to San Francisco (1902), intending to travel around the world on research. He changed his mind, however, and decided to settle down and write, but he developed appendicitis and quickly died of gangrene and peritonitis.

In his short life, Norris wrote seven novels, two of which were published posthumously. They are varied in content and style. *Moran of the Lady Letty: A Story of Adventure off the California Coast* (1898) is a silly melodrama about a college man turned atavistic hero when shanghaied, a Wagnerian heroine named Moran Sternersen, their violent relationship, and her murder by a Chinese thief.

*McTeague: A Story of San Francisco** (1899, dedicated to Gates) is one of America's first naturalistic novels and remains a compelling example of that form. *Blix* (1899) stars a heroine nicknamed Blix (patterned after Norris's wife Jeannette) who leaves dull San Francisco high society to have a fling with a journalist who wants to write seriously; their love may survive her going to a New York medical school when he is offered an editorial position on a magazine staff—also in New York. *Blix* has obvious autobiographical overtones. *A Man's Woman* (1900) takes the hero and his woman, a nurse, through several conflicts, ending not only with her being subdued but also helping to finance his expedition to the North Pole. *The Octopus: A Story of California** (1901) begins Norris's wheat trilogy, which *The Pit: A Story of Chicago* (1903) continues. (The third book was never begun.) *Vandover and the Brute* (1914), started in 1894 when Norris was in Harvard, was left unrevised. Discovered after his death, *Vandover* was edited and touched up by Norris's younger brother, novelist Charles Norris (and husband of novelist Kathleen Norris), and published much later. This volume describes the downward spiral of the partly autobiographical Vandover, who wants to be a painter but lacks the requisite self-discipline and even the self-knowledge. He carelessly seduces a girl whose subsequent suicide causes the death of Vandover's father, gambles away his inheritance, and degenerates partly owing to the fatal influence of lycanthropy.

Norris also wrote a juvenile narrative in verse, entitled *Yvernelle: A Legend of Feudal France* (1892), and several so-so short stories, collected in *A Deal in Wheat and Other Stories* (1903) and in *The Third Circle* (1909). Death prevented him not only from finishing his wheat trilogy but from even starting a planned second trilogy. The first book in the wheat trilogy begins with the epic task of growing wheat in California and getting it to market (*The Octopus*); the second volume (*The Pit*) continues with grain-market speculation in Chicago; the third (to be called *The Wolf*) was to describe its distribution to and consumption by hungry hordes in Europe. The second trilogy was to have dealt with the Battle of Gettysburg. Norris is a major novelist because of *McTeague*, *The Octopus*, and *The Pit*. In his best writing, he combines—sometimes confusingly, but always vigorously—modernity and tradition, pessimism and optimism, naturalism and romanticism. His uncertainty as to whether fiction should be romantic or realistic is reflected in several of his critical essays, including "Zola as a Romantic Writer" (1896), "The True Reward of the Novelist" (in *World's Work*,* October 1901), "A Plea for Romantic Fiction" (1901), and "The Responsibilities of the Novelist" (1902). In theory, Norris advocated combining the idealism and melodrama of romanticism with the truthful details of actuality found in realism. His best critical writing is assembled in *The Responsibilities of the Novelist and Other Literary Essays* (1903).

Through his New York publishers, Norris met Hamlin Garland,* William Dean Howells,* and many other established or emerging writers. Norris "discovered" and recommended Theodore Dreiser* and his *Sister Carrie** to Doubleday, Page. While in Cuba, Norris met Richard Harding Davis,* Stephen

Crane,* and Frederic Remington,* among other notables. Norris had many other literary friends.

Norton, Charles Eliot (1827–1908). Scholar, critic, editor, translator, and educator. He was born in Cambridge, Massachusetts. His father was a Harvard professor of sacred literature. In due time the son also became an influential, conservative figure in Boston's intellectual community, and he knew most of the leading American and European writers of his epoch. After he graduated from Harvard (1846), he went into business, traveled, and married Susan Ridley Sedgwick in 1862 (the couple had six children). Soon after his wife's death in Germany (1872), Norton began his long professional career at Harvard (1873–1898). In addition to publishing important books on Italy and Italian art, Norton edited letters by Ralph Waldo Emerson (1883, 1886), George William Curtis (1893–1894), James Russell Lowell (1894), Anne Bradstreet (1897), and several British writers. He also translated Dante Alighieri's *Divine Comedy* (1891–1892). Norton was a personal influence on many of his contemporaries, too numerous to list but including Bernard Berenson,* Henry Blake Fuller,* Henry James,* Frederick L. Olmsted,* and Edith Wharton.*

O

Ochs, Adolph Simon (1858–1935). Newspaper publisher. Born in Cincinnati, Ohio, Ochs moved with his family after the Civil War to Knoxville, Tennessee, where he worked for various newspapers (1869–1875, 1876) and in Louisville, Kentucky (1875–1876). He cofounded the *Dispatch* in Chattanooga, Tennessee (1877), bought a controlling interest in the Chattanooga *Times* (1878), improved it over the years (to 1896), and finally acquired the bankrupt *New York Times* (1896). His main competitors were William Randolph Hearst* and Joseph Pulitzer.* Avoiding the sensationalism practiced by his leading rivals, the *Times* published government news, real estate news, out-of-town buyers' names, book reviews, and letters to the editor. When the paper lacked the money to cover the Spanish-American War* thoroughly, it suffered from low circulation (25,000 in 1898), and Ochs cut the price from 3¢ to 1¢ (1898). Circulation immediately improved (to 100,000 by 1901), and with increased circulation came better advertising revenue. Ochs bought the Philadelphia *Times* (1901) and the Philadelphia *Public Ledger* (1902) and merged the two. For $2,500,000 he built the Times Tower on Broadway, in Times Square, in New York City (1904). (He sold the merged Philadelphia papers in 1913.) Ochs married Effie Miriam Wise in 1883. Their only child, Iphigene Bertha Ochs, married Arthur Hays Sulzberger, who became publisher of the *Times* (1935–1961), as did their son Arthur Ochs Sulzberger (in 1963).

The Octopus: A Story of California (1901). Novel by Frank Norris.* *The Octopus* pits hardworking wheat ranchers in the San Joaquin Valley of California against the Pacific and Southwestern Railroad, which is imaged as an octopus attempting to strangle the independence of the growers. The railroad owners set ever-higher rates, control ranch land for their rights-of-way, and bribe rate-setting commissioners and even the judges to whose courts the farmers go vainly for justice. Magnus Derrick, and old-style ranch owner and ex-California governor, ruins his good name permanently by becoming involved in a bribery scheme with the railroad commissioners. Derrick and his good but shy wife Annie, formerly a teacher, have two sons: Lyman Derrick and Harran Derrick. Lyman, an ambitious, hypocritical lawyer, lets the railroad owners use him in his effort to become governor of California. The ultimate result is that the railroad has him in its tentacles. Harran, the other son, who manages the family's ranch, is willing to condone bribery to help his father but is killed when a pro-railroad federal posse tries to evict the ranchers from land "legally" belonging to the railroaders. Also killed are Annixter, a farmer whose ingrained selfishness is altered to a sense of decency and cooperation when he marries good Hilma Tree, his dairy worker; Hooven, an idealistic German who rents land from the Derricks and wants to love his adopted country (his widow subsequently starves in San Francisco); and Osterman, a nearby rancher who tries but fails to persuade the railroad commissioners to reform.

A young man named Presley, Magnus Derrick's guest and also a writer, is Norris's ideal observer and spokesman in *The Octopus*. Presley becomes anguished at the seeming inevitability of evil but comments objectively on events as they unfold. S. Behrman, the villainous banker and railroad representative, squeezes the ranchers by callously demanding as freight rates "all that the traffic will bear," but he gets his comeuppance when he is drowned in a titanic, strangling flood of wheat as it pours into the vast hold of a ship scheduled to deliver its life-sustaining cargo abroad. A curious minor character is nature-loving, mystical old Vanamee, who carelessly allows his flock of sheep to wander into the steel path of the relentless locomotive, which hideously kills and scatters them. Vanamee, now a telepathic loner, dwells on the fate of his fiancée, flower-girl Angèle Varian, who eighteen years earlier was raped, gave birth to a glorious daughter, and died. Her grown child suddenly appears, like a resurrection, and loves and comforts Vanamee, who thus uniquely triumphs in the story. Presley would like to write an epic (of the sort that Norris began in *The Octopus* and continued in *The Pit*) about wheat, a gift from nature which not only sustains life but also symbolizes truth and even goodness emerging from and thus ending strife, lies, and evil.

In its grandeur, ruggedness, imagery, and social message, *The Octopus* has a considerable sweep. A real-life armed confrontation between grasping railroaders and oppressed ranchers that occurred at Mussel Slough in 1880 provided one inspiration for Norris's story. Poetic Presley rings changes on Edwin Markham,* author of "The Man with the Hoe."* Norris's 1899 interview of Collis P. Huntington, one of The Big Four* California railroad magnates, is recalled when Presley interviews Shelgrim, the *Octopus* railroad president who rationalizes in terms of social Darwinism.

An Old Town by the Sea (1893). A book of sketches by Thomas Bailey Aldrich.* This seven-chapter work touches on historical events concerning Portsmouth, New Hampshire (and its Piscataqua River), where Aldrich was born. It describes "the waterside" and takes the reader on a stroll through the town, calling special attention to the old houses. Aldrich also profiles several colorful local personalities from Colonial and Revolutionary times and closes with personal reminiscences. References to Nathaniel Hawthorne and Henry David Thoreau clearly indicate the kind of New England prose Aldrich aims to emulate here.

Olmsted, Frederick L. (1822–1903). (Full name: Frederick Law Olmsted.) Landscape architect. Born in Hartford, Connecticut, the son of a wealthy merchant, Olmsted would have entered Yale in 1837 but for eyes weakened by a case of sumach poisoning. He traveled a great deal in the northeastern United States and in Canada with his father, studied privately (1837–1840), worked for a New York importer (1840–1842), informally attended lectures in science and engineering at Yale (1842–1843), took a trip to China (1843), practiced scientific farming, and did editorial and publishing work (1845–1857). Olmsted traveled in the United States and abroad during much of this time, going, for example, extensively through the antebellum South, about which he published valuably (1857, 1860). He was general secretary of the U.S. Sanitary Commission during part of the Civil War (1861–1863); he resigned because of worsening lameness caused by an old accident. He then went to California as first commissioner of Yosemite National Park (1863–1865), after which he settled in New York (1865–1878).

The first to call himself a landscape architect (rather than a landscape gardener), Olmsted did a phenomenal amount of work in his chosen field. He did much of the planning for what became Central Park in New York City (from 1857; his partner in this work was British architect Calvert Vaux), was landscape designer for New York north of 155th Street (1860), and went on to be landscaper for areas and parks in Albany, Boston, Brooklyn, Buffalo, Chicago, Detroit, Hartford, Louisville, Milwaukee, Montreal, Niagara Falls, Philadelphia, Staten Island, Tarrytown, and Washington, D.C. Of specific importance here, Olmsted planned the Stanford University campus (1888) and the Biltmore estate outside Asheville, North Carolina (1890; John Singer Sargent* painted his portrait outdoors there), and was chief landscape planner for the World's Columbian Exposition* in Chicago (1893). While in Chicago, Olmsted worked closely with Daniel Hudson Burnham.* Olmsted's main aesthetic model was the eighteenth-century English garden. His main ecological value lay in his skillful use of open areas and natural watersheds.

Olmsted married his brother John Olmsted's widow Mary Cleveland Perkins Olmsted in 1859 (John had died in 1857), became stepfather to her three children, and fathered two more children. Some years before his death, Olmsted's mind began to fail (1896). His professional papers were coedited by his son Frederick Law Olmsted, Jr. (2 vols., 1922, 1928).

Olympic Games. *See* Sports.

"The Open Boat" (1897). Short story by Stephen Crane.* In this artistic redacting of Crane's being shipwrecked in January 1897 off the Florida coast, a dingy and its four occupants are threatened by choppy seas. The four—the injured captain, the cook, Billie the oiler, and a newspaper correspondent—row and row. An onshore wind seems to help but does not. A seagull threatens them. The cynical correspondent is warmed, however, by the thrill of "subtle brotherhood." The four men make a sail out of a coat. They see a lighthouse, then the shore, and hear the surf. No one comes to rescue them. Fearful of swamping, they head to sea again. Night falls, and the correspondent ponders the irony of death in life. Nature seems malevolent, with its darkness and cold, a nearby shark, and a distant star. Dawn breaks. The men must try to run through the surf. They back the boat in, jump, and struggle to get ashore. Rescuers on the beach suddenly do what they can, but Billie drowns. What the three survivors learn is that nature, apparently hostile, is merely indifferent. "The Open Boat," perhaps Crane's finest story, is a masterpiece of naturalism.*

The Open Boat and Other Tales of Adventure (1898). A collection of short stories by Stephen Crane.* The best of these seventeen stories are "The Open Boat,"* "The Bride Comes to Yellow Sky,"* "Death and the Child," and "An Experiment in Misery." "Death and the Child" is the one solid artistic fruit of Crane's experiences in Greece during the Greco-Turkish War. In it, Peza, an Italian war correspondent (whose father was Greek), visits Greek soldiers in the trenches at Velestino and is romantically eager to fight and learn. Soldiers accommodate him by arming him and pointing him forward. Meanwhile, a little child, deserted by his parents, is playing with sticks, flocks, and dogs on a mountain near his empty house, above the battlefield. In the end, Peza, who ran away but is mortally wounded now, comes upon the curious child. "An Experiment in Misery" is a Bowery sketch, in which a young man decides to sample the life of a bum. He dresses in rags, walks in the rain, and joins a beggar in a flophouse. Next morning the two share coffee and rolls and sit on a park bench, where they are surrounded by tall, indifferent buildings. These and the other stories are notable for dry-eyed objectivity, charnel-house imagery, and acidic humor. Crane's tone here is regularly sarcastic.

Open Door Policy. This diplomatic strategy was devised by John Hay,* when he was secretary of state during the presidency of Theodore Roosevelt.* Hay sought the advice of William Woodville Rockhill,* an expert in Far Eastern affairs. The political and military weakness of China, as evidenced by the Sino-Japanese War (1894–1895) and its aftermath, left the country open to commercial and political inroads by various foreign countries, including France, England, Germany, Italy, Japan, and Russia, as well as the United States. America, which had little trade with China, rejected invitations by England (1898–1899) to agree to share and share alike in exploiting China commercially. Still, America was uneasy at the prospect that more aggressive foreign countries would step in, do more and more business there, and ultimately erect tariffs disadvantageous to America's possible future interests. So Hay asked the appropriate officials in Berlin, London, Paris, St. Petersburg, Rome, and Tokyo to agree to an "Open Door" policy by which their governments would guarantee "equal and impartial trade" within their respective spheres of influence in China, and also guarantee to preserve "Chinese territorial and administrative" integrity (1899). The equivocal response of the various governments did not deter Hay from announcing his policy a success.

A military event soon tested the solidity of the policy. The Boxers, a loosely organized secret society of antiforeign Chinese militants officially entitled I Ho Ch'uan (The Righteous and Harmonious Fists), fomented a series of killings and riots (the so-called Boxer Rebellion) in Peking (now called Beijing). Abetted by imperial Chinese army units and with the tacit approval of T'Zu Hsi, the dowager empress of China, the Boxers surrounded various European diplomats and nationals, as well as about 3,000 Chinese Christians, and pinned them down in the legation quarter for two months (June–August 1900). The Boxers, estimated to number about 140,000, announced that their plan was first to cut the telegraph wires, then to tear up the railroads, and at last to decapitate all foreigners. This rebellion caused the governments of England, France, Germany, Japan, and the United States to mount an international military force of 19,000 to rescue foreign legation personnel (August 1900). Some 2,500 American soldiers, including veterans of the occupation of the Philippine Islands in the aftermath of the Spanish-American War,* participated in lifting the siege and punishing the Boxers. (The German army was far more harsh in its measures.)

In the uneasy aftermath, Britain acknowledged Japan's special and dominant interests in China; tensions between Russia and Japan in Manchuria resulted in the Russo-Japanese War in 1905 (peace terms were mediated by Roosevelt at Portsmouth, New Hampshire); a secret agreement was struck by Japan and Russia to divide Korea, Manchuria, and Mongolia into dual spheres of influence (1907); and, finally, the Root-Takahira Agreement was signed in 1908 (Elihu Root was Roosevelt's secretary of state and Baron Kogoro Takahira was Japan's ambassador), which publicly recognized Japan's unique influence in the Far East and thus closed a diplomatic "door" never more than partly "open."

Operettas. The 1890s saw the production of numerous operettas, some successful but many not. Seven of the most successful were *Robin Hood* (1891), *King Rene's Daughter* (1893), *Rob Roy* (1894), *Prince Ananias* (1894), *The Wizard of the Nile* (1895), *El Capitan* (1896), and *The Fortune Teller* (1898). The music for *Robin Hood* was composed by the distinguished Reginald De Koven, with libretto by the prolific Harry Bache Smith. Principal songs were "Brown October Ale" and "Oh, Promise Me." *Robin Hood* is now regarded as the first American operetta properly defined as contemporary in style. The music for *King Rene's Daughter* was composed by Julian Edwards, libretto based on a drama by Henrik Hertz. The music for *Rob Roy* was composed by De Koven, libretto by Smith. The principal song was "The Merry Miller." The music for *Prince Ananias* was composed by the famous Victor Herbert,* libretto by Francis Neilson. The best song was the haunting "Amaryllis." The music for *The Wizard of the Nile* was composed by Herbert, libretto by Smith. The cleverest composition was "Stonecutters' Song." The music for *El Capitan* was composed by the famous John Philip Sousa,* libretto by Charles Klein, lyrics by Sousa and Tom Frost. The principal songs were "El Capitan's Song," "Sweetheart, I'm Waiting," and "A Typical Tune of Zanzibar." The music for *The Fortune Teller* was composed by Herbert, book and lyrics by Smith. The principal songs were "Gypsy Love Song," "Romany Life," "Only in the Play," and "Always Do as People Say You Should." Herbert is now widely regarded as the best American operetta orchestrator. Smith wrote over 300 libretti and wrote or coauthored lyrics for about 3,000 songs. American operettas in the 1890–1891 season began to outnumber imports substantially. The end of the 1896–1897 season, however, marked the beginning of a decline in the popularity of operettas in the United States.

Our National Parks (1901). Book of essays by John Muir,* reprinted from earlier *Atlantic Monthly** sketches. After personal, poetic, geographic, and philosophical introductory material, Muir discusses the four major national parks in the West: the Yellowstone National Park, the Yosemite Park, the Sequoia, and the General Grant. (The General Grant is no longer a national park.) Upon first seeing Yellowstone Park, the biggest of the four, one is "hushed and awe-stricken before phenomena wholly new," Muir says. He especially likes Yosemite, and writes about it in great detail concerning its forests, "wild gardens," animals and reptiles, birds, and fountains and streams. Muir reveres the gigantic redwoods, "standing bravely up, millenium in, millenium out, to all that fortune may bring them, triumphant over tempest and fire and time, fruitful and beautiful, giving food and shelter to multitudes of small fleeting creatures dependent on their bounty." He closes with a section on American forests and an appeal for ecological sanity: "God has cared for these trees, saved them from drought, disease, avalanches, and a thousand straining, leveling tempests and floods; but he cannot save them from fools,—only Uncle Sam can do that." Part of *Our National Parks* duplicates material from Muir's earlier book *The Mountains of California.** For example, Muir again is fascinated by the Douglas squirrel—"a firm, emphatic bolt of life, fiery, pungent, full of brag and show and fight." Muir's book about America's national parks is full of accurate, modest, thrillingly poetic word pictures. (*See also* National Parks.)

P

Page, Thomas Nelson (1853–1922). Fiction writer, lawyer, and diplomat. Born in Oakland Plantation, Hanover County, Virginia, later the scene of three memorable Civil War battles, he enrolled (1869) in Washington College (later named Washington and Lee), where he was materially aided by its president, Robert E. Lee. Page left college without a degree because of a lack of funds (1872). He tutored for a while and also read law in his father's office, attended law school at the University of Virginia (1873–1874), passed the bar (1874), and combined law practice (in Richmond, from 1876) with writing for publication. All of his life, he was obsessed by the romance of the antebellum South, the Civil War, and Reconstruction miseries. He romanticized the Old South, and his sentimental fiction was extremely popular. He sold "Marse Chan," his most famous short story, in accurate black dialect, to the *Century** (1881; it was published in March 1884). Idealistic and sentimental, it is also a gripping depiction of the most romantic, heroic traits of both Southern whites and African Americans before and during the Civil War. Page married Anne Seddon Bruce in 1886, but she died two years later. He quickly published *In Ole Virginia or Marse Chan and Other Stories* (1887), undoubtedly his best collection; *Befo' de War: Echoes in Negro Dialect* (1888), dialect verses coauthored with A. C. Gordon; and *Two Little Confederates* (1888), a sentimental war yarn with realistic details, written for juvenile readers.

The decade of the 1890s was especially important for Page. He married Florence Lathrop Field, the widowed sister-in-law of Chicago merchant genius Marshall Field* (1892), discontinued his law practice and moved to Washington, D.C. (1893), became a popular man about town, and published eleven books, mostly of fiction. They are *Among the Camps or Young People's Stories of the War* (1891); *Elsket and Other Stories* (1891), of which the title story is a moody fantasy of unconsummated love set in a Norwegian mountain village; *On Newfound River* (1891, enlarged in 1906), a North-South love story novel set in antebellum Virginia and including political and race-relations local color; *The Old South: Essays Social and Political* (1892), chauvinistic, conservative, nostalgic essays on antebellum and postbellum Southern social life, politics and law, race relations, and literature; *The Burial of the Guns and Other Stories* (1894), in which the title story symbolizes the defeat but not the ruin of Confederate heroism; *Pastime Stories* (1894), redactions of insignificant anecdotes and sketches about African Americans and lawyers; *The Old Gentleman of the Black Stock* (1897), more juvenile fiction; *Social Life in Old Virginia* (1897), more romantic, idealistic essays; *Two Prisoners* (1897, rev. ed. 1903); *Red Rock* (1898), a bitter, pro-Southern novel depicting Northern and freed African-American excesses during Reconstruction days, but sweetened by love interests; and *Santa Claus's Partner* (1899).

In the early twentieth century, Page published more fiction designed to bring the North and South closer together and also an ultralaudatory biography of Robert E. Lee (1908, rev. ed. 1911). Page became active in national politics and was appointed ambassador to Italy (1913–1919). While in Italy, he studied Dante in his ample spare time; later he wrote *Dante and His Influence* (1922). Page returned to America, was widowed in 1921, and died back home in Oakland Plantation, Virginia.

Page, Walter Hines (1855–1918). Journalist, publisher, and diplomat. Born in Cary, North Carolina, he studied at Trinity College (1871, now Duke University) and transferred to Randolph-Macon (1873) and then to Johns Hopkins, which he left without a degree (1878). He became a reporter for and then the editor of the *Gazette* in St. Joseph, Missouri (1880–1881). He quit to tour the South and report on conditions there to the New York *World* (1881–1883). Resigning when Joseph Pulitzer* took over the *World*, Page gained control of and edited the Raleigh *State Chronicle* (1883–1885), hoping to help reconstruct the South by deploring nostalgia and advocating realistic education, especially for African Americans, and improved roads and farm conditions. He joined the staff of the New York *Forum* (1887–1895), of which he gained control (1891) and which he soon made highly influential. He moved on to the *Atlantic Monthly** (1895–1898, as editor 1898–1899); became a partner in the publishing firm of Doubleday, Page & Company (from 1899, splitting off the firm of S. S. McClure* and publishing works by Frank Norris*), and founded and edited the liberal *World's Work** (1900–1913).

Page was appointed U.S. minister to Great Britain (1913–1918) by his friend President Woodrow Wilson. Page wrote splendid official and private letters concerning English life and diplomacy. Earlier, he published *The Rebuilding of Commonwealths* (1902), including essays on new vocational training, especially for African Americans, in the South; *A Publisher's Confession* (1905), containing his professional and commercial creed; and *The Southerner* (1909, as by Nicholas Worth). Page's voluminous letters appeared posthumously (3 vols., 1922–1925).

Page knew innumerable significant authors of the 1890s. Page married Alice Wilson in 1880 (the couple had four surviving children).

Painter, William (1838–1906). Inventor. He was born in Triadelphia, Montgomery County, Maryland. His father was a physician and merchant. Young Painter was educated in Quaker schools in Fallston, Maryland, and in Wilmington, Delaware. While working in various manufacturing plants in Wilmington and Fallston (until 1865) and thereafter in Baltimore, he invented, designed, and sometimes patented dozens of ingenious devices. But his only important inventions were bottle stoppers. He patented a rubber stopper (1885), experimented further, and devised a top or cap with a metal flange and a cork seal (1892). Success was immediate and worldwide, establishing factories in Canada, England, France, Germany, and Japan, as well as in Baltimore and elsewhere in the United States. Painter was secretary and general manager of his Crown Cork & Seal Company (1892–1903). One of his employees was King Camp Gillette.* With his considerable wealth, he built an estate near Pikesville, Maryland, maintained a stable of fine horses, traveled occasionally, collected automobiles, and was a generous philanthropist. Painter married Harriet Magee Deacon (1861; the couple had three children).

Painting and Illustration. The 1890s saw a burst of wonderfully creative activity in the realm of pictorial art. Before 1880 or so, American pictures were too frequently either derivative of European religious, allegorical, and historical works, or crude and folksy; and, after about 1910, too often American pictures were nouveau arty, abstract, cubistic, and otherwise not representational. The towering 1890s geniuses in the field of American painting were Thomas Eakins,* Winslow Homer,* John Singer Sargent,* and James Abbott McNeill Whistler.* These artists produced portraits, landscapes, seascapes, and much else. By far the best painters of Western scenes, usually with human and animal occupants, were Charles Marion Russell* and Frederic Remington.* Ralph Albert Blakelock* and Albert Pinkham Ryder* were a pair of tortured pictorial wizards of the time. Mary Cassatt* was the best American female painter active in the 1890s, and Henry Ossawa Tanner,* the most outstanding African-American painter. In a class by himself was the versatile John La Farge.* Several of these painters went abroad for study and subject matter for varied periods of time. When they returned, some of them coalesced into groups, notably The Ten,* led by Childe Hassam,* and then The Eight* (also called the Ash Can School), led by Robert Henri.* The best of numerous illustrators active in the 1890s include Charles Dana Gibson,* Joseph Pennell,* Remington, Russell, and Howard Pyle.* It should go without saying that most of the above-named artists did not confine themselves to painting and drawing. For example, Pyle, Remington, Russell, and Whistler were also writers of considerable merit, as was La Farge, who was also a stained-glass artist of incredible talent. Other versatile artists include Ernest Thompson Seton,* who was also an author, naturalist, and lecturer, and Louis Comfort Tiffany,* who is known to this day for his unique work in glass.

Palmer, Potter (1826–1902). Merchant and capitalist. He was born in Albany County, New York. After routine schooling, he became a clerk in a country store in Durham, New York, and within two years—because of his business genius—he was in charge. Soon thereafter, he started a dry goods store in Oneida, New York, sold it to open a bigger one in Lockport, New York, but remained ambitious for even bigger ventures. He had visited Chicago in 1852 and had liked the vigorous young city; he sold out back home and bought a supply of goods in New York City to stock an establishment in Chicago. At this point, Palmer was financed in part by his prosperous father. Young Palmer, always an innovative merchant, initiated the practice of sending goods to customers on approval, permitting returns for exchange or refund, and having bargain-day sales. Many of these practices were copied by Macy and Company in New York, the Bon Marché in Paris, and elsewhere. Palmer offered his wholesale dry goods firm to Chicago merchant genius Marshall Field* (1865), then of Farwell, Field & Company. The firm of Field, Palmer, and Leiter was formed, from which Palmer withdrew—at a handsome profit—for reasons of worsening health (1867). Thereafter, he traveled extensively. When he returned to Chicago, he invested in downtown real estate, redesigned a major business district, and supervised extensive commercial rebuilding, but he was devastated by the Chicago fire of 1871. He borrowed the huge sum of $1,700,000 from the Connecticut Mutual Life Insurance Company, rebuilt (including the Palmer House Hotel), and recouped magnificently.

Palmer married Bertha Honoré, daughter of a Chicago capitalist and real estate holder, in 1871 (the couple had two children). Palmer became a tireless civic, social, and cultural leader. For example, he was named vice president of the World's Columbian Exposition* (Chicago, 1893). His wife was president of the Women's Commission of the exposition. Their mansion, a Norman-Gothic castle costing $700,000, was located on Lake Shore Drive, an area which Palmer helped to plan and develop. Both before and after her husband's death, Bertha Palmer, a ravishing, small-waisted beauty, was a canny art collector for the seventy-foot picture gallery located in her residence. For example, through her friendship with Mary Cassatt,* the expatriate American painter in Paris, she was able to purchase four Renoirs for $5,000. She also fancied Barbizon school paintings. At her death, her collection went to the Chicago Institute of Art. Henry Blake Fuller* satirized both Palmer and his wife in *With the Procession: A Novel** (1895) and in "The Downfall of Abner Joyce" (part of *Under the Skylights* [1901]).

Pan-American Exposition. Exposition. Held in Buffalo, New York, from 20 May to 2 November 1901, to promote that city's economy and popularity. The idea for the exposition came when some Buffalo businessmen attended the Cotton

States and International Exposition* (Atlanta, 1895) and saw what it was doing for that city. Cheap electrical power from Niagara Falls, available from 1896, inspired them to make the Buffalo exhibit an electrical marvel. An exposition company was formed, and funds were sought (from 1897) by means of a bond sale, local subscriptions ($1,500,000), a grant from the state government ($300,000) and another grant from the federal government, and lavish Latin American exhibits (which proved disappointing). The theme, which was to be revealed by color symbolism and artistic allegory, was nineteenth-century New World progress. The original opening, planned to occur in 1899, was delayed by the Spanish-American War* (1898) and then by the Exposition Universelle (Paris, 1900).

Theodore Roosevelt,* then vice president, appeared on opening day. Structures, mostly in Spanish Renaissance style, included the 375-foot-tall Electric Tower, powered by the Falls, the Electricity Building, the Ethnology Building, the Horticulture Building, the Machinery and Transportation Building, the Manufactures and Liberal Arts Building, the Temple of Music, the U.S. Government Building (featuring, among much else, Filipino artifacts), and many individual foreign-nation buildings. A vivid midway included a Filipino village. Bernhard E. Fernow,* the renowned forester, was an exhibit judge. Geronimo,* the Apache chief, some years after his surrender was induced to display himself at the exposition. Early attendance was poor because of wretched weather. In midsummer, the attendance improved, but then tragedy struck. William McKinley* paid the exposition a presidential visit, where he spoke to tumultuous crowds, but he was mortally wounded by an assassin at the Temple of Music (6 September). Receipts thereafter were adequate, but surely a historic pall was cast over the exposition, which—although it attracted more than 8,000,000 visitors—lost more than $3,000,000, generated many lawsuits filed by unhappy investors, and did little to promote pan-Americanism. The exposition was celebrated by the issuance of American commemorative stamps (*see* Commemorative Postage Stamps). Part of a valuable government exhibit of postage stamps was stolen during the exposition.

Panic of 1893. (Also called the Depression of 1893.) Shortly before the inauguration of Grover Cleveland* as president (March 1893), the most severe depression ever to hit the United States up to that time occurred. Worse than the depressions of 1819, 1837, and 1873, it lasted until 1896 or so. The causes of the Panic of 1893 are still obscure, but major contributing factors were the overexpansion of railroads, banks, and business firms and frequent mismanagement and corruption therein; high tariffs, which ultimately lowered federal income and sales of American goods abroad; inevitable labor unrest and agitation (1,300 strikes occurred in 1892); falling prices for agricultural products (corn, cotton, and wheat prices had been too low in 1892); racism, with 232 lynchings in 1892 (mostly of African Americans); the complicated issue of Free Silver,* panic selling of stocks; and the hands-off philosophy of state governments and the federal government. Here are some specifics. Some 70,000 miles of railroad lines had been built between 1880 and 1890. When the panic began, railroad revenues fell. The Philadelphia and Reading Railroad failed early in 1893; other lines followed. These developments hurt the steel industry first and allied industries soon thereafter. The prestigious National Cordage Company failed and took several other commercial concerns with it. The Sherman Silver Purchase Act (1890) had been requiring the government to buy silver bullion for gold-backed legal tender, and otherwise caused confusion about how to manage currency and the national debt. Foreign investors called in their loans for payment in gold. The federal gold reserves fell below their supposedly safe level of $100,000,000; ultimately, they fell as low as $41,000,000. A monstrous domino effect set in: 15,000 businesses failed; 600 banks closed; 50 railroads became insolvent; and 2,500,000, and perhaps far more, men and women became unemployed. The march of Coxey's Army* and the Pullman Strike* followed. President Cleveland called for the repeal of the Sherman Silver Purchase Act, ordered the sale of government bonds for gold, and later (1895) persuaded John Pierpont Morgan* and a Wall Street syndicate to loan the federal government $65,000,000 in gold (for a $7,000,000 commission). Liberal writers and speakers, including Eugene V. Debs,* William Dean Howells,* and Henry Demarest Lloyd,* began or continued to inveigh against the establishment way of doing business.

Parent-Teacher Associations. (Abbreviation: PTA.) Cooperative, volunteer organizations. The national PTA was organized in Washington, D.C., in 1897, by Alice McLellan Birney and Phoebe Apperson Hearst (wife of ex-Senator George Hearst and mother of William Randolph Hearst*). Called at first the National Congress of Mothers, the organization was renamed Parent-Teacher Associations in 1924. The purpose of the organizations is to bring parents and teachers of their children together, each in a given school. The PTA is a noncommercial, nonsectarian, and nonpartisan organization founded to foster the educational and allied interests of children and teenagers by advocating cooperation between families and school personnel. Although it has undergone many changes in the twentieth century, its aims remain the same: to promote children's welfare in and out of the home, to raise the standards of home life, to press for laws to protect children, to increase parent-teacher cooperation in the training of children, and to educate the public at large in ways to improve opportunities for children to enjoy a better life through mental, social, physical, and spiritual education.

Peary, Robert Edwin (1856–1920). Explorer and author. Although he was born in Cresson, Pennsylvania, Peary grew up in Maine. He graduated from Bowdoin College (1877), was a Coast and Geodetic Survey draftsman and surveyor, was commissioned as a U.S. Navy engineering officer (1881), aided official U.S. surveys for a Nicaraguan canal (1884–1885, again in 1888), and through his reading became curious about Greenland. He journeyed by sledge with Matthew A. Henson, a loyal African-American friend and lifelong associate, into Greenland (1886). Home again, Peary married Josephine Diebitsch in 1888. He mapped the northern coast of Greenland while on navy leave (1891–1892), with his wife, Henson, and Dr. Frederick A. Cook. He voyaged close to the North Pole twice (1893–1895, 1898–1902). The second polar expedition was supported by the Peary Club (formed in 1897) and was made possible when William McKinley* issued the navy a presidential order to grant Peary ample leave time. Taking another ship, named the *Roosevelt*, north yet again (1905–1906), Peary reached a point 174 miles from the North Pole. Trying a final time (1908–1909), he reached the exact pole on 6 April 1909. Peary estimated that the crew was within three miles and crisscrossed to make sure that they had reached the pole.

Peary's wife was with her husband on the west coast of Greenland when she gave birth to their first child, Marie Ahnighito (1893). This birth was the farthest north of any white child in history up to that time. On another occasion, Peary brought back a ninety-ton meteorite (1897). He and his wife had one other child (1903).

A controversy threatened to damage Peary's reputation. In April 1909 Dr. Cook announced that he had stood at the North Pole on 21 April 1908. Cook, however, has been considerably discredited not only because he lacked any evidence to support his claim but also because his boast that he had climbed Mount McKinley in 1906 was proved fraudulent. Peary, who retired as a rear admiral in 1911, is generally named as the leader who first conquered the North Pole. His books detailing his earlier efforts are *Northward over the "Great Ice"* (2 vols., 1898) and *Nearest the Pole* (1907); these works were followed by descriptions of victory in *The North Pole* (1910) and *Secrets of Polar Travel* (1917). Peary was assisted by ghost writers in the preparation of some of these publications.

Pembroke (1894). Novel by Mary E. Wilkins Freeman.* Barney Thayer, the son of Caleb and Deborah Thayer, loves Charlote Barnard, and they are soon to get married and move into a new house built by Caleb for them. But Barney has a big argument with Charlotte's father, who orders him out of the house and forbids the marriage. New England stubbornness sets in, and neither man can be persuaded to apologize. Barney moves into his new house in sullen solitude. Years pass. He does not marry anyone else, nor does Charlotte. Finally, the faithful, aging lovers shed their pride and reunite, in the house that pride kept empty so long. The grim plot of *Pembroke* grew out of a true story in the family of the author, whose name was Mary Eleanor Wilkins before her marriage. Her maternal grandfather, Barnabas Lothrop, built a house in Randolph, Massachusetts, for his son Barnabas Lothrop, Jr. The young man loved and was to wed Mary Thayer, but when he argued with her father about politics, he was ordered away and left town—never to return to his Mary. Barnabas Lothrop, Sr., gave the house to his daughter Elinor and her husband Warren Wilkins, who became the parents of the future writer. *Pembroke* appeared on the 1895 best-seller list. In the preface to an 1899 reprint of *Pembroke*, the author calls her novel the story not only of typical diseased New England wills but also of the curative power of love.

Pennell, Joseph (1857–1926). Etcher and illustrator. He was born in Philadelphia to a Welsh-Irish Quaker family. His father was a teacher and then a shipping clerk. Young Pennell, a moody, sickly, picture-drawing child, attended Quaker schools and became a clerk in a coal company. He studied drawing in night classes at the Pennsylvania School of Industrial Art, but soon he quit classes and opened his own studio (about 1880). He quickly began to sell his illustrations, first to *Scribner's Magazine** (1881). Next he published an article entitled "A Ramble in Old Philadelphia" (*Century*,* 1882) with his drawings and a running text by Elizabeth Robins. Pennell illustrated *The Creoles of Louisiana* by George Washington Cable* (1884) and then went to Italy (1884) to illustrate articles by William Dean Howells* on Tuscany. Pennell married Miss Robins in 1884, and the two honeymooned by bicycle, and with sketch pad and notebook, from London to Canterbury (August 1884), then went by tricycle from Florence to Rome (October 1884). They established a residence in London (1884) in order to prepare material on Europe for a hungry American market. The two eventually composed twelve books devoted to their "holidays," beginning with *A Canterbury Pilgrimage* (1885). Pennell's drawings were featured in *Century*, *Harper's Monthly Magazine*,* and various British journals, and also in books by Cable, F. Marion Crawford,* John Hay,* Henry James,* John Charles Van Dyke,* and other writers, including several in England.

Pennell became the art critic of the London daily *Star* (1888) but soon turned the long-lasting column over to his highly capable wife. He published *Pen Drawing and Pen Draughtsmen* (1889), bought a press (1892) and started printing his own proofs, and instead of fearing the competitive threat of photoengraving studied the new process and adapted to it. Through his close friendship with James Abbott McNeill Whistler,* Pennell developed an interest in lithography (from about 1895), went to Spain to prepare lithographs for Washington Irving's *The Alhambra* (1896), published *Lithographs and Lithographers* (1898), and joined the International Society of Sculptors, Painters and Graphers (about 1898). Pennell and his wife together wrote a biography of Whistler (1908) and later edited Whistler's journal (1921). As the twentieth century wore on, Pennell continued his furious activities: He pioneered in the illustrating of ugly industrial sites; he drew pictures of the Panama Canal and various locales in Western America, Washington, D.C., and Greece; and he depicted scenes of World War I, which seen close up almost caused him to suffer a nervous breakdown. Later, he remained active as an artist, a teacher of etching, a harsh but honest critic, and an art society administrator—all of which wore him out so that an attack of pneumonia proved fatal. In his will, he provided for the enrichment of Library of Congress pictorial holdings. Pennell produced more than 900 etched and mezzotint plates, 620 lithographs, an autobiography (*Adventures of an Illustrator* [1925]), and much else.

Personal Recollections of Joan of Arc (1896). Historical novel in three books by Mark Twain.* To conceal his identity, Twain says that this work is a translation of recollections written in 1492 by Joan's page and secretary Sieur Louis de Conte, whose initials, however, are the same as those of Samuel Langhorne Clemens, Twain's real name.

I. Conte and Joan, two years younger than he, grow up in Domremy, France. Troubled by Burgundian raids and rumors that Henry V of England is taking part of France, Joan hears Voices telling her that she will lead armies to liberate the country. She asks permission at Vaucouleurs to see the Dauphin of France, but she is ordered home.

II. Joan, age seventeen (in 1429), inspires recruits, correctly predicts a military defeat for the Dauphin. With an entourage including her friends, Joan has an audience with the Dauphin at Chinon. When she passes his tests, she is named general in chief of the French armies. She marches to Blois and transforms the sinful, wolfish soldiers into loyal, moral ones. She relieves Orléans and attacks the English at St. Loup and Tourelles. At Tours, Joan suggests that the Dauphin order his coronation promptly; she raises a new army and defeats the British in battles culminating at Patay (18 June). The Dauphin is crowned as Charles VII at Rheims. Vacillating and poorly advised by pro-British Bishop Pierre Cauchon and others, the king with Joan moves toward Paris, but makes a treaty with Burgundy, and allows Joan to be captured near Compiègne (24 May 1430).

III. Bishop Cauchon buys Joan from Burgundy and puts her on trial at Rouen (beginning on 21 February 1431). Inspired by her Voices and parrying all questions, she is nonetheless convicted of heresy, sorcery, and other crimes, and is burned at the stake (30 May 1431). Twenty-three years later, the king appeals to the pope, and Joan is declared spotless and perfect.

Twain long admired Joan of Arc, whom he called "the noble child, the most innocent, the most lovely, the most adorable the ages have produced." He worked for years conducting his research into the Maid of Orléans and her times, wrote his book painstakingly, and called it his best work (which it is not). Its most memorable parts concern the Domremy childhood of Joan and her friends, European folklore, the vigorous battle scenes, and various caustic aspects of the protracted Rouen trial.

Phases of an Inferior Planet (1898). Novel by Ellen Glasgow.* This work relates the confusing, naturalistic story of Mariana Musin, a Bohemian singer, who gives up her profession in New York to marry Anthony Algarcife, a flaccid intellectual. The death of their infant daughter Isolde destroys their marriage. After the couple are divorced, Mariana escapes to sing abroad and to endure a loveless marriage to a rich Britisher; Anthony becomes Father Algarcife, an Anglican priest. The two meet eight years later, but, her career in ruins, she soon dies; he toys with the idea of suicide but resists and undertakes social work instead. *Phases of an Inferior Planet* is not a great novel, but it does indicate Glasgow's developing strength.

The Philistine. (Full title: *The Philistine: A Periodical of Protest.*) Monthly magazine. Founded by Elbert Hubbard* in June 1895, it was edited by him from 1896 through the July 1915 issue ($1 a year). *The Philistine* helped start the vogue of small side-pocket magazines available at newsstands. Its announced purpose was to tilt at the windmills of literary convention; its pages were filled with cheap, vulgar, verbose, sarcastic cracks at the *Bookman*,* Bliss Carman,* the *Century** (edited by Richard Watson Gilder*), Stephen Crane,* Hamlin Garland,* Richard Hovey,* William Dean Howells,* S. S. McClure,* Theodore Roosevelt* (and his "Ruf Writers"), Mark Twain,* and many non-American literary figures as well. Later it became more miscellaneous and epigrammatic. Its biggest success was the 1899 publication of Hubbard's essay "A Message to Garcia."* Hubbard said that by 1900 the circulation of *The Philistine* was 60,000; within five years, double that figure. Though socialistic and antiestablishmentarian at first, *The Philistine* had become protrust and otherwise conservative by about 1910. *The Philistine* died when Hubbard went down with the *Lusitania*.

Phillips, David Graham (1867–1911). Novelist, journalist, and social reformer. Born in Madison, Indiana, Phillips attended DePauw (1882–1885) and became a journalist in Cincinnati (1887) and then for the *Sun* and the *World* in New York City (1890), where he lived with his sister. Owing to his observation and training in the 1890s, he was able to make an important contribution to the muckraking movement a little later not only with magazine articles but also with most of his twenty-three novels. His novels include *The Great God Success* (1901), critical of politics, big business, and materialism; *The Master Rogue* (1902), critical of specific senators; *The Cost* (1904), about Wall Street financial manipulations; *The Deluge* (1905), more about Wall Street chicanery; *The Plum Tree* (1905), about political boss corruption; *Light-Fingered Gentry* (1907), about insurance scams; *The Second Generation* (1907), opposing the concept of inherited wealth; *The Fashionable Adventures of Joshua Craig* (1909), about national political corruption; *The Conflict* (1911), about city political corruption; *George Helm* (posthumously published in 1912), about state political corruption; and *Susan Lenox: Her Fall and Rise* (posthumously published in 1917—Phillips's best), about slum conditions, city corruption, and prostitution. Phillips was shot to death by a lunatic who imagined that his sister had been maligned by Phillips in *Joshua Craig* and who then committed suicide.

Pinchot, Gifford (1865–1946). Forester and public official. He was born in Simsbury, Connecticut. His father, who was French, was a wealthy New York wallpaper merchant. Young Pinchot was educated in America and France and graduated from Yale University (1889). He studied forestry in England, France, Germany, and Switzerland (1889–1890) and returned to the United States to promote scientific forest management. He started America's first systematic forestry work at the Biltmore, the estate of George Washington Vanderbilt* in Asheville, North Carolina (1892). He became a member of the National Forest Commission of the National Academy of Sciences (1896) and headed the Department of Agriculture's Division of Forestry (1898–1910), which was renamed the U.S. Forest Service with Pinchot as chief forester (1905). In 1902 he developed a forestry conservation program for the Philippine Islands. He became the chief advisor of fellow conservationist Theodore Roosevelt* and helped to persuade the president to introduce federal control measures. The two men preferred utilitarian conservation policies, that is, forestry, land reclamation, and private leasing of acreage in the public domain, to mere scenic preservation. Pinchot felt that strictly preserving something in nature benefited only lovers of scenery; that trees, for example, should not be guarded merely for aesthetic reasons but instead should be managed as crops; and that federally held properties should be made productive through scientific development. Therefore, he initially opposed the creation of the National Park Service as a potential enemy of the U.S. Forest Service. (*See* National Parks.) Pinchot, together with his father and brother, founded and endowed Yale's Forest School (1903) and was named professor of forestry there (1903–1936). In his later years, Pinchot was an outspoken critic of government policies, criticized President Howard Taft and his cabinet for their exploitation of Alaskan resources, and was therefore dismissed from the service (1910).

During Pinchot's tenure, the number of national forests increased from 32 to 149, with 193,000,000 acres. Speaking of men in his administration, Roosevelt praised Pinchot as the one who, "on the whole, stood first." Pinchot supported Roosevelt's unsuccessful bid for the Republican presidential nomination in 1912, was appointed forestry commissioner of Pennsylvania (1920–1922), and was elected governor of Pennsylvania (1923–1927, 1931–1935). Grey Towers was the magnificent Pinchot family mansion in Milford, Pennsylvania. Pinchot married Cornelia Elizabeth Bryce in 1914 (the couple had one child). He was the author of numerous books, monographs, government pamphlets, and essays in his field, including *Government Forestry Abroad* (1891), *Biltmore Forest* (1893), "Notes on the Forests of New Jersey" (1895), *The White Pine* (coauthored, 1896), *Timber Trees and Forests of North Carolina* (1896), *The Adirondack Spruce* (1898), "Notes on Some Forest Problems" (1898), "Work of the Division of Forestry for the Farmer" (1898), "Progress of Forestry in the United States" (1899), "The Relation of Forests and Forest Fires" (in the *National Geographic Magazine*, 1899), *A Study of Forest Fires and Wood Production in New Jersey* (1899), "Short Account of the Big Trees of California" (1900), and *The Profession of Forestry* (1901). His posthumously published autobiography is *Breaking New Ground* (1947).

Pink Marsh (1897). Collection of episodes and brief anecdotes by George Ade.* Pink Marsh is a Chicago shoeshine youth who calls himself a "culled boy" and who tells the Morning Customer, his tolerant white straight man, that with "mo' ej'cation" he would "be lawyeh o' someping like 'at." Pink is shrewd, witty, quick, loquacious, and knowledgable about such aspects of city life as craps, numbers, alcohol, boxing, and easy ladies.

Poems (1901). Collection of poetry by William Vaughn Moody.* The four best poems are "An Ode in Time of Hesitation," "Gloucester Moors," "On a Soldier Fallen in the Philippines," and "The Menagerie." Moody's "Ode" (first published in May 1900) is his most frequently reprinted and surely his finest poem. It decries American expansionism following the Spanish-American War.* It is unusual in the light of the fact that Moody initially favored the war but then had his doubts when America became expansionistic. The poem begins with praise of the heroic idealism of Robert Gould Shaw and his glorious African-American Union army regiment, the 54th Massachusetts, in its noble, self-sacrificial attack on Confederate Fort Wagner (18 July 1863). But then doubts that "I dare not yet believe" creep in. Is the American eagle little now but "talons and . . . maw"? The poet closes with a plea to America's leaders not to "stain" our soldiers' chivalry by turning their victories to "gain"—or else their "baffled and dislaureled ghosts / Will curse us." In "Gloucester Moors" (first published in December 1900), Moody enjoys some time off on a New England beach, which he lyrically depicts, but then he protests the dehumanizing economic exploitation of others: "Who has given to me this sweet, / And given my brother dust to eat? / And when will his wage come in?" "On a Soldier Fallen in the Philippines" (first published in February 1901) similarly begins more happily than it ends. Moody first asks that the soldier be thanked and praised for his sacrifice; but then the poet hopes that no whispered message will reach him that his death was accompanied by the death of "his darling land," which "stumbled and sinned in the dark." The person in "The Menagerie," an intelligent drunk, visits real-life Adam Forepaugh's celebrated menagerie and dimly concludes that he and some of the animals are similar though lower on the ladder of living creatures "groping" for "the shape and soul of Man." Look at this end product—"A little man in trousers, slightly jagged." What if the sad beasts sit in judgment of him on that final day? This troubling poem is yet another reaction to the theories of Charles Darwin, which left their residue in tradition-oriented Americans at the close of the 1890s.

Pond, James B. (1838–1903). (Full name: Major James Burton Pond.) Lecture manager. He was born in Cuba, New York. His father was a blacksmith and a farmer, who moved with his family (ultimately including eleven children) to Wisconsin, Illinois, and then Wisconsin again. He failed at farming and homesteading and returned to blacksmithing. Young Pond left home in 1853, became a printer's apprentice in Fond du Lac, Wisconsin (1853–1856), and drifted about as a journeyman printer in Wisconsin, Illinois, Minnesota, Missouri, Kansas, and Colorado (1856–1859). He returned to Wisconsin to publish a newspaper in Markesan (1859–1861). During the Civil War, he was a daring officer in the Union cavalry (1861–1865) and rose to the rank of major. Still restless, Major Pond engaged in newspaper work and the furniture business in Salt Lake City, Utah. When Ann Eliza Young, the nineteenth wife of Brigham Young, left her old husband in 1873 she decided to go on the lecture circuit, and Pond offered to be her manager on her tour by way of Laramie, Wyoming, and Denver, Colorado, to Washington, D.C., and later. He worked in and out of James Redpath's lecture bureau (Boston, 1873–1875), then with a partner named George H. Hathaway bought out Redpath, worked with Hathaway (1875–1879), and finally established his own firm in New York (1879).

Pond managed and traveled widely with Henry Ward Beecher in the United States and abroad (1875–1887); at the same time and later, he steadily expanded his list of clients and professional friends. They include Susan B. Anthony,* George Washington Cable,* F. Marion Crawford,* Frederick Douglass,* Paul Laurence Dunbar,* William Dean Howells,* Elbert Hubbard,* Hamilton W. Mabie,* Joaquin Miller,* Thomas Nelson Page,* Robert Edwin Peary,* James Whitcomb Riley,* Ernest Thompson Seton,* Mark Twain,* Booker T. Washington,* and such foreign celebrities as Matthew Arnold, Sir Arthur Conan Doyle, William E. Gladstone, Rudyard Kipling, and Henry M. Stanley. Pond often made enormous sums of money for the "stars" whose tours he managed. He describes some of his activities with Beecher in *A Summer in England with Henry Ward Beecher* (1887), recalls his childhood in "A Pioneer Boyhood" (*Century*,* October 1899), and sums up the work of his professional career in *Eccentricities of Genius: Memories of Famous Men and Women on the Platform and Stage* (1900). *Eccentricities of Genius* is a mine of anecdotal information. Pond married Ann Frances Lynch in 1859 (the couple had one child, and then his wife died in 1871) and Martha Marion Glass in 1888 (the couple had one child).

Populist Party. Political party. The party was formed in the 1890s because of widespread agrarian discontent going back to post–Civil War years. Earlier farmers' alliances in the South, Middle West, and Far West had urged easing of tax burdens, federal regulation of railroads, and unrestricted minting of silver coins (at the old rate of 16 to 1 against gold). Since many politicians supporting these reforms had been elected on the city, county, and state levels by 1890, their constituents established a national party, officially designated the People's Party but usually known as the Populist Party. It first gained national exposure when it held a huge convention in Cincinnati, Ohio, in 1891. The party organized a national convention in Omaha, Nebraska, in 1892, nominated James B. Weaver* for president, and took heart when Weaver polled 308,000 popular votes on a platform of reforms, including some sensible ones (a graduated income tax, an eight-hour workday in industry, direct senatorial elections, immigration restrictions, and initiatives and referendums) but also some controversial ones (Free Silver* and government control if not ownership of railroads and of telephone and telegraph companies). The Populist Party also proposed a ''subtreasury'' plan to allow farmers to receive federal loans and then hold nonperishable crops from market until their prices rose sufficiently to merit selling.

In the next national elections (1896), many Populist candidates were sent to the U.S. Senate and the House of Representatives. However, Weaver lost in his second bid for the presidency at that time, although he polled more than one million votes. He might have fared better but for the fact that the Democrats nominated William Jennings Bryan* and preempted some of the Populist platform planks; in addition, the Western wing of the Populists favored fusion with the Democrats to support Bryan while the Southern wing resisted. The Populists even made the mistake of supporting Bryan while naming their own vice presidential candidate, which caused voter confusion and a split among Democrats, all of which helped William McKinley* to win. When the plight of the farmers was gradually mitigated later in the 1890s, the Populist cause needed new rallying points. It split into pro- and anti-Democratic camps (1900), with one naming its own candidates for president (Wharton Barker) and vice president (Ignatius Donnelly*). The party was further weakened in the next two presidential elections. In addition, when Theodore Roosevelt* was president, he enacted many Populist proposals, which further limited the appeal of their cause. Hamlin Garland* and Frank Norris,* among others, wrote about the farm conditions that fostered the growth of the Populist Party.

Porter, William Sydney. The real name of O. Henry.*

Powell, John Wesley (1834–1902). Explorer, ethnologist, and conservationist. Born at Mount Morris, New York, he was the oldest of eight children of a licensed Methodist-Episcopalian circuit-riding preacher and his wife. The family moved to and farmed successively in Ohio, Wisconsin, and Illinois (about 1841–1851). Then Powell left home, read on his own, taught school intermittently, and took college classes when and where he could (in Illinois and Ohio), never obtained a degree. He explored the Mississippi Valley region, and was fascinated by the great outdoors. A member of the Illinois State Natural History Society (1854–1861), he collected specimens of flowers, minerals, rocks, and shells. While serving as an artillery officer in the Union army during the Civil War (1861–1865), he lost his right arm at Shiloh, in 1862, but soon returned to active duty and was mustered out at war's end as a major. He taught geology at Illinois Wesleyan College (1865–1867) and Illinois Normal University (1867), conducted geographical and geological expeditions in the mountains of Colorado (1867, 1868), and then led several dangerous surveying expeditions to the Green and Colorado rivers and their plateaus and canyons (1869–1875), which gained him not only national fame and even glory, but also expertise in conservation, ethnology, geology, geomorphology, irrigation, and land reform and reclamation.

Powell published *The Exploration of the Colorado River and Its Tributaries, Explored in 1869, 1870, 1871, and 1872 under the Direction of the Secretary of the Smithsonian Institution* (1875), *Report on the Geology of the Eastern Portion of the Uinta Mountains* (1876), and *Report on the Lands of the Arid Region of the United States, with a More Detailed Account of the Lands of Utah* (1878). He also founded a journal entitled *Contributions to North American Ethnology* (1877). Having moved his base of operations to Washington, D.C., in 1873, and being on amicable terms with important federal politicians, Powell became influential in the formation of the U.S. Geological Survey (1879). He published *Introduction to the Study of Indian Languages* (1880). He was named head of the Smithsonian Institution's new Bureau of American Ethnology (1879–1902) and head of the Geological Survey (1881–1894). He began a program of government publication of bulletins (from 1883), monographs (1890), and detailed atlases (1894). He was always honest and inspiring in supervising budgets, federal and state politicians, experts, and subordinate scientists. In addition, he envisioned a sane development of Western resources (partly through competent irrigation programs and reform of land laws), and opposed efforts of anticonservation exploiters of forests, grasslands, and mineral resources. Opponents of Powell first blocked his hydrographic survey (1890), initially approved by Congress to study the feasibility of water reservoirs and public irrigable land reservations for homesteaders' use; and then they engineered his resignation as Geological Survey director (1894). He returned to work with the Ethnology Bureau, published *Canyons of the Colorado* (1895), and a philosophical, hail-and-farewell volume entitled *Truth and Error; or, the Science of Intellection* (1898).

Powell married Emma Dean, a cousin, in 1862 (the couple had one child). An army nurse, who had helped save his life when he was wounded, his wife accompanied him on some of his expeditions and was pleased when he named his first Colorado River boat the *Emma Dean*.

Presidential Elections, 1888 to 1900. In 1888, Benjamin Harrison,* Republican candidate, received 5,439,853 popular votes and 233 electoral votes, and defeated the following: Grover Cleveland,* Democratic candidate, who gained 5,540,309 votes but only 168 electoral votes; and Clinton B. Fisk, Prohibition candidate, who received 249,506 votes. In 1892, Cleveland received 5,556,918 votes and 277 electoral votes, and defeated the following: Harrison, who gained 5,176,108 votes and 145 electoral votes; and James B. Weaver,* People's candidate, who had 1,041,028 votes and 22 electoral votes. In 1896, William McKinley,* Republican candidate, received 7,104,779 votes and 271 electoral votes, and defeated the following: William Jennings Bryan,* Democratic and People's candidate, who gained 6,502,925 votes and 176 electoral votes; John M. Palmer, Nationalist Democratic candidate, who had 133,148 votes; and Joshua Levering, Prohibition candidate, who had 132,007 votes. In 1900, McKinley received 7,207,923 votes and 292 electoral votes, and defeated the following: Bryan, Democratic and Populist candidate, who gained 6,358,133 votes and 155 electoral votes; John C. Woolley, Prohibition candidate, who had 208,914 votes; and Eugene V. Debs,* Social Democratic candidate, who had 87,814 votes.

The Principles of Psychology (1890). Two-volume work by William James.* This monumental ''textbook,'' which was twelve years in the making, concerns both experimental psychology and the philosophy of the mind; it is grounded in positivistic, dualistic thought. It was the first in its field and, according to many present-day scholars, remains the best. Its twenty-eight long chapters define and discuss the scope of psychology, the functions and activities of the brain, habit and automatism, psychological methods and pitfalls, the relation of mind to other things, stream of thought and consciousness of self, attention, conception, discrimination and comparison, association, time and memory, sensation and imagination, kinds of perceptions (things, space, and reality), reasoning, production of movement, instinct, emotions, the will, hypnotism, and ''necessary truths and the effects of experience.''

James sees the mind as evolving, much as Charles Darwin and Herbert Spencer theorized that living forms and bodies evolve, and with as much spontaneity. The mind has an active job to do; it responds to and modifies the environment of the body in which it is housed, for specific purposes. Mental responses are complex, with thoughts being personal and in flux, having to do with objects both familiar and unfamiliar, involving expectations of pleasure or pain, and resulting in choices. Each thought in the flow of time is slightly or considerably different from all previous thoughts, as it relates itself to both the past and the present. James images consciousness both as a stream and as a bird alternately perching on facts and then flying to novelties, with peripheral twilight ever beyond illuminated spots. From a ''swarming *continuum*'' out there, we thoughtfully accept and relate and reject, through habit, desire, interest, whim, validation by our memory of ''reality,'' and the current appeal of what happens to be near and needful. Willpower is brought to bear, so that we are attentive, affirmative, sensible in making our choices, and sometimes admirably heroic in resolving to face the unwelcome—and even to lead others.

High points of *The Principles of Psychology* include James's pioneering treatment of the consciousness of self, his arresting notion that we are sorry because we cry and are afraid because we tremble (and not, in each instance, the other way around), and his description of the fluidity (not stasis) of the experiential stream.

James published an abridgment of this huge work, as *Psychology: Briefer Course* (1892). James's main sources were not only traditional philosophers, such as George Berkeley, David Hume, Immanuel Kant, John Locke, and Herbert Spencer, but also many psychologists, including Alexander Bain, Hermann Helmholtz, Carl Stumpf, James Ward, and Wilhelm Wundt. In the main, James's massive work was enthusiastically received, by professionals and the public alike. Most colleagues, especially Stumpf and Ward, praised it, although James's eccentric friend and colleague Charles Peirce found fault with it. George Santayana,* philosopher but also man of letters, and William Dean Howells,* man of letters only, were both able to appreciate its stimulating style; Howells went so far as to fear that the work was in danger of becoming a popular success. Its influence on younger philosophers, among them Henri Bergson, John Dewey,* and Josiah Royce,* is incalculable.

Prohibition Party. Political party. This party was formed to outlaw the production, sale, transportation, and consumption of alcoholic beverages. The first convention of the party was held in Chicago in 1869. The first national convention was held in Columbus, Ohio, in 1872, to nominate a presidential ticket. The party did poorly then, and also later (1876, 1880). In the course of time, the party advocated woman suffrage, antimonopoly measures, currency reform, direct popular vote for president and vice president, immigration law reform, and uniform marriage and divorce laws. It cooperated with the Anti-Saloon League of America* and the Woman's Christian Temperance Union. Iowa, Kansas, North Dakota, and South Dakota adopted statewide prohibition during the period from 1880 to 1890. At this time, the Prohibition Party became a one-issue party again, in presidential campaigning (1884, 1888), but without much effect. In 1892 it achieved its greatest impact, when it polled just over 271,000 votes for its candidates out of a total of about 12,000,000 votes (Grover Cleveland* won). The party never did as well again (1896 and later). Although it continued to function both before and after Prohibition became law (1920–1933), it never did so significantly.

PTA. *See* Parent-Teacher Associations.

Puck. Weekly magazine. The magazine, which featured humor, satire, wit, and chromolithographic cartoons, ran from 1877 to 1918. In the 1890s, it sold well at station newsstands along the New York Elevated Railroad. Often gently satirical, *Puck* revealed its serious side when it attacked various forms of political chicanery. The magazine was sold to William Randolph Hearst* in 1917, after which it became lighter and then folded. In its long heyday, *Puck* was edited by H. C. Bunner,* until his death (1896). James Huneker* later contributed essays to it.

Pudd'nhead Wilson, A Tale (1894). Novel by Mark Twain.* The action begins at Dawson's Landing, Missouri, in 1830, with the switching at birth of two babies by Roxana, a young slave. The babies are Thomas à Beckett Driscoll, son of Percy Northumberland Driscoll and his dying wife, and Valet de Chambre, son of Roxy, Percy's white-skinned, blue-eyed "black" slave, who has charge of both infants. When she is threatened with being sold "down the river" by Percy, Roxy exchanges the babies to enable her son to have a life of luxury.

Unfortunately, as it turns out much later, a young lawyer named David Wilson, who had just migrated from New York state to Dawson's Landing, has a hobby of collecting fingerprints, and he adds the babies' prints (before the babies are switched) to his harmless collection. Wilson does not flourish in town, because of a subtle remark he made before some rubes, who nicknamed him "Pudd'n-head." Fifteen years pass. Roxy's child, called Marse Tom, has grown abusive because of his pampered upbringing; the real Driscoll heir, as Chambers, is sturdy but deprived because of his slave environment and mentality. Impoverished and dying, Percy frees Roxy and requests that his childless older brother Judge York Leicester Driscoll aid and make an heir of Tom, who is further spoiled, goes to Yale for two years, and returns addicted to drink, cards, loafing, and even stealing. In June 1853, dark Luigi and fair Angelo Capello, twin Italian musical prodigies, come to Driscoll's Landing to captivate the townspeople. Roxy, who has been a Mississippi River steamboat chambermaid, returns home somewhat crippled and also broke because a bank crash has wiped out her savings. When she appeals to Tom for help but is abused by him, she tells him that he is her son—by the respected Colonel Cecil Burleigh Essex, a member of one of the First Families of Virginia and a recently deceased townsman—and she blackmails Tom into sharing his allowance from the doting Judge Driscoll. Tom, who cannot mend his ways, continues stealing—he even takes Luigi's bejewelled dagger—and one day foolishly insults Luigi, who kicks him. The judge is outraged when Tom declines to challenge Luigi to a duel, and he exchanges shots with Luigi himself. Sad that his uncle has not been killed, Tom goes to Saint Louis to fence some of his loot, but he is robbed. He returns and tells Roxy. She offers to let him sell her back into easy servitude—up the river—to cover his debts. He agrees but sells her down the river to what he hopes will be her doom. She escapes, returns to pounce on Tom, and orders him to tell the judge he sold her and to beg for money and forgiveness. Instead, Tom resorts to his habitual disguise as a woman and sneaks in to rob his uncle. When he is discovered, Tom kills him with Luigi's knife to shift the blame and thus guarantee his inheritance, and leaves the distinctive weapon as evidence.

Luigi is charged with murder, but Pudd'nhead Wilson, his defense attorney, proves not only that Tom's fingerprints are on the weapon but also that Tom is really Roxy's slave-born son. Pudd'nhead becomes a hero. Tom is sold down the river. Chambers, the real Driscoll scion, claims his just inheritance, but he is uneducated and hence useless. Roxy, utterly broken now though pensioned by the real Tom, joins a church.

One of the most striking features of *Pudd'nhead Wilson* is the sequence of mordant aphorisms from Pudd'nhead's "Calendar," which grace the beginning of each chapter. For example, "Why is it that we rejoice at a birth and grieve at a funeral? It is because we are not the person involved." *Pudd'nhead Wilson* began as "Those Extraordinary Twins" (1894), a burlesque starring Siamese twins, but soon grew into its present form. Wilson's jocose remark that earned him his nickname—that if he owned half of a barking dog he would kill his half—symbolically resonates through the novel: Alleged white supremacy and black inferiority are halves of one social and political body, and each half (barking, sick, or otherwise) mortally affects the other half. The novel features an early fictional use of fingerprinting, presents Twain's theory that ''training is everything'' (both Toms are products of conditioning more than of heredity, Roxy is ashamed of her son's ''nigger'' blood, and even Pudd'nhead advocates the Southern duelling code), daringly flirts with miscegenation (Roxy is proud of her white colonel lover), and—though or because flawed—is in many ways Twain's most representative novel.

Pulitzer, Joseph (1847–1911). Journalist. Born in Makó, Hungary, he received a classical education in Budapest and sought military service in Austria, France, and England, but was rejected because of poor eyesight and physical weakness. He immigrated to the United States and joined a cavalry unit of the Union army in New York toward the end of the Civil War (1864–1865). Then he worked at various menial jobs in Saint Louis (1865–1868) and became a reporter for the German daily *Westliche Post* (1868–1869). He was intelligent, energetic, fearless, and eccentric in digging out the news. He entered state politics and soon became a Democrat permanently. He bought and quickly sold an interest in the *Post* (1871, 1873), bought the Saint Louis *Staats-Zeitung* for little and at once sold its Associated Press membership to the Saint Louis *Daily Globe* for a huge profit. He studied law and politics, polished his English to near perfection, was admitted to the District of Columbia bar, became a Washington correspondent for the New York *Sun* (1876–1877), and bought the Saint Louis *Dispatch* at great risk (1878). He merged it with the *Post* to form the *Post-Dispatch*, which, owing to his thorough, courageous, and often sensational reporting and editorializing on the subject of city corruption, soon began to turn a profit (by 1881). When his main editorial writer got some bad publicity for killing a lawyer in self-defense (1882), Pulitzer felt that it would be expedient to sell out in Saint Louis and buy the New York *World* from Jay Gould* (1883).

Pulitzer converted the *World* into a distinguished, liberal newspaper—and the main voice for the Democratic Party. He was elected to Congress from New York (1885), but he soon became disgusted by federal political machinations and resigned (1886). During the 1890s, he reported and interpreted the news honestly, praised laborers as America's only true aristocrats, and advocated a number of causes, among them breaking up monopolies; taxing corporations and taxing the wealthy, their luxuries, and their inheritances; instituting moderate tariffs, for revenue only; and abolishing the habit of political bosses of forcing their employees to contribute to political campaigns. To compete with William Randolph Hearst* and his *Evening Journal*, Pulitzer founded the New York daily *Evening World* (1887), which soon became a money-maker. Pulitzer should be criticized, as should Hearst, for the yellow-journalism techniques that were introduced and augmented at this time. His tricks included scare headlines, sensational reporting (especially of crimes and scandals), gaudy features (including those dealing with sports and women's fashions), contests, wild illustrations and cartoons, comics, and the like. Complicated physical ailments, including weak lungs and a bad stomach, nervous insomnia, sensitivity to all noises, and ultimately total blindness, combined to force Pulitzer to quit editing the *World* (1890), which had financially enriched him vastly. Nevertheless, he built a stately new office structure for $2,500,000 on Park Row in New York (1890), opened it with lavish ceremonies (1891), and continued into the early twentieth century to issue advice and orders relating to both style and content, thus making it a newspaper of national and international stature and influence.

During the Spanish-American War,* Pulitzer's leading writer Stephen Crane* wrote for the *World* even as Hearst's main journalist Richard Harding Davis* wrote for the *Journal*. Over the years, Pulitzer praised Grover Cleveland,* Crane, George Dewey,* Charles Evans Hughes, and David Graham Phillips,* among others, and he lambasted James G. Blaine,* William Jennings Bryan,* Richard F. Croker,* Gould, Hearst, John Pierpont Morgan,* John D. Rockefeller,* Theodore Roosevelt,* and Tammany Hall.* Pulitzer especially deplored American imperialism and inveighed against expansionist moves into Hawaii, the Philippine Islands, and the Virgin Islands. He attacked Roosevelt for his actions in Colombia and the Isthmus of Panama (1908). He was sued for allegedly libeling Roosevelt, Morgan, and others, but he was vindicated when the case was dropped (1909). Pulitzer married Kate Davis in 1878 (the couple had seven children, five of whom survived him). John Singer Sargent* painted a portrait of Kate Pulitzer. In his will, which distributed $18,645,000, Pulitzer left provisions to establish a school of journalism at Columbia University and a sequence of prizes to reward and encourage public service and morals; American literature, music, and journalism; and better education.

Pullman, George (1831–1897). (Full name: George Mortimer Pullman.) Inventor. He was born in Brocton, New York. He worked as a cabinetmaker in Albion, New York (1848–1855), as a contractor in Chicago (1855–1859), and as a mining-town storekeeper in Colorado (1859–1863) and then returned to Chicago, where, with a friend named Ben Field, he designed the Pullman railroad car with folding upper berths (patented in 1864). Pullman then patented extendable seat cushions to create lower berths (1865). He organized the Pullman Palace Car Company (1867) to satisfy the increasing number of orders from railroad companies. He built dining cars (1868), chair cars (1875), and vestibule cars (1887). He also founded the "model town" of Pullman, Illinois (1880), on the northwest shore of Lake Calumet, once outside but now part of Chicago. The town quickly grew, from a population of four (in January 1881) to more than 8,200 (1884). It embraced the factories of the Pullman Palace Car Company, which employed 3,000 in 1884, the Allen Paper Car Wheel Company, the Union Foundry and Pullman Car Wheel Company, the Chicago Steel Works, the Steel Forging Company, the Chicago Steel Horseshoe Company, a brickyard, and smaller manufacturing concerns. The efficiently planned town included macadamized streets, docks, a playground, a scenic Pullman Drive, numerous houses—mostly workers' five-room cottages rented at $17 a month plus water tax—a church, a schoolhouse, a markethouse, a hotel (with the only bar in town), an arcade with a library (6,000 volumes plus numerous periodicals, with a $3 per annum use fee), a theater, a fire station, and stables. The difficulty was, of course, that the company owned the town, even its public works, and the residents, mostly workers (paid $1.30 to $4.00 a day), grew discontent, especially when freely expressed criticism was not tolerated by the supervisors. After the Panic of 1893* had begun, Pullman lowered his employees' wages by 25 percent but did not correspondingly reduce their rents (1894). In time, Chicago annexed his town, although his company retained most of the property until 1910. George Pullman is now remembered mainly because of the bitter Pullman Strike* (June–August 1894).

Pullman Strike. Bitter labor dispute. The strike began in Pullman, Illinois, near Chicago, a town that had been founded in 1880 as a "model town" by George Pullman.* The strike began in June 1894 when Pullman, who was regarded by his workers as paternalistic, refused to discuss their grievances, mainly about wages. Employees in the car shops declared a strike, which soon escalated. The American Railroad Union, led by volatile Eugene V. Debs,* supported the Pullman strikers with funds and an offer to help settle their grievances. When Pullman again declined to arbitrate, Debs's union voted to boycott Pullman cars everywhere. Transportation was halted throughout the North and even into the West. The company, backed by the General Managers' Association of Railroads, appealed for support to President Grover Cleveland,* whose pro-railroad attorney general Richard Olney appointed as U.S. special counsel a railroad lawyer named Edwin Walker. Walker obtained an injunction from the federal circuit court in Chicago against obstructing railroad traffic and thus preventing delivery of the mail. When renegade laborers overturned a mail train and events turned ugly and violent, Walker requested federal troops. Cleveland replied by dispatching a regiment of regular army soldiers, and also cavalry and artillery units, to Chicago on 4 July. This act provoked armed resistance by the more militant strikers. John Peter Altgeld,* governor of Illinois, who had already ordered the state militia out to control disorder during the strike, was opposed to big business, and Walker aimed both to finish him politically and to break the strike. Altgeld called for the withdrawal of federal troops, but in vain. Debs, who disregarded the injunction, was tried for contempt of court, convicted, and sentenced to serve six months in prison. The strike ended in August.

"The Pupil" (1891). Short story by Henry James.* Pemberton, a poor American student who had attended Oxford, gets a position with the Moreens, an American family wandering through Europe. He is to tutor their precocious but sickly son Morgan, age eleven. Pemberton grows very fond of Morgan but dislikes his sleazy parents, his toadying older brother, and his husband-seeking sisters. The group make their way from Nice to Switzerland, Florence, and then Paris. Pemberton does not complain much at receiving no pay, but finally he demands and gets a paltry sum. One day, in Nice again, Morgan, now fourteen, interrupts a lesson to tell Pemberton to abandon the whole shabby family. Instead, Pemberton, though feeling emotionally blackmailed, declines further pay but stays on since he cannot let his friend suffer. The boy says he would rather leave with Pemberton, who, instead, from Venice, accepts a tutoring job in England. When the Moreens cable him from Paris that Morgan is ill, he chucks his work and rushes to the recuperating lad's side, and they resume their friendship. After a long winter's walk, the hungry pair return to find that the whole family has been evicted from their hotel rooms. The parents say that Pemberton can now be the sole guardian of Morgan, who is elated, but when he sees Pemberton hesitate, he dies. Most of James's Americans in England or on the Continent are well-to-do and admirable, but in this story the shabbiness of other Americans abroad is exposed.

Pupin, Michael (1858–1935). (Full name: Michael Idvorsky Pupin.) Physicist, inventor, and educator. Born in Idvor, Hungary, in what is now Yugoslavia, he studied in Prague, Czechoslovakia (1873–1874). He immigrated to the United States, did menial odd jobs and read in the Cooper Union library (1874–1879), graduated from Columbia University (B.A., 1883), and became an American citizen (1883). Pupin then studied physics and mathematics at Cambridge, in England (1883–1885), and at Berlin University (1885–1889), where he earned a Ph.D. He returned to Columbia—as an instructor in mathematical physics (1890–1892), an adjunct professor of mechanics (1892–1901), and a professor of electromechanics and director of research laboratories (1901–1931). Pupin studied discharges at low pressure from vacuum tubes and invented an electrical resonator (1890). He invented a method of tuning oscillating currents (1893) and developed the use of spaced inductance coils to improve long-distance telephonic and telegraphic transmission (1894). This type of coil was later called the Pupin coil. He discovered secondary x-ray radiation, took the first x-ray photographs in the United States, and invented a method of rapid x-ray photography using a fluorescent screen (1896). The Bell Telephone Company and several German telephone companies bought his patent for long-distance transmission (1901). In the controversy over who invented the radio (*see* Radio), Pupin sided with Guglielmo Marconi and criticized Nikola Tesla.*

In all, Pupin patented thirty-four inventions. He served as Serbian consul during World War I. His many publications include *Thermodynamics of Reversible Cycles in Gases and Saturated Vapors* (1894), *The Serbian Orthodox Church* (1918), *Yugoslavia* (1919), his prize-winning autobiography entitled *From Immigrant to Inventor* (1923), *The New Reformation* (1927), and *Romance of the Machine* (1930). Pupin married Sarah Katharine Jackson in London in 1888 (the couple had one child, and Mrs. Pupin died in 1896).

Pyle, Howard (1853–1911). Artist, illustrator, writer, and art teacher. He was born in Wilmington, Delaware, into a Quaker family. Since he showed an early ability in drawing, he did not go to college but instead studied art in Philadelphia for three years (1869–1872). Then he was sidetracked by working in his father's leather business. On an impulse, while reporting on a wild pony roundup in Virginia (1876), Pyle wrote an essay about a small Virginia island and sent it, accompanied by illustrations, to *Scribner's Magazine*,* which accepted it. Encouraged, he studied at the Art Students League in New York (beginning in 1876), published some short stories and illustrations in *Harper's Weekly* and *St. Nicholas* (1877), and was given moral support by some established magazine illustrators (1878), including Edwin Austin Abbott and Charles Reinhart.* Pyle returned to Wilmington to work (1879), where he married Anne Poole in 1881 (the couple had seven children). Pyle drew superbly with pen and ink for several magazines, and he also became noted for accurate and distinctive illustrations for historical books such as Woodrow Wilson's *Washington* (1897) and Henry Cabot Lodge's *Story of the Revolution* (1898). Pyle also illustrated many contemporary novels, for example, *In the Valley* by Harold Frederic* (1890).

In the forefront among artists preparing illustrations in color, Pyle in his prime produced from 100 to 200 illustrations a year. Well before the 1890s, he also began a literary career, by writing as well as illustrating books for children. The first such book was *The Merry Adventures of Robin Hood* (1883). Titles of his writings from the period between 1888 and 1901 include *Otto of the Silver Hand* (1888), a brutally realistic historical novel for children, set in thirteenth-century Germany; *The Rose of Paradise* (1888), Pyle's first novel about pirates, here eighteenth-century Indian Ocean pirates; *The Wonder Clock* (1888), two dozen fantasy yarns for children; *Men of Iron* (1892), a novel about fifteenth-century British castle life, starring a youthful knight; *A Modern Aladdin* (1892), a tale of terror in eighteenth-century France; *The Garden behind the Moon* (1895), an allegorical fairy tale about survival and spiritual maturing after death, inspired by the death in 1889 of Pyle's son Sellers, his reading of the works of Emanuel Swedenborg, and his correspondence with William Dean Howells;* *The Story of Jack Ballister's Fortunes* (1895), a historical novel abut Eastern seaboard pirates; *Twilight Land* (1895), diverse fairy tales; and *The Price of Blood* (1899), a parody of sentimental and romantic fantasy.

Early in the twentieth century, Pyle wrote and illustrated four magnificent books concerning Arthurian legends (1903–1910). He was briefly the well-paid art editor of *McClure's Magazine** (1905–1906). Toward the end of his life, he turned to historical mural painting. Pyle also taught art at the Drexel Institute in Philadelphia (1894–1900) and at Chadds Ford, Pennsylvania, in the summers of 1898, 1899, 1901, and 1902. He also established the Howard Pyle School of Art in Wilmington (1900), where he gave free lessons (1900–1905), and he even commuted to New York City to teach at the Art Students League (winter 1904–1905). His nearly 200 students, many of whom continued his so-called Brandywine Tradition, included Maxfield Parrish and N. C. Wyeth. Pyle went to Florence, Italy, in 1910, to improve his mural technique, but he suddenly died there. He is now regarded as the author of classic stories for children, the best illustrator, especially of black-and-white pen pictures, of books and magazine pieces who ever lived, and an art instructor of unparalleled importance.

R

Radio. Wireless transmission and reception of signals and sounds by electric waves. This immensely significant invention gained enormous impetus as the 1890s ended and the twentieth century began, but it had a lengthy early nineteenth-century background, involving theorists, laboratory technicians, inventors, and popularizers in Denmark, England, France, Germany, Italy, and the United States. Work by such scientists in the field as Wilhelm von Bezold, Edouard Branly, Thomas A. Edison,* Michael Faraday, Wilhelm Feddersen, Joseph Henry, Heinrich Rudolph Hertz, Sir Oliver Lodge, James Clerk Maxwell, Hans Christian Oersted, Auguste Righi, and Nikola Tesla* resulted in the discovery and development of electromagnetic induction, wireless transmission, and receivers.

Guglielmo Marconi, who initially experimented in Bologna, Italy (1895), applied available knowledge to build the first wireless telegraph device, a commercially practical communication system using a key (recorder), a landed aerial, and a coherer (receiver). He patented his process in England in 1896, sent a signal from Spezia to Italian naval vessels twelve miles out at sea in 1897, and capitalized his own wireless and signal company in London in 1897. The year 1899 was a busy one for Marconi: He sent a message thirty-two miles across the English Channel, transmitted a lifesaving message when a British lightship was run down by a steamer, was hired by American newspaper owner James Gordon Bennett* to send reports on the America's Cup races around the Isle of Wight, and visited the United States. Marconi's most popular feat was his sending of a Morse code signal—the letter "s"—from Poldhu, Cornwall, in England, to St. John's, Newfoundland (1901). When Michael Pupin* praised Marconi, Tesla ridiculed the Italian.

Meanwhile, in the 1890s and on into the twentieth century, other scientists were hard at work, although they did not gain the accolades showered on the inventor-hero Marconi. These scientists include Karl Braun, Sir William

Crookes, Lee De Forest, Reginald Aubrey Fessenden, Sir John Ambrose Fleming, Charles Proteus Steinmetz,* and John Stone Stone. They developed alternators, coaxial coils, crystal detectors, diodes, electronic tubes, heterodyne and superheterodyne reception, ionization theories, magnetic detectors, triodes (audions), tuners, and voice-sound transmitters.

Of all the above-named men, the following worked in American laboratories: De Forest, Fessenden, Marconi, Steinmetz, Stone, and Tesla. Lee De Forest (1873–1961) was born in Council Bluffs, Iowa, earned his Ph.D. at Yale, and took out about 300 patents related to wireless telegraphy, telephony, and sound movies. He invented the responder and established the American De Forest Telegraphy Company, but he was dismissed from his company because of a patent dispute. He applied for a patent for the triode (audion), which ushered in the age of electronics. De Forest's autobiography is immodestly entitled *Father of Radio* (1950). Reginald Aubrey Fessenden (1866–1932) was born in Bolton, Quebec, Canada, was educated at Trinity College, Port Hope, Ontario, taught in Canada and Bermuda, was employed by Edison as an engineer and chemist, published articles on electricity, worked for George Westinghouse* (1890), taught at Purdue briefly and then at the University of Pittsburgh (1894–1900), experimented in electromagnetism, patented an improved wireless-signal receiver (1899), was the first to transmit speech by wireless (1900), experimented in wireless telegraphy for the U.S. Weather Bureau (1900), patented an oscillation method used in microphone detection systems (1901), patented a continuous-wave generator (1901), and organized the National Electric Signal Company in Washington, D.C. (1903), broadcast music (1906), and did much else of value in wireless communication, including transmitting underwater signals. Charles Proteus Steinmetz (1865–1923) of the General Electric Company cooperated with Fessenden (beginning in 1901) in manufacturing high-frequency alternators. John Stone Stone (1869–1943) was born in Dover, Virginia, and educated at Columbia and Johns Hopkins. He was a pioneer theoretician in telephone and radio engineering. He patented tuned circuits for transmission and reception (1902), ahead of Marconi. Prolonged litigation finally resulted in establishing Stone's priority (1943). Stone also experimented with short-wave radio and ultrahigh-frequency radio transmission. Nikola Tesla (1856–1943) diagrammed a workable radio (1893), demonstrated wireless communication over a twenty-five-mile distance (1897), built a radio-controlled ship (1898), and in the year of his death was declared by the U.S. Supreme Court to have anticipated all other inventors with his radio patents (1943).

More than any other nineteenth-century inventions and embellishments concerning astronomy, the automobile, electricity, photography, or the telephone, the amazingly complex radio was the result of cooperative efforts by dozens of scientists, culminating at the turn of the century in quick applications of radio technology in the fields of lifesaving, war and peace, journalism, meteorology, transportation, and entertainment; and, of course, it led to that twentieth-century boon and bane, television.

The Red Badge of Courage (1895). Novel by Stephen Crane.* On the eve of his first battle in the Civil War, a young Yankee soldier named Henry Fleming wonders how he will behave under fire. His new friends Jim Conklin and Wilson boast of their steadfast courage. In the morning their regiment, after marching meaninglessly, is attacked. At first Henry does little—he fires away, observes some men being wounded, and experiences a sense of camaraderie—then he notices the silence and the indifferent blue sky above. Another attack surprises the tired men, including Henry, into a retreat. Learning that the enemy has lost this engagement, Henry experiences a sense of guilt, makes his way into a forest, scares a squirrel, comes upon a dead soldier, and joins a procession of men wounded and responding to their battle experiences in various ways. He recognizes his friend Conklin, who, wounded, staggers, falls, and dies. His conscience again bothering him, Henry envies the heroic dead, seeks his own lines, but is swept up in another haphazard retreat. This time he is clubbed on the head by a frenzied fellow soldier. Wandering about in pain, he is led to his unit by an unnamed comrade. He meets up again with Wilson, once a braggart but now so modest that Henry feels superior to him. Next morning, with his head wound washed, Henry participates in another attack; this time he holds his ground and fires like a blind demon so furiously that his lieutenant praises him. During a lull, Henry and Wilson go into the woods for water and overhear two officers ridicule Henry's regiment but say that it must be used in a bloody attack soon to take place. Again Henry fights well, taking a dead color-bearer's flag forward and earning another compliment, although the unit fails to gain its intended objective. Now and a little later, Henry begins to feel like a worthy veteran.

In addition to the anecdotes Crane heard about the Civil War and his incredible imagination, his major source was "Battles and Leaders of the Civil War," published by *Century*.* The unnamed battle in which Henry Fleming participates is remarkably similar to the Battle of Chancellorsville, fought in Virginia, from 1 to 3 May 1863. Crane also may have read and been influenced by John William De Forest's *Miss Ravenel's Conversion from Secession to Loyalty* (1867) and Wilbur F. Hinman's *Corporal Si Klegg and His "Pard"* (1887), as well as several other war novels. *The Red Badge of Courage* occasionally resembles Émile Zola's powerful war novel *La Débâcle* (1892), which Crane denied he ever read. He offered *The Red Badge of Courage*, his second novel (after *Maggie: A Girl of the Streets**), to publisher S. S. McClure,* who kept it for six months without sending word to Crane. Crane then sold an 18,000-word abridgment of it to the Bacheller-Johnson newspaper syndicate for $90. The syndicate published the abridgment in the Philadelphia *Press* (3–8 December 1894) and the New York *Press* (9 December 1894). D. Appleton and Company then published the full novel as *The Red Badge of Courage: An Episode of the American Civil War* (1895, 1896).

The Red Badge of Courage is a tour de force, a superb piece of imaginative writing. Following an age-old plot, it recounts the adventures of a callow youth growing through horrible experience to maturity. This is the first modern war novel. Previous fictional treatments of war were by comparison historical, panoramic, and epic, and were narrated from an omniscient point of view. Action was on a vast scale, and its strategists displayed heroism and intelligence. Crane, on the other hand, avoids the romantic and the epic here; he shows that in ground-level combat few know much about what is going on. In keeping with his times, Crane was naturalistic in *The Red Badge of Courage*, in which environment and chance control people, who behave more like animals than angels, and toward whom Mother Nature is indifferent. This novel is also notable for fine structure; selective detail; impressionistic coloration; graphic religious, animal, and machine imagery; and an ironic, pessimistic tone. Critical opinions, which have been extensive, vary concerning the possible message of *The Red Badge of Courage*. Does Henry Fleming evidence any kind of Christian redemption? Is he more than a beast? Do any of his illusions remain? What kind of final terms does he come to about himself and the world around him?

Red Men and White (1896). Collection of short stories by Owen Wister,* illustrated by his friend Frederic Remington.* The tales are mostly of two types: Indians defeated by white men, and white law opposing lawlessness. The best of the first category is "Specimen Jones," the story of a wandering cowboy who outwits some savage Apaches by feigning insanity. "The General's Bluff" features real-life General George Crook,* who fools enemy Indians by pretending that he has stronger forces at his disposal than he does. Specimen Jones figures in this story too. The best law-and-order yarn is "Salvation Gap." In it, two men vie for the attentions of a dance-hall floozy. She prefers one; so the other kills her. A mob seizes the innocent man, ignores the pleas of a sheriff, and lynches their victim, whereupon the murderer confesses, begs to be hanged, is refused, and commits suicide. "A Pilgrim on the Gila" contrasts praise of the West by politicians in Washington, D.C., plumping for Arizona statehood, with a depiction of the region's tawdry cowboys, businessmen, civic leaders, and lawyers.

Reed, Walter (1851–1902). Military physician. He was born in Belroi, Virginia, but soon moved with his family to Charlottesville (1852). He studied medicine at the University of Virginia (1867–1869), where he received his medical degree at the age of seventeen, and then he studied at the Bellevue Hospital Medical College in New York, where he received a second medical degree in 1870. After private practice in Brooklyn and New York City, Reed entered the U.S. Army (1875), was promoted to captain (1880) and then major (1893), and became professor of bacteriology and clinical microscopy at the Army Medical School and the curator of its museum in Washington, D.C. (1893). Reed and others studied causes of yellow fever (1897–1899). He helped prove that the fever from which soldiers suffered and often died during the Spanish-American War* was typhoid not yellow fever. He headed the Yellow Fever Commission of the U.S. Army to Havana, Cuba (1900–1901), to study the deadly disease, working in the command of General Leonard Wood.* Reed's experiments, using volunteers, proved that yellow fever is transmitted by the *Stegomyia fasciati* mosquito (later classified as *Aedes aegypti*) and not by contact and contagion; furthermore, that the disease agent is a filterable virus. These experiments were the first to prove that a virus can cause a human disease. The army then rid areas of mosquito infestation and thus freed Havana from a disease that had ravaged the city for three centuries. Reed returned to Washington (1901), taught pathology and bacteriology at the Columbian University Medical School (now part of George Washington University), and died of neglected chronic appendicitis. Reed's publications include *The Contagiousness of Erysipelas* (1892), *The Propagation of Yellow Fever: Observations Based on Recent Researches* (1901), *The Etiology of Yellow Fever: An Additional Note* (coauthored, 1902), *Report on the Origin and Spread of Typhoid Fever in United States Military Camps during the Spanish War of 1898* (1904), and many articles. Walter Reed Hospital in Washington, D.C., was named after him (1909).

Reid, Whitelaw (1837–1912). Journalist and diplomat. Born on a farm near Xenia, Ohio, he graduated from Miami University in Oxford, Ohio (1856). He became a school superintendent in South Charleston, Ohio (1855–1857), and then began a career in journalism, first with various Ohio newspapers (1857–1861). During the Civil War, Reid was a correspondent who covered several Union army campaigns and also politics in Washington, D.C. (1861–1865). He was librarian of the House of Representatives (1863–1866); toured, wrote about, and unsuccessfully invested in the postbellum South (1865–1867); and began his association with the pro-Republican New York *Tribune* (1868–1905), where he worked for its editor Horace Greeley, associated with John Hay* and others, and accepted writings by Henry James* and Mark Twain,* among others. Reid supported Greeley's unsuccessful bid for president of the United States (1872), and after Greeley's death he became the *Tribune* editor (1872–1905). Under Reid, both the quality and the circulation of the newspaper improved. During the 1870s, he gathered an excellent staff, moved to a better building, pioneered by introducing Mergenthaler linotype presses, began an annual index, and started a Sunday edition. His news coverage and editorials showed intelligence and tact; William Randolph Hearst* and Joseph Pulitzer* relied more on conflict and sensationalism. Reid favored an open-shop policy but finally agreed to go union (1892). His criticism of President Chester Arthur helped Grover Cleveland* become governor of New York (1883–1885). Reid favored the unsuccessful bid of James G. Blaine* for the presidency in 1884. Reid supported the successful campaign of Benjamin Harrison* for president in 1888, after which Harrison appointed Reid minister to France (1889–1892). When Harrison made an unsuccessful bid for reelection, Reid was his vice-presidential running mate (1892).

Reid supported most of Cleveland's policies, traveled to Asia Minor (1894–1895), and supported the victorious campaign of William McKinley* for president in 1896, vigorously criticizing William Jennings Bryan* and espousing

American expansionism. President McKinley, with the reluctant backing of Hay (the minister to England), commissioned Reid to represent the United States as special ambassador at Queen Victoria's Jubilee in London (1897). When the threat of war with Spain loomed, Reid initially favored buying Cuba instead of freeing it by force of arms; but when war proved inevitable, he supported the policies of McKinley (1898), who after the victory made him a member of the peace commission in Paris (1898). Later in his life, Reid supported Theodore Roosevelt* during his presidency and served him—and America—notably, not least as a popular minister to England (1905–1912).

Reid's writings include *Ohio in the [Civil] War: Her Statesmen, Her Generals, and Soldiers* (2 vols., 1868; Edmund Clarence Stedman* used Reid's description of the Battle of Gettysburg as the basis for a stirring poem), *Some Consequences of the Last Treaty of Paris* (1898), *Problems of Expansion, as Considered in Papers and Addresses* (1900), and the posthumously published *American and English Studies* (1913) and *Making Peace with Spain: The Diary of Whitelaw Reid, September–December 1898* (1965). Reid married Elizabeth Mills in 1881 (the couple had two children). Elizabeth Reid was acting head of the nursing division of the American Red Cross during the Spanish-American War,* was chairperson of the American Red Cross in London during World War I in London, and continued her exemplary humanitarian work later. The Reids' son Ogden Mills Reid edited the *Tribune* (from 1913).

Reinhart, Charles (1844–1896). (Full name: Charles Stanley Reinhart.) Illustrator and genre painter. He was born in Pittsburgh, Pennsylvania, and attended Sewickley Academy outside Pittsburgh (to 1861). He worked as a telegraphist for the Union army's railroad corps during part of the Civil War (1861–1864), clerked in a Pittsburgh steel mill (1864–1867), and studied art in Paris and Munich (1867–1870). Returning to New York, he produced drawings exclusively published by Harper & Brothers (1870–1877). After free-lancing, he returned to Paris (1880–1891), and while there took fruitful trips elsewhere in France and also to England, Germany, Italy, and Spain. Reinhart remained busy drawing for magazines and books published by some of the best American and foreign firms. He was successful through the 1880s and well into the 1890s as a painter in oils and watercolors but mainly as a brilliant black-and-white illustrator; he is considered the best in this field in late nineteenth-century America. He gained popular favor when he sent 153 drawings to a Chicago exhibition (1891), and he and several other artists decorated domes of the World's Columbian Exposition* (Chicago, 1893). He was awarded medals in Philadelphia (1888), Paris (1889), and Chicago (1893). Death prevented his completing a series of Civil War illustrations to be published in the *Century*.* Reid married Emilie Varet in 1873 (three of their children survived the artist). Henry James* knew and admired Reinhart and published a complimentary essay about him in *Harper's Weekly* (14 June 1890).

Remington, Frederic (1861–1909). (Full name: Frederic Sackrider Remington.) Painter, sculptor, illustrator, and author. He was born in Canton, New York. His father, a newspaperman, served in the Union army during the Civil War. Remington moved with his family to Ogdensburg, New York (about 1875), enjoyed hunting in the woods and fishing, read widely, and became adept at drawing. He attended the Vermont Episcopal Institute at Burlington (1875), the Highland Military Academy at Worcester, Massachusetts (1876), and then Yale to study art and play football (1878–1880). He went west to Montana (1881), lamented the passing of the Old West, bought a sheep ranch outside Peabody, Kansas, in 1883, with a $4,000 inheritance from his father's estate, and sold it but soon lost his money by making poor investments (1884). He married Eva Caten in 1884, and tried without initial success to do free-lance artwork for Eastern magazines (1884). Discouraged, his wife left their Kansas City home to return to her parents in New York state (1885). Remington sketched Apaches and U.S. troops in Arizona (1885), attended the Art Students League in New York (1885), and finally succeeded in selling some drawings (1886), partly because the nationwide notoriety of the Apache chief Geronimo* made artwork dealing with the Southwest popular. Remington and his wife resumed married life in New York (1886).

Remington began to write realistic sketches of soldiers, Indians, and horses in the Far West, and in addition he sold nearly two hundred pictures to various periodicals in one year (1888). He also illustrated *Ranch Life and the Hunting Trail* by Theodore Roosevelt* (1888). *The Last Stand*, Remington's oil painting depicting George Custer's troops under fatal attack by the Sioux warriors of Sitting Bull,* earned a silver medal at the Paris Universal Exposition (1889). While covering the Sioux uprising for *Harper's Weekly*, Remington observed the conduct of the U.S. Army in the Wounded Knee* area of South Dakota (1890), and he grew so disgusted that he took himself to Africa, Germany, and Russia for refreshing art inspiration (1891–1892). Upon his return to the United States, he began to study Western cowboys and to treat them artistically. He illustrated new editions of Henry Wadsworth Longfellow's *Hiawatha* (1891) and Francis Parkman's *The Oregon Trail* (1892), and later books by, among others, Emerson Hough, Alfred Henry Lewis, Nelson A. Miles,* and his friend Owen Wister.* Remington held a one-man show in 1893. He hunted in the Dakotas (1894). He filed reports on the Pullman Strike* riots in Chicago (1894) and published his first short story, "The Affair of the —th of July" (*Harper's Weekly*, 2 February 1895), based on those riots and clearly in sympathy with the strikebreakers. He produced his first bronzes, *The Bronco Buster* (1895) and *The Wounded Bunkie* (1896), which shows two mounted cavalrymen, one of whom is wounded and is being supported by the other. With Richard Harding Davis,* Remington went to Cuba (1896) and then again as a *Harper's Weekly* correspondent (1898). Weakened by malaria he grew so disillusioned with military bureaucrats that his writing became gloomier, ironic, and naturalistic. He traveled in Montana and Wyoming (1899). Yale awarded him an honorary degree (1900).

By this time and, indeed, later, Remington's artwork overshadowed his considerable literary production, which is unfortunate. But his pictorial range is phenomenal, in quantity and quality. He made at least 2,739 paintings and drawings—in oil (sometimes in monochrome), watercolor, pen and ink, and crayon. His pictures appeared in forty-one periodicals (including *Century*,* *Collier's*,* *Cosmopolitan Magazine*,* *Harper's Weekly*, *Harper's Monthly Magazine*,* *McClure's Magazine*,* *Outing*, *St. Nicholas*, and *Scribner's Magazine**) and also in 142 books. He created twenty-five bronzes. His varied subjects include Western explorers, trailblazers, and pioneers; Indians and U.S. Army soldiers; cowboys; and buffalo, horses, and cattle. His finest oil paintings include *A Dash for Timber* (1889), presenting mounted soldiers seeking woods as protection from Indians in pursuit; *Antelope Hunting* (1889); *Charge of the Rough Riders at San Juan Hill* (1899); *Caught in the Circle* (1901), showing frontiersmen being attacked by Indians; and *A Cavalry Officer* (1901). Among his finest black-and-white illustration are the pictures he made for an edition of Longfellow's *Hiawatha* (1891); *A Misdeal* (1897), depicting five cardplayers shot dead or wounded in a saloon; *The Pony War Dance* (1897); and *Protecting the Army Train* (1897). His best bronzes, in addition to *The Bronco Buster* and *The Wounded Bunkie* are the following: *The Scalp* (1898), in which an Indian holds up his trophy; *The Norther* (1900), which shows a horse and a rider half frozen in a snowstorm; *The Cheyenne* (1901), which presents an armed Indian on a galloping pony; and *The Buffalo Signal* (1901), which shows an Indian rider holding aloft a buffalo robe on a pole. Remington's pictures are often images as seen by a neutral, sometimes romantic, observer. His statues are more pictorial than sculptural.

Remington's books, all of which the versatile man illustrated himself, are *Pony Tracks* (1895), previously published articles on Western hunting, fishing, ranching, and soldiering; *A Rogers Ranger in the French and Indian War* (1897); *Crooked Trails* (1898), more reprinted Western articles; *Stories of Peace and War* (1899), three reprints; *Sundown Leflare* (1899), nostalgic, interlocking stories told by an Eastern painter-narrator about a heroic half-breed friend; *Men with the Bark On* (1900), bitter Western stories and Cuban war dispatches; *John Ermine and the Yellowstone* (1902), an elegiac, antiprogress Western novel featuring a white male raised by Crow Indians who soldiers in the late 1870s (it was dramatized in 1903); and *The Way of an Indian* (1906), featuring a Cheyenne who regards himself as invincible, ending in the late 1870s.

Remington was well on his way to wealth and professional independence after he negotiated an annual contract with *Collier's* for a dozen new paintings each year for $10,000, beginning in 1903, but he died suddenly, a victim of appendicitis. His theme may be simply summed up as the Old West not won but lost. Remington and Charles Marion Russell* are indisputably the two finest painters of the Old West.

The Reverberator (1888). Short novel by Henry James.* George Flack, who works in Paris for *The Reverberator*, an American newspaper which features gossip, visits his traveling American friends the Dossons in their hotel. They are rich, vapid old Whitney Dosson, his plain daughter Delia, and his pretty daughter Francie. Flack persuades Francie to sit for her portrait with an American expatriate painter, in whose studio she meets Gaston Probert, born in France but into an American family. Gaston and Francie soon fall in love. He tells her many intimate details about members of his family and introduces her to them; with great reluctance they accept her as Gaston's fiancée. Suddenly Flack publishes several horrible but true stories about the Proberts in *The Reverberator*, stories which Francie had innocently told to Flack. The upshot of the ensuing noisy Probert family scene is that the initially outraged but finally loyal Gaston accepts uncomprehending but sweet Francie despite likely denunciation by most of her outraged in-laws to be. James's purpose in this novel is threefold: to present a gauche American girl whose heart is in the right place, to contrast American and French mores, and to vilify sensational American journalism.

Review of Reviews. Monthly magazine. It was founded by William Thomas Stead in London in 1890. Its crusading, goodwill purpose was to unify the English-speaking world spiritually, intellectually, and socially. Its main feature, "The Progress of the World," concerned reforms and reformers, particularly in relation to politics and economics. Also included were other editorials, summaries of reviews worldwide, comments on numerous journals (in English and several foreign languages), condensations of important new books (one per issue), an annotated bibliography of other new books, and a listing of special magazine items. Stead expanded by establishing an American *Review of Reviews*, under the intelligent editor Albert Shaw (1891), and an Australian *Review of Reviews* as well (1892). The American version, the best of the three, sold for 20¢ a copy (25¢ in 1892) and featured superior illustrations, including cartoons from around the world. The American edition was retitled the *American Review of Reviews* in 1897 and grew in circulation to well over 100,000 (partly because of its careful coverage of the Spanish-American War*) and soon far more. Notable American authors represented included Jack London,* Jacob Riis,* and Theodore Roosevelt.* *Review of Reviews* combined with *World's Work**—the two became *Review of Reviews and World's Work* (1932–1937)—then merged into the *Literary Digest* (1937) but failed that same year. *Review of Reviews* excluded fiction and muckraking.

Richard Carvel (1899). Historical novel by Winston Churchill.* Cast in late eighteenth-century America, it features as its title hero an upper-crust colonial Marylander who is reared by his paternal Tory grandfather. Kidnapped through the machinations of a bad uncle who covets the Carvel family estate, he lands, after several sea fights, in Georgian England, where he enjoys a reunion with his coquettish girlfriend Dorothy Manners. She is in England because her father wants her to socialize there and wed herself to a title. While in England, Richard Carvel is a victim, a heroic swordsman, and a debater; by the time he returns to Annapolis, his deceased grandfather's land is in the clutches of the vicious uncle. Richard bides his time by managing a friend's farm until the Revolution breaks out and impels him to go to sea again—and straight into the naval engagement against the *Serapis* by the *Bonhomme Richard*, captained by his friend and commanding officer John Paul Jones. Richard is wounded and must recuperate. Where? In Miss Manners' London home. Soon all is well, with a return to Annapolis, the unmasking of the villain, the recovery of the hero's estate, and marriage. Churchill, who attended the U.S. Naval Academy at Annapolis, knew seamanship and also fencing well and described lively naval and rapier clashes in *Richard Carvel*. The book became such a best-seller that the British Winston Churchill, in the summer of 1899, wrote to the novelist that henceforth he would put his full name Winston Spencer Churchill on his own title pages. *Richard Carvel* was praised by reviewers for its well-researched historical accuracy, although forward-looking critics, for example, William Dean Howells* and Frank Norris,* expressed dislike of its historical-romantic effusions.

Riis, Jacob (1849–1914). (Full name: Jacob August Riis.) Journalist, author, photographer, and social reformer. Riis was born in Ribe, Denmark, the third of fourteen children of a Latin teacher whom he aided in preparing material for a weekly newspaper. Riis was apprenticed to a Copenhagen carpenter for four years, then he immigrated to the United States with $40 in his pocket (1870). He held a sequence of menial jobs in New York, New Jersey, and Pennsylvania, got into newspaper work (1873), bought and wrote for a small Brooklyn newspaper (1875), and worked as a police reporter and feature writer for the New York *Tribune* (1877–1888) and the New York *Evening Sun* (1888–1899). In the late 1880s he began to lecture, showed slides made from his own photographs (often taken at night by the new magnesium-flash process), and wrote about the crowded and filthy living conditions of New York's poverty-stricken tenement dwellers. He was responsible for razing the notorious Mulberry Bend tenement and subsequently built on its site the Jacob A. Riis Neighborhood House (1888).

Riis's major book on the subject of tenement life is *How the Other Half Lives: Studies among the Tenements of New York** (1890). Riis wrote much else on this subject and other works akin to it. When Theodore Roosevelt* became police commissioner of New York City (1895), he accompanied Riis on investigative tours of slum areas. (When president, Roosevelt offered Riis the position of the governor of the Virgin Islands but was turned down.) Riis was named secretary of New York's small-parks commission (1897). With phenomenal energy, he continued to crusade for the poor—for more adequate housing, safer water, better parks, and more playgrounds for children. He helped to close infamous police-station lodging houses, to reform child-labor laws, to start a truants' school, to find housing for vagrants, and to close bakeries in tenement basements because of the hazard of fires. His other books are *The Children of the Poor* (1892), *Nibsy's Christmas* (1893), *Out of Mulberry Street* (1898), *A Ten Years' War* (1900), *The Making of an American* (1901, an inspiring autobiography), *The Battle with the Slum* (1902), *Children of the Tenements* (1903), *Is There a Santa Claus?* (1904), and *Theodore Roosevelt the Citizen* (1904). Riis returned to Denmark briefly and married his Ribe sweetheart, Elizabeth Nielsen, in 1876 (the couple had five children). Riis suffered from a weakened heart (beginning in 1904). After his wife's death in 1905 Riis married his secretary (1907).

Riley, James Whitcomb (1849–1916). Poet and journalist. He was born in Greenfield, Indiana. His father was a lawyer and state legislator. Young Riley held a variety of jobs, as a shoestore clerk, Bible salesman, house and sign painter, assistant to a patent-medicine salesmen, itinerant actor, jingle-writer for minstrel shows, and recitation artist and reader (1870–1878). This background prepared him to become the poet of ordinary people. After publishing poetry sporadically in newspapers (from 1870), Riley began to succeed with some prose humor as well as more poetry (often published in the Indianapolis *Journal* [1877–1885]). He enjoyed national success as a popular reader on tour (Boston and elsewhere from 1882). He traveled to England (1891), the Far West (1892, 1896), and Mexico (1906). He was exceedingly popular and highly honored in his lifetime. His books (more than ninety in number), beginning with *The Ole Swimmin' Hole and 'Leven More Poems* (1883, usually reprinted newspaper and magazine items), include *Rhymes of Childhood* (1890), *A Child-World* (1897), and *Home-Folks* (1900), among the best. His works, which may be divided into the sugary sentimental (for example, "An Old Sweetheart of Mine") and the folksy rural (for example, "The Ole Swimmin' Hole"), are notable for their easy rhythms, clean and simple content, Hoosier dialect, nostalgic picturesqueness, pathos, and clichés. Riley had an alcohol problem.

Robinson, Edwin Arlington (1869–1935). Poet. Robinson, born in Head Tide, Maine, was the youngest of three sons. His father retired from business with savings of $80,000 and moved the family to Gardiner, Maine, a little down the Kennebec River from Head Tide (1870). After Robinson graduated from high school (1887), he stayed at home composing poetry declined by various publishers and suffered from a chronic ear ailment. He entered Harvard in 1891, but his father's unwise investments and his death in 1892, followed by the Panic of 1893,* required Robinson to withdraw. Death took his mother in 1896, one brother in 1899, and the other in 1909. One of his two "successful," but unstable, brothers was a physician who married his poet-brother's fiancée, was addicted to morphine, and committed suicide; the other, a businessman, died of alcoholism. Robinson published *The Torrent and the Night Before* (1896), at his own expense, and then *The Children of the Night** (1897), at a generous friend's expense. When a reviewer of the former little book called it somber and its author's world evidently ''a prison-house,'' Robinson replied (*Bookman*,* March 1897): ''The world is not a prison house, but a kind of spiritual kindergarten, where millions of bewildered infants are trying to spell God with the wrong blocks.''

After living briefly in New York (1897–1898) and clerking for Harvard's president (1899), Robinson began a long residence in New York (from 1899) and associated with an assortment of friends, notably the writer Hermann Hagedorn, the poet-dramatist Percy Mackaye, William Vaughn Moody,* Edmund Clarence Stedman,* and author-editor Ridgely Torrence. Admirers in Gardiner secretly subsidized Robinson's next book of verse, *Captain Craig* (1902), which Trumbull Stickney* reviewed with unique early appreciation (1903). Robinson worked as an IRT subway construction timekeeper in New York (1903–1904), suffered in severe poverty, and had an alcohol problem. Then came his first real break. Theodore Roosevelt* admired *The Children of the Night*, praised it in print, and wangled Robinson a sinecure in New York's federal Custom House. The moderate pay and ample free time enabled him to put together *The Town Down the River* (1910); the town, called Tilbury, was based on Gardiner. Robinson never knew opulence (or marriage); but friends, grants, better sales, and even prizes spelled not only an end to want but also the steady production of short works (including ''The Man against the Sky'' [1916], a popular work that was a turning point in his career), long Arthurian romances in distinguished blank verse (for example, the best-selling *Tristram* [1927]), and several narrative poems of psychological subtlety. Robinson, a careful, traditional craftsman with a unique timbre, dramatizes characters who win over frustration and failure to achieve spiritual triumph through muted stoicism, and he employs restrained humor and an irony bordering on pity.

Rockefeller, John D. (1839–1937). (Full name: John Davison Rockefeller.) Industrialist and philanthropist. His father was a sharp, itinerant, quack-medicine salesman. Young Rockefeller was born in Richford, New York, but moved with his family to Cleveland, Ohio (1853). After high school, where he studied bookkeeping, Rockefeller attended a business college, became a sharp-eyed, outwardly calm bookkeeper, and determined early in life to be a rich man. He encouraged his employer to refine kerosene commercially (1862), then with partners formed one oil company after another (1862, 1866, 1867), bought Cleveland refineries and Pennsylvania oil fields, and established the Standard Oil Company of Ohio (1870, with $1,000,000 in capital; by 1873, $3,500,000). This evolved into the Standard Oil Trust (1882), which, however, after it had dazzled the world by trust- and holding-company manipulating, was dissolved by order of the U.S. Supreme Court in 1892 (*see* Sherman Anti-Trust Act). In the 1890s, Rockefeller's company owned 70 percent of the oil business in the United States. It was the first great American business trust.

Rockefeller married Laura Celestia Spelman, a merchant's daughter from

Akron, Ohio, in 1864. The couple had five children, including John Davison Rockefeller, Jr. (1874–1960), who graduated from Brown in 1897. By 1895 John D. Rockefeller, Sr., had begun sharing decision-making with his son, while he himself expanded into iron-ore mining and banking ventures. The family oil operations were divided into eighteen companies, as Standard Oil of New Jersey (1899); but the Supreme Court defined the result as a monopoly in restraint of trade and required it to be broken up again (1911). The elder Rockefeller wrote *Random Reminiscences of Men and Events* (1909), retired in 1911, turned to philanthropic activities, and eventually dispersed about half of his personal fortune, estimated in 1899 at more than $500,000,000 and at the time of his death at $1,000,000,000. Ida M. Tarbell* wrote *The History of the Standard Oil Company* (2 vols., 1904), a sensational muckraking exposé of Rockefeller and his corporate maneuvers.

John D. Rockefeller is most fondly remembered now for providing funds to establish the University of Chicago (1891), the Rockefeller Institute for Medical Research in New York City (1901, now Rockefeller University), the General Education Board (1902), and the Rockefeller Foundation (1913), and for donating large sums to many schools and churches. John D. Rockefeller, Jr., was later responsible for building Rockefeller Center and the Riverside Church, both in New York City, and for restoring Colonial Williamsburg in Virginia. His five sons all had distinguished careers. John D. Rockefeller III (1906–1978) was in business and philanthropy; Nelson Rockefeller, in politics; Laurence Rockefeller, in business and conservation; Winthrop Rockefeller, in business and politics; and David, in banking. John Davison "Jay" Rockefeller IV (born in 1937), the son of John D. Rockefeller III, is now in politics.

Rockhill, William Woodville (1854–1914). Orientalist and diplomat. Born in Philadelphia, he received an unusual education in France, in philology, languages, and military science, culminating in his graduation from L'École Speciale Militaire of St. Cyr (1873). He then served in the French Foreign Legion in and out of Oran, Algeria. Rockhill lived in the United States (1876–1881), returned to France to continue his study of oriental languages, and then filled diplomatic posts for the U.S. State Department in China and Korea (1884–1888). Under the auspices of the Smithsonian Institution, he explored in China, Mongolia, and Tibet (1882–1892), with some time back in America. At times he was in considerable danger, which was mitigated by his dressing in native garb and speaking oriental languages fluently. Rockhill returned to Washington, D.C., to work for the State Department in ever-more significant posts (1894–1897). During this time, he was also an official representative at the World's Columbian Exposition* (Chicago, 1893) and at an international geographical conference (London, 1895). Next, Rockhill was appointed U.S. minister to Greece, Romania, and Serbia (1897–1899). He then served as director of the International Bureau of American Republics (1900–1905).

Rockhill offered advice to John Hay,* then secretary of state, regarding his

Open Door Policy,* and was also sent by President William McKinley* as plenipotentiary to China (1900–1901) to report on the Boxer Rebellion, represent American interests, and advise the U.S. minister in China. When the minister went on leave, Rockhill was in charge of negotiations and stayed until the Peking Protocol was signed (7 September 1901). It meted out punishment, honored the Chinese killed while opposing rioters, guaranteed future protection of U.S. citizens, respected the "Open Door," and ordered payment by China to the United States of $25,000,000 in indemnities (two-thirds of which was later returned to China). After this, Rockhill served as minister to China (1905–1909), ambassador to Russia (1909–1911), and ambassador to Turkey (1911–1913). Rockhill died in Honolulu, on his way to China on official business. His books written during the 1890s are *Land of the Lamas* (1891) and *Diary of a Journey to Mongolia and Thibet* [sic] (1903). Rockhill married Caroline Tyson in 1876 (the couple had two children; she died in 1898) and Edith H. Perkins in 1900.

Rogers, Henry Huttleston (1840–1909). Financier. Born in Mattapoisett, Massachusetts, he grew up in neighboring Fairhaven, finished high school at age fourteen there, clerked in a grocery store, sold newspapers, and worked on a local railroad. He took $600 in savings and went with a Fairhaven friend to the Pennsylvania oil fields, where the two opened a refining plant at McClintockville, near Oil City (1862). Rogers joined a large oil company in the Allegheny valley (1866), patented his method of separating naphtha from crude oil (1870), and fought against John D. Rockefeller* and his attempts at mergers (1872). But then he and his associates joined Rockefeller's Standard Oil Trust (1874), and Rogers became a vice president (1890) and chairman of the executive committee (1895) of what had become known as the Standard Oil Company. By slick maneuvers, he also helped incorporate the Consolidated Gas Company of New York (1884) and the Brooklyn Union Gas Company (1895); incorporated the Federal Steel Company (1898); and organized the Amalgamated Copper Company (1898, capitalized at $75,000,000), was its president (1899–1909), and helped make it the largest copper company in the world (by 1906). With railroad and insurance company interests as well, he emerged as a combination of magnetic friend, energetic and relentless business leader, and mocker of governmental investigations; he became known as "Hell Hound" Rogers.

In New York, Rogers had a Broadway office, in which Ida M. Tarbell* interviewed him and which vastly impressed Mark Twain,* who met him in 1893. Rogers and Twain instantly delighted each other, and Rogers at once became his financial adviser, helped him avoid bankruptcy (1894–1897), acted as his literary agent, and was allowed to use his own informed judgment in playing the stock market with Twain's money—for example, he once made a profit of 30 percent in two months in 1898 on a $17,500 investment. In his turn, Twain was loyal. He refused to let the publishing company of Charles L. Webster (his niece's husband) print a book critical of Standard Oil (1894); he dedicated *Following the Equator: A Journey Around the World** to Rogers (1897); and he once wrote to his wife that Rogers was his best friend and the only man he "would give a *damn* for" (15 February 1894). Rogers generously endowed numerous buildings in his hometown of Fairhaven and was lavish in his gifts to Helen Keller, Booker T. Washington,* and others. Still, more objective observers of Rogers had reason to be critical. The methods he used to incorporate the Federal Steel Company were ruthless, and his organization of Amalgamated Copper savaged competitors, including Marcus Daly* and F. Augustus Heinze,* and involved watered stock. Rogers is quoted as saying that he was not in business for his health but was out for the dollars. He was a legitimate target of the muckrakers in the early twentieth century. In addition, he was exposed in a Missouri court suit by revelations that Standard Oil had secretly invested in subsidiary companies (1905). John Pierpont Morgan,* his longtime rival, hurtfully denied him needed credit at one point (1907). Rogers damaged himself financially by underwriting construction of the 443-mile Virginia Railroad for $50,000,000. Rogers married his Fairhaven sweetheart, Abbie Palmer Gifford in 1862 (the couple had three children; his wife died in 1894) and widowed Emile Augusta Randel Hart in 1896. At the time of his death, Rogers' $100,000,00 personal fortune had dwindled to a mere $50,000,000.

Roosevelt, Theodore (1858–1919). Twenty-sixth president of the United States, author, outdoorsman, and conservationist. Roosevelt was born in New York City. He graduated from Harvard (1880), where he was a close friend of Owen Wister,* studied law at Columbia University (1880–1881), was a New York state assemblyman (1882–1884), and then ranched and hunted in the Dakota Badlands (1884–1886). He returned to New York City and ran unsuccessfully for mayor in 1886; the machinations of Richard F. Croker* defeated him, as well as Henry George.* He became a member of the U.S. Civil Service Commission (1889–1897), and the assistant secretary of the navy (1897–1898). The Spanish-American War* thrust Roosevelt into greatness. He resigned his position in federal government, helped organize a volunteer cavalry regiment, and served as the Rough Riders' lieutenant colonel, later colonel, in Cuba (1898). His immediate superior was Colonel Leonard Wood.* When he returned to the United States after the war, Roosevelt enjoyed spectacular political successes: He was governor of New York (1899–1900), vice president of the United States (1901, running over the objections of Mark Hanna*) during the presidency of William McKinley,* and—upon that man's assassination—president of the United States (1901–1905; elected in 1904 and serving to 1909).

As president, Roosevelt is remembered for many achievements both domestic and international. On the domestic front, he advocated government reform; reciprocity treaties; trust-busting, to the consternation of Edward Henry Harriman,* James J. Hill, John Pierpont Morgan,* and others; business regulations; and outlawing freight rebates. He also established the Department of Commerce and Labor, regulated railroads, supported conservation and reclamation measures, and instituted the required inspection of foods and drugs. On the international front, he authorized his secretary of state John Hay* to formulate the Open Door Policy,* recognized Panamanian independence from Colombia, started the Panama Canal, and helped end the Russo-Japanese War. Roosevelt felt that such writers as Ray S. Baker, Thomas Lawson, David Graham Phillips,* Charles Russell, Upton Sinclair, Lincoln Steffens,* and Ida M. Tarbell* had laudable aims but sometimes were too sensational. In derogation of them, he quoted, in a memorable speech given on 17 March 1906, from John Bunyan's *Pilgrim's Progress* about "the man with the muckrake . . . who could look no way but downward"; thus was the term "Muckrakers" coined.

Roosevelt hunted and collected specimens of fauna in Africa and also explored in South America, sought the presidency as a Progressive (Bull Moose) candidate without success, and was disappointed when he was not allowed to secure a military command in World War I. Roosevelt married Alice Hathaway Lee in 1880 (they had one child; his wife died in 1884) and Edith Kermit Carow in 1886 (they had five children). Books by Roosevelt, an inveterate author, include biographies of Gouvernour Morris (1888) and Oliver Cromwell (1900); *Ranch Life and the Hunting Trail* (1888, illustrated by his friend Frederic Remington*), about the Dakota Territory cattle industry, frontier types, Indians, sheriffs, and prairie and mountain hunting for meat and trophies; *Essays on Practical Politics* (1888); *The Winning of the West: An Account of the Exploration and Settlement of Our Country from the Alleghanies to the Pacific** (4 vols., 1889–1896); *New York* (1891), a part of the *Historic Towns* series; *The Wilderness Hunter* (1893), about hunting in the Dakotas; *The Rough Riders** (1899), concerning the Spanish-American War; and *The Strenuous Life: Essays and Addresses by Theodore Roosevelt** (1900). Roosevelt also wrote other books earlier and later.

A voracious and eclectic reader, Roosevelt had strong opinions on numerous fellow American writers of the 1890s. He knew several of them personally. In varying degrees, he was sociable with and knew the accomplishments of Henry Adams,* Edward Bok,* John Burroughs,* Bliss Carman,* Stephen Crane,* Richard Harding Davis,* Finley Peter Dunne,* Mary E. Wilkins Freeman,* Hamlin Garland,* Richard Watson Gilder,* King Camp Gillette,* Robert Grant,* Joel Chandler Harris,* Hay, Oliver Wendell Holmes,* William Dean Howells,* Henry James,* Hamilton W. Mabie,* Alfred Thayer Mahan,* William Vaughn Moody,* Frank Norris,* Gifford Pinchot,* Remington, Jacob Riis,* Edwin Arlington Robinson,* Ernest Thompson Seton,* Frank R. Stockton,* Frederick Jackson Turner,* Mark Twain,* Edith Wharton,* and Wister; and he was predisposed in favor of most of them. He deplored the bitterness of Ambrose Bierce* but admired his stories about Civil War combat. He encouraged Carman and Robinson. His early dislike of Davis changed to admiration after the two met in Cuba. He delighted in the writings of Dunne and Freeman. He modified his early distrust of the works of Garland. He bestowed high praise on Grant's *Unleavened Bread.** He revered Harris both as a writer and as a moral influence. Hay was Roosevelt's close friend as well as a valued member of his cabinet. Roosevelt loathed the publications of William Randolph Hearst* and Joseph

Pulitzer.* Roosevelt appointed Holmes as associate justice of the U.S. Supreme Court in 1902 and later regretted having done so. Roosevelt thought Howells's realism was too grim. He regarded James as a miserable snob, although they socialized in the White House and elsewhere. Roosevelt was professionally influenced by the thoughts and writings of Mahan, Pinchot, and Turner. Roosevelt disliked *The Octopus: A Story of California** by Norris, and he admired *How the Other Half Lives: Studies among the Tenements of New York** by Riis. Roosevelt offered Riis the Virgin Islands governship, but the offer was not accepted. Roosevelt was an early admirer of Stockton's writing and enjoyed the books by Twain* featuring Tom Sawyer and Huckleberry Finn, valued *Pudd'nhead Wilson, A Tale** highly, did not appreciate the satire of *A Connecticut Yankee in King Arthur's Court*,* and fortunately did not live to see many of Twain's anti-Roosevelt blasts in print. (Nor did Twain, in some cases.)

Holmes may well have described Roosevelt best. In a letter to Sir Frederick Pollock (9 February 1921) concerning the recently deceased ex-president, Holmes wrote: "He was very likable, a big figure, a rather ordinary intellect, with extraordinary gifts, a shrewd and I think pretty unscrupulous politician. He played all his cards—if not more."

Rose of Dutcher's Coolly (1895). Novel by Hamlin Garland,* revised in 1899. This novel recounts the story of decent Rose Dutcher's sexual, social, and intellectual maturing. Rose, the daughter of fairly well-to-do, widowed John Dutcher, grows up doing unending, monotonous work on the family farm in Wisconsin, near Bluff Siding. She is educated by observation of farm animals to accept the thrilling but dangerous omnipresence of sexuality. As a teenager she is shaken by intimacy with an oafish adolescent named Carl; ecstatically admires the artistry of a lithe circus acrobat named William De Lisle, who performs with a traveling troupe; and escapes oppressive country life by attending the state university. On the train to Madison, she is disgusted by the unwanted attentions of a conductor and then of a brakeman, but is befriended by a peppy woman lawyer, who advises her to prepare for a profession and then marry only if she wants children. Once safely settled in school and rooming with her father's friend Dr. Edward Thatcher and his wife, Rose studies hard and has several near love affairs, but she prefers independence to marriage and motherhood. Interestingly, Dr. Thatcher asks Rose to move to a campus room because he is too much agitated by her great beauty. Slowly maturing into a pure but vibrant young woman, she graduates in the class of 189—, briefly visits her lonely father, who hopes vainly that she will live with him indefinitely, and soon leaves with a gift of $300 from him to go to Chicago to try for a career in writing.

At first this energetic city intimidates Rose, but she is aided by other young tenants in her rooming and boarding house. One such person, a law student from Colorado, knows Joaquin Miller* and John Muir.* Through Dr. Thatcher, Rose meets an unmarried "alienist" (psychiatrist) named Dr. Isabel Herrick and, through her, she meets several interesting and talkative people—writers, scientists, teachers, and artists—including Warren Mason, an experienced, cynical editor (and would-be novelist). Dr. Herrick's friends include the wealthy Harveys, who invite Rose to the symphony. She looks stunning but—more important—is inexpressibly inspired by Wagner's music. Mason talks to her about it and then about her writing. He sees promise in it and encourages her. She meets and soon likes the Harveys' son Elbert, but she and Mason, who is forceful and sad, develop a closer relationship. As love between them matures, so does Rose—personally, socially, and intellectually. She thinks long and hard about the pernicious double standard that denies women their full potential and about art in America, and she wonders whether marriage jeopardizes women's freedom. A fierce Lake Michigan storm, during which ships are crushed and men drown, is observed by Rose, Mason, and Elbert, and it acts as a catalyst for them. Elbert takes the chilled girl home to his mother, and hints about their marriage are soon in the air. But Mason has been humanized by watching rescue work during the storm, and he writes to Rose that being his wife would not foreclose her personal ambitions. She accepts his proposal.

Rose of Dutcher's Coolly may be a kind of fictional picture of what Garland thought his sister might have become if she had not died but had instead been able to obtain a higher education and pursue a career of her choice. The novel, neatly constructed with a gallery of minor characters (some rather static), crisp dialogue, and graphic descriptions, valuably dramatizes problems of concern for sensitive women to this day. When it first appeared, it was criticized for its daring frankness. But like much pioneering fiction of the 1890s, it is now regarded as tame compared to more modern novels, stories, plays, and movies. All the same, it still expresses profound feelings and retains considerable power. Ironically, Garland himself, living into the 1920s and well beyond, branded as licentious much of the fiction his trailblazing helped make possible.

The Rough Riders (1899). War memoirs by Theodore Roosevelt.* This stirring account of Roosevelt's service with the First Volunteer Cavalry Regiment during the Spanish-American War* is composed of six chapters and four appendices. In the first chapter, Roosevelt tells how the regiment was assembled, mainly of two types of men he regarded as heroic: aristocratic, Ivy League students, athletes, and sportsmen (mainly from Harvard and Yale); and rugged Western ranchers, cowboys, hunters, and miners (mainly from New Mexico, Arizona, Oklahoma, and Indian Territory). They trained, broke horses, and procured mule teams, in San Antonio, Texas. In the second chapter, he explains how they moved to Tampa, Florida, where they assembled men, equipment, and livestock, and from where they sailed to Cuba and landed at Daiquiri. (At this point, Roosevelt notes Richard Harding Davis* and Frederic Remington* among hordes of civilians in official and unofficial capacities, and he especially praises Captain William O. "Bucky" O'Neill, his Arizona ideal.) Roosevelt devotes his third chapter to General S.B.M. Young, his old friend from Yellowstone National Park days, and he describes how Young's regular cavalry units fought at Las

Guasimas, with Roosevelt's Rough Riders taking part. Roosevelt stresses weather, terrain, tactics, gallantry, and casualties. The fourth chapter is devoted to the cavalry at Santiago; highlights include the deaths of O'Neill and others, wounds, and the bravery of the Rough Riders in the attack on the San Juan hills. Here is Roosevelt when his troops misunderstood some sudden gunfire: "Listening, I made out that it came from the flat ground to the left, and jumped to my feet, smiting my hand on my thigh, and shouting aloud with exultation, 'It's the Gatlings, men, our Gatlings!' " The fifth chapter, called "In the Trenches," is devoted to "work" on the firing line, food, weaponry, enemy sharpshooters and guerrillas, prisoners, African-American troops, tending to the wounded, truce time, guarding the Caney road, official foreign visitors, and the surrender at Santiago. The sixth chapter tells about policing the camp, yellow fever and other sickness, shipping home to Montauk, disbanding the regiment, and Roosevelt's high opinion of his men. Appendices include detailed muster-out rolls, official letters, reports, and corrections of inaccuracies.

The Rough Riders is a unique book. It recounts events during an important moment in American history from the point of view of a brave participant and a skillful writer. It touches valuably on political aspects of a curious war. And it helped to make the author president. Roosevelt revered the historian Francis Parkman and the battle-hardened memoirist Ulysses S. Grant, and he emulates their narrative style here. All the same, there is much truth in the suggestion by Finley Peter Dunne* that *The Rough Riders* might well have been entitled *Alone in Cubia*.

Royce, Josiah (1855–1916). Philosopher and educator. Royce was born in Grass Valley, a Nevada mining town, to British-born parents who had met in Rochester, New York, and had gone west in 1849 with others seeking California gold. Young Royce attended school in San Francisco (from 1866); graduated from the University of California, Berkeley (1875; his thesis was on the theology in Aeschylus's *Prometheus Bound*); studied in Germany (1875–1876); received his Ph.D. at Johns Hopkins (1878; his thesis was on the possibility of error—if we admit human error, we imply absolute truth); and lectured on logic and literature at Berkeley (1878–1882). He married Katharine Head, a California judge's daughter, in 1880 (the couple had three children). William James,* who had long recognized Royce's ability as a philosopher, offered encouragement and saw to it that the younger man became his temporary replacement at Harvard while he was on leave (1882–1883). Early in his career, Royce wrote a book on California (1886) and in addition a novel entitled *The Feud of Oakfield Creek* (1887), which he always thought more of than the public ever did. (He was always conscious of his Western origin when amid Eastern intellectuals.) After a bitter professional controversy with rival philosophers (1890–1891), Royce became a professor of philosophy at Harvard (1892–1916). During his long tenure there, he enjoyed leave time to lecture at the University of Aberdeen (1899, 1900) and elsewhere.

Beginning in the mid-1880s, Royce argued in favor of monistic idealism, reasoning that there is an Absolute (the permanent, unchanging law of Truth) around and toward which finite and in part necessarily erroneous philosophies posit their points. His publications in the 1890s are as follows: *The Spirit of Modern Philosophy* (1892), arguing that belief in absolute truth is preferable to positivism and social Darwinism; *The Conception of God* (1895, included in rev. ed., with other authors [1897] as *The Conception of God: A Philosophical Discussion concerning the Nature of the Divine Idea as a Demonstrable Reality*), reasoning that experience should teach us that the Absolute is real and that internal meanings (wills, intentions, etc.) require confirmation by external meanings (ideas, ideals, etc.); *Studies of Good and Evil: A Series of Essays upon Life and Philosophy* (1898), on suffering, pessimism, idealism, natural law, self-consciousness, mysticism, and an 1850 California squatters' riot; and *The World and the Individual* (2 vols., 1899, 1901), theorizing that individuals are to a series of numbers as perfect order is to infinity (the Absolute) beyond those persons and numbers, and discussing the relationship of idea and being.

Royce ultimately found comfort in calling himself an absolutistic pragmatist. Both James, who was pragmatic and pluralistic, and George Santayana,* who was torn between naturalism and idealism and whose dissertation Royce directed, disagreed professionally but amiably with such a position. Royce continued vigorously writing until shortly before his death. For years he feared the advent of World War I; worrying over it when it came was partly the cause of his death.

Russell, Charles Marion (1864–1926). Painter, sculptor, illustrator, and author. Born in Saint Louis, Missouri, he was the son of a wealthy businessman. As a lad, Russell so preferred sculpting in clay, sketching, and playing hooky that his parents sent him to a New Jersey military academy (1879–1880). But they soon relented and let him go to Montana, where he had long wished to go. Once there, he worked on a sheep ranch, did chores for a professional hunter, and became a cowboy (1880–1887). He inveterately sketched Western scenes and activities. One tiny painting, called "Waiting for a Chinook [thawing wind]" (1887), depicting an ice- and coyote-doomed steer in winter, was made into hundreds of thousands of postcards, which were sent around the world as a Montana weather report. The picture made Russell famous. He lived in Alberta, Canada, with Blood Indians, and almost went native there permanently (1888). He published illustrations in *Harper's Weekly* (1888) and *Leslie's Magazine* (1889) and then a small portfolio called *Studies in Western Life* (1890). He continued to drift through Montana as a part-time cowboy and itinerant artist, well paid for his paintings but indifferent to money. Lewistown, Great Falls, and Cascade, all in Montana, are now associated with his early-1890s artwork.

Russell visited Saint Louis, accepted a commission from a rich manufacturer for several paintings, and thereafter devoted himself to art (1893). In 1895 he met Nancy Cooper, age seventeen, in Cascade, married her in 1896, and found his free-and-easy ways at an end. His wife kept him out of saloons and at his easel and modeling table; she encouraged him to sell his paintings for more than his customary $25 each (she had raised the figure to $15,000 by 1926); and she supervised his signing of contracts for illustrations in Eastern publications (including Emerson Hough's *The Story of a Cowboy* [1897] and works by Theodore Roosevelt,* Owen Wister,* and others later). She persuaded him to move to Great Falls, where he built a log-cabin studio behind their house. Russell planned his first bronze, a medallion of an Indian's face, and published his second portfolio, entitled *Pen Sketches* (1899). Most of his finest pictures were done in the 1890s and on into the early twentieth century. He worked in oil (on canvas, board, academy board, cardboard, and masonite panel), in watercolors (often combined with gouache, opaque white, and graphite), and with pen and ink (and sometimes graphite).

A selective list of titles indicates Russell's range of pictorial subjects: *Lost in a Snow Storm—We Are Friends* (1888), *Canadian Mounted Police Bringing in Red Indian Prisoners* (c. 1888), *Indians on Bluffs Surveying General Miles' Troops* (c. 1889), *Cowboy Sport—Roping a Wolf* (1890), *Line Rider* (1890), *Crow Indians Hunting Elk* (c. 1890), *Attack on the Mule Train* (1894), *Indian Fight* (1895), *Keeoma* (1896, a reclining Indian maiden), *Bronc in Cowboy Camp* (1897), *The Snow Trail* (1897), *The Picture Robe* (1899), and *Indian Scouting Party* (1900). Two of Russell's most superb works are *Indian Women Moving* (1898), which depicts three Plains Indians—one a hag, another hooded, and the third a mother with cradleboarded baby—being led by a wolfish dog; and *Buffalo Hunt No. 26* (1899), which shows a herd harassed by an Indian lancer on a vividly painted horse, two mounted comrades trailing, hunting activity in the distance, and a rattlesnake in a bush in the foreground. At his best, Russell captures dramatic moments in his Old West, with suspense high and the outcome uncertain. His clever lines and magnificent colors tease and move the spectator's eye about and back to the central subject. Foreground action is usually well delineated, the background rather washed in, and hazy hills and the horizon faint. Russell's bronzes are dated 1903 and after; his collections of short fiction and essays, in the 1920s.

Mention should be made of Russell's endearing habit of illustrating, with pen and ink and often in colors, his personal letters to friends. Many are now priceless collectors' items. Charles Marion Russell and Frederic Remington* are indisputably the two finest painters of the Old West.

Ryder, Albert Pinkham (1847–1919). Painter. He was born in New Bedford, Massachusetts, then the world's major whaling port. His father was a customhouse officer and a dealer in fuel; two of his brothers were sailors. Early in life Ryder painted local scenes with help from an amateur artist nearby. He went to New York City (about 1867 or a little later), was rejected when he first applied to the National Academy of Design, was informally instructed by a painter of romantic religious scenes, and finally was admitted to the Academy of Design (1871–1872). Ryder visited European galleries a few times (1877, 1882, 1887,

1896) but was never much influenced by what he saw there. His early rural landscapes with livestock were generally naive, crudely mystical, and unpraised; so he and a few other young rebels established the Society of American Artists (1877) and exhibited regularly there (to 1887). About 1880, Ryder began a series of loosely depicted biblical and mythological scenes, as well as scenes inspired by his love of works by Lord Byron, Geoffrey Chaucer, William Shakespeare, Edgar Allan Poe, and Alfred, Lord Tennyson; English ballads; and operas by Richard Wagner. For decades Ryder lived in a couple of slovenly rooms, painted with worm-like slowness, and was indifferent to his unsold canvases—lovingly kept and touched up over the years—piles of debris, dirty dishes and clothes, and personal hygiene. When he fell sick (1915), his friends moved him out to Long Island.

A typical Ryder painting is blocked out in masses with slowly rhythmic motions and with elongated, squashed, turbulent, and usually balanced elements, predominantly in ugly browns and dirty yellows. His works often verge on the abstract. His tones are usually bleak but sometimes almost warm. He regularly depicts sea waves and glum clouds, with an eerie sun or moon as the source of uncertain light. He made such wretchedly careless use of his materials (sometimes he used candle grease and wax instead of professional pigments) that many of his works are now almost hopelessly blotched, wrinkled, and cracked. (This deterioration has tempted more forgers to copy his work than that of any other painter of his epoch.) He left about 165 paintings. Among the best are *Marine* (c. 1890), revealing angular brown sails above a quiet black-brown sea in what appears to be moonlight; *Jonah* (c. 1890 or earlier), showing a boiling chocolate and lemon milkshake sea with Jonah out of a twisted boat, a half-yawning, glaring whale approaching him, and God à la William Blake squinting out of a splintered yellow-brown sky holding the sun in His right hand; *Siegfried and the Rhine Maidens* (c. 1890), presenting two young women writhing in yellow-green water and a mounted knight half hidden in attenuated trees with twisted branches under swirling gray-brown clouds, all lit by a sun or a moon above; and *Constance* (c. 1896), depicting Chaucer's queen moorless at sea but divinely guided toward safety. Ryder's famous painting *The Race Track (Death on a Pale Horse)* (c. 1910) he began (about 1895) to commemorate a waiter who bet all of his savings on a horse that lost, after which the waiter committed suicide. Ryder's works have been compared to those of Ralph Albert Blakelock,* but they are better composed if less easily understood.

S

Saint-Gaudens, Augustus (1848–1907). Sculptor. He was born in Dublin, Ireland. His father was a shoemaker from France; his mother was Irish. At age six months, Saint-Gaudens accompanied his family, to escape the Irish potato famine, to the United States—first to Roxbury, Massachusetts, then to New York City. Determined from childhood to become an artist, he was apprenticed at age thirteen to French cameo cutters, took drawing lessons at Cooper Union and the National Academy of Design, and studied in Paris (1867–1870) and then in Rome (1870–1872), where he obtained commissions from a few wealthy Americans traveling abroad. Saint-Gaudens established a studio in New York City (beginning in 1872); returned with more work to Rome (1874–1875), where he admired Donatello's portrait statuary; and began to favor energetic naturalistic modeling to the smooth, effete neoclassical style. Home again, Saint-Gaudens became very busy, often in association with H. H. Richardson, Stanford White,* and John La Farge* (ultimately his closest friend). In 1877 Saint-Gaudens, La Farge, and fellow artist Louis Comfort Tiffany* organized the Society of American Artists in reaction to the conservative National Academy of Design in New York. Saint-Gaudens met Augusta F. Homer in Rome, married her in Roxbury in 1877 (the couple had one son), and went with her to Paris and then Rome to work on medallions, portraits, and other sculpture (1877–1878). His masterful bronze *Admiral David Farragut* (1881, New York) uses selective naturalistic detail to reveal the subject's tough personality. Its marble base was designed by White, who also did other later pedestals for Saint-Gaudens.

Magnificent success followed. Saint-Gaudens, back in his New York studio, helped revitalize American sculpture, then in decline because of its insipid neoclassical imitativeness. He opened a second studio on an old farm in Cornish, New Hampshire (1885–1907), which he named Aspet, after his father's hometown in France. Saint-Gaudens's bronze *Abraham Lincoln* (1887, in Chicago) presents the heroic, tall, harrowed president rising to deliver the Gettysburg

Address. His bronze *Puritan* (1887, Springfield, Massachusetts) captures the essentials: a massive, grim-featured figure with a Bible in his left hand, a cudgel in his right. Saint-Gaudens's *General John A. Logan* (Chicago, 1887) is a skillful equestrian. Henry Adams,* a close friend, commissioned Saint-Gaudens to execute a seated bronze figure for the grave of his wife (1891, Rock Creek Cemetery, Washington, D.C.). Untitled, it was called *The Mystery of the Hereafter* by the sculptor and *The Peace of God* by the distraught Adams; it is now often known as *Grief*. It is of a draped, hooded figure sitting on granite, serene, reposeful but enigmatic, poignantly abstract. White designed its architectural setting. It caused some dismay when it was first set in place, because it seemed unchristian to many. This statue is one of the abiding masterpieces of nineteenth-century American sculpture. Saint-Gaudens created only one nude: a copper *Diana* (New York, 1892). His high-relief bronze the *Colonel Robert Gould Shaw Memorial* (Boston, 1897) presents the Union army officer on horseback accompanying his brave African-American troops, with a flying female allegorical figure encouraging them from above, and holding laurel for victory but also poppies for death. The sculptor worked for years on a low-relief, bronze, seated *Robert Louis Stevenson* (Edinburgh, 1887–1902), whom the sculptor knew well. His bronze group *General William Tecumseh Sherman* (New York, completed 1903 after much work) depicts the hero on horseback riding through Georgia preceded by a slim, winged maiden representing victory. Saint-Gaudens did some of the work on this statue in Paris (1897–1900), where he associated with Trumbull Stickney* and also Adams.

In addition to major statues and groups, Saint-Gaudens designed many items ordered by Congress, bronze and marble low-relief plaques, church and mansion decorations, and low-relief portraits of friends (including John Hay,* William Dean Howells* and his daughter, and Henry James*). Saint-Gaudens won the Grand Prix at the Paris Salon (1900). In response to a presidential order from Theodore Roosevelt* (1905), Saint-Gaudens designed new gold $10 and $20 gold pieces (1907). (*See* Coins.) He was remembered by his innumerable friends, including Daniel Chester French,* Hay, Howells, James, La Farge, John Singer Sargent,* Stevenson, Roosevelt, and White, as considerate, hardworking, and touched by genius. His Cornish estate, partly ruined by a fire (1904), contains much of his work. His autobiography is *The Reminiscences of Augustus Saint-Gaudens* (2 vols. 1913), which was amplified by his son Homer Saint-Gaudens.

Saltus, Edgar (1855–1921). (Full name: Edgar Everston Saltus.) Prolific, decadent author. Born in New York City, he was enrolled at St. Paul's School, Concord, New Hampshire (1871–1872), studied intermittently at Yale (1872, 1873), accompanied his indulgent mother abroad (1873) and stayed to study (in Paris, Heidelberg, and Munich to 1878), and then studied successfully for a law degree at Columbia University (1878–1880). He published a biography of Honoré de Balzac (1884), translations of several French short stories, and a pair of gloomy books: *The Philosophy of Disenchantment* (1885), deriving from Arthur

Schopenhauer and Eduard von Hartmann; and *The Anatomy of Negation* (1886), tracing antitheism through the ages. Saltus then wrote a series of esoteric and deliberately shocking novels—ultimately sixteen in number (1887–1922)—notable for epigrammatism and preciosity, and for espousing hedonism, exoticism, eroticism, and rebellion against American society's materialism, provinciality, and hypocritical morality. Intertwined with these books were two volumes of short stories, enough poems to make up a posthumous collection, and eleven historical and biographical works. Saltus married Helen Sturgis Read in New York City in 1883 (they were divorced in 1891); Elsie Welsh Smith in London in 1894 (the couple had one child and then separated in 1901; the second Mrs. Saltus died in 1909); and Marie Giles in Montreal in 1911. After Saltus died, Marie Saltus wrote an overly appreciative, incomplete biography of him (1925).

Saltus's many works in the 1890s include *Love and Lore* (1890), *Mary Magdalen, A Chronicle* (1891), *Imperial Purple* (1892), *Madam Sapphira: A Fifth Avenue Story* (1893), *Enthralled: A Story of International Life Setting Forth the Curious Circumstances concerning Lord Cloden and Oswald Quain* (1894), and *When Dreams Come True: A Story of Emotional Life* (1895). *Love and Lore* contains essays ridiculing modern etiquette in courtship and society when compared to behavior in medieval courts of love, and it includes comments on fiction, which is best, in Saltus's view, when it stylishly presents thrilling sensuality and criminal conduct. *Mary Magdalen* is a combination of vague doctrinal commentary, a redaction of the biblical account of Jesus Christ and Mary Magdalen, and fiction, in which Judas falls in love with and attempts to blackmail Mary before his betrayal of Christ. *Imperial Purple* is a series of flashy essays describing the horrible (and therefore to Saltus sublime) behavior of Roman emperors from Julius Caesar forward; all is supported by historical research hidden under hypnotic, shudder-producing descriptions of pomp and crime. It ends with the advent of Christianity. *Imperial Purple* is regarded as containing Saltus's best writing. (Saltus tried to repeat its success with his 1920 *Imperial Orgy: An Account of the Tsars from the First to the Last*, depicting the bloodthirstiness of the Russian czars.) *Madam Sapphira* is an ungentlemanly novel based on the breakup of Saltus's first marriage and the divorce that ended it. In the fiction, the author is less blameless than he was in real life. The novel *Enthralled*, fin-de-siècle decadence personified, is powered by a grotesque plot involving a money-seeking monomaniac, a patricide, a faked suicide, the surgical transformation of the villain's face and form, and an heiress saved from incest with that villain. *When Dreams Come True*, the main characters of which are ludicrously named, features Tancred Ennever as an autobiographical hero. Of good parentage, well educated, and now a writer, he selfishly loves Edenic Sylvia Marsh, dallies with widowed Madame Bravoura, loses Sylvia to Prince Sappia, and returns to Bravoura. Oddly, Saltus here warns his readers that selfish love can be dangerous.

Saltus may be regarded as an example par excellence of the disenchanted, avant-garde dilettante, dandy, poseur, iconoclast, and erotic, exotic skeptic in fin-de-siècle America. Although his favorite American writer was Henry James,* Saltus himself was an American combination of Joris-Karl Huysmans and Oscar Wilde. Always writing at a furious pace, Saltus hit his peak about 1895 and thereafter was weaker though never quiet. He is presented as a minor figure in *Painted Veils*, the 1920 novel by James Huneker.*

Santayana, George (1863–1952). (Real name: Jorge Agustín Nicolás de Santayana y Borrás.) Philosopher, poet, novelist, and professor. Santayana, who was born in Madrid, Spain, of Spanish parentage, remained a lifelong Spanish citizen. His mother had been married earlier to a Bostonian who died in 1857, leaving her at age thirty with two daughters and a son. Santayana's father was about fifty at the time of his son's birth. Santayana's mother took her first three children to Boston with her in 1868, and his father took George Santayana to Boston four years later (1872) and soon left him there with his mother. Santayana, who grew up in Boston, was educated at the Boston Latin School, Harvard (he graduated in 1886, having spent the summer of 1883 in Spain with his father), the University of Berlin (1886–1888), and Harvard again (Ph.D., 1889 in philosophy under Josiah Royce* and William James*). Santayana taught philosophy brilliantly—but reluctantly, it seems—at Harvard (1889–1912), with frequent released time spent elsewhere, for example, Cambridge, England (1896–1897), where he met Bertrand Russell, and later Italy and the Far East (1904–1905) and Paris (1905–1906). Santayana contributed to the *Harvard Monthly*, which he helped found in 1885, until 1903. Editors, fellow contributors to the magazine, and student friends included George Pierce Baker,* Bernard Berenson,* Bliss Carman,* W.E.B. DuBois,* William Vaughn Moody,* and Trumbull Stickney.* (Santayana and Stickney disliked each other. Santayana evidently had homosexual tendencies.)

When his mother died and left him a legacy (1912), Santayana quit teaching. He felt that he no longer had an American home and retired to a life of interpretive contemplation and genteel expression in France, England, and finally Italy. During his formative years, he was troubled by having a Mediterranean outlook on life in a New England puritan environment. Although his major writing was accomplished in the twentieth century, Santayana published earlier works: *Sonnets and Other Verses* (1894, enlarged ed. 1896), *The Sense of Beauty: Being the Outline of Aesthetic Theory* (1896), *Lucifer: A Theological Tragedy* (1899), *Interpretations of Poetry and Religion* (1900), and *A Hermit of Carmel and Other Poems* (1901). *Sonnets and Other Verses* was published by Stone and Kimball, the firm established by Herbert S. Stone* and Ingalls Kimball. The first edition contains twenty-nine sonnets (some published earlier), other short poems, a verse-play fragment, and a dramatic poem called "Lucifer: A Prelude." The most famous sonnet begins "O world, thou choosest not the better part!" and continues "It is not wisdom to be only wise, / And on the inward vision close the eyes, / But it is wisdom to believe the heart." The 1896 edition added another thirty sonnets, many of which express renunciation of earthly mutability in favor of transcendental essences. To satisfy his department, which was troubled by having a poet in its midst (and, to boot, an unmarried one who associated with and made disciples of young male undergraduates), Santayana lectured on the theory and history of aesthetics (1892–1895) and published the results as *The Sense of Beauty*. After an introduction defining the three main approaches to aesthetics (didactic, historical, and psychological), Santayana discusses the nature of beauty, the materials of beauty, form, and expression. He theorizes that ingredients constituting art are located when one tries to satisfy desire and to improve life by placing it in harmony with human aspirations. Beauty may be best understood and analyzed as human pleasure objectified. It exists in the attributes of material things insofar as they please in a way that enriches and harmonizes aspects of life.

Lucifer: A Theological Tragedy, an expansion of Santayana's "Lucifer: A Prelude," is a long blank-verse closet drama presenting a conjunction of Jesus, Hermes, Lucifer, Mephistopheles, and Zeus. In *Interpretations of Poetry and Religion*, Santayana argues that religion is comparable to poetry. Although neither can rightly be interpreted as an exact, successful presentation of actuality, both should be understood as attempting through the use of the imagination to depict elements of the mysterious, craved ideal. Santayana insists that all we can really know is what we experience. This book annoyed the New England intellectual establishment by criticizing Robert Browning as a poet of barbarism (it did not mind his linking Walt Whitman with Browning), Ralph Waldo Emerson for lacking any system and for being vague and elusive at bottom, and even William Shakespeare for ignoring the religious impulse. William James called the philosophical position of Santayana "a perfection of rottenness" (i.e., not pragmatic), but he delighted in its cool style. The title poem of *A Hermit of Carmel and Other Poems* is a drama, mostly in Keatsian blank verse, cast in medieval times, featuring a hermit and a knight who are brothers separated as children by war. They meet again, but the hermit must do penance for a sinful past by not identifying himself to the uncomprehending knight. In "The Knight's Return," the sequel, the knight (now named Palmerin) goes home to his faithful girlfriend Flerida, pardons a sinful rival Ulric, and patiently waits for sunrise and his wedding hour. Santayana coined the phrase the Genteel Tradition* in *The Genteel Tradition at Bay* (1931). *The Last Puritan* (1935) by Santayana was a best-selling novel. His excellent autobiography is *Persons and Places* (3 vols., 1944, 1945, 1953).

Sargent, John Singer (1856–1925). Painter. He was born in Florence, Italy. His father, a Philadelphia physician, was a reluctant expatriate; his mother, a cultivated, restless, domineering musician. Sargent showed artistic tendencies early, studied art in Florence, sketched in various parts of western Europe, and became a formal art student in Paris (beginning 1874). He first visited the United States in 1876, partly to establish his American citizenship. He studied the works of Diego de Silva Velázquez in Madrid, went to Morocco, and then to Haarlem to view paintings by Franz Hals. Sargent's electrifying *El Jaleo* (1882), a consequence of his time in Spain, magically catches a dancer swirling in front of a long row of seated musical accompanists. *The Daughters of Edward D. Boit* (1882) is an elegantly posed, Velázquez-like study of Sargent's expatriate artist friend's four little girls. Next, Sargent exhibited his most sensational work, the controversial *Madame X* (a portrait of courtesan Madame Pierre Gautreau), in the Paris Salon (1884). The ensuing notoriety encouraged him to go to London, where he established a permanent studio (1885) and soon achieved international acclaim. Thereafter, he visited the United States often (1887, 1890, and almost every year from 1895), in search of subjects for his costly portraits, which he also made of celebrated European subjects—actors and actresses, aristocrats, artists, bankers, diplomats, musicians, princes and princesses, statesmen, writers, and beautiful and homely members of their families. He became an associate member of the Royal Academy (1894), sent five portraits to it in one year (1895), and was soon voted full membership (1897). Portraits by him, though often sought, on occasion displeased their subjects, because Sargent was a profound observer and recorder of character, and was said to highlight unpleasant traits. He was best at catching the delicacy of the innocent young and the cunning and dignity of the old.

The 1890s were Sargent's greatest years. His paint became thicker, his colors clearer and bolder. Sargent captured his subjects in tense balance and made their faces uniquely expressive. Fast and efficient, he was demanding of himself, sometimes curt with sitters, and dazzlingly brilliant. In the early twentieth century, he created even more portraits, averaging more than sixteen annually (1900–1907). Thereafter, he tapered off as a portraitist slightly. He did, however, paint a superb portrait of his close friend Henry James* (1913), which was enormously admired by their mutual friend William Dean Howells,* toward the end of James's life. Sargent also painted portraits of John Hay,* S. Weir Mitchell,* Joseph Pulitzer,* James Whitcomb Riley,* John D. Rockefeller,* presidents Theodore Roosevelt* and Woodrow Wilson, the wives of William James,* Pulitzer, and Whitelaw Reid,* and the young son of Augustus Saint-Gaudens.* (The character Charles Waterlow, the painter in James's novel *The Reverberator** [1888], may be based in part on Sargent.)

Sargent's major works executed between 1888 and 1901 are numerous. The following are perhaps the best:

Isabella Stewart Gardner[*] (1888): The subject is standing full face front, with her famous pearls in two strands around a slim-enough waist, her arms down, and her hands clasped low. In the background, a tapestry pattern oddly suggests a halo. Gardner mistakenly called this work the best of Sargent, who painted her again in her muffled, old-age misery (1922).

Ellen Terry as Lady Macbeth (1889): The famous actress appears in a flowing robe with monstrous sleeves. She holds a crown with both hands above her head; her face is pale, her eyes glazed. Sargent delighted in Terry's London performances.

Mrs. Adrian Iselin (1888), which was painted during Sargent's American visit (1887–1888): The subject is an austere, hard-eyed New York society lady, wearing a dark dress and standing with her right little finger pressed firmly against a table edge.

A Morning Walk (c. 1888): This Impressionistic picture presents a young woman, with a light parasol, against a vague garden background.

Japanese Dancing Girl (1889): This painting is a stylized depiction of a passionless Oriental performer, seen from rear left.

Paul Helleu Sketching, and His Wife (1889): This beautifully harmonized, oddly angled, Impressionistic study features Sargent's young friend and his wife. The straw-hatted, bearded artist is painting beside a reed-hidden boat; his teenage bride is reclining next to him but is looking the other way.

Vernon Lee (1889): This pencil sketch hints at the obviously weird personality of the subject, who was a controversial writer. Her real name was Violet Paget. Sargent's earlier portrait of her (1881) exposes an even more eldritch physiognomy.

La Carmencita (1890): This sensational presentation of the famous Spanish dancer shows her robed in a glittering orange and gold dress with her hands on hips, in a cocky pose. Sargent, who met Carmencita in New York (1890) and helped popularize her, gives her a Goya-like treatment here.

Joseph Jefferson (1890): This hasty oil shows the popular American actor's mobile face and ebullient nature.

Mrs. Edward Davis and Her Son Livingston (1890): The wife and son of a businessman and ex-mayor of Worcester, Massachusetts, are the subjects of this portrait. Mrs. Davis, who seems overdressed, has a pleasant but plain face, and is almost furtively holding the hand of a pasty lad in a sailor suit and huge hat.

Nude Egyptian Girl (1891): This portrait presents a long-limbed young woman with her buttocks toward the viewer, with her left breast in profile and with a small and haughty head; she is casually braiding her long hair. Sargent painted her in glowing orange during a happy time spent in Egypt (1890–1891).

Eleanora Duse (c.1893): This Impressionistic, hasty, unfinished work shows sincerity and tragic stoicism in the famous actress, who gave Sargent one brief sitting.

Lady Agnew (c. 1893): This exquisite portrait of Sir Andrew's delicately gorgeous wife shows her seated on a chair with material of a flowery design, against a dreamy blue background. She has raven hair, a rich dress with a silky mauve sash, and hauntingly beautiful dark eyes.

Coventry Patmore (1894): This work depicts the feisty English poet, with his wavy gray hair, floppy moustache, firm lip and chin, and a glint in his right eye. Sargent was much impressed by his subject's biblical face, and he painted Patmore again one year later.

Ada Rehan (1894): The Irish-born, American actress is depicted standing before some rich tapestry in massive, heavily dressed majesty, holding a fan of white feathers.

Gardiner Greene Hammond (1895): This portrait presents a rich Bostonian stuffed shirt par excellence, with half-closed eyes, pug nose, indifferent moustache, soft mouth, and all. Sargent also obtained a commission for Mary Cassatt* to paint Hammond's children.

Frederick Law Olmsted[*] (1895): The sweet old landscaper is depicted standing with his cane in the Biltmore garden, owned by George Washington Vanderbilt* (whose portrait Sargent also painted in 1895).

Mrs. Carl Meyer and Her Children (1896): The British banker's wife is shown seated, tilting forward and half-smiling. Two of their children stand behind her big settee, on which is an upended book about to flop over. Pearls and gilt edges suggest wealth. Henry Adams* wrote to his deceased wife's niece Mabel Hooper La Farge (2 May 1897) about this picture: "The art of portrait-painting of Jewesses and their children may be varied but cannot be further perfected. Nothing better ever was done, or can be.")

Asher Wertheimer (1898): The distinguished London art dealer is depicted with thinning hair, semi-satanic eyes, a black moustache, a gold watch chain gleaming in front of his dark clothing, and a cigar teetering in his left hand; at the lower left is a black, tongue-lolling dog. (Adams called this painting a crucifixion of its subject.)

Mr. and Mrs. Isaac Stokes (1897): The bearded New York banker, with his arms folded, appears in the shadowy background; his jaunty, grinning wife appears in the foreground. Evidently just off a tennis court, she holds a straw hat. Both figures are elongated à la El Greco, whose works Sargent admired.

Henry Gurdon Marquand (1897): In this portrait, the frosty old philanthropic New York banker, with much inner fire remaining, is seated with his legs apart; his right arm is thrown casually over a chair back, and his left hand props up his head; he refuses to admit his apparent fatigue. He has a grim, firm, no-nonsense mouth.

An Interior in Venice (1899): In this portrait, an old, seated couple (American expatriates Daniel and Ariana Curtis) is shown with a younger, standing pair (their son Ralph and his wife Lisa); the old man peruses a propped-up folio volume, his wife stares at the viewer, and the younger two prepare tea. Chandeliers, framed paintings, and other objets d'art ooze wealth all about.

The Wyndham Sisters (1899): This painting, lavishly praised and sold in the 1920s to the Metropolitan Museum of New York for £20,000, shows two women seated on a puffy couch and another one standing behind; all three wear dresses resembling cumulous clouds, and all three are reputedly beautiful and bright.

The Sitwell Family (1900): Sir George and Lady Ida Sitwell, and their to-be-famous children Edith, Sacheverell, and Osbert, are shown with accessories in the form of expensive furniture (borrowed for the sittings). Sir George grew annoyed with Sargent for posing everyone as he did but paid Sargent £1,500 for the work anyway.

Ena and Betty, Daughters of Mr. and Mrs. Asher Wertheimer (1901): A young woman is depicted on the left in a dark dress with her mouth closed; another young woman is shown on the right in a light dress with her mouth ajar—both have exaggerated expanses of brawny shoulders above low-cut gowns. The two are forcefully posed, and the result was highly popular.

Ethel Smyth (1901): This bold charcoal, right-profile portrait shows the composer-feminist, with her eyes alert and her chin bravely tilted up.

Mrs. William Crowninshield Endicott (1901): This portrait presents a rich, seated dame, with a tight neck band, much lace, and a firm but powdery elegance. She was the wife of the secretary of war, from Salem, Massachusetts, during the first term of President Grover Cleveland.*

By 1910, Sargent had lost much of his zest for portrait work. Sargent had well-invested funds aplenty, and he became ambitious to concentrate on huge murals and to return to Impressionistic watercolor work. He had established a studio in Boston (1903) and resumed work on his ambitious *History of Religion* murals for the Boston Public Library (1890–1916). He remained active his entire life. His graphic *Gassed* (1919, twenty feet long) depicts British military casualties following a World War I German poison gas attack. Of his portraits, Sargent said, "I chronicle: I do not judge." He was indifferent to expressions of criticism and envy from his fellow painters, and he grew dismayed at his influence on younger painters. (Cassatt once foolishly described Sargent as a "buffoon"; James Abbott McNeill Whistler* regarded his paintings as ordinary.) Sargent, who never married, knew almost everyone of consequence in the high-toned international society of his day and was much in demand socially, despite his overgruff, often inarticulate, big-bear manners.

Schumann-Heink, Ernestine (1861–1936). (Full name: Ernestine Roessler Heink Schumann Rapp.) Operatic contralto. She was born Ernestine Roessler at Lieben, near Prague (then in Bohemia). Her professional name came about because she married Ernest Heink (1882) and then Paul Schumann (1893). She first appeared professionally in Graz, Austria (1876), toured with German opera companies, and starred in Hamburg (1888). She debuted in Chicago in Richard Wagner's *Lohengrin* (1898) and sang with the Metropolitan Opera Company (until 1903), made concert and operetta appearances (1903–1905), and then returned to grand opera (1905–1914). She also married William Rapp, Jr. (1905; they were divorced in 1914). Schumann-Heink was pro-American during World War I and remained active as a popular singer to 1935.

Schwab, Charles M. (1862–1939). (Full name: Charles Michael Schwab.) Industrialist. He was born in Williamsburg, Pennsylvania. After attending local schools at Loretta, Pennsylvania, he graduated from St. Francis College there (1878), and then he obtained work at the Edgar Thomson Steel Works (owned by Andrew Carnegie* and his brother) in Pittsburgh (1881), where he became assistant superintendent (1882). He was appointed superintendent at Carnegie's Homestead Steel Works (1887–1889), but he returned to Thomson Steel in 1889 (until 1892). After the bloody Homestead Lockout* occurred in 1892, Carnegie sent Schwab back to the Homestead factory to restore peace, harmony, and efficiency there (1892–1897). Schwab was named president of the Carnegie Steel Company (1897–1901), helped negotiate the sale of Carnegie's steel holdings to John Pierpoint Morgan* (1901), and became president of the resulting United States Steel Company (1901–1904). Schwab then headed the Bethlehem Steel Company, in which he bought a controlling interest. During World War I, this firm filled enormous military contracts. Some of Schwab's later injudicious investments, coupled with generous philanthropic donations and endowments and the Depression (beginning 1929), caused the financial titan to die almost insolvent.

Scovel, Sylvester (1869–1905). (Full name: Henry Sylvester Scovel.) Journalist and engineer. He was born at Denny Station, Allegheny County, Pennsylvania. After schooling in Pittsburgh and a Michigan military academy, Scovel attended the University of Michigan for parts of four years, supporting himself as a timekeeper in construction plants. He then worked in several states as an engineer, then was hired by both the Pittsburgh *Dispatch* and the New York *Herald* (1895) to report unrest in Cuba. He was seized by Spanish authorities in Havana (1896), escaped confinement, became a daring prorevolutionary reporter for the New York *World* (owned by Joseph Pulitzer*), and lived and worked dangerously with Cuban insurgents for several months. Early in 1897 he was imprisoned again and condemned to execution by the Spanish government, but the United States government successfully demanded his release. Scovel was sent by the *World* to cover the Greco-Turkish War, but he was soon recalled and reassigned to Cuba to report pre-war tensions and then to cover the Spanish-American War* as head of the *World* staff in Florida and Cuba (1898–1899). At first, he was attached to the American forces, and he soon caused himself and others many difficulties because of his recklessness, bluntness, and disobedience of army regulations. In July 1898, Scovel got into trouble when he punched General William R. Shafter, whom he had much reason to despise. Scovel became a consulting engineer to the Cuban customs service of the American military government established in Cuba (1899–1902), remained in Havana to undertake commercial ventures, and died there. Scovel married Frances Cabanné in 1897. While in Greece (1897), Scovel met fellow war correspondent Stephen Crane,* and in England on his way home and to Cuba he was entertained by Crane and his so-called wife Cora Taylor. Scovel was Crane's editorial superior in Cuba during the war and associated closely and dangerously with him, and also with correspondent Richard Harding Davis* and photographer James H. Hare.*

Scribner's Magazine. Superb monthly magazine. Founded in 1887 (25¢ a copy), it was excellently edited by Edward L. Burlingame from that date until 1914. From the start, it was designed to compete with *Century*,* to which *Scribner's Monthly* had been sold in 1881. In no time, *Scribner's Magazine* was numbering among its contributors many of the best writers in the United States. It featured excellent serial novels (by George Washington Cable,* Richard Harding Davis,* Harold Frederic,* William Dean Howells,* and a few tip-top English authors), short stories (by H. C. Bunner,* Stephen Crane,* Robert Grant,* Joel Chandler Harris,* Bret Harte, Robert Herrick,* Henry James,* Sarah Orne Jewett,* and Edith Wharton*), a variety of nonfictional prose (concerning autobiography, biography, ecology, fine arts, history, labor, railroads, and travel by Charles Francis Adams, Jr. [the brother of Brooks Adams* and Henry Adams*], Davis, Grant, Henry Cabot Lodge [the father of George Cabot Lodge*], Alfred Thayer

Mahan,* Jacob Riis,* and Walter A. Wyckoff*), poetry (by Richard Hovey* and Edwin Markham,* for example), and good, then great, illustrations (for example, by Howard Pyle;* however, it was not until the twentieth century that the work of Pyle, Frederic Remington,* N. C. Wyeth, and so on and full-color plate techniques made *Scribner's Magazine* preeminent). As for circulation, in 1891 it was 100,000; by 1900, half again more than that figure. *Scribner's Magazine* continued to be one of the finest magazines of its kind, though with vicissitudes, until it began to slide under a left-leaning editor (1930), which slowly led to the demise of the magazine (1939).

Sculpture. After the Civil War, American sculpture gradually began to shake off some of the debilitating effects of effete neoclassicism, which had been practiced too often by expatriate sculptors—trained mostly in Rome. By the 1890s, several magnificent artists were bringing more realism and naturalism to American statues, partly by going back to certain sturdy sculptors of the Renaissance for inspiration, partly by fastening upon American subjects, but mostly by being more independently creative. The leader in the field was indubitably Augustus Saint-Gaudens,* but others almost as skillful include Daniel Chester French,* Lorado Taft,* John Quincy Adams Ward,* and Olin Levi Warner.* Government commissions and contracts for decorative work for new American buildings and several expositions provided many opportunities for the display of their talents. Mention should also be made of Frederic Remington* and Charles Marion Russell,* who, though perhaps better known as painters, found ample time and had the skill to sculpt Western figures, often in energetic action, in enduring bronze.

Seaman, Elizabeth Cochrane. *See* Nellie Bly.

Secret Service (1895). Play by William Gillette.* Lewis Dumont, of the U.S. Secret Service, is known as Captain Thorne of the Confederate army, inside Richmond, Virginia, under siege during the Civil War. His mission is to help break down city defenses. He and Edith Varney, daughter of a Confederate general, have fallen in love. A Southern War Office official named Arrelsford tries while in her home to prove to Edith that "Thorne" is a spy but fails. In the Confederate telegraph office, Arrelsford tries again; he hides and peeks with Edith when Thorne starts to wire an order that will weaken a Confederate defense sector, but he is delayed by Arrelsford's call to the guards. Thorne foils his foe by ordering the guards to arrest Arrelsford! Edith steps forward with a document of aid to Thorne—a commission as a Confederate major. She admirably attempts thus to save her lover, who, however, just as admirably resumes his wiring of the rest of the order. But then he revokes the order, destroys the commission paper, and escapes. Later he makes his way to Edith's home and explains his spy mission. He is captured and goes with Arrelsford to be executed, but is saved when word comes that Thorne's order was not received in full, and the hero is merely put under arrest. He and Edith will await war's end. *Secret Service* opened in Philadelphia (1895), was revised and moved to New York, and played there for five months (1896) with Gillette in the leading role. He then took it to London and starred there (1897). A French version was also performed (1897).

Seton, Ernest Thompson (1860–1946). (Birth name: Ernest Evan Thompson: pen names: Ernest E. Thompson, Ernest Seton-Thompson, and Ernest Thompson Seton. Seton was an eighteenth-century family name on his father's side. Legal name: Ernest Thompson Seton, from 1901.) Naturalist, author, illustrator, and lecturer. He was born in Durham, England, the twelfth of fourteen children of a dour Calvinist and his meek wife. The family immigrated to Canada, first to a farm at Lindsay, Ontario (1886), then to Toronto (1870). Seton preferred nature around Lindsay to urban Toronto. Because his father wanted Seton to become an artist he studied art in Toronto (1876–1879) and then in London (1879–1881), where he concentrated on mammalian anatomy. He returned sick and nervous to Canada and sought to improve his health by homesteading, exploring, doing field research, and sketching in remote regions of Manitoba (1882–1886), during which period he also returned briefly to Toronto and studied at the Art Students League in New York. Seton published *The Birds of Manitoba* (1891) and illustrated and coauthored ornithologist Frank M. Chapman's *Handbook of Birds of Eastern North America* (1895) and *Bird-Life* (1897). Seton went to Paris to study anatomy (1890–1892), then returned home sick again. His famous painting of a sleeping wolf was exhibited in Paris (1891). He was hired as a wolf killer in New Mexico (1893) and followed that experience with an animal story entitled ''The King of Currumpaw'' (*Scribner's Magazine** 1894), about a huge wolf named Lobo that was killed only because of his loyalty to his mate Blanca. Seton published *Art Anatomy of Animals* (1896), traveled extensively in the Northwest (1897, 1898), and published *Wild Animals I Have Known* (1898), with 200 of his own illustrations. This popular work was quickly translated into Danish, Dutch, German, and Swedish. It helped set a pattern for modern animal stories, in which beasts are considerably humanized. Seton published *Wild Animal Play for Children* (1900), *The Biography of a Grizzly* (1900), *Lobo, Rag and Vixen* (1900), and *Lives of the Hunted* (1901). He traveled to Norway (1900) and also to the Arctic region (1907).

Seton founded the Woodcraft Indians (1902), which helped lead to the establishment of the Boy Scouts, in which organization he was deeply involved. Seton also continued to travel, write, and lecture well into the twentieth century. He applied for U.S. citizenship (1930), sold his Eastern property, and moved to New Mexico, where he built his magnificent ''Seton Castle'' to blend with the landscape and to house his 13,000 books, 8,000 paintings and drawings, and 3,000 bird and animal skins. Among his many friends may be named John Burroughs* (who charged him with describing animal behavior inaccurately), Hamlin Garland,* William Dean Howells,* Theodore Roosevelt* (whom he criticized for wanting to give Boy Scouts training in weapons), and Mark Twain.* Seton married California heiress Grace Gallatin in 1896. The couple had one child and were divorced in 1935, owing partly to her having a divergent career as an author and feminist. Seton immediately married decades-younger Julia M. Buttree in 1935 (the couple adopted a child). Seton was a skillful illustrator, a popular writer, and a restless, opinionated, testy eccentric.

Sewanee Review. Literary and critical quarterly magazine. The magazine was founded in 1892 by William Peterfield Trent while he was a professor of English and American literature at the University of the South in Sewanee, Tennessee. At first the journal was privately financed, and Trent was both editor (to 1900) and a frequent anonymous contributor. Most of the articles published in it concern literature, history, education, book reviews, and current issues. The journal, priced at 75¢ a copy and with low circulation figures through the 1890s, exerted a considerable positive influence in academic and allied circles. Theodore Roosevelt* praised it on occasion. The *Sewanee Review* is still a leader in a field now crowded with numerous other academic magazines. Incidentally, the *Yale Review** was also founded in 1892.

Sheldon, Charles M. (1857–1946). (Full name: Charles Monroe Sheldon.) Clergyman and author. Sheldon was born in Wellsville, New York, graduated from Brown (1883) and then Andover Theological Seminary (1886), was ordained as a Congregational minister (1886), became a pastor in Waterbury, Vermont (1886–1888), and then founded the Central Congregational Church in Topeka, Kansas (1889–1919). He once disguised himself in old clothes and a battered hat and pretended to seek work in order to learn firsthand about poverty. To promote Sunday evening church attendance and to appeal to young people worshipping at evening services, Sheldon began to read suspenseful chapters of his own didactic fiction instead of preaching regular sermons. This technique proved highly successful and led to the publication of his "sermon-serials." Much later, he moved to New York City to edit the *Christian Herald* (from 1920). His religious books include *Richard Bruce* (1891), *The Crucifixion of Philip Strong* (1894), *His Brother's Keeper; or, Christian Stewardship* (1896), *In His Steps: What Would Jesus Do?** (1897), *The Narrow Gate* (1902), *The Heart of the World* (1905), *All the World* (1918), *In His Steps Today* (1921, a sequel to *In His Steps*), *Let's Talk It Over* (1929), and *He Is Here* (1931). His autobiography is *Charles M. Sheldon: His Life Story* (1925); his booklet *The History of "In His Steps"* (1939) discusses his most popular work. *In His Steps* has been translated into more than twenty languages and has sold worldwide anywhere from eight to twenty-five million copies, making it perhaps the most popular novel in American literary history, until *Gone with the Wind*, by Margaret Mitchell, was published in 1936. Owing to a defective copyright in its 1896 serial form, *In His Steps* was widely pirated and Sheldon enjoyed only meagre royalties.

Sherman Anti-Trust Act. Law passed in 1890 to prohibit commercial trusts and combinations that restrain trade between and among states or between the United States and foreign countries. The guiding force behind the act was John Sherman, a senator from Ohio and the brother of Civil War hero General William Tecumseh Sherman. Much of the act, however, was written by George Franklin Edmunds, a distinguished constitutional lawyer and a senator from Vermont. It became the responsibility of the Department of Justice to enforce provisions of the act, which superseded any and all state laws regulating trusts and monopolies. The act represented the first attempt by Congress to stop big business from centralizing power and monopolizing markets, often through conspiracies by chronically dishonest corporate officers to fix prices, blacklist, rig freight rates, and so on. The act decreed that size alone does not constitute restraint of trade, but combinations designed to coerce or attack sources of competition do. At first, decisions by the U.S. Supreme Court favored big business. For example, the Court ruled in *United States v. E. C. Knight Company* (1895) in favor of the so-called Sugar Trust, on the grounds that no transaction had taken place across state lines. This, despite the fact that the American Sugar Refining Company had purchased four other companies, including E. C. Knight, and thus had gained control of 98 percent of the sugar-refining business in the United States. Ironically, a decade after the passage of the Sherman Anti-Trust Act, Andrew Carnegie,* John Pierpont Morgan,* and Charles M. Schwab* formed the United States Steel Corporation (1901), the largest corporate structure in the world; it was the result of a merger of most of the existing steel firms in the United States and controlled 75 percent of American steel production. Theodore Roosevelt* during his presidency ordered the Department of Justice (1902) to prosecute the Northern Securities Company, a railroad monopoly in the Northwest. Later targets of trustbusting activities included the American Telephone and Telegraph Company, the DuPont Company (manufacturers of explosives), and Swift and Company (meat packers). In one of his whimsical opinions, Oliver Wendell Holmes,* associate justice of the U.S. Supreme Court, characterized the Sherman Anti-Trust Act as an instrument designed to punish successful competition encouraged by the national habit of praising American initiative and the free enterprise system.

Shore Acres (1892). Play by James A. Herne.* Earlier titles were *The Hawthornes*, *Shore Acres Subdivision*, and *Uncle Nat*. The scene is Frenchman's Bay, near Bar Harbor, on the coast of Maine. Gentle, tolerant Nathaniel ''Nat'' Berry lets seemingly important successes go by unsought. His stiff younger brother Martin Berry manages their property, which includes valuable acreage along the shore—hence the title *Shore Acres*. The two brothers argue when Martin wants to sell the hallowed family property to a land developer. More important for the plot, however, is the fact that Martin, who married the woman of Uncle Nat's dreams, has a daughter named Helen, who loves Dr. Sam Warren. The young physician's liberal ideas bother Martin but not serene Nat. Martin and Sam argue over such touchy topics as evolution. Nat hopes that the young couple can have happiness of the sort he missed; so he helps them elope by boat. The two brothers fight at a lighthouse when Martin unavailingly tries to keep the beacon unlit so that the lovers will be shipwrecked. The famous final scene of *Shore Acres* poignantly shows old Nat, having come to an understanding with his brother and with Helen, Sam, and their child—back for a pleasant visit—silently locking up the snug homestead against a wintry storm.

"The Significance of the Frontier in American History" (1893). Essay by Frederick Jackson Turner.* Turner begins by quoting an 1890 census bulletin to the effect that up to 1880 the United States had an open frontier but that by 1890 it was closed because of various "isolated bodies of settlement" along its line. Until 1890, Americans by expanding westward provided a "vital force" which created unique institutions and constitutional forms. As the frontier moved westward, such institutions had to be modified to meet specific needs of settlers who were taming the wilderness and establishing patterns of community life. All nations have expanded and developed in this fashion, but European countries, among other non-American ones, have pushed into each other's "fortified boundary line," causing conflicts which only the strongest are able to survive. America is unique because its institutions, not having "Germanic origins," which historians have stressed for too long, evolved in sparsely populated regions. As pioneers moved from a given settled community farther west, they retrogressed to primitive stages, assessed specific needs, reevaluated institutions, and adapted them to meet new requirements. Each pocket of settlement thus developed a little differently.

Hence the diverse "American character," which has evolved from this "perennial rebirth," this "beginning over again," this "fluidity" and constantly recurring contact with frontier savagery, and the establishment of one "primitive society" after another. It is time for historians to study the overriding importance of "the Great West" and stop emphasizing Eastern events. The vaguely defined American "frontier," unlike borders elsewhere, was neither fortified nor heavily populated, but always had free land beckoning from the other side. Although the Atlantic coastal frontier was European in nature, waves of western frontier lines were ever less European and more American, and Americanization occurred fast and well out there. The "colonist" might be dressed and equipped like a European, but "the wilderness . . . [took] him from the railroad car and put . . . him in the birch canoe" or in "the log cabin of the Cherokee and Iroquois" and made him a self-sufficient primitive in a trice. New communities, with new institutions, soon developed. The advancing frontier, separated from the Atlantic coastal region, paused at the Allegheny Mountains, then at the Mississippi and Missouri rivers, pushed to the Rocky Mountains, stopped at "arid tract[s]," then surged forward to the Pacific Ocean.

The first frontiersmen traded with the Indians and later established lonely ranches, only to be evicted by nesters and farmers. As waves of people proceeded westward, farms evolved into towns, cities, and manufacturing centers. In the process, the frontier created the American mentality, the first ingredient of which was British, to be sure; but then into "the crucible" went Scotch-Irish, Pennsylvania Dutch, former indentured servants of various racial backgrounds, and Germans. Those who were pushing westward required manufactured goods, and some who stayed to become farmers sent their produce east. Since "[m]obility of population is death to localism," this constant western movement weakened sectionalism and fostered nationalism, and "the democracy of Jefferson" gave way to "the national republicanism of Monroe and the democracy of Jackson." Rugged frontiersmen relied on themselves for survival, hence valued personal liberty; so when they clustered into primitive communities, they demanded democracy, encouraged democratic suffrage policies, and tolerated only a minimum of governmental interference—especially from Eastern politicians who ineffectually expressed fear of "an unregulated advance of the frontier." "The New England preacher and school-teacher" enjoyed a measure of success among Westerners, who, however, influenced them as well. Life on the frontier over the centuries created important and typically American "intellectual traits" and personal "characteristics," including "coarseness and strength combined with acuteness and inquisitiveness, that practical, inventive turn of mind, quick to find expedients; that masterful grasp of material things, lacking in the artistic but powerful to effect great ends; the dominant individualism, working for good and for evil, and withal that buoyancy and exuberance which comes from freedom." Four centuries after America was discovered, and after a century of constitutional democracy, "the frontier has gone, and with its going has closed the first period of American history."

Sources of Turner's "The Significance of the Frontier in American History" are many, including environmental determinists, biologists and geographers, census bulletins, documents by western travelers, and publications of political economists. Turner read his essay at the World's Columbian Exposition* in Chicago, on 12 July 1893, as the fifth and final learned paper to be delivered to a tired audience of historians and reporters. They were unimpressed. He read it again before the State Historical Society of Wisconsin and republished it in the society *Proceedings* (December 1893). The essay was frequently reprinted in the immediately ensuing years. John Fiske* and Theodore Roosevelt,* among others influential in the 1890s, praised it if only briefly. Turner adapted its theory in many related articles, and he was soon much sought after. Critics of his position concerning the frontier were immediately active and have continued to be so since. Nevertheless, today, despite no little residual controversy, "The Significance of the Frontier in American History" is regarded as the most important historical document ever written by an American.

Silhouettes of American Life (1892). Collection of short stories by Rebecca Harding Davis.* These thirteen short stories originally appeared in various magazines during the 1870s and 1880s. Rebecca Harding Davis was the mother of

Richard Harding Davis,* the more famous but less able writer. She was an unappreciated pioneering realist, in reality a pre-naturalist. By the 1890s, she had become somewhat conventional, sentimental, and didactic, but the stories in *Silhouettes of American Life* are readable and poignant; their sentimentality is saved by an understated, wry humor. The stories carefully present an almost nationwide variety of characters, with a stress on frustrated but stoical women. "The Doctor's Wife" features a Philadelphia doctor's sad second wife's life stoically if briefly endured. "An Ignoble Martyr" explains that a New England woman declines marriage to serve a widowed, tyrannical mother who believes in nothing but work, but the heroine daringly changes as time advances: "She visited her neighbors; she read novels; she joked in a scared way."

Sister Carrie (1900). Novel by Theodore Dreiser.* Carrie Meeber, age eighteen, inexperienced, and pretty, leaves her small-town home in Wisconsin to live with her married sister in Chicago and to find work there. She attracts the eye of gamy but decent Charles H. Drouet, a traveling salesman for a Chicago company. She finds a dreary job in a shoe factory but soon loses it. Drouet persuades her to let him set her up in a small apartment, and she casually becomes his mistress. Through Drouet, Carrie meets George W. Hurstwood, who is almost forty, has an enviable position as a saloon manager, and is the husband of a shrewish wife and the father of a pair of teenage children—a self-centered son and a backbiting daughter. Hurstwood falls in love with Carrie and visits her while Drouet is out of town. Hurstwood attends a theatrical performance in which Drouet has persuaded timid Carrie to act, and he is intrigued by her natural flair for the stage. Hurstwood urges Carrie to leave Drouet for him; he even promises to marry her. Mrs. Hurstwood discovers the liaison, demands vacation money, and then begins divorce proceedings. Hurstwood grows desperate. One night, after drinking with friends in the saloon where he works, he chances to find the safe door open when is alone. He cannot resist the temptation to take the $10,000 he finds in the safe.

Hurstwood rushes to Carrie, who has been temporarily deserted by Drouet following a spat, tells her that Drouet is in the hospital, and, instead of taking her to him, he spirits her out of Chicago on a train to Montreal. Once there, Carrie demands that Hurstwood marry her, and he does so—illegally. His employees send detectives after him, and he returns most of the money he stole. He and Carrie move to New York City. He changes his name to George W. Wheeler, and the couple rent a small apartment. He buys a partnership in a bar. A few dreary years pass. His business fails. He and Carrie move into cramped quarters. Unable to find steady work, he becomes a has-been. On the other hand, Carrie develops a little ambition, obtains a job as a chorus girl, and moves up to the position of a minor actress. Through the friendship of a neighbor, Carrie chances to meet Bob Ames. He pays her the unique compliment of saying that her mind is worth cultivating. Sadly, this only makes her conclude, once she begins to achieve material security, that money cannot buy happiness. Meanwhile, Hurstwood has obtained employment as a scab laborer during a trolley-car strike, but he is shot at by disgruntled union workers and quits in terror. Now he can find nothing.

Working steadily, Carrie gives him her spare cash, explains in a note that she cannot support him further, and leaves him. She feels a pang of guilt but begins to room with a fellow actress and soon enjoys high pay. As she rises, Hurstwood slides to the status of a Bowery bum. Drouet, unchanged over the years, happens to turn up in New York as a branch office manager. He seeks out Carrie to congratulate her on her stage success, and he is puzzled when she seems to see nothing attractive in her former lover and helpmate. He tells her that Hurstwood left Chicago as a thief, and she momentarily feels sorry for the wretched fellow. When Hurstwood finds her at the theater later and begs for money, she cannot avoid regarding him as a criminal. Still, she gives him a little money, and he turns away. One cold winter night, Hurstwood miserably concludes that the game is up; he turns on the gas in his flophouse room, dies, and is buried in Potter's Field. By coincidence, at this very time his wife, their daughter, and the girl's well-to-do husband are passing through New York on their way to sunny Rome; furthermore, Carrie, back from a successful London tour, is sitting bemused in an opulent hotel room in a rocking chair by the window.

Sister Carrie has a simple time line; the action starts in August 1889 and concludes in January 1897. Dreiser's main themes here are all naturalistic: the overriding importance of money and sex, mutability and incomprehensible confusion in life, the impermanence of joy, and the presumptuousness of any moral judgments. *Sister Carrie* is noteworthy for its power, not its style, which is marred by clumsy writing, too much detail, clichés, and jumps in point of view. Dreiser based a pivotal part of this novel on an episode in the life of his sister Emma, whose married Chicago lover in 1886 stole money from the safe of his company, which owned saloons, and decamped with her to Canada. Dreiser submitted his novel to Doubleday, Page & Company. It was recommended by their reader Frank Norris* and was accepted. When Frank Doubleday, senior partner, returned from a vacation in Europe and read it, he—and, according to legend, his wife as well—tried to require changes. When Dreiser argued, the company decided to print the book but not advertise it; it sold fewer than five hundred copies—to Dreiser's profound discouragement. An abridged edition of *Sister Carrie* was published in London (1901). The novel was republished in the United States (1907), was denounced by conservative critics, praised by others, and began selling well. Curiously, in 1981 a full edition was published for the first time; this edition restored some 36,000 suppressed words and the original form of the last two chapters. In the complete edition, Carrie's world becomes bleaker and even more naturalistic, Carrie more uneasy, and the three main males—Hurstwood, Drouet, and Ames—more credible.

The Sisters' Tragedy, with Other Poems, Lyrical and Dramatic (1891). Collection of poems by Thomas Bailey Aldrich.* The short title poem, in heroic couplets, explains that Muriel and her sister Agläe both love one man. Muriel marries him. When he dies, the widow tells her long-pining sister that he was an unloving husband.

Sitting Bull (c. 1831–1890). (Native American name: Tatanka Iyotake.) Teton Sioux Native American chief and holy man. He was born near Grand River, in what is now South Dakota. As a youthful brave of the Hunkpapa subtribe, he fought in several battles against the Crows. He became the unifying chief of the Sioux Nation in the late 1860s. He did not lead any attacks against U.S. Army units in the 1870s, but he was the canny strategist behind many warrior chiefs who did. After General George Armstrong Custer's defeat at the Battle of the Little Big Horn (June 1876), the victors dispersed; Sitting Bull took his followers to Canada, which, however, declined responsibility for them. They returned to surrender to the army at Fort Buford (in northern Dakota Territory, 1881), and Sitting Bull was imprisoned at Fort Randall (in Montana, 1881–1883), then released to Standing Rock (in southern Dakota Territory). He later toured in Western shows, including one owned and starred in by William F. Cody* (1885). On 15 December 1890, Sitting Bull, then living in his Grand River cabin, was murdered by Native American police who had been ordered by Standing Rock agent James McLaughlin to arrest him in connection with the Ghost Dance "insurrection," which had actually been masterminded by the visionary Wovoka.* In addition to Sitting Bull, his young son, six of his bodyguards, and six Indian policeman were killed. Many of his Hunkpapas fled, some as far as Wounded Knee,* where several were victims of the massacre there (29 December 1890). Although Sitting Bull has been denigrated by several commentators and legendized by others, he was in truth a versatile Native American genius.

Smart Set. Monthly New York society magazine. It was founded in 1890 by William D'Alton Mann, whose weekly *Town Topics*,* in which he enjoyed a controlling interest (from 1891), had long proved popular. *Smart Set* was priced at 25¢. From the start a cleverly written, witty journal, it soon enjoyed a wider readership than the snobbish upper-crust New York society at which it had been originally aimed. It is noteworthy that *Smart Set* published the first short story by O. Henry* to see print. Mann sold his magazine in 1901 to John A. Thayer, who started it on the way to real eminence in succeeding years, especially when H. L. Mencken and George Jean Nathan began to edit it (1914). When these two men grew tired of the *Smart Set*, they started the more substantial *American Mercury* (1924).

Soldiers of Fortune (1897). Novel by Richard Harding Davis.* Robert Clay, a civil engineer, has been a soldier in Africa and a bridge builder in Central America. Although he was born poor and has known hardships, he remains a romantic neoaristocrat at heart. When businessman Langham hires Clay to manage his Valencia Mining Company in a country called Olancho, on the South American northern coast, Clay carries with him a photograph of Langham's older daughter Alice, met in New York, for inspiration. He quickly shapes up the mine. Langham comes to inspect progress and brings his younger daughter, Hope, for company. The government of Olanchan President Alvarez is threatened by a revolutionary leader named Mendoz. Alvarez is killed. Clay, remembering what he learned as an officer in Egypt and Algeria, leads the loyalists to remove Mendoz. Clay, who declines the presidency, becomes a hero endowed with all the attributes of the romantic adventurer: fighter, leader of men, perfect gentleman with ladies, and exploiter of nature. Alice soon pales in his eyes. She is too conventional, constricted by moneyed society, and timid. But Hope is romantic, and regards Clay as finer than "her heroes and princes in fiction." She repudiates her sister as a role model—Hope even helped Clay rescue Alvarez's widow—and participates in Clay's fulfillment of the American dream, which includes the spread of American civilization abroad and with it American exploitation of the lazy Latin Americans' natural resources. Olancho is Venezuela thinly made over. Langham's mining company is based on the Juragua Iron Company, which Davis saw in Cuba while he was a college student. Details of Olancho and aspects of the action grew out of Davis's 1895 visit to Venezuela and his *Three Gringos in Venezuela and Central America*, the 1896 book, which came out of that visit. In several respects, Clay is probably Davis's notion of himself at his best. Certainly the two shared the same Manifest Destiny philosophy. *Soldiers of Fortune* was immensely popular. Davis was paid $5,000 by *Scribner's Magazine** for serial rights. When it was published in book form, the public bought almost 100,000 copies the first year. Its London edition (1897) was a smash hit, and Davis, who was in England when it was the talk of the country, basked in the glow. Davis went to Cuba (1913) to help produce a movie based on the novel. Two years later, he and his second wife Bessie named their daughter Hope after its heroine. From the date of its publication, however, *Soldiers of Fortune* has had severe critics; they regard the hero's accomplishments as impossible and his philosophy as dangerously jingoistic.

Songs. The period from 1888 to 1901 saw the composition of innumerable popular songs. The best include "Bedouin Love Song," music by Ciro Pinsuti, words by Bayard Taylor (1888); "Oh, Promise Me," music by Reginald De Koven, words by Clement Scott (1889); "Tenderly Calling," music by Ira David Sankey, words by Frances Jane Crosby (1890); "Thy Beaming Eyes," music by the distinguished Edward MacDowell,* words by William Henry Gardner (1890); "Little Boy Blue," music by the distinguished Ethelbert Nevin,* words by the popular Eugene Field* (1891); "The Pardon Came Too Late," music and words by the prolific Paul Dresser, brother of Theodore Dreiser* (1891); "Ta-ra-ra-bom-der-e," music and words by Henry J. Sayers (1891); "The Man That Broke the Bank at Monte Carlo," music and words by Fred Gilbert (1892); "The Side Walks of New York," music and words by Charles B. Lawlor and James W. Blake (1894); "America the Beautiful," words by Katherine Lee Bates, music from "Materna" (1888) by Samuel Augustus Ward (1895); "The

Band Plays On,'' music by Charles B. Ward, words by John E. Palmer (1895); ''The Hand That Rocks the Cradle,'' music by William H. Holmes, words by Charles W. Berkeley (1895); ''All Coons Look Alike to Me,'' music and words by Ernest Hogan (1896, containing the first use of the word ''rag,'' in a description of the syncopated accompaniment calling for ''negro rag''); ''A Hot Time in the Old Town,'' music by Theodore M. Metz, words by Joe Hayden (1896); ''Laugh and the World Laughs with You,'' music by Louis F. Gottschalk, words by the prolific Ella Wheeler Wilcox (1896); ''Love Makes the World Go 'Round,'' music by William Furst, words by the playwright Clyde Fitch* (1896); ''Sweet Rosie O'Grady,'' music and words by Maud Nugent (1896); ''Asleep in the Deep,'' music by H. W. Petrie, words by Arthur J. Lamb (1897); ''Danny Deever,'' music by the distinguished Walter Damrosch, words by Rudyard Kipling (1897); ''On the Banks of the Wabash Far Away,'' music and words by Paul Dresser; ''Gypsy Love Song,'' music by Victor Herbert,* words by the prolific Harry Bache Smith (1898); ''The Rosary,'' music by Ethelbert Nevin, words by Robert Cameron Rogers (1898); ''A Stein Song,'' music by Frederic Field Bullard, words by the popular Richard Hovey* (1898); ''Who Dat Say Chicken in Dis Crowd?'', music by Will Marion, words by the popular Paul Laurence Dunbar* (1898); ''My Wild Irish Rose,'' music and words by Chauncey Olcott (1899); ''A Bird in a Gilded Cage,'' music by Harry Von Tilzer, words by Arthur J. Lamb (1900); ''I Can't Tell You Why I Love You, But I Do,'' music by Gus Edwards, words by Will D. Cobb (1900); and ''Mighty Lak' a Rose,'' music by Ethelbert Nevin, words by Frank L. Stanton.

Sousa, John Philip (1854–1932). Bandmaster and composer. Sousa, born in Washington, D.C., was trained to be a violinist, but he could also play the piano and several wind instruments. He became a young member of the U.S. Marine Band (1867–1872). He then played the violin in various theater orchestras. Next, he was appointed bandmaster of the Marine Band, which he polished into America's finest band (1880–1892). Sousa then organized his own excellent band of about sixty top-notch musicians, in showy dress, and took it on tour in the United States—giving many captivated audiences their first taste of music by the finest foreign composers—and in Europe (four times, and including ragtime), and finally around the world (1910). He composed more than 100 spirited marches, the best of which are *Semper Fidelis* (1888), *Washington Post March* (1889), *Liberty Bell* (1893), *King Cotton* (1897), *Stars and Stripes Forever* (1897, with an innovative piccolo obbligato melody), and *Hands across the Sea* (1899). Typically, a Sousa march begins with a flourish or fanfare; then come the main section and a trio section in the subdominant key; only sometimes does a return to the main section provide the close. The best of Sousa's eleven comic operas are *El Capitan* (1896) and *The Bride-Elect* (1897). Sousa also wrote music of other sorts, including a symphonic poem, suites, and waltzes, and he inspired the 1908 invention of the sousaphone (a tuba with a flaring, adjustable bell). His autobiography is *Marching Along* (1928). (*See also* Operettas.)

South Carolina Inter-State and West Indian Exposition. This exposition was held just outside Charleston, South Carolina, along the Ashley River, between 1 December 1901 and 1 June 1902, to promote the port, nearby agricultural activities, and Caribbean trade in the wake of the Spanish-American War.* The exposition was housed in fourteen buildings varied in architecture from Mexican mission style to Spanish Renaissance style. In addition, a local plantation served as the Women's Building (with silk exhibits). The huge, domed Cotton Palace (with products from regional mills) was attractive, as was a 4,000-seat auditorium. Exhibits in the Machinery and Transportation Building, in the Negro Building, and along the midway, as well as the appearance of Theodore Roosevelt* on President's Day in April 1902, helped draw enough crowds to enable the exposition to break even and even turn a small profit.

Spanish-American War. Armed conflict between the United States and Spain. The war was caused by the pressure of American investments in and policies toward Cuban sugar, tobacco, and mining industries; by increasing American chauvinistic imperialism in and beyond the Caribbean region; and by American journalistic sensationalism. The announced purpose of the United States, however, was to liberate Cuba, Puerto Rico, and the Philippine Islands from oppressive Spanish domination. Native Cuban insurrectionists became especially active (1895), whipped up American sympathy, lobbied for money and supplies in New York City, fed to newspaper owners William Randolph Hearst* and Joseph Pulitzer* lurid accounts of Spanish atrocities, and inspired American political leaders of every party to call for recognition of Cuban belligerency and even American military intervention in Cuba. Business and labor organizations joined in the clamor, as did Latin American groups and even isthmian canal advocates. Their goal was not the amelioration of conditions for non-Spanish people in Cuba, Puerto Rico, and the Philippines, but rather profits through the opening of new markets, the exploitation of raw materials and cheap native labor, and the building of naval bases to defend merchant fleets in the Caribbean and the Pacific.

After William McKinley* was elected president in 1896, Theodore Roosevelt,* always jingoistic, became even more so. Military planners took the theories of sea-power advocate Alfred Thayer Mahan* more seriously. Spanish brutality in Cuba (1896–1897) evoked an official American protest (27 June 1897). Pulitzer's *World* published a purloined letter in which the Spanish minister in Washington, D.C., belittled McKinley for weakness and vacillation (9 February 1898). The U.S. battleship *Maine* was mysteriously blown up in Havana harbor (15 February), killing 266 men, whereupon Congress unanimously voted $50,000,000 to be used by McKinley for defense (9 March). An American board of inquiry reported that the *Maine* had been destroyed by an exterior mine (21 March). The State Department delivered an ultimatum to Spain to declare an armistice in Cuba and to permit home rule there (29 March). Spain agreed to comply (10 April). McKinley approved a resolution demanding that Spain withdraw from Cuba (20 April); but before this resolution could be delivered by the American minister in Madrid, Spain had expelled him. McKinley declared a blockade of Cuban ports (22 April). Spain declared war on the United States (24 April). Congress declared (25 April) that the war had been in effect from 21 April.

Hostilities and their ugly aftermath followed, in this sequence. The U.S. Asiatic naval squadron of six vessels under Commodore George Dewey* sank, silenced, or captured the entire Spanish Pacific fleet of ten vessels (Manila Bay, 30 April–1 May); 381 Spaniards were killed, and eight Americans were wounded. Seven U.S. Naval vessels blockaded the Spanish Atlantic fleet of seven vessels in Santiago de Cuba harbor (from 29 May). U.S. Army regulars and volunteers, numbering some 17,000, and poorly trained and equipped, disembarked in Cuba (beginning 22 June). American forces were victorious at the Battle of El Caney and the Battle of San Juan Hill (1 July). When the Spanish fleet attempted to leave Santiago harbor, American naval units destroyed it (3 July); 474 Spaniards were killed and 1,750 were captured, and one American was killed and one was wounded. Wake Island was taken during the Philippine campaign (4 July; formally occupied in 1900). Hawaii (not sought by Grover Cleveland* during his presidency but wanted by McKinley) was annexed by joint resolution of Congress (7 July; on 30 April 1900, Congress granted Hawaii territorial status, effective 14 June 1900). The Spanish garrison at Santiago, numbering 24,000 soldiers, surrendered (17 July) after being threatened by American artillery bombardment. U.S. Army units under General Nelson A. Miles* invaded Puerto Rico with no significant opposition (25 July). Spain made peace overtures in Washington, D.C., through the French embassy (26 July). Disease and food poisoning in the American ranks in Cuba required evacuation of troops to Long Island (beginning 4 August). A peace protocol was signed (12 August). Spanish troops in Manila surrendered to assaulting American forces, then numbering 10,700 men, aided by Filipino resistance leader Emilio Aguinaldo and his guerrillas (13 August).

A peace commission met in Paris (beginning 1 October). The Treaty of Paris was published (10 December), by which Spain agreed to free Cuba, assume liability for a $400,000,000 Cuban debt, cede Puerto Rico and Guam to the United States, and cede the Philippine Islands to the United States for a payment of $20,000,000. When Aguinaldo, who had been leading rebel Filipinos against Spain and had established a native provisional government (12 June 1898), learned the terms of the treaty, he called upon his forces to declare independence (5 January 1899). Hostilities broke out between American forces and Filipino guerrillas (4 February 1899). Meanwhile, American imperialists (most Republicans) and antiimperialists (Democrats, Populists, and some Republicans) had been arguing about the Treaty of Paris in and out of the U.S. Senate, which finally ratified it (6 February 1899) by a two-vote margin. McKinley signed an army appropriations bill (4 March 1901) which included an amendment requiring Cuba, before being granted independence, to allow the United States to supervise its finances, to intervene when necessary (U.S. forces did intervene 1906–1909), and to make no treaties without U.S. approval (Cuba agreed 12 June). Aguinaldo, long a resistance leader against American forces, was captured (23 March 1901). American forces withdrew from Cuba (20 May 1902). Congress passed the Philippine Government Act (also called the Organic Act), which permitted the Philippines to be governed as an American territory by officers appointed by the U.S. president (1 July 1902). Filipino-American hostilities ended (4 July). It was also decreed that Puerto Rico and Hawaii would be similarly governed.

Of the more than 274,000 officers and men serving in the American army during the Spanish-American War and its immediate aftermath, 5,462 died in the Caribbean region, in the Philippines, and in American camps; but combat casualties accounted for only 379 of those deaths. In addition, 1,604 were wounded. The direct cost of the war has been put at $250,000,000. American military heroes of the Spanish-American War include Dewey, Charles Vernon Gridley, Miles, Walter Reed,* Roosevelt, and Leonard Wood.* War correspondents included Stephen Crane,* Richard Harding Davis,* and Sylvester Scovel.* A daring combat photographer was James H. Hare.* Many distinguished authors wrote about the conflict, some profoundly, others only in passing, but almost always in opposition. They include Jane Addams,* George Ade,* Ambrose Bierce,* William Jennings Bryan,* W.E.B. DuBois,* Paul Laurence Dunbar,* Finley Peter Dunne,* B. O. Flower,* Henry Blake Fuller,* Benjamin Harrison,* John Hay,* William Dean Howells,* William James,* William Vaughn Moody,* George Santayana,* William Graham Sumner,* and Mark Twain.* In a letter sent from London to Roosevelt, Hay said, "It has been a splendid little war; begun with the highest motives, carried on with magnificent intelligence and spirit, favored by that Fortune which loves the brave" (27 July 1898). On the other hand, Ernest Howard Crosby (1856–1907), a minor poet, put it differently in the "Real 'White Man's Burden' " (in *Swords and Plowshares*, 1902): "We've made a pretty mess at home, / Let's make a mess abroad." American expansionism, fed by the success of the Spanish-American War, led to diplomatic, commercial, and military consequences involving the United States in China, The Hague, Samoa, Colombia, and Panama—consequences obviously felt to this day.

Sports. The United States has always been a sports-minded country. In the 1890s Americans enjoyed participating in or watching archery, baseball, basketball, bowling, boxing (*see* James J. Corbett* and John L. Sullivan*), cycling, fishing, football, golf, harness and horse racing, hiking and mountain climbing, hockey, hunting, rowing, skating, skiing, soccer, swimming, target shooting, tennis, wrestling, yachting, and various track and field events. A fuller list of popular sports would also include fencing, lacrosse, rodeo events, and still other athletic activities.

Baseball and football, the two preeminently popular sports in the United States in the 1890s, got their start at about the same time. An early form of baseball was played in England and in the United States for some years before Abner

Doubleday supposedly invented the game at Cooperstown, New York (1839). The first baseball game to take place between rival teams was played in Hoboken, New Jersey (1846). Thereafter the game evolved slowly. The first curve pitch appeared in 1867. The Cleveland Red Stockings were the first semiprofessional team (from 1869). Professional baseball began with the organization of ten teams in the National Association of Professional Baseball Players (1871) and expanded to eleven teams (1872), then thirteen (1875). The standard size and weight of the baseball were adopted in 1872; gloves and masks were introduced in 1875. The National League of Professional Baseball Clubs was formed in 1876. The American Association was formed in 1882 and quickly expanded to twelve teams (1884). Rival clubs agreed—only temporarily—to respect one another's territorial rights and not to raid each other (beginning in 1883). The Union Association, the so-called outlaw league, was formed in 1884, but lasted only a short time. The first chest protector was designed in 1885; and the three-strike rule was made official in 1887. In 1888 an early version of the World Series was played, with the National League's New York team defeating the American Association's Saint Louis team. When National League club owners annoyed their players by grading them A to E and paying them accordingly, in 1888, the Players' League was formed but, unfortunately, in such a way that all leagues were hurt (1889). The four-ball walk was instituted in 1889; the National League formed a twelve-club circuit in 1892; and the pitching distance was lengthened to 60 feet 6 inches in 1893. After many changes, the National League emerged with eight teams—in Boston, Brooklyn, Chicago, Cincinnati, New York, Philadelphia, Pittsburgh, and Saint Louis (from 1900 well into the twentieth century). The present American League (from 1901) grew out of the Western League, which was formed (1893) out of the Western Association, an outgrowth (1888) of the old Northwestern League. The American League was composed of teams in Baltimore, Boston, Chicago, Cleveland, Detroit, Milwaukee (soon replaced by Saint Louis), New York, Philadelphia, and Washington D.C. (by 1904). Many colleges formed splendid baseball teams and supported them well; college football, however, was always more popular.

Football grew out of British rugby and was established on an informal basis on American college campuses in the 1840s. Princeton and Rutgers played the first intercollegiate game (1869), with twenty-five men on each team. In the 1870s Columbia, McGill (in Montreal, Canada), and Yale scheduled matches and formed what became the Intercollegiate Football Association (1876). Rules were modified to limit teams to eleven on a side (1880). Soon there were other changes. In the last decades of the nineteenth century, Walter Camp, a Yale football player and then a Yale graduate, became a recognized and respected leader in recommending modifications to various aspects of the game, including formations, motions, scoring, and refereeing. (Changes continued well into the twentieth century.) The first All America team was named in 1889. The shape of the football, that of a prolate spheroid, was adopted in 1896 and modified until 1912. The first Rose Bowl game, featuring Michigan and Stanford, was held in 1901. Meanwhile, professional football was evolving. The first professional game, played in Latrobe, Pennsylvania, pitted town teams from Latrobe and nearby Jeannette (1895). (Professional football, however, did not gain great popularity until the establishment of the national Football League in 1921.) At first, the game played on college gridirons was entirely too brutal; the so-called flying wedge (outlawed 1894) was the most lethal of several innovative maneuvers, and protective gear was almost nonexistent. College players were killed on an alarmingly regular basis; no fewer than eighteen died in one year alone (1905). In 1906 Theodore Roosevelt,* then president of the United States, summoned athletic directors from Harvard, Princeton, and Yale to the White House for a conference to make the game safer. To this day, however, football is almost as violent as boxing.

Golf, which got its modern start in fifteenth-century Scotland, was quite popular in the United States by 1888; matches were held that year in Florida, Illinois, Iowa, New York, West Virginia, and perhaps elsewhere. The St. Andrew's Golf Club was founded in Yonkers, New York (1888), from which its headquarters subsequently moved to Grey Oaks, New York (1894). There were at least seventy-five golf organizations in the United States by 1895; five of them established the Amateur Golf Association of the United States (1895). The first championship tournament was held in Newport, Rhode Island, in 1895. Thereafter the popularity of the game spread like wildfire. (America's Professional Golfers Association was formed in 1916.)

Tennis was imported from Bermuda to the United States in 1874, and the rules for the game were soon formalized (1880). The U.S. Lawn Tennis Association was formed in 1881 and the first national championship was held, at Newport, Rhode Island, in the same year. The first international tournament featured American and British players at Chestnut Hill, Massachusetts, in 1900. (Professional tennis did not begin until 1926.)

Basketball, invented by James Naismith* in 1891, grew rapidly in popularity as a winter indoor sport. At first it was called Naismith ball. Yale soon had a basketball team (1892–1893); then Cornell and the University of Chicago formed teams (1893–1894). The first basketball competitions for women pitted the University of California, Berkeley, against Leland Stanford University, in 1896, and the University of Washington against Ellensburg Normal School, also in 1896. Columbia, Harvard, Princeton, and Yale established the Eastern Collegiate League in 1901. Basketball was exported to Europe by American soldiers during World War I, after which it quickly spread around the world. The game has been considerably modified since then.

A few other sports popular in the United States in the 1890s may be discussed more briefly. Horse racing, because it attracted gamblers, was chronically corrupt; reformers demanding honest controls accomplished little until the Jockey Club was formed in 1894. Ice hockey, which evolved out of field hockey, gained its start in the United States when a group of American college students visited Canada in the winter of 1894–1895, fell in love with the game, and imported it back home. Soccer, perhaps the most popular athletic game in the world, did not gain a foothold in the United States until the twentieth century.

The first modern Olympic Games were held in Athens, Greece, in 1896. Participants represented only eight countries—Denmark, England, France, Germany, Greece, Hungary, Switzerland, and the United States. America sent men mostly from the Boston Athletic Association. The following Americans won gold medals: Thomas Burke (100-meter dash, 400-meter dash), Ellery Clark (running high jump, long jump), James Brendan Connolly (triple jump), Thomas Curtis (110-meter hurdles), Robert Garrett (16-pound shot put, discus throw), and William Hoyt (pole vault). To the next Olympic Games, held in Paris, France, in 1900, the United States sent fifty-five men. The following won gold medals: Ray Ewry (standing high jump), John Flanagan (16-pound hammer throw), Alvin C. Kraenzlein (long jump), George Orton (2,500-meter steeplechase), and Jon Tewksbury (400-meter hurdles). Confusion over when to start the 1900 games, however, marred them, and some records were flawed. The next games were held in Saint Louis, Missouri, in 1904. Women were not allowed to compete in the games held in Athens in 1896. They did compete in golf and tennis in the games in Paris in 1900. Margaret Abbott of the United States won the first gold medal for women, in the women's nine-hole golf competition. No women were allowed to enter the official games in Saint Louis in 1904, but they were permitted to be ''unofficial'' competitors in women's archery. Lidia Howell, an American woman, won the gold medal in that event.

Stanford, Leland (1824–1893). (Full name: Amasa Leland Stanford.) Railroad builder, politician, and one of The Big Four.* (The other three are Charles Crocker, Mark Hopkins, and Collis P. Huntington.)

Stanton, Elizabeth Cady (1815–1902). Reformer. She was born in Johnston, New York, the daughter of a judge. She attended a girls' academy in Troy, New York (1832), studied law in her father's office but, because she was a woman, could not be admitted to the bar. She became active in antislavery and temperance movements. She married Henry Brewster Stanton, a lawyer, journalist, and abolitionist (1840); she insisted at the time of the wedding ceremony that the word ''obey'' be omitted from their vows. The Stantons attended an international antislavery convention in London in 1840; however, because she was a woman, Mrs. Stanton was not admitted to the meetings. While living in Boston (from 1846), she helped organize the Seneca Falls Convention (1848), which was the first American group to assemble for woman's rights. One plank of their platform was woman's suffrage. She also argued for more rational divorce laws (to stop condoning brutality and drunkenness, for example), coeducation, and a married woman's right to hold property. She persuaded Susan B. Anthony* to join the movement in 1851. Stanton was the first president of the National Woman Suffrage Association (1869–1890) and the first president of the National American Woman Suffrage Association (1890–1892). She was also an editor and a prolific writer. She coauthored (with Anthony and Matilda Joslyn Gage) *History of Woman Suffrage* (4 vols., 1881–1902). The fourth volume covers the period from 1883 to 1900. (Two additional volumes, in which Stanton obviously was not involved, bring coverage up to 1920.) The Stantons had seven children. Her autobiography is entitled *Eighty Years and More (1815–1897)* (1898).

Statehood. The following seven territories became states between 1888 and 1901: North Dakota, 2 November 1889; South Dakota, 2 November 1889; Montana, 8 November 1889; Washington, 11 November 1889; Idaho, 3 July 1890; Wyoming, 10 July 1890; and Utah, 4 January 1896.

Stedman, Edmund Clarence (1833–1908). Poet, critic, editor, and stock broker. Stedman was born in Hartford, Connecticut. His father died when the boy was only two years of age. He moved a year later with his mother and younger brother to her parents' home in New Jersey, and he was subsequently reared by his great-uncle in Norwich, Connecticut (from 1839). His mother remarried in 1841 and became poetess-novelist Elizabeth Kinney. Stedman attended Yale (1849–1851), until his expulsion for misbehavior; he was awarded an honorary M.A. in 1871. He edited the Norwich *Tribune* (1852–1853). He eloped with and married Laura Woodworth in 1853 (the couple had two sons). On reaching the age of twenty-one, he learned to his surprise that he had been disinherited. Stedman tried a variety of jobs—publisher, clockmaker, real estate broker, and railroad clerk (1854–1859). In 1860 he published *Poems, Lyrical and Idyllic* and became day editor of the New York *Evening World*. During the Civil War years, he worked as a Washington correspondent (1861–1863), a clerk in the attorney general's office (1863), a banker (1863), and finally an independent broker (1864). Thereafter Stedman combined success on Wall Street and success as a man of letters—poet, editor, critic, and mentor to younger and better writers. Stedman's volumes of poetry, which were once considered more important than they are now, culminated in *Poems, Now First Collected* (1897). His most important editorial work includes *A Library of American Literature* (11 vols., 1888–1890, coedited with Ellen Mackay Hutchinson), showing that by 1890 America already had a bright and sweeping national literature; *The Works of Edgar Allan Poe* (10 vols., 1894–1895, coedited with George E. Woodberry); *A Victorian Anthology* (1895), immensely popular; and *An American Anthology, 1787–1900* (1900), including much recent poetry. His best criticism appears in *Poets of America* (2 vols., 1885), which anticipates early twentieth-century critics by focusing on the text and, in addition, deploring the didacticism so pervasive in establishment literature. He also wrote a conservative book formulating his aesthetic principles: *The Nature and Elements of Poetry* (1892). Stedman was too much of an exemplar of the Genteel Tradition,* most of the defenders of which (notably Thomas Bailey Aldrich* and Richard Watson Gilder,* and most of the established authors associated with them) he knew intimately but against which the younger writers of the 1890s were rebelling. Yet it must also be emphasized that Stedman was friendly and helpful to many of those very same rebels, including Hamlin Garland,* Richard Hovey,* Emma Lazarus, Percy MacKaye, Harriet Monroe, William Vaughn Moody,* Edwin Arlington Robinson,* and Charles Warren Stoddard.* Furthermore, an 1880 essay by Stedman praising Walt Whitman marks the beginning of Whitman's acceptance by the establishment.

Stedman remains a curious figure in literary annals. He wanted to be a poet but was only a third-rate one, and he knew it. He wanted to break free of Victorian restraints but remained partly fettered. His older son embezzled from his father's firm (1883), and the two men were estranged for twenty-three years thereafter. Stedman was a member of the New York Stock Exchange for thirty years, had financial problems partly owing to his son's crime, sold his seat on the Stock Exchange (1900), wrote and edited part of a history of the Exchange (1905), suffered the deaths of his wife (1905) and then his reconciled son (1906), had two heart attacks (1899, 1908), and died in the knowledge that he had never become the significant poet he had wanted to be.

Steffens, Lincoln (1866–1936). Muckraking journalist, social reformer, and socialist. Born in San Francisco, Steffens graduated from the University of California, Berkeley (1889), studied abroad for three years, worked on the New York *Evening Post* (until 1898), and became an editor of the New York *Commercial Advertiser* (until 1902). One of his New York mentors was Jacob Riis.* Steffens did editorial work and writing for S.S. McClure* and his *McClure's Magazine** until he resigned (1906) to become a free-lance journalist. He and several other journalists developed the *American Magazine*, beginning in 1906. His most important work began as "The Shame of the Cities," a *McClure's* series (1903, 1904–1905). He expanded this material and published it in book form, as *The Shame of the Cities* (1904), and then wrote *The Struggle for Self-Government* (1906) and *Upbuilders* (1909). Steffens studied Marxism and Russian revolutionary activities, visited the Soviet Union, where he met Nikolai [Vladimir Ilich Ulyanov] Lenin (1911), and was impressed by the Communist experiment in Russia, opining somewhat inaccurately, "I have seen the future and it works." His autobiography was published (1931); his letters appeared posthumously (1938). Steffens significantly exposed graft and corruption in boss-run American cities and reasoned that successful businessmen were wrongly admired for their wealth, which too often they used to put politicians in office and to keep them there as long as they were quietly subservient. Steffens's vast range of friends included, among many others, Mary Austin,* Abraham Cahan,* Finley Peter Dunne,* Norman Hapgood,* John Reed, and Ida M. Tarbell.*

Steinmetz, Charles Proteus (1865–1923). (Original name: Karl August Rudolph Steinmetz; nicknames: Proteus, Loki.) Electrical engineer. Born a hunchback in Breslau, Germany, he soon displayed precocity in literature, mathematics, and physics. He was educated at the University of Breslau (1883–1888), became a socialist and edited a radical newspaper, wrote critically of the government, and was obliged to escape to Switzerland, where he studied at the Polytechnic Institute at Zurich (1888–1889). He then immigrated to New York City and changed his name (1889). He became a draftsman in an electrical shop in Yonkers, New York (1889–1893) and began to study ways to increase efficiency in alternating current motors and to publish essays on electricity. (He opposed the theoretical preference of Thomas A. Edison* for direct current.) Steinmetz's lectures on how to calculate hysteresis (that is, power loss in electrical devices owing to conversion of magnetic action into useless heat [1892]) and on certain alternating current phenomena (1893) attracted respectful but baffled professional attention. Steinmetz joined the General Electric Company in New York as a consulting engineer (1893) and remained with the company in that capacity after its move to Schenectady, New York (1894–1923). Through him, the company obtained more than 200 patents (for example, aluminum lightning arresters, improved arc lamps, and better generators and motors).

Steinmetz collaborated with Reginald Aubrey Fessenden to build a one-kilowatt alternator for use in radio research (*see* Radio). Steinmetz was president of the American Institute of Electrical Engineers (1901–1902) and was also a professor of electrical engineering at Union College (from 1902). Later in his life, he studied and produced electrical transients, that is, exceptionally brief changes in electrical circuits (for example, lightning). His publications include *Theory and Calculation of Alternating Current Phenomena* (1897), on how to predict the performance of electrical machinery at the design stage; *Radiation, Light and Illumination* (1909); *Engineering Mathematics* (1910); and *America and the New Epoch* (1916), arguing via historical data that individualism and competition must soon be regarded as outmoded. He also dabbled in Schenectady politics (from 1911). Unmarried, Steinmetz legally adopted a brilliant young engineering associate at General Electric.

Steinway, William (1836–1896). Piano manufacturer. He was born in Seesen, Germany. His father, Henry Engelhard Steinway, was a piano manufacturer. Young Steinway was well educated, spoke English and French as well as German, had a fine tenor voice, played the piano well, and was adept at piano tuning. He accompanied his family to New York City in 1851 where his parents offered him a choice of a musical career or a business career. Steinway chose a business career and was accordingly apprenticed to a New York piano maker. He helped his father and his brothers Charles and Henry, Jr., found the piano-manufacturing firm of Steinway & Sons in 1853. With a few assistants, they built a piano a week and moved to better quarters (1854, 1859) as business improved. When Charles and Henry, Jr., both died (1865), William Steinway persuaded his oldest brother, Christian Friedrich Theodore Steinway, to leave Germany and become his partner in New York. Theodore Steinway handled scientific and manufacturing aspects of the company, while William Steinway managed the finances and aggressive advertising. To promote music appreciation in America (and hence interest in buying pianos), Steinway and his father built Steinway Hall on 14th Street in New York City and opened it with a distinguished concert (1867), the first of many the Steinways encouraged (and partly financed). Steinway incorporated (1876), became president, and bought 400 acres of land on Long Island Sound, where he founded the town of Steinway, Long Island, and built a factory. By the 1890s, the company was producing 3,000 pianos a year and exported them widely. Steinway was proud that his instruments were acclaimed the finest in the world. The company also had facilities in Hamburg and London. Steinway supported the arts, was generous in other ways, was a civic leader, served on several municipal boards, and was chairman of the commission that planned the first subway in New York City. He married Johanna Roos in 1861 (the couple had two children) and Elizabeth Raupt in 1880 (the couple had three children).

Stickney, Trumbull (1874–1904). (Full name: Joseph Trumbull Stickney.) Poet. He was born near Geneva, Switzerland. His father was a Harvard graduate (1852) who taught classics at Trinity College, in Hartford, Connecticut, and traveled with his family on inherited wealth. He and his domineering wife had two daughters and then two sons. With his family, Joseph lived in Italy, Switzerland, New York, Germany, France, and England (1874–1885); he went to boarding school in England (1886); then lived with his family again in New York, New England, France, and England (1886–1891). He attended Harvard, where he concentrated on classics (graduating in 1895). At Harvard, he was taught by several influential teachers, including Lewis E. Gates* and George Santayana;* made friends with fellow students George Cabot Lodge,* Robert Morss Lovett,* and William Vaughn Moody;* published precious and gloomy verse, naive short fiction, and antimodernist essays and reviews in the Harvard *Advocate* and the *Harvard Monthly* (1892–1895); and became aloof during his junior and senior years.

Stickney studied at the Sorbonne for the *Doctorat ès Lettres* (1895–1903); traveled expensively; composed (1896–1899) his *Eride* sonnets to an unidentified love and *Prometheus Porphoros* (1900), which expressed his defiant search for unattainable perfection; enjoyed friendships abroad with Henry Adams* (and Adams's intimate friend Elizabeth Sherman Cameron, wife of Senator James Donald Cameron—did Stickney love her?), Henri Hubert (French social anthropologist), Lodge, and Augustus Saint-Gaudens;* translated part of the *Bhagavad-Gita*; and published reviews in Italian (1900–1901), essays on art for the *Nation*, *Dramatic Verses* (1902), and *Les Sentences dans la Poésie Grècque* (his Sorbonne thesis, Paris, 1903). Stickney's was the first Sorbonne doctorate awarded to an English or American student. Stickney returned to America, favorably reviewed Edwin Arlington Robinson* (1903), taught Greek at Harvard (1903–1904), did some unfinished translating, and died at the age of thirty of a brain tumor. Lodge, his brother John Lodge, and Moody assembled and published *The Poems of Trumbull Stickney* (1905), which contain melancholy, stoical, pagan lyrical and dramatic verse, the energy of which hints at a future which death nullified. One line affirms that "Error loves and nourishes thy soul."

Stieglitz, Alfred (1864–1946). Photographer, editor, and gallery director. Born in Hoboken, New Jersey, he studied engineering and photographic techniques at the Berlin Polytechnic Institute (1882–1890), returned to New York and worked for a photoengraving firm (1890–1895), and then began to advance the cause of amateur photography. He edited the *American Amateur Photographer* (1893–1896) and *Camera Notes* (1897–1902) and then founded and edited *Camera Work* (1903–1917), thus advancing the careers of many emerging photographers. Stieglitz popularized German avant-garde work and also organized an exhibit of work by members of the National Arts Club (New York, 1902). This show led to the organization of the Photo-Secession, a group of photographers led by Stieglitz, Edward Steichen, and C. H. White (1902). Stieglitz went on to exhibit works by modern European painters and sculptors, was the first to exhibit children's art (1912) and black African sculpture (1914), returned to photography, then directed photographic galleries (1925–1946) to call attention to first-rate photographers and also painters, including Georgia O'Keeffe (whom he married in 1924). Stieglitz's timeless photographs are especially sensitive to clouds, shadows, and snow. All his life, Stieglitz fought to make photography recognized as a legitimate creative art form.

Stockton, Frank R. (1834–1902). (Full name: Francis Richard Stockton.) Fiction writer. He was born in Philadelphia, one of nine children of an elderly Methodist writer and his young, second wife. After high school, Stockton became a wood engraver in Philadelphia and New York City (to 1866). He married Marian Edwards Tuttle of South Carolina in 1860, published a good bit (beginning 1860), and from 1867 devoted himself full-time to writing (newspaper and magazine articles, children's stories, a household handbook, novels) and editing. His *Ting-a-Ling* (1870), now regarded as a children's classic, and his *Rudder Grange* volumes (beginning in 1879), which at first featured a young married couple living in a canal boat with a talkative maid, helped to charm wide audiences. But it was his short story "The Lady or the Tiger?" (*Century*,* November 1882) that made the name Stockton known around the world. Stockton let his readers everywhere wonder whether the princess would signal her unavailable lover to open the door to the woman he has been ordered by the king to marry or to open the door to a man-eating tiger. (An operetta based on the story was produced in 1888.)

Stockton continued to be immensely popular. Of his forty-seven or so books, eighteen were published in the 1890s. Realism encroaches on fancy, Stockton's supreme virtue, in several of them. All the same, many became best-sellers, notably *The Adventures of Captain Horn* (1895), which concerns a shipwreck on the Peruvian coast and which was so popular that Stockton, as was often the case, happily provided a sequel. His last years were somewhat sad. From the late 1870s his eyesight had been poor, and by the 1890s he had to dictate much of his fiction. He moved to New Jersey (1890) and then to Virginia (1899). He decried America's increasing imperialism after the Spanish-American War.* He sensed, rightly, that his brand of fiction was being shouldered aside by the realists and naturalists. Even so, his popular works filled a crying need in the America of his era. He had an engaging personality, a fanciful imagination, and literary fecundity. It is unfortunate that he is remembered today only for "The Lady or the Tiger?"

Stoddard, Charles Warren (1843–1909). Author and educator. He was born in Rochester, New York. His father failed in business there, relocated in San Francisco, and in time sent for his family (1854). Stoddard loved the Pacific Coast and did not want to be shipped back to Rochester for more schooling (1857–1859). He returned to the West Coast to become a San Francisco bookstore handyman, a poet, a friend of journalists and show people, and a student in San Francisco and Oakland, California. In the 1860s, he visited friends and relatives in Hawaii, indulged his homosexual proclivities with native lads there, published *Poems* (1867), converted to Roman Catholicism, and wrote travel sketches concerning Hawaii. In the 1870s, he visited Tahiti, published "A Prodigal in Tahiti" (*Atlantic Monthly*,* 1872), joined San Francisco's Bohemian Club (presided over by Ina Coolbrith*), published *South-Sea Idyls* (1873), went as a traveling correspondent to Europe—where he met Ambrose Bierce,* Joaquin Miller,* Mark Twain,* and other writers—and the Middle East (1873–1877), and relaxed back in the United States, where he often borrowed from and sponged on friends, for example, Edmund Clarence Stedman.* In the 1880s, Stoddard did editorial work in Honolulu, visited the Molokai leper colony, taught at Notre Dame, grew sick, traveled on the Continent with a rich widow and her son (1888–1889), and began to teach English literature at the Catholic University of America in Washington, D.C. (1889–1901). Stoddard numbered among his acquaintances Henry Adams,* Mary Austin,* Hamlin Garland,* John Hay,* William Dean Howells,* and Henry James.* Stoddard grew corpulent, was sought out for his stunning conversation, but became an increasingly irresponsible teacher, and was finally released. Toward the end of his life, he stayed with friends and family members, was given a regular income by a rich Ohio couple, wrote sporadically, and settled in Monterey, California, where he died.

Stoddard wrote travel books, religious books, and miscellaneous items. His 1890s books are *Hawaiian Life: Being Lazy Letters from Low Latitudes* (1894), local-color essays on Hawaii as a lost Eden combined with lushly styled autobiographical bits; *The Wonder-Worker of Padua* (1896), a devout biography of St. Anthony of Padua; *A Cruise under the Crescent: From Suez to San Marco* (1898), spotty but often shimmering local-color and reminiscent pieces, but less admirable than his earlier *Marshallah! A Flight into Egypt* (1881); and *Over the Rocky Mountains to Alaska* (1899), a blend of humorous observations and literary and historical references. Stoddard's strangest book is *For the Pleasure of His*

Company: An Affair of the Misty City: Thrice Told (1903). A shapeless, weirdly plotted roman à clef, it details real-life, post–Civil War Bohemians and their hedonistic, abnormal artiness. In it, the scintillating but unselling poetess Elaine is a thinly veiled portrait of Coolbrith.

Stone, Herbert S. (1871–1915). (Full name: Herbert Stuart Stone.) Publisher and magazine editor. He was born in Chicago. While he was still a Harvard undergraduate, Stone and his classmate Hannibal Ingalls Kimball, Jr., began to publish fine books, including works by Bliss Carman,* Eugene Field,* Hamlin Garland,* and George Santayana.* Stone compiled and published "Popular Guide to Chicago and the World's Fair" (1892) to cater to the masses of tourists visiting the World's Columbian Exposition* (Chicago, 1893). Stone and Kimball continued publishing together in Chicago, where they also started the *Chap-Book** (1894), a literary magazine edited by Stone. Stone knew literature; Kimball, printing and finance. Their biggest success was *The Damnation of Theron Ware** by Harold Frederic* (1896). Stone and Kimball split up in 1896. Kimball took the firm's properties to New York; H. S. Stone & Company kept the *Chap-Book*. A year later Stone bought back all of the unsuccessful Kimball's assets at auction (1897). The *Chap-Book* became *House Beautiful* in 1898. Among other authors, Stone published George Ade,* Kate Chopin,* Robert Herrick,* Richard Hovey,* Henry James,* and George Barr McCutcheon,* whose *Graustark: The Story of Love behind a Throne* became a 1901 best-seller. Stone sold his business in 1906 but continued to edit *House Beautiful* until 1913. Stone was drowned when the *Lusitania* was sunk.

The Strenuous Life: Essays and Addresses by Theodore Roosevelt (1900). Collection of magazine articles and speeches given by Theodore Roosevelt* on a variety of occasions. Later editions of *The Strenuous Life* (1901, 1902, 1910, 1918) include later pieces. Roosevelt delivered the title speech in Chicago on 10 April 1899. In it, he exhorts individuals and the nation to avoid sloth, and instead to accept challenges and to press beyond timid limits. America must remember the example of England and her imperial reach and must advance with a strong army and navy. He concludes: "I preach to you, my countrymen, that our country calls not for the life of ease but for the life of strenuous endeavor. . . . Above all, let us shrink from no strife, moral or physical, within or without the nation, provided we are certain that the strife is justified." Other essays and speeches are along similar lines: Be aware that a "good boy" becomes a good man, let your goals match your zeal, perform what you promise, balance study and athletics and socializing, be resolute and vigorous (as in football, "hit the line"), apply ethics instead of merely studying ethics, avoid stealing and bearing false witness, do not idolize professional athletes, encourage "fellow-feeling" among all citizens, help the needy to help themselves, do not let the "best" be the enemy of the merely "good," and be aware that political corruption and "lawless violence" are America's greatest dangers. In other pieces in *The Stren-*

uous Life, Roosevelt praises George Dewey,* Ulysses S. Grant, Alfred Thayer Mahan,* George Washington, the YMCA, and the YWCA; advocates fair labor-management practices; criticizes China's dangerous policy of ethical passivity; expresses hope for friendship between North America and South America; and defends American policies with respect to the Philippine Islands.

Sullivan, John L. (1858–1918). (Full name: John Lawrence Sullivan; nicknames: The Boston Boy, The Boston Strong Boy, The Boy, John L., and The Strong Boy.) Professional heavyweight boxer. Sullivan, the son of Irish-born parents, was born in Roxbury, Massachusetts. He completed grammar school and attended night classes (but not classes at Boston College, as he later claimed); worked as plumber, tinsmith, and mason; and played semiprofessional baseball. Then Sullivan became a professional boxer. He was five feet, eleven inches tall and weighed 193 pounds in 1878. He boxed first in Boston, next in New York and Cincinnati, and soon in many other cities—winning all the way. At this time, all such fights were illegal, but the authorities usually looked the other way. He took the London Prize Ring (bare-knuckle) championship title from Paddy Ryan after nine rounds in Mississippi City, Mississippi (1882) and then defeated English champion Charlie Mitchell in New York (1883; they later fought to a draw after thirty-nine rounds in France, in 1888). In the 1880s Sullivan went on tour conducting profitable four-rounders against all comers, sparring shows in circuses, and similar theatricalities in England and Australia. He won constantly, but he also became dissipated and regularly broke training. He successfully defended his bare-knuckle title for the last time in a grueling bout of seventy-five rounds, which lasted two hours and fifteen minutes, against Jake Kilrain in Richburg, Mississippi, in 100-degree plus temperature, on 8 July 1889. Western hero Bat Masterson was timekeeper. The record-breaking purse was $20,000, but it cost Sullivan more than that to keep out of jail—since bare-knuckle fights were illegal—and he was extradited from New York to Mississippi, where he was indicted, tried, and convicted, but later acquitted on appeal.

Sullivan went on tour as a wretched actor in a miserable play in America and Australia (1890–1891). Back home again, he published a challenge to one and all in March 1892. James J. Corbett* answered the call. The Sullivan-Corbett bout, held in New Orleans on 7 September 1892, was the first heavyweight championship contest to be sponsored by an athletic club rather than by gamblers, to be held in a legal urban ring, and to be fought under the Marquis of Queensbury rules (that is, with gloves, for three-minute rounds, with ten-second knockouts, and so on). Masterson was again timekeeper. Corbett, younger, lighter, and more scientific, defeated Sullivan by a knockout in the twenty-first round. Throughout his career, the most severe critic of Sullivan was Richard Kyle Fox,* proprietor of the *National Police Gazette*, which ran stories and cartoons vilifying him. After his 1892 defeat, Sullivan ballooned to almost 300 pounds, drank more excessively than usual, remained cheery but sometimes grotesquely so, became a classic "has-been" athlete, drifted into poverty, declared bankruptcy, and died (solvent again) of heart trouble and cirrhosis of the liver. Sullivan married Mrs. Annie Bates Bailey in 1883 (the couple had a son who died at age two; they separated in 1884 and were divorced in 1908) and Katherine Harkins in 1910 (she died in 1916).

In his heyday, John L. Sullivan was generous, patriotic, convivial, impulsive, self-confident, and as quick with his tongue as with his fists; he was the workingman's friend and a role model for the feisty among the downtrodden. He was the most popular nineteenth-century sports hero in the world. On the dark side, he was also a thoughtless, flashy, brooding, brutal, vengeful, hedonistic, adulterous and wife-beating alcoholic. His enviable professional prize-bout record was forty-seven victories (twenty-nine by knockout), fourteen decision wins, three draws, and one loss by knockout. Sullivan is notable for helping to move prizefighting from its shadowy place in the counterculture to the brightly lit world of commercial entertainment. He earned well over 1 million dollars in the ring, on tour, as a vaudeville performer, and on the lecture circuit. A ghostwriter helped him write his vivid but often unreliable autobiography, entitled *Life and Reminiscences of a Nineteenth Century Gladiator* (1892); it was promptly parodied in *De Recomembrances of a 19-Cent Scrapper* (1892), by someone using the pen name John L. Sluggervan. It is of interest that Theodore Roosevelt* was one of Sullivan's admirers, welcomed him in the White House, and corresponded with him.

Sullivan, Louis (1856–1924). (Full name: Louis Henri Sullivan.) Architect. He was born in Boston to Irish and Swiss-French parents. He studied at the Massachusetts Institute of Technology, with a Philadelphia architectural firm (1873), with a Chicago firm (1873) that created skeletal-steel designs, and then at L'École des Beaux-Arts in Paris (1874). When he returned to Chicago, Sullivan began an independent practice (1875), became the design partner in his own firm—associating with engineer Dankmar Adler (from 1881)—and was responsible for many buildings internationally acclaimed for their functional form, for their attractive and humanizing embellishments (often plantlike in appearance), and for helping in the evolution of modern skyscrapers. Examples include the Auditorium Building in Chicago (1889), influenced by famous architect H. H. Richardson; the Opera House in Pueblo, Colorado (1890); the Wainwright Building in Saint Louis (1891), a pioneering skyscraper, with vertical piers emphasizing its loftiness; the Transportation Building at the World's Columbian Exposition* in Chicago (1893), which foreshadowed and later long dominated modern architecture; the Bayard Building in New York (1894); the Chicago Stock Exchange (1894); the Guaranty Building in Buffalo, New York (1895), now the Prudential Building; the Schlesinger and Meyer Store in Chicago (1899, extended 1903–1906 and now called the Carson, Pirie, Scott Building); the National Farmers' Bank in Owatonna, Minnesota (1908); and the Merchants' National Bank in Grinnell, Iowa (1914).

It should be mentioned that after Sullivan and Adler went their separate ways

(1895), Sullivan's popularity waned to a degree. His influential *Kindergarten Chats* (1901–1902), serialized in the *Interstate Architect & Builder*, was later published as a book with the same title (1918). In it and in his *Autobiography of an Idea* (1924), Sullivan advocates making American architecture express American life and aspirations. He always tried to have form follow function (stressing skeletal structure and acoustics), argued for organic architecture, and rooted his buildings in nature and democracy. He is famous for combining science (employing a mechanistic, technological, massive, realistic style) and nature (including elements of an organic, curvilinear, ornamental, democratic, romantic style). His most famous pupil, one-time assistant and associate, and professional follower was Frank Lloyd Wright.* Sullivan died in poverty.

Sumner, William Graham (1840–1910). Economist, sociologist, and educator. He was born in Paterson, New Jersey, to which his father, born in England, had immigrated in 1836. Young Sumner soon moved with his parents to Hartford, Connecticut, where his father became a railroad repair shop employee. After attending public schools in Hartford, Sumner entered Yale University (graduating in 1863), studied theology at Geneva, Göttingen, and Oxford (1863–1866), tutored at Yale (1866–1869), and was ordained as an Episcopal priest (1869). He preached in New York City (1869–1870) and in Morristown, New Jersey (1870–1872); then he became a professor of political and social science at Yale (1872–1910). In his classes and outside lectures, he reasoned in favor of a sound monetary system, big business and even trusts, realistic laissez-faire, and civil service reform, and in opposition to protective tariffs, governmental interference, socialism, and the Spanish-American War.* He saw that war as an expression of America's wrong-headed imperialistic adventurism. Sumner published with great conservative force. His works include *A History of American Currency* (1874), *American Finance* (1875), and *A History of Banking in the United States* (1896). In his famous lecture entitled "The Forgotten Man" (1883; published in a much later collection of his essays [1919]), he sympathized with the person he called C, because A and B decide how C will support useless D. That is, C, the "forgotten man," is the self-supporting person who works, saves, and then pays the costs of other people's political and social stupidity. Also active in nonscholarly ways, Sumner was a member of the New Haven Board of Aldermen (1873–1876) and a member of the Connecticut State Board of Education (1882–1910).

Beginning in about 1890, Sumner, who could read a dozen foreign languages effectively, began to broaden his intellectual range to include research in anthropology, custom (i.e., folkways and mores), marriage, politics, religion, and sociology; in addition, he published biographies of Alexander Hamilton (1890) and Robert Morris (1892). His *Folkways* (1907), a study of custom—that fundamental aspect of life underlying much else—is considered a classic in the field of social science. His *Science of Sociology* (4 vols., 1927) was the result of notes of his which were assembled, polished, and considerably rewritten by his Yale successor Albert G. Keller.

Sunday, Billy (1862–1935). (Full name: William Ashley Sunday.) Revivalist. Born in Ames, Iowa, he was reared in orphanages, worked his way through high school, held odd jobs in his early youth, and played professional baseball (1883–1891). He experienced a religious conversion in 1887, married Helen A. Thompson in 1888 (the couple had four children), and became a Presbyterian. Sunday worked for the YMCA in Chicago (1891), was active as a popular evangelist's assistant, started his own career as a revivalist (1896), was licensed by the Chicago Presbytery to preach (1898), and was ordained without examination (1903). Sunday, the most widely known evangelist of his era, espoused a fundamentalist creed together with denunciation of saloons and alcohol. During the first two decades of the twentieth century, his flamboyant, acrobatic, noisy manner of preaching gained him an estimated 300,000 converts and sizable contributions to his coffers. Thereafter, his influence waned to a considerable degree.

Symphony Orchestras. Among the earliest symphony orchestras in the United States were those established in Chicago, 1891; Cincinnati, 1895; Los Angeles, 1897; Philadelphia, 1900; and Pittsburgh, 1900. Only two symphony orchestras were organized before the 1890s: the New York City Symphony (1842) and the Boston Symphony (1881).

T

Taft, Lorado (1860–1936). (Full name: Lorado Zadoc Taft.) Sculptor. Taft was born in Elmwood, Illinois. His father was a liberal Congregational minister, then a geology professor (beginning in 1871) at the Illinois Industrial University (which later became the University of Illinois), and finally a Kansas banker; his mother was a music teacher. From the moment young Taft saw plaster casts of statues unloaded for the university's new museum (1874), he was determined to be a sculptor. He attended the university (B.A., 1879; M.A., 1880), went to Paris to study sculpture at L'École des Beaux Arts and to enjoy atelier life (1880–1883, 1884–1886), and established a studio in Chicago (from 1886). He received commissions and became an active sculptor, teacher—at the Chicago Art Institute from 1886 to 1906 and occasionally at the university—and traveling lecturer on art. He entered into the cultural life of the booming city of Chicago, making friends with such fellow residents as painter Charles Francis Browne and novelists Henry Blake Fuller* and Hamlin Garland,* among many others. Garland became Taft's brother-in-law when he married Taft's sister Zulime. Taft was hired to superintend all the sculptural work at the World's Columbian Exposition* (held in Chicago, 1893) and created some of the sculptured pieces there himself, including *The Sleep of the Flowers* (1892) and *The Awakening of the Flowers* (1892) for the Horticultural Building. Taft went as art critic for Chicago's *Interocean* newspaper to Paris to cover the 1900 exposition there. Taft's early work, in addition to the ones just mentioned, include *General Ulysses S. Grant* (Leavenworth, Kansas, 1889), *Despair* (1898), and a nymph fountain (Chicago, 1898). Taft also created several monumental fountains, portraits, and medallions, including one honoring James Whitcomb Riley* (1916).

Taft's best later group compositions include *Solitude of the Soul* (Chicago, 1901); *Fountain of the Lakes* (1903), a bronze allegorical representation of the five Great Lakes; and *The Blind* (Urbana, Illinois, 1908). His *Black Hawk* (Oregon, Illinois, 1911) is an enormous, fifty-foot concrete figure of an illustrious

Native American. One of Taft's most lasting contributions was his promoting and popularizing of art education in the public schools. His most famous lecture, called "Clay Talk," combined a discussion of the processes of sculpture with a quick hands-on demonstration; Taft first gave this demonstration in 1891 and repeated it 1,500 times all over the country. Taft was a splendid speaker, a generous friend, and a dignified professional. He was awarded many honors. Because of his background, he was pro-French in his sculpture and combined graphic naturalism with mystical touches, but never any modern Impressionism. Taft's writings include *The History of American Sculpture* (1903) and *Modern Tendencies in Sculpture* (1920), which evolved from University of Chicago lectures. Taft married Carrie Bartlett in 1890; she died in childbirth in 1891. He later married his first wife's cousin, Ada Bartlett (1896); the couple had three daughters, one of whom married Senator Paul H. Douglas of Illinois.

Tales of Soldiers and Civilians (1891). (English title *In the Midst of Life: Tales of Soldiers and Civilians*, 1892; rev. and enlarged American and British ed., *In the Midst of Life: Tales of Soldiers and Civilians*, 1898.) Collection of short stories by Ambrose Bierce.* Fifteen of these stories derive from the Civil War; eleven concern civilian life. Most are reprinted from earlier periodical publication. The best are based on Bierce's harrowing Civil War experiences. All are gruesome, including the following especially memorable examples. "Chickamauga" features a deaf-mute child playing happily among gorily wounded casualties of a battle near his home. In "The Coup de Grâce," a captain kills his mortally wounded sergeant to end the fellow's horrible suffering, then looks up and sees that the dead man's brother, a major and the implacable enemy of the captain, has observed the act while approaching with a stretcher. In "A Horseman in the Sky," a Virginian in the Union army kills an enemy cavalryman to prevent his reporting the Union position, and then reveals that the man he killed was his own father. "An Occurrence at Owl Creek Bridge," Bierce's most celebrated story, conveys the thoughts, feelings, and sensations racing through the consciousness of a Confederate civilian spy as he mistakenly believes he has escaped at the precise moment that he is actually being hanged. Finally, the titular hero of "Parker Adderson, Philosopher," a Union army sergeant, is caught by the Confederates and is sentenced to be shot as a confessed spy. He philosophizes wittily, stoically, and bravely—until, at the last moment, he turns to hopeless and cowardly begging. The most frequently cited "civilian" tale is "The Boarded Window." In it, a frontiersman prepares his wife's body for burial next morning, dozes, is awakened by a commotion, and drives a hungry panther from their little cabin through the window—only to discover a bit of the animal's ear beneath his wife's teeth.

It may be added that Bierce's other stories are equally scary, with cleverly prepared surprise endings, and almost always involving death. In fact, of his sixty-eight stories, sixty-six concern death. His short works have been compared to those of Nathaniel Hawthorne and Edgar Allan Poe, but in truth Bierce was, though technically brilliant, always limited and often disgusting.

Talks to Teachers on Psychology: And to Students on Some of Life's Ideals (1899). Collection of lectures by William James.* Two-thirds of the book consists of fifteen informal public speeches James gave to teachers in Cambridge, Massachusetts (1892) and repeated at various institutions and schools. They concern the art of teaching, the stream of consciousness, children, behavior and reactions, habit, the acquisition and association of ideas, interest and attention, the memory, apperception, and the will. The talks to teachers are largely self-help and pep talks. The rest of *Talks to Teachers on Psychology* comprises three additional lectures written out for delivery to students (primarily women): "The Gospel of Relaxation," "On a Certain Blindness in Human Beings," and "What Makes a Life Significant?" The last two are classics. "On a Certain Blindness in Human Beings" concerns "the blindness with which we all are afflicted in regard to the feelings of creatures and people different from ourselves." James urges us to be sensitively responsive to the value not only of all other living creatures, whether they are dogs, pig farmers, Walt Whitman loafing on a bus, or stargazers, but also of "the mere spectacle of the world's presence." "What Makes a Life Significant?" It is struggling against "the powers . . . of darkness"; it is "getting through alive"; and it is enjoying "human life in its wild intensity."

Tammany Hall. Popular name for the Democratic Party machine in New York. It controlled city, county, and state politics throughout the nineteenth century and beyond, by the exercise of bribery, favoritism, fraud, intimidation, patronage, showy charity, and the power of dishonestly obtained money. Founded as the Society of St. Tammany, in New York City (1789), it was named after the benevolent, freedom-loving, and wise Native American Delaware chief Tammenend or Tammany. At first its aim was to combat the restrictive, aristocratic, Federalist form of government. It was incorporated as the Society of Tammany in 1805. Its membership and philosophy began to change (about 1817) when Irish immigrants first gained entry to the society. As early as the 1820s, the society was politically corrupt. In the 1850s, Fernando Wood was the dishonest Democratic mayor of New York. He commanded street gangs and dispensed bribes. But the worst Tammany leader was "Boss" William Marcy Tweed, whose Tweed Ring, by the late 1860s, threatened to gain dictatorial control not only of the city and the county but also of the state itself. Tweed was arrested (1871), was convicted of criminal conduct, and was imprisoned (1873). In the 1890s, after the death of corrupt anti–Tweed Democrat Mayor John Kelly, his even more corrupt protégé Richard F. Croker* gained control. Among brave crusaders in the 1890s against the baleful influence of Tammany Hall, Joseph Pulitzer* was foremost. But it was not until the early 1930s that Tammany influence was destroyed by investigations and court action. It has been estimated that the thievery of the Tweed Ring cost New York City taxpayers at least $100,000,000.

Tanner, Henry Ossawa (1859–1937). African-American painter. Born in Pittsburgh, Pennsylvania, Tanner was the son of an author and a bishop in the African Methodist Episcopal Church. Young Tanner moved with his family to Philadelphia (1866), studied painting under Thomas Eakins* at the Pennsylvania Academy of the Fine Arts (1880–1882), was an illustrator, taught at Clark University in Atlanta, Georgia (1888–1889), and went to Paris for further study (beginning in 1891). Although he left the United States partly to avoid racial prejudice, his teetotaling ways and his keeping of the Sabbath marked him as different yet again from his Bohemian art student friends. Tanner visited the Holy Land twice (1897, 1898) to do research for paintings of dramatic Old and New Testament events. He gradually evolved from an Eakins-like brooding realism into more vague, impressionistic, and subjective work. He visited the United States (1902–1904) but then returned to Paris, where he eventually died. His best works include *The Banjo Lesson* (1893), which presents an old African-American man patiently showing a little black lad how to play, in a naturalistically sketched cabin setting; *Daniel in the Lion's Den* (1896); and *The Raising of Lazarus* (1897).

Tarbell, Ida M. (1857–1944). (Full name: Ida Minerva Tarbell). Author, editor, and lecturer. Tarbell was born in Erie County, Pennsylvania. She first gained fame as a muckraker, along with Lincoln Steffens,* both of whom published in *McClure's Magazine** (founded by S. S. McClure*), as did Finley Peter Dunne,* who in his Mr. Dooley's pieces called Tarbell ''Idarem.'' She helped increase the circulation of *McClure's* with her essays published in it on Napoleon Bonaparte (1894–1895) and Abraham Lincoln (1895–1896, 1898–1899). Her *Life of Abraham Lincoln* was published in book form (2 vols., 1900). Her most significant work is her exposé of the business practices of John D. Rockefeller* and his Standard Oil Company associates. Researched and written over a period of four years and costing McClure almost $50,000, this sensational work first appeared serially in *McClure's* (1902–1904) and was republished as *The History of the Standard Oil Company* (2 vols., 1904). Since Tarbell's father was an oil pioneer who had been ruined by the oil company, Tarbell had personal reasons for writing her exposé. Remaining objective, however, she slowly read through court records, legislative reports, and newspaper accounts; interviewed officers of the company and also their victims; and composed a detached but damning account, which remains one of the best muckraking documents ever written. Tarbell later wrote for *Collier's** and *Cosmopolitan Magazine*.* Her autobiography is *All in the Day's Work* (1939).

Tarkington, Booth (1869–1946). (Full name: Newton Booth Tarkington.) Novelist, short-story writer, playright, and autobiographer. Born in Indianapolis, Indiana, he attended Phillips Exeter Academy (1887–1889), Purdue University (1890–1891, no degree), and then Princeton University as a special student (1891–1893, no degree). At Princeton, he was a bass soloist for the glee club, an actor, and a campus editor and writer. After college, he returned home, tried his hand at creating pen-and-ink drawings for publication, and wrote steadily but without initial success until the end of the 1890s. He published *The Gentleman from Indiana* (1899), concerning the fight a country editor wages against political corruption, and *Monsieur Beaucaire* (serialized in *McClure's Magazine*,* December 1899, January 1900, then appearing in book form in 1900), a highly popular eighteenth-century historical romance about a French duke who disguises himself in England as a barber and has an affair with a titled English lady who is then exposed as a cheat. Tarkington later wrote the popular novel *Penrod* (1914) and its sequels, two prize-winning novels—*The Magnificent Ambersons* (1918) and *Alice Adams* (1921)—memoirs entitled *The World Does Move* (1928), and almost sixty other books of fiction and drama long and short.

Tarkington married Louisa Fletcher in 1902; the couple had one child who predeceased him, and they were divorced in 1911. Tarkington then became a teetotaler and married Susanah Keifer Robinson in 1912. Tarkington knew George Ade* and George Barr McCutcheon,* from their days at Purdue University together, and also Hamlin Garland,* William Dean Howells* (whom he regarded as America's best writer), Henry James,* James Whitcomb Riley,* and other important writers of his time.

The Ten. A group of painters. (Full name: The Ten American Painters.) The Ten include Frank W. Benson, Joseph De Camp, Thomas W. Dewing, Childe Hassam,* Willard Metcalf, Robert Reid, E. E. Simmons, Edmund C. Tarbell, John H. Twachtman (who was after his death replaced by William M. Chase), and J. Alden Weir. All were successful New York and Boston Impressionistic painters. They exhibited together (beginning in 1898), were best in the early years of such shows, and later turned somewhat precious. The Ten presaged the advent of The Eight,* a different, more dynamic, and more influential group.

The Ten American Painters. *See* The Ten.

Tennessee Centennial and International Exposition. The purpose of this exposition, held in Nashville, Tennessee, from 1 May to 31 October 1897, was to popularize frontier life, post–Civil War pride and patriotism, and modern technology. Built just outside of town, near Lake Watauga, the exposition featured a replica of the Parthenon in which were shown art exhibits. Other buildings, mostly classical in style also, were the Agriculture Building, the Auditorium (seating 6,000), the Commerce Building, the U.S. Government Building (with diverse federal exhibits, including some from the Smithsonian Institution), the Machinery Building, the Negro Building, the Minerals and Forestry Building, the Transportation Building, and five specific state and four specific city buildings. Many foreign countries also sent personnel and cultural exhibits. The exposition sold almost 1,200,000 tickets and broke even.

Tennis. *See* Sports.

Tesla, Nikola (1856–1943). Inventor. He was born in Smilijan, Croatia, in what was once Yugoslavia. His parents were Serbians. His father was a clergyman; his mother, a needleworker and home-implement inventor. At age five, young Tesla built a waterwheel without paddles. The death of two of his brothers during his childhood probably helped cause the numerous fears, obsessions, and behavioral quirks that marked his later life. From childhood, he was troubled by sharp mental images, including flashes of light that interfered with his normal vision. At an early age, he developed an incredible photographic memory and the ability to imagine constructions without drawings or models. After attending classes at the Austrian Polytechnic School in Graz (1875–1876) and evidently undertaking some irregular schooling in Prague, Czechoslovakia (to about 1880), Tesla worked for a telegraph office in Budapest, Hungary (1881) and suffered a brief but puzzling nervous breakdown. In 1882, suddenly in a flash, he imagined the principle of his alternating current motor. He was employed as a troubleshooter by the telephone subsidiary of the Continental Edison Company in Paris (1882–1883). He built an alternating current induction motor but, when he failed to secure financial backing from the Germans he approached (1883), he migrated to the United States with a laudatory letter of introduction to Thomas A. Edison* himself (1884).

Communication was no problem for Tesla, who spoke English, French, German, and Italian, as well as various Slavic languages. Edison, however, was a considerable problem. Tesla worked well for the Edison Company, but the cranky Edison was adamantly opposed to Tesla's insistence on the applicability of alternating current, and Tesla soon quit. He formed an electric light company in Rahway, New Jersey, was eased out by his financial backers, and formed a more solid one (1887). He was invited to lecture to the American Institute of Electrical Engineers (1888). His reputation spread quickly, and he began to be popular among Manhattan's elite. By 1891 he had taken out forty patents, with many more to follow. At about this time, George Westinghouse* paid Tesla an uncertain sum for rights to the alternating current dynamos, motors, and transformers of his design. (The million-dollar payment, often mentioned, is incorrect; $40,000 plus royalties on power sold is more likely.) As a consultant for Westinghouse in Pittsburgh, Tesla modified Westinghouse's 133-cycle current to 60 cycles. (Sixty-cycle current is standard to this day.) John Pierpont Morgan* also financed many of Tesla's experiments. In his own New York laboratory, Tesla refined his induction motors and polyphase system (to 1896), which made it possible to generate electrical power in one place and to transmit it over great distances. He experimented with high-frequency alternating current to develop efficient lighting (1889). He invented a high-frequency coil (1891), which was later applied to uses in heating, diathermy, and radio (*see* Radio), and which ultimately led to neon and fluorescent lighting.

Tesla became an American citizen and then visited his widowed mother back in Croatia (1891). He lectured to spellbound scientists in London and Paris, saw his dying mother a final time in Croatia, fell sick there himself, and at the moment of her death had an extrasensory vision of her passing (1892). His alternating current system illuminated the World's Columbian Exposition* (Chicago, 1893). By 1893 Tesla had thought out the principles of what became radio, and he designed a wireless transmission system. (Not until 1943 did the U.S. Supreme Court reverse an initial finding favoring Guglielmo Marconi and rule that Tesla had anticipated Marconi and others with his own basic radio patents.) Tesla helped develop the first hydroelectric generating plant to harness the power of Niagara Falls (1896). He developed unmanned, radio-guided torpedoes and boats (1898). He built a 12-million-volt generator in Colorado to transmit power without wires (1899–1900).

Tesla continued to be productive well into the twentieth century. Some of his theorizing helped lead to atom smashers, computers, cosmic-ray research, electron microscopes, microwave ovens, missiles, nuclear fusion, plasma physics, radar, and robots. Tesla was a confirmed bachelor but had, in addition to innumerable professional admirers, many social friends, including Robert Underwood Johnson* and Mark Twain.* Unfortunately, Tesla was often careless in the manner in which he took and preserved notes concerning his thoughts and experiments; many of his ideas, therefore, have been forever lost. His autobiography, "My Inventions" (*Electrical Experimenter*, May, June, July, October 1919; reprinted in Zagreb, Yugoslavia, in 1977), provides some clues as to his methods and successes. It is of unparalleled significance that many of Tesla's formerly so-called missing papers, evidently requisitioned by U.S. military intelligence officers in 1947, are contained in a classified file in the library of a U.S. defense research agency. Do they concern rumors of Tesla's research into energy transmission through the earth and experiments with disintegrator-beam weapons? The term "tesla" was officially adopted to indicate the magnetic-flux density unit (1956).

Their Silver Wedding Journey (1899). Novel by William Dean Howells.* Basil March has edited *Every Other Week*, a New York magazine, for nine years, and is now tired and a bit sick. So he and his wife Isabel sail off for a European vacation. They observe, comment on, and converse with several fellow passengers, of various backgrounds and social strata. General E. B. Triscoe is with his daughter Agatha. Handsome, unattached L. J. Burnamy is traveling to become the secretary for Stoller, a Chicago newspaper owner now in Carlsbad. These and several less important passengers figure in subsequent land action. After Plymouth and Cuxhaven, the Marches visit Hamburg, Leipzig, and Carlsbad, where Burnamy meets Agatha and rather likes her. He loses his job when Stoller is embarrassed by the socialistic tinge of some of the young man's dispatches, but he gets a job reporting on German theaters. The Marches proceed to Nürnberg, Ansbach, and Würzburg, where Stoller pops up, and go on to Weimar, where Burnamy appears. They visit cold Berlin and proud Potsdam.

In Weimar, Agatha's father gets sick, and the girl and Burnamy plan their engagement. When Agatha finds out about a flirtatious young woman for whom Burnamy bought flowers, she breaks it off. The Marches continue their travel so assiduously—to Frankfort, Mainz, Cologne, Düsseldorf—that they grow tired and homesick. They console sad Agatha in London, then return to New York. Burnamy, ready for a new job, calls on them. Agatha appears, by happy coincidence, and all is well.

The Marches' itinerary in *Their Silver Wedding Journey* parallels that made by Howells and his wife in July–October 1897. In the resulting book, Howells is more attractive as a travel writer than as a novelist. He never lost his ability to sketch tourist attractions and cultural sites deftly. But here his cast of characters is somewhat mechanical, and the plot, while smoothly managed, is contrived. Howells in *Their Silver Wedding Journey* capitalizes on the popularity of Basil and Isabel March, who appeared in four of his earlier novels—*A Hazard of New Fortunes** 1889, *Their Wedding Journey* (1872), *The Shadow of a Dream* (1890), and *An Open-Eyed Conspiracy* (1897)—as well as in three short stories.

The Theory of the Leisure Class (1899). Sociological tract by Thorstein Veblen.* Its purpose is to castigate snobbery and high-society pretentiousness by ridiculing not only a love of material things but also chew-it-up-and-spit-out consumption practices. Veblen, a lifelong critic of American capitalist economy, explains that long ago the leisure class emerged when primitive savagery evolved into barbarism, and when a peaceful way of life changed into chronic social bellicosity. At first, savages were contented and had few needs. But population increased, feeding grounds and females were competed for, men dominated domestic units, and women became drudges. Many weapons and multiple wives became evidence of an individual male's prowess. War and hunting challenged the "best" man, who idled the rest of the time, left productive work and other ordinary jobs to women and inferior men, and took conspicuous pride in his superior leisure. Farming, manual labor, and industry were consigned to subordinates. The elite preferred government work, religious activities (with temples, holidays, and no manual work), dangerous sports, weaponry, nobler types of animals (horses, dogs, and falcons), and the supervision of routine community workers. Leaders oppressed, injured, and killed inhabitants of rival communities. Stopping competition, human or otherwise, was honorable.

Victorious leaders must not merely be successful; they must evidence their status by showy possessions. As societies stabilized, a given ruler could elevate his wife (or one of several wives) and even exemplary servants from lowly industrial labor but still demand arduous subservience from them. In modern times, wives and domestic staffs help the conspicuously successful man of the house reveal his free time for friendship, parties, clubs, and charity work, and help him show off his estate, residence, and property therein—including fancy clothes and jewelry, furniture, objets d'art, utensils, and meals. Consumption of things must also be conspicuous, for example, exotic foods and expensive drinks. One must also conspicuously waste, by hunting what one does not eat, living in a museum-like home, employing a visible excess of servants, buying something expensively handmade when a mass-produced equivalent would do as well, preferring thoroughbred horses and unclean dogs to efficient cats, and even sustaining obvious financial loss without evident suffering. One must also demonstrate vestigial remains of the predatory instinct by going into conservative grab-and-hold banking, litigious law, violent sports, and gambling. Veblen castigates university life (priestly robes, ranks, and courses leading to fraudulent, unproductive leisure) but optimistically sees conservatism countered by scientific training for industrial vocations.

The Theory of the Leisure Class, in which such useful and now popular phrases as ''absentee ownership,'' ''conspicuous consumption,'' ''conspicuous leisure,'' ''conspicuous waste,'' ''pecuniary emulation,'' and ''price system'' figure prominently, was adversely reviewed by orthodox critics but pleased sharper ones, including William Dean Howells.* Veblen followed his often-reprinted classic with *The Theory of Business Enterprise* (1904), *The Higher Learning in America: A Memorandum on the Conduct of Universities by Businessmen* (1918), and other works. For Veblen, history was the story of the immemorial defeat of the lowly, industrious artisan by the ruthless predator. In modern times, the robber baron hinders progress by his conservative ways, which include favoring obsolete modes of production and wealth distribution. Veblen writes about conduct to which the best American novelists, dramatists, and poets of the 1890s were holding up the mirror; and his influence, usually indirect, in the next decades was enormous.

The Third Violet (1897). Short novel by Stephen Crane.* (Before publication, it was tentatively entitled ''The Eternal Patience''; it was serialized in October and November 1896 in *Inter Ocean* and in the New York *World*.) Billie Hawker, a struggling artist in New York City, leaves his Bohemian studio to visit his hardworking old parents, his two young sisters, and the family dog Stanley, back on the farm. He also plans to do some painting while he is there. At the train station, he meets rich, aristocratic Miss Grace Fanhall, on her way to a nearby resort hotel called Hemlock Inn. In the morning Hawker encounters his friend George Hollanden, a writer, who is also at the inn, and learns from him that in addition to some stuffy old female guests, Grace is vacationing there with her deceased brother's wife and two children. Present also are the young Worcester sisters, chaperoned by their placid mother. The young people get together, play some tennis, climb hills, and go picknicking and boating. Hawker and Grace do not hit it off very well. When the rather gauche fellow comments about her heiress status, she cannot help gently reproving him. When she praises his artwork, he ridicules it. A rich rival named Jem Oglethorpe drifts in and plays a little tennis too. When he departs temporarily, Hawker awkwardly expresses his relief to Grace, whom Hawker's father delights by giving her an ox-wagon ride to the inn.

The scene shifts to the rooms in New York City of a group of impoverished artists: Wrinkles, Grief (Warwickson, a.k.a. Great Grief), Penny (Pennoyer), and Purple Sanderson. They exchange banter about work, money, and food. In comes a peppy model named Florinda ''Splutter'' O'Connor, who loves Hawker—with resentful hopelessness. Hawker returns to his studio, across the corridor from the other painters. They kid him about the two violets he has been mooning over, given to him by Grace on separate occasions at the Hemlock Inn. Hawker calls at her brownstone home in Manhattan, but she is out; so he returns to his Bohemian friends for supper, wine, and cigarettes. He walks Splutter to her mother's Third Avenue home, with no effective talk. Hollanden pops in on the artists and reveals Hawker's interest in Grace. Ignoring Splutter, Hawker calls on Grace, and they discuss artists. He says that his poverty is shameful, but she prefers to define him as brave. Later, near the artists' place, Penny consoles Splutter, when both of them must honestly admit that Grace, who with Hollanden has just visited Hawker, is beautiful. After moping about, Hawker one snowy day calls on Grace, says he treasures his two violets, is surprised when she thrusts a third one at him, calls her serene and cruel, says he is going far away but stays, and is called ridiculous.

This partly autobiographical novel is quite ineffective. Hollanden is Crane's light but unflattering sketch of himself. The Art Students League typecast figures are patterned on Crane's Bowery friends. Hawker in particular derives from the Manhattan painter Corwin Knapp Linson,* on whom Crane sponged off and on (1891–1894). Grace Fanhall owes much to Helen Trent and Lily Brandon Munroe, two of Crane's early loves (1891–1892). The country scenes, including the Hemlock Inn, partly mirror the Hartwood Club and its Sullivan County environs outside Port Jervis, New York, and could also be said to resemble the hills, forests, and lakes in the nearby Catskills and Poconos—familiar areas to Crane. His lawyer brother William Howe Crane had a financial interest in the club. Stanley is the fictional picture of the orange and white setter belonging to Crane's brother Edmund Brian Crane. If Stephen Crane needed to reinforce his personal notions of the world of impoverished artists, he could recall *A Hazard of New Fortunes** and *The Coast of Bohemia* (1893), both by William Dean Howells,* and many other such works, and even grand operas. *The Third Violet* is marred by puppet characters, immature and repetitious dialogue, and jumpy shifts in point of view. It is redeemed only by Crane's painterly handling of outdoor scenes, his acid portraits of gossiping old dowagers, and by lovable Stanley.

Tiffany, Louis Comfort (1848–1933). Painter, designer, and glassmaker. Born in New York City, he was the son of wealthy jeweler Charles Louis Tiffany, the founder of Tiffany and Company. Young Tiffany studied painting, visited Paris and Morocco (1868), and became permanently enamored of French art glass and Islamic art. He concentrated on his painting through the early 1870s, then evinced interest in decorative arts. He experimented with glass (1875), organized with John La Farge* and Augustus Saint-Gaudens* the Society of

American Artists (1877) in reaction to the conservative National Academy of Design in New York, and established a glassmaking plant in Cirona, New York (1878). Tiffany devised his own method of producing what he called Favrile glass (i.e., "handcrafted," from the Latin word *faber*, meaning "craftsman") but which is now known as Tiffany glass. He founded Louis C. Tiffany and Associated Artists in New York (1881), and he quickly became famous for decorating private residences, clubs, and theaters. He designed the chapel for the World's Columbian Exposition* (Chicago, 1893). He made stained and iridescent glassware (from 1893), including beautiful household items—bowls, pottery, vases, lampshades, and bibelots featuring asymmetrical forms, floral patterns, and glowing colors. He reorganized his firm at Tiffany Studios (1900), built a gorgeous villa for himself called Laurelton, in Oyster Bay, Long Island (1904), and founded and endowed the Louis Comfort Tiffany Foundation for deserving art students nearby (1918). Tiffany's creations fell out of fashion in the 1930s, have been greatly admired and much in vogue since the 1950s, and are now widely regarded as America's most outstanding contribution to the Art Nouveau style.

Town Topics. Fortnightly women's magazine. The magazine was started by W. R. Andrews as *Andrews' American Queen: A National Society Journal* in New York in 1879. At $3 a year, it featured society notes from fifty cities—in the East, the South, and the Middle West—and became a weekly in 1880 ($4 a year, 10¢ a copy). Thereafter it included foreign correspondence, short fiction, humor, literary and music reviews, and illustrations. It was retitled *American Queen* (1883–1884; society notes were restricted to the Northeastern seaboard), then *American Queen and Town Topics* (1885), and finally *Town Topics* (1885–1937). Ownership, editors, and editorial policy changed over the years to include a wittily written scandal column called "Saunterings." By 1890 circulation was over 50,000 copies. William D'Alton Mann bought a controlling interest in *Town Topics* (1891) and later became the publisher of the similar monthly *Smart Set** (1900). Mann augmented his income by blackmailing high-society people to pay him for keeping details of their affairs out of *Town Topics*. Those who paid included New York millionaires John Warne Gates, James R. Keane, John Pierpont Morgan,* William Kissam Vanderbilt, and William Collins Whitney. But the feisty mother of John Jacob Astor IV* refused and was accordingly often vilified. *Town Topics* is now regarded as especially valuable for its criticism and fiction. James Huneker* wrote annual music reviews, among other items (1897–1902).

Trans-Mississippi Exposition. This exposition was held in Omaha, Nebraska, in the summer of 1898, to show the world that the failure of trans-Mississippi area pioneers to convert grazing land into one vast farming region had been followed by certain agricultural successes (mainly a patented corn planter, agricultural schools, and an enormous local meat-packing industry), as well as success in cultural ventures. Structures at the exposition, usually classic in architectural style, included the Agriculture Building, the Fine Arts Building, the Machinery Building, the Manufacturing Building, and the Mining Building. Two special attractions, one admirable, the other less so, were the Arch of States (made of twenty-three Western states' adjoining coats of arms) and a hootchy-kootchy "Streets of Cairo" midway dance show. A controversial attraction was a large teepee in which were Native American tribal exhibits and outside which were numerous Native American camps and even mock battles between redskins and whites. Geronimo,* the Apache chief, some years after his surrender, was even induced to display himself at the exposition. African-American, Chinese, and Filipino villages, and a Venetian-style lagoon, among other features, provided still more variety and helped to promote the exposition, which rang up a creditable attendance figure of some 2,700,000. The exposition was celebrated by the issuance of American commemorative stamps. (*See* Commemorative Postage Stamps.)

Travel and Travelers. After the Civil War ended, Americans began to travel in greater numbers, but not until several decades later did transoceanic voyages become comfortable enough and cheap enough for hordes of middle-class Americans, including those who lived west of the Atlantic seaboard, to set sail. In addition, better tourist services (notably the well-trained employees of Thomas Cook and Company) and improved Continental rail travel to the major capitals, museum cities, and spas enticed ever-increasing numbers of Americans abroad. Artists, scholars, the wealthy, travel writers, war correspondents, and diplomats left American shores in record numbers. The young, the adventuresome, and the less wealthy took to buckboards and even bicycles in England and on the Continent, especially along the good roads and colorful byways of England, France, Germany, and Italy. Especially newsworthy travelers and culture-vultures of the 1890s were the money-loaded robber barons and their free-spending wives, nubile daughters, and spoiled sons. In 1900 alone, 100,000 Americans went to Europe. Impressive, though fewer, numbers also went to the Caribbean, South America, Africa, the Pacific islands, and the Far East. The motives of these travelers were varied. Some sought relaxation, cultural enlightenment, or recovery from fatigue, ennui, or sickness; others, adventures in strange locales; a few, subject matter for essays, poems, books, and paintings; many, titled husbands for their daughters.

Writers who recorded the actions of these restless Americans are too numerous to name, but any short list would include Henry Blake Fuller,* Hamlin Garland,* John Hay,* Lafcadio Hearn,* William Dean Howells,* Henry James,* Charles Warren Stoddard,* Mark Twain,* and Edith Wharton.* Other writers vacationed, and occasionally resided briefly, in Europe and elsewhere abroad, but did not leave especially valuable written records of their time away from home; these include Ambrose Bierce,* Robert Herrick,* Sarah Orne Jewett,* Jack London,* Joaquin Miller,* and Booth Tarkington.* Painters availing themselves of the

European experience include Mary Cassatt,* Childe Hassam,* Robert Henri,* Winslow Homer,* John La Farge,* John Singer Sargent,* and James Abbott McNeill Whistler.* Sculptors include Daniel Chester French* and Augustus Saint-Gaudens.* Musicians include Edward MacDowell* and Ethelbert Nevin.* Scholars include Edward Bellamy,* Bernard Berenson,* W.E.B. DuBois,* John Fiske,* Lewis E. Gates,* G. Stanley Hall,* William James,* George Cabot Lodge,* Orison Swett Marden,* S. Weir Mitchell,* Charles Eliot Norton,* Josiah Royce,* George Santayana,* William Graham Sumner,* and Henry Van Dyke.* Among the fewer Americans who voyaged on Pacific Ocean waters were Henry Adams,* Ernest Fenollosa,* Hearn, La Farge, and Stoddard. Two Americans who were important in the 1890s and who had significant experiences in South America were William James and Theodore Roosevelt.* The best war correspondents of the decade were Stephen Crane* and Richard Harding Davis.*

Some Americans significant to an understanding of the 1890s were born abroad (some to American parents) and then visited or migrated to the United States; they include Berenson, H. H. Boyesen,* Abraham Cahan,* F. Marion Crawford,* Samuel Gompers,* Hearn, Jacob Riis,* Santayana, Sargent, and Trumbull Stickney.* The most notable art collectors who raided European markets were Isabella Stewart Gardner* (counseled by Berenson), William Randolph Hearst* (who often used poor judgment), John Pierpont Morgan* (who had superb taste), and Bertha Honoré Palmer (who was the wife of Potter Palmer*).

International marriages, most of which linked daughters of American millionaires and aristocratic European males, make up a fascinating part of the story of the 1890s. It has been estimated that five hundred such uppity marriages, including many before 1890 and many after 1900, cost the United States half a billion dollars in dowries, ceremonies, and annual allowances. (The skillful illustrator Charles Dana Gibson* skewered these pretentious, title-seeking young American women in superb drawings.) In one year alone, 1895, Anna Gould, Mary Victoria Leiter, Consuelo Vanderbilt, and Pauline Whitney were married to European aristocrats. In addition, Julia Grant married Prince Michael Cantacuzene of Russia, in Newport, Rhode Island, in 1899.

Anna Gould was the daughter of vicious financier Jay Gould,* recently deceased. Attractive, penniless, absurd, witty Boniface (nicknamed Boni), the Marquis of Castellane, pursued her, vacationed with her family, proposed in Quebec, married poor Anna (age nineteen) in New York City, took her to France, lived with her in and out of Paris in palatial splendor, spent Gould wealth on objets d'art, became a father (of three in time), bought and sailed in a 1,600-ton yacht, threw lavish parties, fought two foolish duels, collected race horses, committed adultery, ran up bills, was sued for nonpayment in New York, was criticized bitterly and openly by the Gould family, and was divorced by his long-suffering wife in 1906. She then married (1908) Helie de Talleyrand-Perigord (later Duc de Talleyrand) and had two more children.

Mary Leiter was the beautiful daughter of multimillionaire Levi Zeigler Leiter, former partner of Chicago merchant genius Marshall Field.* She caught the eye of George Nathaniel, Lord Curzon of Kedleston (later viceroy of India) at a party in London (1890). Workaholic Curzon was well educated, bright, stiff (with a crippled and corseted spine), not wealthy at all, scholarly, enamored of politics and travel, and ambitious to marry a rich and intelligent woman. He and Mary struck up an acquaintance, corresponded, saw each other again in London (1891) and in Paris (1893). After he had traveled to Persia and Afghanistan on research they announced their engagement in London (1895), and they were married in Washington, D.C. (1895). Her father gave the couple $1,000,000, an annual stipend of £6,000, and the promise of at least $1,000,000 more for each child if and when they had a family. Curzon and his lady bought fancy residences in England and were beatifically happy together; soon they had two children. Curzon rose in politics, became undersecretary for foreign affairs (1895) and viceroy of India with elevation to baron (1898). He went to India with his family and a nurse (1899). Lady Curzon loved India, admired her husband's pro-Indian diligence, hated the heat, and began to summer in England in 1901. She was sad when after political squabbles he resigned in 1905 and they returned to England. She died there in 1906. Lord Curzon was wretched for a long while, but later he realized that he could not control the legacy old Levi Leiter had bequeathed to Curzon's children once they came of age, and he married Grace Hinds Duggan, a rich American widow (1917).

Consuelo Vanderbilt, the great-granddaughter of Cornelius Vanderbilt, was dragged around India, Paris, and London (1893–1894) by her dictatorial mother, who was in the process of getting divorced from her wealthy but passive husband William Kissam Vanderbilt, brother of George Washington Vanderbilt.* More important, the mother was seeking a title for Consuelo. Suitors flocked about her, and the mother picked the ninth Duke of Marlborough (nicknamed "Sunny," good-looking, but pale, frail, and dainty), whose family also was pressuring him to marry money and thus preserve the family name and estate which was being jeopardized by insufficient funds. Despite the fact that she was, and he had been, in love elsewhere, poor Consuelo, age eighteen, and Marlborough were married in New York (1895). Her father settled $2,500,000 on the couple and also pledged an annual stipend of $100,000 to each of the two. Shortly after the wedding, the New York *World* published a picture of every remaining eligible English duke, with the caption, "Attention, American heiresses. What will you bid?" Marlborough and Consuelo had two sons, which pleased the duke's grandmother, the dowager duchess. After Queen Victoria's death (1901), Consuelo helped officiate at Edward VII's coronation. The couple decided on a legal separation in 1906, by which time $10,000,000 of Vanderbilt money had gone into improving their residences, mainly Blenheim Palace but also their home in London. Consuelo did war-relief work during World War I, obtained a divorce (1918) and then an annulment (1921), and she remarried in 1921.

Pauline Whitney was the daughter of widowed William Collins Whitney, who was a lawyer, politician, and secretary of the navy during the first administration of Grover Cleveland* (1885–1889). She married Almeric Hugh Paget (Lord

Queensborough), in New York, in 1895 (Cleveland attended), and she brought to the bridegroom some $4,000,000, counting her wealthy mother's estate, her father's gift, and her rich bachelor-uncle Oliver Payne's present. She invested so well that at her death in 1916, her husband inherited $15,000,000. He remarried and kept all U.S.–generated funds in England; his and Pauline's daughters Dorothy and Olive subsequently became British high-society disgraces.

Julia Grant was the daughter of Frederick Dent Grant and the granddaughter of Ulysses S. Grant.

Other international marriages of the late nineteenth century include those of May Goelet, niece of William Kissam Vanderbilt's brother Cornelius Vanderbilt's wife Grace Wilson Vanderbilt, to the Duke of Roxburghe; Jennie Jerome of Baltimore to Lord Randolph Churchill (their son was Sir Winston Churchill); and the daughter of Levi Parsons Morton, vice president during the administration of Benjamin Harrison,* to the Duc de Valençay et de Sagan.

A Traveler from Altruria (1894). Utopian novel by William Dean Howells.* Aristides Homos (representing Christian Socialist Howells) travels from his native Altruria (island of altruism), which practices an equality of the sort Americans merely preach, to be the guest of novelist Twelvemough (representing conservative Howells) in a New Hampshire summer hotel in "Egoria" (land of egotism, i.e., America). During his stay, Homos meets various American types: a banker (Mr. Bullion), a minister, a physician, an attorney, a teacher (Professor Lumen), high-society ladies (notably Mrs. Peggy Makely), vacationers, servants, and workers from nearby. He talks with many of these people after dinner his first evening. He is taken (by wealthy society lady Peggy Makely) to the home of a poor farm family (owned by Mrs. Camp and her children Lizzie and Reuben), is persuaded to lecture to a large open-air crowd, and then leaves for New York. The action is less important than the knotty social, economic, and political questions that Homos asks. They concern ecology, farming, money and credit, property rights, labor relations, social classes, marriage, unemployment, education and the professions, art, poverty, exercise and other leisure activities, and successful big business (the current American ideal). Homos also reveals that Altruria is a combination of Hellenic and early Christian cultures. It seems that St. Paul brought true Christianity to its once-heathen shores, but civil unrest and economic strife followed, religion promised happiness in the next world rather than in this world, competition and accumulation jeopardized life itself, and might made right. But then altruism slowly triumphed over all obstacles. Homos identifies Altruria's present-day idealistic beliefs and practices with regard to manufactured goods, culture centers, peace, nondenominational Christianity, absence of money, and, therefore, absence of crime and vice. Only the down-to-earth members of his audience believe Homos, who soon leaves for New York—to the relief of the skeptical Twelvemough and his associates.

A Traveler from Altruria grew out of a series of letters of the same title, which Howells published in the *Cosmopolitan Magazine** (November 1892–October

1893). A second series, entitled "Letters from an Altrurian Traveler," appeared in the same magazine (November 1893–September 1894). Howells published a revision of the last six of these letters as *Through the Eye of the Needle* (1907). This second utopian novel, in which the satirical tone is softened, presents more adventures of and lectures by Aristides Homos, who marries a rich young New York widow and takes her back (without her millions) to Altruria, from which she happily writes informative letters back home. Howells was sincere in his liberal beliefs, but he also sought to capitalize on the popularity of utopian fiction, especially *Looking Backward: 2000–1887** by Edward Bellamy.* Howells's Altrurian romances caused critical controversy, but the author reported receiving countless letters of praise from ordinary readers.

"The Turn of the Screw" (1898). Long short story by Henry James.* In this story, the narrator, an unnamed governess, is hired in London, for her first assignment, by the indifferent uncle of Miles and Flora, two beautiful and precocious little orphaned siblings, to oversee their education at the lonely British estate of Bly. The nervous young woman sees, or thinks she sees, the ghosts of Peter Quint, former steward at Bly now reportedly dead, and Miss Jessel, the children's former governess, also deceased. The governess thinks that this nefarious pair are trying to corrupt the children; so she endeavors to shield them. She enlists the moral support of Mrs. Grose, the evidently simple housekeeper at Bly. The governess hopes to impress her absent employer, the children's uncle, but does not want to disturb him. As the climax nears, she challenges Flora to admit that she has been with Miss Jessel down by the lake; but the girl denies it, will not see the governess again, and is taken away to London by Mrs. Grose. Meanwhile, the governess and Miles share a tense last supper; when she sees Quint just outside the window, she embraces the boy protectively, but he dies in her arms.

"The Turn of the Screw" may well be the finest ghost story ever written. James makes it unique by his special brand of ambiguity, and in his several comments on it he never gives away the secret. Are the ghosts real? Or are they figments of the governess's imagination, inflamed both by Victorian sexual repression and her late-night reading? Or did James want readers to consider both possibilities?

Turner, Frederick Jackson (1861–1932). Historian, scholar, and educator. Turner was born in Portage, Wisconsin. His father was a newspaper editor and politician. After young Turner graduated from high school, he worked as a typesetter for his father (1878–1880), then he attended the University of Wisconsin (B.A., 1884). He worked as a correspondent for Chicago and Milwaukee newspapers (1884–1885), tutored rhetoric and oratory at the University of Wisconsin (1885–1888), earned his master's degree in history there (1888), and began to study at Johns Hopkins (1888). Turner taught at the University of Wisconsin (1889–1910) and earned his Ph.D. at Johns Hopkins (1890). Turner made a unique name for himself as an American historian when he read his paper entitled "The Significance of the Frontier in American History"* during the 12 July 1893 session of the American Historical Association, held at the World's Columbian Exposition* in Chicago. The contents of this controversial paper have been debated ever since, but no historian doubts its towering importance. Turner continued to do research into and publish on aspects of American history, and to teach at Wisconsin and then at Harvard (beginning 1910). He became president of the American Historical Association (1910) and was visiting lecturer and scholar at various institutions, even after his retirement from Harvard (1924). Of his dozens of publications, long and short, after "The Significance of the Frontier in American History," the most important are *The Rise of the New West, 1819–1829* (1906), *The Frontier in American History* (1920), and *The Significance of Sections in American History* (1932). Turner married Caroline Mae Sherwood in 1889 (the couple had three children).

Twain, Mark (1835–1910). (Real name: Samuel Langhorne Clemens.) Journalist, humorist, novelist and short-story writer, satirist, travel writer, and lecturer. Clemens was born in Florida, Missouri, but soon moved with his family to Hannibal, Missouri (1839). After the death of his father in 1847, Clemens left home to become a journeyman printer and neophyte newspaperman (1853–1857), Mississippi River steamboat pilot (1857–1861), Western journalist (1861–1866), and traveler to the Mediterranean Sea area and the Holy Land (1867). He married Olivia Langdon in 1870. Twain maintained a residence in Elmira, New York (1870–1871), Hartford, Connecticut (1871–1896), Europe and London (1891–1895, 1897–1900), New York (1900–1908), Florence, Italy (1903–1904), and Redding, Connecticut (1908–1910). He was obviously very unsettled. Over the years, he lectured in various places in the United States, in England (1872, 1873), and then literally around the world (1895–1896—see *Following the Equator: A Journey around the World**).

Twain's major works, with emphasis on those of the 1890s, include *The Innocents Abroad* (1869), *Roughing It* (1870), *The Gilded Age* (1873, coauthored with Charles Dudley Warner), *The Adventures of Tom Sawyer* (1876), *The Prince and the Pauper* (1882), *Life on the Mississippi* (1883), *Adventures of Huckleberry Finn* (1884), *A Connecticut Yankee in King Arthur's Court** (1889), *The American Claimant* (1892), "Extracts from Adam's Diary" (1893), "The £1,000,000 Bank-Note" (1893), *Tom Sawyer Abroad* (1894), *Pudd'nhead Wilson, A Tale** (1894), "Fenimore Cooper's Literary Offenses" (1895), "What Paul Bourget Thinks of Us" (1895), *Personal Recollections of Joan of Arc** (1896), *Tom Sawyer Abroad, Tom Sawyer, Detective, and Other Stories*, (1896), *Following the Equator: A Journey around the World** (1897), "Concerning the Jews" (1899), "The Man That Corrupted Hadleyburg"* (1899), "China and the Philippines" (1900), "Dinner to Hamilton W. Mabie [*]" (1901), "To the Person Sitting in Darkness" (1901), *What Is Man?* (1906), *The Mysterious Stranger* (1916, other versions published later), and *Letters from the Earth* (1963).

Although he turned fifty-five in 1890, Twain shared with the younger writers of the 1890s a diminution of religious faith (to put it mildly in his case), awareness from firsthand observation of the importance of the Far West, hatred of "Gilded Age" robber barons and corrupt politicians, sympathy for oppressed laborers and the victimized poor, and disgust at American expansionism. In a few of his lectures and minor writings, Twain mentions Thomas Bailey Aldrich,* whose 1870 novel *The Story of a Bad Boy* influenced his depictions of Tom Sawyer and Huckleberry Finn, Harold Frederic,* and Theodore Roosevelt.* Although they were kindred spirits in many ways, Twain and Ambrose Bierce* were never friends. Twain blasts away at Mary Baker Eddy* in *Christian Science with Notes Containing Corrections to Date* (1907) and "Secret History of Eddypus, the World-Empire" (1872). He met Charles Warren Stoddard* in California in the 1860s, hired him as a live-in secretary while he lectured in London (1873–1874), and followed his activities later, often through correspondence with their mutual friend William Dean Howells.*

Twain was hilarious with most of his friends and was happy in his home life—that is, until tragedy struck. He and his wife had four children. But his only son died in infancy. Then one daughter died, in 1896, his wife in 1904, and another daughter in 1909 (a few months before his own death). Four of Twain's closest friends were George Washington Cable,* with whom he lectured on a tour managed by James B. Pond* (1884–1885); John Hay;* Howells, whom he regarded as America's greatest novelist; and Henry Huttleston Rogers,* a Standard Oil robber baron. It was Rogers who counseled him on financial matters, so successfully in the 1890s that Twain moved from an indebtedness of more than $100,000 in James W. Paige's typesetting machine (1894) to assets equal to more than $300,000 five years later.

Two Bites at a Cherry, with Other Tales (1894). Collection of short stories by Thomas Bailey Aldrich.* The title story tells how Bostonian Marcus Whitelaw meets Rose Mason, still a lovely woman, in the cathedral of Naples, Italy, while they are attending the May ceremony of the liquifaction of the blood of Saint Januarius. Some fifteen years have passed since Whitelaw unsuccessfully proposed to Rose, and she married a California railroad "despot," who Whitelaw (though traveling afar) has heard is now dead. Whitelaw, glad Rose is not hiding her beauty in widow's black, is smitten anew; and she seems responsive. Determined not to delay, he proposes again. But she says that she has already remarried. The surprise ending of this richly detailed, well-paced story is cleverly led up to, but its title has its drawbacks. A better story in the collection is "For Bravery on the Field of Battle," in which a quiet New Englander fights well in the Mexican War, loses a leg saving his captain's life, and returns to the plaudits of his hometown. He is soon forgotten and in time dies alone.

Two Years in the French West Indies (1890). Travel essays by Lafcadio Hearn.* The two volumes are entitled "A Midsummer Trip to the Tropics" and "Martinique Sketches." "A Midsummer Trip to the Tropics" is divided into thirty-three usually short fragments. There is almost no narrative structure. The narrator moves through blue and bluer waters, to Martinique, where first he dilates upon interracial sexual unions (Hearn had an illegal African-American wife in Cincinnati) and then slobberingly depicts native flesh in ten shades of black. He also draws vivid word pictures of lush foods, coastal and fishing scenes, an abandoned British town, and especially the fer-de-lance, the poisonous native viper. "Martinique Sketches" is divided into fourteen longer sections, often interlinked. One sketch, called "Un Revenant," concerns Père Labat, who named Martinique "le Pays de Revenants," sought in vain to return there, and became the subject of Creole ghost tales. "La Guiablesse" describes a female zombie. "La Pelée" takes the reader on an arduous climb up the famous volcanic mountain. "Bête-ni-pié" catalogues a variety of insects and reptiles, ending with the huge and repulsive bête-ni-pié centipede itself. "Pa Combiné, Ché!" [Don't think that way] is a potpourri discussion of local and Creole fruit, cooking, talk, beliefs, sickness, and sorrows—ending in cynical bitterness. *Two Years in the French West Indies* is memorable for incidental stylistic splendors, is marred by Hearn's boredom amid nature's dangerous largesse, and lacks the virtue of having its parts add up to a whole.

U

Unguarded Gates and Other Poems (1895). Collection of poems by Thomas Bailey Aldrich.* In the title poem, Aldrich opposes the immigration policy of America, on the grounds that swarms of eastern and southern Europeans are bringing "unknown gods and rites," "tiger passions," and "strange tongues" into a land which "Liberty, white Goddess" ought to guard more carefully. Aldrich went further in a letter to critic George Woodberry (14 May 1892), in which he called his poem a "protest against America becoming the cesspool of Europe."

Universities. By about 1885, the better American universities had introduced the elective system and also graduate schools. Thereafter, enrollments increased. Successful immigrant families, predominantly of northern European origin, began to see the social, commercial, and professional advantages of higher education, as well as the snob appeal of academic degrees. State legislatures and private donors supported universities and colleges more substantially. Schools became increasingly institutionized, with authoritative presidents, more active deans, ever-increasing bureaucracy, distinct ranks with faculties, and new, separate, and competing departments. By the end of the nineteenth century, the greatest American universities certainly included the following endowed ones: Chicago, Columbia, Cornell, Harvard, Johns Hopkins, Pennsylvania, Princeton, Stanford, and Yale. And they included the following state universities: California, Illinois, Michigan, Minnesota, and Wisconsin. By comparison, other institutions of higher learning may have been significant but overall, and regardless of the measures used, somewhat less so. (The Carnegie Foundation for the Advancement of Teaching listed, as of 1908, the above universities as the top fourteen in terms of money spent annually on instruction.)

All but Stanford and Chicago were well established by the 1890s. Stanford was in its infancy as the decade began. Leland Stanford Junior University, to call it by its full name, was founded in 1885 by Leland Stanford, one of The Big Four,* and by his wife Jane Stanford, following the early death of their only child. It was built on their country estate on the San Francisco Peninsula. David Starr Jordan was the first president. He had an M.D. from Indiana Medical College, taught in Indiana, and was president of Indiana University (from 1885) when Stanford lured him away in 1891. Classes at Stanford University first began in October of that year. The faculty of seventeen was expanded to twenty-nine by the second year. Graduate instruction was available from the start, and faculty members were engaged in research as well as in teaching. Jordan, who headed the university until 1916, installed a major system, and the only required entrance subject was English. The aim of the school was to strengthen its students to assume leadership roles in a free society unfettered by moribund tradition.

The University of Chicago was founded as a private, nonsectarian institution, by an initial gift in 1891 from John D. Rockefeller* of $600,000, and it was built on grounds donated by Marshall Field,* Chicago wholesale and retail dry goods merchant. The American Baptist Education Society also helped establish the university. William Rainey Harper was the first president of the University of Chicago. Harper had earned a Ph.D. in biblical studies from Yale at the age of eighteen and had taught at Denison University (Ohio), the Baptist Union Theological Seminary in Chicago, and Yale before he went to the University of Chicago, which he headed until his early death in 1906. Classes opened in 1892. The first faculty, all well paid, included eight former university and college presidents. In time, they were joined by John Dewey,* Robert Herrick,* Robert Morss Lovett,* William Vaughn Moody,* and Thorstein Veblen.* The Panic of 1893* caused much concern for a time. The trustees raised and contributed $1,000,000 and also cooperated well with Harper, who introduced the quarter system (including a summer school), a university extension, and downtown classes; founded a university press; and insisted on faculty control of athletic programs. In the first decade, Harper supervised the erection of twenty-nine buildings, costing $4,000,000. During this time, the Divinity School was well established and the Law School substantially so, plans for a medical school were well under way, and schools in technology, music, and the arts were all in the offing.

Two other distinguished institutions of higher learning got their start in the 1890s. They are Clark University and the California Institute of Technology. Clark University, in Worcester, Massachusetts, was founded in 1887 as a private, nonsectarian institution by the endowment of Worcester merchant Jonas Gilman Clark to make graduate studies in sciences available at low cost to New Englanders (men only, at first). From its inception, research was stressed. G. Stanley Hall,* the eminent psychologist, was the first president of Clark University. He helped to recruit an excellent faculty and to build its reputation. The California Institute of Technology began as the Throop Polytechnic Institute, a trade and crafts school founded in Pasadena, California, by Amos G. Throop in 1891. It moved to its present campus in 1910 and changed its name in 1920 to the one by which it is now known. Cal Tech is a privately supported coeducational center for study and research in astronomy, biology, chemistry, engineering, physics, and seismology.

Unleavened Bread (1900). Novel by Robert Grant.* Selma White is a social climber, unaware of her own hypocrisy, which makes her a complex bad heroine. She opportunistically marries Lewis J. Babcock, a varnish dealer in the western city of Benham. Getting involved in plans for a new Episcopalian church, she soon admires Wilbur Littleton, the New York architect retained for the project. While she is attending a feminist meeting in Chicago, her husband gets mixed up with a woman at a country fair. Selma welcomes his infidelity as an excuse for divorce, which causes the local minister to conclude that she lacks "the leaven of feminine Christian charity." (Hence the title *Unleavened Bread.*) She steps up by marrying Littleton and goes with him to New York, but soon she becomes discontent with her plight there. Her new husband has insufficient income and she dislikes his nice sister; although three years pass, at least they have no children. The couple argue but do not get divorced. When Littleton is named architect to design some college buildings back in Benham, Selma is happy at the thought of leaving New York, but overworked Littleton declines, contracts pneumonia, and dies.

Though ambitious to go it alone, perhaps as a lecturer or an actress, Selma accepts the invitation of Mr. Parsons, a rich, sick resident in Benham, to be his housekeeper and friend. Then, through some ensuing school board activity, she meets sturdy widower James O. Lyons, a local lawyer turned politician. Parsons names Lyons his executor, dies, and leaves Selma considerable money and the city even more, for a new hospital, plans for which throw Lyons and Selma together. She accepts his proposal of marriage—on condition that he get elected to Congress. He does, but Washington society is yet another source of frustration for her. The pair return to Benham, and Lyons runs for governor. He wins when influential Horace Elton offers aid in return for a promise that Governor Lyons will support a bill giving him a cushy gas franchise. Selma is pleased at being in the social limelight—until a moral crisis looms. When a senator dies and Lyons wants to be elected as his replacement, it becomes clear that he can win only if he vetoes the bill Elton requires. Selma floridly persuades her husband that he must violate his pledge, veto the bill, and rise politically. And he does so.

Selma is a typical modern bad heroine, somewhat unusual in 1890s fiction. She has fierce energy and cruel cleverness, but she lacks depth. Hence her story reveals that gaining wealth is a useless undertaking if, in the process, one loses or fails to make use of moral responsibility. *Unleavened Bread* was a best-seller, turned Grant into a serious writer, was praised by William Dean Howells,* was admired by Theodore Roosevelt* for showing the dangers of the feminist movement, and influenced Edith Wharton* when she wrote *The Custom of the Country* (1913). Grant helped Leo Ditrichstein adapt *Unleavened Bread* for the stage

(1901), and he resurrected the vicious Selma in two later novels—*The Undercurrent* (1904) and *The High Priestess* (1915).

Up from Slavery: An Autobiography (1901). Autobiography by Booker T. Washington.* In his preface, Washington explains that his book grew out of articles published in *Outlook* magazine and was written at odd moments while he was traveling or otherwise working to advance the cause of his beloved Tuskegee Normal and Industrial Institute. He regrets its imperfections. *Up from Slavery* contains seventeen chapters and is mostly a straightforward, simple, unpretentiously eloquent narrative in chronological order about his being born a slave, his childhood, his struggle for an education, his poverty while he was a student at the Hampton Institute, his brief time as a seminary student in Washington, D.C., his teaching Indians and night school at Hampton, the founding of the normal and industrial school at Tuskegee and his early difficult days there, his fund-raising activities in the North, and his participation in the Cotton States and International Exposition* at Atlanta. The last three chapters, which are more discoursive, deal with Washington's success as a public speaker, his travels in Europe, and his "Last Words."

Up from Slavery skillfully combines personal reminiscence, specific anecdotes, generalizations, important letters to and from Washington, long quotations about him from newspapers and other sources, and—throughout—a combination of modesty and inevitable self-praise. Two of the most revealing passages are the following: "In this address [to the National Education Association, Madison, Wisconsin, summer 1884] I said that the whole future of the Negro rested largely upon the question as to whether or not he should make himself, through his skill, intelligence, and character, of such undeniable value to the community in which he lived that the community could not dispense with his presence. I said that any individual who learned to do something better than anybody else . . . had solved his problem, regardless of the colour of his skin." And this: "I had never sought or cared for what the world calls fame. I have always looked upon fame as something to be used in accomplishing good. I have often said to my friends that if I can use whatever prominence may have come to me as an instrument with which to do good, I am content to have it. I care for it only as a means to be used for doing good, just as wealth may be used." *Up from Slavery* should be read in conjunction with Washington's more hasty, amateurish, and commercially oriented autobiography, *The Story of My Life and Work* (1900; rev. eds. 1901, 1901, 1915). In both works, Washington includes mention of his contacts, brief or otherwise, in person or by correspondence, with such 1890s notables as Alexander Graham Bell,* Andrew Carnegie,* Grover Cleveland,* Frederick Douglass,* Benjamin Harrison,* William Dean Howells,* Collis P. Huntington,* Hamilton W. Mabie,* William McKinley,* Thomas Nelson Page,* Walter Hines Page,* John D. Rockefeller,* Augustus Saint-Gaudens,* and Mark Twain.* It should be noted that most of Washington's books were ghostwritten, at least in part. Max Bennett Thrasher helped Washington with *Up from Slavery*.

To be specific, it evolved from a series of articles suggested by S. S. McClure,* Walter Hines Page* (of Doubleday, Page and Company), and Lyman Abbott, editor of *Outlook*, in which it appeared serially (3 November 1900–23 February 1901). Page published it in book form (March 1901). It was a substantial critical success but at first only a moderate sales success. However, it was reprinted in England and circulated worldwide, and was soon translated into at least fifteen foreign languages. More important, it raised the spirits of African-American readers and also helped whites to a better understanding of the plight of American blacks. Howells wrote a complimentary review essay in the *North American Review* (August 1901). *Up from Slavery* is now considered a classic.

V

Van Dyke, Henry (1852–1933). Clergyman, author, educator, and diplomat. He was born in Germantown, Pennsylvania, but he grew up in Brooklyn, where his father, a Presbyterian pastor, preached. Van Dyke graduated from Princeton (1873) and its Theological Seminary (1877), and then he studied in Berlin (1877–1878). He became a Congregational minister in Newport, Rhode Island (1879–1883) and a Presbyterian minister in New York City (1883–1899). Having published *The Poetry of Tennyson* (1889) and other critical studies, Van Dyke taught English literature at Princeton (1899–1913). He lectured at the Sorbonne in Paris about American culture and society (1908–1909) and was appointed U.S. minister to the Netherlands and Luxembourg (1913–1916), but he resigned because of America's neutrality during the early years of World War I. Van Dyke married Ellen Reid in 1881 (the couple had nine children, five of whom survived their father). Van Dyke knew many persons significant in the 1890s, including Grover Cleveland,* William Dean Howells,* Hamilton W. Mabie,* Walter Hines Page,* James Whitcomb Riley,* and Mark Twain.* Van Dyke was a lovable author on a variety of subjects. His main works include "Is This Calvinism or Christianity?" (1890), an early address defining his centrist theological position; *Little Rivers* (1895), about fishing, Van Dyke's favorite sport; *The Gospel for an Age of Doubt* (1896), based on conservative lectures delivered at Yale; *The Other Wise Man* (1896), a popular fable, originally a long sermon and later widely translated, about the influence of a fourth "wise man" at the time of Christ's birth; *The First Christmas Tree* (1897), another sermon turned into a booklet; *Fisherman's Luck* (1899); *The Ruling Passion* (1901), a collection of romantic tales; and numerous other later works, once popular but no longer highly valued.

Van Dyke, John Charles (1856–1932). Art critic and librarian. Van Dyke was born in New Brunswick, New Jersey. His father served in the U.S. Congress and was a New Jersey supreme court justice. Van Dyke moved with his family to Minnesota (1868), where he was conventionally educated but also became an able horseman. He attended law school at Columbia, was admitted to the bar (1877) but did not practice, and became a librarian at the New Brunswick Theology Seminary (1878–1932). In his ample free time, Van Dyke studied art, often traveling widely to do so, wrote books on the subject, lectured on modern art at Rutgers (1889), and became a professor of art history there (1891–1929). He was a contributing essayist to *Century** on art (1884–1904) and wrote from a highly personal point of view. Van Dyke also spent much free time in Arizona, California, and Montana, developed a profound love of natural beauty, and often wrote on the subject. He was an observant, determined, and personally gracious man. His books include *How to Judge of a Picture: Familiar Talks in the Gallery with Uncritical Lovers of Art* (1880, reprinted in the 1880s and 1890s), *Art for Art's Sake: Seven University Lectures on the Technical Beauties of Painting* (1893; 12th ed., 1901), *A Text-book of the History of Painting* (1894; 5th ed., 1901), *Nature for Its Own Sake: First Studies in Natural Appearances* (1898; 4th ed., 1901), and *The Desert: Further Studies in Natural Appearances* (1901). Van Dyke wrote later works based on extensive visits to art galleries in Austria, Germany, Hungary, Madrid, Paris, Rome, and Russia, and also more books attesting to his love of the Far West. Van Dyke feels that nature is best appreciated when the ego is suppressed, when details are observed and harmonized, and when the mind accepts mutability and beauty as beyond understanding.

Vanderbilt, George Washington (1862–1914). Vanderbilt family scion, agriculturalist, and benefactor. Born in New Dorp, Staten Island, New York, he was the youngest of the four sons of William Henry Vanderbilt and hence the grandson of fabulously wealthy Cornelius Vanderbilt. Young Vanderbilt was educated by and traveled extensively with private tutors, and was shy as a youth. Inheriting vast wealth, he became a multimillionaire art collector, agriculturalist, forestry pioneer, linguist, and public and university benefactor. When he grew enamored of the mountains of western North Carolina (from 1888), he started to acquire some 125,000 acres just southwest of Asheville (1889) and commissioned architect Richard Morris Hunt and landscape architect Frederick L. Olmsted* to design a classic European-style estate. Gifford Pinchot* helped Vanderbilt introduce scientific agriculture and silviculture throughout the extensive grounds surrounding Biltmore. The main building echoed the architectural lines not only of the residences of Francis I of France but also of certain Loire Valley chateaux, but it was modified somewhat to suit American taste. The result was Vanderbilt's fantastic country home, called Biltmore. Built at a cost of about $3,000,000, it was formally opened on Christmas Eve 1895. Vanderbilt lived there with the help of eighty servants, and he directed various experiments in agriculture, forestry, stockbreeding, and wine making. Biltmore features a banquet hall—seventy-two feet by forty-two feet—a breakfast room, a salon, a ninety-foot art gallery, a 20,000-volume library, central heating, refrigerators, electric lights and appliances, lavish bedrooms, and indoor bathrooms. Guests enjoyed a billiard room, a bowling alley, and an indoor swimming pool. Nearby was a model village containing cottages resembling houses in Cheshire, England.

Vanderbilt married Edith Stuyvesant Dresser in 1898; the couple had one child. Vanderbilt and his wife knew many persons important in the 1890s and later. James Abbott McNeill Whistler* painted portraits of both Vanderbilt (1898) and his wife (started in Paris in 1899, finished in 1902). John Singer Sargent* also painted Vanderbilt (1895). One of their most articulate guests was Henry James,* who slept at Biltmore for a few days (1905) and called the place "a gorgeous practical joke" in a letter to Edith Wharton* (8 February 1905).

Veblen, Thorstein (1857–1929). (Full name: Thorstein Bunde Veblen.) Social scientist, economist, and educator. His parents migrated from Norway to a fertile farm near Cato, Wisconsin (1847), where Veblen was born into a family that ultimately included nine children. They all moved to Minnesota (1865), and Veblen graduated from Carleton College Academy (1880; now Carleton College) with a major in philosophy. He studied briefly at Johns Hopkins, and he earned his Ph.D. at Yale (1884). Failing to find employment as a teacher, he returned to Minnesota, read widely, wrote, and studied economics, partly at Cornell (1891–1892). He began teaching for poor pay at the University of Chicago (1892–1906), Stanford (1906–1909), the University of Missouri (1911–1918), and the New School for Social Research in New York (from 1919). During World War I he was a consultant in Washington, D.C., on industrial aid, but his unorthodox opinions caused his early release.

Veblen's morose and egocentric nature and also his behavior in his private affairs militated against his professional success. He married Ellen May Rolfe, the bright niece of the president of Carleton College, in 1888. She wrote a popular children's book entitled *Goosenberry Pilgrims* (1902). Publicizing his infidelity (1904), she caused his departure from Chicago, joined him again in Stanford (1906), separated thereafter, obtained a divorce (1911), subsequently died (1926). Veblen married Anne Fessenden Bradley, a divorced woman with two children, in 1914. Their marriage was not happy; he neglected her, and she developed serious mental problems and later died (1920). Meanwhile, he lost job after job because of his conduct. Toward the end of his life, he survived on the charity of friends, and he lived in an increasingly slovenly way. He finally died of tuberculosis in sad loneliness.

Veblen's works include *The Theory of the Leisure Class** (1899), his most important book; *The Theory of Business Enterprise* (1904), continued as *Absentee Ownership and Business Enterprise in Recent Times* (1923); *The Instinct of Workmanship* (1914), which he called his best book; *The Higher Learning in America: A Memorandum on the Conduct of Universities by Businessmen* (1918); *The Vested Interests and the State of the Industrial Arts* (1919); and several books on Germany, Aryan culture, and peace. Veblen's mind was sharp and profound, uncompromising and harsh; his writing style—not to mention his life-style—proved somewhat baffling to most would-be followers inasmuch as it was long winded, caustic, ironic, and satirical. But he must be regarded as a uniquely creative author of works on social thought. He coined such useful and now popular phrases as "absentee ownership," "conspicuous consumption," "conspicuous leisure," "conspicuous waste," "pecuniary emulation," and "price system."

The Voice of the People (1900). Novel by Ellen Glasgow.* This novel presents a credible range of social groups—aristocrats, poor-white farmers, common villagers, and disadvantaged African Americans—all in postbellum flux. Several minor characters are especially well limned. The heroine, Eugenia Battle, does not marry Nicholas "Nick" Burr, the man she should, because she comes from wealth, whereas he springs out of peanut-farm poverty. Therefore, well-born (and well-named) Eugenia gets married properly—to Dudley Webb, a juiceless, amoral descendant of a once-proud antebellum Virginia family. Meanwhile, amid vicissitudes, Nick rises by hard work and is determined to study to become a lawyer, a politician, and Virginia's liberal, untouchable governor. His unsuccessful opponent is none other than Webb. Nick suffers a bad-luck death when he tries to rescue an African American from a lynch mob. Yet Nick spiritually survives as a voice for liberalism, while Eugenia's superficial happiness is an occasion for Glasgow's fine irony.

This fine fictional work, with events occurring between 1870 and 1898 in Kingsborough, Virginia, is the first of many novels by Glasgow concerning the cultural history of her native state. Interestingly, Kingsborough is based on Williamsburg, the colonial capital of Virginia restored by John D. Rockefeller, Jr., son of John D. Rockefeller.* Although it is better than her two earlier novels—*The Descendant** (1897) and *Phases of an Inferior Planet** (1898)—*The Voice of the People* is not a great novel. It does, however, give promise of superb fiction yet to come.

W

Walker, Lewis (1855–1934). Manufacturer. Born in Wellsville, Ohio, he graduated from Allegheny College, in Meadville, Pennsylvania (1877). At first he practiced law but soon entered the world of business. While visiting the World's Columbian Exposition* in Chicago (1893), Walker saw an early form of a new type of fastener invented in 1891 by Whitcomb L. Judson.* Over many years, Walker aided Judson and financed a company to develop his fastener, which by 1912 was perfected. A year later Walker and others refinanced the company as the Hookless Fastener Company, in Meadville. In 1928, the fastener, by then called a zipper, was renamed the Talon; in 1937 the company became Talon, Inc. Walker was a progressive businessman and also an admirable civic leader.

Wallace, Lew (1827–1905). (Full name: Lewis Wallace.) Lawyer, soldier, author, and diplomat. He was born in Brookville, Indiana, and was admitted to the bar in 1849. He served as a Union army general during the Civil War (1861–1865), was governor of the New Mexico Territory (1878–1881), and was U.S. minister to Turkey (1881–1885). Wallace, following his first love, which was literature, wrote three sweeping historial novels. *The Fair God: A Story of the Conquest of Mexico* (1873) is based on research and the author's observation of Mexico. *Ben Hur: A Tale of the Christ* (1880), a worldwide best-seller, is the most famous novel in English about the early Christian era; it was dramatized by William Young (1899) and enjoyed a run of two decades. *The Prince of India; or, Why Constantinople Fell* (1893) makes use of Wallace's time in Turkey and features the Wandering Jew. Wallace, who was a painter and a lecturer, also published a biography of Benjamin Harrison* (1888) and an autobiography (1906).

War Is Kind (1899). Collection of poems by Stephen Crane.* In style and content, these poems resemble the ones in Crane's earlier collection, *The Black Riders and Other Lines.** The ironically named title poem begins with mock romantic diction: "Do not weep, maiden, for war is kind. / Because your lover threw wild hands toward the sky / And the affrighted steed ran on alone, / Do not weep. / War is kind." The other poems in the little book inveigh against God, the indifference of pretty nature, and humankind's silly illusions. The most famous poem in the collection is the one in which a man tells the universe that he exists, to which the universe answers that "the fact has not created in me / A sense of obligation."

Ward, John Quincy Adams (1830–1910). Sculptor. He was born on a farm near Columbus, Ohio, attended school regularly but much preferred to model clay figures in a nearby pottery, studied with and worked for realistic sculptor Henry Kirke Brown in Brooklyn (1849–1856), and established his own studio in Washington, D.C. (1857–1859) and then in New York (from 1860). Ward produced much realistic portrait statuary (often of military and political celebrities), as well as other statues, in the next decades. He achieved his greatest successes before 1890, but his bronze statue of seated editor Horace Greeley (New York, 1890), his truculent bronze statue of abolitionist clergyman Henry Ward Beecher (Brooklyn, 1891), and his energetic bronze bust of politician Roscoe Conkling (New York, c. 1892)—not to mention other works—were ample reason for Ward's being elected first president of the National Sculpture Society (1893). Though aging, Ward in the early twentieth century received and executed new commissions, including equestrian statues of General Philip Sheridan (Albany, 1908) and General Winfield Scott Hancock (Philadelphia, 1910; the horse was done by assistants). Ward will be remembered for valuably introducing specific naturalistic detail in American portrait sculpture. Ward married Anna Bannan in 1858 (she died in 1870), Julia D. Valentine in 1878 (she died in 1879), and Rachel M. Ostrander Smith in 1906.

Ward, Lester Frank (1841–1913). Sociologist and paleontologist. Born in Joliet, Illinois, Ward was the youngest of ten children. His father was an ingenious mechanic; his mother, a scholarly and versatile woman. Young Ward moved during his childhood with the family to Buchanan, Iowa, where he enjoyed a rugged frontier youth. He went to Myersburg, Pennsylvania (1858), to be with his brother Cyrenus Osborne Ward, a wagon-hub manufacturer and later a distinguished labor leader. Lester Ward attended Susquehanna Collegiate Institute, at Towanda, Pennsylvania (1861–1862), joined the Union army during the Civil War (1862–1864), and was honorably discharged because of wounds received in action. He worked for the U.S. Treasury, in Washington, D.C. (1865–1881), successively in the navigation, immigration, and statistics divisions. During this same period of time, he studied at Columbia College (now Georgetown University), where he earned his B.A., 1869; law degree, 1871; and M.A, 1872.

(In 1897 he was awarded an LL.D there.) He joined the U.S. Geological Survey (1881–1892), traveled widely then and later in the United States and abroad, and was also a dogged amateur linguist, mastering several languages (French, German, Greek, and Latin), and learning to read others (Hebrew, Japanese, and Russian). He published innumerable articles on aspects of anthropology, biology, botany, paleontology, psychology, and sociology. His botanical studies include *The Flora of Washington* (1881), *Sketch of Paleontological Botany* (1885), *Synopsis of the Flora of the Laramie Group* (1886), *Types of the Laramie Flora* (1887), and *Geographical Distribution of Fossil Plants* (1889). He also wrote the entries on botany in the *Century Dictionary* (1888–1890).

Ward brought his admirable versatility to bear on the subject of evolutionary sociology, of which he became the first American scholar of genuine merit. His books in this then-emerging field include *Dynamic Sociology* (1883), *The Psychic Factors of Civilization* (1893), *Outlines of Sociology* (1898), *Pure Sociology* (1903), *The Text-book of Sociology* (1905, coauthored), and *Applied Sociology* (1906). In these works, Ward assumes the existence of differences in people owing to heredity and race, and he argues that humane democracy should seek to eradicate poverty and should provide public education suited both for exceptionally gifted students and for persons of ordinary and differing talents, thus improving the social environment of all people so as to achieve progress and enlightenment. Ward taught sociology at Brown University (1906–1913). His intellectual autobiography is *Glimpses of the Cosmos* (6 vols., 1913–1918). Ward married Elizabeth Carolyn Vought in 1862 (the couple had one child who died in infancy, and then the mother died in 1872). Ward then married Rosamond Asenath Simons in 1873.

Warner, Olin Levi (1844–1896). Sculptor. He was born in Suffield, Connecticut. His father was an itinerant Methodist preacher. The family moved to Amsterdam, New York, in 1846. Young Warner received the usual schooling in that area and then in Brandon, Vermont, where he also lived with his family (to 1863). He developed a hobby of carving chalk, at which he became adept. He supported himself as a telegraphist in New York State and in Georgia, saved what money he could, and sailed for Paris to study sculpture at L'Ecole des Beaux-Arts (1869–1870). Augustus Saint-Gaudens,* who was already studying there, helped Warner feel at home. Warner joined the French Foreign Legion (1870–1871) and then returned to art classes in Paris (1871–1872). Home again, he established a studio in New York (1872–1876), which failed, and he returned to his father's Massachusetts farm. But then he obtained some orders for portrait medallions and busts, and he began to exhibit his work to admiring New York viewers (1878). Thereafter, Warner was successful, especially in the 1890s. He created profile medallions of Native American chiefs whom he met during a long trip through the Northwest (1889–1891) and a Mozart head (Buffalo, 1892). For the World's Columbian Exposition in Chicago,* in 1893, he created a souvenir coin and heads of European artists, statues of Henry Hudson and Christopher Columbus, and busts of New York governors Dewitt Clinton and Roswell P. Flower (for the New York State Building) at the exposition. He also made a statue of Governor Charles Devens of Massachusetts (Boston, 1894) and idyllic figures, portrait medallions of friends, and much else.

Warner was awarded a huge commission to produce three sets of bronze doors for the Library of Congress. He completed one set (Washington, D.C., 1894), but before the other two could be executed, a carriage hit and killed him while he was bicycling through Central Park in New York. Warner married Sylvia Martinache in 1886; the couple had two surviving children.

Washington, Booker T. (1856–1915). (Full name: Booker Taliaferro Washington.) African-American educator, author, and social reformer. Washington was born on a plantation in Franklin County, Virginia, to a white father and an African-American slave mother. Young Washington attended night school while, during the day, he worked in a salt furnace and a coal mine at Malden, West Virginia (from about 1865). After working as a servant in a home whose owners encouraged his desire to learn, he walked and hitchhiked some 500 miles to Hampton, Virginia, where he enrolled at the Hampton Normal and Agricultural Institute in 1872. He worked as a janitor for his board, graduated (1875), taught school back in Malden (1875–1877), attended Wayland Seminary in Washington, D.C., briefly (1878–1879), taught Native Americans at the Hampton Institute, and supervised the night school there (from 1879). Then came the opportunity that changed his life. In 1881 he was selected to organize what became the Normal and Industrial Institute for Negroes at Tuskegee, Alabama, chartered by the state legislature and initially funded at $2,000 per annum. The school began in a shanty and a church, with thirty students. Washington did spectacularly well. By the time of his death, he had supervised the building of more than 100 structures, mostly by student labor; moreover, the school had an endowment of $2,000,000 and a faculty of 200 and an enrollment of 1,500, owned 2,000 acres locally, had been granted by the federal government some 25,000 additional acres in northern Alabama, and offered classes in 38 trades and professions. (It should be noted that Washington's theory of combining mechanical and theoretical education predated similar thinking by John Dewey.*)

Meanwhile, Washington had evolved into the leading advocate in the United States for African-American education, and he spoke nationwide on race relations, for example, at the opening of the Cotton States and International Exposition* in Atlanta in 1895. He developed and espoused his theory on the need for African Americans to learn agricultural, industrial, and domestic skills and the need for their gradual absorption into national society. Furthermore, he kept commentary to a minimum on political activity and civil rights, and he espoused accommodationist policies. Washington was given honorary degrees by Harvard (1896) and Dartmouth (1901). Washington's many writings include *The Future of the American Negro* (1899), *Sowing and Reaping* (1900), *The Story of My Life and Work* (1900), *Up from Slavery: An Autobiography** (1901), *Character*

Building (1902), *Working with the Hands* (1904), a biography of Frederick Douglass* (1907), *The Story of the Negro* (1909), and much else. Washington married Fannie Norton Smith in 1882 (the couple had one child; his wife died in 1884), Olivia A. Davidson in 1885 (the couple had two children; that wife died in 1889), and Margaret James Murray in 1893.

Most of Washington's books were ghostwritten in part. Washington was criticized in his lifetime by more militant African Americans, for example, W.E.B. DuBois.* Since his death he has sometimes been labeled an "Uncle Tom" for his temporary, pragmatic acceptance of a "separate but equal" status for African Americans. The essential fact remains, however, that Booker T. Washington was a spokesman, of unparalleled significance and influence in America, for African Americans.

Weaver, James B. (1833–1912). (Full name: James Baird Weaver.) Politician. Weaver was born in Dayton, Ohio, graduated from the Cincinnati law school (1856), served in the Union army during the Civil War (1861–1865, rising from lieutenant to brigadier general), and went to Iowa to become a district attorney and a federal assessor of internal revenues for the Republican administration. In the mid–1870s, Weaver joined the Greenback Party, which favored the issuance of more currency to ease the debt burdens of Midwestern and Western farmers and workers. He was elected to the U.S. House of Representative (1879–1881) as a Greenbacker. He was nominated for president on the Greenback ticket (1880) and received more than 308,000 popular votes. He was reelected as a Greenback-Labor and Democratic representative (1885–1889). He ran for president again on the Populist Party* ticket (1892) and received twenty-two electoral votes and more than 1 million popular votes. Weaver helped found the Populist Party and became its most outstanding leader.

Westinghouse, George (1846–1914). Inventor and manufacturer. He was born in Central Bridge, New York, and worked in his father's machine shop as a boy. During the Civil War, he served as a soldier in the Union army (1861–1864) and then as an engineer with the Union navy (1864–1865). After attending Union College briefly (1865–1867), he returned to work with his father, and he patented a rotary steam engine, a machine to place derailed railroad freight cars back on track, and, in 1866, a reversible steel railroad frog to enable the wheels on one rail of a track to cross an intersecting rail. More important, he patented a centralized airbrake system for railroads (1869). He organized the Westinghouse Air Brake Company (1869) and improved braking devices for use throughout the United States, and in Canada and Europe (1870). Westinghouse was the first major employer in the United States to introduce the idea of Saturday half holidays for his workers (1871). He continued to be amazingly inventive. He organized his own company to make high-speed steam engines (1880); worked on railroad signals and interlocking switches, bought relevant patents owned by others, and established the Union Switch and Signal Company in Pittsburgh

(1882); founded the Westinghouse Electric Company in Pittsburgh (1884); and began to distribute electric power by the alternating current method being developed by Nikola Tesla,* whom he employed and treated honorably, and whose various rights (to alternating current transformers, motors, and transformers) he bought (1888, 1889). At about this time Westinghouse disputed with Thomas A. Edison,* who impractically favored distribution of electricity by direct current. Westinghouse drilled natural gas wells near Pittsburgh, experimented with pipe apparatus to distribute gas safely (1884), began to supply gas to Pittsburgh homes (1885), and organized the East Pittsburgh Improvement Company (1888).

There was no letup in the 1890s. Westinghouse assembled the equipment for the vast Westinghouse Air Brake Company in Pittsburgh (1890), organized the Pittsburgh Meter Company (1891), helped light the World's Columbian Exposition* (Chicago, 1893), founded the Westinghouse Electric and Manufacturing Company (1894), built huge gas engines (1895), erected ten generators to harness the water power of Niagara Falls (1894) which furnished power to Buffalo (1895–1896; Buffalo was the first major city to be electrified from a central power station), bought Parsons steam turbines and modified them substantially (1896), competed with Edison's General Electric Company, but also licensed that organization to use some of his patents (1896). The industrial companies that Westinghouse controlled are too numerous to list. He also earned many honors, and he was a member in many societies, leagues, and clubs. His various commercial organizations were capitalized at $120,000,000 in 1900, but the Panic of 1907 caused him to lose control. He retired from the company (1911) and turned to other professional interests. In all, Westinghouse owned some 400 patents, having worked, for example, on safety devices for natural gas pipelines, shock absorbers for railroad cars, marine steam turbines, electric trolley-car motors, electric-powered brakes for subway trains, and automobile shock absorbers. Westinghouse married Marguerite Erskine Walker in 1867; the couple had one son. His wife, a notable sculptress, designed two of their lavish homes, was active in many charities, and died three months after her devoted and beloved husband did.

Wharton, Edith (1862–1937). (Full name: Edith Newbold Jones Wharton. Nickname: Pussy.) Novelist, short-story writer, travel writer, critic, essayist, and poet. She was born in New York City into a rich and prominent family which owned Manhattan land, had residences in New York and Newport, Rhode Island, and also lived at times in Europe. Miss Jones read widely in her childhood, was privately tutored, began juvenile writing, and first enjoyed publishing success in the late 1870s. After her father died (1882), she remained with her mother in New York and in Newport. She met and greatly admired Walter Van Rensselaer Berry (1883) but unfortunately married Boston socialite Edward Robbins Wharton instead (1885). Twelve years her senior, he became an unstable, insensitive, and generally miserable husband. The couple lived and entertained in New York and Newport, cruised in the Aegean Sea (1888), spent spring seasons in Italy, and bought a Newport estate (1893). (They were divorced in Paris in 1913.)

When Mrs. Wharton periodically suffered from nervousness and melancholy (1894–1896, 1898, and later), she turned to writing more seriously, as a form of therapy prescribed (1898) by S. Weir Mitchell,* among other neurologists. During these years, she also found European travel beneficial. When Berry was a house guest, he helped Edith Wharton write *The Decoration of Houses* (coauthored with Ogden Codman, Jr., 1897). This popular book, often reprinted, helped to promote anti-Victorian interior designs. Her three earliest books of fiction were *The Greater Inclination* (1899), a collection of short stories; *The Touchstone* (1900), a short novel; and *Crucial Instances* (1901), a collection of short stories. *The Greater Inclination* comprises stories about sensitive, independent-minded Americans at home and in Europe. "The Muse's Tragedy," perhaps the best tale in the group, presents a woman who is thought to have sexually consummated an intellectual relationship with a poet but who did not and wishes she had. *The Touchstone* dissects the troubled conscience of a man who sells the love letters written to him by a famous woman novelist, now deceased, so that he can afford to marry the woman he really wants. A significant tale in *Crucial Instances* is "The Recovery," in which a New England painter judges New England to be aesthetically starved once he gets to European museums.

Superficially judged at first to be too imbued with fin de siècle cynicism, Wharton began to be recognized as a major, highly sophisticated writer beginning with the appearance of her first big novel, *The Valley of Decision* (2 vols., 1902). She went on to publish well over thirty other books, in various genres, and she is now regarded as perhaps the greatest woman American novelist, for her keen observation of high society, her thematic range, and her commitment to technique. She especially valued her personal and professional friendships, most commencing after 1900, with the following significant Americans: Henry Adams,* Bernard Berenson,* W. C. Brownell* (her editor at Charles Scribner's Sons), Clyde Fitch* (the two collaborated on an unsuccessful 1906 play based on her 1905 runaway best-selling novel *The House of Mirth*), William Morton Fullerton (her longtime lover), Richard Watson Gilder* (her *Century** editor), Robert Grant* (whose *Unleavened Bread** she admired), William Dean Howells,* Henry James* (whom she regarded as her "wisest" friend), William James,* Charles Eliot Norton,* and Theodore Roosevelt,* among countless others.

Whilomville Stories (1900). Collection of thirteen interconnected tales by Stephen Crane.* The fictitious village of Whilomville is based on Crane's memories of drowsy towns in New Jersey and of Port Jervis, New York, where he had lived as a boy. *Whilomville Stories* include episodes of inept hunting, African Americans and their hard menial labor and watermelon thefts, school kids' pranks and fights, racism, puppy love, and children imitating the uppity affectations in adults. Dr. Trescott and his son Jimmie figure in several of the tales, as they do in "The Monster," the title story of *The Monster and Other Stories.* *Whilomville Stories* may owe something to *The Story of a Bad Boy* by Thomas Bailey Aldrich* and the escapades of both Tom Sawyer and Huckleberry Finn by Mark Twain.*

Whistler, James Abbott McNeill (1834–1903). Painter, etcher, lithographer, and dry-point artist. He was born in Lowell, Massachusetts. Soon after his father, an ex-army officer and then a civil engineer, went to Russia to supervise building a railroad between St. Petersburg and Moscow (1842), the family followed (1843). While still a boy, Whistler, energetic, self-centered, and ambitious, showed talent in drawing, but he also had a heart condition. He attended the Imperial Academy of Fine Arts in St. Petersburg (1843–1849). His study there ended when his father died of cholera (1849). The family returned to Stonington, Connecticut. Whistler attended West Point (1851–1854) but was dismissed after he failed chemistry. He became a draftsman and cartographer for the U.S. Coast and Geodetic Survey (1854–1855), during which time he mastered etching techniques. He accepted an allowance from his indulgent mother Anna Mathilda McNeill Whistler and went to Paris (1855), never to return to America. Becoming a dandified Bohemian, he was somewhat influenced by realistic painters; by the Impressionists, several of whom he knew personally; by the Pre-Raphaelites—he liked their languid, dreamy, feminine subjects but avoided their religious and literary overtones—and by exhibitions of Japanese prints—with their asymmetrical composition, oddly angled perspectives, and economical, flexible lines. Mostly, however, he followed his own eclectic genius.

Whistler published many of his etchings (French subjects, 1858; Thames scenes, 1860; Venetian locales, 1880 and later) and began to prefer London to Paris. He painted his half sister Deborah Whistler Haden in *Portrait of Lady Seymour Haden at the Piano* (1859); her husband was the British surgeon and etcher, with whom Whistler had a permanent falling-out in 1867. Whistler caused a sensation with his *Symphony in White, No. 1: The White Girl* (1862), which was exhibited at the Salon des Refusés in 1863; the model was his longtime, Irish-born mistress Joanna Hiffernan, who was replaced by Maud Franklin, his second mistress, in the 1870s. He later exhibited many more controversial paintings, including the famous portrait of his mother, who had moved to London, with failing eyesight, to live with her beloved son (1863). The work, first entitled *Arrangement in Gray and Black No. 1* (1872), is skillfully structured along rectangular lines; it was purchased by the French government (1891) and now hangs in the Louvre. Another portrait patterned similarly was *Arrangement in Gray and Black No. 2: Thomas Carlyle* (1873). Whistler also produced a series of so-called crepuscular *Nocturnes* (from 1872), followed by *Arrangements*, *Etudes*, and *Harmonies*. These titles suggest his awareness of the relationship of painting to music. He explicitly defined painting as "the poetry of sight." He excelled in arranging harmonious patterns and colors, not in representing nature, people, and buildings with naturalistic correctness.

Critics and the public alike failed to realize that Whistler was a pioneer in the

Aesthetic Movement which adopted an art-for-art's sake philosophy and thus led to even more modern abstract art. When John Ruskin, the powerful and didactic art critic, published harsh criticism of Whistler's perspectiveless, undetailed, nonnarrative, nonsymbolic, almost colorless work (1877), the artist sued (1878) and nominally won; but the ligitation expenses caused him to declare bankruptcy (1879). Whistler became a member of the Society of British Artists (1884; president 1886–1888) and a chevalier of the French Legion of Honor (1889), mounted a large retrospective exhibition in London (1892), and sent a selection of etchings to the World's Columbian Exposition* (Chicago, 1893). Charles Lang Freer, Detroit railroad multimillionaire, visited Whistler's Paris studio, introduced himself as a collector, impressed the artist (1894), and became his friend and patron. Whistler was the first president of the International Society of Sculptors, Painters, and Gravers (1897), and he received gold medals at the Paris Exposition (1900). By this time the British and Americans were vying for the honor of claiming Whistler as their own.

Three of Whistler's most notable late paintings are *Mother-of-Pearl and Silver: The Andalusian* (c. 1894), *George W[ashington] Vanderbilt*[*] (1898), and *Brown and Gold: Self-Portrait* (c. 1900). The first presents a proud woman in Spanish garb, in a manner reflecting the work of Diego de Silva Velázquez, whom Whistler admired. The second is a controversially planned composition, in which rich, shy Vanderbilt stands elongated between a dark foreground and a gloomy, unfurnished background. The third, which is but one of many depictions of his oddly attractive cocky self, is a quick, flat, and gloomy portrait highlighted by a plume-like tuft of white hair, a monocle, and a Legion of Honor rosette—stressing the favorite colors of Rembrandt, whom Whistler also admired. Among less impressive portraits are *Arrangements in Black No. 8: Portrait of Mrs. Cassatt* (1885), of Lois B. Cassatt, sister-in-law of Mary Cassatt;* *Arrangement in Black and Gold: Comte Robert de Montesquiou-Fezensac* (1892), a portrait of the bizarre French homosexual writer and acquaintance of Whistler's friends Henry James* and John Singer Sargent;* *Brown and Gold: Portrait of Lady Eden* (1894), showing a messy, shadowy figure perched on a long couch, with an unrecognizable face, against a streaky background; *Robert Barr* (1895), a portrait of the novelist friend of Stephen Crane;* and Vanderbilt's glum-looking wife (1902). Whistler could have made far more money from his portraits if he had chosen to flatter his subjects, which he never did.

Somewhat late in life, Whistler married Beatrix Godwin, the widow of an architect friend (1888) and resided mostly in Paris with her (early 1890s); he was devastated by her death in London (1896). Whistler tutored at the Académie Carmen (1898–1901), sought to improve his worsening health by trips to North Africa, Corsica, and elsewhere, but returned no better to a series of London hotel residences. Whistler, who used a butterfly image as a signature, was eccentric in dress, acidly witty in conversation, admired by his many friends (including James, Dante Gabriel Rossetti, Algernon Charles Swinburne, and Oscar Wilde), and clever in articles and books. His writings include *Ten O'Clock*

(1888), based on an 1885 lecture on aesthetics; *Propositions* (1888), also about his art creed; *The Gentle Art of Making Enemies: As Pleasingly Exemplified in Many Instances, Wherein the Serious Ones of This Earth, Carefully Exasperated, Have Been Prettily Spurred on to Unseemingliness and Indiscretion, While Overcome by an Unique Sense of Right* (1890), partly about Ruskin; *Eden Versus Whistler, The Baronet and the Butterfly* (1899), about another lawsuit, this time with the Edens; and his posthumously published *Journals* (1921). Sculptor Augustus Saint-Gaudens* designed the memorial for Whistler at West Point. His friends Joseph Pennell* and his wife Elizabeth published a two-volume biography of Whistler (1908).

White City. *See* World's Columbian Exposition.

White, Stanford (1853–1906). Architect. He was born in New York City. His father was Richard Grant White, literary and music critic, essayist, and editor. Young White apprenticed in the office of the famous architect H. H. Richardson (1872–1878) and was his chief assistant in constructing the Romanesque Trinity Church in Boston (1872–1877). White studied in Europe (1878–1880), partly with Augustus Saint-Gaudens,* and he returned to join and help create the architectural firm of McKim, Mead, and White (1880), which became famous for structures in the Italian Renaissance style. White applied several of Richardson's techniques with respect to textures, details, ornaments, and colors, and to interior finishes and furnishings. He enjoyed abundant success through designing town and country mansions for New York's rich and famous and, in addition, the Washington Arch (1889), the original Madison Square Garden (1890), and the Herald Building (1894)—all in New York City. Most of these structures, as well as other White creations, have since been razed to make way for so-called progress. White designed the pedestals for Saint-Gaudens's *Farragut*, *Lincoln*, *Logan*, and the tomb for the wife of Henry Adams;* he also designed churches and university and military buildings; the stables, tennis courts, and swimming pool for the Astor estate in Rhinebeck, New York; and even magazine covers and picture frames. Although White also worked on skyscrapers, he deplored their concept on aesthetic grounds.

White inspired younger artists, hoped for the evolution of a distinctly American architecture, and lived life with ruthless exuberance. Unfortunately, it was this very zest for life that cost him his life. Although he was married to Bessie Smith, a New York judge's daughter (1884; the couple had one son), White also dallied with Evelyn Nesbit, a pretty showgirl who modeled for drawings by Charles Dana Gibson.* She later married Harry Kendall Thaw, a railroad mogul. When Thaw learned about Evelyn's previous liaison with White, Thaw shot and killed him in defense of her alleged premarital honor. The murder occurred on the Madison Square Garden roof at the opening of a roof show. After a sensational trial, Thaw was acquitted on the grounds of temporary insanity. White's varied accomplishments in the 1880s and 1890s, and later, have been cast into shadow by his lurid death.

White, William Allen (1868–1944). Journalist. Born in Emporia, Kansas, he attended Emporia State University (1884–1886) and the University of Kansas (1886–1890). He bought the weekly Emporia *Gazette* in 1895 and made it into a nationally respected, American small-town newspaper, renowned for its conservative editorials. White's most famous editorial, "What's the Matter with Kansas?" (15 August 1896), opposed the Populist Party,* thus aided William McKinley,* and was syndicated nationally. White's one book to be published in the 1890s was *The Real Issue and Other Stories* (1896). White rose to great prominence in the early twentieth century as a respected spokesman on social and political matters.

The Will to Believe, and Other Essays in Popular Philosophy (1897). Collection of essays by William James.* All ten of these essays had been previously published, some as early as 1879. The assumption underlying all of them is the probability of a life above mankind's level of consciousness. It therefore makes sense to have faith despite inadequate proofs. The act of faith is a moral one. Faith is useful in the practical world of feeling, thought, and free will. If we did not take some things on preliminary trust, we could never act or gain knowledge. So it is proper to adopt a tentative religious faith, despite rational doubts. Wishing and willing will make faith stronger. Doubting can cause the thinker to lose out in his search for truth; furthermore, acting on faith will validate that faith. A faithful person's actions have moral consequences. The two most significant pieces in this collection of essays are "The Will to Believe" (1896), in which James exhorts his readers to decide "yes" passionately, if they cannot prove "no" intellectually; and "Is Life Worth Living?" (1895), the answer being "certainly," if one believes it is and acts accordingly.

Willard, Frances Elizabeth Caroline (1839–1898). Educator, reformer, lobbyist, and orator. She was born in Churchville, New York. Her parents were both teachers. She moved with her family to Oberlin, Ohio, then to a farm near Janeville, Wisconsin, where she grew up loving both reading and outdoor activities. She graduated from Northwestern Female College (1859); taught near Evanston, Illinois, in Pittsburgh, Pennsylvania, and in Lima, New York (1860–1868); then she traveled in Europe (1868–1870). When she returned to the United States, she gave public lectures on her experiences abroad (1870) and discovered her immense talent for public speaking. She became president of Evanston College for Ladies (1871–1874); when this institution was absorbed by Northwestern University (1873), she became dean of women there (1873–1874). Willard joined the temperance movement in 1874, became corresponding secretary of the National Woman's Christian Temperance Union (1874), and then served as its president (1879–1898). Under her leadership, the organization grew to a total of 10,000 locals and a membership of 250,000. She helped to found the World's Woman's Christian Temperance Union (1883) and later became its president (1891). This organization was ultimately active in fifty countries with a membership of 2,000,000. Willard joined the woman's suffrage movement and helped to organize the Prohibition Party (1882). One of her tactics was to invade saloons, sing hymns, kneel in the sawdust, and pray aloud. She lectured in every state of the Union and in all American territories. Her fixed philosophy was that temperance was the salvation of the home, the family, and the Christian way of life. Willard also advocated safety codes for female industrial workers; lobbied for better home protection, nutrition, kindergartens, schools, and prisons; and spoke in favor of labor and police reform. Her other notable achievements included establishing a temperance hospital, a publishing outlet, and a lecture bureau. Frances Willard wrote *Woman and Temperance* (1883), *Glimpses of Fifty Years* (1889), *A Classic Town: The Story of Evanston* (1892), and many pamphlets and articles. She also coedited *A Woman of the Century* (1893) with Mary A. Livermore.

Winnemucca, Sarah (1844?–1891). (Native American name: Thocmetony [Shell Flower].) Interpreter, lecturer, and educator. She was born into the Paiute tribe, near Humboldt Sink in Nevada. Admiring the ways of white men and women, her grandfather took friends and relatives, including Winnemucca, to do ranch work in the San Joaquin Valley in California. She learned English and Spanish, lived with a white family back in Nevada, became a nominal Christian, went to a white school briefly where she received the name Sarah (1860), then attended classes in a convent in San Jose, California. Trouble between whites and the Native Americans caused strife, during which one of her brothers was murdered (1865). Sarah became an interpreter at Camp McDermott, Nevada (c. 1868–1871). She married but left an abusive white army officer (1871), married but left an abusive Native American, and lived and worked as an interpreter at a reservation in southeastern Oregon (1872–1876). She aided the U.S. Army during the Bannock War (1878), after which she lectured persuasively in San Francisco to plead for better treatment of the mistreated pacifist Paiutes. She even appealed to officials in Washington, D.C. (1880). Winnemucca taught Native American children at Vancouver Barracks, in the state of Washington (1880–1881), and, in 1881, married an army lieutenant, L. H. Hopkins, who accompanied her on the lecture circuit in the Northeast (1881–1884). Disillusioned with promises broken by federal officials, she founded a school for Paiute children (1884–1887) on ranch land near Lovelock, Nevada, donated to her brother by wealthy Leland Stanford, one of the Big Four.* Sick and widowed (from 1886), Winnemucca lived with her sister in Monida, Montana, and died there of tuberculosis. Her *Life among the Piutes: Their Wrongs and Claims* (1883) is a splendid personal and tribal history.

The Winning of the West: An Account of the Exploration and Settlement of Our Country from the Alleghanies to the Pacific (1889–1896). Four-volume history by Theodore Roosevelt.* Volume I (1889) details events between the

French exploration of the Ohio Valley (beginning in 1763) and the organization of Kentucky (1776). Volume II (1889) concerns machinations on an international scale (1777–1783). Volume III (1894) traces migrations and settlements (1784–1790) and discusses conflicts with Indians, various separatist activities, and the organization of the Northwest Territory and the Southwest Territory (1787, 1788). Volume IV (1896) analyzes frontier difficulties, with emphasis on land speculation, the Louisiana Purchase (1803), and continued pioneering into the Far West (1791–1807). Roosevelt's plan combines a general movement forward chronologically and essays on democratic settlements, Indians, steady currents of immigration, family life on the frontier, and modes of travel. Roosevelt clearly loves to romanticize the exploits of his heroes, including Daniel Boone, George Rogers Clark, Andrew Jackson, Kasper Mensker, James Robertson, John Sevier, and Mad Anthony Wayne. Especially notable is Roosevelt's treatment of frontier activity during the American Revolution, the Moravian Massacre, the villainous James Wilkinson, the Battle of Fallen Timbers, Aaron Burr's conspiracy, and the daring pioneers "of the Western waters."

Roosevelt was undoubtedly inspired by the monumental histories of Francis Parkman, to whom he dedicated *The Winning of the West*. He was also impressed by *The American Commonwealth* (1888), James Bryce's significant and influential study. In addition, he was encouraged to write this Western history by his personal observation of racial diversity during his ranching and hunting days in the Dakota Territory (1884–1886). He made careful use of original source materials and presented his narratives with great literary skill, but he romanticized certain heroes and was—at least according to Frederick Jackson Turner*—too eager to preach the lesson that the forces of good regularly defeat those of evil. At one time, Roosevelt planned to carry his history through later volumes to include the taking of Florida and Oregon, the history of the Republic of Texas, and the acquiring of New Mexico and California. Hamlin Garland* provided an introductory essay for one of the volumes of the 1924 reprint of *The Winning of the West*.

Wister, Owen (1860–1938). Lawyer, musician, and author. Born in Philadelphia, he was an only child. His father was a prominent physician; his mother, the aristocratic and art conscious daughter of actress Fanny Kemble. Owen Wister traveled with his parents in Europe and attended schools in Switzerland and England (1870–1873), studied in St. Paul's School (Concord, New Hampshire, from 1873), and graduated from Harvard (1882), where his classmates included Charles Townsend Copeland* and Shakespearean scholar George Lyman Kittredge and where he was a close friend of Theodore Roosevelt.* Wister then studied music in Europe (1882–1883), returned home (1883) for business, and, to improve his health, vacationed on orders from his physician S. Weir Mitchell* in Wyoming (first in 1885). Wister then studied law at Harvard (1885–1888) and passed the Pennsylvania bar (1889). By this time he realized both that he had fallen in love with the Far West—to which he returned fourteen times—and that he was going to write Western fiction. He published short stories set in the West (beginning in 1892) and also a significant essay entitled "The Evolution of the Cow-Puncher" (1895). Collections of his short fiction include *Red Men and White** (1896) and *The Jimmyjohn Boss and Other Stories** (1900), as well as later titles. These stories helped Wister to prepare the way for his novels *Lin McLean** (1897) and *The Virginian: A Horseman of the Plains* (1902). Roosevelt read parts of *The Virginian* in magazine form and criticized them for their harshness, but *The Virginian* made Wister famous and became the paradigm of countless later formulary Western novels—with the tight-lipped, chivalric hero; the pliant heroine, usually from the effete East; a melodramatic adventure plot against an accurate local-color setting and spiced with restrained Western humor; and the inevitable gunfight in which plain good triumphs over obvious evil.

The Virginian, a runaway best-seller for years, was dedicated to Roosevelt; one popular edition was illustrated by Frederic Remington,* who had also illustrated earlier fiction by Wister. Although his finest work was composed between 1892 and 1902, Wister sporadically continued writing well into the twentieth century. He wrote another novel—*Lady Baltimore* (1906), a careful depiction of genteel manners in turn-of-the-century Charleston, South Carolina—more short stories, political essays, books for children, and biographical studies of Ulysses S. Grant (1901), George Washington (1907), and Roosevelt (1930). Wister's journals and letters (1885–1895) have also been published (1958). Among Wister's close friends, in addition to Roosevelt, were Henry Adams,* Henry Mills Alden,* Oliver Wendell Holmes,* William Dean Howells,* Henry James,* Remington, Mark Twain,* and other significant figures of his day. Wister married his cousin Mary Channing "Molly" Wister in 1898 (the couple had six children; Mrs. Wister died in childbirth in 1913). She was the model of Mary Stark "Molly" Wood, the peppy, proper heroine of *The Virginian*.

With the Procession: A Novel (1895). Novel by Henry Blake Fuller.* The place is Chicago; the time, 1893–1894. Honest, wealthy, old Chicago wholesale grocer David Marshall has a pushy young associate named Belden, whose business methods are successful, even necessary, but also less than honorable. David's wife Eliza is as old-fashioned and as frugal as he. They have five children (partly stereotypical): Alice Marshall Robinson, married and with a busy social life; Roger Marshall, a hard-driving lawyer interested in real estate speculation; Jane Marshall, unmarried, quaint, restless, and honest; Richard Truesdale Marshall, just back from four dilly-dallying years in Europe, and doomed to become a dilettante; and Rosamund Marshall, back from school in the East, discontent with the Middle West, and willing to have herself placed on the international marriage market. Jane, who wants to push the rusty old Marshalls into society's current procession, is happy when she meets frank, glittering Susan Lathrop Bates, who happened to know old David Marshall when they were both young, who helped propel her business pioneer husband Granger Bates to their present wealthy position, and who now through Jane draws the Marshalls into "the procession'' of Chicago's modern high society. Susan Bates admirably spends money on fine art, music, and buildings—to outdo her social rivals—but at the same time she criticizes her son for studying art himself. Art is for leisure-class women. Susan Bates and Jane Marshall combine first to get Rosy Marshall into the social swing, then to urge David Marshall, with only limited success, to join it—by obtaining a new carriage, a better house, and a self-aggrandizing philanthropic hobby. David and his wife agree to start building a mansion, and, at about the same time, David lets Belden weaken the old business by becoming a partner. David dislikes the tide of immigrants not of Chicago's old Anglo-Saxon strain, will not agree to underwrite them by charity, and then grows fatally debilitated. The momentum of the procession finally scatters the Marshalls: Roger takes the family fortune into real estate ventures; Truesdale finds Chicago culturally unsuitable and plans to leave the country; Rosy marries and also plans to depart; and Jane, though loyal to the old ways, is rendered uneasy by the knowledge of the changes she has helped to precipitate.

David Marshall is based in part on Fuller's own father; Susan Bates and her weirdly colorful mansion are patterned after real-life Chicago social leader Bertha Honoré Palmer, wife of Chicago merchant Potter Palmer,* and their outlandish lakefront residence. In an 1895 review of *With the Procession*, William Dean Howells* commended Fuller for the incomparable quality of his work and especially relished the depiction of Susan Bates. James Huneker* in an 1895 review pronounced it better than works by either Howells or Hamlin Garland.* Many other Eastern reviewers, however, found the novel too negative, that is, too realistic. And well they might, since one of its themes is the inevitable ruin of Chicago's old settlers (sometimes elitist, sometimes hypocritical) by pushy and successful immigrants (too often corrupt and corrupting).

Women and Economics: A Study of the Economic Relation between Men and Women as a Factor in Social Evolution (1898). Tract by Charlotte Perkins Gilman.* In this tract, this monumentally significant feminist argues that the traditional family, dominated by a patriarchal authority figure since caveman times and sanctioned by religion and government, has subjugated women, who by participating in an artificial division of the sexes have been required to preserve contradictions and confusions within male and female personalities which result in lifelong difficulties. These problems include placing women in an inferior status psychologically and sexually (parasites in society, domestic animals at home), and also economically and politically. The patriarchal family structure guarantees the subservience of women, because they are obliged to perform domestic service, are dependent financially, feel emotionally and sexually dominated, and have turned submissive through the ages. It is time, Gilman says, that women quit subscribing to a slave mentality, stop being servants to men, and demand ''economic equality and freedom.'' Meanwhile, women must not be blandished by such superficial ''cures'' of basic ills as merely gaining the vote, being handed somewhat more varied jobs and a little more money, and being allowed to support superficially helpful legislation. Instead, women must demand true sexual equality, in and out of marriage, and psychologically satisfying employment outside the home. Toward this end, homes might well become kitchenless, with persons hired to prepare food; furthermore, day-care centers could care for the little children of working mothers.

Too optimistically, Gilman theorized that once women humanized the brutal, male-dominated work force, capitalism would disappear. Gilman, when asked, said that her two main influences for *Women and Economics* were "Our Better Halves" by Lester Frank Ward* (in *Forum*, November 1888) and *The Evolution of Sex* (1889) by Sir Patrick Geddes and J. Arthur Thomson. Not that this independent thinker needed much in the way of source material for her radically original thinking. *Women and Economics* was well received, was enthusiastically reviewed in the United States and in London, was occasionally praised as the best treatment of its subject since John Stuart Mill's 1869 "Subjection of Women," sold very well, and made its author internationally known and welcome. In its first quarter-century of life, *Women and Economics* enjoyed seven editions and was translated into seven foreign languages.

Wood, Leonard (1860–1927). Surgeon and soldier. Born in Winchester, New Hampshire, he attended Harvard (1880–1884; M.D., 1884) and pursued an unremunerative, dull private practice in Boston briefly. He was then commissioned in the Army Medical Corps and began his military career with the cavalry in the Arizona Territory. He served bravely under General Nelson A. Miles* during the campaign to capture Apache chief Geronimo* (1885–1886); once he carried a dispatch 100 miles through hostile territory, and later he helped escort surrendered Apaches out of Mexico to Miles's headquarters. Wood was promoted to the rank of captain and assistant surgeon (1891) and was later reassigned to Washington, D.C. (1895), where President William McKinley* became one of his patients and Theodore Roosevelt* became one of his closest friends (from 1897). During the Spanish-American War,* Wood served as colonel of the First U.S. Volunteer Cavalry Regiment, known as the Rough Riders; Roosevelt was his second in command. Once in Cuba, Wood led his unit during the Battle of Las Guásimas, was promoted to brigadier general (1898), and was appointed military governor of Santiago (1898) and then military governor of Cuba (1899–1902). He imposed invaluable order, justice, and sanitation improvements on the island. At the time, Wood's medical associate Walter Reed* was busy eradicating the yellow fever plague in Cuba caused by mosquitoes. Wood rose in rank from brigadier general (1901) to major general (1903); was reassigned to the Philippines as governor of Moro Province, Mindanao, and adjacent islands (1903); and became commander in chief of U.S. forces in the Philippines (1906–1908).

In later life, Wood was commanding officer of the Department of the East, U.S. Army (1906–1908, 1914–1917) and then Chief of Staff, U.S. Army (1910–1914). He was regarded as a possible Republican Party presidential candidate

(1916, 1920) and was governor general of the Philippines (1921–1927). Wood loved the strenuous life and was admirably courageous, but he was also personally cool and somewhat aloof. He married Louisa A. Condit Smith in 1890 (the couple had three children). He died after being operated on a third time for a brain tumor.

The Workers: An Experiment in Reality: The East (1897). Book by Walter A. Wyckoff.* Wyckoff, identified on the title page as an assistant professor of political economy at Princeton University, explains in his preface that a friend suggested what became his experiment to gain "practical knowledge" so as to refine his theoretical knowledge. He adds that his narrative is factual, although he changed some names to protect living persons. In July 1891, Wyckoff leaves the comfortable confines of academe and becomes an itinerant, unskilled laborer in order to see what the have-nots of America are like and how they survive. He fails at selling magazines, mows a lawn for his supper, saws wood for permission to sleep in a barn, saws more wood for a minister for food the next day, bothers the minister's congregation by attending church service in his shabby clothes, walks near the Hudson River, is depressed by rain, notes the speech and reading habits of persons who grudgingly offer hospitality, gets a kitchen job at a tavern near West Point, and then is hired to help raze an old building at the Academy—at $1.60 a day for "five working-days of nine hours and a quarter each, less the 'called time' eaten out by . . . rain." He shovels dynamited debris, loads it with bleeding hands into carts, fantasizes while working to pass the time, and chokes on the lime dust. He rooms and boards with an Irish woman and her family, as do some of the other workers. Wyckoff includes character sketches of his fellow laborers, comments on their backgrounds, physical condition, complaints, profanity, camaraderie, and hopelessness through being unskilled and unorganized in a supply-and-demand economy. Bidding farewell to this landlady, he watches the West Point "sunset parade," admires the efficient military use of manpower, and laments the absence of a similar "organization for industrial ends."

For three weeks in August, Wyckoff works as a hotel porter in Orange County, New York, from 5 A.M. to 11 P.M., at the "menial drudgery" of scrubbing floors, washing windows, sweeping the veranda and walks, cleaning and filling and lighting oil lamps, helping the hot-tempered chef, brushing the billiard tables, acting as bellboy, sorting mail, carrying linen and blankets, and cleaning cuspidors. He eats leftovers from guests' tables with the other overworked help. He observes their quarrels and sleeps in a room behind the proprietor's office. He compares his West Point work, which "seems to harden [men] . . . into slaves," with porterage, which he preferred because "initiative and . . . pride" were involved, but he feels that factory girls have prospects for better marriages than do demeaned hotel maids. He pockets a profit of $4.02 and moves on.

His next job is at an insane asylum at Middletown, New York, where he digs a sewer ditch and hauls milk, laundry, swill for pigs, ashes, and vegetables for a few days in September—at $1.50 per nine-hour day. After getting his shoes repaired by a talkative old cobbler, he takes his $6 and trudges to Wilkes-Barre, Pennsylvania, where he observes the autumn colors, the landscape, different houses, lonely farms, and little villages, and talks with a variety of people, mostly poor. He rents a room, fails to find employment, and escapes for a few hours of reading in the free library (like one feeding an addiction, he says). Then he goes back "into the gas-lit street, and into our modern world, with its artificialities and its social and labor problems." He travels on to Pleasant Hill, where he is hired by a prosperous, thoughtful farmer, for 75¢ a day plus board and permission to sleep on a cot in the wagon-house loft. He works well for five days; he repairs a pond dam and picks apples, goes to church with the family, meets the neighbors, and listens to his employer on the subject of farming. The man theorizes on hard toil, the drain of labor off to cities, "shiftless" landowners and workers, "scientific" improvements, and the coming of competition.

Wyckoff passes through a poverty-stricken farm area and then better land to a lumber camp west of Williamsport, where in October he joins a crew of about twenty strong, free, happy, attractive men, who, however, are violently profane, and in their sparse leisure seek "liquor and lust." His first job is loading strips of hemlock bark onto wagons and cutting paths for the wagons to the tannery. His boss at first curses him, but soon senses his intelligence, and asks him to help the ill-trained camp bookkeeper. Wyckoff sketches several of his coworkers: an uneducated but heroic overseer, a handsome favorite back from time off, an Irish lad with a gift of song, luckless Civil War veterans, the alcoholic son of a lumberman, a debauched widower, a Swede injured by an axe, and a rheumatic old man. Wyckoff works a little more than two weeks and accepts pay of 75¢ a day. During his last Sunday, he goes to a nearby town, where he is asked to preach at a homely church to ordinary people weakened by poverty and sin but still seeking "the Bread of Life," and he does so. Then he heads out, curious to learn the latest news of the wide world beyond the work camp.

Wyckoff narrates his adventures with attention to detail, reveals great powers of observation and profound sympathy, and often quotes from the Bible and from literary texts. Though occasionally employing humor and irony, he never demeans his fellow workers. He continues the story of his life as an unskilled itinerant worker in *The Workers: An Experiment in Reality: The West.**

The Workers: An Experiment in Reality: The West (1898). Book by Walter A. Wyckoff.* Here, Wyckoff continues the narrative that he began in *The Workers: An Experiment in Reality: The East** (1897). In his previous work, Wyckoff described his experiences as an unskilled, itinerant worker in New York State and Pennsylvania. Now he is "pressing westward through a land unknown." In Chicago, beginning in December 1891, he is hungry and tired, finds no work, attends a gospel meeting, and goes for the night to a station house with a few hundred other "bums." He survives on odd jobs, buys cheap food, and watches swarms of city workers. He shovels snow, and he is paid and fed for doing so by an Irish woman who inveighs against the influx of Italian workers. He attends a meeting of talkative socialists, visits the room of a ragged family, and fails to obtain a job at a factory. After applying without success to be a slaughterhouse owner's private handyman, Wyckoff at last finds a job. He works in a factory ten hours a day (at $1.50 per day) for seven weeks packing and shipping mower, reaper, and harvester parts, and he eats and sleeps in a tenement nearby. He observes his fellow workers, his landlady and her family, and the weekend ''public gayety'' of his new friends. Unemployed again, his savings amount to $17.50. One Sunday, he attends a workingman's church, where he ponders Christianity and poverty. He goes to a socialist meeting where sundry men assail religion, espouse communistic anarchism, and defend true Christianity. He summarizes their speeches at great length, then he goes home with a young German mechanic to share dinner with his family and talk about Marxism. Next day, Wyckoff meets a man who is trying to unionize sweatshops and who takes him through foul streets to a crowded, filthy home where hordes of people of all ages are sewing cloaks for a dollar a day. In April 1892, Wyckoff begins a job as an unskilled road builder, for from $1.50 to $1.75 a day, at the World's Columbian Exposition.* He works near the Transportation Building and the Manufacturers Building; he eats and sleeps with 400 other men in an adjacent temporary ''hotel,'' made of fragrant but vermin-infested wood; he is encouraged by his fellows to work slowly; and he observes the varied personalities of his new associates and their different responses to the work here. He takes a conservative friend to a union meeting, where labor-capital relations and the principles of organization are discussed.

The narrative moves from Chicago to his arrival in Denver, Colorado. Wyckoff works at a steel company in Joliet, Illinois, for a week in May, attends the National Republican Convention in Minneapolis, Minnesota, in June, talks politics with men giving him rides through rich farmland, and then works for a week for a hospitable, hardworking, devout farm family. He hears about recent changes in rural life. He makes his way to Council Bluffs, Iowa, where he takes a two-week livery-stable job, for $10 and meals. On to western Nebraska, then a railroad job (12.5¢ an hour for three weeks), and so to Denver (September). By January 1893, he is in Phoenix, Arizona. But first he failed to find work in some Rocky Mountain mining camps and beyond into the Southwest; accepted hospitality from free and easy homesteaders, courteous prospectors, engineers, and frontier lawyers; and got a job ($2.50 a day) helping drive a team of burros 600 miles through New Mexico into Arizona (November and December). Wyckoff's final report is from San Francisco and is dated I February 1893. The last leg of his odyssey was up the Pacific slope through orange groves, past mission churches, and to cities by the sea.

In *The Workers: The West*, Wyckoff combines, as he did in *The Workers: The East*, memorable graphic observations of squalid working conditions, praise of the workingman's spirit, and an unquenchable love of nature. His political theories come to the fore to a greater degree in his second volume. The most terrifying passage in either work appears early in the narration of Wyckoff's western experiences: "Suddenly there dawns upon you an undreamed of significance in the machinery of social restraint. The policeman on the crossing in his slouching uniform . . . is . . . ready to lay hold on you, should you violate . . . the rules of social order. Behind him you see the patrol wagon and the station-house and the courts of law and the State's prison and enforced labor, the whole elaborate process by means of which society would reassimilate you, an excrement, a non-social being and a transgressor of the law, into the body politic once more, and set you to fulfilling a functional activity as a part of the social organism."

World's Columbian Exposition. (Also known as the Chicago World's Fair of 1893, the Great White City, and White City.) The largest, and most elaborate nineteenth-century public exposition held in the United States, perhaps in the world. It was some years in the planning. A corporation was established (1889), headed by professional and business leaders who amassed $5,000,000 in funds; $5,000,000 more was added in 1890, and an additional $2,500,000 was generated through federally minted souvenir coins in 1893. The project was debated in the U.S. Congress (1890), and presidential approval was given by Benjamin Harrison* (1890) to open the exposition in 1893 (instead of 1892, as first hoped). A city corporation and a national commission were formed to make the necessary decisions (1890). The national commission decided that the following types of exhibits would be presented: agriculture, electricity, ethnology, fine arts, fisheries, horticulture, liberal arts, livestock, machinery, manufactures, mines and metallurgy, transportation, and miscellaneous. Jackson Park was chosen as the site (1890). Many prominent individuals cooperated to make the exposition a success. Marshall Field,* among others, made generous donations. Potter Palmer* was named vice president and director; his wife Bertha Honoré Palmer was named president of the Women's Commission. Daniel Hudson Burnham* supervised the architecture for the exposition, employed almost 20,000 men (including Walter A. Wyckoff,* who wrote about the experience in *The Workers: An Experiment in Reality: The West**), and was responsible for expending some $20,000,000 in construction costs. Burnham asked Frederick L. Omsted,* the distinguished landscape architect, to work with him. Construction included a large lagoon, an island with trees, a Court of Honor with a big basin, canals and little lagoons, and buildings around the main lagoon and basin.

It was decided that the basic style of the major buildings would be neoclassical, stressing formality, balance, and massiveness. Major buildings included the Administration Building, the Agriculture Building, the Art Building (which uniquely survives as the Museum of Science and Industry), the Electricity Building, the Fisheries Building, the Horticulture Building, Machinery Hall, the Manufactures and Liberal Arts Building (the biggest enclosed structure ever built [787 feet by 1687 feet], containing statues and paintings in more than seventy galleries), the Mines and Mining Building, and the Transportation Building (designed by Louis Sullivan*). Spectacular use of electric lighting, planned by Nikola Tesla,* on many of the gleaming white structures caused the exposition to be called "White City." Nineteen foreign countries, among eighty-six non-American entities, and thirty American political governments (notably Illinois), set up their own buildings. Some 65,000 exhibits were ultimately assembled. A Department of Publicity and Promotion was formed (1890) to make known the name and location of Chicago to attract the necessary visitors from the Eastern seaboard and Europe. Sculptor Augustus Saint-Gaudens* was enlisted as an art adviser. Daniel Chester French* created a statue symbolizing the Republic to stand beside the main basin. Olin Levi Warner* provided statues to beautify the New York Building and did other work for the exposition. Louis Comfort Tiffany* designed the chapel. Other artists and sculptors, including Mary Cassatt,* Charles Reinhart,* and Lorado Taft,* provided artwork and decorative details of various sorts. James Abbott McNeill Whistler* sent a selection of his etchings for exhibit. At the World's Congress Auxiliary, the following nationally known intellectual leaders gave lectures: William Jennings Bryan,* George Washington Cable,* John Dewey,* John Fiske,* Hamlin Garland,* Henry George,* Samuel Gompers,* Mary Elizabeth Clyens Lease,* Josiah Royce,* and Lester Frank Ward.* Henry Adams,* agog when he first saw the exposition, was chairman of a Congress of Historians, members of which heard Frederick Jackson Turner* read a short version of his essay entitled "The Significance of the Frontier in American History."* Countless other figures important to an understanding of the 1890s visited the exposition for various reasons. They include Paul Laurence Dunbar,* Bernhard E. Fernow,* Henry Blake Fuller,* Scott Joplin,* Leslie Enraught Keeley,* Eadweard Muybridge,* Lewis Walker,* and Wyckoff. The World's Parliament of Religions held a colossal, week-long conference. Women were of outstanding importance at the exposition, especially at the Women's Building and during meetings of the World's Congress of Representative Women, the guiding minds behind which included those of Jane Addams,* Susan B. Anthony,* and Elizabeth Cady Stanton;* twenty-seven countries sent delegates. A main money-making feature of the exposition was a spectacular midway. Located between Jackson Park and Washington Park, it featured all kinds of sideshow attractions, including the gigantic ferris wheel of George Ferris.* William F. Cody,* better known as Buffalo Bill, performed with his Wild West show at the exposition.

The World's Columbian Exposition closed on 30 October, in the black. More than 21,500,000 admission tickets had been sold. It was a cultural and patriotic success, as well as a commercial one. It explained America to the waiting world. Later historians have properly criticized the exposition, however, as having certain deleterious effects: American imperialistic jingoism was often embarrassingly strident, Native Americans and African Americans received insufficient coverage, and incipient American architectural innovation was stifled by government-sponsored classicism. The exposition was celebrated by the issuance of the first American commemorative stamps ever authorized by the United States Postal Service. (*See* Commemorative Postage Stamps.)

World's Work. Monthly magazine. Founded in 1900 (25¢ a copy, illustrated), the magazine was partly owned, and edited (to 1913) by, Walter Hines Page,* who from the start planned to make it an optimistic, chest-thumping journal explaining to the world the success of the American way of life—in big business, industry, politics, social reform, and international influence. A little after the muckrakers had made their greatest impact, *World's Work* began to attack abuses by powerful industrialists and financiers. Still, it published the reminiscences of John D. Rockefeller* and otherwise preferred to analyze "success" rather than the social causes behind "failure." *World's Work* merged with *Review of Reviews** in 1932.

Wounded Knee. The name of a creek twenty-five miles west of Marlin, South Dakota, the site of a dreadful massacre. On 29 December 1890, eight troops (500 soldiers) of the Seventh Cavalry of the U.S. Army attempted to disarm a group of about 350 Native American Miniconjou Sioux camped along Wounded Knee Creek, on the Pine Ridge Reservation, and to herd them back to Standing Rock, South Dakota. The army was under the command of Colonel James W. Forsyth. The Sioux were led by Big Foot, old and suffering from pneumonia. On 15 December, at Standing Rock, Sitting Bull,* his young son, six of his bodyguards, and six Native American policemen had been killed in a fight occasioned by an order for Sitting Bull's arrest. The Miniconjou Sioux had recently heard of his death and were reluctant to be disarmed. A shot was fired—by which side is still a matter of dispute. In the ensuing confusion, more shots were fired, four army Hotchkiss rapid-fire guns opened up on the Native Americans, hand-to-hand fighting followed, and the Native Americans broke through the army circle. More fighting occurred in the village and gullies, and more Native Americans and members of their families were pursued and killed. One reputable authority lists casualties as 146 Native Americans and 25 soldiers killed, and 51 Native Americans and 39 soldiers wounded. (Figures, however, vary widely.)

Historians are not in agreement as to the immediate cause of the massacre. Big Foot's band, surrounded by soldiers with superior weapons, including artillery, was not likely to have initiated any provocative action. Furthermore, the Seventh Cavalry, General George Armstrong Custer's old outfit, after a quarter of a century, may still have itched for revenge. Surely reasons for long-standing resentment in the Native Americans' minds and hearts included their loss of traditional lands, their miserable mistreatment for decades, untrained and dishonest white agents, and the belief by many Native Americans that their Ghost-Dance religion, led by Wovoka,* made them invulnerable. Charles Eastman,* the Pine Ridge agency physician, cared for the massacre survivors. Frederic Remington,* covering the Sioux uprising, was an almost on-the-scene illustrator of the massacre. Immediately after the massacre, about 4,000 frenzied Pine Reservation Native Americans retreated fifteen miles north. They were pursued and surrounded on orders from General Nelson A. Miles* by units of the Seventh Cavalry and the Ninth Cavalry, and they surrendered without gunfire on 15 January 1891. The perhaps inevitable tragedy at Wounded Knee spelled the end of organized Native American resistance in the Old West.

Wounds in the Rain: A Collection of Stories Relating to the Spanish-American War of 1898 (1900). Collection of tales by Stephen Crane.* The best of these twelve sketchy tales are ''The Price of the Harness,'' ''Marines Signaling under Fire at Guantanamo,'' and ''War Memories.'' ''The Price of the Harness'' narrates a death-marked soldier's unsung courage during the Spanish-American War,* specifically at the time of the American attack on Kettle Hill, in Cuba (1 July 1897). An often-quoted line from the story is this: ''He laid his face to his rifle as if it were his mistress.'' Joseph Conrad and Richard Harding Davis* regarded the story as especially excellent. ''Marines Signaling under Fire at Guantanamo'' contains honest, graphic reporting. ''War Memories'' summarizes Crane's varied experiences in the conflict, with basic veracity plus some obvious fiction here and there, all neatly touched with topographical accuracy, grotesque imagery, grim humor, self-deprecation, and understatement. For example, Crane closes his detailed ''War Memories'' with this confession: ''I have told you nothing at all.'' One other piece deserves mention. It is ''This Majestic Lie,'' which concerns the dishonesty of yellow-press journalism during the war.

Wovoka (1854–1932). Native American Paiute. The son of a Paiute prophet, he was born in Nevada Territory and lived for a time with a white rancher and his family, who called him Jack Wilson and taught him about the Bible. An unspecified sickness (1889) caused him to have visions in which he figured as a Native American Messiah who had died, seen God in heaven, and returned to life. Wovoka began to preach a message of love and neighborliness, but he also encouraged the five-day Ghost Dance. The practice of this peaceful dance spread rapidly from Nevada into the North Plains, was written about by alarmed journalists, and was discussed apprehensively by army commanders, especially when the Sioux began to convert it into a war dance. Native Americans participating in the Ghost Dance, as modified by the Sioux, regarded themselves as invulnerable to army gunfire when wearing Ghost Shirts, which were made of buckskin and were decorated with buffalo and thunderbird paintings. It was thought that Sitting Bull* offered encouragement to both the Ghost Dance and to Native American restiveness in Nebraska and the Dakotas. His arrest and murder in 1890 led to the massacre at Wounded Knee,* after which Wovoka faded into obscurity and died many years later in Nevada.

Wright, Frank Lloyd (1869–1959). Architect. He was born in Richland Center, Wisconsin. His father was a minister and musician; his mother, a Welsh-born schoolteacher. The Wright family moved to Iowa, Rhode Island, and Massachusetts, then returned to Wisconsin. After his parents were divorced in 1885 his father abandoned the children. Young Wright worked for a local builder and was a part-time civil engineering student at the University of Wisconsin (1885–1886). He went to Chicago in 1887 and began to work (1887–1893) for his ideal, famed architect Louis Sullivan,* doing residential designs and helping with plans for the Victorian Hotel (Chicago, 1893). When Sullivan discovered that Wright was developing a private practice by working late at night, the two parted company. Wright's popular houses in the 1890s and a little later were influenced by Japanese architecture (an example of which Wright saw at the World's Columbian Exposition* [1893]), Mayan and Mediterranean peasant homes, and cubism. His work became famous for low planes (including exaggerated eaves), hipped and multileveled roofs, wide windows, balconies, curving terraces, and memorable overall appearance. Wright developed town plans (1900) for clusters of homes, four in each group. He published plans in the *Ladies' Home Journal** (1901) for what was known as the prairie house (a modification of Sullivan's version of the shingle style). These typically two-storied homes featured wide-eaved roofs with or without gables, wing walls, accentuated horizontal lines, casement windows in bands, rooms connected by wide openings, and occasionally tall basements. Modifications which included main rooms on the second floor led indirectly to the modern split-level residence.

Wright's lecture entitled "The Art and Craft of the Machine" (1901, often repeated) is a modern architecture manifesto. In the twentieth century, Wright built modified prairie houses in Chicago and its environs, elsewhere in Illinois, and gradually in other states. Later, he developed inexpensive, flat-roofed, one-story "Usonian homes" on heated concrete slabs. He accepted commissions to design company buildings, banks, and hotels. His work is too extensive to list here, but it does include the Larkin Building (Buffalo, 1904), the Imperial Hotel (Tokyo, 1922), his own home and office and school (Taliesin East, at Spring Green, Wisconsin, 1909; burned and rebuilt in 1914, hit by lightning and rebuilt in 1925), Falling Water (Mill Run, Pennsylvania, 1938; now widely regarded as the most beautiful structure to be designed in the last 100 years), Johnson's Wax Building (Racine, Wisconsin, 1936), Taliesin West (another home, office, and school near Scottsdale, Arizona, 1938), the Florida Southern College chapel (Lakeland, 1940), and the Guggenheim Museum (New York, 1959). In all, Wright designed nearly 1,000 buildings.

Wright married Catherine Lee Tobin in 1889; the couple had six children and were divorced in 1922. Meanwhile, he openly lived, in Germany, Italy, and the United States, with Mamah Cheney, whose husband reluctantly gave her a divorce. While she, her two children, and four friends were staying in Taliesin East and Wright was temporarily in Chicago, a demented cook-houseman set fire to the structure, murdered all seven occupants, and killed himself (1914). Wright married his sculptress companion Miriam Noel in 1923; she left him in 1924 and agreed to a divorce in 1927. He had a child by Olgivanna Hinzenberg (also called Olga Lazovich), who was thirty-nine years younger than he and who later became his third wife (as of 1928). Wright wrote *Experimenting with Human Lives* (1923), *Modern Architecture* (1931), *An Autobiography* (1932, rev. 1943), *The Disappearing City* (1932, arguing that automobiles were causing urban decay), *An Organic Architecture* (1939), *An American Architecture* (1955), and *A Testament* (1957). He merits his unique fame as an architect for using materials, on site where possible, so as to show their character; for developing organic and democratic forms, plasticity and interrelationship of materials and lines, and spatial openness and continuity; and for subordinating everything to human needs. Olgivanna Wright wrote a somewhat unreliable memoir concerning her deceased husband (1966).

Wrigley, William, Jr. (1861–1932). Industrialist. Born in Philadelphia, he worked for his father's soap-manufacturing company (beginning in 1874), moved to Chicago (1891) to distribute his father's products, and inaugurated the idea of offering premiums, including chewing gum, with purchases. Gum immediately became more popular than soap; so he concentrated on manufacturing and selling gum instead. The business grew fast, as his early gum brands, including Pepsin, Sweet-Sixteen, and Vassar, spread across the United States. More brands followed. He incorporated as the William Wrigley, Jr., Company (1910), capitalized at $9,000,000. He obtained chicle, the essential ingredient in chewing gum, from Mexico and elsewhere south of the border, and flavors from Michigan spearmint farms. The gum manufacturing process went on in factories in Chicago and elsewhere in the United States and abroad. Wrigley retired as company president in 1915 but remained board chairman and helped direct other commercial organizations as well. He was principal owner of the Chicago Cubs, a baseball team in the National League, and encouraged other athletic endeavors in many ways. He is to be commended for much philanthropic generosity. Wrigley married Ada E. Foote in 1885 (the couple had two children).

Wyckoff, Walter A. (1865–1908). (Full name: Walter Augustus Wyckoff.) Educator, sociologist, and author. He was born in Mainpuri, India, the son of an American missionary, of Dutch ancestry, and his wife. He was educated in America, first at the Hudson Academy and the Freehold Institute, and then he graduated from the College of New Jersey (1888), which later became Princeton. He attended the Princeton Theological Seminary for one year, traveled abroad, and then decided to augment his theoretical knowledge of social problems by practical experience to be gained through becoming an itinerant, unskilled laborer (1891–1893) in Connecticut, New York State, Pennsylvania, Chicago (where he worked at the World's Columbian Exposition*), Denver, the Southwest, and finally California. After this period, Wyckoff went around the world tutoring. Once back at Princeton, he was less interested in abstract theology, and he became a lecturer in sociology and then an assistant professor of political economy there (until 1908). He wrote up his adventures as a manual laborer, his observation of a variety of fellow workers, and his socialistic conclusions in *The*

*Workers: An Experiment in Reality: The East** (1897), *The Workers: An Experiment in Reality: The West** (1898), and *A Day with a Tramp and Other Days* (1901). He was a member of the [Robert Edwin] Peary* Auxiliary Expedition in 1899. Wyckoff married musician Leah Lucille Ehrich in 1903 (the couple had one child).

Wyndham Towers (1890). Narrative poem, mostly in blank verse, by Thomas Bailey Aldrich.* Wyndham Towers, an old structure in Devonshire, is the scene of a family tragedy in Elizabethan times. Vicious Richard Wyndham and his attractive brother Darrell both love Griselda. Richard kills his brother, but, while he is trying to hide the body, he is trapped in an airless chamber. Griselda soon dies. Before a later owner can bring his bride to the Wyndham Towers, he wants to renovate it. During reconstruction, a workman finds the dusty skeletons and then the towers burn. In a letter to a friend (4 June 1900), Aldrich called this work his "best long poem." Its archaic, richly imagistic style has much to recommend it.

Y

Yale Review. Quarterly journal. Founded in May 1892, the original purpose of the journal was to replace Yale's theologically oriented *New Englander*, which discontinued publication in 1892. The new review featured essays on economics, history, literature, and politics and excellent book reviews. It was edited (1892–1911) by Henry Walcott Farnam, professor of economics at Yale and the son-in-law of the last editor of the *New Englander*. Material on international politics was especially notable, and a conservative, anti-imperialistic American policy was steadily advocated. When the *American Historical Review** began publishing in 1896, the *Yale Review* stopped including historical essays. When a group of economists announced plans to establish a journal devoted to essays on economics (1911), the *Yale Review* commenced a new series (October 1911), edited by the illustrious Wilbur Lucius Cross and publishing shorter essays, lighter items, and some poetry. Incidentally, the *Sewanee Review** was also founded in 1892.

Yekl: A Tale of the New York Ghetto (1896). Short novel by Abraham Cahan.* The novel concerns Yekl, a blacksmith from the Old World who has left his wife Gitl and their child to migrate ahead of them to New York City, where he has become Jake Podgorny, a tailor in a sweatshop. He professes to like boxing and baseball (ultra-American activities), impresses the female workers, and reluctantly sends for his family. When they arrive, Jake now regards Gitl as frumpy and divorces her. He strives for American materialistic improvement by marrying Mamie, even as pathetic little Gitl weds decent, scholarly young Bernstein. Cahan is here satirizing the American "success" story by revealing the corruption of Jake. Cahan showed his manuscript to William Dean Howells,* who had met him earlier and who found a publisher for it, but only after such a delay that Cahan translated his story into Yiddish, as *Yankel the Yankee*, and serialized it in the *Arbeiter Tseitung* (beginning on 18 October 1895). The novel was a popular and a critical success.

"The Yellow Wall-paper" (1892). Short story by Charlotte Perkins Gilman.* The narrator, a young wife and new mother named Jane, is suffering from an undefined nervous disorder, and is taken to a rented mansion in the country by her husband John, a well-meaning but misguided and gently domineering physician. Jane wants to write in a meaningful and therapeutic way, but she is pressured not to do so by John, by her brother (also a physician), and by S. Weir Mitchell.* Jane secretly continues to keep a diary of her impressions, while she is largely confined in a nailed-down bed in a garret-nursery room with barred windows and peeling yellow paper on the walls. Its pattern is hideous, dull, and confusing, with irregular lines which "curve . . . for a little distance . . . [and] suddenly commit suicide— . . . destroy themselves in unheard-of contradictions." Days pass, and Jane begins to identify the outline of "a woman stooping down and creeping about behind that pattern." This imagined woman can leave the mansion and escape into the sunshine, but on moonlit nights she is imprisoned and shakes the paper. One night the demented narrator and her alter ego in the wallpaper lines cooperate to peel and shake off long strips of the paper. At the end, John rushes in and finds his wife on all fours, crouching the way her doppelgänger did and becoming that creature. The woman boasts that she has freed herself—from John and Jane!—by destroying the paper; when John faints, she creeps over him.

In real life, Gilman, married in 1884, became a mother in 1885, suffered a nervous disorder thereafter, and was patronizingly treated in 1887 by Dr. Mitchell, who prescribed exclusive devotion to domesticity and motherhood, regular rest after meals, a maximum of two hours daily of intellectual activity, no use of the imagination, and no more writing or drawing ever again.

As early as 1890, Gilman tried to publish "The Yellow Wall-paper." *Scribner's Magazine** rejected it. She then sent it to William Dean Howells,* who passed it on to his successor at the *Atlantic Monthly*.* He also rejected it, on the grounds that it would make readers miserable. Gilman finally sent it to the *New England Magazine*, where it was published (January 1892). It caused a pro-and-con stir, may have inspired Dr. Mitchell to alter his treatment of neurasthenia, was reprinted as a chapbook in 1899, figured in a 1920 anthology of American stories assembled by Howells, and has been reprinted and overanalyzed to this day.

Youma: The Story of a West-Indian Slave (1890). Novella by Lafcadio Hearn.* Its plot is based on a real-life event that occurred during the bloody 1848 Martinique slave insurrection. Youma is a slave girl. Her best friend is a Creole named Aimée Desrivières. Aimée marries, has a daughter named Mayotte, and dies. Beautiful Youma, who becomes Mayotte's loyal servant, attracts the attention of Gabriel, the black plantation overseer, who wants her to elope with him. But Youma remains to serve and guard Mayotte. During the ensuing slave rebellion, the endangered Desrivières family escapes to town for protection in a friendly family's home, which the rebels set on fire. Although some of the white occupants jump out of the windows to safety, Youma refuses to leave without Mayotte, defies the rebels, and burns to death. The story is told in Hearn's usual impressionistic style, with colorful vividness and graphic detail. The enslaved heroine gives up her lover, remains devoted to the white child in her care, and perishes.

A NINETIES BIBLIOGRAPHY

WORKS CONCERNING HISTORICAL AND CULTURAL BACKGROUND

Ammons, Elizabeth. *Conflicting Stories: American Women Writers at the Turn into the Twentieth Century*. New York: Oxford University Press, 1991.

Bailyn, Bernard, et al. *The Great Republic: A History of the American People*. Boston and Toronto: Little, Brown, 1977.

Berman, Jeffrey. *The Talking Cure: Literary Representations of Psychoanalysis*. New York and London: New York University Press, 1985.

Berthoff, Warner. *The Ferment of Realism: American Literature, 1884–1919*. New York: Free Press, 1965.

Bordman, Gerald. *American Operetta from* H.M.S. Pinafore *to* Sweeney Todd. New York and London: Oxford University Press, 1981.

———. *American Musical Comedy from* Adonis *to* Dreamgirls. New York and London: Oxford University Press, 1982.

———. *American Musical Revue from* The Passing Show *to* Sugar Babies. New York and London: Oxford University Press, 1985.

Bresnahan, Roger James. *The Literature of the Spanish-American War: An Anti-Imperialist Anthology*. Ann Arbor, MI: Xerox University Microfilms, 1974.

Brooks, Van Wyck. *The Confident Years: 1885–1915*. New York: E. P. Dutton, 1952.

Browne, Turner, and Elaine Partnow. *Macmillan Biographical Encyclopedia of Photographic Artists & Innovators*. New York: Macmillan Co., 1983.

Chronicle of America. Mount Kisco, NY: Chronicle Publications, [1989].

Clark, Patrick. *Sports Firsts*. New York: Facts on File, 1981.

Conn, Peter. *Literature in America: An Illustrated History*. Cambridge, England: Cambridge University Press, 1989.

Craven, Wayne. *Sculpture in America*. New York: Thomas Y. Crowell, 1968.

Current, Karen. *Photography and the Old West*, New York: Harry N. Abrams, 1986.

Davidson, Abraham A. *The Story of American Painting*. New York: Harry N. Abrams, 1974.

Day, Martin S. *History of American Literature from the Beginning to 1910*. Garden City, NY: Doubleday, 1970.

Douglas, Susan J. *Inventing America Broadcasting: 1899–1922*. Baltimore and London: Johns Hopkins University Press, 1987.

Downs, Robert B. *Famous American Books*. New York: McGraw-Hill, 1971.

Dulles, Foster Rhea. *Americans Abroad: Two Centuries of European Travel*. Ann Arbor: University of Michigan Press, 1964.

Dynes, Walter R. *Encyclopedia of Homosexuality*. 2 vols. New York and London: Garland, 1990.

Emery, Edwin. *The Press and America: An Interpretative History of the Mass Media*. 3rd ed. Englewood Cliffs, NJ: Prentice-Hall, 1972.

Ferré, John P. *A Social Gospel for Millions: The Religious Bestsellers of Charles Sheldon, Charles Gordon, and Harold Bell Wright*. Bowling Green, OH: Bowling Green State University Popular Press, 1988.

Grun, Bernard. *The Timetables of History: A Horizontal Linkage of People and Events*. New York: Simon and Schuster, 1979.

Hamm, Charles. *Music in the New World*. New York and London: W. W. Norton, 1983.

Hart, James D. *The Oxford Companion to American Literature*. 4th ed. New York: Oxford University Press, 1965.

Hickok, Ralph. *New Encyclopedia of Sports*. New York: McGraw-Hall, 1977.

Hitchcock, H. Wiley. *Music in the United States: A Historical Introduction*. 3rd ed. Englewood Cliffs, NJ: Prentice-Hall, 1988.

Hook, Andrew. *American Literature in Context, III: 1865–1900*. London and New York: Methuen, 1983.

Hoopes, Donelson F. *The American Impressionists*. New York: Watson-Guptill, 1972.

Howard, John Tasker. *Our American Music: A Comprehensive History from 1620 to the Present*. 4th ed. New York: Thomas Y. Crowell, 1965.

Hoyt, Edwin P. *The Whitneys: An Informal Portrait 1635–1975*. New York: Weybright and Talley, 1976.

Izod, John. *Hollywood and Box Office, 1895–1986*. New York: Columbia University Press, 1988.

Jaher, Frederic Cople. *Doubters and Dissenters: Cataclysmic Thought in America, 1885–1918*. New York: Free Press of Glencoe, 1964.

John, Arthur. *The Best Years of the Century: Richard Watson Gilder*, Scribner's Magazine, *and the* Century Magazine, *1870–1909*. Urbana, Chicago, London: University of Illinois Press, 1981.

Josephson, Matthew. *The Robber Barons: The Great American Capitalists, 1861–1901*. New York: Harcourt, Brace & World, 1934.

Knight, Grant C. "The 'Pastry' Period in Literature." *Saturday Review of Literature* 27 (16 December 1944): 5–7, 22–23.

———. *The Critical Period in American Literature*. Chapel Hill: University of North Carolina Press, 1951.

Kunitz, Stanley J., and Howard Haycraft, eds. *American Authors 1600–1900: A Biographical Dictionary of American Literature*. New York: H. W. Wilson, 1938.

Lauritsen, John, and David Thorstad. *The Early Homosexual Rights Movement (1864–1935)*. New York: Times Change Press, 1974.

A Literary History of the American West, sponsored by the Western Literature Association. Fort Worth: Texas Christian University Press, 1987.

Lloyd, Norman. *The Golden Encyclopedia of Music*. New York: Golden Press, 1968.

Logan, Rayford W., and Michael R. Winston, eds. *Dictionary of American Negro Biography*. New York and London: W. W. Norton, 1982.

Loggins, Vernon. *The Negro Author: His Development in America to 1900*. New York: Columbia University Press, 1931.

Lovell, John, Jr. *Digests of Great American Plays: Complete Summaries of More Than 100 Plays from the Beginnings to the Present*. New York: Thomas Y. Crowell, 1961.

Martin, Jay. *Harvests of Change: American Literature 1895–1914*. Englewood Cliffs, NJ: Prentice-Hall, 1967.

Mattfeld, Julius. *Variety Music Cavalcade 1620–1969: A Chronology of Vocal and Instrumental Music Popular in the United States*. 3rd ed. Englewood Cliffs, NJ: Prentice-Hall, 1971.

Metzger, Linda, et al., eds. *Black Writers: A Selection of Sketches from Contemporary Authors*. Detroit: Gale Research, 1989.

Moody, Richard, ed. *Dramas from the American Theatre: 1762–1909*. Cleveland and New York: World Publishing, 1966.

Morris, Richard B., ed. *Encyclopedia of American History*. New York: Harper, 1953.

Mosley, Leonard. *The Glorious Fault: The Life of Lord Curzon*. New York: Harcourt, Brace, 1960.

Mott, Frank Luther. *Golden Multitudes: The Story of Best Sellers in the United States*. New York: Macmillan, 1947.

———. *A History of American Magazines, 1885–1905*. Cambridge, MA: Belknap Press of Harvard University Press, 1957.

———. *A History of American Magazines, 1905–1930*. Cambridge, MA: Belknap Press of Harvard University Press, 1968.

Panek, LeRoy Lad. *Probable Cause: Crime Fiction in America*. Bowling Green, OH: Bowling Green State University Popular Press, 1990.

Pattee, Fred Lewis. *A History of American Literature since 1870*. New York: Century, 1915.

Pearson, Hesketh. *The Marrying Americans*. New York: Coward-McCann, 1961.

Pfaelzer, Jean. *The Utopian Novel in America 1886–1896: The Politics of Form*. Pittsburgh: University of Pittsburgh Press, 1984.

Pizer, Donald. *Realism and Naturalism in Nineteenth-Century American Literature*. Carbondale and Edwardsville: Southern Illinois University Press, 1966.

———, ed. *American Thought and Writing: The 1890's*. Boston: Houghton Mifflin, 1972.

Postero, Leonard (Postosties), and Jim Koger. *The Calendar of Sports History*. Athens, GA: KP Sports Enterprises, 1981.

Quinn, Arthur Hobson. *A History of the American Drama from the Civil War to the Present Day*. 2 vols. New York: Appleton-Century-Crofts, 1927, rev. ed., 1936.

———. *American Fiction: An Historical and Critical Survey*. New York: Appleton-Century-Crofts, 1936.

Roberts, Peter. *The New Immigration: A Study of the Industrial and Social Life of Southeastern Europeans in America*. New York: Macmillan Co., 1912.

Rogal, Samuel J. *A Chronological Outline of American Literature*. Westport, CT: Greenwood Press, 1987.

Rood, Karen L., ed. *American Literary Almanac: From 1608 to the Present*. New York and Oxford: Facts on File, 1988.
Runte, Alfred. *National Parks: The American Experience*. 2d ed., rev. Lincoln and London: University of Nebraska Press, 1987.
Russell, Sandi. *Render Me My Song: African-American Women Writers from Slavery to the Present*. New York: St. Martin's Press, 1990.
Sanders, Ronald. *The Downtown Jews: Portraits of an Immigrant Generation*. New York: Harper & Row, 1969.
Schlereth, Wendy Clauson. *The Chap-Book: A Journal of American Intellectual Life in the 1890s*. Ann Arbor: UMI Research Press, 1982.
Schneider, Herbert W. *A History of American Philosophy*. New York: Columbia University Press, 1946.
Slosson, Edwin E. *Great American Universities*. New York: Macmillan Co., 1910.
Sparhawk, Ruth M., Mary E. Leslie, Phyllis Y. Turbow, and Zina R. Rose. *American Women in Sport, 1887–1987: A 100-Year Chronology*. Metuchen, NJ: Scarecrow, 1989.
Story of the Great American West. Pleasantville, NY, Reader's Digest Association, 1977.
Sung, Betty Lee. *Mountain of Gold: The Story of the Chinese in America*. New York: Macmillan Co., 1967.
Treat, Roger, with revisions edited by Pete Palmer. *The Encyclopedia of Football*. 15th ed. South Brunswick, NJ: A. S. Barnes, 1977.
Utley, Robert M., and Wilcomb E. Washburn. *The American Heritage History of the Indian Wars*. New York: American Heritage, 1977.
Vanderbilt, Arthur T., II. *Fortune's Children: The Fall of the House of Vanderbilt*. New York: William Morrow, 1989.
Veysey, Laurence R. *The Emergence of the American University*. Chicago and London: University of Chicago Press, 1965.
Wagenknecht, Edward. *Cavalcade of the American Novel*. New York: Holt, 1952.
Weisberger, Bernard A., et al. *The Life History of the United States*, vol. 7: 1877–1890. *The Age of Steel and Steam*. New York: Time, 1964.
———. *The Life History of the United States*, vol. 8: 1890–1901. *Reaching for Empire*. New York: Time, 1964.
Whitlow, Roger. *Black American Literature: A Critical History*. Chicago: Nelson Hall, 1973, rev. 1976.
Williams, William James. *A Heritage of American Paintings from the National Gallery of Art*. Maplewood, NJ: Rutland Press and Hammond, 1981.
Yellen, Samuel. *American Labor Struggles*. New York: Harcourt, Brace, 1974.
Ziff, Larzer. *The American 1890s: Life and Times of a Lost Generation*. New York: Viking, 1966.

WORKS ON AUTHORS

Agosta, Lucien L. *Howard Pyle*. Boston: Twayne, 1987.
Anderson, David D. *Ignatius Donnelly*. Boston: Twayne, 1980.
Bennett, James D. *Frederick Jackson Turner*. Boston: Twayne, 1975.
Bergmann, Frank. *Robert Grant*. Boston: Twayne, 1982.
Bickley, R. Bruce, Jr. *Joel Chandler Harris*. Boston: Twayne, 1978.

Billington, Ray Allen. *Frederick Jackson Turner: Historian, Scholar, Teacher*. New York: Oxford University Press, 1973.

Bishop, Ferman. *Henry Adams*. Boston: Twayne, 1979.

Blansfield, Karen Charmaine. *Cheap Rooms and Restless Hearts: A Study of Formula in the Urban Tales of William Sydney Porter*. Bowling Green, OH: Bowling Green State University Popular Press, 1988.

Bonner, Thomas, Jr. *The Kate Chopin Companion*. Westport, CT: Greenwood Press, 1988.

Bowman, Sylvia E. *Edward Bellamy*. Boston: Twayne, 1986.

Bowron, Bernard R., Jr. *Henry B. Fuller of Chicago: The Ordeal of a Genteel Realist in Ungenteel America*. Westport, CT: Greenwood Press, 1974.

Briggs, Austin, Jr. *The Novels of Harold Frederic*. Ithaca, NY: Cornell University Press, 1969.

Brooks, Van Wyck. *Fenollosa and His Circle with Other Essays in Biography*. New York: E. P. Dutton, 1962.

Brown, Maurice F. *Estranging Dawn: The Life and Works of William Vaughn Moody*. Carbondale and Edwardsville: Southern Illinois University Press, 1973.

Buckingham, Willis J., ed. *Emily Dickinson's Reception in the 1890s: A Documentary History*. Pittsburgh: University of Pittsburgh Press, 1989.

Budd, Louis J. *Robert Herrick*. New York: Twayne, 1971.

Butcher, Philip. *George Washington Cable*. New Haven, CT: College & University Press, 1962.

Carrington, George C., Jr., and Ildikó de Papp Carrington. *Plots and Characters in the Fiction of William Dean Howells*. Hamden, CT: Archon, 1976.

Cary, Richard. *Sarah Orne Jewett*. New York: Twayne, 1962.

Cobbs, John L. *Owen Wister*. Boston: Twayne, 1984.

Coyle, Lee. *George Ade*. New York: Twayne, 1964.

Current-Garcia, Eugene. *O. Henry*. New Haven, CT: College & University Press, 1965.

Dorfman, Joseph. *Thorstein Veblen and His America*. New York: A. M. Kelley, 1966.

DuBois, Paul Z. *Paul Leicester Ford: An American Man of Letters, 1865–1902*. New York: Burt Franklin, 1977.

Eble, Kenneth E. *William Dean Howells: Second Edition*. Boston: Twayne, 1982.

Erisman, Fred, and Richard W. Etulain, eds. *Fifty Western Writers: A Bio-Bibliographical Sourcebook*. Westport, CT: Greenwood Press, 1982.

Etulain, Richard W. *Owen Wister*. Boise, ID: Boise State College, 1973.

Filler, Louis. "Introduction" to Finley Peter Dunne, *Mr. Dooley: Now and Forever*. Stanford, CA: Academic Reprints, 1954.

Franchere, Hoyt C. *Edwin Arlington Robinson*. New York: Twayne, 1968.

Frederic, Harold. *The Correspondence of Harold Frederic*, ed. by George E. Fortenberry, Stanton Garner, and Robert H. Woodward. Fort Worth: Texas Christian University Press, 1977.

French, Warren. *Frank Norris*. New York: Twayne, 1962.

Frost, O. W. *Joaquin Miller*. New York: Twayne, 1967.

Gale, Robert L. *Plots and Characters in the Works of Mark Twain*. 2 vols. Hamden, CT: Archon, 1973.

———. *Charles Warren Stoddard*. Boise, ID: Boise State University, 1977.

———. *John Hay*. Boston: Twayne, 1978.

———. *A Henry James Encyclopedia*. Westport, CT: Greenwood Press, 1989.

Gish, Robert. *Hamlin Garland: The Far West*. Boise, ID: Boise State University, 1976.

Greenslet, Ferris. *The Life of Thomas Bailey Aldrich*. Boston and New York: Houghton Mifflin, 1908.

Grenander, M. E. *Ambrose Bierce*. New York: Twayne, 1971.

Gross, Theodore L. *Thomas Nelson Page*. New York: Twayne, 1967.

Haldane, Seán. *The Fright of Time: Joseph Trumbull Stickney 1874–1904*. Ladysmith, Québec: Ladysmith Press, 1970.

Halpern, Martin. *William Vaughn Moody*. New York: Twayne, 1964.

Henson, Clyde E. *Joseph Kirkland*. New York: Twayne, 1962.

Hills, Mary A. *Charlotte Perkins Gilman: The Making of a Radical Feminist, 1860–1896*. Philadelphia: Temple University Press, 1980.

Holzberger, William G., ed. *The Complete Poems of George Santayana, A Critical Edition*. Lewisburg, PA: Bucknell University Press, 1979.

Kirk, Clara Marburg. *W. D. Howells, Traveler from Altruria 1889–1894*. New Brunswick, NJ: Rutgers University Press, 1962.

Knapp, Bettina L. *Stephen Crane*. New York: Ungar, 1987.

Kunitz, Stanley J., and Howard Haycraft, eds. *American Authors, 1600–1900: A Biographical Dictionary of American Literature*. New York: H. W. Wilson, 1938.

Langford, Gerald. *The Richard Harding Davis Years: A Biography of a Mother and Son*. New York: Holt, Rinehart and Winston, 1961.

Lazarus, A. L. *The Best of George Ade*. Bloomington: Indiana University Press, 1985.

Lazarus, A. L., and Victor H. Jones. *Beyond Graustark: George Barr McCutcheon, Playwright Discovered*. Port Washington, NY: Kennikat, 1981.

Leary, Lewis, ed. *Mark Twain's Correspondence with Henry Huttleston Rogers 1893–1909*. Berkeley and Los Angeles: University of California Press, 1969.

Lewis, R.W.B., and Nancy Lewis, eds. *The Letters of Edith Wharton*. New York: Scribner's, 1988.

Linneman, William R. *Richard Hovey*. Boston: Twayne, 1976.

Linson, Corwin K. *My Stephen Crane*. Edited by Edwin H. Cady. Syracuse, NY: Syracuse University Press, 1958.

Lyon, Thomas J. *John Muir*. Boise, ID: Boise State College, 1972.

McCullough, Joseph B. *Hamlin Garland*. Boston: Twayne, 1978.

McDermott, John J., ed. *The Writings of William James: A Comprehensive Edition*. New York: Random House, 1967.

———. *The Basic Writings of Josiah Royce*. 2 vols. Chicago and London: University of Chicago Press, 1969.

Macdonald, Allan Houston. *Richard Hovey: Man & Craftsman*. Durham, NC: Duke University Press, 1957.

Moran, John C. *An F. Marion Crawford Companion*. Westport, CT: Greenwood Press, 1981.

Morris, Lloyd. *William James: The Message of a Modern Mind*. New York: Scribner's, 1950.

Myers, Gerald E. *William James: His Life and Thought*. New Haven and London: Yale University Press, 1986.

Nagel, James, ed. *Critical Essays on Hamlin Garland*. Boston: G. K. Hall, 1982.

O'Connor, Richard. *Ambrose Bierce: A Biography*. Boston and Toronto: Little, Brown, 1967.

Osborn, Scott Compton, and Robert L. Phillips, Jr. *Richard Harding Davis*. Boston: Twayne, 1978.

Pearce, T. M. *Mary Hunter Austin*. New York: Twayne, 1965.

Perry, Ralph Barton. *The Thought and Character of William James*. 2 vols. Boston: Little, Brown, 1936.

Pilkington, John, Jr. *Francis Marion Crawford*. New York: Twayne, 1964.

———. *Henry Blake Fuller*. New York: Twayne, 1970.

Revell, Peter. *James Whitcomb Riley*. New York: Twayne, 1970.

Rhodehamel, Josephine DeWitt, and Raymund Francis Wood. *Ina Coolbrith: Librarian and Laureate of California*. Provo, UT: Brigham Young University Press, 1973.

Rideout, Walter B. "Introduction." Ignatius Donnelly, *Caesar's Column: A Story of the Twentieth Century*. Cambridge, MA: Belknap Press of Harvard University Press, 1960.

Ridge, Martin. *Ignatius Donnelly: The Portrait of a Politician*. Chicago: University of Chicago Press, 1962.

Ross, Edward J. *Henry George*. New York: Twayne, 1968.

Rouse, Blair. *Ellen Glasgow*. New York: Twayne, 1962.

St. Pierre, Brian, ed. *The Devil's Advocate: An Ambrose Bierce Reader*. San Francisco: Chronicle Books, 1987.

Samuels, Charles E. *Thomas Bailey Aldrich*. New York: Twayne, 1965.

Samuels, Ernest. *Henry Adams*. Cambridge, MA: Harvard University Press, 1989.

Scambray, Kenneth. *A Varied Harvest: The Life and Works of Henry Blake Fuller*. Pittsburgh: University of Pittsburgh Press, 1987.

Scharnhorst, Gary. *Horatio Alger, Jr*. Boston: Twayne, 1980.

———. *Charlotte Perkins Gilman*. Boston: Twayne, 1985.

Scholnick, Robert J. *Edmund Clarence Stedman*. Boston: Twayne, 1977.

Schwab, Arnold T. "James Huneker's Criticism of American Literature." *American Literature* 29 (March 1957): 64–78.

Shepherd, Jean, ed. *The America of George Ade (1866–1944): Fables, Short Stories, Essays*. New York: Putnam's, 1961.

Smith, Herbert F. *Richard Watson Gilder*. New York: Twayne, 1970.

Spiller, Robert E. "Introduction." Hamlin Garland, *Crumbling Idols: Twelve Essays on Art and Literature*. Gainesville, FL: Scholars' Facsimiles and Reprints, 1952.

Sprague, Claire. *Edgar Saltus*. New York: Twayne, 1968.

Stallman, R. W. *Stephen Crane: A Biography*. New York: Braziller, 1968.

Stephens, Donald. *Bliss Carman*. New York: Twayne, 1966.

Stevenson, Elizabeth. *Lafcadio Hearn*. New York: Macmillan Co., 1961.

Stineman, Esther Lanigan. *Mary Austin: Song of a Maverick*. New York and London: Yale University Press, 1989.

Stuart, David. *O. Henry: A Biography of William Sydney Porter*. Chelsea, MI: Scarborough House, 1990.

Thiébaux, Marcelle. *Ellen Glasgow*. New York: Ungar, 1982.

Titus, Warren I. *Winston Churchill*. New York: Twayne, 1963.

Turner, Arlin. *George Washington Cable: A Biography*. Durham, NC: Duke University Press, 1956.

Wertheim, Stanley, and Paul Sorrentino, eds. *The Correspondence of Stephen Crane*. 2 vols. New York: Columbia University Press, 1988.

Westbrook, Percy D. Rev. ed. *Mary Wilkins Freeman*. Boston: Twayne, 1988.

Winston, George P. *John Fiske*. New York: Twayne, 1972.
Woodress, James. *Booth Tarkington: Gentleman from Indiana*. Philadelphia and New York: Lippincott, 1955.

WORKS ON ARTISTS, COMPOSERS, AND SCULPTORS

Agosta, Lucien L. *Howard Pyle*. Boston: Twayne, 1987.
Dippie, Brian W. *Looking and [Charles Marion] Russell*. Fort Forth, TX: Carter Museum, 1987.
Downes, William Howe. *John S. Sargent: His Life and Work*. Boston: Little, Brown, 1925.
Erisman, Fred. *Frederic Remington*. Boise, ID: Boise State University, 1975.
Gale, Robert L. *Charles Marion Russell*. Boise, ID: Boise State University, 1979.
Gilman, Lawrence. *Edward MacDowell: A Study*. New York: Lane, 1909.
McCracken, Harold. *Frederic Remington: Artist of the Old West, with a Bibliographical Check List of Remington Pictures and Books*. Philadelphia and New York: Lippincott, 1947.
Ormond, Richard. *John Singer Sargent: Paintings, Drawings, Watercolors*. New York and Evanston: Harper & Row, 1970.
Taft, Ada Bartlett *Lorado Taft: Sculptor and Citizen*. Greensboro, NC: Privately printed, 1946.
Young, Andrew McLaren, Margaret MacDonald, Robin Spencer, and Hamish Miles. 2 vols. *The Paintings of James McNeill Whistler*. New Haven, CT: Yale University Press, 1980.

WORKS ON OTHER PERSONS

Alberts, Robert C. *The Good Provider: H. J. Heinz and his 57 Varieties*. Boston: Houghton Mifflin, 1973.
Carnes, Cecil. *Jimmy Hare, News Photographer: Half a Century with a Camera*. New York: Macmillan Co., 1940.
Cheney, Margaret. *Tesla: Man out of Time*. Englewood Cliffs, NJ: Prentice-Hall, 1981.
Cherny, Robert W. *A Righteous Cause: The Life of William Jennings Bryan*. Boston and Toronto: Little, Brown, 1985.
Cowles, Virginia. *The Astors*. New York: Knopf, 1979.
Garraty, John A., ed. *Encyclopedia of American Biography*. New York: Harper & Row, 1974.
Gates, John D. *The Astor Family*. Garden City, NY: Doubleday, 1981.
Isenberg, Michael T. *John L. Sullivan and His America*. Urbana and Chicago: University of Illinois Press, 1988.
Lewis, Oscar. *The Big Four: The Story of Huntington, Stanford, Hopkins, and Crocker, and of the Building of the Central Pacific*. New York: Knopf, 1938.
Merrill, Ginette de B., and George Arms, eds. *If Not Literature: Letters of Elinor Mead Howells*. Columbus: Ohio State University Press, 1988.
Stern, Gerald Emanuel, ed. *Gompers*. Englewood Cliffs, NJ: Prentice-Hall, 1971.
Swanberg, W. A. *Pulitzer*. New York: Scribner's, 1967.
Swetnam, George. *Andrew Carnegie*. Boston: Twayne, 1980.

Tharp, Louise Hall. *Mrs. Jack: A Biography of Isabella Stewart Gardner*. Boston: Little, Brown, 1965.

Washington, Booker T. *The Booker T. Washington Papers*. Edited by Louis R. Harlan and John W. Blassingame. *Volume I: The Autobiographical Writings*. Urbana: University of Illinois Press, 1972.

Wagenknecht, Edward. *The Seven Worlds of Theodore Roosevelt*. New York: Longmans, Green, 1958.

MISCELLANEOUS

Arlott, John, ed. *The Oxford Companion to World Sports and Games*. London: Oxford University Press, 1975.

Cribb, Joe, Barrie Cook, and Ian Carradice. *The Coin Atlas: The World of Coinage from Its Origins to the Present Day*. New York: Facts on File, 1990.

Danzig, Allison, and Joe Reichler. *Baseball: Its Great Players, Teams and Managers*. Englewood Cliffs, NJ: Prentice-Hall, 1959.

Ely, Richard T. "Pullman [the town]: A Social Study." *Harper's New Monthly Magazine* 70 (February 1885): 452–66.

Eidelberg, Martin. "Art Pottery." In *The Arts and Crafts Movement in America 1876–1916*, edited by Robert Judson Clark, 119–86. Princeton, NJ: Princeton University Press, 1972.

Findling, John E., and Kimberly D. Pelle, eds. *Historical Dictionary of World's Fairs and Expositions, 1851–1988*. Westport, CT: Greenwood Press, 1990.

Fried, Lewis F. *Makers of the City*. Amherst: University of Massachusetts Press, 1990.

Gorn, Elliott J. *The Manly Art: Bare-Knuckle Prize Fighting in America*. Ithaca, NY: Cornell University Press, 1986.

Holbrook, Stewart H. *The Story of American Railroads*. New York: Crown, 1947.

Kane, Joseph Nathan. *Famous First Facts: A Record of First Happenings, Discoveries, and Inventions in America*. 4th ed., exp. and rev. New York: H. W. Wilson, 1981.

Kimble, Ralph A. *Commemorative Postage Stamps of the United States*. Rev. ed. New York: Grosset & Dunlap, 1936.

Krisciunas, Kevin. *Astronomical Centers of the World*. Cambridge, England: Cambridge University Press, 1988.

Lamar, Howard R., ed. *The Reader's Encyclopedia of the American West*. New York: Thomas Y. Crowell, 1977.

Mandel, Leon. *American Cars*. New York: Stewart, Tabori & Chang, 1982.

Montville, John B. *Mack [Trucks]*. Newfoundland, NJ: Haessner Publishing, 1973.

Nicholson, Margaret. *A Manual of Copyright Practice for Writers, Publishers, and Agents*. 2d ed. New York: Oxford University Press, 1956.

Rae, John B. *The American Automobile*. Chicago: University of Chicago Press, 1965.

Reinfeld, Fred, and Burton Hobson. *Catalogue of the World's Most Popular Coins*. 12th ed., ed. Robert Obojski. New York: Sterling, 1986.

Sammons, Jeffrey T. *Beyond the Ring: The Role of Boxing in American Society*. Urbana and Chicago: University of Illinois Press, 1988.

Scott 1991 Specialized Catalogue of United States Stamps. 69th ed. Sidney, OH: Scott, 1990.

In addition, the usual invaluable encyclopedias and standard desk reference books, including the *Academic American*, the *American*, the *Britannica*, *Collier's*, the *Dictionary of American Biography*, the *World Book*, and various volumes edited by Frank N. Magill of plot summaries and biographical essays; and shorter biographical dictionaries such as *Webster's*, *Who's Who*, and *Who Was Who* publications.

CLASSIFIED APPENDIX: BIOGRAPHICAL ENTRIES IN KEY OCCUPATIONAL AND PROFESSIONAL CATEGORIES

ACTIVISTS, LABOR ORGANIZERS, AND REFORMERS

Addams, Jane
Anthony, Susan B.
Bellamy, Edward
Cahan, Abraham
Catt, Carrie
Comstock, Anthony
Debs, Eugene V.
Flower, B. O.
George, Henry
Gillette, King Camp
Gompers, Samuel
Harper, Frances
Hubbard, Elbert
Lloyd, William Demarest
Phillips, David Graham
Riis, Jacob
Stanton, Elizabeth Cady
Steffens, Lincoln
Washington, Booker T.
Willard, Frances Elizabeth Caroline

ARCHITECTS

Burnham, Daniel Hudson
Olmsted, Frederick L.
Sullivan, Louis
White, Stanford
Wright, Frank Lloyd

CONSERVATIONISTS

Burroughs, John
Fernow, Bernhard E.
Muir, John
Olmsted, Frederick L.
Pinchot, Gifford
Vanderbilt, George Washington

CRITICS: LITERARY, ART, AND MUSIC

Berenson, Bernard
Boyesen, H. H.
Brownell, W. C.
Crawford, F. Marion
Fuller, Henry Blake
Garland, Hamlin
Hapgood, Norman
Howells, William Dean
Huneker, James
James, Henry
Mabie, Hamilton W.
Norton, Charles Eliot
Stedman, Edmund Clarence
Van Dyke, Henry
Van Dyke, John Charles
Wharton, Edith

ECONOMISTS

George, Henry
Sumner, William Graham
Veblen, Thorstein

EDUCATORS, LECTURERS, AND ORATORS

Adams, Henry
Baker, George Pierce
Boyesen, H. H.
Brann, William Cowper
Bryan, William Jennings
Carver, George Washington
Copeland, Charles Townsend
Crawford, F. Marion
Dewey, John
Douglass, Frederick
DuBois, W.E.B.
Fenollosa, Ernest
Fernow, Bernhard E.
Fiske, John
Gates, Lewis E.
Giddings, Franklin Henry
Gilman, Charlotte Perkins
Hall, G. Stanley
Herrick, Robert
James, William
Lovett, Robert Morss
Moody, William Vaughn
Naismith, James
Norton, Charles Eliot
Page, Thomas Nelson
Page, Walter Hines
Pupin, Michael
Pyle, Howard
Reid, Whitelaw
Rockhill, William Woodville
Royce, Josiah
Santayana, George
Seton, Ernest Thompson
Steinmetz, Charles Proteus
Stoddard, Charles Warren
Sumner, William Graham
Sunday, Billy
Taft, Lorado
Tarbell, Ida M.
Tesla, Nikola
Turner, Frederick Jackson
Twain, Mark
Van Dyke, Henry
Van Dyke, John Charles
Veblen, Thorstein
Washington, Booker T.
Willard, Frances Elizabeth Caroline
Wyckoff, Walter A.

EXPLORERS

Huntington, Ellsworth
Muir, John
Peary, Robert Edwin
Powell, John Wesley

HISTORIANS

Adams, Brooks
Adams, Henry
Crawford, F. Marion
Fiske, John
Ford, Paul Leicester
Kirkland, Joseph
Mahan, Alfred Thayer
Roosevelt, Theodore
Tarbell, Ida M.
Turner, Frederick Jackson

HUMORISTS

Ade, George
Burgess, Gelett Frank
Dunne, Finley Peter
Field, Eugene
Twain, Mark

INDUSTRIALISTS, MANUFACTURERS, FINANCIERS, MERCHANTS, AND PHILANTHROPISTS

The Big Four
Candler, Asa Griggs
Carnegie, Andrew
Clark, William A.
Coxey, Jacob Sechler
Crocker, Charles
Daly, Marcus
Dow, Herbert Henry
Eastman, George
Edison, Thomas A.
Field, Marshall
Frick, Henry Clay
Gould, Jay

Harriman, Edward Henry
Heinz, Henry John
Heinze, F. Augustus
Hopkins, Mark
Huntington, Collis P.
Morgan, John Pierpont
Palmer, Potter
Rockefeller, John D.
Rogers, Henry Huttleston
Schwab, Charles M.
Stanford, Leland
Westinghouse, George
Wrigley, William, Jr.

INVENTORS

Astor, John Jacob IV
Bell, Alexander Graham
Burroughs, William Seward
Dick, A. B.
Eastman, George
Edison, Thomas A.
Ferris, George
Gillette, King Camp
Judson, Whitcomb L.
Naismith, James
Painter, William
Pullman, George
Pupin, Michael
Tesla, Nikola
Westinghouse, George

JOURNALISTS, EDITORS, AND PUBLISHERS

Ade, George
Alden, Henry Mills
Aldrich, Thomas Bailey
Bennett, James Gordon
Bok, Edward
Brann, William Cowper
Brisbane, Arthur
Bunner, H. C.
Burgess, Gelett Frank
Copeland, Charles Townsend
Davis, Richard Harding
Donnelly, Ignatius
Dreiser, Theodore
DuBois, W.E.B.
Dunne, Finley Peter
Flower, B. O.
Gilder, Richard Watson
Hapgood, Norman
Harris, Joel Chandler
Hearst, William Randolph
Heinemann, William
Howells, William Dean
Hubbard, Elbert
Johnson, Robert Underwood
Lovett, Robert Morss
Lummins, Charles F.
Mabie, Hamilton W.
McClure, S. S.
Marquis, Albert Nelson
Moody, William Vaughn
Munsey, Frank A.
Norton, Charles Eliot
Ochs, Adolph Simon
Page, Walter Hines
Pulitzer, Joseph
Stedman, Edmund Clarence
Stieglitz, Alfred
Stone, Herbert S.
Tarbell, Ida M.

LAWYERS

Bryan, William Jennings
Chesnutt, Charles W.
Grant, Robert
Holmes, Oliver Wendell
Kirkland, Joseph
McAllister, Ward
Major, Charles
Page, Thomas Nelson
Wallace, Lew
Wister, Owen

MILITARY AND PEACE OFFICERS

Crook, George
Dewey, George
Earp, Wyatt
Lea, Homer
Mahan, Alfred Thayer
Miles, Nelson A.
Reed, Walter
Roosevelt, Theodore

Wallace, Lew
Wood, Leonard

MUSICIANS AND COMPOSERS

Garden, Mary
Herbert, Victor
Joplin, Scott
MacDowell, Edward
Nevin, Ethelbert
Schumann-Heink, Ernestine
Sousa, John Philip

ORIENTALISTS

Fenollosa, Ernest
Hearn, Lafcadio
Lea, Homer
Rockhill, William Woodville

PAINTERS AND ILLUSTRATORS

Beard, Dan
Blakelock, Ralph Albert
Burgess, Gelett Frank
Cassatt, Mary
Eakins, Thomas
The Eight
Gibson, Charles Dana
Hassam, Childe
Heaton, Augustus George
Henri, Robert
Homer, Winslow
La Farge, John
Linson, Corwin Knapp
Pennell, Joseph
Pyle, Howard
Reinhart, Charles
Remington, Frederic
Russell, Charles Marion
Ryder, Albert Pinkham
Sargent, John Singer
Seton, Ernest Thompson
Tanner, Henry Ossawa
The Ten
Tiffany, Louis Comfort
Whistler, James Abbott McNeill

PHILOSOPHERS

Dewey, John
Fiske, John
Hall, G. Stanley
James, William
Royce, Josiah
Santayana, George

PHOTOGRAPHERS

Fly, Camillus S.
Hare, James H.
Muybridge, Eadweard
Riis, Jacob
Stieglitz, Alfred

PLAYWRIGHTS

Ade, George
Aldrich, Thomas Bailey
Belasco, David
Daly, Augustin
Davis, Richard Harding
Fitch, Clyde
Fuller, Henry Blake
Garland, Hamlin
Herne, James A.
James, Henry
Moody, William Vaughn
Tarkington, Booth

POETS

Aldrich, Thomas Bailey
Bunner, H. C.
Carman, Bliss
Chopin, Kate
Coolbrith, Ina
Crane, Stephen
Dickinson, Emily
Field, Eugene
Fuller, Henry Blake
Garland, Hamlin
Gilder, Richard Watson
Gilman, Charlotte Perkins
Grant, Robert
Harper, Frances
Hay, John
Hovey, Richard

Lodge, George Cabot
Markham, Edwin
Miller, Joaquin
Moody, William Vaughn
Riley, James Whitcomb
Robinson, Edwin Arlington
Santayana, George
Stedman, Edmund Clarence
Stickney, Trumbull

POLITICIANS, DIPLOMATS, AND STATESMEN

Altgeld, John Peter
Blaine, James G.
Bryan, William Jennings
Clark, William A.
Cleveland, Grover
Coxey, Jacob Sechler
Croker, Richard F.
Donnelly, Ignatius
Douglass, Frederick
Hanna, Mark
Harrison, Benjamin
Hay, John
Herrick, Robert
Lovett, Robert Morss
McKinley, William
Pinchot, Gifford
Reid, Whitelaw
Rockhill, William Woodville
Roosevelt, Theodore
Stanford, Leland
Van Dyke, Henry
Wallace, Lew
Weaver, James B.

SCULPTORS

French, Daniel Chester
Remington, Frederic
Russell, Charles Marion
Saint-Gaudens, Augustus
Taft, Lorado
Ward, John Quincy Adams
Warner, Olin Levi

WRITERS: FICTION

Adams, Henry
Aldrich, Thomas Bailey
Alger, Horatio, Jr.
Austin, Mary
Baum, Lyman Frank
Bierce, Ambrose
Boyesen, H. H.
Bunner, H. C.
Cahan, Abraham
Chopin, Kate
Churchill, Winston
Crane, Stephen
Crawford, F. Marion
Davis, Rebecca Harding
Davis, Richard Harding
Donnelly, Ignatius
Dreiser, Theodore
Dunbar, Paul Laurence
Ford, Paul Leicester
Frederic, Harold
Freeman, Mary E. Wilkins
Fuller, Henry Blake
Garland, Hamlin
Gilman, Charlotte Perkins
Glasgow, Ellen
Grant, Robert
Harper, Frances
Harris, Joel Chandler
Hay, John
Hearn, Lafcadio
Henry, O.
Herrick, Robert
Howells, William Dean
James, Henry
Jewett, Sarah Orne
Kirkland, Joseph
London, Jack
McCutcheon, George Barr
Major, Charles
Mitchell, S. Weir
Norris, Frank
Page, Thomas Nelson
Phillips, David Graham
Pyle, Howard
Remington, Frederic
Russell, Charles Marion
Saltus, Edgar
Sheldon, Charles M.
Stockton, Frank R.
Stoddard, Charles Warren

Tarkington, Booth
Twain, Mark
Wallace, Lew
Wharton, Edith
Wister, Owen

WRITERS: NONFICTION

Beard, Dan
Brann, William Cowper
Burroughs, John
Eastman, Charles
Eddy, Mary Baker
Farmer, Fannie Merritt
Fenollosa, Ernest
Hearn, Lafcadio
Heaton, Augustus George
Holmes, Oliver Wendell
Hubbard, Elbert
Johnson, Robert Underwood
La Farge, John
Lea, Homer
Linson, Corwin Knapp
Lummis, Charles F.
Muir, John
Peary, Robert Edwin
Riis, Jacob
Rockhill, William Woodville
Seton, Ernest Thompson
Wyckoff, Walter A.

INDEX

Page numbers in italics refer to main entries. Written or artistic works are usually indexed only if they were produced in the period 1888–1901.

About the Author

ROBERT L. GALE is Emeritus Professor of American Literature at the University of Pittsburg. He is the author of many books and articles on a range of American literary and cultural figures, including Francis John Hay, Richard Henry Dana, Jr., Mark Twain, Edgar Allan Poe, Herman Melville, Thomas Crawford, Matt Braun, Luke Short, Will Henry, and Louis L'Amour. He has published two previous reference books with Greenwood Press, *A Henry James Encyclopedia* (1989) and *A Nathaniel Hawthorne Encyclopedia* (1991).